CHAMPION REDOUBTABLE

The Diaries and Letters of
Violet Bonham Carter
1914–1945

Friday 10th May B. got trunk to see on a trunk call for Rugby before I was called — He said "Have you heard the news?" I said "No —" "has Chamberlain resigned?" He replied "Holland & Belgium were invaded early this morning —

There was not a word yet in the papers — but the wireless had announced it at 8 & reports came through during the day that the Dutch & Belgians were fighting hard — in spite of bombing attacks & parachute troops — helped at by Fifth Column in Holland — He had an immediate meeting of Air-Raid Wardens & B. & I took the 8—12 watch at the Post & decided not to go

Violet's diary entry for 10 May 1940, recording the dramatic news of the German invasion of Belgium and Holland

CHAMPION REDOUBTABLE

The Diaries and Letters of
Violet Bonham Carter
1914–1945

Edited by
Mark Pottle

'Her father – old, supplanted in power, his Party
broken up, his authority flouted, even his long-
faithful constituency estranged – found in his
daughter a champion redoubtable even in the
first rank of Party orators.'

Winston S. Churchill, *Great Contempories* (1937)

Weidenfeld & Nicolson
LONDON

First published in Great Britain in 1998
by Weidenfeld & Nicolson

© 1998 Jane Bonham Carter,
Virginia Brand, Eliza Bonham Carter
Editorial Text © 1998 Mark Pottle
Introduction © 1998 John Grigg

A CIP catalogue record for this book is available
from the British Library.

ISBN 0 297 81650 0

Typeset by Selwood Systems, Midsomer Norton
Set in Stone Serif
Printed in Great Britain by Butler & Tanner Ltd
Frome and London

Weidenfeld & Nicolson

The Orion Publishing Group Ltd
Orion House
5 Upper Saint Martin's Lane
London, WC2H 9EA

Dedicated to Raymond Bonham Carter

CONTENTS

List of Illustrations   ix

Preface   xi

Editorial Note   xiv

List of Christian Names and Nicknames   xvi

Family Tree   xviii

Introduction by John Grigg   xxi

PART ONE   The Great War
  ONE   1914–1915: *The Outbreak of War*   5
  TWO   1915: *Rupert Brooke*   24
  THREE   1915: *Gallipoli*   45
  FOUR   1915–1918: *Marriage and War*   67

PART TWO   The Inter-War Years
  FIVE   1919–1921: *The Paisley Election;*
  The Anglo-Irish War   105
  SIX   1922–1924: *Liberal Schism and Reunion;*
  The Ruhr Crisis   136
  SEVEN   1924–1939: *Liberal Decline;*
  Anti-Appeasement   161

PART THREE   The Second World War
  EIGHT   1939–1942: *The Home Front*   203
  NINE   1943: *Mother and Son*   251
  TEN   1944: *Reconstruction*   289
  ELEVEN   1945: *Victory and Defeat*   324

Appendices
  A. Glossary   370
  B. Biographical notes   380
  C. Notes on houses   397

Select bibliography   401

Index   405

ILLUSTRATIONS

A selection of photographs appears between pages 226 and 227

Unless otherwise indicated all photographs come from the Bonham Carter family archives

Frontispiece: a page from Violet's diary for 10 May 1940

Violet, November 1915
Cyril Asquith, c. 1915
Raymond Asquith, c. 1916
Rupert Brooke, 1913[1]
Officer of the Hood Battalion, Royal Naval Division, Blandford, February 1915[2]
Arthur Asquith, Bernard Freyberg and Violet, Alexandria, June 1915
H. H. Asquith and David Lloyd George, 1916
Violet at the Paisley by-election, 1920
David Low cartoon depicting Paisley politics
Violet with Paisley milliners
Asquith camp savours victory
Sir Maurice Bonham Carter and 'Butter', late 1920s or early 1930s
Mark Bonham Carter at Winchester
Sir Maurice, Cressida and Laura Bonham Carter at Stockton
Cressida, Laura and Violet, early 1930s, Stockton
Mark and Raymond, Stockton 1932
Violet, Raymond and Laura, Stockton
Violet and wireless set, c. 1945
Churchill, Christmas 1941
Mark Bonham Carter and parents, October 1943
Sir William Beveridge, Violet and Dingle Foot, February 1945
Violet as the new president of the Liberal Party, April 1944[3]
David Low cartoon depicting the return of party politics, February 1945[4]
George VI, Taw-Taw Glimour, [unidentified], Princess Margaret, Queen Elizabeth, Mark Bonham Carter, [unidentified].

[1] The Rupert Brooke Estate
[2] The Trustees of the Imperial War Museum
[3] The Illustrated London News Picture Library
[4] David Low/*Evening Standard*

PREFACE

This volume covers the years during which Violet and Maurice Bonham Carter's four children were born. Cressida, Laura, Mark and Raymond all went on to have children of their own, and my greatest debt in producing *Champion Redoubtable* goes to this extended family. To the Bonham Carters, Grimonds and Ridleys, for their kindness and assistance, I am more thankful than I can adequately express. With their help another step has been taken towards completing the work that Mark Bonham Carter began. His plan to produce an edition of his mother's papers took shape several years before his untimely death in September 1994. It is fitting that he should have a central place in the concluding chapters of this volume, which like its predecessor *Lantern Slides* owes its existence to him.

Since his death I have had constant support and encouragement from his widow Leslie. I have also been greatly helped by their three daughters Jane, Virginia and Eliza. They have the trenchancy, wit and humour of their grandmother, and have dealt nobly with the burdens of administering the Violet Bonham Carter MSS, for which they are now responsible, and on which this work is based. Raymond Bonham Carter has provided much of the organizational drive that has kept up the momentum to my research, and both he and his wife Elena have been vital to my progress. Cressida Ridley has also generously given of her time, helping with important background information. Outside the family, Michael and Eleanor Brock have offered tireless support, patiently advising and encouraging, and offering me the great benefit of their years of editorial experience. Mark Bonham Carter would have appreciated the efforts of them all.

Every family member that I have talked to has had a particular reminiscence of Violet, but for the most part it is not the wife and mother who emerges from these pages. Rather, it is the political animal. I have tried to balance what is significant in terms of understanding her life, with what is likely to be of most historical interest, and inevitably more of the public than the private person has emerged. I have aimed at making the editorial unobtrusive (though some sections of the text have required quite extensive annotation) and have kept the highest possible ratio of source material to supplementary text. The period 1914–45, though it is still within the memory of many now alive, is rapidly passing from our view and I hope that this work serves as an authentic record of a part at least of what is disappearing. It is a different world in many respects from today's, and as with everything historical the opinions expressed in these diaries and letters need to be read in context.

The research on which this volume is based has been made possible by generous support from the Joseph Rowntree Reform Trust; the Leverhulme Trust; and the Wolfson Foundation. To the trustees of these three institutions, I am most grateful. I would also like to express thanks to the Bonham Carter family for their assistance, and also to the donor who requested anonymity. The Warden and Fellows of Nuffield College, Oxford, have provided valuable support for my research, and the President and Fellows of Wolfson College, Oxford, have been particularly generous with their assistance. To all members of Wolfson, including of course all staff, I am deeply indebted.

A work such as this could not be produced without the co-operation of individuals who hold copyright. Their broad-minded generosity makes a vital and often unrecognized contribution to the writing of history, and it is with special feeling that I acknowledge the kindness of: Lady Freyberg; Grizelda, John and Magnus Grimond; Lord Kilbracken; Alexander Murray; Hon. Mrs Mary Rous and the Hon. John Rous; Lady Soames. For permission to quote from the Harold Nicolson diaries I am grateful to HarperCollins Publishers. The letters of Rupert Brooke to VA of 8 September, 2 and 16 December 1914, and those of his mother of 28 April and 1 June 1915, all fall under the copyright of the Rupert Brooke Estate 1997: for permission to publish these, the editor thanks the trustees of the Estate. The other letters involving Brooke have been published unexpurgated in Geoffrey Keynes (ed.) *The Letters of Rupert Brooke* (1968): I am grateful to Faber and Faber Ltd for licence to publish the extracts reproduced here. The letters from Winston Churchill are reproduced with the permission of Curtis Brown Ltd, London, on behalf of the Estate of Sir Winston S. Churchill, copyright Winston S. Churchill.

For their support in applications for funding I would like to thank: Lord Blake; Lord Bullock; Lord Jenkins of Hillhead; Lord Wolfson of Marylebone. For their assistance with specific queries, and for their thoughtful encouragement, I am grateful to: Lord and Lady Airlie, Kate Barker, Mats Bergquist, Helena Bonham Carter, Sue Boothby, Charles Brand, Ron Chernow, Lady Dundas, Heather Dutch, Rachel Edge, Matthew Evans, Lady Freyberg, Caroline Fryer, Milton Gendel, Lord Gladwyn, Henry Hardy, Brian Harrison, Jonathan Hope, Air Vice-Marshal J. E. Johnson, Lord Kilbracken, Modupe Labode, Anne Langslow, Nigel Nicolson, Barbara Rashbass, Mary Rous, John Rous, Kate Shearman, Lady Judith Swire. Comments made by Mark Curthoys, Mike Edge, David Langslow, Isabelle Phan, John Regan, Fiona Ryan, Jon Stallworthy and Ned Wakeman have been especially helpful. Cassia Joll and Rachel Leyshon at Weidenfeld have smoothed the path towards production. The staff of the following institutions have given valuable assistance: Balliol College Library; the Bodleian Library; British Library Newspaper Library, Colindale; Churchill Archives Centre, Churchill College, Cambridge; Harry Ransom Humanities Research Centre,

Texas; Imperial War Museum; Nuffield College Library; Wolfson College Library. I would also like to thank Jackson and Dennett of Oxford, book-binders.

I have valued very highly the comments made on this volume and the last by John Grigg, and I was delighted when he agreed to write the introduction to this work. He has a wonderful sense of the history of this period and knew many of the protagonists, including of course Violet herself. His introduction, like that of Roy Jenkins in the previous volume, offers a unique perspective of the subject matter that is as much a piece of history as the diaries and letters themselves. Peter James has undertaken an expert job of copy-editing the text. For his valuable contribution, and for the safety net that his skill provides, I am grateful. Almost my final acknowledgement goes to Ion Trewin, publisher. Ion has given excellent advice as to the best handling of the material, and has ensured that these sheaves of history have been appropriately bound and are now ready to be dispatched to posterity. Many sets of hands have helped put them together and I have not been able to acknowledge the efforts of everyone involved. Nonetheless I am deeply appreciative and to none more so than my family and friends. I would like to end by thanking again Raymond Bonham Carter and Michael Brock, two 'champions redoubtable'. Any faults in this publication are my own.

Mark Pottle, August 1997
Wolfson College, Oxford

EDITORIAL NOTE

Champion Redoubtable comprises about 175,000 words, of which 25,000 are preliminaries and appendices, and 150,000 edited diaries and letters. Of the latter, roughly four-fifths are source material and the remainder editorial text. The diary entries, comprising around 66,000 words, have been selected from eight journals that between them contain around 250,000 words. They cover the years: 1915 (February–June), 1921 (March–April), 1923 (March), 1940 (May–June), 1942, 1943, 1944, 1945. Outside of these years there is either no diary at all, or else all that exists is a 'journal of motherhood' – a record of the children growing up, with very little reference to politics and public life. The correspondence that has been selected comprises around 51,000 words, and has been chosen from around two thousand letters, perhaps in excess of half a million words. The extant correspondence is spread fairly evenly, though thinly, over the period with a concentration around 1914–15 and 1943–5. The relative paucity of material for the 1930s, a decade of great importance in Violet's public life, has been dealt with by an extended editorial link. This makes use of selected quotations from the transcripts of the public speeches that Violet gave in this period.

In short, around one page in every six or seven from the source has been published. The basic principle employed in the selection of material has been that it should illuminate 'life and times'. Letters and diary entries have been selected on the basis of their broad biographical and historical significance. It is impossible to include every word on any given theme, but an attempt has been made to present a fair and representative sample. The editor's intention has been to present an authentic picture of an age, by allowing the participants to tell their own story in their own words. It is an approach that is complementary to, but different from, biography. The first volume of diaries and letters, *Lantern Slides*, deals with the Edwardian Age, a world that quickly vanished with the outbreak of European war in August 1914. *Champion Redoubtable* covers the three great epochs immediately following: the Great War, the inter-war years and the second world war. Sub-divisions in the volume reflect this content.

The transcriptions of diaries and letters included here are faithful to the source, with necessary concessions to intelligibility. Errors in spelling, grammar and punctuation have for the most part been silently corrected. Exceptions have been made where the error in some way expresses the individuality of the author, or the context in which they wrote. For example, Violet made frequent use of the dash as a kind of halfway house between a full stop and a comma, and this has been retained, for it gives an indication of the spontaneity of her writing. Words that have been added by the editor, because they are necessary to the sense, are enclosed in square brackets. Where it has not been possible to discern a word, a query has been enclosed in square brackets '[?]'. Excisions that occur at the beginning of a paragraph are marked by a three point ellipsis, which may also indicate that one or more paragraphs have been omitted from the beginning of a letter or diary entry. Omissions in the middle of a sentence are marked by a three-point ellipsis, while a four-point ellipsis marks an omission occurring at the end of a sentence; this may include the following sentence[s] and paragraph[s]. The material that has been excised has been left out because it was felt that it does not contribute significantly to the narrative of 'life and times', or else would need too much editorial commentary for it to be readily understood by all but a few experts in the given field.

An attempt has been made to identify all individuals appearing in the text, and to provide biographical information on them. Notes on the principal characters appear in the appendix of 'Biographical notes'. Lesser characters are given a short note that in the main appears at the foot of the page on which they first appear. The index can be used to locate both forms of reference. Where there is neither a note in the appendix, nor a footnote, it can be assumed that nothing could be discovered for the individual in question. The effective dates of the volume, for the identification of individuals by title, are 1 August 1914 to 31 December 1945: thus, Lady Violet Bonham Carter, and not Lady Asquith of Yarnbury (cr. 1964).

The dates given for the diary entries are contemporaneous, unless otherwise indicated (compare, for example, 7 January 1945 with 22 February 1915). In order to keep footnotes to a minimum, the biographical and historical information given herein has been made deliberately concise. This applies also to the narratives in the editorial linking passages, and the entries in the appendix of biographical notes. Cultural reference points (e.g. 'Yeats', 'Heine') and prominent figures mentioned only in passing (e.g. 'Haig', 'Foch') have not been elucidated where they can be found in *Encyclopaedia Britannica*.

LIST OF CHRISTIAN NAMES, INITIALS AND NICKNAMES APPEARING IN THE TEXT

Aga   H. H. Asquith
AJB   Arthur James Balfour
AMA   Arthur ('Oc') Asquith
Anthony   Anthony Eden
Archie   Archie Sinclair
Atty   Anthony Corbett
Austen   Austen Chamberlain
B.   Bongie; Betty Asquith (rarely)
Baffy   Blanche Dugdale
Barbara   Barbara Freyberg/Barbara Sykes
B.D.   Bloody Duck (= VBC)
Beaver   Lord Beaverbrook
Beb   Herbert Asquith
Bernard   Bernard Freyberg
Bett/Betty   Betty Asquith
Bev.   Sir William Beveridge
Billy   Billy Grenfell
B.L.   Andrew Bonar Law
Bluey   H. T. Baker
Bob   Bob Boothby/Lord Robert Cecil
Bongie[/y]/Bonge   Maurice Bonham Carter
Brendan   Brendan Bracken
Brigid   Brigid Balfour
Bubbles   Jasper Ridley (jnr)
Budge   John Evelyn Firth
C.   Cressida Ridley; Clementine Churchill
Canon, the   Revd. J. O. Hannay
Charles   Charles Lister
Christine   Christine Asquith
Clemmie   Clementine Churchill
Cony   Constantine Benckendorff
Crinks   Harcourt Johnstone
Cynthia   Cynthia Asquith
Cys   Cyril Asquith
Denis   Denis Browne
Desmond   Desmond MacCarthy

Diana   Diana Grey
Dingle   Dingle Foot
Donald   Donald Maclean
Duff   Alfred Duff Cooper
Dunn   James Dunn
Eddie[/y]   Eddie Marsh
Edgar   Edgar Vincent
Elizabeth   Elizabeth Bibesco
Ettie   Lady Desborough
Evan   Evan Charteris
E.W.   Ellen Wilkinson
Father   H. H. Asquith
F.E.   F. E. Smith
Frank   Frank Sykes
French   Sir John French
Friz[z]   Bernard Freyberg
Gelda   Grizelda Grimond
Goonie   Gwendeline Churchill
Hamar   Hamar Greenwood
Harold   Harold Nicolson
Hatchie   Harold Nicolson
H.P., Sir   Horace Plunkett
Hugh   Hugh Godley
Jag   Andrew Grimond
Jan   Jan Masaryk
Jasper   Jasper Ridley (snr)
Jean   Jean Asquith
Jimmy   Jimmy Rothschild
Jo   Jo Grimond
John   John Manners
Julian   Julian Grenfell
K.   Katharine Asquith/Lord Kitchener
Kelly   Frederick 'Cleg' Kelly
Laura   Laura Grimond
Law   Rose Law
L.G./Ll.G.   David Lloyd George
M.   Margot Asquith
McK   Reginald McKenna

McKennae, the Reginald & Pamela McKenna
Marigold Marigold Sinclair
Mark Mark Bonham Carter
Maurice Maurice Baring
M.B.C. Maurice Bonham Carter
Megan Megan Lloyd George
Micky Roderick Meiklejohn
Monica Monica Grenfell
Monty General Montgomery
M.R.B.C. Mark Bonham Carter
Nigel Nigel Nicolson
Oc Arthur Asquith
Ombrello Neville Chamberlain
Ottoline Ottoline Morrell
Parkie[/y] Dr Parkinson[?]
Patrick Patrick Shaw-Stewart
Percy Percy Harris
Phillipps Vivian Phillipps
Priscilla Priscilla Bibesco
Puff[lin] Anthony Asquith
R./Raymond Raymond Asquith/ Raymond Bonham Carter

Ray Raymond Bonham Carter
R.B.C. Raymond Bonham Carter
Rufus Rufus Isaacs
Sigele Grizelda Grimond
Simon Sir John Simon
Stephen Stephen Tennant
Sue Sue Asquith
Thomas Thomas Balogh
Tom [Mosley] Oswald Mosley
Toto Alphonse Morhange
V. Violet Asquith/Venetia Stanley
V.A. Violet Asquith
V.B.C. Violet Bonham Carter
Veronica Veronica Morhange
Victor Victor Cazalet
W. Winston Churchill
Wilf[rid] Wilfrid Roberts
Winston Winston Churchill
Wu Edwin Montagu
Y.B.s Yeatman Biggs
υ Hugh Godley

Asquith and Bonham Carter family tree, 1945

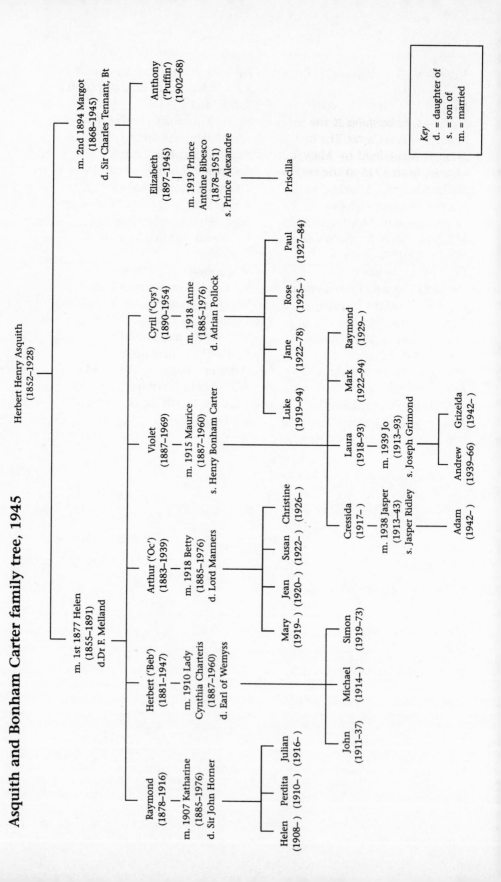

Champion Redoubtable is the second volume of the diaries and letters of Violet Bonham Carter. The first, *Lantern Slides*, covered the period 1904 to 1914. It was edited by Mark Bonham Carter and Mark Pottle. A third volume, from 1945 to the end of Violet Bonham Carter's life, in 1969, is planned.

INTRODUCTION
John Grigg

In *Lantern Slides*, the first volume of Violet Asquith's diaries and letters, we see her launched in Edwardian high society and responding to its opportunities with all the brilliance and emotional intensity of her nature. She was the only girl among the five remarkable children of H. H. Asquith's first marriage, and in some ways the most gifted of them all. Her mother died when she was four, and three years later her father – already politically important as home secretary in the Liberal government then in office – married Margot Tennant, and so brought his family into a socially more exalted sphere. His own background was middle-class, as was that of his first wife, Helen Melland. But Margot's was emphatically, if recently, upper-class.

Because of her sex Violet was not, like her brothers, sent to school or university, but was taught at home by governesses before being sent to France and Germany for 'finishing'. She had a powerful and inquisitive mind, allied to a temperament of overwhelming force. Her friend Winston Churchill described her, in later life, as 'a woman of such *vehement* intelligence' (stressing the adjective). She was also acutely sensitive to beauty, visual and musical, and a lover of literature, with a command of language that enabled her to write most colourfully and expressively from her teens onwards. In the period covered by the present volume it enabled her, as well, to become one of the finest orators of her time.

Her literary talent must have been stimulated by her stepmother, Margot, who had a notable flair for words. Violet's style as a writer owes more than a little to Margot. Was that the limit of her influence? In his Introduction to *Lantern Slides* Roy Jenkins says that Violet would allow Margot to 'pronounce on matters like how to curtsey or dress or which was the best hotel', but would never have dreamt of 'consulting her on any serious matter of the heart or politics'. The second statement is certainly true, but I would suggest that Margot's social influence on Violet was not confined to trivialities. While she largely shared her brothers' wariness towards their stepmother (which in the case of the eldest, Raymond, amounted to implacable dislike), as the only girl she was necessarily more involved with her and susceptible to her. And the effects are scarcely less apparent on the social than on the literary side. Without acknowledging the fact in her diary – without, probably, being conscious of it herself – Violet essentially took her stepmother's view of Society (as distinct from society). Margot, who was a 'Soul', revelled in privilege while feeling herself much superior to run-of-the-mill members of the privileged world. Much the same could be said of Violet.

Privileged she was, to a degree now almost unimaginable. Her father was at the political summit of a nation and empire that still constituted the world's only superpower. In 1905, when the Liberals returned to office after ten years in opposition, he was appointed chancellor of the exchequer, and in the spring of 1908 he became prime minister, a post he was to hold, in peace and war, until the end of 1916. As his daughter, Violet was the equivalent of a princess while he remained in Downing Street. At home she inspired special interest, and the doors of the grandest houses were open to her. When she travelled abroad the red carpet was rolled out for her, metaphorically if not literally, wherever she went. Visiting Washington DC on her own in 1913 (aged twenty-five) she stayed at the British embassy and attended a lunch party in her honour, given by the US attorney-general, at which all present rose and sat down when she did. Those were heady times for an opinionated and impressionable young woman. She made the most of her advantages, but also did regular work in the East End of London giving practical help to people who had none of her luck, without moral pride or condescension. In *Lantern Slides* we are made marvellously aware of her own evolving character, and of the elite society to which she belonged – a society on the brink of catastrophe.

The new volume begins with her reactions in the early days of a war that was to prove the most comprehensive and devastating ever known. It ends with her reflections at the conclusion of a second, even more terrible, war. The period covered is much longer than in *Lantern Slides*, as well as more momentous. At the start Violet is still a young unmarried woman; by the end, she is a grandmother. There are many gaps in the record, for reasons explained by Mark Pottle in his Editorial Note. Violet was at best an intermittent diarist throughout the period, and the decade of the 1930s, of the greatest significance for her as well as for the country, is a particularly unfortunate gap, which however Dr Pottle has done his admirable best to fill with commentary of his own and quotation from Violet's magnificent speeches.

In one sense Violet was made for politics; in another sense, not at all. She was passionately committed to liberal values, of which she never ceased to regard the Liberal Party as, in Britain, the only true exponent. She was also absorbed in the drama of political life, ever since, as a child, she had eagerly awaited her father's return from the House of Commons, to hear his account of the day's business there. Yet there was little, if anything, of the New Woman in her. The feminist attitude to politics, and to life generally, repelled her, partly no doubt because the father whom she worshipped took a traditional view of the role of women. Two themes are strongly apparent in *Champion Redoubtable*. The first is her natural inclination to associate loyalty to a political cause with loyalty to a male hero; her father, above all, but also increasingly Winston Churchill. The other is her belief that even politics must be subordinated to the duties of home-making and motherhood.

In November 1915 she married Maurice ('Bongie') Bonham Carter, her faithful suitor for many years, and her father's equally faithful private secretary. She thus became Mrs Bonham Carter until, in December 1916, Bongie received a knighthood in Asquith's resignation honours, when she became Lady Bonham Carter. In 1925, when Asquith took an earldom, she assumed the courtesy title by which she was to be known for nearly forty years – and will always best be known – of Lady Violet Bonham Carter. (It is as such that she appears in the *Dictionary of National Biography*, in an entry written by William Haley.) But near the end of her life, in 1964, she reverted to her maiden name when she went to the House of Lords as Lady Asquith of Yarnbury.

The critical moment at which she had to decide between active politics and family life – feeling, rightly or wrongly, that the two were incompatible – was after the by-election at Paisley in early 1920, when Asquith regained a seat in Parliament (having been defeated in 1918) with Violet as his most effective supporter in the campaign. As Churchill later put it in *Great Contemporaries* (in words that provide the title for this volume), Asquith 'found in his daughter a champion redoubtable even in the first rank of Party orators'. After Paisley a career in Parliament seemed to beckon. In a diary entry written at the time to Gilbert Murray (pp. 114–15) she said that she had received fourteen invitations to stand, and felt 'terribly tortured' as to what she should do. At a time when Liberalism was, she admitted, in supreme need of 'standard bearers', it was difficult for any true believer like herself to refuse to play a part. Yet she had only to think of her two children (two more were to follow) to know that by allowing any other claim to encroach on what was theirs 'by divine right' she would be 'forfeiting not only the simplest & most intense form of happiness' but also her most imperious duty in life, 'if yielding to an ecstasy of nature' could be called a duty.

It is clear from this and other passages that domesticity was her strongest motive for staying out of politics. She believed that a woman's place was in the home. But there may also have been another, supplementary reason. When Margot urged her to stand in 1924, using the artful argument that she should 'win a seat for father', she writes to Bongie that Margot has 'no conception of what any sort of work means – let alone the aeons of drudgery involved in being in Parlt' (p. 162). Was she perhaps reluctant to face the humdrum life of a backbencher, having experienced life at the top when her father was prime minister? Whatever the balance of motives, she devoted herself almost exclusively to private life until the mid-1930s, when the Nazi threat to freedom and civilization stirred her to renewed political activity.

As a mother she was conservative in many of her attitudes. In his Introduction to *Lantern Slides*, already quoted, Roy Jenkins observes that, despite 'having herself been deprived of a university education by the class and sex prejudices of Edwardian England, she proceeded to do exactly the same with her own daughters thirty years later'. For them, too, she regarded general culture rather than formal qualifications as necessary, if they were to fulfil their natural destiny as women. For her sons she was more ambitious, and the elder, Mark, whom she described to Churchill – when she thought she had lost him in the second world war – as 'the light of my eyes, my pride & hope & Morning Star', felt always (as he wrote) that she had invested in him 'many ambitions & many of the high hopes which for her, as for so many of her generation, had been frustrated by the slaughter in the trenches'. Mark's excellent letters from abroad, before and after his escape in Italy, form a notable contribution to Part Three of this volume. (It was he who conceived the idea of publishing his mother's diaries and letters, and he was the joint editor, with Dr Pottle, until his sudden, lamented death in 1994.)

Violet's marriage to Bongie ended only when he predeceased her by nine years in 1960. Throughout this long period he was a rock of stability to her, as he had been during the emotional *Sturm und Drang* of the years before 1914, particularly during her long infatuation with Archie Gordon, to whom she became engaged while he was dying in hospital after a motor accident in 1909, and to whom for several years afterwards she addressed her diary in the form of a personal letter (see *Lantern Slides*). Bongie's patience and devotion were further tested in the inter-war years, when Violet became emotionally involved with another man, O. T. ('Foxy') Falk. Falk was an economist, who had been a treasury delegate at the Paris Peace Conference. He was also an all-round aesthete, intellectually exciting and athletic (an Oxford golfing Blue) – all attributes to which Violet tended to be strongly drawn. In addition, Bongie had business dealings with him, which did not always turn out advantageously. Between 1927 and 1934 the Bonham Carters spent holidays and many weekends with him at his house in Wiltshire, Stockton House, in the Wylye Valley.

Falk was married, but separated from his wife. The exact nature of Violet's relationship with him is hard to determine, though it may well have been in the strict sense platonic (as was, reputedly, an earlier love affair of his with Pavlova). But it was certainly passionate enough on her side to cause great and prolonged distress when he fell for her children's Swiss governess, Anna Elizabeth Hubler, better known by her nickname 'Cuffy'. With his backing Cuffy later established a girls' finishing school at Oxford, but meanwhile she left the Bonham Carters' service and he left Stockton. A Calvinist turned Christian Scientist, Cuffy did not, her pupils maintain, become his mistress but would gladly have married him had he asked her when his wife eventually died. In any case his affections were transferred to Cuffy for the rest of his life, and for several years Violet suffered acute jealousy. These must have been very difficult years for her, and no doubt also for Bongie, but their partnership survived the experience and was probably fortified by it. They did not turn against Wiltshire but in 1935 acquired the lease of Tilshead Lodge on Salisbury Plain. The Yarnbury of her title as a life peer was taken from a prehistoric site in the area. (Only a few unimportant letters from Falk to Violet have been preserved among her papers. If any from her to him exist, they have not been traced.)

Violet's occasional infatuations are not to be compared with her lifelong worship of her father, which is evident throughout the present volume. In May 1915 Asquith had to bring the Tories into a coalition government under his leadership, just after he had suffered the personal blow of hearing that his intimate friend Venetia Stanley was to marry Edwin Montagu, a junior minister and trusted member of his circle. The book throws fascinating light on these developments, and on Violet's attitude to them at the time. Venetia was a close friend of hers, and she reacts with amazement and disgust to the news of the engagement, particularly to Venetia's decision to convert to Judaism. But was she aware how much Venetia meant to her father? Roy Jenkins records that, after she had read the text of his 1964 biography of Asquith – for which, in collusion with her son Mark as his publisher, he had used Asquith's letters to Venetia as a prime source, and in which he had quoted from them in such a way as to leave Asquith's feelings for Venetia in no doubt – Violet claimed that 'she had not hitherto had the slightest idea of any special relationship between her revered father and Miss Stanley'. Despite his initial feeling that this denial was implausible, Jenkins was nevertheless convinced by the terms in which she justified it: 'It cannot be true. Venetia was so plain.'

Readers of this volume will be forced to conclude that she was a victim of selective memory or self-deception. Even if pictures of Venetia gave support to her disparaging comment (as many would dispute), there can be no escaping the written evidence that proves, almost beyond a shadow of doubt, that Violet knew the truth at the time. In a letter dated 7 June 1915 (pp. 62–63), Margot writes to her: 'Father is happier over V's marriage tho' not converted – he thinks he wd mind less were it anyone else but I tell him whoever she married he wd mind deeply *as he has been very much in love*' (my italics). It is surely inconceivable that Violet could have overlooked those words, or that she would have failed to be outraged by them – and to have left some record of her outrage – if she had felt them to be untrue. Indeed one cannot seriously suppose that Margot would have written in such terms had she not known she was referring to a situation of which Violet was fully aware. Moreover, in her diary covering the personal and political crisis of spring 1915, Violet quotes her father as saying (p. 53), 'this has been the unhappiest week of my life', and she merely remarks 'I believe it has.' If she had been unaware of his feelings for Venetia, she must have been dumbfounded by such language – because even the sacrifice of an old friend, Haldane, in the process of forming the new government could not have made the week unhappier for him than that in which his first wife, Violet's mother, had died of typhoid on the Isle of Arran in 1891. Only a comparable, or greater, personal blow could explain his use of the word 'unhappiest'.

These disturbing events must have helped her to take, at long last, the decision to marry Bongie. But her love for her father remained supreme. The day after her marriage she writes to him (admittedly in response to an appeal from him to keep their 'divine companionship as it has always been'): 'You lie at the very bottom of my heart – nothing can ever get beneath you – or that deep and absorbing love of you which has always been the first principle of my existence.' While saying that she feels 'very, very safe' with Bongie, and acknowledging his 'strong, tender & self-controlled devotion', she makes it all too clear that her acceptance of him owes much to his willingness to treat their partnership as subordinate to the father–daughter link. 'It is the greatest comfort to me that he understands my love for you so perfectly & loves you so deeply himself' (p. 87).

Asquith's fall in 1916 changed Violet's life. She felt, as Asquith himself did, that his position had been usurped, and she could never forgive the man who took his place. The fact that many of her father's warmest admirers could see that his powers were failing towards the end of 1916, and that a change of war direction was vital in the national interest, did not influence her at all. In her eyes he was the noblest of rulers, ignobly deposed, and her detestation of his successor blinded her almost totally to Lloyd George's merits, while causing her relentlessly to exaggerate his defects. When she 'accidentally & rather dramatically' lunches with him on a train in 1923, she cannot deny that they have 'an excellent talk', but brings herself to acknowledge a virtue in him only by pairing it with a profound fault: 'Having no fidelities he also has no rancours – & no embarrassment at encountering people with both' (p. 156). Her rancour was certainly as undeviating as her loyalty to her father. Megan Lloyd George, who had a similar father-fixation but would have liked to be friends with Violet, once told me that she had tried to break down the barrier, but ultimately without success. And she added, rather touchingly, 'If only she could realize it, there's nobody in the whole world who can sympathize with her more than I do.'

Both daughters deserve *our* sympathy, but it is harder to sympathize with those historians who can only praise Asquith while damning Lloyd George, or vice versa. Such partisanship is absurd. It should be obvious that the achievements of both men were outstanding, and that much of their best work was done while they were colleagues in government and next-door neighbours in Downing Street. Many of their talents and strengths were complementary, and they also had more in common than is generally acknowledged. For instance, both were from Nonconformist backgrounds from which each, in his own way, largely escaped; and both were natural rulers, with bold and adventurous temperaments. The breach between them that occurred in 1916 was a tragedy for both of them, for the Liberal Party and for the country.

Between 1924 and 1926 they were formally reconciled, but as uneasy partners. After Asquith was defeated at Paisley at the end of 1924, and then accepted a peerage, Lloyd George became Liberal leader in the Commons. In 1926, after their disagreement over the General Strike, Asquith withdrew altogether and Lloyd George became outright leader of the party. At this time Violet writes to Gilbert Murray (p. 172): 'I feel ... that you & I & others like us are disfranchised – perhaps for our lives ... to serve a party that half-believes in Lloyd George ... seems to me wholly impossible.' When Asquith died in 1928 she became the guardian of his shrine, and as such felt herself to be also keeper of the true Liberal flame.

Soon after her father's death she had a sharp passage of arms with the other political hero in her life, Winston Churchill. In recent years he had not been behaving at all heroically from her point of view, having joined Lloyd George's Coalition in 1917 and served in it until the end, and having in 1924 accepted office as chancellor of the exchequer in Baldwin's Tory government. His name had appeared in a list of 'renegades' in a posthumous work by Asquith, and he was so stung by this word, as applied to himself, that he seems to have sent her no word of condolence on what she describes (p. 176) as *'the greatest sorrow that can ever come to me'* (my italics). Her letter of reproach brings a flowery one from him in return: 'I never for a moment forgot you & I am ashamed that I did not set out my feelings. . . . In the circumstances you are quite right in what you say.' She then promptly forgives him, as she would have forgiven nobody else with such a record of backsliding: 'Thank you for your most sweet & generous letter. It was entirely like you to write it' (p. 177).

The origins of their friendship are well documented in *Lantern Slides*, though Roy Jenkins draws attention to the curious fact that her account of their first meeting, given long afterwards in her book *Winston Churchill as I Knew Him* (1965), does not appear in her contemporary diary. She reminds Churchill of the occasion in this volume, in a letter written in 1942 (p. 239): 'I always remember your saying to me at a dinner at Mary Elcho's – at which I first met you – "we are all worms – but I do believe that I am a glow-worm". You never said a truer word – but oh! for more glow-worms!' (We do not know if he shared her memory of the occasion.

In any case, he could hardly have objected to her attributing such a good remark to him). Though she was probably not much attracted by him physically – he was not her type, in that sense – it is a fair surmise that she would have married him if he had proposed to her while he was still a bachelor in her father's government. She had boundless faith in him and invariably defended him against critics. On the other hand she felt that a good wife would criticize him privately and so help him to make the best of himself. Discussing his engagement, in 1908, to Clementine Hozier (in a letter to Venetia Stanley, *Lantern Slides*, p. 162), she writes: 'He did not *wish* for – though he needs it badly – a critical, reformatory wife who would stop up the lacunas in his taste etc. & hold him back from blunders.' We can sense that she felt some chagrin – perhaps great chagrin – about not having been offered the role herself. (The accident that befell her in Scotland while the Churchills were on their honeymoon was not, I believe, a suicide attempt, though her willingness for it to receive wide publicity may have reflected a desire to cause him a pang.)

Her impassioned opposition to the dictators in the 1930s, and to the policy of appeasing them, brought her close to Churchill again. But she was ahead of him in her crusading zeal. As Dr Pottle says: 'Violet campaigned vigorously . . . first under her own banner and later as part of a cross-party alliance led by Winston Churchill.' At the Liberal Party conference only three months after Hitler came to power she showed how clearly she understood the significance of what had happened: 'In Germany freedom as we conceive it seems to have perished . . . in the twinkling of an eye, almost without a struggle, & given place to a nightmare reign of force.' But she warned that the threat to freedom came not just from Nazism and fascism but from Soviet communism as well (p. 181). In the same year, supporting an appeal on behalf of Jewish refugees from Nazi persecution, she said: 'I want to make clear my profound conviction that this is not a matter which concerns the Jewish community alone. It concerns all who believe in justice and our common humanity.' And she added: 'I suppose if this were Germany most of us would be behind barbed wire. I can only say for myself that I should be ashamed to be anywhere else.' Knowing her, one cannot doubt that she meant what she said.

In 1936 she joined an inter-party and non-party group to fight appeasement, under Churchill's leadership. It was called 'Focus in Defence of Freedom and Peace'. At a rally in the Albert Hall she described Churchill as 'that brilliant political phenomenon who eludes all categories and defies classification'. In the same speech she produced a wonderful phrase: 'Democracy – that great army that needs no uniform' (p. 189). It is most unfortunate that she kept no diary during this period, but Dr Pottle quotes from a post-war diary entry her recollection of an incident at the time of Munich. Leaving a Focus lunch meeting at the Savoy, she says, 'with a lump in my throat [I] met Eddie [Marsh] coming jauntily in on the ball of the foot with bristling eyebrows "Isn't it glorious?" he piped "we are *not* going to be bombed after all". I replied with fury "Glorious. Where do you see glory? You think of nothing but your own skin" – the only unkind word I had ever said to Eddie and it made me feel afterwards as if I'd hit a child' (p. 191).

For the absence of a diary in the 1930s we have the compensation of superb diary material for much of the period 1940–5. But there is one deprivation that covers the whole period – that Violet was not in Parliament. In August 1941 she would have been willing to stand for Berwick when a vacancy occurred in that Liberal seat. Her children were old enough for her to feel no longer constrained by domestic duty (the girls grown up, and even her younger son, Raymond, at boarding school). Under the wartime party truce she would have been elected then as a matter of course, and her presence in the House of Commons would have been electrifying. Her old friend Churchill, now prime minister, might have found it hard to deny her a place in government – might even have wished to have her as a colleague – despite his distaste for women in politics. Sadly, she was not chosen as the Liberal candidate, and her last opportunity to have a serious career in Parliament was lost. (Wells in 1945 and Colne Valley in 1951 would have led nowhere in particular, even if she had won either seat; and her appointment to the House of Lords was too late to be of any value.) She was very disappointed about Berwick, as we can see from a letter at the time to Bongie (p. 233).

Nevertheless, her life during the second world war was exciting, not least because she and Bongie were both air-raid wardens. Her descriptions of the Blitz in London, combined with her record of work as a governor of the BBC and of conversations with people near the centre of affairs – above all, with Churchill – make Part Three of this book an important contribution to the history of the war.

For obvious reasons, the volume as a whole contains fewer records of travel than *Lantern Slides*, but after the first world war she paid interesting visits to Ireland (March–April 1921) and Germany (March 1923). Her accounts of both show her power of observation and, also, her prejudice. In the former she looks through Green spectacles, neither visiting Northern Ireland nor showing much understanding of the Unionist position. She is appalled by the (Lloyd George) government's counter-terror, while seeming to regard the IRA's terror as an inevitable consequence of British misrule in Ireland. She believes in her father's policy of dominion status for the Twenty-Six Counties, which was indeed the basis of the Treaty signed at the end of the year. But would it have been possible for Lloyd George to secure the compromise he did, involving the agreement of both the Irish negotiators and leading Unionists, if the disgust of British public opinion at the methods used against the IRA had not coincided with its effective defeat by those very methods (as admitted by Michael Collins)? The timing was all-important.

In Germany her attitude is predetermined by hostility to (Lloyd George's) Versailles Treaty and by uncritical acceptance of Keynes's arguments against the reparations clauses. She is unmoved when Rudolf Breitscheid, leader of the Independent German Socialists, replies 'Yes' to her question 'Could Germany honestly make a repayment that would satisfy the French?' Yet her German diary is fascinating, and never more so than when she meets Konrad Adenauer in Cologne (p. 153), describing him as 'an oldish rather tired man of great ability'. His remarks to her are of extraordinary interest in view of what he was to achieve when he was much older, and after another World War.

My own memory of Violet, which is vivid and affectionate, is mainly of her later years. Though I met her occasionally from (my) childhood onwards, it was only during the Suez crisis in 1956 that I got to know her well. In that episode – which will doubtless feature prominently in the next (and last) volume – we were on the same side and appeared together on platforms, though to her pitying incomprehension I was, at the time, a member of the Conservative Party. For the rest of her life she never ceased to be very kind to me, despite occasional disagreements.

The worst occurred when, in a review of Roy Jenkins's biography of her father, I ventured to say that Asquith, like Madame Bovary, was deluded by the mirage of aristocratic freedom. She sent me at once a long and blistering letter about this, which I treasure. But I treasure still more her reply when, soon afterwards, I congratulated her on her life peerage. 'In choosing my title,' she wrote, 'I was torn between Asquith and Bovary, but played for safety & plumped for Asquith in the end.'

John Grigg
6 October 1997

ONE

The Great War

1914–1918

CHRONOLOGY OF EVENTS 1914–1918

1914	August	3 – cabinet authorizes mobilization of regular army; 4 – German army invades Belgium; Britain declares war on Germany; 22 – BEF engages German army at Mons
	September	5–9 – battle of the Marne; 16 – Gen. French issues instructions for trench warfare
	October	10 – fall of Antwerp; 12 – first battle of Ypres (to 11 November)
	November	3 – Turkey declares war on Allied powers
1915	January	28 – war council approves naval attack on Dardanelles
	February	28 – Royal Naval Division embarks for Dardanelles
	March	16 – 29th Division begins passage to Dardanelles; 18 – Naval bombardment of Dardanelles Straits begun, and suspended
	April	22 – second Ypres (to 25 May); first use of gas, by Germans near Ypres; 25 – first Gallipoli landings
	May	7 – sinking of the *Lusitania*; 15 – Fisher resigns as first sea lord; 17 – Asquith accepts Coalition; 23 – Italy enters war on Allied side; 26 – new cabinet announced; 31 – Zeppelin bombs London
	June	4 – attack on all fronts in Gallipoli
	August	6 – landings at Suvla Bay in Gallipoli
	October	14 – decision taken to replace Hamilton by Monro as c-in-c Gallipoli
	December	18–19 – evacuation of Suvla Bay and Anzac Cove, Gallipoli; 19 – Haig replaces French as c-in-c on Western Front
1916	January	8 – evacuation of Cape Helles, Gallipoli; introduction of conscription of single men aged 18–41
	February	21 – battle for Verdun begins (to December)
	June	5 – Lord Kitchener drowns in sinking of HMS *Hampshire*
	July	1 – battle of the Somme (to 18 November); 4 – Lloyd George made secretary for war
	September	15 – tanks used in battle for the first time, on the Somme

1916	December	5 – Asquith resigns; 7 – Lloyd George becomes premier; forms a Coalition government
1917	April	6 – America declares war on Germany; 9–14 – battle of Arras
	July	31 – third Ypres, or Passchendaele (to 13 October)
1918	February	Representation of the People Act
	March	21 – beginning of German offensive on western front
	April	11 – Haig's 'backs to the wall' order of the day
	August	8 – beginning of Allied counter-offensive
	October	30 – Turkish government signs armistice of surrender
	November	9 – Kaiser flees to Holland, and abdicates; republic proclaimed in Berlin; 11 – German delegation signs armistice of surrender
	December	14 – general election: 339 Coalition Unionists; 134 Coalition Liberals; 73 Sinn Féin; 59 Labour; 48 Unionists; 26 Liberals; 28 others

ONE

The Outbreak of War

August 1914–February 1915

As the London Season of 1914 drew to a glorious close, the likelihood of a major war breaking out on the Continent hardened into certainty. With conflict looming between Germany and France, British public opinion was divided over intervention. Despite the 1904 Entente with France many believed that the country should remain neutral unless directly attacked itself. Against this there was widespread feeling that it would be both dishonourable and unwise to stand aside and witness the probable defeat of France. This rift was closed when on 4 August Germany invaded Belgium, as a preliminary to its attack on France. It was an act of aggression in flagrant violation of international treaty, and the spectacle of gallant Belgian resistance presented the British public with a moral cause behind which it could unite. When Asquith heard of the German invasion he wrote, 'this simplifies matters', and Sir Edward Grey later commented that without it the country 'would have been split from end to end'. Amid an upsurge of patriotic feeling, Britain declared war. The massive cost in human life of the conflict that ensued has tended to obscure from later generations the romantic idealism prevalent in Britain in August 1914. It can be seen in the letter that Violet wrote to her pacifist friend Ottoline Morrell, shortly after the outbreak: 'you <u>cannot</u> think I am in favour of war as such. It is only that I feel there are some things worse than death & all the horrors we are living in now.' Violet wrote then that she felt this conviction 'more strongly every day', but it was to be severely tested in the years ahead, which took such a heavy toll of her generation. Several of her close friends were involved in the early fighting in northern France, where the French armies and small British Expeditionary Force mounted a desperate defence against the massive German onslaught.[1]

---

[1] M. and E. Brock, *H. H. Asquith: Letters to Venetia Stanley*, 150; MBC to VBC, 8 October 1917; VA to Ottoline Morrell, 29 August 1914.

Hugh Godley to V.A.   *Monday 24 August 1914*
                                           Office of the Parliamentary
                                           Counsel, Whitehall, S.W.

My dearest,

I am afraid there is no chance of my being able to get up to the north next week, I have just been away in a remote place for a week, & next week I shall have to be on duty. I should have loved to come.

It is extraordinary I think how little the people in the country districts seem to know or think about all that is going on. Even in the north, where they occasionally see a newspaper, and where they have a few glimmerings of intelligence, they are really much more interested in their every day affairs, and down at Hartfield, where they never see a paper of any kind, they seem hardly to know that a war is going on at all.

I find it almost impossible to read anything except newspapers myself. One reads the same account of the same thing in about 6 different papers in a sort of vague hope of being able to squeeze something new out of them. The merciless accession of casualty lists is almost unbearable, though personally I have I think only two people left at the front whom I am directly interested in. I never knew anything more characteristic of Aubrey than just to turn up, more or less all right, just after a very circumstantial, and apparently quite hopeless, story had been generally circulated about him.[1] I hope very much that he will not go out again; it is simply suicide, and quite unnecessary.

My colleague (Hulton) at the office has spent the last month going from recruiting office to recruiting office, & being always turned away because of his sight. He has now at last been accepted as a private in the Territorial Army Service Corps, which I suppose means that he has to wash up the dishes for the troops. It is most gallant of him I must say; by the way you w^d like him I think; he is very clever & quite amusing.

I have just met a man whose daughter was married on Aug. 23rd to a man who was killed in action on August 27th. I think really such cases are not nearly so bad as some. I remember after the Boer War all the young widows married again at once. I remember you saying to me before the fighting began that the two people for whom you feared most were Percy Wyndham & John.[2] I must go now. Bless you Dear, always H.

---

[1] Aubrey was wounded in the retreat from Coeuvre, 1 September, captured by the Germans, given medical aid and later liberated by a French advance. Raymond Asquith wrote to him on 20 September: 'It was thoroughly characteristic of you to be shot and lost but equally characteristic to be found and healed. I would always put my last shilling on your luck in these little things' (John Jolliffe (ed.), *Raymond Asquith: Life and Letters*, 195).

[2] Both were dead within a month. John Nevile Manners (1892–1914), a Balliol contemporary

M.B.C. to V.A.   *Friday 28 August*
10 Downing Street,
Whitehall, S.W.

Beloved

You will see your Father's statement in the Press.... Our troops have no doubt lost heavily as they had to retire in the face of a very heavy artillery fire & I fear that some of our guns have been lost. Do not mention this. I expect by this time that we must have had about 10,000 casualties but this is merely a guess. One thing is satisfactory, we have got support now on each of our flanks. I do not think that one need take a too gloomy view of the situation, the thing that makes one uneasy is that the French have shown such bad strategy, & have been outmanoeuvred. Our people have done wonders & have really I think saved the situation for the French.[1] I hope before long they will have an opportunity of attacking something like their own numbers of enemy.... My love darling. B.

V.A. to Venetia Stanley   *Saturday 29 August*
Stanway, Winchcombe,
Gloucestershire

Darling – So sweet of you to ask me to Penrhôs & I shall avail myself without fail of your kind offer! – just for the moment every plan is in a haze. London is exhausting to a degree but one feels hopelessly restless anywhere else. Father & I had a very healthy & delicious Sat. to Mon. at Lympne last Sunday & on Thursday I came down here. It is divinely green & sleepy & remote & lulling. Lord Elcho has just issued an abrupt ultimatum to all his employees servants etc.– to join the Army or leave his service – & then gone off to London leaving poor Lady Elcho to cope with the situation – which he created without consulting her in any sort of way. It is too cruel as the people here have hardly heard of the war. Lady Elcho is at present concocting an explanatory speech with Eliza Wedgewood's assistance to make this evening in the barn....[2]

of Cys Asquith, was killed in action (at Landrecies) on 1 September, and Percy Wyndham (1887–1914), son of George Wyndham, on 15 September.

[1] The French had not anticipated that the Germans would attack in force through Belgium, and had concentrated their strength to the south, along their border with Germany. The Germans thus had an overwhelming superiority of men in the north, and only a desperate rearguard defence by the BEF at Le Câteau, 26–27 August, checked the German advance.

[2] Hugo Charteris, Lord Elcho (1857–1937) and his wife Mary *née* Wyndham (1862–1937). Violet refers to these old friends by their Elcho name, even though Hugo had succeeded as 11th Earl of Wemyss (June 1914). Of his 'abrupt ultimatum' Violet wrote to Bongie: '[Lady

This long wait for the casualty list is most cruel.... The whole thing is like living in a nightmare. I go back next week as I am enmeshed in one or two forms of activity – equipping hospitals – distress-committees etc. Father poured very cold water on all nursing suggestions.

... I haven't read or written a line – & feel a permanent <u>sick</u> apprehension of the lists. I imagine they must be out to-day or to-morrow. Goodbye darling write again, yr V.

V.A. to M.B.C.   *Monday 31 August*
                                                Stanway, Winchcombe,
                                                   Gloucestershire

I write one line to say I'm not coming home till Wed. morning.... I was so reassured by your letter & the Press Bureau statement this morning. Sunday's Times simply froze one's blood with terror. It must have been as you say ignorant correspondents who met stragglers....[1]

We had a most amusing meeting in the barn on Sat. night at which Lord Elcho's edict of dismissal was temporarily remitted & she [Lady Elcho] & Beb & a woman called Miss Eliza Wedgewood made impassioned speeches asking for voluntary help. Beb quoted 'England expects every man to do his duty' in firm & ringing tones – & Miss Wedgewood announced that <u>Father</u>, through tapping the German wireless, had discovered that all the Belgian atrocities were true![2] Also that owing to our Fleet having all been sent to 'somewhere in the North' the Germans could come over here in 2 hours from Ostend. This was by way of inspiring panic.

I do really think that <u>some</u> of the boys should enlist. Father will be asked why he doesn't begin his recruiting at home....[3] Are you rested? & missing me? Yr V.

Elcho] is miserable about it – the creed of her life being the liberty of the individual' (28 August 1914; see, too, Jane Ridley and Clayre Percy (eds.), *The Letters of Arthur Balfour*, 311–12).

[1] A special edition of *The Times* on Sunday 30th carried the 'Amiens despatch', written by Arthur Moore, who had been swept along with the BEF in its withdrawal from Mons and Le Câteau. Its last sub-heading read 'Need for Reinforcements'.

[2] The influx of Belgian refugees to Britain stimulated rumours, many of them untrue, of German atrocities on civilians in occupied territories.

[3] Lord Kitchener, newly appointed secretary of state for war, foresaw a long conflict and proposed to raise an army of 100,000 by voluntary recruitment. The appeal was launched on 7 August, and by the end of September 750,000 had responded. All of Asquith's adult sons had enlisted by the end of the year.

M.B.C. to V.A.   *Monday 21 September*
                                      10 Downing Street,
                                      Whitehall, S.W.

Beloved ... The latest telegram from French says that they have repulsed
successfully several counter attacks but have suffered rather heavy casualties....[1] I do not think that we know enough yet to say whether our
position is becoming more favourable. I cannot help feeling that the
Germans must be looking for a weak place in our line for a counter attack.
Stalemate cannot be their game.[2]

There are persistent rumours of John Manners's death. I have just been
speaking to Mary Herbert about them & we agree in thinking that it is not
yet time to give up hope. The story is just the same as what Aubrey told &
indeed I think is his story gaining credence from repetition. It apparently
rests on the evidence of five privates, who say that [they] saw him killed
but it does not seem certain whether they mean actually dead on the
ground or merely that they saw him bowled over. The action was in a
thick wood & at night & apparently the rest of the platoon has disappeared
so there still I think is a chance that he is a prisoner. However Lady
Manners has been told the story that he is dead. I will send some books
for your journey tomorrow, if I can collect something suitable. Bless you
always, this is a hopeless letter but I have been continuously interrupted.
My love darling   B.

V.A. to H.H.A.   *Sunday 18 October*
                                           St Omer

My darling Father – So far I have had the most wonderful & intensely
interesting journey. We got to Boulogne about lunch-time after a very
rough & cold crossing – the atmosphere of the place was very strange &
abnormal.[3] Soldiers everywhere – the French ones just like toys – in their
red trousers – ours in khaki about two feet taller – gaga-looking doddering
old French generals covered with stars – & masses of Red X people many
of whom crossed with us. Nearly all the hôtels shut – we got lunch at one,

---

[1] Field Marshal Sir John French, commander-in-chief of the BEF; see biographical notes.

[2] It was thought that in a long war the weight of Russian numbers would inevitably tell, so
that the Germans had to go for a quick knock-out blow in the west.

[3] Violet had organized a small party consisting of her brother Beb, his wife Cynthia, and a
family friend, Sir James Dunn, for a week-long visit to British military hospitals in France. For
this she had the permission of the British and French governments. They left London on
Saturday 17 October travelling in Dunn's Daimler, driven by his chauffeur, Beston.

full of soldiers, but were told beds for the night would be quite out of the question . . . .

I thought of going on to Calais but was strongly advised against it by some Red X people coming from Dunkirk – who said (quite untruly) that the Germans were just going to occupy it (Dunkirk) & were fast coming south – also that he had heard we had been 'rolled up'. Beb was very much alarmed![1] We decided to come on here for the night & were just trying unsuccessfully to wire to you at the Post-Office when who should I see but <u>Maurice</u>! looking marvellously well & <u>responsible</u> in a khaki Holbein coat trimmed with possum.[2] I nearly died of delight & surprise – he was so like himself. 'I've just come over to buy a lobster for the Flying Corps' he said – & got into our motor – bought the lobster & we all went off together. Soon we saw a lovely B.E. overhead – which had just arrived from England. The road to St. Omer was perfectly lovely – rolling down country – we passed large camps of horses & soon began to see green rockets going up – this was the Flying Corps Headquarters – they send up rockets at night to show them the way home. We dropped M. & motored on in the dark to St. Omer – constantly challenged but our passes got us through . . . .

This morning French sent round for me to come & see him at 8.30. I found him well but <u>absolutely</u> changed in appearance – responsibility hanging round him like a cloud. He showed me all his maps & seemed extraordinarily confident. He says they take boys of 16 & men of 50 from the Germans now & is sure they cldn't spare any for invasion – he sent you all sorts of messages & was perfectly sweet to me.[3] He says Foch is <u>much</u> the best of the French Generals. He is rather perturbed by the fall of Antwerp as he says we shall have to mask it, which will mean such a lot of men.[4] I was shown the Hospital – not a <u>general</u> one – the first place men are brought to by motor ambulance from the firing-line. The men were pathetic & so brave . . . .

Aeroplanes constantly come over this place – a German Taube dropped

---

[1] Violet and her companions had landed in northern France during the 'race to the sea', in which each side tried to turn the other's northern flank. The channel ports were an obvious target, and on 15 October Ostend fell to the German army. That Sunday, however, the German advance was held, and Dunkirk was not in imminent danger.

[2] Maurice Baring (1874–1945), writer and critic; lifelong friend of the Asquiths; served with the Royal Flying Corps, 1914–19.

[3] It was said of the German army at the first battle of Ypres (12 October–11 November) that the men were too young, and the officers too old. Kitchener feared German 'invasion raids' on Britain – that his commander in France, Field Marshal Sir John French, decries this is early evidence of the tension between them.

[4] Antwerp fell on 10 October, and its loss intensified the German pressure on the northern part of the Allied line.

bombs into the Headquarter Staff's <u>courtyard</u> a week or two ago, & three women were killed in the street the day before yesterday. It is a <u>lovely</u> little old Town with a huge square market place & hôtel-de-ville. The streets absolutely full of English soldiers. The Indians or some of them are due here to-day & I am passionately keen to see them. We go on probably to Amiens this evening. Will you wire or write me to the <u>Ritz</u> Paris. We may not stay there – but will call for letters.

Our party are very odd. Beb more <u>absolutely</u> useless & befogged & shy than anything you can imagine – he has no practical instinct or enterprise of any kind & does not remember or even carry! a thing. Dunn <u>very</u> good tho' a little ignorant of ropes.[1] Cynthia passive but very sensible & calm & unfussed. I wish Oc could have come. So far the verdict of everyone I meet is strongly against the amateur. They say cars if turned into ambulances & sent <u>without their owners</u> are acceptable – but in huge masses & without professionals they simply cumber & block the roads. The conditions of life are quite indescribably different from anything one has ever experienced or even imagined.

Goodbye – bless you – Yr V – <u>Extraordinary</u> optimism here.

V.A. to H.H.A. *Monday 19 October*
Amiens

Darling Father – Everything that has ever or <u>can</u> ever happen to me pales & shrivels before the thrilling interest of this expedition. How I long for you to have been with me all the time.... We passed miles of our transport waggons going on towards the front – huge motor lorries with City of Westminster stamped on them[2] – covered with the most splendid men who all waved their hands & shouted with joy when they saw us – knowing we were English – I have never felt more moved. At one point I stopped the car & offered some of them cigarettes. You <u>should</u> have seen them! they <u>swarmed</u> round the car like bees with outstretched hands & caps & it needed great self-control not to give them every peppermint & cigarette & Daily Mirror we had in the motor. Then they all cheered like no election crowd I have ever seen.

We reached Béthune just before dark – one could hear the guns thundering away in the distance only 3 to 5 miles off – & great quivers of light in the sky like summer lightning – no flame. This Hospital was the very

---

[1] (Sir) James Dunn (1875–1956), cr. Bt, 1921; Canadian-born financier; gave Violet and Bongie as a wedding gift a portrait of Violet by Sir William Orpen.

[2] Public transport vehicles were commandeered in the early stages of the war and appeared in France in their original livery.

first place they are brought to from the front by motor ambulance – they are not undressed but lie about on stretchers on the ground in their uniforms – bandaged – or operated upon if the case is very urgent. It seemed so strange to see them lying about in their dirty & often blood-stained clothes – but they say the hospital has to be so mobile they cannot carry bed-clothes or night-shirts – & in any case it wld. tire them to be undressed & redressed in 48 hours – & they never stay there for longer – as the hospital usually moves on wherever the firing line moves & they are sent off by train to a general hospital. They were all marvellously brave & pathetic – some dying (these mostly under morphia) with bullets through the lung or shrapnel in the head – & a good many slighter arm & leg wounds – painful but not dangerous. They all wanted cigarettes above all things.

One poor man was badly hit by one of our own shells – 'I'd rather it had been the Germans – I would – but I daresay it was our own fault or rather the officer's that took us too near. I've been all thro' it since Mons & never had a scratch till now. Well if I'm sent back again I suppose I must try & do my best.' – I cld. see he was <u>haunted</u> by the thought of going back. There were some very jolly Scotchmen amongst them – they mostly looked a good colour & seemed not at all nervously shattered tho' one poor man cried from sheer nervous exhaustion. None of them I spoke to had had their clothes off since they started. I was surprised at their not having their boots off now – but the R.A.M.C. Dr. said they didn't seem to want to. The staff seemed small – only 8 Drs & 40 men attendants to deal with 2 or 3 hundred wounded – & more pouring continually in & one felt if a few really <u>great</u> surgeons like Cheyne were in these clearing Hospitals many lives might be saved....

Next day (Monday) we went off to Bailleul via Cassel – through our lines all the way – transport, ammunition – gun-carriages – & a lot of tired-looking Infantry of the 3rd division coming from the Aisne – they were so white & jaded poor things – I nearly broke up their order by throwing them cigarettes. We were the <u>only</u> thing on the roads besides soldiers – & at one point in our progress were whizzed past by Gen. French & the Headquarter Staff on their way to the firing line! They carry a small Union Jack on their motor which no one else is allowed to do.

At Bailleul – about three miles from the fighting – we saw some German prisoners being marched away – our soldiers guarding them, trying in vain to conceal their pleasure, smiling all over their faces. The French populace jeered openly at them. 'Eh! Guillaume qui n'est pas habillé – Guillaume qui a perdu ses culottes de velours' – I remonstrated heygately 'il ne faut pas se moquer des prisonniers' – 'Eh dame! il faut bien! que voulez- vous? Les Allemands c'est un sale peuple – des brigands – des barbares – ils ont tout pillé – tout ravagé' etc. etc. with eloquent gesticulations. They all say

'Les Anglais – c'est nous'[1] (I wish I felt the same about them!) & the impression the north of France gives now is that <u>we</u> have invaded & occupied it.

Bailleul hospital was on the same lines as Béthune but still nearer the front – men coming in all the time – mostly so tired they went straight to sleep however bad their wounds. I talked to 4 German wounded prisoners – one had the Iron Cross – rather a trumpery looking thing – not at all solid or massive as it sounds – with a large W in the middle. He was 'verlobt' – & depressed by the German indifference to casualties. 'Für Menschenleben geht's bei uns nicht an'.[2] He said the Germans cld. put 15 million into the field if they liked – I doubt this. Another was terribly worried about his symptoms (he had an abdominal wound) & begged me to translate them to the Dr. which I did – this reassured him much. Dunn, an acharné patriot, was deeply shocked at my giving him a pack of cards to play Skat with![3] We motored off towards Amiens – starting on the Armentières road – stopped to help 2 Army motorbicyclists, <u>delightful</u> men, who needed a spanner – & punctured ourselves.

Streams of refugees came by with their pathetic bundles on their backs. I cross-examined one old woman in hopes of atrocities 'Les Allemands se sont mal conduits dans votre village?' '<u>Très</u> mal – ils ont tout ravagé etc.' – – 'Ils étaient cruels?' – '<u>Très</u> cruels – ils ont tué un cochon'![4] – I felt relieved at the death of a pig having loomed so large in the category of horrors! but there's no doubt these poor people have suffered terribly. We heard very loud firing all that afternoon. One town – Merville – we passed through was full of Turcos – I've never seen such low savage faces. They are extraordinarily Oriental & all have Arab horses. We saw many dead horses & trees blasted by shells by the wayside – & in one field – delicious sight – a lot of our men tently – concentratedly – <u>wildly</u> – playing football! Gradually as we got south our soldiers ceased & the French ones began – just like pictures of the Napoleonic wars – they look rather sad & tired & their horses in poor condition. Not at all gay or Latin or demonstrative. One town we reached very hungry hadn't a crumb of bread in it, only

---

[1] 'Eh! William who is not dressed – William who lost his velvet pants' ... 'One should not make fun of prisoners' – 'Well, lady! One has to! what do you want? Germans, they are a nasty people – thieves – ruffians – they have pillaged everything – devastated everything' ... 'The English – it's us.'

[2] 'engaged' ... 'We are not concerned about human life'.

[3] Dunn had been told stories of German atrocities, including the enemy's use of white flags to lure British troops to their deaths: 'From all I can judge from the German wounded and prisoners I have seen they are a cruel barbarous people. On the other hand I feel I never till now realized what a fine race of men our fellows are....'.

[4] 'The Germans have behaved badly in your village?' 'Very badly – they have devastated everything' – 'Were they cruel?' – '<u>Very</u> cruel. They have killed a pig.'

pastry! Tonight we are in very civilised quarters – my bed was previously occupied by French & before that by the German Commander in Chief![1]

Love to you beloved – this is a terribly diffuse letter but I cannot concentrate these torrents of experience. Please give my news to Cys & Bongie & Margot. Yr V.

The Royal Naval Division

It was a characteristic of the response in Britain to the outbreak of war in 1914 that groups of friends volunteered to fight together, and by late November a small constellation well known to Violet had assembled in the Hood Battalion of the Royal Naval Division. They included her brother Oc, their friends Patrick Shaw-Stewart, Charles Lister and Rupert Brooke, and Brooke's friend Denis Browne. An outsider to the circle who became an intimate was the young New Zealander Bernard Freyberg. The Naval Division had been established in August 1914 by Winston Churchill, for the purpose of providing the navy with an infantry force capable of carrying out restricted land operations. Churchill stated that if at some future point the Division's 15,000 men were not needed by the navy they would be handed over to the army for general service, and this is ultimately what happened. The force thus had a dual identity, which was reflected in outward signs: while junior officers and other ranks took naval titles (i.e. 'stokers' and not 'privates'), there were army lieutenant-colonels among the senior ranks. Active service came quickly for this young force, which was thrown into the defence of Antwerp early in October even before it had finished basic training. The bulk of three battalions were captured during the retreat from the city, and Churchill came under serious criticism for committing his force to so risky a venture. After its return to England the Division completed its interrupted field training at Blandford in Dorset, in preparation for an unknown destination overseas the following year.[2]

---

[1] Amiens had been on the western edge of the massive southwards turn executed by von Kluck's 1st Army, 30 August–3 September, in response to which French had evacuated his forward base in the town, 28 August.

[2] James W. Fry and Thomas McMillan, *The Complete History of the Royal Naval Division.*

V.A. to Rupert Brooke
Sunday 29 November
The Wharf, Sutton Courtenay,
Berkshire

My dear Rupert ... I have spent a very strange 10 days in Winchester Hospital. My first 2 or 3 days were almost pure nausea – & overfatigue – but after that I found I rather liked it – at least a good many aspects of it. It is difficult at first to withstand a simultaneous assault on all one's senses – sight – hearing – smell – touch – smell much the worst. 'The comfortable smell of friendly fingers' – which I spent hours trying to disperse or mitigate with 'the benison of hot water' but in vain. 'Clean sheets' were also rare – the 'male caress of blankets'?? common![1] – & I never saw a newpeeled stick all the time I was there. I abhorred the dressings (all septic shrapnel wounds in my ward) but didn't turn a hair at operations. If I go abroad it will be the beginning of the week after this (7th 8th 9th) experimentally till Xmas – & then if I find I am filling any real gap I shall go back directly afterwards.[2]

When Oc & all of you go I shall like being away – but I don't like missing the last weeks of you all – & I shall hate leaving the knowledge of home. But this is the one moment of my life when I do feel faintly ascetic stirrings – that it's almost wrong to be lapped in cosy normality while a few people face unutterable horror for us all. It is quite a false & sentimental reflex – & does not mean that I mean to treat the poor wounded as a moral gymnasium & hair-shirt for myself!...

We have had a damp-ish Sunday down here by the river – 'the beautiful & deathstruck year' in a state of lovely decay. I went over to tea with the poet laureate who asked me to apologize profusely to Father for him for not having written more on the war.[3] I hastily begged him not to mention it. Raleigh was there trembling & spitting & talking the most utter nonsense, bless him.[4] He is drilling & learning to shoot – how dangerous isn't it.... I must stop. Everywhere there are beech leaves whirling in blue Whistlerish river-mists – & lying in thick crackly carpets – they are exactly the colour of Cys's hair. He has now got a commission in the Queen's Westminsters & drills all day in Dean's yard.

Have you read the new Wells or the new Sinister Street?[5] Can I send you

---

[1] Misquoted phrases from Brooke's poem 'The Great Lover': 'Then, the cool kindliness of sheets, that soon / Smooth away trouble; and the rough male kiss / Of blankets ... '.

[2] Violet did not pursue her VAD nursing work beyond this trial spell at Winchester.

[3] Robert Seymour Bridges (1844–1930), poet laureate, 1913–30.

[4] Sir Walter Alexander Raleigh (1861–1922), professor of English literature at Oxford, and fellow of Magdalen College; greatly affected by the outbreak of the war, which dominated his life thereafter.

[5] The second volume of Compton Mackenzie's *Sinister Street* was published in 1914, the first having appeared in 1913; the Wells referred to is probably *The War That Will End War* (1914).

anything – books? food or a compass?! Tell me directly you join Oc – Yours
Violet A.

Rupert Brooke to V.A.   *Wednesday 2 December*
                                              Royal Naval Division, Blandford,
                                                                    Dorset

                                                        Hood Battalion aha!
My dear Violet,
   Behold! Hoch! εὐοι vive l'Eddie (or somebody). D. Browne comes today.[1]
Oc joins us on Saturday – by last report. So if you were in Blandford on
Sunday, you might catch a glimpse of us. I hope you will be, if you are
going to the front directly....
   ... Oc is in C company: not very distinguished. I am in A. My company
are all stokers: very violent men. My fellow officers come from the South
Pole, mostly. We live in a muddy hell. You cannot imagine the persistence
pervasion & muddiness of the mud. (You can bring a motor up the road a
mile away to take Oc out to dinner.)...
   If you come, do bring a book & an account of the Dynasts.[2] Any book
except Compton Mackenzie & Bridges's poems. I see Beb gazetted. Has
he gone to the Palace? I wish Cys was with us instead of the Queen's
Westminsters. This between platoon drill & a lecture. Please warn me if
you come. I don't want to be duty officer that day. RB

V.A. to Rupert Brooke   *Sunday 20 December*
                                                      10 Downing Street,
                                                       Whitehall, S.W.

My dear Rupert –
   We had such a wonderful Sunday – & I did so long for you to be there.
Mise-en-scène – Walmer moated! crenellated, battlemented, bastioned,
buttressed, littered with sham cannons & neat piles of those trim croquet-
balls (can they ever have been ammunition?) & telescopes & Wellington's
boots – with a whole sea full of ships outside.

---

   [1] (William) Denis Browne (d.1915), a Rugby and Cambridge contemporary, and close friend,
of Rupert Brooke; musician and music critic; joined RND, September 1914; killed in action,
Gallipoli, 4 June 1915.
   [2] Thomas Hardy's epic-drama of the Napoleonic War, *The Dynasts* (3 pts, 1904–8), was
staged at the Kingsway Theatre in London by Harley Granville-Barker, in the winter of 1914–
15.

Personnel Father, me, Bongie[1], Davies (new delightful private secretary), Hugh, Cys, Lord D'Abernon (so far rather grey & uneventful you will think) – supplemented on Sunday by Kitchener & – $\Phi\rho\epsilon\nu\chi^c$ – <u>so</u> secret that I put it in a cypher – the only one I know – & which I pray the able-bodied as a class can't read.[2] Don't breathe it to <u>anyone</u> on pain of having your tongue torn out – he sailed across to see Father.

It was so thrilling – he & K furnished the sharpest contrast imaginable – being one the biggest ruffian & the other the smallest (in stature I mean) gentleman ever born – Φ was amazingly optimistic about things, much more so than either Father or K. He detects great signs of 'strain' in the Germans – says he has taken practically nothing but professors prisoners for the last 3 weeks! It is cheering to think they have already been driven back onto their Raleigh line of reserve. He thought it quite on the cards sudden collapse might take place & the whole thing might be over in April or May without anyone getting anywhere sensational – like Berlin! . . . Goodbye – Yrs Violet

Rupert Brooke to V.A.   *Christmas Day,*
                                                 Friday 25 December
                                    Royal Naval Division, Blandford,
                                                            Dorset

My dear Violet ... Never say we're not a hilarious nation. Christmas Day in the Naval Division is a revelation. The Battalion C.P.O., a very fat man, who has been drunk since dawn, is conducting the band in an Irish jig in the middle of the parade-ground. He can't beat time, but he dances very convincingly. He's slightly like Pelissier. Half my stokers are dancing half-naked in their huts. They spent the night on cheap gin. The surrounding woods are full of lost & sleeping stokers. I expect most of them froze over-night. Pathetic creatures.

Your Walmer week-end sounds too thrilling for belief. I wish I'd been there. But one can't get away from this mud-heap very easily. My throat collapsed again and left me voiceless. I can only communicate with the other world by Morse or Semaphore. Which do you prefer?

[1] At the outbreak of war Bongie was principal private secretary to the prime minister, and though he made enquiries early on about volunteering for the Royal Flying Corps he continued in this post until the fall of the coalition government in December 1916. Asquith placed great reliance upon Bongie and would have been reluctant to part with him.

[2] Violet's rudimentary Greek spells [Sir John] 'French'. Her lax attitude towards secrecy, evident here, was common of London Society during the early stages of the war (see M. and E. Brock (eds.), *H. H. Asquith: Letters to Venetia Stanley*, 419–20).

I've discovered that this is the site of a <u>Roman</u> camp. Does that move you? It overwhelms Ian & me. I gave my platoon the slip yesterday morning (they were out gathering holly): & went a delicious country walk, descanting drops of a poem (don't report me).

> ... 'And drowsy drunken seamen
> Straying belated home,
> Meet with a Latin challenge,
> From sentinels of Rome – '

> 'In dreams they doff their Khaki,
> Put greaves & breast plate on:
> In dreams each leading stoker,
> Turns a centurion – ' etc ...

Good luck for next year, Rupert

Rupert Brooke to V.A.   *Saturday 9 January 1915*
Royal Naval Division, Blandford,
Dorset

My dear Violet,

I'm sitting in the ante room before dinner: & you can't, and I shouldn't like you to, imagine, precisely what that's like. But it's worlds away – universes away – from last Saturday evening, or the almost-as-great happiness of Sunday evening (my poor military brain!)[1] It was fun. Or, <u>was</u> it, at all? Not '<u>was</u> it <u>fun</u>'? but, '<u>was</u> it?' The continuity of this mud is too convincing. I can't imagine that all my evenings since Antwerp weren't in here, and all my mornings on parade, & my afternoons lecturing sleepy, clotheless, embedded stokers. There was a dream of leave, & London, & lovely things. But it was no more: I woke to my servant's voice, 'Six-thirty, and you're orderly officer today, Sir,' and the corpse-like light that precedes these queer green chalky dawns....

The conviction grows that we stay here for months, till the Division's completed. Hell. And many say we then go out in an Army with the Canadians & the Ulstermen. What a fate! And how bored one'll become here. Still, the months may bring another leave.

I must retire to my cabin to write the remainder of my promised sonnets. One more is turning out <u>fairly</u> good. It's rather like developing photographs. Forgive the dreariness of this letter. Shall I ever see you again? Goodnight.   Rupert

---

[1] Brooke had spent the previous weekend with Violet and Oc at Walmer Castle, where there was a large house party.

V.A. to Rupert Brooke   *Monday 11 January*
                                             Walmer Castle, Kent

My dear Rupert – Our swan-revel seems such aeons away – & I am wondering so much about you all – specially (in fact, really only) you & Oc – & longing to hear how you found the mud-heap & Quilter[1] – & whether you have been dry at all since I saw you last – & whether the new road is made – or any new plans about your future? ...

We were <u>flooded</u> with people over Sunday – there was hardly space to plant a pounce table – the McKennae – <u>poisoning</u> the atmosphere within a huge radius; Beb (the half-wit) & his wife Cynthia; Norton (do you know him? an infinitely cultured ex-diplomatic dilettante – half-alive); Winston, Clemmie & Goonie.[2]

W. in marvellous form. I'm afraid his sinister hint about the impending job for the Naval Brigade meant nothing. I urged him to go down & review you but he wants to wait for a frost. We relevé-d you – & both agreed there was strangely little wrong with you. He is anxious we shld. leave Walmer as he says there is real risk there with no anti-aircraft guns – he wld. back himself to pot any given house at Zeebrügge within 24 hours. However the Germans may think Father an asset to them – as we do the Kaiser – & spare us.

A really <u>dead</u> secret – mind you keep it – Bonar Law's brother, the head of their firm, has been caught 'trading with the enemy' & that in the form of supplying <u>Krupps</u> with iron. Isn't it amazing & horrible? Everyone is doing their damnedest to keep it dark – but they seem to think it ultimately must leak out thro' the legal proceedings.[3]

Didn't you think our answer to the American note splendid – & quite unanswerable?[4] I was so glad it was crisp & stiff – & said to Father 'I'm sure one oughtn't to fawn on & slobber over the Americans – it's much better policy to kick them' – to which he replied 'Yes – in the stomach'! How much do you think Derenberg would give one for that?

[1] Lieutenant-Colonel Arnold Quilter (d.1915), ex-Grenadier Guards; commander of the Hood Battalion, RND, 1914–5; killed in action, Gallipoli, 6 May 1915.

[2] Lady Gwendeline Churchill (1885–1941), 'Goonie', Winston's sister-in-law.

[3] The facts became publicly known in May 1915, when two of the partners in the firm William Jacks & Co. were prosecuted for supplying the German armaments manufacturers Krupps with iron. John Law, a third partner, was not held responsible and and was not prosecuted (Robert Blake, *The Unknown Prime Minister*, 257–60).

[4] The American Note of 26 December protested at the effect of the British naval blockade of Germany on American trade. War materials bound for Germany were undoubtedly carried by American vessels, and this prejudiced Asquith against that country. Grey was more realistic, realizing the dependency of the Allies on America for their own munitions (M. and E. Brock (eds.), *H. H. Asquith: Letters to Venetia Stanley*, 346–7; 382).

I have been reading & re-reading your poem – it <u>is</u> good.[1] I love 'Frost, with a gesture, stays the waves that dance.' Every word of the last 6 lines seems to me perfect – 'gone proudly friended' is the only thing I <u>might</u> criticize & that with no certainty. Touches like 'sat alone' – bring home the destruction of an <u>individual</u> extraordinarily poignantly & intimately to me. Please write a <u>lot</u> more.

<u>Wed 13th</u> In London for 2 nights I have just got yr. letter – sent on from Walmer – it was heavenly hearing from you. I have felt such a strong & insistent desire for your society since you returned to Blandford! – present conditions do not offer much scope for its satisfaction . . . .

. . . How I loved our evening – & how I hate the thought of the wetness & flatness of Blandford for you – only – forgive me – but I can't help preferring you to be bored than killed. Can I send you anything such as books or a hot water bottle? it would be quite virile if it had a khaki cover – Oc has got one. Goodbye.   Yrs Violet

I wish Walmer had been just a shade emptier – I felt oddly as if I had never met you before, which is a pity – as I'm never going to meet you again.

Rupert Brooke to V.A.   ***Sunday 24 January***
                    Royal Naval Division, Blandford, Dorset

My dear Violet,   Your letter was a great pleasure. The days have flowed by since: and though I've occasionally had the time, I've never had the mental life to write to you. If you knew how indistinguishable from Quilter (even in robustness!) I'm getting. The only chance of possessing the last muddly drilled-upon corner of one's soul, & entertaining the remotest thin ghost of an idea, is to withdraw to one's cabin, roll up in the brown sleeping-bag, forget that one's Officer of the Day tomorrow, & – write to you.

(Some days later) at that point I slept. And now – after days – & <u>nights</u> of toil, I've deplorably got a cold again.[2] I'm in bed with it, stupid beyond military crassness, irritable, depressed & uncomfortable. And, this time, no chance of you swooping down in a car on Saturday to ravish me away to champagne & sheets & Lady Wimborne & all things light & lovely. My only glimmer of a malingering & unpatriotic hope, is that if I develop (as

---

[1] While staying with Violet at Walmer Castle at the beginning of the month Brooke had copied out for her his sonnet 'The Dead', to which she here refers, one of the five 'war sonnets' published in the new year of 1915.

[2] With reference to his earlier remarks about 'robust' health, Brooke added a marginal note, '*observe the penalty of ὕβρις [hubris]*'.

I so feebly <u>couldn't</u>, before, you remember?) a TEMPERATURE, I shall be packed off out of Camp promptly. They've discovered that no one <u>ever</u> gets better in these miasmic huts. In that case, instead of going through to Rugby, I think I should be wiser to turn Eddie's into [an] R.N.D.M.C. depot, & wheeze there, swathed, in the great chair before the fire. Would you come one afternoon & read Shakespeare to me? I'm sure London's the cure for a bad cold – that they spring from the absence of anything one likes – except exercise – & that to be happy & amused is the remedy....

I don't want a hot water bottle, thanks. My feet are always feverish. But I <u>do</u> want a book. One which is as amusing as Sterne & Jacobs & France & strong as Dr Johnson & lovely as Marvell and the Anthology, & Shakesperian as Shakespeare. Can you find it? It's the only thing that could tempt me to interest enough to read it, this evening.

Forgive my immense stupidity. I'll write when this present cloud lifts. Write to me of you & London.   Rupert.

V.A. to Rupert Brooke   *Monday 1 February*
Walmer Castle, Kent

My dear Rupert – I am <u>so</u> sad that you are feeling wretched – & that I have missed you this whole Sat. to Monday in London....

I was glad to get your letter ... you do write the best of anyone. (Of course I've never heard from Quilter.) After you went to Blandford & the mud swallowed you up again I felt as if you'd dropped thro' a hole in the world – & <u>that</u> without even knowing it was <u>you</u> – just a vague sense of leakage somewhere – located & stanched by the arrival of yr. letter....

Henry James was here 2 Sundays ago – & rather amusing about you & <u>another</u> Rupert Brooke – did you know there was one? also a poet – also a soldier – also at Cambridge (& consequently also presumably thinking 'wog' funny.) I do <u>hope</u> you are the best of the two. H. J. seemed on the whole to think so.

He & Winston were a most incongruous & infelicitous combination – W. never listening to the end of <u>one</u> of his sentences....[1] Yrs   Violet

---

[1] Violet later remembered this disastrous meeting: 'I longed to show Winston off at his very best – but unfortunately he was at his very worst. He had never heard of Henry James & he cld. not think why we all listened with such reverent attention & such misplaced patience to this rather long-winded old man. He disregarded him, he contradicted him, he interrupted him, he showed him no consideration whatsoever.... When Monday morning came & time

Rupert Brooke to V.A.   *Thursday 18 February*
Royal Naval Division, Blandford, Dorset

My dear Violet,

We're 'standing off' this morning, to 'mark & mend'. So, you see, I've time to write. I'm incredibly healthy. You were an angel to me. I've never so much enjoyed being ill. Those last three days at Walmer were heavenly. Did you like them? It was such a moment of peace, against the pleasant excitement of London, & the remoter background of this dream-like war. It seemed a divine & Paradisal interlude, somehow, where hour flowed into hour unmarked by bugles, & never bringing one nearer anything, or further away from anything.

Now I'm three days gone in reality – or this different dream. I came with quite a zest for it, I find with astonishment. Even yesterday – Winston's visit – barely damped me. What a day! Perhaps you'll have heard of it. A real Blandford day of the milder kind, mud rain & a hurricane. First old Paris put the review off, because of the weather (but that was after we'd stood out a battalion of Lears, in the pitiless storm for half an hour).[1] Then Winston turned up & demanded something. We were hurried out to an extemporized performance, plunging through rivers & morasses. It was like a dream. At one point I emerged from the mud, with my platoon, under the wheels of a car, in the midst of a waste. And in the car were what I thought were two children, jumping about clapping their hands shrilling & pointing. It was Eddie & Clemmie. Goonie was there; but I didn't see her. Eddie came to luncheon ... & was divinely civilian. He told us all the jokes from the Times & all the atrocity stories: things we never hear. The wardroom was fascinated by him, & said, in chorus, when he left 'what odd eyebrows'.

It is rumoured Winston was 'pleased', & impressed by our superiority to the other Brigades: & that we shall go out as a Brigade. Which gives us more chance of survival ....

This is the letter of a sublieutenant – as dull as ditchwater. I wish I had even my civilian bright little interest in anything. I'm a machine, a clod, a platoon officer, a Jim Barnes, a tittle, an omicron, a jelly, a dry anatomy, a less-than-protoplasm .... There's a fine sun & a clean wind. When are you coming near, or to, Camp? Come & view my buffalo-like health, your handiwork.   Rupert

---

to say goodbye Henry James drew me aside & speaking in his very slow, deliberate hesitating way ... he said: 'My dear child – it has been a very interesting – er – a very encouraging experience to meet that young man. It has brought home to me very vividly – very forcibly – the limitations by which men of genius purchase their ascendancy over mankind.'

[1] Major-General (Sir) Archibald Paris (1861–1937), cr. KCB, 1916; general officer commanding the RND at Antwerp, Gallipoli, and in France; severely wounded 1916; retired, 1917.

V.A. to Rupert Brooke

Saturday 20 February
Walmer Castle, Kent

My dear Rupert ... I loved getting your letter – & hearing you were well & happy. Happy I want you always to be – & well, nearly always – only sometimes just ill enough to come & stay in that curious inland room – & for me to order your meals & bring you an occasional Mexican handkerchief.

You don't know how I miss talking to you – about 10 times a day the first 3 days I thought of something quite <u>vital</u> to say to you – but even more I miss just having you in the room – like a hyacinth bulb! And seeing things through your eyes as well as my own – you have made me see so many funny & lovely things thro' your lens. 'Hullo ragtime' was the first (& perhaps the greatest) – & 'some bull' comes high in that category – & the way seagulls fly is another. And now I look out of my dull-(ish) eyes at a dull though hectic world....

The Dardanelles began Friday morning early ... 40 ships were engaged – all out of range – the biggest blazing away at the forts, Carden in command.[1] Yesterday alas they had to discontinue the attack temporarily because of bad weather. We got the news about 1.30 at night, there was a great ringing of bells – & pattering down passages. I think it not at all outside the range of possibility that you might be sent out there as reserves later on. I asked for yr. poems at Bumpus's yesterday & was shown an account of them in a catalogue with recommendations by the Times & Spectator 'A rich nature – eager sensuous, brave – & Mr Brooke shows an uncanny' etc etc!!! <u>very</u> funny I thought.

<u>Monday</u> D. St. I have just got here & heard you are <u>going</u> on Sat.[2] I can feel nothing but grey, iced terror for you all – but I know how happy you & Oc will be & try to feel glad for you – it is very difficult. I have wired to Oc asking which day wld. be best to come down & say goodbye or will you be allowed to come here? Tell me if there is anything I can get for you – Violet.

---

[1] Admiral (Sir) Sackville Hamilton Carden (1857–1930), cr. KCMG, 1916. In January the war council authorized a naval attack on the Dardanelles Straits with the Turkish capital, Constantinople, as the ultimate objective. On 19 February the Turkish forts guarding the approaches to the Straits were damaged by Royal Navy bombardment; on 25 February the attack was resumed, and the forts destroyed. This was not by any means the end of Turkish resistance – see below, p. 45.

[2] As part of the plan to seize Constantinople the Naval Division was despatched to the Dardanelles to support the naval operation there. It left on Sunday 28 February 1915.

TWO

Rupert Brooke

February–April 1915

Rupert Brooke's reaction to the news that the Royal Naval Division was to be sent to the Dardanelles was one of unsuppressed excitement. Schooled in the classics, he regarded the prospect of a campaign close to the site of ancient Troy as the subject matter for a latter-day Iliad. *His enthusiasm found a general echo. Maurice Bonham Carter wrote to Violet on the day of departure: 'I think that this expedition is a good solution for the Naval Division from their friends' point of view. It will be amusing for them & I hope not perilous.' The aim of the expedition was to gain control of the Dardanelles Straits, which would lead to the capture of the Turkish capital, Constantinople, and possibly the end of the war for Turkey. Great prizes were on offer, and the operation was widely seen as an attractive alternative to the deadlock on the Western Front. Complacency about the reported military incapacity of the Turks, however, created a misplaced sense of optimism. The Royal Navy proved unable to take control of the Straits, and so the attack aimed at Constantinople had to be pursued through an invasion of the Gallipoli Peninsula instead. The Naval Division played a central role in the brutal campaign that followed, which Brooke did not live to witness. Had he done so it is inconceivable that his reaction to the war would have been unchanged. He had not wanted the conflict, the onset of which had depressed him, but he found in the self-sacrifice of his generation something worthy of expression. Violet later remembered his companionship as 'pure delight ... nothing ever missed him that was beautiful or funny', and this is an image of him that is worth keeping, the image of a poet not of war, but of 'laughter, learnt of friends'.*[1]

---

[1] MBC to VA, 28 February 1915; see Jon Stallworthy, 'Who Was Rupert Brooke?' in *Critical Survey*, volume 2, number 2, 185–193.

Diary – Monday 22 February 1915 – written 22–23 May, in Marseilles

On Monday 22nd Feb – I heard – quite accidentally through Lady Essex at lunch – that the Naval Division were going abroad – Patrick, on laryngitis leave, had telephoned to her that he was ordered back at once – & though both he & she were quite sceptical I somehow felt it was true.[1] I rang up Eddie who confirmed it – & that night at dinner at the Admiralty elicited details from Winston. He was in the throes of a 'low' Influenza – rather piano – & dressed in dark green plush – but thrilled at the prospect of the military expedition & full of plans for landing them in Gallipoli when the teeth of the situation had been drawn by the ships – marching them into Constantinople 'That will make them sit up – the swine who snarled at the Naval Division'. This reflection seems to afford him even more balm than the prospect of the impending downfall of the Ottoman Empire.[2]

He was in very good & characteristic form after dinner – patches of purest nonsense & crudest fun – alternating with really purple breaks of speech & thought. Very amusing about K's psychology & the way he had jockeyed Lord Curzon out of India[3] – 'I would never have resigned. I wld have abandoned my policy if people at home were against it. I would have waived everything. I wld have been studiously uncivil to him in public – but resign – never. I would have waited my time & fought him on some other issue & beaten him. Never resign.' He discussed every aspect of the strategy, military & naval, with zest & suddenly breaking off said quite seriously 'I think a curse should rest on me – because I love this war. I know it's smashing & shattering the lives of thousands every moment – & yet – I can't help it – I enjoy every second of it'.[4] He said (what I have often thought) that when one watches the extraordinarily arbitrary & haphazard way in which death & destruction are meted out by Providence – no guiding principle of justice or expediency apparently at work –

---

[1] Patrick Houston Shaw-Stewart (1888–1917), Balliol contemporary of Charles Lister and Cys Asquith; fellow of All Souls, 1910; joined RND, September 1914; served Gallipoli, 1915; killed in action, France, 30 December 1917.

[2] Churchill had been stung by criticism following the Division's involvement in the unsuccessful defence of Antwerp.

[3] Curzon had resigned as viceroy of India in August 1905 over a dispute involving Kitchener's powers as commander-in-chief of the Indian army.

[4] On 28 July 1914, shortly after he had mobilized the fleet, Churchill had written to Clementine: 'Everything tends towards catastrophe and collapse. I am interested, geared up and happy. Is it not horrible to be built like that? The preparations have a hideous fascination for me. I pray to God to forgive me for such fearful moods of levity. Yet I wd do my best for peace, and nothing would induce me wrongfully to strike the blow ...' (Martin Gilbert, *Churchill*, 268).

one feels more than ever convinced of the unimportance of life. It <u>cannot</u> matter as much as one thinks whether one is alive or dead. The <u>absolute</u> planlessness here makes one suspect a bigger plan elsewhere.

Rupert Brooke to V.A.   *Monday 22 February*
                                          Royal Naval Division, Blandford,
                                                            Dorset

Oh Violet it's too wonderful for belief. I had not imagined Fate could be so benign. I almost suspect her. Perhaps we shall be held in reserve, out of sight, on a choppy sea for two months. Yet even that.

But I'm filled with confident & glorious hopes. I've been looking at the maps. Do you think <u>perhaps</u> the fort on the Asiatic corner will want quelling, & we'll land & come at it from behind & they'll make a sortie & meet us on the plains of Troy? It seems to me strategically so possible. Shall we have a Hospital Base (& won't you manage it!) on Lesbos! Will Hero's Tower crumble under the 15″ guns? Will the sea be polyphloisbic & wine dark & unvintageable (you, of course, know if it is)? Shall I loot Mosaics from St Sophia ... & Turkish delight? & Carpets? Shall we be a Turning Point in History?

Oh, God! I've never been quite so happy in my life, I think. Not quite so <u>pervasively</u> happy; like a stream flowing entirely to one end. I suddenly realise that the ambition of my life has been – since I was two – to go on a military expedition against Constantinople. And when I <u>thought</u> I was hungry, or sleepy, or falling in love, or aching to write a poem – <u>that</u> was what I really, blindly, wanted.

This is nonsense. Goodnight. I loved your letter. But even more the news (in an arrangementary telegram of Eddie's) that I may see you on Thursday. I think I shall wire to you tomorrow for a book. I'm very tired, with equipping my platoon, Rupert

Diary – Thursday 25 to Saturday 27 February – written 22–23 May, in Marseilles

[Thursday 25th] ... a brilliant sun sparkling on frost – air like crystal – we started early for the review. Clemmie & I got on horseback & cantered down the lines. They were drawn up in battalions on a lovely sweep of downland – Oc – Rupert – Johnny Dodge & Patrick standing like rock before their men.[1] Rupert looked heroic – & others less well-proportioned,

---

[1] John Bigelow ('Johnny') Dodge (1894–1960); born in New York; joined Hood Battalion of

extremely funny. When Winston & 'the Board' – that phantom body – full of a mystic significance but whose functions are as difficult to detect & apportion as those of the Trinity – had gone by, the formations melted out of their military rigour & we talked to them – I feeling rather high up on my horse, & the superiority of cavalry over infantry. I thanked my <u>stars</u> I was riding & not plodding with the others in the clay.[1] Poor little Eddie was heartbroken at losing the 'Hood' – & a rather pathetic figure – George Peel galloping up & down very affairé but 'serviable' – Goonie drooping deliciously – Lady Wimborne firmly ensconced on a motor box – Margot nipping feverishly in a very short Russian ballet skirt & snowboots.[2]

Clemmie & I cantered about till the King came – then there was a formal march past – they all looked quite splendid sweeping past in battalion formation – & I had a great thrill when the Hood came on preceded by its silver band – & Quilter roared like a lion '<u>Eyes Rrright</u>' & all their faces turning. I hadn't realized before what a different colour men of the same race can be – Patrick was arsenic green – Oc primrose – Kelly slate-grey – Rupert carnation pink – Denis Browne the most lovely mellow Giorgione reddish-brown.[3] The King looked rather mesquin in a Khaki coat with a fur-collar – but was more forthcoming & agréable than I have ever known him – making quite gratuitous & <u>good</u> conversation.

After a second march past we rode up to lunch with the Hood. I sat next Freyberg – Rupert's company commander who had fought under Villa in Mexico – left there on the outbreak of war & struggled back across America to find himself penniless at San Francisco – where a swimming competition was fortunately just going to take place. He won this & got home on his prize money. In Antwerp he got caught on a live rail. He quite frankly

RND, September 1914; at Antwerp, Gallipoli, and France (1916–19; DSO, DSC); naturalized British subject, June 1915; afterwards a member of the London stock exchange, and served 1939–45 war; according to Brooke, 'a young and very charming American ... who turned up to fight "for the right"' (Christopher Hassall, *Rupert Brooke*, 474).

[1] Violet and Clementine's riding was witnessed, critically, by Margot: 'they neither of them looked quite horsemen to my professional eye. Violet with a bad flat wide brimmed hat & her pretty hair very untidy & unbusiness-like & elbows tight to her sides. (She has never had a lesson & does not like being coached or criticized in anything poor darling.) Clemmy with perfect hat & tie but shortish stirrup & toe down. Both of them riding with short reins wh. gives a curiously amateur look to all riders men and women ...' (Diary of Margot Asquith, vol. October 1914-May 1915).

[2] (Arthur) George (Villiers) Peel (1868–1956), temporary major, Royal Marines, 1915; Liberal MP for Spalding, Lincolnshire, 1917–18. Lady Wimborne was probably Cornelia, widow of the first Baron Wimborne; she was then aged sixty-eight, and in need of 'ensconcing' on such a cold day.

[3] Frederick Septimus ('Cleg') Kelly (1881–1916), musician; born in Sydney; an Oxford contemporary of Oc Asquith; three times winner of the Diamond Sculls at Henley; joined RND, 1914; wounded, June 1915; killed in action, Beaucort-sur-Ancre, 13 November 1916.

wants to make his own fortune as well as England's out of the war. On my other side I had Kelly – Rupert opposite – every form of delicacy such as grapefruit – marron glacés – foie gras & champagne had been procured by Patrick. It somehow wasn't <u>quite</u> the fun it ought to have been. I had a tightening of the heart throughout....

[Saturday 27th] I came up for the last time ... the camp had disintegrated a good deal overnight. Great waggons packed with blankets & packing cases lay across the road – becalmed in a sea of mud – mules still rioted – stokers tore about – officers whistled – thick formations of men stood about here & there – being counted & equipped. Oc was doing up his little green canvas suite of bath-chair etc. – & we had a table laid in his little deal room & lunched together. Rupert joined us later – <u>very</u> tired – & the bubble of excitement momentarily gone off him. He had had his hair cut very short – by order – & his sun-helmet was too small for him & wldn't go on.

He complained bitterly that <u>Kelly</u> had got hold of his sonnets & was spreading them among his mess-mates. He gave me all his things to take back with me – futurist curtains & books – I also took Oc's & Patrick's. Patrick I have never liked so much as I did this time – he was much less aggressively on the crest of the wave than I have ever known him – rather gentler & humbler & generally more muted – possibly merely the result of a poisoned throat. Rupert was marched off before I left. I said goodbye to Oc & motored back ... then bed & wrote a long letter to Rupert.

V.A. to Rupert Brooke

early morning,
Sunday 28 February
Lake House, Hamworthy, Poole

I write you a letter to read on the high seas – because you will get none from anyone for so long – & because it will give me a little illusion, a very pale one, of going on talking to you after you're gone. After-you're-gone is a bleak thought – the green fades from the grass whenever I think it – & the sky comes down & turns into a ceiling – but yet I feel – (with the best attempt at disinterested emotion I've ever made) – <u>glad</u> – (which is not for one moment to be confused with <u>happy</u>) that you're going. For it is so <u>very</u> 'mete & right' for you (of all people) so to do.

I see it all for you – the journey – cold at first & uncomfortable – sometimes calmly & sometimes feverishly speculative – then one morning the gliding into strange – bright seas – strewn with shining islands – then the first sound of our ship's guns – the landing on a tongue of foreign soil – & you leading your whiskered stoker children against the Paynims. The <u>luck</u> of there being such an adventure left in the world! & you there to have it – things usually happen to the wrong people. And yet – you didn't really <u>need</u> the Dardanelles. Patrick needed them – <u>badly</u> – & Kelly. But you cld. have done without.

When I have asked myself in (rare) moments of introspection in the last 2 months – <u>why</u> I loved being with you so – one of the reasons I disentangled from a skein of unanalysable & indefinable ones was that I have <u>never</u> spent a moment with you anywhere – not at a pounce table – or a music hall – or a Downing St lunch! – that wasn't permeated by & shot through with <u>colour</u> – & a sense of <u>adventure</u> – the feeling one lives for – the Dardanelles in fact. I <u>knew</u> you hadn't got it – the very reverse in fact – you felt with luck warm – a little less comfortable probably than if I'd been Eddie, a little comfier perhaps than if I'd been Flora Guest – principally <u>warm</u> – but that didn't matter to me. I was too happy to have any vanity about it. . . .

I know you'll do glorious things – & I want them for you – & I suppose it's no good saying don't get killed. There are so many excellent reasons why you shouldn't – much better ones than my minding. But I should mind. Write to me please uncensored letters & be business like about sending them off & if anything shld. <u>happen</u> – like wound or illness to you or Oc let me know & if possible come. I shall write often again of course – but it is so uncertain when & whether you'll get my letters. Goodbye beloved Rupert – bless & keep you – if thoughts could save you should be very safe – Always yrs, V

Written in bed – very late & rather tearfully – so forgive possible 'soppiness' which morning light may reveal. I start at crow of cock for Bristol.

Diary – Sunday 28 February – written 22–23 May, in Marseilles

I started off before 8 in Dunn's car driven by Beston – picked up Agnes Peel at the Portman's House near Blandford & started for Avonmouth.[1] We motored back through lovely sleepy Hardy country – stone villages & walls all-overgrown with moss & lichen. . . . We went thro' Bristol & out the other side along the Severn, winding thro' steep banks – then a little town began, built round the docks – a great door opened & let us through & I saw huge watery pans in which great ships stood – moored – & alongside on the quays a confusion of soldiers – trucks mules – packing-cases gangways – sound & movement. I went past several ships till I reached the

---

[1] The Hood Battalion left its base at Blandford on the evening of Saturday 27 February, boarding the *Grantully Castle* at Avonmouth docks the next day; the ship was a Union Castle liner, converted into a troop transport.

Grantully Castle. I waited till I saw a Hood cap & then asked for Oc.

He was on board shaving – then Denis Browne came up & took charge of me – said he wld. go for Oc. . . . [Rupert] just managed to exchange his watch with Kelly & was free till 4. Oc came & we went off to an hôtel Montagu had recommended in the environs of Bristol. . . . After lunch Rupert's main idea as usual was to get as warm as possible – he is a real lizard – & we coiled ourselves almost in the fire-place – till it was time to go out & have a prescription made up for Patrick's throat which was more than usually poisonous that day. The streets had a very grey empty Sunday look – & the chemist had to be knocked up with some difficulty. Rupert & I sat outside talking – it was impossible to go near any of the things one was thinking of – & difficult to keep up a bright cardboard interchange. He showed me a lovely little new poem of his, beginning 'When colour is gone home into the eyes'. He said in his usual intensely quite modest-eyed way – '"A" (I) think the first line's perfectly divine'. . . .

. . . I went on board the transport with them. It was a not bad Union Castle boat & they were only 2 in a cabin. I went in to see poor Patrick who was lying in his bunk amongst cough mixtures & bandages looking I must confess rather septic. I dawdled about with them – with a terrible pre-operation feeling – the suspended knife seemed just above us all – then the dull muffled siren booms & hoots began, charged with finality, & I knew it was falling. Rupert walked with me along the narrow crowded decks – down the little plank stairs – then I said goodbye to him. I knew by his eyes that <u>he</u> felt sure we should never see each other again.

Oc took me over the gangway – & we talked a few moments feverishly – he gave me messages & telegrams to send – then another imperious hoot & he had to hurry back. The gangway was raised & the ship moved slowly out – the Hood trumpeters playing a salute on their silver trumpets as it passed the mouth of the harbour. The decks were densely crowded with splendid Khaki figures with happy confident faces – the thought of the Athenian expedition against Syracuse flashed irresistibly thro' my mind.[1] I saw Oc's face to the last – Rupert's not at all – I think he purposely stayed away.

I watched them till they became a blur – then picked my way mistily among ropes & packing cases back along the quays. I met George Peel who spoke to me – it was like a voice in a dream. I said rather dazedly aloud – to Beston – I wonder when the next train to London goes – & a stranger with a time-table told me. I had just time to catch it. I had a

---

[1] The Athenian expedition against Sicily, launched during the Peloponnesian War, was synonymous with disaster; set against a background of political discord at home, it ended with the complete destruction of the invading force (October 413).

carriage to myself & tried to read the 'Triumph of Time' – through tears.[1]
Bongie met me. He & I & Cys spent the evening together.

Rupert Brooke to V.A.   ***Thursday 4 March***
                    S.S. Grantully Castle, *bound for Malta*

Four days out.

All day we've been just out of sight of land, thirty or forty miles away – out of sight, but in smell. There was something earthly in the air, & warm – like the consciousness of a presence in the dark – the wind had something Andalusian in it. It wasn't that wall of scent and invisible blossom & essential spring that knocks you flat, quite suddenly, as you've come round some unseen corner in the atmosphere, fifty miles out from a South Sea Island. But it <u>was</u> the good smell of land – & of Spain, too! And Spain I've never seen, & never shall see maybe. All day I sat & strained my eyes to see, over the horizon, orange groves & Moorish buildings & dark eyed beauties & guitars & fountains & a golden darkness. But the curve of the world lay between us. . . .

Another day; <u>off Africa</u>. My dear, I don't know when, after Malta, I shall be able to get a letter through. We're in the dreamiest, most utter, most Trustful, ignorance of what's to come. Some even say it'll all be over before we get there. I hope not: & certainly think not. Impossible. I rather figure us scrapping forlornly in some corner of the Troad for years & years. Everyone will forget all about us. We shan't even be told when peace is declared. . . .

One's so entirely 'surrounded by the horizon of the day', even – perhaps more – in this odd little respite from war. I've not the strength of mind to withdraw myself from the current, & think. Perhaps I never have, even in peace. I'm a hand-to-mouth liver, God help me.

It has been very good being with you. I had rather be with you than with anyone in the world. And you've been very kind to me. Do not care much what happens to me or what I do. When I give thought to it at all, I <u>hate</u> people – people I like – to care for me. I'm selfish. And nothing but harm ever seems to have come of it, in the past.

I don't know. In some moods that thought seems wrong. Generally right. I don't know the truth about that – or about anything. But somewhere, I think, there's bad luck about me. There's a very bright sun, & a lot of comedy in the world; so perhaps there's some point in my not getting shot. But also there's point in my getting shot. Anyway, you're very good to me. The Staff-Captain is going to seal up the mail-bag. Goodbye. Rupert

---

[1] *The Triumph of Time*, or *Pandosto*, an Elizabethan prose romance written by Robert Greene, and now best known as the source for *The Winter's Tale*.

V.A. to Rupert Brooke

Friday 12 March
10 Downing Street, Whitehall,
S.W.

I was so <u>afraid</u> of parting from you all that last strange day in Bristol – that when we'd said goodbye I felt as one does after an operation – 'at any rate <u>that's</u> final – it will be better now' – but it wasn't – it was worse – & I longed so terribly just to <u>see</u> you again once – as the ship moved away – & I mistily gazed & gazed searching all the Khaki bodies for your face – & not finding it. They were <u>all</u> other people – they were none of them you – not one!...

... I must try & tell you anything I've heard about your prospects 'as a unit'! First – Ian Hamilton is going to command you – & it is by him that I am sending this letter as being the most likely way of reaching you quickly....[1] His going was Father's idea – & I was passionately keen he shld while it hung in the balance (K. had suggested Leslie Rundle who starved the Guards Brigade in the S. African war – but this is <u>deadly</u> secret).[2] He is very brave & gallant & has just the right dash of irregularity I think for this expedition (of soul I mean – of course he is otherwise regular to the finger tips) – he has a really romantic Crusading feeling about it & has seen more fighting than almost any other soldier in the Army....

I had two long talks with Ian Hamilton about it – one rather uncomfortable one when he was aching to go but hadn't been sent for yet – & the other last night when it was clinched. I put you & Oc very prominently on the tapis both times – & he swore to look after you both – which I hope means the maximum opportunity with the minimum danger. He said he wld. love to have you (Rupert) on his staff but I expect this is the last thing you wld. enjoy.[3]

The authorities still seem to think it quite possible that if all goes well at sea Turkish resistance might collapse & that there may be no serious fighting only a formal entry into Constantinople – but if there <u>is</u> to be

---

[1] General Sir Ian Standish Monteith Hamilton (1853–1947), chief of staff to Kitchener in the Boer War; commander MEF, 1915. Asquith wrote to Venetia Stanley, September 1914: 'He is a sanguine enthusiastic person, with a good deal of *superficial* charm ... but there is too much feather in his brain' (M. and E. Brock (eds), *H.H. Asquith: Letters to Venetia Stanley*, 257). Violet's letter did not leave with Hamilton, who departed for the Dardanelles at once following his appointment on 12 March.

[2] General Sir (Henry Macleod) Leslie Rundle (1856–1934), governor and commander-in-chief of Malta, 1909-15; nicknamed 'Sir Leisurely Trundle', possibly because of the delays associated with his command during the Boer War.

[3] Violet had met Hamilton shortly before his appointment was confirmed: 'He said the first thing he wld. do if he was sent wld. be to offer Rupert a place on the staff. This from literary freemasonry!' Hamilton's *The Ballad of Hadji, and other poems* had appeared in 1892.

any bloodshed I shall move Heaven & earth to be there to stanch it on a yacht....

... Grey as life seems now my prevailing feeling when I think of you is one of deep thankfulness to Fate – for the many patches of pure delight it has given me in the last few months – a 'scented store' – to feed on in my heart with thanksgiving (as the Communion service says). Bless & keep you safe, always – all-ways Yrs Violet

V.A. to Rupert Brooke   *Wednesday 31 March*
                                             10 Downing Street,
                                             Whitehall, S.W.

Getting my first, stampless, Expeditionary letter from you was <u>heavenly</u> – & such a perfect one....[1] I wonder if there is anything you want to hear from here. Nothing happens....

Gradually every man with the (rough) average number of limbs & faculties is being sucked out to the war – & I feel as if I were sitting on a beach at low tide amongst old boots & wreckage. Those who have remained have acquired an artificially inflated value – Montagu & Duff Cooper the only two men left in London – from whom in peace women with aesthetic sensibilities shuddered & shrank – now swoon on divans surrounded by troops of odalisques – Ruby [Peto] – Diana [Manners] – Viola [Tree] – Katharine – Nancy [Cunard] – Ly Essex – Ava Astor etc. etc. etc. A <u>real</u> Scheherazade – the favourite negroes creeping out when the white men are gone to the war.

Raymond may go any day now (he wld have gone last week only he hadn't finished his musquetry) & K & I are seriously thinking of going into a Hospital when he does. It is rather a weak thing to do as I regard the prospect with genuine abhorrence – but life outside is becoming impossible & also there is a real want of nurses – appeals in the paper – which I <u>can't</u> <u>help</u> seeing – though I clap the glass on to my blind eye every time. I'm afraid it may be one of the regrettable cases in which 'one <u>ought</u> to go' – (though <u>hating</u> to lose oneself – more than one's ever hated losing anyone else)....

You tell me not to care what happens to you. If it is for my sake – I have made my hedonistic calculus & am ready to take the risk of yr. bad luck & its possible reflex action on me. But if it is for yours – if I don't fill any hole in your life – & if you are bothered by the responsibility – for it is a responsibility always – of people who care for you – then I can do as you say. As to being 'selfish' – what good is one's <u>unselfishness</u> to anybody –

---

[1] Rupert's letter of 4 March, above.

but a leper? (or God perhaps?) <u>Promise</u> <u>never</u> to do anything unselfish in yr. relations with me. You don't know what a delicious warmth it gave me when you said you liked being with me. You rarely give one warmth – but more <u>light</u> than anyone in the world -- -- --

Just back from St. Paul's where I heard the Bach Passion Music <u>in the dome</u> with Cys. You don't know how lovely it was. Leaning right up against a golden rail & gazing over & down through mists into a dim vastness where men – like insects crawled & prayed amongst yellow candle flames – & the sound <u>leaping</u> up in shrill bursts as from a choir of (Paradise Lost) archangels – & then wandering softly round & round – in echoes & re-echoes. I longed for you to be there. Shall I soon get another letter from you? How I wish you were here & I was here. As it is you're there & I'm nowhere.

Goodbye – love from Violet

Diary – March – written 22–23 May, in Marseilles

I have never had such a sense of living in a vacuum as I did during March – letters from Rupert & Oc seemed the only real things – there was some disagreement between W. & K. as to the sending out of the 29th Division – a necessity from the very first. . . .[1] K. is like a screw who feels economical so long as he is spending money slowly – he doesn't like parting with his reserves – & held the 29th up using the bad Russian knock in the East as a pretext. This delayed things considerably. Talking to him one night after dinner I said: 'If the Dardanelles come off W. will deserve full & almost <u>sole</u> credit. He has shown great courage in taking the responsibility – rather over the head of Fisher & the experts.' K – indignantly 'Not at all I was always <u>strongly</u> in favour of it. No one who has seen as much of the East as I have cld. fail to appreciate its importance'. I said as I was glad to hear it – as if it went wrong he wld. be there to support & stand by W. (I don't see him doing it!)

W. speaks sanguinely of the whole thing being a picnic – & Oc writes afraid they will get there too late – but Hankey thinks it will be a tough job. He has maintained from the very first that it cldn't be done without men. . . .

[Friday 5 March] I went down to Walmer with Father Edgar & B on

---

[1] The 18,000-strong 29th Division was assigned to the Dardanelles campaign by the war council on 16 February. On 19 February Kitchener argued that it should be held back to cover the western front, after Russian setbacks in the east, and he only released the Division on 10 March. The delay severely limited the options available in the Dardanelles (M. and E. Brock (eds), *H. H. Asquith: Letters to Venetia Stanley*, 373–5, 438–50; and see below, p. 45).

Friday night ... we had a rather interesting talk after dinner about peace-terms.[1] Father said that his own instinct was against <u>any</u> territorial acquisitions on our part – we had as much as we cld. manage well as it was – & ought not financially to burden ourselves with any more liabilities. On the other hand if Russia & France proved too greedy we might be obliged to take a wedge somewhere in self-defence. ...

The Russians getting Constantinople seemed to be regarded with equanimity – a home for the Turks in Asia was under consideration & the fate of Palestine was some difficulty. Herbert Samuel issued a strong minute to the Cabinet urging that it be made over to the Jews for their repatriation – to which [Edwin] Montagu replied with a really witty wail (which was <u>not</u> circulated) imploring that the Jews shld. be given no abiding home or dwelling place lest it be taken as an excuse by the other nations for driving them out! & representing the unfittedness of himself & his race-mates to lead a peaceful rural life tending flocks under olive trees in the cedars of Lebanon.

... Father & Montagu had a rather interesting talk one night late in the Pillar room – about ammunition.[2] K. has certainly been culpably apathetic about it ... & besides that being generally passive & secretive & treating the whole thing rather as his private show & no one else's business much. The idea on the tapis is to set up a Committee including Lloyd George (& possibly AJB) also to deal with munitions. ... Father anticipated, however, strong opposition to the idea from Kitchener, in which he was quite right. It was finally put through – almost a month later ... & only after a squalid bogus intrigue against Father had been cooked up by the Tory press – & exploded with some difficulty by ours ... & also after a fishwife row had taken place between Ll.G. & McKenna in Father's presence.[3]

He was much amused when they came to him hand in hand a few days

[1] Anticipating victory in the Dardanelles, Britain and France recognized future Russian control over the Straits and Constantinople, in return for territorial gains elsewhere. This was the most important of the 'secret treaties' made by the Allies during the war (A. J. P. Taylor, *Struggle for Mastery*, 542).

[2] Probably at Walmer Castle, Saturday 20 March. The heavy expenditure of shells on the western front and problems in production led to a 'shell shortage' in April, potentially damaging to Asquith's government. Earlier in March decisions had been taken to create a new munitions committee, with executive powers to expedite production, but this threatened to encroach on Kitchener's control of the war office and was resisted by him (M. and E. Brock (eds), *H. H. Asquith: Letters to Venetia Stanley*, 460–2).

[3] The row took place on 30 March. Asquith wrote to Venetia Stanley that he had quietened the pair by threatening to resign: 'I wish you cd. have seen them! Their mutual anger dissolved like a frost under a sudden thaw: and they both with a united voice exclaimed: "The day you leave that chair, the rest of us disappear, never to return!" And I am sure they meant it. Wasn't it rather a fine moment for me?' (M. and E. Brock (eds), *H. H. Asquith: Letters to Venetia Stanley*, 522–4).

later to press upon him a scheme for buying the brewers out & taking over
the public houses by the State. Father thinks this scheme costly & quite
impracticable as well as uncalled for in the present situation. Ll.G. on the
other hand sees drink at the bottom of all the munition shortage – &
wishes for the most drastic remedy possible. The poor King was finally
victimized, a letter being wrung from him by Ll.G. publicly pledging
himself – if the Govt. thought wise – to touch no alcohol till the end of
the war. In this course he was followed by Lord K. – whose temper has
since been very trying, Haldane – who looks on the verge of complete
collapse in consequence, & (I think) Runciman.[1]

Father gave a pathetic account of his visit to Windsor shortly after the
temperance régime set in – almost complete silence prevailed at meals –
broken only by Margot's hunting stories – 'She'd had her jorum of brandy
before coming down' Father wld. explain. The poor Queen who usually
enjoys a small bottle of sparkling moselle said to Father, looking wistfully
at her substituted Perrier, 'We have been carted'.

We spent a peaceful Easter at the Wharf – guests R. K. Evan & Montagu.[2]
I had divine walks along the river with R & K – & went over with K. on
Sunday afternoon to see the Masefields.[3] Only she was there with an
odious feminist called Mrs Sanger who said 'when people ask me how I
teach Sex-Questions I say keep a cat'. We had been very far from asking
her. We had the usual earnest talk with poor 'Con' – Russia, Kropotkin[4]
etc. all the problems which had confronted one for the first time at 12
thrashed heavily & conscientiously out.

V.A. to Arthur Asquith   *Tuesday 6 April*
                                                  10 Downing Street,
                                                  Whitehall, S.W.

Beloved Artie – I so loved getting your letter from Lemnos & was much
amused by the utterly futile & <u>imbecile</u> attempt at excision by the censor.
Do in future write under cover to Father as they could hardly wish to
censor your communications with him....

     ... The last thing I heard was that land operations were going to be

---

[1] Walter Runciman (1870–1949), cr. Baron, 1933; Viscount, 1937; Liberal MP 1902–31;
Liberal National, 1931–7; president of the board of trade, 1914–16, 1931–7; lord president,
1938–9.

[2] Evan Charteris (1864–1940), barrister, and uncle of Cynthia Asquith.

[3] John (1878–1967) and Constance 'Con' Masefield were friends of Violet, and lived at
Cholsey in Berkshire, about seven miles from the Wharf.

[4] Prince Peter Kropotkin (1842–1921), eminent Russian theorist of anarchism.

begun on 15th April (my birthday) simultaneously with another attack by the ships. I wonder if this means that you will be brought into action then? It all seems so remote & incredible. I can only realize in waves which ebb & flow that a continuous & organized series of attacks on your life will be made from then onwards! I wonder how much you realize it yourself & how excited you all are about it.

I am writing to you at the Club & enclose a letter which they wish me to send you – they send one out monthly now to all the different members who have enlisted. Price has grown nearly a foot & put on a stone in 3 months – Ronald Glover has joined the Fusiliers at the age of $15\frac{1}{2}$! – & was taken. They all seem to love being in the Army & will loathe being herded back into their stuffy professions after the war.

Father was very much amused by your telegram – he has not yet given up his own liquor & doesn't I believe intend to do so.[1] This course should make him very popular with one strata of his fellow countrymen. Poor Bongie is terribly harassed by the Press who bombard him for an expression of intention & can only reply lamely 'It isn't quite settled yet.' I must stop this now as Eddie has just told me a pouch is going at cock-crow to-morrow. I'm afraid it's very dull – but there isn't a syllable of news.

All my love darling, from V –

Rupert Brooke to V.A.   *Friday 9 April*
                                             Port Said, Egypt

I'll try to write you a good account of things sometime – when there's anything to write about. Or when, & even, I'm just a bit more energetically cree-ative about the various shades & degrees of non-happening through which we loiter. But just now – for these six days – I've been a victim to the sun. He struck me down, all unaware, the day before Sir Ian inspected us. I lay, racked by headache & diarrhoea, under an awning on the sand, while the stokers trudged past. Afterwards, Sir Ian came to see me a moment.[2] A notable meeting, it was generally felt: our greatest poet-soldier & our greatest soldier-poet. We talked blank verse. He looked very

---

[1] Oc had sent a telegram on behalf of the Naval Division reading 'Reported spread of temperance alarms and amazes us. Stand fast.' (M. and E. Brock (eds.), *H. H. Asquith: Letters to Venetia Stanley*, 525, n. 1).

[2] Hamilton recalled: 'Asked Brooke to join my personal Staff ... as enabling me to keep an eye on the most distinguished of the Georgians. Young Brooke replied, as a *preux chevalier* would naturally reply, – he realised the privileges he was foregoing, but he felt bound to do the landing shoulder-to-shoulder with his comrades. He looked extraordinarily handsome, quite a knightly presence, stretched out there on the sand, with the only world that counts at his feet' (Sir Ian Hamilton, *Gallipoli Diary*, i, 71).

worn & white-haired. I thought him a little fearful – not <u>fearful</u>, but less than cock-sure – about the job. Later, they took me out of Camp to this hotel, where I've been cool & starving & convalescent.... I wished you were here: with your experience of internal disease in Egypt & of my morose invalid manner. Couldn't you have cured – or, certainly, <u>healed</u> – me more swiftly?

Anyhow, here I am, well up on that difficult slope that leads from arrowroot past chicken broth, by rice puddings, to eggs in milk, & so to eggs, & boiled fish, & finally (they say) chicken & fruit & even real meat. But that is still beyond the next crest. On! on! But while I shall be well, I think, for our first thrust into the fray (unless senility overtakes me), I shall be able to give my Turk, at the utmost, a kitten's tap. A diet of arrowroot does not build up violence. I am as weak as a pacifist. The better able to survey & note, maybe....

We're a gay enough little party in the Hood. A softened Colonel. Oc is well & patient. Charles I like more as I see him more. I didn't realise what an awareness & subtlety he concealed under that equine madness. Imagine what an extraordinary, an unprecedented, conglomeration of sound Oc & I & Denis Browne put up with, when you learn that Patrick with his loud titter, Cleg Kelly with his whinny, & Charles with his great neigh, are all in the same tent. The sound from it frights the Egyptian night, & sends the ghosts of Antony & the gypsy scudding away across the sand....

... I've written nothing. I've made two or three faint attempts at an Ode or Threnody: a very serene affair, full of major chords & layer outlooks, like an English lawn at sunset. But I haven't, even loitering in the Aegean, even on our world-forgotten laughing little island, had just the necessary detachment. I suppose it won't be finished. Perhaps if I'm wounded......

I fasten my eyes on the horizon for your hospital ship. Bring out a delicious lot of books. But I fear none of us'll be wounded for a long long time yet. Ever Rupert

M.B.C. to V.A.   *Friday 16 April*
                                                    10 Downing Street,
                                                    Whitehall, S.W.

My Beloved, You have been quite divinely sweet to me these last days & have filled me with happiness. The immediate result is that I am missing you more than ever – when you are away I have a feeling of loss & emptiness of which I am always conscious. The second result is that I want more and more to marry you and find the delay increasingly hard to bear with patience....

... There appears to have been a bit of a breeze between K & LG in the

Cabinet today over Munitions. Your father told me that LG really said some things that he would find it impossible to forgive had they been said to him. It is a great pity as in the main I think he is right, but it makes it very difficult for your father to set things straight. Of course the Committee cannot work unless K & the war office work with it & K has apparently an insuperable objection to giving it any detailed information whatever. Darling I do wish that I were with you.... B

Diary – Sunday 18 April – written 22–23 May, in Marseilles

... we had our last Walmer Sunday – rather a good one. Ld Crewe – whose amazing <u>informality</u> of mind, skulking within that wooden formal manner, astonishes one every time afresh. Soveral – brilliant, gentian-blue & brimming over with the International gossip of the last 50 years. John Morley – frail & exquisite – poisonously malignant (about war etc.) – tenuous-voiced – it was like hearing the last notes of a Stradivarius....[1] I had marvellous à trois both nights after dinner with J. Morley & Soveral. Of course they cldn't keep off the war & J.M. proceeded to reveal a depth of wrongness & bitterness about it I hadn't suspected him of. At the time he resigned I imagined it had been mainly from age overfatigue & the feeling that this wasn't the kind of thing he had ever believed in or gone in for & it was too late to begin now.[2]

But now he believes – or pretends to – that the whole Cabinet had been let in about the Entente – kept in the dark & deceived – that Belgium was only a pretext – we shld have to have backed up France anyhow – that '<u>All Wars</u> are <u>evitable</u>'.[3] This was the great axiom he harped on. Soveral was

[1] Robert Crewe-Milnes (1858–1945), succeeded 1885 as 2nd Baron Houghton; earl of Crewe, 1895; Marquess, 1911; secretary of state for India, 1910–15. Marquis de Soveral (1862–1922), Portuguese ambassador in London, and a popular figure in Edwardian society. John Morley (1838–1923), cr. Viscount, 1908; lord president, 1910–14; resigned in protest against British entry into the European war, 3 August 1914.

[2] 'According to Charles Hobhouse, Morley informed the cabinet: "You all know my views, those of a lifetime, I cannot renounce and if you persevere in intervention, I cannot return to this room". As he had said the same thing about once a month for 3 years, no one took this very seriously'. (Edward David (ed.), *Inside Asquith's Cabinet*, 179–80).

[3] Morley was arguing that secret military 'conversations' between the British and French staffs, beginning in 1906, committed Britain to the defence of France regardless of the German invasion of Belgium. Sir Edward Grey, the author of British policy, could not agree. While he believed that Britain should not 'stand aside' in August 1914, and was ready to resign if it did, he had made absolutely clear in his dealings with the French that the decision for war lay with parliament alone. In his view the invasion of Belgium provided a *casus belli* for the majority of Britons, and not a pretext for their government. (Viscount Grey of Fallodon, *Twenty-Five Years*, i, 312).

excellent & took him on really well. It was strange [to] have our national ethics defended by a Portugee. J.M. became so caught up in the wheels of his Anti-English case as to be involved in a pro-German one – & before he knew where he was, defending their conduct in 1870 – saying the French had caused the war.... The hot championing of, & sentimental weakness for, Germany entertained by the extreme left anti-militarist Liberals is one of their strangest & most astonishing qualities at this moment.

It is such a paradox that the dreamers & idealists – the Arthur Ponsonbys,[1] J. Morleys etc. – should at this juncture take up such a materialistic point of view – saying 'the principle may be vital – it may be at stake – but we haven't the right to squander our national resources or shed <u>our</u> national blood in safeguarding it'. As against that the crasser genus – the materialists who have never stood for much except concrete expediency – with one voice say 'what matter if we lose <u>all</u> our money – if <u>all</u> our sons are killed? we must keep our word'....

His (J.M.'s) intellectual courtesy is extraordinary. I have never met anyone so appreciative or delightful to talk to. But his vanity is extreme. As Simon said to me 'he is always eavesdropping on what the world is saying about him – & it was hard for him, when after his exit he stood in the wings listening for the audience's demonstration, to receive not one bouquet – & not even a boo'. (It's true.) His exit from the stage passed quite unnoticed & I think he is wounded by it.[2]

Eddie Marsh to V.A.   *Friday 23 April*
                                                Admiralty, Whitehall

Dearest Violet,[3] I have very alarming news from Mudros – a telegram to say that our beloved Rupert is in the French hospital ship Duguay Trouin with septicaemia – 'condition very grave'. Winston has telegraphed asking to be kept fully informed. I will tell you what comes. I have telegraphed to his mother. The suspense will be hard. Yours Eddie

[1] Arthur Augustus Ponsonby (1871–1946), cr. Baron Shulbrede, 1930; radical Liberal MP for Stirling Burghs, 1908–18, who later migrated to the Labour Party.

[2] Morley had expected more defections from the cabinet than occurred. Only three other ministers planned on 2 August to resign with him – John Burns (1858–1943), Sir John Simon and Earl Beauchamp (1872–1938). The latter two changed their minds after news had arrived of the German ultimatum to Belgium, and a 'strong appeal' had been made to them by Asquith. They resumed their places in cabinet, Beauchamp even succeeding Morley as lord president of the council (5 August).

[3] Violet was staying at the Vice Regal Lodge in Dublin.

M.B.C. to V.A.   *Friday 23 April*
10 Downing Street,
Whitehall, S.W.

Beloved. Eddy told me of Rupert's death tonight. You are minding it very much I know, as indeed must everyone who knew him.[1] Eddy naturally is stricken by it.... Your father minds it very much. We have heard nothing except that he was on a hospital ship at Lemnos.

Eddy thinks that he may very likely have gone with the rest from Alexandria before he was really well, not wishing to be left out of it. He was said to be ill of septicaemia which means blood poisoning, but how contracted we do not know. The [naval] operations have been postponed owing to bad weather & there is no news.

I have been thinking of you all day, beloved. Bless & comfort you. B.

Arthur Asquith to V.A.   *Friday 23 to Sunday 25 April*
S.S. **Grantully Castle,**
bound for Gallipoli

My dear Violet, We may be off at any time now, so I will set down the details of Rupert's case....

Friday April 2nd, we were reviewed by Sir Ian Hamilton. Rupert had been sick twice in the night, had a headache & was altogether out of sorts. He did not get up for the Review, but lay on his camp-bed under a green canvas awning. It was a hot day. Sir Ian came to see him, and I now know – he did not tell us – asked him to join his Staff. Rupert refused. Sir Ian's parting words to our Colonel were 'Mind you take care of him: his loss would be a national loss'....

Last <u>Tuesday, April 20th</u>, we all landed on this island [Skyros] for a Divisional field day. It was a hot sunny day. Rupert had been Officer of the Watch for four hours of the preceding night. He left the ship with his men about 8.a.m. and was walking or sitting in the sun 'till 5 or 6 p.m. Charles, Freyberg and I swam off to the ship, about one mile, in the evening. Rupert was on the beach and said to me he wished he could join us but he did not feel strong enough yet....

Next morning, Wed. 21st, I found him in bed in his cabin. His upper lip was a good deal swollen: and he complained of pains in his back and head.... Yesterday, Thursday, morning, R.'s temperature was higher and the swelling was extending up the side of his face, and down the side of

---

[1] A telegram from Eddie Marsh late that evening broke to Violet the news that Rupert Brooke had died at five o'clock in the afternoon, local time.

his neck.... There was a well-equipped French hospital ship, the Duguay Trouin, lying in our bay. The Doctors arranged for him to be moved there....

[Saturday 24 April] Next morning, Friday 23rd, Denis and I were over at the Duguay Trouin soon after nine. McCracken came with us.[1] We found the French surgeons just going to operate....

Denis and I agreed each to stay with Rupert half the day. He was unconscious – at least, twice, when I spoke to him, he seemed to make an effort in his throat to speak: but no words came. I left Denis with him.... When I came back after lunch he had taken a turn for the worse. A wireless inquiry came from Sir Ian: the chief French surgeon told me to answer 'Etat désespéré'. We were to sail at dawn next day: I left Denis with him, and went off to make alternative arrangements in case he died before or after our sailing. By the time I returned, 5.15. p.m., he had been dead half an hour.

He died unconsciously and without pain, after an illness lasting less than three days. We buried him last night at about eleven o'clock. Charles Lister commanded the digging party: Patrick the firing party: they and the bearers were all Petty Officers and men of his Company. The French provided a fairly solid plain oak coffin, on which I burned his name and the date with a hot iron. Denis and Charles had chosen the most lovely spot for his grave: in a small grove of wild olive trees, up an unfrequented glen, about three quarters of a mile from the sea: the moon thinly veiled: a man carrying a plain wooden cross and a lantern leading the way: some other lanterns glimmering: the scent of wild thyme: a dim group of French and English officers: the three volleys: the Last Post.

Then some of us stayed and covered his grave with big lumps of white and pinkish-white marble. We had little time. We agreed that whoever survived would come back and make a wall round the grave.[2] Denis and I have been sifting Rupert's effects all day today.

We left Skyros at dawn today – or rather yesterday – it is 1.15 a.m. [Sunday 25 April] – I must go to bed. Our escorting battleships open fire on the Turks at 5 a.m. today. Love. Yours Oc.

P.S. Charles has no compass, and was very fond of Rupert: so I have handed on to him the compass you gave Rupert. I hope this was right? Ys Oc

---

[1] W.J. McCracken, staff-surgeon to Hood battalion, RND; DSO in France, 1916 (bar, 1917).

[2] Of the five who decorated the grave, only Oc Asquith and Bernard Freyberg survived: Denis Browne and Charles Lister died at Gallipoli that summer, while 'Cleg' Kelly was killed in France the following year.

Diary – Friday 23 to Sunday 25 April – written 22–23 May, in Marseilles

[At the Vice Regal Lodge, Dublin] ... Just before dinner I got a wire from Eddie saying 'there is bad news of Rupert – he is ill with blood-poisoning on French hospital ship. Condition grave. I am hoping & will wire you directly I hear more.' I felt frozen with terror at first & then – I don't know why – a causeless reaction of relief – & sort of wave of trust that Life wld. recognize Rupert's preciousness – that Fate itself wld. recoil before so cruel a platitude as his death wld. be. I sent off 2 wires to Eddie & Bongie – then dressed & came down to dinner. It was like having to take part in a play till 11 – & not really very difficult....

... [after dinner] the telephone bell rang.... I stood in Ly Scott's room waiting & with a half sense that it might be for me. Nathan came out with a very grave face & said gently 'It's bad news I'm afraid' – I asked – is he <u>dead</u>? He said 'yes.'[1]

I went back next evening – after a nightmare day of trying to live outwardly decently....

Bongie that angel was up & waiting whitely about the house for me. I lay down & he came up to see me. He said nothing but his love & his dumb, solid, minding, strong presence comforted me a little. I think it is the best selfish sorrow I have ever had – it was not only for me I minded but for the world – that this perfect thing should be no more – this being without compare. It was like Spring being dead – or music – or flowers – like seeing some marvellous vase shattered before one's eyes. And I wanted so much much more of him for myself. Never to be able to dip into his mind – never to be able to look into his eyes again.

I went alone to St Paul's at 12. It rained all day. After tea I saw Eddie – quite broken poor darling. It is the first thing that has given me control – the feeling that he was feeling it <u>for</u> me – it somehow seemed to lighten the weight & dull the edge.

---

[1] Lady Scott (1878–1947), widow of the Antarctic explorer, and from 1915 a close friend of H. H. Asquith. Lieutenant-Colonel Sir Matthew Nathan (1862–1939), under-secretary to the lord-lieutenant of Ireland, 1914–16. Margot wrote to Oc: 'Poor Violet has felt Rupert's death deeply & has <u>behaved very well</u>. Every-one here has been saddened by this death ...' (2 May 1915).

Mrs Brooke to V.A.   ***Wednesday 28 April***
                                                 24 Bilton Road, Rugby

My dear Miss Asquith

I am not going to <u>thank</u> you for your letter for I know your sorrow too is very great, you want no thanks for telling me. Mine is more than I can express to anyone. Knowing him as you did you can understand what a son he was. I have had two great sorrows before this in both of which Rupert was my one consoler – 8 years ago my eldest son died away from home.... Rupert did everything possible to help. Then 5 years ago my husband died unexpectedly; again Rupert did everything. Now I feel as if I must have him to console me in this terrible grief. He spoke to me often of you & also of your brother 'Oc'. He was so pleased to have him in the same battalion.

I have had 4 letters from him since he left England; all but the last were full of delight in his surroundings.... I mean presently to see about photographs & you certainly shall have one. The last that I know of are what Schell took just before he went [on] his tour. I don't think he was taken in Khaki, we did talk of it but he put it off & personally I never cared for him in Khaki though others did.[1]

My Rupert hated the idea of war; I shall never forget his misery when he came home last July 31. He had been dining at your house the night before & had felt very strongly that war was on us; he wouldn't go anywhere & sat almost in silence. I think Antwerp impressed him enormously & helped to write those sonnets which I have always been happy to think that he finished & sent off from my room on Jan.1. He sat with me all morning doing them.

I must not write more. I do hope if you hear anything from your brother that you think would interest me you will let me hear it. You will be feeling anxious on his account now. Perhaps my Rupert has been spared much by going now. His tender heart would have been torn in pieces if he had seen his friends wounded or killed.

                    With love, ever yours, M R Brooke

---

[1] Brooke was photographed by the American photographer Sherrill Schell in London in April 1913, shortly before he left for America, and was also pictured with his battalion at Blandford: see the illustrations below.

THREE

Gallipoli

April–June 1915

The campaign to capture Constantinople and knock Turkey out of the war was conceived in December 1914 as a combined naval and military operation. There were however difficulties in raising an army for a major land campaign early in 1915. When Churchill argued that a naval force alone could accomplish the mission he was too readily believed, and on 28 January the war council approved his plan of a naval attempt to force the Dardanelles Straits. Gradually, though, general recognition grew that a substantial military force was needed, if only to consolidate the navy's gains. There were long delays before this force was finally sent, on 16 March, only two days before the naval attack began. When this attack was suspended on the same day, after three warships were lost to mines, there was no option but to wait. It took a month before the army was ready to mount an invasion, and in this time the Turks trebled their strength on the peninsula, offering fierce resistance to the landings of Sunday 25 April. Only at great cost were beachheads established at Cape Helles in the extreme south, and at Anzac Cove fifteen miles to the north. Ironically, given the original hopes for a breakthrough at Gallipoli, both sides now entrenched and there was a repetition of the deadlock on the western front, with its attendant high casualties. By the time of the Allied withdrawal that winter more than 140,000 men had died. Much criticism has subsequently been levelled at Churchill over the failure of Gallipoli. In reality few of the planners emerge with any credit, in stark contrast to the soldiers themselves, who were given an almost impossible mission.

Arthur Asquith to V.A.   **Thursday 29 April 1915**
S.S. Grantully Castle, *off Gallipoli*

Dearest Vizie ... Of our Division only the unhappy Anson took part in the first landing of the 29th Division at the Point [Cape Helles]. We hear nothing but praise of their behaviour. Meanwhile we were being used for a bloodless demonstration, threatening Bulair and the mainland opposite.

You will probably have heard of Freyberg's swim. The first idea was to land a platoon to make a noise and to make the Turks think we were really going to attack them there. Freyberg had spoken to me before of swimming ashore to reconnoitre: it was to have been a two man 'stunt'; and I was to have been his companion. Charles also wanted to come: and Cleg. We had some long practice swims in the bay at Skyros. Freyberg put his idea to the Staff: they thought what a good plan to let him swim ashore and light flares, with a destroyer behind to do some firing, instead of sending a platoon to almost certain death. The Colonel would not be persuaded into risking another officer: so Freyberg swam alone, pulling a little canvas-boat full of flares, food and a revolver.[1] The boat, which was to take him within $\frac{1}{2}$ mile off shore, misjudged his distance from the shore, and he swam his hardest from 1 a.m.–2 a.m. – perhaps two miles – bitterly cold – and a dolphin gave him a fright by coming along side: he saw its fin within reach, and mistook it for a shark: a shark had been seen about. From the bridge of this ship we, at 2 a.m. saw his flares 5 miles away: then heard a spitting of machine-guns, and gunfire. The flashes seemed to us to come from the shore: really it turned out to be only the destroyer's fire which we had seen. He swam safely back and picked up his boat again.[2]

That was early morning of the 26th. That evening we sailed South again, and breakfasted 1 a.m. 27th morning as we had been told we were to be landed immediately in support of the 29th Division's landing. We arrived off the point to find we were not wanted yet & all through a beautiful hot day watched the bombardment of Krithia and Achi Baba Hill, and the gradual advance of our men. It was a wonderful sight.

That was Tuesday: the same evening we were sent North as we were told we might be wanted to support the Australians.[3] They had landed at the base of a great hill, about 900 ft. high covered with low scrub except where there are great sandy cliffs: gorges every 50 yards or so down the face: a narrow strip of beach at its foot. This hill commands the surrounding country. The Australians seem to have made a most gallant landing: and charged straight up the hill – like looseplay of a Rugby football scrum a man told me who saw it.... Two battalions of Marines were landed to support them: there was great dissatisfaction in this Battalion: people began to wonder whether we were to be spectators for ever. Tonight we

[1] 'When the plan was accepted Freyberg then asked that Oc Asquith accompany him. This [Colonel] Quilter refused, saying that he was prepared to risk the life of one New Zealander, but was damned if he was going to be held responsible for drowning the son of the Prime Minister!' (Paul Freyberg, *Bernard Freyberg*, 54).

[2] For this feat Freyberg was awarded the DSO, the first of many high honours for bravery.

[3] The Australian and New Zealand Army Corps landed at Ari Burnu, 'Anzac Cove', a cape beneath the Chunuk Bair heights. It was about a mile to the north of the intended landing place at Gaba Tepe, which offered much greater strategic potential.

have been moved back to the point, and we really are going to land at last. We hope to take part tomorrow in the storming of Achi Baba: but I never count on anything coming off now 'till it has actually happened.

Collins' battalion is disembarking at present.[1] You cannot conceive anything more spectacular than the scene outside tonight. A reddish moon, quite full, and a bigger fleet of warships and transports than I have ever seen, lying off this Point. Two hospital ships – green brilliance from end to end: a lull in the shelling. It was almost too Earls' Court.

I think we shall have a very hard time, and probably want more troops. Accounts of the first landing of the 29th Division are thrilling: the first hundred to rush at the barbed wire killed to a man: second hundred ditto: third hundred over and up the cliff. . . .

I have been busy censoring men's letters: it brings home the responsibility of having even 50 of them on one's hands. But I feel happily fatalistic about it all. Poor Rupert; to have died as he did and without seeing all this and taking part in it. Love to all. Ys Oc.

Diary – Friday 7 to Monday 17 May, written 22–23 May, in Marseilles

[Friday 7 May] . . . as I was having my bath, Margot rushed in with a telegram in her hand making loud sobbing noises & saying 'He's not dead! he's not dead! he's not dead.' I of course concluded that Oc tho' not killed was in an all but hopeless condition & was infinitely relieved to find a rather satisfactory telegram from Ian Hamilton saying 'wounded in knee no loss to life or limb'.[2] We afterwards heard that tho' it had gone right thro' the knee the bullet had miraculously missed the bone.

I went off that afternoon to the Masefields for the night. He met me at the station & we motored from Cholsey in divine evening sunlight. Lollingdon was looking perfect – very world-forgotten tucked into its fold of downland. The cocks & hens seemed to have multiplied enormously since I was there last. Jan was as usual – gentle, melancholy & exquisitely flavoured. We went out after dinner & walked along the chalky road up onto the downs – past wonderfully smelling brierbushes. We talked a lot of Rupert. Masefield feels very strongly that he cldn't have lived long –

---

[1] Lieutenant-Colonel G. G. Collins, commander of the Howe Battalion.

[2] Margot was annoyed that Violet took this so calmly: 'Henry came into the bedroom in his dressing gown his eyes streaming with tears holding a telegram in his hand. . . . I saw Henry in front of me & felt sure Oc had been killed. . . . I ran to tell Violet who was in her bath poor darling! she was surprised more than moved. Surprised that I cd. feel emotion over a mere escape & almost put about that I had frightened her, tho' she too adores Oc – "Goodness I thought by yr. face & manner he was dead! you gave me an awful fright!"' (Diary of Margot Asquith, vol. of October 1914–May 1915).

'his hold on life was never a sure one'. He wants to write something about him & wants me to do so too....

Masefield & I agreed that Rupert was essentially undynamic – he <u>exhaled</u> his work – it blossomed on him naturally – he was never travailing or convulsed by the work of creation.....

He [Masefield] thought one shld. pay a scanty toll to death – which surprised me rather as I shld. have suspected him of a brooding fidelity to the past. You shld. wring the pith & marrow out of every moment of the present. He admitted Rupert had no 'magic' for him. Yeats had – but he had broken with Yeats as not having a very delicate conception of friendship – by which I suspect that he crabbed Mrs M. I dropped him at Bridges & then flew back to find Lloyd George & Rufus arriving at home.[1]

We had rather an amusing Sunday [9 May] with them [at Downing Street] – Ll.G. in marvellous form. Much speculation as to whether the loss of the Lusitania wld. lead to America coming in – & if so how much good she wld. be to us.[2] It was mostly agreed she cld. organize munition making on a huge scale & have a large army ready for next year. Ll.G.'s estimate of duration was more than a year more....

Monday I had arranged to go over to France with Venetia who was going into the Norman Hospital. Since Rupert's death life at home had become intolerable to me & I thought seriously of joining Rachel Dudley at Wimereux. My idea was to go over for a week – see the place & conditions as I cld. never bear to commit myself finally to any prospect I hadn't visualized – & then come home with my mind made up – for aprons caps outfit etc....

Oc's wound & my desire to go out to him threw my French plans into chaos. It was difficult to discover quite where he was – & whether I might miss him on the way if I started at once.... [on] Tuesday evg. we heard definitely he wld. not be sent home so I made hasty arrangements to sail Sat. from Marseilles on a Japanese ship. It involved a terrible rush – being photographed for passport etc. ... trying in vain to find a shady hat – & Thursday morning [14 May] Coates being ill, & forbidden by Parky to start, & no other maid in the house having the nerve to travel with me, <u>Father also wishing me to stay</u>, I put off for a week.[3]

[1] Sir Rufus Isaacs (1860–1935), 1st Baron Reading, 1914; lord chief justice of England, 1913–21; a lifelong friend of the Asquiths.

[2] The British liner *Lusitania* was torpedoed off southern Ireland by a U-boat on 7 May, with the loss of 1,198 lives, 124 of them American. The ship was carrying American munitions to Britain. The United States did not join the war for almost another two years.

[3] Coates was Violet's maid, and Parkinson ('Parky') the Asquith family doctor.

The Montagu marriage and the May 1915 Coalition

In mid-May Violet's father faced setbacks in his public and personal affairs that combined to make one of the most unhappy periods in his life. On Wednesday 12th he learned that Venetia Stanley, with whom he was in love, was to marry his protégé Edwin Montagu. Beyond his immediate family these were the two people to whom he was closest. He had not suspected their affair and news of the engagement came as a hurtful surprise. Asquith had come to rely greatly on the solace of Venetia's company, and he was deprived of her love at a time when he most needed it. Two days later on Friday 14th Lord Fisher, the first sea lord, literally walked away from the admiralty over a disagreement with his chief, Churchill. This precipitated a crisis that led to the end of the Liberal government. Armed with the knowledge of Fisher's resignation, and backed by Lloyd George, Bonar Law demanded a Coalition government. Asquith had little option but to agree. Violet witnessed his distress and was deeply angry with Edwin and Venetia for adding so heavily to his sorrows. She was also shocked that Venetia was prepared to convert to Judaism in order to marry Edwin, who would otherwise lose the income that he derived from his father's will. At a time when their friends were 'fighting muddledly enough for some idea called England' it seemed impossible that Venetia could thus 'renounce England and Christianity'. Relations between these once close friends were never properly restored. Against this troubled background she decided at long last to marry Bongie, her mainstay in so many crises. She confided this secret to her father before leaving to visit the wounded Oc in a hospital in Alexandria.[1]

[*diary continued*] Curious & disturbing news reached us on Wed. evening of Montagu's engagement to Venetia. Montagu came round to say goodbye to me on Wed. evening after Club etc. – I knew something was up – & half suspected what had happened. He told me of it with extraordinary calm – leaning against the mantelpiece in Micky's room. I am bound to confess that the thought of it – much as I love him – & clearly as I recognize his points – filled me with horror.

The reasons against are too obvious to require definition – & I had reason to believe from things she has said to me in the past that she was fully alive to them. M.'s physical repulsiveness to me is such that I wld. lightly leap from the top story of Queen Anne's Mansions – or

---

[1] Of the effect of the personal crisis on the political, see Roy Jenkins, *Asquith*, 358–66; M. and E. Brock (eds), *H. H. Asquith: Letters to Venetia Stanley*, 595–9; for criticism of Violet over the Montagu marriage, see John Jolliffe (ed), *Raymond Asquith: Life and Letters*, 202.

the Eiffel Tower itself to avoid the lightest contact – the thought of <u>any</u> erotic amenities with him is enough to freeze one's blood. Apart from this he is not only very unlike an Englishman – or indeed a European – but also extraordinarily unlike a man. Father once defined him as a 'bundle of moods & symptoms'. He is a little more than this – but he has no robustness, virility, courage, physical competency – he is devoured by hypochondria – which if it does not spring from a diseased body must indicate a very unhealthy mind. As against this he has imagination, ambition, fire in his stomach (my favourite quality!) & real generosity & powers of devotion. A better friend than lover I shld. say....

Apart from one's personal almost nervous recoil at the prospect I cldn't help regarding it as an unambitious & disappointing solution for Venetia's life. She is désoeuvrée & bored by her milieu – she wants a 'cadre' for her life – not being a spider who spins her own web. She loves the scope which money & interest give her for making happiness for others – this has always been her own principal & favourite occupation. M. gives her all this – but at what a price....

... I asked M. about the religious difficulty – he replied 'we can get round that'. I have since learned that by getting round it – he meant V. going through it. This shocked me to the marrow. To renounce England & Xianity – even if one has never held it – at the dead bidding of foul old Swaythling & to secure his filthy 10,000 £ a year[1] – for <u>that</u> to renounce one's religion & take on a new one – become a <u>Jew</u> – seems to me the most impossibly, squalidly cynical antic.

It is true that Venetia believes nothing – has no spiritual 'apprehension' whatever – but she then is not entitled to masquerade as a believing Jew.... I saw her Thursday morning – without knowing then of this aspect of the case. She seemed quite calm – rather cheerful than happy – admitted she felt no 'glow' about it & used one phrase which haunted me 'there was nothing else much there'. I cannot help feeling she wld. have done anything else if there had been....

[Saturday 15 May] We went in the morning to Geoffrey Howard's wedding.... When Father had signed the register & we got back he called me & told me a most astonishing piece of news in these words – 'Fisher has levanted'. He had simply <u>run away</u> from the Admiralty – leaving his post, his work etc. – pulling down all the blinds of his London house, & leaving a red herring trail in the direction of Scotland.[2] Grave as the

---

[1] Much later in life Violet struck through the words '– scraped up discreditably in some Ghetto or other –' which came at this point.

[2] Fisher's letter of resignation to Churchill, delivered 15 May, ended 'I am off to Scotland at once so as to avoid all questionings'. He was later discovered in the Charing Cross Hotel, a short distance from the admiralty.

situation was Father cldn't help laughing at its extraordinary comic aspects. Masterton expected him to be making for France & was out after him with a troop of beagles scouring the Continental railway stations & expresses[1] – Lloyd George was off on a another track & Bongie on a 3rd. We (F. & I.) were to have driven down to the Wharf Sat. afternoon – so imagine our despair as we sat thro' hours of glorious sunshine waiting. Finally however he – Fisher – was caught – carried in in one of the retriever's mouths & dropped bloodshot & panting at the door of the Cabinet room! Father had armed the beagles with a paper saying 'Lord Fisher in the name of the King I command you to return to your post'! This writ was served on him! Father spent about an hour in conversation with him – he was very mellow & friendly but said he found W. quite impossible to work with. He was always doing things without consulting him (F) – was overbearing etc. etc.

Father told him that if he wished to resign he must do so in the proper way & put his reasons for doing so in writing. This I have no doubt will tax him severely. Personally I suspect him of inspiring the recent poisonous press campaign against W. . . . & right & left giving the impression that he had been from the outset opposed to the Dardanelles, had fought it tooth & nail & been overridden. The truth being that though he was never keen about it he didn't lift up his voice against it in the War Council – signed every order for it with his own hand – & if it had come off at the start wld have claimed his full share of credit for it. It wld then have been 'the Fisher touch'.[2] I consider he has behaved in a lower – more cowardly and more unworthy way over this than any Englishman since the War. Winston may have been exasperating to work with but F. had no right to desert him at this juncture. It was his post of duty – & he ran away from sheer funk. . . .

Sunday morning I drove with Father to see Puffin – we talked mostly of M. & V.[3] It is so wonderful to feel he really needs me & that I make a difference to him (I was deeply moved by meeting him coming away from my bedroom last week in London one night late – having left a little note on my pillow saying 'don't go away from me now – I need you'). Bongie came down after lunch – having spent the morning with the King in a low blue turned down collar & golfing things – bless him! The King had

[1] James Masterton-Smith (1878–1938), private secretary to the first lord of the admiralty, 1908–17.

[2] At the war council meeting of 28 January, at which approval was given for Churchill's Dardanelles plan, Asquith recalled that Fisher kept 'an obstinate and ominous silence', though the plan was 'warmly supported by Kitchener and Grey, & enthusiastically by A.J.B.' (M. and E. Brock (eds), *H. H. Asquith: Letters to Venetia Stanley*, 405).

[3] The Asquiths had driven to the Wharf, Sutton Courtenay, late on Saturday, where they stayed until the Monday morning.

been very anxious to discuss W.O. affairs which aren't going too smoothly either – K & French being constantly at loggerheads. The King is a strong Kitchenerite & wld like him to be made Commander-in-Chief & have military authority over French. Bongie said he (the King) talked <u>incessantly</u> the whole time & he had to be constantly interrupting.

McKenna had telephoned [that] he was driving down at 5.30 – so we (B & I) were in rather a pother when Masterton rang up about 5.30 to say Winston wanted to come & was then starting. We didn't much want them to coincide – & told Masterton to try & postpone & delay him by hook or crook.

Bongie & I then went out for a little walk down the bridlepath to Abingdon – sat in a meadow with our backs to a tree & picked armfuls of marsh marigolds. When we came back the McKennae were there ! Pamela sitting in neat blue serge at tea – McK. closeted with Father upstairs & Prince Paul of Servia loose in the garden![1] I had a longish talk with him – & gathered that they dreaded being absorbed by Russia more than anything & hoped to goodness we shld. keep Constantinople if we got it (not much hope I'm afraid !) – also, that the Grand Duke Nicholas was an awful old Knurd & debauchee & he had constantly carried him home dead-drunk at night![2] The McKennae were tucked up in their motor & speeded off & then I went out with Edgar & Bongie in a boat for half an hour's relaxation after this & when we returned Winston was standing at the bottom of the lawn on the river's brink looking like Napoleon at St. Helena. I walked up & down with him in my dressing gown later on while the others were dressing for dinner. He was very low I thought poor dear.

I asked him if he knew he was on the edge of a volcano in his relations with Fisher – he said no – they had always got on perfectly well – differed on no principle – he had always supposed him perfectly loyal etc. <u>Poor</u> Winston – there is a very naïve disarming trustfulness about him – he is quite insensitive to climatic conditions. Poor Clemmie was actually a good deal upset & this fateful Sunday closed with their departure – & Bongie's after dinner. I motored up with Father next morning [17 May] – he saw Bonar Law before lunch.

I went to the play with Edgar & Cys. . . . When I got in I heard Father wanted to speak to me. I went into the Cabinet room. He was sitting at the table writing – with a <u>heavy</u> look of unhappiness I have rarely seen on his face before. It rent me. Open beside him on the table was a letter from

---

[1] Prince Paul Karageorgevitch of Serbia (Violet uses the older spelling) had arrived in London on 5 May in a private capacity.

[2] Grand Duke Nicholas (1856–1929), Russian commander-in-chief; by 'Knurd' Violet means 'drunk' (i.e. drunk spelt backwards).

Haldane. I had a sudden flash of knowledge. 'Father is it a Coalition?' – 'I'm afraid so.' We both sat there in despair. 'All this butchery I've got to do.' '<u>Must</u> poor Haldane go?'[1] 'Yes – one must harden one's heart about it all.' 'Was there <u>no</u> other way out?' 'No – we cldn't have had a public brawl between W. & Fisher at this moment – with Italy on the brink of coming in. Besides things aren't very happy at the W.O. either – K & French can't get on.'

We sat on & talked. I implored him not to have Ld. Curzon in – mischief making & swollen headed & I shld. think not wanted by either side. He said before I went to bed 'this has been the unhappiest week of my life'. I believe it has.[2]

Diary – Wednesday 19 to Thursday 20 May – written 22–23 May, in Marseilles

[Wednesday 19th] ... Father made a statement about Coalition – which was received in black & angry gloom by the supporters of both sides. I had to rush off directly afterwards ... but met Winston in the passage – he took me into his room.

He sat down on a chair – as I have never seen him, really despairing for the moment – with no rebellion or anger even left. He never even abused Fisher – simply said 'I'm finished'. I bubbled with bromide protestations – but he waved them aside 'No – I'm done. What I want above all things is to take some active part in beating the Germans. But I can't – it's being taken from me. I'd go out to the front at once – but these soldiers are so stuffy – they wldn't like my being given anything of a command. No I'm finished.'

Then quite at the end he said – very gently & not really reproachfully 'I think yr. Father might perhaps have stuck to me – with Wilson & the Board – <u>if</u> there was going to be a Coalition.[3] If there wasn't – it was another matter – party capital cld. have been made. But with a Coalition – I think he might have done it.'[4]

I felt heart-broken for him – for he has done his very damnedest. One

---

[1] Re-reading her diary in the 1960s Violet inserted two sentences here, which she attributed to her father: '<u>I</u> feel <u>strongly</u> tempted to resign. This would lead to a general break-up'.

[2] Violet added in the 1960s, 'I have never seen him nearer throwing in his hand.'

[3] Sir Arthur Knyvet Wilson (1842–1921), 3rd Bt, 1919; retired as first sea lord, 1912; returned to admiralty at Churchill's behest to assist first sea lord, 1914. Churchill proposed that Wilson be Fisher's replacement, and in this he had the support of the admiralty board.

[4] There was implacable Unionist opposition to Churchill continuing at the admiralty, which was communicated to him by Bonar Law on 21 May (Martin Gilbert, *Churchill*, 316–20).

thing he said however I cldn't help smiling at. It could so well have been used 'in evidence against him'. Speaking of Fisher & his ingratitude – W. said quite ingenuously: 'That's why I took him – because I knew he was <u>old</u> & <u>weak</u> – & that I shld be able to keep things in my own hands. My plans – that's what I'm anxious about – my plans – that they shld. be carried out if I go.' He also said he thought the Coalition 'in a dangerous condition now as the Tories were trying to make the Cabinet a political vantage ground & <u>not</u> a non-political perfect war-machine.'

... Edgar came in to see me after dinner – & we talked about the situation etc. then I went down to see Wu – & was just in the middle of, & at a rather heated moment in, a conversation about Venetia's embracing of the Jewish faith when we were interrupted by Margot. For once in his life Wu talked a good deal of rot – pretending that there were only two alternatives – for V. to become a Jewess or else to break off the engagement & that he had tried to break it off that afternoon, <u>had</u> broken it off in fact, & then become re-engaged because they had both discovered that they cldn't exist for 10 minutes without one another etc. He reiterated again & again how passionately in love with him Venetia was – I can't think how she has made him feel so sure of this. He waved away the money issue saying it was not <u>that</u> he minded losing, but estrangement from his people. It is the first time he has shown anything but abhorrence of them to me.

I went in to see Father who told me with tears of a wonderful scene in the House that afternoon. After his statement he was told that all the cream of the party, who were meeting in a room upstairs, were in open revolt at the Coalition – wldn't stand it at any price & were passing hot resolutions against it – saying it was the 2 Tories in the Cabinet W. & K. who had brought us to ruin as it was.

Father went up to them & asked every one of them to hold up their hands as a mark that he was addressing them in strictest confidence. He then made a personal appeal to them to support him – in this course which he hated as much as any of them. He said 'I can't tell you the truth. I can only ask you to trust me. I can only ask you to believe me when I say that this course was an absolutely necessary one. I can only appeal to you to stand by me as you have always done in the past'. He said they were all in tears – they cheered him to the echo & backed him to the last man. It was a very wonderful personal triumph & he was deeply moved by it.[1]

---

[1] Charles Hobhouse recalled that Asquith was summoned to this meeting by Oswald Partington (1872–1935), Liberal whip, who had grown alarmed at its angry mood: 'With great difficulty he induced him [HHA] to attend the gathering, but in an address of great tact and cunning, for there was as much of the one as of the other, he completely placated the angry assembly' (Edward David (ed.), *Inside Asquith's Cabinet*, 245–6).

He came up into my bedroom later on & talked to me till nearly 3 about every sort of thing politics – Venetia – Margot. Poor darling he said: 'I have sometimes walked up & down that room till I felt as tho' I were going mad. When one needed rest to have a thing like the Morning Post leader flung at one – all the obvious reasons for & against things more controversially put even than by one's colleagues'. Venetia rested him from all this. We spoke to my own affairs. He was infinitely wonderful. No two people have ever so completely & perfectly understood one another – been so inside one another as he & I. I felt it a great wrench leaving him – but I have made all my plans now & Oc will be expecting me.

I left very early the next morning Thursday 20th. It was grey & drizzling – Margot & Bongie came to see me off. . . .

V.A. to M.B.C.   *early morning*
Wednesday 19 May
10 Downing Street,
Whitehall, S.W.

Dearest –

One line of goodbye to post to you before I leave England – I felt a great wrench of parting at my heart as I faced you over that chasm – & a great wave of committal. You know me well enough to know that I am already wondering how long it will persist – but there it is for the moment – & perhaps for life.[1]

Bless you for all you do for me & are to me. I shall be very homesick away from you. Egypt somehow feels so much farther away now than in peace – but I am right to go I think & see Oc before he plunges back into that cauldron of horror at Gallipoli – & if I can start my Office successfully I shall feel something has been done by me worth doing.[2]

Take care of yourself for my sake – take no risks of accidents – don't oversmoke – go to bed early – ride or try & take some form of early morning exercise during the summer – I'm sure you ought to with yr. athletic body. Send me all the bouquet of the papers & gossip & forward 90 per cent of my correspondence either to the Hôtel Majestic or the Agency, Alexandria. Try & protect Father from worry & pad him with as much duvet as possible. God bless & keep you, Yr V.

---

[1] Violet refers to her secret engagement to Bongie, made shortly before her departure.

[2] Violet had undertaken, on behalf of the admiralty, to set up in Alexandria an information bureau that would collate details of Royal Naval casualties in the region.

M.B.C. to V.A. *Thursday 20 May*
10 Downing Street,
Whitehall, S.W.

Beloved. You gave me a solid foundation of happiness on which to rest during the dreary weeks that you are away but do not dally on your homecoming. Your father needs you & so do I most bitterly. Please telegraph as soon as you reach Egypt. I have had another busy day & shall be very glad when everything is settled & we can return to something like our normal life which will certainly seem like a holiday. As far as I know not much progress has been made though I think it is clear that neither W.S.C. nor F. can stay at the Admiralty. W. is struggling hard against such a decision, which shows how little he grasps the situation. Meanwhile we are getting resolutions from Liberal MPs against his inclusion in the Cabinet at all. They think that he is the author not merely of this crisis but also of the Curragh crisis too.[1] Poor man I am sorry for him for he is on tenterhooks. . . .

Darling be happy & do not forget me in the newness of your life. I love you so. B.

M.B.C. to V.A. *Friday 21 May*
10 Downing Street,
Whitehall, S.W.

Beloved. It is a little difficult for me so to date events in my mind, so that I may be sure what you know and what you do not. At first as you know the Tories would have been content with about six members of the Cabinet but now they have stiffened in their demands and ask for their numerical proportion at least. . . . Haldane I fear goes, the Tories appear to insist on this and your father is not going to fight it. Grey minds his exclusion bitterly, so does the King who takes a very right view of his merits. It makes one wonder what would happen if your father were to put his foot down.[2] I suppose he thinks that once having undertaken to form a

---

[1] In March 1914 Churchill became the standard bearer of the government's Home Rule bill, then entering its final stages in parliament. His involvement further intensified Unionist opposition to the measure, the depth of which was made clear by an incipient rebellion of army officers at the Curragh garrison in southern Ireland at the end of the month.

[2] Haldane had been educated in Göttingen, spoke German fluently, had a passion for Hegel, a sheepdog named 'Kaiser' and had once unguardedly described Germany as his 'spiritual home'. He thus became the victim of anti-German prejudice during the war. The Unionists demanded his exclusion from the coalition, and Asquith acquiesced, 'sadly and self-critically, but relatively easily' (Roy Jenkins, *Asquith*, 362).

Coalition Government he must go through with it on lines which give it the most favourable chance of working. Winston of course poor devil has been struggling hard to keep his office, but once he received the final decision that it was impossible, accepted it really well & wrote to say that he would accept to take any office that might be offered him. Whatever may be his faults, personal pettiness & rancour are not of them....

[22 May] Clemmie wrote your father a most amazing letter before W's fate was decided. She said 'Why do you part with W? unless indeed you have lost confidence in his work & ability? But I know that cannot be the reason. Is not the reason "expediency" – to restore public confidence. I suggest to you that public confidence will be restored in Germany by Winston's downfall. There is no general desire here for a change, but it [is] certainly being fostered by the press who have apparently made up their minds. I trust they are not making up yours for you. All you have to do is to stand by Winston & the Board of Adm^y & Sir A. Wilson. If you throw Winston overboard you will be committing an act of weakness & your Coalition govt will not be as formidable a war machine as the present Govt. etc etc.' The question at once arose as to whether this was Winston or Clemmie. I say that W. ununderstanding as he is of personalities, could not have perpetrated such a bêtise, & I now learn that he did not inspire it, though he allowed it to go (perhaps without learning its contents). Of course he himself is without an inkling of what the party feels towards him....

Your father L.G. Crewe & McK had a discussion with B.L. & AJB this morning on the composition of the Cabinet & it is gradually taking shape & much you will dislike it.... The chief interest of these discussions has I gather been the attitude of the Tories one to the other. B.L. not [at] all stomaching the idea of Austen getting a Secretaryship of State without some corresponding office coming to him.... B.L. has no illusion about his own position in the party frankly recognising that he is a compromise....

... Darling go on missing & do not falter or regret now that you feel you have made a decision. I do not fear but that we can have a glorious life together

My love always & bless & keep you safe. B.

V.A. to M.B.C. *Monday 24 May*
Hôtel Splendide, Marseilles

I am really off to-morrow.[1] We went down to the ship this afternoon &

---

[1] Violet arrived in Marseilles on Friday 21st, expecting to leave the following day on board the S.S. *Herefordshire*; the ship, however, was delayed until Tuesday 25th; faced with this delay, she came close to abandoning her voyage.

saw the 1st officer who told me to be on board by 9 as they hoped to sail at noon. So this is a line of goodbye to you most dear & good & near to me.

I hate going so far away from you this time. I don't know why – it gives me a real lump in the throat – a feeling of loneliness & insecurity – as tho' I shld. never find my way back again. But you tell me I shall & you are always right about me – aren't you? And when I do come back – who knows what mayn't happen? That all seems very fabulous & remote, but what is real & vivid & very true is the sense of you – & your nearness to me – & your essentialness to my life. We are too close for anything ever to find its way between us.

I couldn't do without you. You are a rock under my feet – & the air I breathe – & the bread I eat – & I trust your goodness & your strength beyond all things. They are firmer than the stars. And your love. I can only feel the pain when it is not there.

Stretch it out towards me over lands & seas – I need it. Goodbye beloved – Your V –

M.B.C. to V.A.   *Thursday 27 May*
                                                       10 Downing Street,
                                                       Whitehall, S.W.

Beloved. I found waiting for me this morning at Downing Street your letter written from Marseilles the night before you sailed. It is a wonderful message that you have given me, it has built a foundation of rock for my life....

Darling I have no fear for the future. I believe I can give you happiness, something essential & solid to build upon, so that things which have seemed to you difficult about marriage – restrictions in scope – limitations on liberty – will prove to [be] unreal, in fact I hope that you will not remember having imagined them.... It terrifies to think of these days of waiting, remember this & come back to me as soon as you possibly can, and pray God keep well & safe.

The Cabinet met for the first time today, and made not a sound. There was a certain amount of discussion as to seats beforehand but eventually they just tumbled into them as they found them & it has worked out pretty well. Curzon I am told held a sort of reception & shook all our men by the hand as they came in. I arranged that Carson & Henderson should mind the doors.[1] I do not know what they discussed, or how they fared.

---

[1] Arthur Henderson (1863–1935), Labour MP for Barnard Castle, Durham, 1903–18; president of board of education, May 1915.

Now that they have got to work, I expect that your father will extract some enjoyment out of the revelation of personalities and interchange between new characters or old characters in an unexperienced rôle. He is happier I think. He saw Venetia before she went off to France last Saturday which perhaps was a bad experience well got over. He has I understand made up his mind that she will marry Montagu. I am inclined to think so too, and am inclined to believe that she wants to apart from any impersonal & external reason, though without being in love in any sense of the word that I understand. Your letter touched Montagu up to some resentment I think, he has not of course told me what you said....

... God bless you beloved, be happy but do not get out of touch with me. I feel very close to you. B.

Mrs Brooke to V.A.   *Tuesday 1 June*
                                                 24 Bilton Road, Rugby

My dear Violet

I found my poor little cook in bitter tears this morning because she had just heard that her young man was wounded somewhere in The Dardanelles. She knew no details whatever except that it happened on <u>May 11</u>. I dare say you can't do anything but she was decidedly cheered when I said I would write & ask you to make enquiries. I wonder how you are getting on; it seems to me that your job is a very big one. Eddie did send me your brother's letter.

Will you thank him for it very much & tell him that his & Denis Browne's letters have been an absolute revelation to me as to how far men's love for each other can go; that they could collect their thoughts & write such letters just as they were entering on the most important action of their lives, is marvellous. It especially touches me of course as it was my son who inspired such love. I never thought for a minute that I should get such complete records of his life for 2 or 3 weeks. I hope your brother's leg is going on well. I am feeling very anxious as my boy Alfred went into the trenches on May 25 & 4 of his fellow officers have been killed since, it is terrible work....[1]

It was a very beautiful but also a heartbreaking thing to read all those letters. I seemed to see the procession going in the dark & then to open the coffin & see in it my boy Rupert, no soldier poet but just my boy, my heart almost broke but I daren't go on.

With love I remain Yours affec^ately, M. R. Brooke

[1] Alfred Brooke (1891–1915); like his elder brother, he enlisted in the first months of the war; killed in action at Vermelles, 14 June 1915, serving with the Post Office Rifles.

**Diary – Wednesday 2 June – Summer Palace Hôtel, Glymenopoulo,
Egypt**

I have been here 3 days. In the middle of a stifling journey from Port Said
to Alexandria I got a wire from Oc saying he wld. meet me at Sidi Gaber – &
sure enough when I put my head out of the window there he was hopping
down the platform in the white glare like a lame jackdaw. He came at a
<u>great</u> pace poor darling – hobbling & sliding stick in hand – & I was thrilled
at seeing him again – withdrawn safely from that cauldron of horror. I
shudder to think of his being plunged back there again....

V.A. to M.B.C.
                                               Thursday 3 June
                                          Summer Palace Hôtel,
                                          Glymenopoulo, Egypt

I have just <u>this instant</u> got yr. letter dated 23rd May forwarded on from
Marseilles – urging me not to go on but to come back & marry you. I hope
you didn't think I got it before starting.... I wld have come back I think
if I had got it & if the ship had waited any longer – but a 3 days delay
seemed just too little to give up for – tho' I was uncomfortably & unac-
countably haunted by the feeling that I was <u>risking</u> our life together.
I don't know why. I wasn't thinking of anything as definite as submarines[1] ....

Oc's wound is quite healed & the mark <u>tiny</u> ... he is still very lame but
extremely agile. I don't think he will go back this next week. They had a
hard time on shore & <u>never once</u> had their advance covered or prepared
by artillery. They were continually being left absolutely in the air by the
French on their right – & quite out of touch with the English on their left.
Slazenger says the 'converted transports', on one of which Oc came back,
are a scandal – disgracefully understaffed – no towels on board so that
men can't be washed – no milk for the typhoid cases – nothing but bully
beef & biscuits for men with broken jaws. Oc didn't suffer much as he
wasn't bad – but he says the staff cldn't possibly cope with the wounded –
3 Drs & 19 orderlies for 850 wounded – 640 of which were stretcher cases.
All thro' bad organization. The actual Hospital ships are excellent.

Do make the W.O. send out anti-gas protections here as they are <u>sure</u>
to start it & it wld be so much better to get the masks before & not
after....[2]

---

[1] The *Herefordshire* was disguised by its captain 'to look as nearly as possible exactly like an
iron-clad! in the naive expectation that it wld. "frighten away the submarines"' (VA to MBC,
29 May 1915).

[2] In fact neither side used gas during the Gallipoli campaign; see below, p. 74.

... Love to you very Dear – write to me – I feel rather excited about going back to you this time – in a new way – as if I were even more Yours.

M.B.C. to V.A.

Friday 4 June
10 Downing Street,
Whitehall, S.W.

Beloved. We got back at about two o'clock last night being very late owing to a fog in the Channel.... We spent practically the whole of our time going round to the various Headquarters where your father had the chance of talking to generals in command. We never went nearer the actual front than about four miles and as throughout the whole of our visit everything was very quiet, we saw little to give us the impression of the reality of war. The weather was quite lovely, the country was at its best green & wonderfully cultivated wherever we went & for the most part, seemingly, we might have been watching the progress of some great manoeuvres in a time of profound peace.

The hospitals at Boulogne, which were the last thing which we saw, quickly and permanently destroyed this impression of unreality and sent me away with an indelible memory of the loss & pain & hideousness of war. Wounds & maimings I can look on & remember almost without horror, but it is the faces of the ill men struggling often without hope for life & suffering from fatigue & pain which I cannot forget. They seemed to belong to a different race, not to the jolly vital Englishmen whom one knows.

We went to Boulogne yesterday afternoon & saw the officers' hospital which Edward Horner had left two days before on the road to recovery. He had a very bad wound through liver & kidney which had to be removed. The doctor seems to think that he will recover satisfactorily however.[1] We also saw the Casino Hospital.... We were taken into the operating theatre & saw the end of a remarkable operation performed by Sergeant who operated on Julian Grenfell.[2] He had by means of a powerful magnet removed a piece of shrapnel embedded in a man's brain. He said that he would recover. Julian, he said, would have got better had not his wound been

---

[1] Edward William Horner (1888–1917), brother-in-law of Raymond Asquith, and a Balliol contemporary of Cys Asquith and Charles Lister. After convalescence at home, Horner was given a staff position in Egypt, but like Raymond and Oc Asquith he successfully engineered a return to his regiment; killed in action, France, November 1917.

[2] Julian Grenfell (1888–1915), a Balliol contemporary of Cys Asquith and Edward Horner, and eldest son of Violet's close friend Ettie Desborough; a career soldier, he was wounded on 13 May 1915 near Ypres, and died of wounds in hospital at Boulogne on the 26th.

septic.... Francis Grenfell was killed almost on the same day that Julian was wounded. My cousin Guy, whom Oc knows, was also killed then.[1]

We met Venetia in Boulogne, she seemed very well but I had little talk with her, as she saw your father for some time & then had to go back to her hospital. I was rather beastly to her I am afraid but I was rather angry that she had turned up & should want to see your father, though I daresay it may have done no harm. I cannot help feeling that having cut herself adrift I do not want anything to be done which may reopen relations, save on a permanent and satisfactory basis, and unless this can be done it is wrong & cruel to attempt it....

I have not heard from you for nearly ten days & I suppose I cannot get a letter for nearly another week.... Keep very well & come back very soon. I ache for this. God bless you & keep you safe. B

Margot Asquith to V.A.   *Monday 7 June*
                                              10 Downing Street,
                                              Whitehall, S.W.

Darling I've not had one line from you since y^r first <u>dear</u> little letter. Here all the xcitement of cabinet-making has gone & things are settling down as usual xcept that it is of course all terribly sad as everyone we meet almost has lost someone dear....

Father went to St Omer Sunday 30th ... he found all our Generals furious with the 'want of shell' campaign in Daily Mail & Times.... Northcliffe will try & run Ll. George against father now! I see tiny signs of it.[2] I think Winston's speech <u>admirable</u>. Poor poor Winston – I <u>am</u> sorry for him & Clemmie. She has hardly been out of tears since & they are going to leave admiralty & live in a Wimborne house lent to them by Ld Wimborne....[3]

I've not seen them since you left, but Masterton begged me to go & see her & forgive her – as you may imagine I flew round as I always forgive every-one every-thing but she was out – they dine this week & I do hope I shall cheer her up. If Winston lives up to the spirit of his speech, sees no

---

[1] Guy Bonham Carter (1884–1915), Winchester and Magdalen contemporary of Oc Asquith; captain in 19th Hussars; killed in action, France, 14 May 1915.

[2] Margot wrote to Oc the following month: 'Politics have been <u>very</u> sad here. Ll. George has allowed Northcliffe & his swine to run him in every way against y^r father ... our rank & file & others w^d have shot Ll.G. any day the last 5 weeks. I with my usual distressing candour told Ll.G. that Northcliffe was <u>going</u> to do it – I saw it like a fish in a glass bowl (I'm really a sort of political clairvoyante). I warned him <u>not</u> to see Northcliffe or be run by him. He has an odd kind of passion for prominence & incapacity to run straight' (18 July 1915).

[3] Ivor Guest (1873–1939), 2nd Baron Wimborne; viceroy of Ireland, 1915–18; Churchill's cousin.

Press men & works silently & loyally he is absolutely <u>sure</u> to get up to the top again, he has a supreme chance if he only knew it father says.... The war news is poorish. Dardanelles last offensive not <u>quite</u> a success tho' <u>so</u> nearly. Ian Hamilton writes praising the Naval Brigade <u>very</u> much. <u>I think of you all out there a great deal</u>. Your work must be deeply interesting & absorbing – it is so much more interesting to see the real thing. I expect you see heaps of poor devils & cheer them up. I often think you are a natural nurse as you move quickly & quietly. Sitting on committees you can do in times of peace, it's dusty unimaginative work & adds nothing to xperience. This tragic war Jasper says we have quite underestimated.[1] We are in for a very long & heart shrinking affair – one can only pray that those we love may lose a limb as I almost feel no one will return alive to us....

Father is happier over V's marriage tho' not converted – he thinks he w^d mind less were it any-one else but I tell him whoever she married he w^d mind deeply as he has been very much in love – he says if she had only told him he w^d have felt it less. That want of candour w^h I've always [?] in V. is what has hurt him but she has suffered tortures of remorse poor darling & I feel very sorry for her. I think Montagu <u>quite</u> right not to give up his mother.... I <u>quite</u> see his point. He is <u>wonderful</u> over it all – courageous, convinced & <u>very</u> humble. They were both old enough to know their own minds & no one must tease them now. There's a good deal of bosh in the religion campaign au fond, tho' superficially it takes one in....[2] It is Montagu's physique that I c^d <u>never</u> get over not his religion....

I feel well but sad.... Oc will have left you. I bear <u>all love</u>. Y^r Margot

Diary – Wednesday 2 to Monday 7 June – written in Alexandria, Tuesday 8 June

... I have been grinding over the preliminaries to the establishment of my Naval Enquiry Office which are going very well.... We are all hectically

---

[1] Jasper Nicholas Ridley (1887–1951); served European war, 1914–18; chairman, Coutts and Co.; married, 1911, Countess Nathalie Benckendorff (d. 1968). The parents of Violet's future son-in-law, Jasper 'Bubbles' Ridley.

[2] Bongie discussed the Montagu marriage with Katharine Asquith that autumn: 'K & I had a long discussion about Venetia & Edwin.... She thinks that we are behaving very badly & unfriendlily. The more one cares for them the more ought one to help them out. Venetia has done on the whole a courageous thing & the objections to her action are actually based much more on racial prejudice, which is unjust than on the suggested sacrifice of conviction for money. I put the various answers to this point of view clumsily no doubt, but still the points were put' (MBC to VA, 8 September 1915).

Indexing at present. It is <u>such</u> a relief to be working with hard headed, busy, professional men instead of soft hearted, idle, fuddled women....

Oc goes up every morning to the Abbassia Hospital to have massage for his knee which is still fairly stiff. In his room is a poor Australian Colonel paralysed from the waist downwards by a bullet which hit him in the spine before even he had disembarked from the boats in the landing. The wounded are very pathetic lying here in endless rows in the heat with the flies crawling all over them....

Wednesday [2 June] we lunched at the Residency with the McMahons....[1] We were later on joined by Lord Edward Cecil with whom however I had no truck except to almost make a bad Church floater – à propos of the canonization of Charles I which he referred to – it was on the tip of my tongue to say 'Yes – the only thing the Church has done since the War – with characteristic irrelevance' or words to that effect.[2] I just stopped in time, forewarned by danger signals from Oc. It is so difficult to remember anyone has any nerves about the Church.

We entertained Wacher & Devaux to dinner that night at the Savoy in Alexandria.... Later on we all went on together to the great Alexandrian after dinner occupation 'Pelota'. It is a Spanish game played in a vast black court – about 3 times the length of an ordinary tennis court with hard white balls which are swiped huge distances by men with figures like Haldane & names like 'Ansola' – wielding huge hooked instruments like buffalo's tusks – made of basket.[3] Betting goes on briskly the while. We sat in a little box & watched – then looked in on lamentable dancing & singing in the Kursaal next door – the only point of which was the wild appreciation with which it was greeted by the Australians in the hall – who yelled encores & full-lunged & rounds of applause after the dreariest & tawdriest performances.

Their spirits & élan vital are no doubt attractive & their physique & appearance is quite magnificent. Gigantic creatures – riding (usually at full gallop on an iron road) with beautiful seats – of the 'Wild West' rather than the Leicestershire type – bare armed, bare-necked, bare chested – wearing Khaki knickerbockers – shirts belts & lovely broad-brimmed felt hats – in which the New Zealanders stick a wild bunch of emu feathers for distinction.

---

[1] Colonel Sir (Arthur) Henry McMahon (1862–1949), cr. GCVO, 1911; high commissioner in Egypt, 1914–16; married, 1886, Mary *née* Bland; the Residency was the official dwelling of the high commissioner.

[2] Colonel Lord Edward Cecil (1867–1918), financial adviser to the Egyptian government. Convocation had moved on 28 April that the name of Charles I be added to the calendar of saints of the Church of England. Two rather solemn letters to *The Times* pointed out that he had already been canonized. A 'Floater' is a *faux pas*.

[3] Violet once described Haldane as having a 'spheroid silhouette'.

They are unanimously loathed for their wealth – insolence – crudity & lack of any sort of discipline manners or consideration. Ego told me the most their officers could do was to ring up the Colonels of other barracks & say 'I think it my duty to warn you that my men are going to raid you to-night'.[1] They dig up graveyards & pull the women's veils off. Any act of crass 'Unsittlichkeit' is immediately explained away by the word 'Australian'. At Gallipoli on the other hand they fight with extraordinary dash & courage – advancing without any order like a football scrum. There is one ghastly story of their going thro' the Turkish prisoners' pockets & then pushing them one by one over the cliffs. But they were I believe on this occasion influenced by atrocities committed on their own men by the Turks, who are said to have lit fires under their wounded etc....[2]

We saw a good deal of Freyberg in these days.... I liked his simplicity, singleheartedness, eagerness, ambition, & a quality of firsthandness which impregnated all he said & thought. Also a sort of intuition very sensitively tho' directly conveyed – without questions or answers or apologies or explanations – of how things stood between me & Rupert. He really loved Rupert – & felt him to the bone.

We bathed together at Stanley Bay several times – a crowded, confined little inlet of sea containing alas! all Alexandria but also the biggest waves I have almost ever seen. Terrifying to my water-cowardice which is as great as ever. Freyberg used to take me in – right in – & then as they came towering darkly <u>feet</u> above us he wld. give a great leap lifting me right off my feet & over it & we would be borne in together in a swirl of foaming surf! My terror never failed nor the succeeding thrill of relief – he is the only person who has ever given me water confidence. It really was his element – he went bounding & shooting through the very centre of the waves like a porpoise when unhampered by me – letting himself be carried in & cast up like a pebble on the beach....

Monday 7th – we dined with Freyberg at the Savoy. Schlesinger who is I think in a very excited overwrought state brought us terribly bad news of the R.N.D....[3] Freyberg whose brother was in the Collingwood – said he didn't want to ask or know anything more about it, as this was his last evening & he wanted to enjoy it. I could see tho' that he was very upset &

---

[1] Hugo Francis 'Ego' Charteris, Lord Elcho (1884–1916), eldest son of 11th Earl of Weymss, Cynthia Asquith's elder brother; killed in action, Katia, 23 April 1916.

[2] Oc Asquith wrote to Violet early in the campaign: 'The Turks have been playing low tricks on the Australians, dressed in our men's uniforms, and using the white flag to make men show themselves. They will get very little change out of the Colonials now' (29 April 1915); but see below, p. 74.

[3] Dr Schlesinger, surgeon attached to the Howe Battalion.

felt his brother was dead....[1] Freyberg was sailing the next day & asked me to go for a drive with him first in the Nassa gardens which I agreed to do.

... We drove round & round & he told me all about his life. He had been wandering ever since he was 15 – knew the South Sea islands well & partly thro' this knowledge & understanding of them felt so close to Rupert.... Swimming is the passion of his life. He dropped me at my Bank & went off to find out about his sailing. When he came back he said to me 'I need you very badly – my brother's killed.' I went out with him – poor poor thing. He was so inarticulate – & so wretched. His brother had come out with the new battalions – he'd only landed 2 days before. We met Oc at the Regine & all lunched together. Afterwards we tried to get things to send back to Patrick & the others. Freyberg went on saying to me stunnedly – 'It's odd I've never cared for people before. I've never had any friends – & now I do for the first time in my life – they're all being killed'. I drove with him again & he dropped me at Glymenopoulo. We sat for a time on the crowded beach. He showed me a little talisman round his neck & said he wld. send it me if he got killed. We said Goodbye.

[1] During the attack on Krithia, 4 June 1915, the Collingwood Battalion was decimated, and afterwards both it and the Benbow were absorbed into the six remaining naval battalions of the RND. Freyberg's elder brother Oscar (1881–1915) was killed in the engagement of 4 June.

FOUR

Marriage and War

June 1915–October 1918

Violet once described herself as a 'fluctuater', and soon after her secret engagement to Bongie in mid-May she expressed doubts about her decision to marry. She wrote to him during her journey to Egypt, 'I cannot imagine it in a practical form. . . . I feel a terrible slipperiness about it.' Before long, though, she had settled her doubts. Bongie had been a close friend for a decade and she had come to feel that she could not live without him. It was a sensation less acute than conventional romance, but also 'bigger – deeper – more absolutely invulnerable'. Their engagement was made public on 5 July and met with a mixed reaction from their friends, some of whom were disappointed at the apparent absence of risk, by which love is often measured. Reginald Farrer wrote to Aubrey Herbert of the 'baleful' news of 'Violet's very insipid engagement', while Aubrey himself found it difficult to congratulate her on something that was so 'tepid'. Cynthia and Katharine Asquith agreed that the marriage seemed 'almost incestuous', and were critical. But in her diary Cynthia also wrote that she was glad of Violet's decision, thinking her 'wise'. Margot, she noted, was 'over the moon'. Given the perpetual strain in relations between step-mother and daughter this was perhaps to be expected. At last Violet would be leaving Downing Street for a marital home. But there is no doubting Margot's genuine happiness about a union that she had long advocated. Her joy was fully shared by her husband, and for both there was a sense of relief. Margot wrote to Oc: 'I was really nervous about V. & thought she had thrown her life away & w^d never have the resolution to marry, but I must say Bongie has shown a great deal of character.'[1]

---

[1] VA to MBC, 24 May 1915 (a.m.); VA to Ettie Desborough, 2 July 1915; Margaret Fitzherbert, *Greenmantle*, 163, 156; Cynthia Asquith, *Diaries*, 49; Margot Asquith to AMA, 18 July 1915.

M.B.C. to V.A.   *Thursday 10 June 1915*
                                                10 Downing Street,
                                                Whitehall, S.W.

Beloved. I am sore that your Father should have had a letter from you to-day & I nothing. That is not right and you can have no excuse as you must have had plenty of time on the voyage to write to me. However it is a blessing to see your dear handwriting again although addressed to someone else. . . .

[11 June] . . . The interesting part of the present situation in the Press is the way in which the Times is running Lloyd George. I enclose some cuttings from today's which are of interest from that point of view.[1] I do not think that this is a campaign which has in any sense [been] engineered by him, but he is such an odd man that he would I think make friends with the devil if he backed any scheme in which at the time he (L.G.) were interested. . . . Margot is very pleased because the London Mail accused her of playing lawn tennis with the German prisoners at Donnington Hall & they have been made to publish an apology for the lie & pay £100 to the Red Cross.[2] I think that it was right to take this up. . . . Bless you always. B.

V.A. to M.B.C.   *Sunday 13 June*
                                            Summer Palace Hôtel,
                                            Glymenopoulo, Egypt

It was delicious getting yr. 2 wires this week – the Mails are very irregular. . . .

We have been very sad here at the terrible R.N.D. casualties, the Howe is practically wiped out – all except Collins – who they say is a positive danger – & who was the only C.O. in the 2nd Brigade who didn't personally lead his battalion in the charge against the Turkish trenches. Our Artillery – which they all groan under – shelled a dummy trench for several hours, they were then told to advance, found it was a dummy, went on to the next which was intact, drove the Turks out with terrible loss to themselves & captured several machine guns, were then shelled by our own

---

[1] 'It is a good augury for the success of the Munitions Ministry that Mr Lloyd George did not wait for the formal establishment of his office. . . . He has shown that he knows what has to be done, but none of his colleagues has as yet given any signs that they do, and some have shown signs that they do not' (*The Times*, 11 June 1915).

[2] Margot won a similar action against the *Globe* magazine in March 1916, which had alleged that she fed German prisoners with 'every dainty and comestible'. Among the stories that circulated was one that Asquith had shares in Krupps, and another that his daughter Elizabeth was engaged to Admiral Tirpitz's son (diary of Margot Asquith). Pro-German slanders resurfaced during the Paisley by-election in 1920; see below, p. 110.

artillery as well as the Turks, heavily counter-attacked by the Turks, had no supports & were obliged to retire with fearful loss, leaving the captured guns behind them. All the C.O.'s were killed or wounded & most of the officers.

Poor Denis Browne – who had only gone back again the day before I got here, & Freyberg's brother in the Collingwood, who had only landed 2 days before – are both dead. It is heart breaking, & I somehow feel nearer it all here than I ever have before, with the ships coming in laden every day – & going out again with these poor heroic patched-up beings. Even Oc said to me quite seriously – it is simply a choice between being killed & being disabled for life – one or the other must happen in time.

Cleg is here, & last night Charles turned up from Malta – but he has gone off again to-day back to Gallipoli. Oc probably gets his discharge to-morrow – which ices my blood rather. I suppose he is bound to be sent back towards the end of the week.... I long to be home in a thousand ways – but feel a faint dread of M.'s nerves. I got a typical letter from her in yr. last envelope.... Goodbye bless you – very Dear – Yr V.

M.B.C. to V.A.
Tuesday 22 June
10 Downing Street,
Whitehall, S.W.

Darling darling darling you have sailed and I am writing to you to Marseilles. I pray that you may be brought there safe & soon. Hurry past week, hurry hurry hurry. I tick off the days like a schoolboy waiting for the holidays....

... Margot has not changed. Instead of having big dinner parties of 20, she has frequent ones of 12, her clothes seem still very new & her bridge not less expensive, but I may be unjust as I really have seen very little of her, since you have been away. Your father will be marvellously glad to have you back. I do not quite know what are his hobbies now, Sylvia to some extent I think, & I know that he has written to V. from time to time.[1] My impression is that he is not unhappy....

Politics are going quite fairly well. The House since your father's speech is settling down. Yesterday McKenna introduced the Bill for the New War Loan & had a great success.[2] He really made a very good speech. Tomorrow

---

[1] Sylvia Henley *née* Stanley (1882–1980), Venetia's elder sister, who became Asquith's chief correspondent and confidante after the break with Venetia.

[2] *The Times* of 22 June praised McKenna's 'admirably clear and businesslike speech'. The war loan offered a high rate of interest in the hope of attracting the large sums necessary to financing the war.

comes L.G.'s much delayed Munitions Bill.[1] He has I think got the agreement of the Trades Unions over it, which is the important thing, & his
tone, which at one time was rather flamboyant and over-acceptable to
Northcliffe, has much improved & frightens his late party less. He was of
course accused of deep intrigue with N, but that I never believed – but he
certainly was playing with fire....

Bless you always, come to me safe & happy. My love follows you
everywhere. B

V.A. to Hugh Godley   *Thursday 1 July*
                                                  10 Downing Street,
                                                  Whitehall, S.W.

Beloved $\dot{v}$[2] – I have been trying & meaning to get hold of you ever since I
got home late on Monday night – but when I tell you what has been
happening to me since I think you will understand. I have been becoming
engaged to Bongie.

Dearest $\dot{v}$ – I wonder what you will think of this. I have no idea what I
do – except that it doesn't correspond to any solution of my life I have
ever imagined – & yet seems strangely natural & inevitable.

It is nothing as sudden – as vivid – as specialized as a mere love-affair –
it covers more ground – it is entangled with the fibres of every experience
I have ever had – & I have for some time been unable to imagine life on
any terms which do not include it....

I should like to feel that you – my dearest & closest & best friend – were
happy for me & with me. Bless you – Yr V.

Hugh Godley to V.A.   *Friday 2 July*
                                                  29 Chester Street, S.W.

My dearest, You will have known how deeply moved I was by what you
wrote me yesterday. You know how deeply, indeed vitally, I am affected
by anything which affects you, whether joyful or sorrowful, & although,
as I think of it by myself, I cannot help looking back into the past, &

---

[1] The bill addressed the fact 'that victory in the war depends on the output of munitions,
and that output in turn depends on the supply and efficiency of labour'. Its success depended
in large measure upon Lloyd George's handling of organized labour (*The Times*, 24 June 1915).

[2] Violet sometimes addressed Hugh (and also referred to him in diaries) by the Greek
character $\dot{v}$, which is pronounced 'hyū', in the same way as his name. This pun dates from
the early years of their friendship, when Violet acquired rudimentary Greek.

thinking of things which might have happened, I do most earnestly & sincerely, & without any reserve whatever, wish you all the joy in the world.... I think your trouble has been, if I may say so, that you have continually involved yourself in relations with people, which, although you were not prepared to marry them, made it impossible, or very difficult, for you to marry anyone else. This tendency became so concentrated in Bongie's case that it could only lead to one end, namely the end to which it has led. I am very glad you are going to be married, & I am very glad you are going to marry Bongie. Even apart from what has happened, I don't think there is anyone to whom I w^d sooner see anyone I cared for married. At the same time he is, without question, a lucky devil.

It is, as you say, very different from any solution of life problems which you have from time to time propounded to yourself; but then those solutions were, almost without exception, wild & fanciful, & sh^d have been dismissed long ago.

I won't write more to you dear, although there is much more to be said. I hope you will let me come & see you when you are not better employed. Without your friendship & company I really believe that I could not continue to exist.

Bless you, now as always, Yr H.

Arthur Asquith to V.A. *Saturday 24 July*
Cape Helles, Gallipoli

My dear Vizie, I wonder on which of these days you are to be wed.[1] I have been rather out of sorts these last three days since I came down from the trenches. It has been blowing a hot tornado of dust: and I have the menace of a septic throat: and am fallen into indescribable lassitude. We had five tiring but exciting nights in the most advanced trenches of the most advanced sector of the line....

... the last evening, it was decided to deal with a sniper's post about 100 yds. to our front, and connected with our front by a tortuous old Turkish communication trench. One of our new officers and some of our men had been sniped from this post, the officer being killed. After some bombardment by French guns, a party led by Charles was to put up barricades at various points in the old Turkish communication trench: so that from one of these barricades we might deal with the sniper by bomb or mortar if he continued his malpractices.

---

[1] Violet and Bongie planned to be married at the end of July, but shortly after her return from Egypt she fell ill with a mild case of typhoid, and the wedding was postponed; it finally took place on 30 November. She spent that summer and autumn mostly in convalescence on the south coast.

Unluckily in the course of the preliminary bombardment, Freyberg had a finger broken and got a shrapnel ball in the stomach: and Charles was hit, slightly, in about six places by splinters. When I came up, Freyberg was collapsed on the ground, calm and conscious but helpless, and thinking that he must be done for: while Charles was careering about in the open in front of our trench, covered with blood, and tarrying on the barricading party.

The congestion at the debouching point of the trench became a perfect nightmare. Sandbags, bandoliers and waterbottles being passed up to the barricaders: Freyberg collapsed in the gangway, with a dead man beside him. Water and ammunition parties arriving from the supports: and then a man to extend the telephone – all at the junction of three trenches 3 ft wide.

Then the officer who had brought up water from the supports was shot in the head, and died soon after in the gangway. By this time Freyberg had been moved in a blanket, and Charles had been persuaded to go to the rear for treatment. I was senior officer left in the firing-line – and second senior in the Battn. We were warned to be prepared for a Turk counter-attack. Happily they did not come: it was most difficult to keep the men awake for this – their fifth – arduous night running. Next morning we were very glad to be relieved and to get back here to our Rest camp....

... There is a rumour here that Clemmy's husband is now on this Peninsula. I hope it is true. I wonder where Bonge and you will honeymoon? I hope you have had delicious presents: for mine you must wait till my return.... Your loving Oc

V.A. to Arthur Asquith   *Friday 6 August*
                                                   10 Downing Street,
                                                   Whitehall, S.W.

Beloved Artie ... Life sounds a perfect nightmare out there now. I sent you out a letter by Hankey which I hope has reached you all right. His first report home has just arrived, a very good one. He had only been to what he calls the Anzac position (Gaba Tepe) when he wrote – so presumably hadn't seen you at the Cape Helles end.

By the time you get this I imagine the big 'push' will have been made – upon which so much depends.[1] Pray God it will be successful. I wonder

---

[1] Violet refers to the landings that took place that day at Suvla Bay, at the northern end of the Gallipoli Peninsula. These were covered by advances on the old frontlines further south at Anzac Cove and Cape Helles. It was hoped that the new front would be a turning point in the campaign; see Oc's letter, below.

how the rumour about 'Clemmy's husband' got afloat.[1]

It was curiously enough founded upon fact. It had been arranged that he was to go out & report on the situation to the Cabinet. Bonar Law being quite agreeable & K. really keen he shld. go. He was inoculated, got a large tropical trousseau & was starting at 10 the next morning when at 8 o'clock at night Curzon & Austen Chamberlain came round & said they had never been consulted & strongly disapproved of his going! Father of course thought B. Law had spoken as their accredited representative....[2]

Arthur Asquith to V.A.   ***Sunday 22 August***
Rest camp, Cape Helles, Gallipoli

My dear Vizie, You and Bonge have been good about writing: I have just had your letters of Aug 6th....

I was interested about Winston, and showed Charles that part of your letter. I only saw Hankey once, for about three minutes. I am sure you all know more than I could tell you about the general trend of operations here. The [?] gossip here is that the surprise was perfect, but that the force landed at Suvla wasted invaluable time waiting for guns instead of pushing.[3] If there is one lesson that one could have learnt in this war, you would think it was to push forward as far as possible as quickly as possible in new country before things can settle down into trench warfare. I hope plenty more troops are on their way out....

I have grown fond of Cleg – laugh and all. He is very vital and his readiness to challenge any and every statement leads to good fun arguments. Freyberg (with rather Colonially over-enthusiastic sentiment) 'By G-d, T. died a very game death.' Cleg (immediately and furiously) 'Why?' Charles and I in fits of laughter. Cleg explains that T. was leading his platoon and doing no more than his duty when he was shot: so why go into superlatives about it. Also T. was insufferable when alive. Argument follows about 'de mortuis'.

I must go to tea. I wish I could be at your wedding but see no likelihood

---

[1] Churchill had been asked by Kitchener to assess the situation in the Dardanelles in advance of the August offensive. After the Unionists objected to his going, Hankey was sent out instead.

[2] The end of this letter is missing.

[3] The initial landings at Suvla Bay were highly successful, but a combination of hesitation and delay 7–8 August allowed the Turks to reinforce their positions. As a result a real chance of making a breakthrough was lost. Leadership, and not planning, was this time judged to be at fault; General Stopford, commanding the 9th Corps, and two divisional generals were subsequently relieved of their commands.

of being home – at any rate until the end of this campaign. Love to all.
Yours Oc.

M.B.C. to V.A.　　　　　　　　　　　　　　　　*Monday 30 August*
　　　　　　　　　　　　　　　　　　　　　　　　　10 Downing Street,
　　　　　　　　　　　　　　　　　　　　　　　　　Whitehall, S.W.

Beloved ... I dined with Hankey & had a long talk with him on the
Dardanelles.... He comes back full of admiration as you know for Birdwood & the Australians and also for the Navy which he thinks does its
work incomparably better than the Army....[1] He says that the Turk is a
clean fighter, they never fire on the hospital ships, nor intentionally –
though the ground is very confined – on our clearing stations, & of course
they have not used gas (& nor therefore shall we) & are ready to arrange
armistices for burying the dead & so on.

On the whole he thinks our men have rather an affection for the Turk.
He saw Oc as you know & said that he was very cheerful & was doing very
well. He thinks that he should have got the command of the battalion &
may yet do so. Of course Hankey is very disappointed at the recent failure
to achieve a big success but he thinks that it may still be done & is ready
to face a winter campaign. I am very glad to have him back.

Tomorrow of course we have a meeting of the Dardanelles Committee &
I suppose that I must be ready to face Margot. I think that I shall ask her
to stop lobbying people about the conscription question.[2] She is doing
no one any good. I wish she were not coming down.... My love darling, B.

Grey is circulating a minute to the Cabinet asking for greater discretion &
mentioning that he has been surprised to hear open discussion of secret
things at luncheon tables. Can he be thinking of No 10?

---

[1] Field Marshal William Riddell Birdwood (1865–1951), cr. Baron, 1938; general officer
commanding Australian and New Zealand Army Corps, 1914–18.

[2] Conscription became the dominant political issue of the day. It was against the instincts
of many Liberals, who believed that the war was being fought precisely to oppose this kind
of 'Prussian' militarism. On the other hand, the long duration of the conflict seemed to
demand wholesale mobilization of the nation's resources, specifically manpower. Margot
Asquith shared her husband's opposition, but not his political adroitness in allowing room
for manoeuvre: 'I'm a passionate voluntary service person & don't believe the men who wait
to be fetched are worth a d–n' (MA to AMA, 24 September 1915).

V.A. to Arthur Asquith   *Thursday 2 September*
Colerne House, Sandwich, Kent

Beloved Artie – I have just been moved down here to the sea – after 7 weeks bed & sofa. It is heavenly to be out of doors again & out of London. I am still very weak & lead the life of a shrimp – a dead one – lying out in the sand all day – reading a little but mainly just breathing. The windows of this house (Anne Islington's) shake all night long from the guns in France. They have been having the most terrific bombardment there. Beb is back on 3 days' leave very strained & tired – a brother officer of his has gone out of his mind....

Hankey is at present being examined by the Cabinet Committee. His letters to Father from Gallipoli were quite excellent. He praised Birdwood & the Anzac forces very highly – & censured the Suvla operations under Stopford – thro' whom the whole coup failed.... It seems incredible to me, <u>however</u> stupid Stopford was, that he should have dawdled on the beach & entrenched 2 miles inland if he had been given definite orders to race across the Peninsula as hard as ever he cld. go. (The landing was admittedly unopposed.)... Here the air is rent by the screams for conscription of the Northcliffe press – almost the wickedest of all his campaigns – as he has now put on to a thoroughly controversial party basis what ought to have been treated as a matter of purely military expediency. There seem no practical arguments in its favour just now as K. is getting all the men he wants & more than he can arm by voluntary methods. They continue to come in at 20,000 a week....[1]

... Everything there (in London) is pretty stale & exhausted – & people in bad spirits over the Russian retreat – & the Dardanelles coup manqué. It is raining so hard onto this page that I must stop. Goodbye my dearest. God bless you.... All my love from V.

Bernard Freyberg to V.A.   *Monday 6 September*
Rest Camp, Cape Helles, Gallipoli

I wonder [if] you like my almost inarticulate scrappy at random notes – they are not exactly literary or spelling masterpieces.... Poor old Charles has been hit by another shell – it is heartbreaking – he was most gallant over it and wanted to walk down instead of being carried.

---

[1] Margot Asquith wrote to Oc, 15 June: 'That vile paper the Times (& Daily Mail) is running conscription for all it is worth.... Father says we c^d not manage another man & that it is a wicked cry to start an anti-war agitation over here.... Northcliffe ought to be shot but it's too good a death.'

We had a hard time last week in the trenches but did not have many casualties – we had to dig in the open to complete a new firing line and it entailed a lot of night digging under fire. Did you hear the story about Oc's sniper? He was making a night reconnaissance of a trench a few yards to our front when he came onto a sniper's post with the sniper asleep in it. He couldn't shoot him while he was asleep & still he felt he couldn't leave him – so he grabbed him by the throat at the same time placing a pistol to his ear – only to find he had been shot a day or two before. . . .

A week later 12th Sept. Trenches. I had to finish abruptly & have not had the chance to write since. I have just heard of Charles' death – it has plunged all of us into the deepest grief. We have got extraordinarily fond of all the Old Hood's and as each one goes it hurts like nothing else. We are all wondering now if this is to be an all winter job or if another big push is to be made soon. . . .

About marriage – I hardly know what to say. I rejoice that you are to be happy – after all the happiness and the good opinion of our women folk is the main thing that keeps us going out here. I envy people who love and marry more than I can tell. I will never marry. A soldier must be able to go to Hellish places if he is sent, if he is to have a career at all – besides it may occur to me to get killed some time which would be troublesome. I wonder if I will see you when I come to London. . . . Love & Bless you, B.

Please answer this as it helps one a lot to hear things B.

V.A. to Eddie Marsh   *Tuesday 7 September*
                                          Colerne, Sandwich, Kent

Dearest Eddie – I am here – in Anne's little house on the sea . . . lying out in the sand all day long, reading & writing a little – mildly – but mainly just breathing. The sea is wonderful to-day as smooth as oil & just flecked here & there with whiteness – of the wings of birds – & foam – & the glimmering white cliffs at the other side of the bay.

My reading has been froth – not to say scum – & my writing pure letters of thanks to lists of people like The Aga Khan, the Archbishop of Canterbury (not allowed letters I see – so how unnecessary!), Devlin, Mrs. Drew, Sir Arbuthnot Lane, Ava Astor, Sir George Askwith, etc! Of people – I have seen none except the Henderson's & B. from Sat to Mondays. . . .

What an angel you are to offer to give me a first edition of Coleridge. I should love it above all things – but you musn't give me anything that ruins you Eddie darling.

Charles's death is the last touch in the devastation of our poor stricken generation. I loved him the best of all his stratum – most beloved & unique being. Thank God I saw him so much & so perfectly in Alexandria just before he went back. But since Rupert's death I've had a sort of numb feeling as if nothing could really ever <u>hurt</u> me again – or bring me ecstasy – but I suppose it might. One feels too the living so mixed with the dead just now – one hardly knows them apart. The living are so absent & the dead so present.

... Goodbye & bless you Eddie dear – I am getting better very, very gradually – my heart gives me some discomfort which is I believe a post-typhoidal platitude – but came quite as a bright surprise to me. My love to W. Yrs V

M.B.C. to V.A. *Monday 13 September*
10 Downing Street,
Whitehall, S.W.

Beloved ... Drummond lunched with L.G. and discussed the conscription problem with him. D. was convinced of two things – that L.G. advocates conscription from a wholly sincere belief that this is the only method by which the war will be won, & that disloyal as his methods may be, he is not personally disloyal to your father, but wants to work with him. He is apparently prepared for this extent of compromise, that an announcement should be made in Parliament that it is necessary to raise such & such a number more men, that this will be done by voluntary enlistment if possible, but that in order that there may be no delay, the Govt. will forthwith introduce a bill giving the necessary compulsory powers to be made use of only when it shall be shown that voluntary enlistment has failed to produce them....

L.G. is apparently prepared if his compromise is not accepted to resign & to stump the country in favour of it. Winston & Curzon would doubtless go with him. I think that, even, should if possible be avoided. Montagu is right in saying that a split at this time would be disastrous, so some way out should be found & I think that it is possible....

Bless you always, please write to me as you did last week. B.

V.A. to Arthur Asquith *Thursday 16 September*
Colerne House, Sandwich, Kent

Beloved Artie – I loved getting your last excellent letter. I'm afraid Charles's death will be a terrible sorrow to you – & leave a great empti-ness in your life out there.... How cruel it seems too that after 2 escapes he shld have been fatally wounded the 3rd time. We have heard no details as yet (you possibly will write them in your next letter) only that he died on the Hospital-ship & that his wound was in the pelvis. I'm afraid this means terrible pain. . . .

I got a letter from him only last Friday – well & happy & just going into the trenches again. . . . How curious & tragic it is to look back on the Hood as it was when it went out & then to think of what is left of you – Rupert & Denis & Charles & poor Quilter gone – & many others you knew & I didn't. . . .

The only incident of any kind here was the Zeppelin raid on London last Wednesday. I – of course – missed it being down here. Father & Bongie were giving a small dinner at D. St. – which was proving rather a failure as they were short of women & there was an empty place. After dinner just as Father had settled to Bridge & B. was talking to Goonie in the drawingroom they heard the deafening report of the Foreign Office gun going off – rushed to the window & there – in the sky – revealed by a white fingered searchlight the Zeppelin was moving very slowly – very high (about 6000 ft. B. thought) with the shells bursting below it like falling stars.

They were all too low & it wasn't hit. There were lots of big fires in the City – one between the Guildhall & the Post Office. One shell dropped just by St Bartholomew's Hospital & made a cavity almost as big as the record one at Ypres.[1] Eddie writes to me 'Raymond Buildings had a narrow escape – there were bombs on each side within 20 yds of it. Just fancy if all the Rupert things that are there had been destroyed.' Isn't it characteristic?

The House met again yesterday & the National Service issue was raised on the vote of credit. That brute Northcliffe has put the whole thing on such a thoroughly controversial basis now & has so inflamed Organized Labour – that I anticipate trouble whether we have it or not.[2] I imagine when the National Register forms are compiled it will give a more accurate idea of how big a margin of 'slackers' (that much exploited body) there are.[3]

They are sending out people after much shorter training now – the Cairene Carter has just gone out after about 2 months – which I suppose

---

[1] Probably a reference to the mining of Hill 60, on the southern edge of the Ypres salient, 7 April 1915; an eye-witness recorded the sight of the hill 'rising straight up into the sky and bursting into pieces' (Malcolm Brown, *The Western Front*, 71–2).

[2] At its conference in 1916 the Labour Party opposed conscription as being 'against the spirit of British democracy and full of danger to the liberties of the people', sentiments that many Liberals would have shared (J. A. Spender and Cyril Asquith, *Life of Lord Oxford*, ii, 208).

[3] There was a general belief that 650,000 men eligible to serve were not volunteering.

means Raymond will go before long.[1] Poor little Bimbo Tennant – that baby – is out at the Front.[2] How I wish you could get leave for a little rest – you must be so tired. I see poor Jack Tennant is killed – the one we met in le Jardin de Rosette. . . .[3] Goodbye – bless you – I will write again. Yr V

Alfred Price[4] to V.A.   *Sunday 26 September*
                                                    17th Divisional Artillery, B.E.F.,
                                                                          France

Dear Miss Violet

I have the greatest pleasure in answering your most kind and welcome letter I received hoping you have recovered from your illness. Well Miss I have nothing to complain about at present everything going steady up to the time of writing.

I didn't quite hear what Martin was discharged for, but I have wrote him asking the reason. I have also wrote to Alec Carmichael but had his letter returned say[ing] he did not live there none. Well Miss before we left England I was given a stripe and by the way things look, promotion is quick here. My work here is setting the fuzes for the shells, which is only a matter of quickness, not hard work. We expect to give them a warm time shortly, and the sooner the better. I must say that it is a lot better out here than some people imagine. You ask if I require anything, well Miss I should be ever so pleased if you would be kind enough to send me some stationery as that is the thing we need most. So now Miss I think I must conclude with best respects to one and all. I remain,

                                                           Yours Sincerely, Fred Price

Would you be kind enough to send Alec's <u>address</u>

V.A. to M.B.C.   *Wednesday 6 October*
                                                The Manor House, Mells, Somerset

Dearest – I have been disappointed in not hearing from you to-day & they tell me there is no post in. I am sorry as I feel just a shade desolate. . . . R. left this morning. I was almost surprised at <u>how</u> sad I felt at parting with

[1] Frederick George Bonham Carter (1877–1968), 'the Cairene Carter', chartered accountant based in Cairo before the war; later secretary to Lazard Bros. & Co.

[2] Edward Wyndham Tennant (1897–1916), Margot Asquith's nephew, killed in action on the Somme the following year.

[3] Possibly John Amherst Tennant (1889–1915), a cousin of Margot Asquith.

[4] Alfred Price was one of the original members of the Archie Gordon Club.

him – there was something so pathetic & incongruous in seeing so perfect & highly finished a being going off into that raw brutal primitive hurly-burly – & in seeing so shy & complicated a one saying goodbye to his children, with real sweetness & emotion I thought.[1]

I felt very moved & sad. K. looks wretched poor darling. Do be sweet to her & try & express in some way how much you feel for her.... Goodbye bless you Darling   Yr V.

V.A. to Arthur Asquith

Friday 8 October
The Manor House, Mells, Somerset

Dearest dear Artie – I haven't heard from you for some time – I wonder how you are & whether there is any chance of your all being given a rest in winter quarters for a time. I'm sure you must need one. As I write to you things look very black – but I daresay the horizon will have cleared before this letter reaches you. Bulgaria as you see is going in against us & Greece, which invited us to land men at Salonica, now looks like backing out – at least the King has again refused to endorse Venizelos' policy.[2]

It <u>may</u> of course come right as it did in Italy when the Prime Minister resigned – but it certainly is a gloomy outlook just now – it is terribly depressing for all of you. Charles's death must be a terrible sorrow & loss to you – there are now no Listers left. Biggish casualty lists are coming in from the offensive in France.[3] Agar-Robartes Myles-Ponsonby & either Essiekoff or Essievitch – I don't know which – have been killed.[4] Raymond goes out to France this week & he & K. came down here to say goodbye to Frances & the children.

He rather happy & excited – poor K. of course quite wretched. Cys was to have gone last week but was again rejected as medically unfit. Beb is back on leave having been very strained & overdone by the bombardment....

[1] Raymond's daughters Helen and Perdita were then aged seven and five; when Raymond left, Katharine was pregnant with their third child, Julian, born 22 April 1916.

[2] The Central Powers and the Allies both attempted to gain Bulgaria's support in the war. After the former made a better territorial offer, Bulgaria entered the war on their side, 5 October 1915. British and French attempts to draw Greece into the war, with a campaign in Salonica aimed at defending Serbia, had the support of the prime minister, Venizelos, but not of King Constantine (A.J.P. Taylor, *Struggle for Mastery*, 548–9).

[3] The battle of Loos, 25 September–13 October, in which the British suffered 50,000 casualties, with very little gained; the engagement was decisive in ensuring that French would be replaced as commander-in-chief.

[4] Hon. Thomas Charles Agar-Robartes (1880–1915), Liberal MP for St Austell, Cornwall, 1908–15; lieutenant, Royal 1st Devon Imperial Yeomanry. Hon. Cyril Myles Brabazon Ponsonby (1881–1915), captain Grenadier Guards.

I am continuing my very slow convalescence at Mells – which is lovely & lulling as ever – the garden flaming with hollyhocks – red hot pokers – Michaelmas daisies – dahlias – & that delicious half rotten autumn smell in the air – the lichen peacefully creeping on over the old stone churches & walls. It is all so calm & normal & undisturbed it is almost impossible to imagine the horror that is shaking the world – & you poor darling far away hanging on to the edge of your grim & bloody Peninsula – amongst flies & half-buried Turks. How I long to get you back again. I got such an amusing letter from our dear little Soudanese night porter addressed to 'Respectable Miss Violet Asquith' the other day!

Bobbetty Cranborne is engaged to Betty Cavendish – which seems an ideal engagement – otherwise there is no gossip. Margot – having signed the Women's War Economy League – has characteristically started by buying a new house! the cottage next the Wharf! I don't know how the devil she will pay for it. There has been a new frontier incident there with the Lindsays I believe & terms are as strained as ever.[1] Let me know what I can send you – Yr lovingest <u>V.</u>

V.A. to Aubrey Herbert   *Saturday 9 October*
10 Downing Street,
Whitehall, S.W.

Dearest Aubrey – You wrote me <u>such</u> a delightful letter – it was heavenly getting it & most sweet of you to think of me from your grim & bloody Peninsula. . . .

. . . I hear from Oc – alive thank God – that is one's highest hope for anybody now. Our poor generation – how its blossom has fallen – <u>Rupert</u> – to me the greatest sorrow of the war – & one of the greatest of my life – Charles – Julian – Billy[2] – John Manners. The living & the dead are curiously mixed in one's mind.[3] Hell & Heaven seem not much further than Gallipoli.

Here things are fairly normal – loathing of Northcliffe is the strongest & most prevalent emotion. The conscription storm is in abeyance for the

---

[1] Henry (1866–1939) and Norah Lindsay (1873–1948), who owned the Manor House in Sutton Courtenay.

[2] Billy Grenfell (1890–1915), younger brother of Julian; killed in action, Hooge, 30 July 1915.

[3] Cynthia Asquith was friendly with all of those mentioned above, and echoed Violet's sentiments: 'Oh why was I born for this time? Before one is thirty to know more dead than living people? Stanway, Clouds, Gosford – all the settings of one's life – given up to ghosts. Really, one hardly knows who is alive and who is dead' (Cynthia Asquith, *Diaries*, 97, entry 11 November). Her younger brother Yvo was killed in action in October 1915.

moment.... The Prime preserves his mellowness & balance throughout. Bonar Law is now an habitué of Downing St. – & fills the place in our lives (once occupied by Waxworks) of Scotch Funny.[1] Winston paints all day in oils & is soon going to have an Exhibition – isn't it all curious?

I understand so well what you say about the war making you wish you could be married again. It <u>does</u> make one want the <u>realest</u> & soundest & intensest & most <u>essential</u> things – & I think it was this feeling that made me suddenly decide to marry Bongie....

Goodbye & bless you dear Aubrey. I can only echo Gabriel's pertinent wish 'I hope you are not killed in the War'. Yrs ever <u>Violet</u>

M.B.C. to V.A.   *Saturday 9 October*
                                                    10 Downing Street,
                                                    Whitehall, S.W.

Beloved ... Hankey and I had an interesting talk with your father at lunch.... He said that he has it in mind to make K. C-in-C of all the forces in the field & to send him out in the first case to the Aegean to deal with the situation there. K. is rattled & tired & in need of a holiday. He [HHA] said that the only person who can undertake the duties of S of S [for war], is himself....

... He has not mentioned what is in his mind to anyone so do not speak of it. If an assistant is chosen who will take the responsibility of dealing with the routine I think your father can do the work with great advantage. His duty will be to preside over the General Staff & the broad conduct of the War. It encourages me to see him in this spirit. If only he will assert himself it will make an enormous difference to the conduct of the war. He & AJB are the only people who really have the clearness of vision & detachment of judgement which is absolutely essential now. All the rest are panicky or have some peculiar prejudice in favour of one plan or another, or simply lack the brains & judgement to enable them to deal with the situation. Love. B.

---

[1] 'Waxworks', so named because of his complexion and 'cotton-wool' side whiskers, was Sir Reginald Macleod (1847–1935), under-secretary of state for Scotland 1902–8. This jocular allusion is an example of Asquith's fatal complacency with respect to Bonar Law, 'the most formidable giant-killer of the century. Balfour, Asquith, and Lloyd George all fell beneath his reluctant axe' (A. J. P. Taylor, *1914–1945*, 15–16).

V.A. to M.B.C.   *Sunday 10 October*
The Manor House, Mells, Somerset

Dearest – I send you a line to go up by Eddie. I was thrilled by the contents of your two letters this morning & am <u>delighted</u> to hear of Father's contemplated move....

... I welcome it because quite apart from W.O. administration it will bring him to closer grips with the <u>war</u> itself & give him a more <u>personal</u> sense of responsibility about it. I have felt sometimes lately as if his clutch hadn't got in – as if the full force of his mind was not in it & driving it forwards....[1]

I heard you beautifully on the telephone this afternoon – it was fun talking to you. When I am away from you I <u>still</u> cannot quite reconstruct you – & the world of warmth & comfort & <u>perfect</u> understanding that closes round us when we are together. I thought your minute to Father <u>very</u> good. I like to think of you using your brains nicely! – you have got very good ones – which used at one time to be in intermittent use – but are now more constantly on the go....

I am getting thro' a few letters – not many. I do feel <u>very</u> tired & slack – & can hardly keep my attention thro' a rubber of bridge. It's odd.... Let me know as soon as you can Father's plans – & E.'s & K.'s & tell me any developments. Ever most dear & good   Yr V.

M.B.C. to V.A.   *Tuesday 12 October*
10 Downing Street,
Whitehall, S.W.

Beloved. I shall send you a hasty line by the evening post which may reach you tomorrow morning. The Cabinet started to discuss conscription today, a most unlucky time it appears to me, as the military situation requires all the consideration which can be given to it & not a method of raising men which can [have] no military effect for many months & only a bad political effect now. The result was not good. Runciman said to me as he came out, 'Well we remain a united Cabinet for another 24 hours'. The discussion will be continued tomorrow & I think that perhaps the conscriptionists may by that time see the futility of pressing the issue at this time.

I need hardly say that L.G. Curzon & Winston are the protagonists.

[1] See the critical account of Asquith's management of the cabinet in Austen Chamberlain's *Down the Years*, 111: 'It was not unknown of the Prime Minister to be writing letters while the discussion proceeded....'.

Their lack of judgement & eye over it is tragic. It brings out Winston['s] worst faults. He has the imagination to grasp ends but his eye is blurred as to means. In this case I think he is wrong in his primary view that man power is the important factor, but even accepting that, the obstacle of providing officers, non-commissioners & equipment for them is not envisaged at all. I think that if he were S. of S. for War he would have his extra 1,000,000 enrolled & divided up into Divisions & would at once reckon on them as equipped, officered & disciplined like the Guards division....

... I must send this at once. Bless you dearest. B.

Arthur Asquith to V.A.   *Thursday 28 October*
                                                              Dardanelles

My dear Vizie, Thank you very much for your letter from Mells, of Oct. 8th; and will you thank Bonge for his of about the same date from D. Street? I am very sorry to hear that you are having such a tiresomely slow convalescence, and have not yet – so Bongy says – recovered your former goatlike strength of leg....

Our work here now is rather like garrison duty in a town – without the town.... I envy those who have gone to Salonica: at any rate they should not suffer from monotony. Please tell Bonge not to allow phrases such as 'The Balkan situation is complicated and difficult at present', to creep into his letters to me. Let him keep those for the Press Bureau: and for North-cliffe: and say to me instead 'Bulgarian political action is complicated on the one hand by M. Radoslavoff's intrigue with Fraülein Wederkund, the famous 'Dresdene Nachtingal' and on the other by M. Cadoslavoffs notorious attachment to La Belle Otero'. Let him in fact adopt the Bystander, not the Spectator, as his model.

Bonge asks if any parcels have reached me yet. I have had one with cigars, two plum puddings and some preserved fruit from Margot.... Would you see Fortnums, and see if they are sending in my weekly parcels a good proportion of chocolate, chickory, biscuits and cake (in tins)? and would you send me a couple of knitted Khaki silk neckties?... Love to all. Yrs Oc.

'Thronging crowd outside and everyone one had ever heard of inside':
the wedding of Violet Asquith and Maurice Bonham Carter,
30 November 1915

There was immense public interest in 'the Asquith wedding', which took place at St Margaret's Church in Westminster on Tuesday 30 November. Cynthia Asquith recalled without exaggeration that there was a '*Thronging* crowd outside and everyone one had ever heard of inside'. A number of the guests were in uniform, and it was inevitable that the war should cast its shadow. Asquith had requested a guard of honour of wounded soldiers, and the week before had observed that at a time of such widespread bereavement even wedding-bells rang with 'a muffled and sombre sound'. In keeping with this the ceremony was toned down, with no reception afterwards. With some justification the Liberal *Daily Chronicle* observed that 'the normal panoply of a marriage of such intense social and public interest was conspicuously absent'. But the occasion could not wholly escape grandeur, and against the backdrop of the war Cynthia Asquith thought it 'unnecessary and irrelevant'. It was a view echoed with some bitterness in the left wing press. The socialist *Herald* carried an editorial 'The Human Comedy: that Asquith Wedding', commenting: 'If we except the Baghdad defeat, which occurred on the same day, the outstanding feature of last week was the marriage of one of Mr Asquith's daughters to one of Mr Asquith's secretaries'. The paper was highly critical of the wealth displayed on this occasion, and discordant notes were also sounded in rural Essex, where the Reverend Andrew Clark recorded the feeling of the villagers of Great Leighs: 'if extravagance is sinful (as the Government says) why did Mr Asquith not check it in the case of his daughter's marriage?' None of this was likely to have made an impact on Asquith, who disregarded the political effect of any trace of extravagance from 10 Downing Street. Meanwhile the newly-weds were *en route* to their honeymoon in northern Italy, leaving behind the inevitable reverberations following a society wedding in wartime.[1]

H.H.A. to V.B.C.   *Tuesday 30 November*
                                                   10 Downing Street,
                                                   Whitehall, S.W.

My Darling Violet – It is your wedding day. How much it means to me you can guess, but can never realise. For 20 years (ever since you were 8 years old) you have been to me the most perfect of companions, & I have tried to be to you not a Father, but an intimate & understanding friend. During all that time we have never failed one another: thank God! I can't remember even one moment when we have ever been apart. You have

[1] Cynthia Asquith, *Diaries*, 106; *Daily Chronicle*, 1 December; *Herald*, 11 December; James Munson (ed.), *Echoes of the Great War*, entry for 7 January 1916, 106.

always understood me, & I believe I have always understood you. It has been a perfect relationship.

And now that you are leaving me, in a time of great strain & stress, I could not bear to think that you should ever be far away. Do not ever let us break or even suspend the chain wh. has always bound us together. Let us maintain the old close intimacy – as it always was & always ought to be. My life wd. be impoverished without you. I beg and pray of you to keep our divine companionship as it always has been. Something has to be sacrificed: but let the essential & true thing be always there.

Your loving & devoted & <u>dependent</u> Father

Margot Asquith to V.B.C.   *Tuesday 30 November*
                                                10 Downing Street,
                                                Whitehall, S.W.

My darling – one line thro' very tired eyes from tears & headache to say I thought you were <u>very</u> brave & <u>wonderfully</u> good all this time – the most trying any woman can go through. You looked delicious both outside & going away.

1st Dec. 1915 6 a.m. I c^d not finish this last night as I was so very tired.... You have been with me – at least in the same house – since you were 6 & I have often been clumsy & tactless & un-understanding but darling you will forgive all this now & remember & believe that I have never failed you nor will I ever fail you (s^d you want me) in times of stress, but I daresay (poor darling!) & I also hope you will want no one but only Bongie. If I ever see an unimaginative female daring to cast even a shadow between you & Bongie I will kill her with my own hand. You shan't have a moment's depression or neglect if I can prevent it – the pain is too great.

Let me know in a written order what you want done in y^r home so that you can get into it whenever you like. I will do anything & everything you want. God keep you both my dear darlings – your Margot

V.B.C. to H.H.A.   *Wednesday 1 December*
                                              Wilsford Manor, Salisbury,
                                              Wiltshire

Most Beloved – I read your precious letter in the train with many tears – but also with a great & deep pride that I shld. have meant anything to <u>you</u> – who have always meant <u>everything</u> to me – since I can remember & are still the <u>closest</u> – the most passionately loved of all human beings to me. You lie at the very bottom of my heart – nothing can ever get beneath you – or that deep & absorbing love of you which has always been the first principle of my existence.

I have lived by its light & strength through many & variegated experiences – thro' times of black anguish – when it was the only thing left to live for – & radiant happiness – nothing has ever dwarfed it – nothing has ever <u>compared</u> with it. 'Being alone' with you has always been my wildest – most thrilling joy – from old Maresfield Garden days[1] – when we slept together – & our little lunches tête à tête in yr. Mount St. rooms ... to now-adays when we motor off together to the Wharf – or one of our Nests – or you come & say goodnight to me in my room. It has been the <u>romance</u> of my life – but a romance built on so deep & steadfast a foundation – that its colours can never fade nor its glamour wane....

... There has never been such a Father – there has never been such a friend – & lacking in many things as I am, & may have been, this thing I have not lacked: to know & realize & thank God for it every hour that it has lasted – never to waste a <u>minute</u> that might be spent with you – never to miss a word you ever said – at meetings or H. of C. or meals – <u>anywhere</u>. And Beloved what I want you to <u>know</u> & <u>realize</u> is that I need you now, not only as much but <u>more</u> than ever before – every hour – ill or well – happy or sad. All sorts of new problems & experiences are opening before me – & how <u>could</u> I face them without you....

I feel very, very safe with B. There are many more 'remarkable' men I might have married in the vulgar sense of the term – but none so utterly sound & true through & through – nor with such strong, tender & self-controlled devotion....

It is the greatest comfort to me that he understands my love for you so perfectly & loves you so deeply himself.... Goodbye – God Bless you – don't ever forget me for an instant – your most deeply loving & needing –
V

H.H.A. to V.B.C.   *midnight, Thursday 2 December*
10 Downing Street,
Whitehall, S.W.

My Darling Violet,

Though it is late, & I have still a lot to do, I must send you one line to thank you for your divine letter, which touched me more than I can say, and which I shall always treasure. I believe our relationship has been

---

[1] 27 Maresfield Gardens, Hampstead, was the Asquiths' home from the year of Violet's birth until 1894; the intimacy that she shared there with her father, following her mother's death in 1891, was broken when he remarried and the family moved home.

unique, and I share to the full your wish that the change in the framework of your life shall not in the least degree impoverish or spoil it. We must devise ways & means to ensure that, in essentials, it shall always be the same.

For the moment, what I want most for you is that you should get free (would that I could do the same!) from the evil of agitating memories and surroundings: and have a perfect holiday of untroubled peace.

The ground-swell of the wedding still pervades this house, but it is subsiding. Outside there is a lot of perturbing factors: Dardanelles, Salonica, Sir J. F. French, &c &c &c....[1] Go on writing to me. Your ever loving Father

Love to Bongie.

V.B.C. to Eddie Marsh   *Friday 17 December*
                                    La Mortola, Ventimiglia, Italy

My dearest Eddie. It was such a joy to me to get your excellent letter two days ago. Very few sounds of the outer world – except muffled echoes in New York Herald etc – reach us in the midst of our boscage. We are living rather like two birds in a <u>vast</u> bush. The garden is really rather wonderful – like one's childhood's conception of Eden – with a dash of Kubla Khan....

... the best thing is to lie down by the sea under the orange trees on a bed of wild rosemary – & this <u>would</u> be perfect but for the grim necessity of writing all the time to thank the Brazilian Minister for his gold chain purse – or Sir Robert & Lady Parks for their silver candlesticks – or the Ulster Liberal Association for the Sod of Turf they so kindly sent me. This is the poison which impregnates every hour for me – as surely as a Baba its rhum.

We have been up the hills a good deal – me on a donkey with eyes like an Osborne – B. on foot – & two charming guides – brunettes (or brun<u>ets</u> – men) with manners more <u>convincingly</u> insincere than AJB's. Not till they praised B's Italian did I find them out....

It feels very strange being away alone like this – with everything different & new ... all my letters addressed to a stranger – at times my own identity seems quite to elude me – & I wonder if I really am myself? (a speculation which only Alice in Wonderland or Bertrand Russell wld. think it worth while indulging in).

One curious thing I have discovered is that B. <u>isn't</u> himself – or rather

[1] Asquith wrote to Violet from Munstead House a little later: 'I came here to escape colleagues & others. I wish I could put a longer distance between myself & some of them' (12 December 1915).

that there were lots of things I didn't know about him before – (a fact which I couldn't have believed possible) – & by this I mean essential & intrinsic things – (not just that he was married at Eton! – like Strickland). It is rather like <u>walking into</u> a picture – one had always known on the wall – quite flat – & finding all sorts of new perspectives – not just the one it presented while one was outside it. The fact of my being able to feel this about <u>him</u> after our <u>great</u> intimacy – opens up wonderful vistas of insecurity & hazard about the (apparently) safest undertakings which gives one an 'up' with life. . . .

Love – write again – we <u>may</u> go to Rome for a few days – then home

yr V.

V.B.C. to Alfred Price   *Christmas Eve,*
Friday 24 December
La Mortola, Ventimiglia, Italy

My dear Price – I was so <u>very</u> glad to get your letter & post-card – & do trust your wound is not a serious one.[1] Perhaps you may even welcome it to give you a little rest & change. I can imagine these dark & icy months of damp & cold must have been very depressing. It has really been almost as bad at home. I can <u>never</u> remember such a cold winter in my life. I was married on the 30th November – all the Club who were at home managed to get leave & come. . . . We were very lucky in being lent this beautiful place on the Italian Riviera to come to for our honeymoon. We have had a delicious fortnight of sunshine. . . .

We have seen lots of French & Italian soldiers – as this place is just on the Frontier between France & Italy. The Italians are having terribly difficult fighting in most rocky & mountainous country. They are all conscripts of course, & not half so highly paid as our soldiers. They say Lord Derby's appeal has been wonderfully responded to at home & that the numbers who have joined are enormous.[2] How proud you must be of having gone when you did & done such splendid service to England. I feel sure that come what may you will never regret it. I feel I have reason to be very proud of the way the Club have come up to the scratch in the war. . . .

---

[1] Price was serving with the 17th Divisional Artillery in France; Violet's letter did not reach him, and was returned to her at Downing Street.

[2] Edward George Villiers Stanley (1865–1948), 17th Earl of Derby, director of recruitment, 1915. Derby's 'appeal' called upon men of military age to 'attest' their willingness to serve, thus negating the need for conscription. Asquith agreed that if insufficient numbers 'attested' then conscription would be introduced, and in January the necessary legislation covering single men aged 18–41 was passed, extended to married men the following May.

With all Xmas love from Mr Bonham Carter & myself I am ever your friend

Violet Bonham Carter

My new address will be Dorset House, Dorset St London W. but of course Downing St. will always find me.

M.B.C. to V.B.C.   *New Year's Eve, Friday 31 December*
                                       10 Downing Street, Whitehall, SW

Beloved. It was delightful to hear your blessed voice on the telephone, I had given you up for the evening & so it was doubly delightful. Edwin proposed to your father that he should dine with him to meet L-G & Rufus tomorrow night, the object being to nobble L-G who is very amenable to this sort of treatment. He always complains now that he never has a chance of seeing your father in such a way as to give them the opportunity for a general talk. This is no doubt true & it is true also that such talks are of great value in keeping L-G sweet....

This afternoon the Cabinet again met & spent its time in an amicable though contentious discussion of the details of the Compulsion Bill. The antagonism between McKenna & L-G is very high, [and] as Edwin had forecasted McK could not forbear from having a dig at L-G & practically accused him of concealing figures, while he was Chancellor of the Exchequer. One cannot help being angry at this sort of attitude; that ministers whose sole thought should be how the war may best be won, should allow their vision & judgements to be so distorted by personal animosities is really tragic; & I feel that though McKenna is right on his case, he almost damns himself to perdition by his animus against his opponents....

You have been so precious to me since our wedding. I cannot tell you how I feel your goodness to me, it has made me happy to the innermost core, & provided such a fund of contentment that I feel impervious to anybody other than the loss of you. It gives me the position of a god in the world & master of my fate so long as you are with me to hold my hand. Bless you always, B.

Bernard Freyberg to V.B.C.   *Friday 7 January 1916*
                                          Cape Helles, Gallipoli

We go tomorrow evening from here if we are lucky, my feelings are very mixed about it, I don't think sentiment can win any war, so I suppose it

is a step in the right direction.[1] I wonder what will be the fate of the R.N.D.
I wonder if you could let me know. I hear we are to stay in the Greek
islands to look after them.[2] I do hope we get to a place where there is
plenty of movement and fighting – say to the zone of operations round
Baghdad, I think there will be plenty to do after we have left here.

Oh! I am miserable tonight – we have just come from a short service held
at Backhouse Post over a cairn (with a cross) which has been consecrated to
the memory of all our fellows whose remains were never found. It was
most impressive, faintly moonlit with Achi Baba (lit at intervals by the
Chanak searchlight) snarling at us from above, while behind us were the
trenches and beaches we have paid so much to get, and beyond are the
hospital ships – the one splash of colour in the whole picture; I wonder if
you can understand what a comfort the sight of the hospital ships have
been to us here during our harder times, of a wet night when things were
very depressing the sight of the hospital ships picked out in green and red
made one glow with a feeling of comfort.

We may get leave for a week in England, I wonder would you care
to see me if I ever come back – don't forget the insignificant platoon
commanders.[3] Your letters to me have been a great joy. You must excuse
my writing as it is in semi-darkness I am doing this. I wonder what the
ones we leave here will think of us tomorrow night when we leave them.
Kia Ora & bless you   B.

Arthur Asquith to V.B.C.   *Tuesday 18 January*
                                                        Mudros

My dear Vizie. I send you two photographs taken by Chrystal – do you
remember – at the Glymenopoulo hotel – it seems long ago.[4] Patrick went
off on leave today and will give you my news, and I have written Father
an account of our last weeks on that damned Peninsula. The suspense as
to whether we should get off before the weather broke was considerable:
and the Turk supply of guns and shells grew and our lives became increasingly disagreeable daily – while our guns were being shipped off and few

[1] Sir Ian Hamilton had been replaced, in October, by General Sir Charles Monro (1860–
1929), and one of his first acts on taking command was to advise evacuation of the peninsula.

[2] After its evacuation from Gallipoli the RND reassembled at Mudros, the harbour town on
Lemnos. The 1st brigade then had the pleasant respite of three-months' garrison duty on the
Greek Islands. On 24 April, the eve of the first anniversary of the Gallipoli landings, the
Division sailed for France, where it played a significant role in the latter stages of the Somme.

[3] Freyberg, Oc and Cleg Kelly were all given leave, and left Mudros for England on 27
February, a year after their departure from Avonmouth docks.

[4] See the illustration below.

counter-batteries remained. It is a great relief to be away from shell-fire for a time: our part of the line was an easy and popular target. I hope Birdwood will get a big share of the credit for the evacuation.[1] The immediate destination of the Hood is an island of which it has been said 'Est in conspectu': Cyril will elucidate – I believe even your husband can.[2]

Our Iliad is over: our Odyssey beginning: I hope it may take me soonish for a spell in the Hesperides....[3]

I have a mass of letters to answer. Love to Bonge. Yours Oc.

Raymond Asquith's death, and his father's fall from power,
September and December 1916

On 15 September 1916 the 3rd Battalion Grenadier Guards participated in a dawn attack on the village of Lesboeufs, on the Somme. Without reaching its objective, the battalion suffered exceptionally heavy losses, with seventeen of its twenty-two officers either killed or wounded. Raymond Asquith was shot in the chest almost at the outset, leading no. 4 company in the attack. He died while being carried to a dressing station at the rear. Five months previously Raymond had secured a return to his regiment at the front, leaving the security of the headquarters staff. Though the staff position had been arranged without his knowledge and against his will, it naturally invited the conclusion that he had used his influence to escape the expected spring offensive. By returning to his regiment Raymond had set the record straight. News of his death reached his father on Sunday the 17th. Asquith's feelings for his eldest son were deep but undemonstrative. During the ten months that Raymond spent at the front his father did not once write to him, at a time when he corresponded frequently with women friends. Guilt about this was compounded by an awareness that he had never been able to reconcile his eldest son to his second marriage. Weighed down by grief, Asquith was given scarcely any respite from the Northcliffe-led press campaign which clamoured for his replacement by Lloyd George. For several weeks he was withdrawn and remote, and it became an effort to speak again in the Commons. Violet kept no record of the events surrounding her father's resignation on 5 December 1916, which can

---

[1] Though General Birdwood was personally against evacuation, he played a central role in the successful operation, and his reputation was considerably enhanced.

[2] The island of Tenedos; from Vergil's *Aeneid* 2. 21–3, '*In sight* of Troy there's an island, a well-known island, Tenedos....'

[3] In Greek mythology the inviting 'garden of the Hesperides' lay at the western extremity of the ancient world – Oc is hoping for home leave, a wish soon granted.

be followed in detail in the published accounts of the protagonists. The episode, though, was one of the defining moments in her life. After Raymond's death J. M. Barrie had written to her, 'of all the war-work you can possibly do now, the best will be to try to help your father in his sorrow ... you can do a great deal, and it is a great part for you'. Her 'part' was made infinitely greater by the events of December.[1]

Hugh Godley to V.B.C.   *Tuesday 19 September*
                             29 Chester Street, S.W.

My dearest, I simply can't begin to tell you what I feel about Raymond; I had kept telling myself all through that it <u>could</u> <u>not</u> happen; anything but that. And yet it has happened again, as it seems always to happen, that if there is one precious life of which one thinks more than another that it <u>must</u> be spared, so surely will the fatal day come. No one was so loved as he was, no one was a necessary ingredient in the lives of so many people; it was impossible to be dull if he was in the same house. I simply cannot imagine life without him.

I know my dear what torture it will be to you; I have so often heard you speak, as of an unheard-of horror, of what you w^d feel 'If something should happen to one of the boys' & I am sure it is no less bad than you would have expected. Quite apart from one's own feelings I think it is a more tragic event that a man like Raymond should be killed in war, than someone like John or Billy. If one had ever given it a thought one w^d have foreseen that it was certain that all the God-like young athletes were certain to fall at once. But Raymond was so absolutely unmilitary, & when the war came, he went into it not with any burning enthusiasm, but just as a sort of matter of course, & he went on with his soldiering just as he went on with his own profession before, in the conscientious methodical way which was so characteristic of him (oddly enough) rather grumbling & yet rather enjoying it, fully realizing what the end might be, but never to all appearances in the least conscious of it. And then when the time came the same devoted service, & the same supreme sacrifice, as in the case of those who went through the whole thing as if it might be a football match.[2]

---

[1] Captain Wilfrid Miles, *Military Operations: France and Belgium, 1916*, ii, 310–13; Sir Frederick Ponsonby, *The Grenadier Guards in the Great War*, 86–107; L. Cope to VBC, 27 June 1954; John Jolliffe (ed.), *Raymond Asquith: Life and Letters*, 236; 286–7; Roy Jenkins, *Asquith*, 414–15; J. M. Barrie to VBC, 30 September 1916.

[2] In July 1916 *The Times* carried a series of uplifting 'stories from the front', designed to reassure the public about the Somme engagement. One, entitled 'Like a football scrum',

I keep thinking of your father, & of the intolerable burden he has to bear. His pride in Raymond was always most touching. Of course there never was a more absurd idea than that R. was 'cynical' or 'unfeeling', he was most tenderhearted & affectionate. But no one was ever more shy about his enthusiasms, & in twenty years of very close & intimate association I never heard him speak with emotion of anyone but his Father & his mother, & of them only on about two occasions.

My dear I can't write about it, though I can think of nothing else. It is just heartbreaking. Look where you will there is nothing but agony & death, & hideous preparation of engines of death, & brutal exultation over deaths. Can anything in the world be worth it? I should like to see you; talking is easier; but I know nothing of your movements. Let me know when I can come. H

Arthur Asquith to V.B.C.   *Wednesday 20 September*
                                      Royal Naval Division, France

Dearest Vizie, I had a telegram from Day today saying that R. has been killed. I have been trying to write to poor Katharine but could find nothing to say. Her desolation is appalling. 'After the war' becomes daily a more parched and flowerless prospect for most of our generation: and the killing of Bosches less unpalatable. I should like any details of R's death which may reach you. At least one can feel that his life was full of fun and enjoyment for himself and others while it lasted.

And he died the best sort of death. I left England May 4th – the day he was due to come home on leave: so have only once seen him in uniform – when he was in the Queen's Westminsters, and we met in St. James St. round a corner and were nearly surprised into saluting and greeting one another. I am afraid Father will be terribly cut up about this, and only hope busy-ness may help him. There is little of the old world of fun left to us.... Love to Bongy. Yr <u>Oc</u>.

---

quoted a captain in the Rifle Brigade: 'the Hun machine-guns were their [the enemy's] only salvation; but wasn't it marvellous the way our chaps laughed at that fire! I've seen them pay far more heed to a sharp shower of rain. Oh, they're the salt of the earth. I've not heard of one single case of shirking. They went into it as though it was a football scrum. And begad, they came out the other side in the same spirit, even a lot who'd got popped' (6 July 1916).

V.B.C. to Hugh Godley   *Friday 22 September*
The Wharf, Sutton Courtenay,
Berkshire

Beloved ʋ – You wrote me such a perfect & understanding letter – as only you could.

My heart feels broken – I can't can't realize that our beautiful – beloved Raymond is gone – with all the laughter & delight & joy he brought to us – that I shall never in this life & world – of which he seemed such an integral & inalienable part – see him again.

I had been rather anxious all last week at Glen – knowing the Guards were on the verge of going in – but never for an instant then – or ever – as I now realize – faced this. Then Monday morning I opened a quite ordinary looking telegram with the usual trivial expectation & read 'Have just heard Raymond was killed on the 15th'.

It is very difficult to bear for oneself – but to see Father suffering so wrings one. Raymond's life was always a romance to him – & he watched it with thrilling pride & expectancy. Also R. belonged to his early idyllic beginnings – to his youth with my Mother & all the freshness & surprise of that part of his life. I showed him your letter & he loved it & read it again & again....

I suppose one shouldn't think of any life given now as wasted – & yet a sense of waste sweeps over me in spite of myself – that that rare, subtle, exquisite being – that inspired combination of atoms – that mind of finely-tempered steel – shld be shot down – dispersed & scattered before even he got over the parapet. He was shot thro' the chest & carried back to a shell-hole where there was an improvised dressing station. There they gave him morphia & he died an hour later. God bless him. How he has vindicated himself – before all those who thought him merely a scoffer – by the modest heroism with which he chose the simplest & most dangerous form of service – & having so much to keep for England gave it all to her with his life.... Yr V

Arthur Asquith to V.B.C.   *Tuesday 24 October*
4th Casualty Clearing Station,
Vth Corps, B.E.F., France

My dearest V. Four nights ago five others and I were buried at varying depths by a 'Minnie' – or heavy mortar bomb. I realized that something odd had happened to my ears, but thought this might pass. Then, two days ago, a cynically unkind order bade me to report at once for attachment to a Staff.[1] I obeyed, and then – my ears being no better but rather worse – I saw a Doctor who says both drums are perforated – that they may heal in three or four weeks, and that I may or may not be deafer as a result. I am to be evacuated by tonight's train....

I doubt whether anyone, except Friz. or Cleg, can realize what a very bitter disappointment it is for me not to be with them just now.[2] In case I may appear as a Casualty under the heading Shell Shock, will you please tell Father how things really stand – that I am perfectly well except for my ears, and that I do not mind Shells any less or any more than I did before? If I get to England, I must scheme to be treated at home: I am not in bed. Love. Yrs Oc.

I was thrilled by your news about the Bongino: I had been wondering when that would happen.[3] Yr Oc.

V.B.C. to Bernard Freyberg   *Tuesday 21 November*
                                    Dorset House, Portman Square, W.

I was so distressed to hear of your wound – as I know quite apart from the pain & discomfort how exasperated you will be by being whisked away to Havre[?] just when things were so exciting for the battalion.[4] However it probably happened after the crucial attack was over & you will have been comforted by the knowledge of how splendidly it & the whole division did. I hear nothing but its praises. We are all very sad to-day at the tragic news of dear Kelly's death. I have not yet seen Oc but I can guess by my own sorrow what a terrible loss he will be to him – & you – & all who served with him. He seemed made for life....

Oc arrived here very deaf & looking rather strained & shattered I thought – tho' he hasn't had a trace of shell-shock – & now hears almost perfectly again. He is of course moving Heaven & Earth to get out again & back to the battalion & has I think wired to the Brigadier to apply for him. Whether there will be any Staff hanky-panky about it I don't know. It is hard on Oc I do think & was not in any way prompted or inspired from home tho' of course it would be a relief to us to know him safe.... Goodbye – & write & tell me how you are. Ever yrs Violet

[1] As his brother had done, Oc fought a running battle to stay at the front with his regiment, and avoid staff posts.

[2] The Naval Division was then preparing to attack German defensive positions north of the Ancre, in one of the final engagements of the Somme, 13–15 November.

[3] Violet was expecting her first baby; (Helen Laura) Cressida was born on 22 April 1917.

[4] Freyberg had in fact been wounded four times, leading the successful attack on Beaucourt, 13 November 1916. For this he was awarded the Victoria Cross.

M.B.C. to V.B.C.   *Friday 1 December*
10 Downing Street,
Whitehall, S.W.

Beloved, L.G. came to see your father this morning and made this proposal. That a new War Committee be formed of which the Secretary of State for War & the 1ˢᵗ Lord of the Admiralty must be members. It should have sole authority to conduct the war, save for the right of appeal to Cabinet. The P.M. should not be a member, but should decide when any matter should be referred to the Cabinet. He wants Bonar to replace AJB at the Admiralty & the Committee to consist of himself as Chairman, Bonar Law, Carson & Montagu (perhaps).

The point of the scheme is obvious. He knows that he cannot replace your father, so he wants to run the war under his aegis – retaining therefore the support of the Liberals, the presence of Bonar Law & Carson will secure the support of the Tories. It is a quite wild scheme, which of course cannot be accepted. It remains to be seen, whether if it is or not, he will resign. Meanwhile Curzon and the [?] Board will resign unless they get their way. The whole situation is as full of difficulty as it has ever been in these recurrent crises.

Saturday – You will see from today's Times & Daily Chronicle, the whole of LG's plan exposed. LG as I have said I think really would prefer the P.M. to stay at the head of the Government – though as a cipher – but of course the Northcliffe Press & the Morning Post wish to clear out both him & Grey. Hugh will take this, so I send it with all my love. B.

V.B.C. to Hugh Godley   *Friday 22 December*
Easton Grey, Malmesbury, Wiltshire

Dearest dear ὁ – I was inexpressibly touched by your generous suggestion – & indeed I promise you that if ever I feel my back really against the wall financially <u>you</u> would be & <u>will</u> be the first person I shall turn to – because I love you enough not to mind depending on you or being under any obligation to you – however delicate. . . .

We are all down here together in <u>deep</u> snow under rather lovely skies grey & flocculent – with breaks of pale clear green & orange at sunset. Rather a sad little party – M. worn & feverish & her nerves sticking out of their sheathes & indeed out of her body altogether – Father – to me infinitely poignant – he looks so jarred & <u>shaken</u>. . . .

About B's honour![1] I'm not surprised you were amused! So were we – &

---

[1] Maurice Bonham Carter was made a KCB in Asquith's resignation honours list.

still more at the seriousness with which it has been taken by the world at large – telegrams & letters of the most serious & 'senti' congratulations pouring in! We were both <u>very</u> averse to having it – he much more even than I – as he is neither a soldier nor a Civil Servant, in both of which professions it is a recognized symbol & 'rung' on the ladder. <u>But</u> on consultation with Edgar & one or two men of low City cunning I <u>was</u> told that it <u>wld</u>. materially enhance his chances of making money in the City & this – coming at the moment when I most felt the need of it – persuaded me to advise him to accept it – which he was all along <u>strongly</u> against on the grounds of funniness & tiresomeness. (To both of us the prefix suggests nothing so much as Sir Jesse Boot[1] & his class – tho' I suppose a K.C.B. does imply some necessary merit – unlike baronetcies etc – which usually <u>just</u> mean money.) I can honestly say except O.M. & V.C. there is no order or honour which has the slightest <u>sentimental</u> value for me. P.C. I would have preferred him to have if he had to have something but this we were told wld be of <u>no</u> use in the City whatever....

I must stop. I have no Xmas present for you. I had such a hellish rush Thursday & Friday. But I send you all my love for the New Year – Yr V.

V.B.C. to Mary Herbert   *Boxing Day, Tuesday 26 December*
                                              Dorset House, Portman Square, W.

Darling – You wrote me such a beloved letter which I have been meaning to answer daily – but I cannot trust myself to write about this. I am so afraid of being hysterical & bitter & violent & all the things one should avoid like the plague. What I <u>feel</u> about it is beyond expression. I would like above all things to see you.

The actual 'crisis' itself could easily have been weathered, as so many other really graver ones have been – by compromises & readjustments – but it was the <u>root</u>-cause & chronic condition from which they have one & all sprung which made it impossible for Father to go on. He couldn't go on facing the odds without – & tackling the superhuman task of the War – whilst his closest & most trusted colleague was working all the while – from within – against him, in close co-operation with his deadliest assailant Northcliffe outside. This sudden recognition of Ll-G's consistent treachery combined with poor Bonar's <u>terror</u> of Carson is what they ship-wrecked on.

How I long for the whole story to be told & known in all its sordidness.

---

[1] Sir Jesse Boot (1850–1931), businessman and philanthropist, the founder of the retail chemists. He was knighted in 1909 and made a baronet in 1916.

But Father's magnanimity & bigness about it all is a heavy trial in some ways! He will hit always 3ft above the belt at least. The best humour of the situation so far has been Ll.G. sending for Bongie & begging him quite seriously to continue to run D.St for him! B. is of course going into the Army at once & I fear we shall have to let our house – rather a bad moment for us to do it.[1] I'm sure I shall never be able to perch & cuckoo with Cynthia's aplomb & addresse! I do so hope B. won't be sent out before my baby comes. My great dread now is that it will be born looking exactly like Lloyd George! whose face & personality has been branded deeper on my soul during the last weeks than any other human being's!. . .

Goodbye Mary darling bless you, Violet

Victory and defeat – the end of the war and the 1918 general election

After the birth of her first child, Cressida, in April 1917, Violet spent much less time writing. There are few letters and virtually no diary for the remainder of the war. She must, though, have dwelt at length upon the years during which 'her brother Raymond had been killed, Beb psychologically damaged, [and] Oc severely wounded'. Less than a fortnight after Cressida's birth Bongie's elder brother Norman was killed, during the battle of Arras. Such a weight of bereavement inevitably took its toll. In August, while the battle of Passchendaele was in progress, Violet wrote to Hugh Godley: 'The thought of the offensive does make one feel sick at heart – the thought of all those precious – indispensable people being pounded out of life by heavy artillery to gain another few bare miles. I suppose the feeling we have both got is what is called "losing morale".' There is no suggestion that Violet's morale collapsed, though the war still had fifteen months to run. Even before the armistice of 11 November 1918 the Coalition leaders, Lloyd George and Bonar Law, were planning a general election. They aimed to capitalize on the credit they would be given for 'winning the war'. This strategy paid predictably high dividends, and at the polls on 14 December Asquith's independent Liberals were annihilated in a massive Coalition victory. Every former Liberal minister lost his seat. Violet felt the heartbreak of her father's defeat 'swallowed up and lost in the great tragedy of seeing all one has loved and believed in disappearing in this vast land-slide'. All marks of 'loyalty, decency and independence' in politics

---

[1] After declining to serve under Lloyd George, Bongie applied to join the Life Guards and later the Royal Air Force, but was rejected from both as being medically unfit (he suffered from varicose veins). As a senior civil servant he was soon found work in the ministry of reconstruction, later transferring to the air ministry.

had been swept away. After four years of intense struggle it was with a complete absence of elation that she looked towards the post-war world.[1]

---

[1] MRBC unpublished autobiographical fragment; VBC to Hugh Godley, 3 August 1917 – the offensive referred to is 3rd Ypres, or Passchendaele; MBC to VBC, 24, 25 October 1918; J. A. Spender and Cyril Asquith, *Life of Lord Oxford*, ii, 311; VBC to Mary Herbert, December 1918, in Margaret Fitzherbert, *Greenmantle*, 216.

TWO

The Inter-War Years

1919–1939

CHRONOLOGY OF EVENTS 1919–1939

1919	January	21 – Paris Peace Conference begins; first meeting of Dáil Éireann; beginnings of guerilla war in southern Ireland (to July 1921 truce)
	June	28 – Treaty of Versailles signed
1920	February	25 – Asquith wins Paisley by-election
	March	first 'Black and Tans' arrive in Dublin
	July	'Auxiliaries' begin to arrive in Dublin
	November	21 – 'Bloody Sunday'
	December	11–12 – Crown forces set fire to city of Cork
1921	July	9 – truce in Anglo-Irish war
	October	11 – Anglo-Irish treaty negotiations in London
	December	6 – 'articles of agreement' for Anglo-Irish treaty signed in London
1922	January	7 – Treaty ratified by Dáil Éireann, 64–57
	June	16 – general election in Irish Free State results in pro-Treaty majority
	October	19 – Conservative MPs vote 185–88 to fight next election as independent party; 23 – Lloyd George resigns, succeeded by Bonar Law
	November	15 – general election: 345 Conservative; 142 Labour; 62 National Liberal (Lloyd George); 54 Liberal (Asquithian)
	December	6 – Irish Free State established
1923	January	23 – French and Belgian troops occupy Ruhr
	December	6 – general election: 258 Conservative; 191 Labour; 159 Liberal
1924	January	23 – first Labour government takes office
	October	8 – government defeated in debate on 'Campbell Case'; MacDonald resigns; 29 – general election: 419 Conservative; 151 Labour; 40 Liberal
1926	May	4–12 – General Strike
	October	15 – Asquith relinquishes leadership of Liberal Party
1928	February	15 – Asquith's death

1929	May	30 – general election: 288 Labour; 260 Conservative; 59 Liberal
1931	August	24 – formation of National Government under MacDonald
	October	27 – general election: 473 Conservative; 13 National Labour; 35 Liberal National (= 521 National); 33 Liberal; 52 Labour
1935	October	3 – Italian invasion of Abyssinia
	November	14 – general election: 432 Conservative; 154 Labour; 20 Liberal
1936	January	20 – death of George V; accession of Edward VIII
	March	7 – German troops enter the Rhineland
	July	16 – beginning of the Spanish Civil War
	December	11 – abdication of Edward VIII, accession of George VI
1937	May	28 – Baldwin resigns as premier, succeeded by Neville Chamberlain
1938	September	29–30 – Munich Conference on Czechoslovakia
	October	3–6 – Munich debate – government majority of 219; thirty Tories abstain
1939	March	15 – German troops enter Prague; 31 – British guarantee to defend Poland

FIVE

The Paisley Election
The Anglo-Irish War

October 1919–April 1921

The Paisley election of 1920

Following his defeat at the 1918 general election Asquith found himself cut adrift politically, and the following year was one of 'bitter exile'. While he was understandably reluctant to submit to the trial of a by-election, he knew that if he was to lead the fight against the Coalition it could be done only by regaining a seat in the Commons. In January 1920 he therefore embarked upon the 'hazardous adventure' of contesting Paisley, an industrial constituency near Glasgow. The seat became vacant on the death of the independent Liberal Sir John McCallum. McCallum's majority had been only 106 in 1918, and there was every prospect of a close contest in 1920, especially since Asquith's 'come-back' attracted considerable attention. Violet campaigned for her father during the three weeks that preceded polling day, on 12 February. There were encouraging signs of early support, though Asquith viewed with concern 3,000 Irish electors 'ordered by their bosses to vote Labour', and 15,000 recently enfranchised women, 'for the most part hopelessly ignorant of politics, credulous to the last degree, and flickering with gusts of sentiment like a candle in the wind'. In winning the women's vote Violet came into her own at Paisley. She made it her task to 'reveal' her father, to show him to be a 'great human personality'. By dramatizing him she dramatized his cause. They both revelled in the sophisticated appreciation of the packed Paisley audiences: 'If some phrase, some sentence pleased them . . . you would hear a whisper behind you on the platform "Weel turned". They treated us just as though we were the Russian Ballet.' Violet contributed significantly to a famous victory, which was hailed as a new 'Midlothian'. But although Asquith showed vision in attacking coercion in Ireland, and the harsh terms of the Versailles Treaty, this proved a false dawn for Liberalism. The muted reception that Asquith was given when he returned to the Commons on 1 March was a more accurate indicator of the Liberals' standing.[1]

---

[1] HHA to Mrs Hilda Harrisson, 30 January 1920, in *Letters to a Friend*, 124–6; J. A. Spender and Cyril Asquith, *Life of Lord Oxford*, 330–1; Harris interview, Violet Bonham Carter MSS.

V.B.C. to Arthur Asquith　　　　　*Saturday 18 October 1919*
　　　　　　　　　　　　　　　　　　Drummond Castle, Crieff

I've been meaning to write to you every day for the last 3 weeks – but the
strike & an intimate knowledge of Spanish posts deterred me for a time. . . .[1]
I long to hear all about yr. Pyrrenean time. I loved yr. letter you wrote just
before starting. I've had a <u>very</u> long & very amusing stretch of nomadic
life – I've never felt so completely cut off from my moorings since I married
(B. didn't get away to join me till last week). First a week at Holker – which
you know – a <u>perfect</u> atmosphere. (Didn't we agree once that if we had to
eliminate from our many & variegated milieus – the two we wld. <u>keep</u>
wld. be the Cavendish world of <u>crystal</u> goodness & greyhound breeding – &
the intelligentsia – Desmond, Clifford Sharp,[2] Gilbert Murray, Masefield,
Winston etc. etc. etc.)

They were at their very best – active as antelopes – & we led a delicious
life of picnics on the edge of lakes & hills, & long walks through tawny
grasses & over rose-coloured moss – & blackberrying – & tennis on a hard
court – & <u>beloved</u> Ld. Bob was there & flavoured every talk & meal for me
with his pungent brain.[3] How I enjoy his keen blade cutting through the
general fluff. His 'slant' on things interests me very much. It isn't mine –
but it has moved much nearer mine since the war. (I can hear you snort a
little over this!). . . .

I spent one night at the Haldanes' on the way up – & admired Haldane's
moral courage for <u>still</u> calling his Newfoundland dog Kaiser! Then on to
Balmoral which was a <u>really</u> amusing experience. I was the guest of the
Stamfordhams[4] (rather like staying in the housekeeper's room) but we
dined most nights with the King – & as I was the only strange doe I sat
next to him every night – & we exchanged hours of what can only be
described as <u>Jaw</u>. I found to my delight that he <u>loathes</u> French (regards
himself as mainly responsible for his displacement) & as you may imagine
I fanned this flame for all I was worth. However I was sorry to find him
strongly in favour of the Russian expedition, passionately against a levy
on capital – & slightly attracted to Ld. Inverforth! He was rather pathetic
about the possibility of a Labour govt. 'They may want to get rid of <u>me</u>' – &

---

[1] Violet had holidayed with her father in Spain in March 1919, and Oc had just returned
from there.

[2] Clifford Dyce Sharp (1883–1935), journalist and editor of *New Statesman*, 1913–31.

[3] (Edgar Algernon) Robert ('Bob') Gascoyne-Cecil (1864–1958), cr. Viscount Chelwood,
1923; a creator of the League of Nations; Nobel Peace Prize winner, 1937; president, LNU,
1923–45.

[4] Arthur John Bigge (1849–1931), 1st Baron Stamfordham, 1911; private secretary to George
V, having previously served Queen Victoria; he married, 1881, Constance *née* Neville (1849–
1922).

me murmuring reassuringly 'Oh no – nonsense – fiddle de dee – what an idea' etc. etc. He then asked how they wld. manage about his household (Ld Chamberlain etc.) who <u>must</u> be peers – & go in & out with a change of Govt. – as there are no Labour peers. This point had never occurred to me & <u>is</u> rather an amusing one.

A squad of 7 pipers suddenly walk round the table towards the end of dinner making a noise such as you can't imagine. The King wears a kilt – also all the boys – & they stalk all day & shoot extraordinarily well. The Queen wears a sky blue tweed & takes constitutionals in Xmas woods – tapping fircones with a walking stick. The mise en scène is <u>pure</u> Victoria & Albert – Diary in the Highlands (Lytton Strachey shld go there).[1] Tartan curtains, glass door-handles, Landseer watercolours of Queen Victoria opening dispatch boxes on the back of a Shetland pony – & Prince Albert deer-stalking in a tight grey frock coat. Soveral & 'John Revelstoke' were my only fellow guests – both great fun....[2]

Love to Betty & bless you. Ever yr V

V.B.C. to Hugh Godley　　　　　　　*Saturday 27 December*
　　　　　　　　　The Wharf, Sutton Courtenay, Berkshire

I send you for Xmas Keynes's book which I think <u>quite</u> brilliant – an unanswerable indictment – which should be a historical work....[3] There is a portrait of Ll.G. ... which he himself censored & cut out – possibly wisely.[4] He read it aloud to us yesterday afternoon. It is <u>extraordinarily</u> good but I think it is perhaps better that he [Lloyd George] should be read between the lines all the time, like the Arlesienne dominating the whole tragedy & yet never 'coming on' herself....

... We have really had the <u>greatest</u> fun & the most excellent talks. Yesterday a bombshell was hurled by Keynes who suddenly accused Margot of neither understanding nor caring for <u>pictures</u>![5] Scene – which can be

---

[1] Lytton Strachey's (1880–1932) *Eminent Victorians* had been published the previous year, and his *Queen Victoria* appeared in 1921.

[2] John Baring (1863–1929), 2nd Baron Revelstoke, and a partner in the Baring Brothers bank; Violet knew him from pre-1914 society.

[3] John Maynard Keynes was a treasury representative at the Paris Peace Conference 1919, but resigned in opposition to its terms; he returned to England and wrote *The Economic Consequences of the Peace* (1919) in protest, which became a bestseller, establishing his international reputation.

[4] 'he compares Ll.G.'s mind to glass – having no colour of its own – but receptively catching any shade in the prism which is thrown across it at a given angle...' (VBC to Hubert Henderson, June 1926; in Robert Skidelsky, *The Economist as Saviour*, 253–4).

[5] Margot had inherited from her father an appreciation of fine art and generally took pride in her aesthetic sense.

better imagined than described. The tragedy of the party is the displacement of Sharp from the intellectual prima donna-ship by Keynes, round whom we all snobbishly cluster.

... All my love bless you ... My love to yr. Father <u>please tell me his opinion</u> of Keynes' book. If you've got it please return as the 1st edition is sold out – V.

V.B.C. to Gilbert Murray   *Saturday 24 January 1920*
                                           Dorset House, Portman Square, W.

Dear Professor Murray – Thank you so much for your letter – & its news. Et tu Judas! I didn't know that it was in me to form an even lower estimate of Montagu's character than I held already – but it has happened.[1] That he should offer himself as the catspaw for Ll.G. to undercut the position of the Free Liberals generally – & Father in particular – in what is – largely thanks to you – one of our few strongholds – is really <u>incredible</u> – especially as whenever he meets any member of our entourage (as he did Elizabeth at a dinner party 6 weeks ago) he pours out to them a plaint about his present leader & political environment – insists that Father is his 'spiritual home' & that he is on the verge of resigning & returning to the fold. His <u>cant</u> & cringing dishonesty make me quite sick. Give me Winston's frank–candid cynicism any day.

As to what reply should be returned <u>I</u> should of course like the stiffest possible negative couched in courteous but pointed language. It might be pointed out that the brand of Liberalism professed by the Oxford Liberal Club is of quite a different character to that practised by the Prime Minister & his Govt. – e.g. his policy in Ireland – Russia – etc. & of course his action at Spen Valley.[2] You will of course make allowance for the fact that my outlook is perhaps blurred by family passions & prejudices – but I do really & honestly feel that, putting all personal issues aside, Ll.G. has betrayed every principle he has ever professed – & has no right to speak as the mouthpiece of <u>any</u> creed – to young people whose faith & convictions are still intact. Anyhow whatever you say – <u>do</u> refuse.

Father had a splendid meeting at Cambridge last night. We (he I & Margot) go up to Paisley Sunday night. I am full of doubt as to the issue – but I feel it must be made a magnificent fight – whatever the outcome. <u>Do</u>

---

[1] The two sides in the Liberal Party schism were then vying for control over constituency associations: Montagu appears to have been part of a Coalition Liberal (Lloyd George) attempt to win Oxford from the Free Liberals (Asquithian).

[2] At the Spen Valley by-election in December 1919 a 'couponed' Coalition Liberal was run against the independent Liberal Sir John Simon, ensuring victory for the Labour candidate.

come & help us once we get our bearings. At present the whole place is a strange unbroken country. I shall feel your good wishes with us. Ever yrs, Violet B.C.

Diary – late January and early February – written in early March, at Dorset House

[Sunday 25 January] We left – Father, M., Vivian Phillipps & myself by the night train & were seen off by little Davies, Lord Lambourne, McKenzie Wood & a few others.[1] There followed nearly 3 weeks – the strangest & most memorable experience of my life. I can only describe it as a nightmare with streaks of ecstasy. We lived in the Station Hôtel (our bedrooms – Margot's & mine – opening onto the platform itself) never leaving it except to get into a motor to go to Paisley. I spoke once or twice every day the whole time we were there – & the blaze of publicity we lived in prevented one ever repeating a <u>sentence</u>. I was feeling ill all the time – & never went to sleep before 4 or 5 – but I was helped partly by an overwhelming sense of the issues at stake – which made one recklessly unselfconscious about one's own part – & also by some arsenic pills, provided by Parkie, which certainly carried me thro' the first week, but afterwards prevented me from sleeping.

I don't think I have ever, since they were born, given so few thoughts to the children.[2] Mercifully I was quite free from anxiety about them – but sometimes I would admit to myself with amazement that I had gone through the day without having time to rest my mind & heart once on the blessed thought of them.[3] The search for mental provender was a very fevered one, especially towards the end. Luckily McKean the Coalitionist gave us many openings – of which I availed myself fully – & the Paisley people were <u>wonderful</u> material to work upon – an extraordinary combination of cool heads & warm hearts. They wld. listen for <u>hours</u> to slabs of solid facts & figures from Father, admirably handled & presented of course, but quite undiluted by gas, fluff or claptrap of any kind – appraising it all clearly – coolly – critically. But they are capable at the same time of the enthusiasm of revivalists. . . .

---

[1] (Henry) Vivian Phillipps (d. 1955), private secretary to Asquith, 1917–22; Liberal MP for West Edinburgh 1922–4; chief Liberal whip 1923–4. Amelius Richard Mark Lockwood (1847–1928), cr. Baron Lambourne, 1917; Unionist MP for Epping, 1892–1917. Major (Sir) Murdoch McKenzie Wood (1881–1949), cr. Kt 1932, Liberal MP for Central Aberdeenshire, 1919–24; Banffshire, 1929–35; Liberal whip, 1923–4, 1932–4.

[2] Violet and Bongie's second child, Laura, had been born on 13 October 1918.

[3] Violet placed great trust in the children's nannie, Ada Bentley, a devout Congregationalist and a passionate Liberal. She was highly intelligent, and the only woman of whom Violet ever admitted being afraid.

V.B.C. to M.B.C.   ***Wednesday 28 January***
                                        Central Station Hotel, Glasgow

Dearest – We have had 2 <u>very</u> busy days. I can't remember whether I wrote
to you before or after Father's adoption meeting – I think before. We
motored out of Glasgow Monday night along dark tram lines through a
patch of Low-land country into Paisley (about 20 minutes' run) a hard
Scotch industrial town – first granite villas – then dark stone houses – then
tramlines – shops – cinemas etc. – & all round factory chimneys – &
women with shawled heads – an industrial atmosphere.

We went first to Father's agent's office. . . . He took us on to the Lib. Club
where the entire Association was mustered – about 300 keen – clever –
foxy old Scotchmen – who gave Father a <u>good</u> but not an enthusiastic
reception.[1]

The Chairman made quite a good opening speech but alluded respect-
fully to Ll.G. & various Liberals – like Munro – within the Coalition. There
was however practically no applause at Ll.G.'s name. Father then made an
admirable speech & really <u>got</u> them all when at the end he said he had
never lowered their colours. They were obviously won round & <u>some</u> of
course were frenzied partisans from the start. . . . The adoption was then
carried with great enthusiasm. Father replied – Margot was called on – got
up & said 'Go in & win' – which was warmly cheered – & they then called
for me & I spoke for about 6 or 7 minutes – (I thought it well to take the Age &
Pro German calumnies <u>tightly</u> by the throat – the latter is <u>very</u> rampant &
poisonous here)[2] & everyone seemed pleased & amused – especially the
journalists who are like birds of prey – thirsty for 'cheap' copy.[3]

Next day Donald Maclean turned up – & we had our first big public
meeting.[4] The hall had been up to a point 'packed' with Labour people
led by 2 discharged soldiers who made very bad street corner speeches
about sep. allowances ('Cld <u>yr.</u> wife live on 12/6 a week' <u>addressed to
Father</u> was a question which went home to <u>me</u>!!). . . .

---

[1] A substantial number of those present would have regarded themselves as supporters of
Lloyd George; Asquith won adoption at Paisley only by a 92–75 vote of the full membership
of the local Liberal Association.

[2] The 'age calumny' must refer to Asquith's declining physical powers, though this only
really became an issue later – in 1920 he was only sixty-seven. For the pro-German calumnies,
see above, p. 68.

[3] *The Times*'s correspondent observed that from Violet the audience got 'a really effective
fighting speech, which confirms an opinion I have already expressed that in his daughter Mr
A. will find his most useful lieutenant in the election'.

[4] Sir Donald Maclean (1864–1932), cr. KBE, 1917; Liberal MP 1910–22 and 1929–32; chairman of the Liberal Parliamentary Party, 1919–22; a close family friend, godfather to Mark
Bonham Carter.

I found to my horror that no women's committee or women's organization of <u>any</u> kind <u>existed</u> – & none is being formed till to-night. No arrangements have <u>yet</u> been made for Women's Meetings & the canvass is only just being mapped out & organized. I naturally feel a delicacy in thrusting myself on them – but I'm sure it is <u>fatal</u> not to get more of a hustle on. I feel the women's vote is the dark horse & that Labour is stealing a march on us every hour.... They don't want one to do much I can see – one must go <u>very</u> carefully.... They <u>hate</u> the thought of strangers from England....

Love – bless you, yr V

Love to Nannie – tell her I will write

Gilbert Murray to V.B.C.   ***Wednesday 11 February***
                                     Yatscombe, Boar's Hill, Oxford

Dear Lady Bonham-Carter,[1]

Well, you have been making history at Paisley, and we have all been hanging on the news from day to day. Everyone I have seen agrees that, whatever the result, the whole political atmosphere is changed. I am inclined to think what I thought after the General Election is beginning to come true, that there is a tremendous reaction of popular feeling coming in favour of your father....

Your speech about the necktie was awfully good.[2] And the only two methods he had of winning votes! I tell myself not to hope; firmly. But I am buying one or two fireworks for Stephen to let off if things go well. Yours very sincerely, Gilbert Murray.

---

[1] After Bongie was knighted in December 1916 Violet became 'Lady Bonham Carter' (without the hyphen used by Murray).

[2] McKean had accused Asquith 'of shaking the bloodstained hands of Sinn Féiners' while wearing a green tie, symbolic of support for their cause. The story first circulated in May 1916 when Asquith spoke to Sinn Féin prisoners in Dublin after the Easter Rising (VBC to MBC, 31 January 1920; Stephen Koss, *Asquith*, 210). Violet later joked that McKean tried to make her father's ties 'the real issue at the election': 'This caused me great alarm because he wore during the contest a series of ties that would easily have lost him the safest seat in Scotland' (Address to NLC, 20 March 1920).

'A Paisley Woman' to V.B.C.   *Thursday 12 February*
                                                              Paisley

Dear Lady Bonham Carter,

I have such a desire to shake hands with your father and wish him a sweeping majority, but knowing from my experience of always being on the outside of the hall – with one single exception – when he was speaking, that there is no chance of speaking to him, I write to you instead. A friend said to me lately 'Surely you are not going to vote for Mr Asquith' and I said 'I am. I don't know anything about politics but his hair curls like my dear old dad's (the best man that ever lived and I have no doubt your father is a close second) and that is quite a good enough reason for voting for him, for me.'

I really do know a little more about politics than that and have read your addresses both with great amusement and interest. I have read some of Mr Asquith's too and am sorry that I have neither the time nor the strength to canvass for him today. He is lucky in having you to speak for him and I am sure you have won the hearts of Paisley Liberals and the admiration of those who are voting on the wrong side.

With all best wishes of a Paisley woman

Diary – Thursday 12 to Friday 27 February – written in early March, at Dorset House

... The demonstration at the Liberal Club on our last night [12 February] was one of the most extraordinary things I have ever seen – & one of the most deeply moving. It was a marvellous joy & consummation of my deep & passionate love for Father – a thing born in the marrow of my bones – to feel I had really been able to help him, as I believe I was. When he said what he owed to me & they all stood up & cheered I felt it really too great a joy for my heart to hold.[1]

We were almost killed at St Pancras on our first return home – by a mob 3000 strong – worked up ... into a state of Dervish-like enthusiasm. They broke down the enclosure prepared for us in which Buckmaster[2] had been waiting with a speech, a flashlight photographer & two bouquets, & we were engulfed in a surging crowd – crushed & battered almost to bits until ultimately a great human wave flung me up onto the roof of a 4-wheeler

---

[1] 'Sneers about the "Asquith circus" are not sufficient to counteract the influence exerted by the wit and political skill of the Liberal leader's daughter' (*The Times*, 5 February 1920).

[2] Stanley Owen Buckmaster (1861–1934), cr. Baron, 1915; Viscount, 1933; lord chancellor, 1915–16.

on which Father was delivering a speech – excellent but quite inaudible!

We were ultimately shipped off in the motor – I shaking hands with Whelan our parlour maid (amongst other thousands!) without recognizing her! – dashed home & found my little angels sleeping so peacefully with a lovely flush on their darling faces. Nannie told me rather shame-facedly that the 'Daily Mirror people' had been round & extracted photographs from her & then pretended she had seen the children – which she never had as they were asleep.[1] When asked by someone where I was Cressida said 'Mama's in Scotland – talking'. . . .

V.B.C. to Gilbert Murray   *Tuesday 17 February*
Dorset House, Portman Square, W.

Dear Professor Murray – Thank you a thousand times for your letter – it was nice of you to write. I have returned exhausted – threadbare in body & mind but full of hope. One daren't promise anything – because one is so much on one's guard against that microbe of optimism that always invades the by-electioneer – but every sign in the political skies favoured Father when we left Paisley. For one thing he became there, what he has never before been in his life, the 'popular' candidate, the darling of the crowd! I am quite sure that the non-political vote – which exists in every con- stituency – was cast solid for him. We 'got' the Women – & I noticed on polling day a very significant fact – that 10 to 1 – or at least 6 to 1 – of the children had red ribbons on (our colours) – & this is symptomatic of the atmosphere of the homes. He fought magnificently – improving in vitality & spirit as the days went on. . . . The most useful part I performed in the struggle was making 'personal remarks' (as they are called in the nursery) about him – & this was useful – as his danger – through shyness – decency – & complete absence of any consciousness of self – is to be too impersonal. . . . Ever yrs, Violet B. C.

[*diary continued* . . .] [We went] up again to Paisley Tuesday night [24 February]. . . .[2] About 12 [midday Wednesday] we drove into Paisley – covered with red carnations & rosettes. Large crowds already in front of the Sheriff's Court house where the counting took place.

Only Father & McNair were admitted to the counting room & M. I &

---

[1] Bongie had written to Violet on 10 February: 'Nanny confessed to me rather anxiously & at the same time excitedly that a lady from the Daily Mirror had called & asked for photographs & induced her to give her the only ones available viz her Littlehampton ones. I said even the children had to be sacrificed today in the interests of the election . . . .'.

[2] To allow time for the votes of 'absent' electors to be included, a fortnight elapsed between the close of the poll and the declaration, in the early afternoon of Wednesday 25th.

Vivian Phillipps agonized next door in a vast municipal sort of room.[1] I started very confident – much more so than M. but after an hour & a half's wait begun to feel rather a needle. . . . Then Phillipps put the lid on our certainty by saying he had just seen Father shake hands with Biggar & congratulate him![2] I felt as if the whole bottom had been knocked out of the future. And outside we heard hoarse impatient outbursts of cheering from the crowd – about 15,000 strong – howling for their prey to be flung to them. That prey was failure – us! I was leaning weakly against the double door when a tiny paper was pushed through – by whom we do not & shall never know. On it, in a hurried pencil scribble, were written the figures . . . I couldn't believe it – I couldn't trust it.[3] It was too wonderful – too good. It was like being shot up from under the sea into the clouds!

We staggered out onto the balcony & waved – then back again – & into the next room where I hugged Father & told him of our agonized suspense, of which he hadn't had one moment! – then a wonderful reception as he went out onto the balcony. Biggar was delightful & did his best to get F. a hearing – but the cheers drowned it all. On to the Liberal Club where we had a rapturous 10 minutes . . . & home for a short rest before our big meeting in the Clark Town Hall – one of the most wonderful meetings I have ever seen. Five thousand white hot people. I was given a most lovely Paisley shawl. F. & I both spoke. Down south again the same night – after being within an inch of our lives at the hands of 3000 Glasgow students who saw us off at the station. We were met at the other end by a group of faithfuls who had been waiting ever since 6 (our train was 3 hours late) with an adjournment for breakfast.

Cressida went round to see Father with Nannie that morning & found him talking to Donald Maclean about the fate of Constantinople. She had red ribbons on her coat & he asked her 'why are you wearing red ribbons?' But she resolutely refused to reply in a 'topical' vein – 'Cos it makes me look smart – that's why'. . . .

I have had 14 different invitations to stand for various constituencies – & I did – & do – feel terribly tortured both as to what I want & what I ought to do. I feel this is a moment when Liberalism needs above all things standard bearers & it is difficult for anyone who believes in it – & has its future as much at heart as I have – to refuse to put any little jot or tittle of réclame or anything else however undeserved into the pot to help it. At

[1] T. Dun McNair, a Paisley printer, and Asquith's election agent; 'a sensitive little Scotchman with a beautiful little head . . . . He always wears a top hat (a curious contrast to Father in his old Homburg rat-catcher & hair well over his collar)'.

[2] J. M. Biggar, unsuccessful Labour candidate at Paisley in 1918.

[3] The figures were: Asquith 14,736, Biggar 11,902, McKean 3,795.

the same time I have only to <u>think</u> of the children to know that by allowing any other claim to encroach on what is theirs – by divine right – if ever there was such a thing – I shall be forfeiting not only the simplest & most intense form of happiness it lies in me to feel, but also surely my most imperious 'duty' in life – if yielding to an ecstasy of nature can be called a 'duty'. What shall it profit a woman to gain or even to save the whole world if she lose her own child? At the <u>bottom</u> I feel my mind is made up – but I feel there are many intermediate layers of struggle to work through....

Lord Kilbracken to V.B.C.   ***Thursday 11 March***
              36 Lower Belgrave Street, S.W.1

My dear Violet,

Your letter was very interesting. As you ask my advice, I must say at once that I very much hope you will give Parliament a trial. I don't believe that you would find it incompatible with the care of your children – which of course I fully admit to be one's first duty. How often people think, before undertaking some new duty, 'I can't possibly find time for it', and yet, when they try the experiment, it turns out somehow that it can be fitted in quite well. Look at the cases of men in Parliament who are barristers, managers of great businesses, or what not – if their work can be run together with Parliament, why not yours?

I need not write down the commonplaces about the duty which lies upon those who have special gifts for a certain kind of work, much as you now know you have, to use it to the best of their ability : nor about the pleasure & help which it surely would be to your father to have you in the House, because with that I have no business to intermeddle.

But remember that, mainly owing to your father's being what he is, but partly also to the position which you have won for yourself, your decision is an important one for many besides yourself. If, with all the advantages which you have, you refuse to go into Parliament because you have young children, you will be doing something by your example towards establishing an unwritten law that such women should not go into the House; a law which w^d deprive your sex of a very large number of its best potential representatives, in the prime of life and at an age when their presence in Parliament would be specially useful.

I certainly – as you ask me – reply, 'Give it a trial'; and if you find that it interferes at all seriously with your domestic duties, the stewardship of the Chiltern Hundreds is open to you under the act that was passed the other day.[1] But I don't think you will have any occasion to apply for it.

It would be very unfortunate if women had to be content with spinsters or elderly matrons as their spokeswomen and administrators.[2] Yrs ever, Kilbracken

'We are witnessing in Ireland today a competition in frightfulness':
the Anglo-Irish war

In Violet's memory of childhood Irish home rule loomed as large as any nursery rhyme. She was seven when Gladstone's government introduced the 2nd Home Rule Bill, providing for limited self-government in Ireland, and late in life she still vividly recalled plying her father with questions on his return from the House: 'What did the Irish do?' Twenty-five years after the defeat of the 1893 bill, by which time Violet had children of her own, this 'Irish question' remained unanswered. The debate, though, had moved on. During the Great War Sinn Féin emerged as the majority party in Irish politics, committed to an independent republic. Following the 1918 general election the party's seventy-three representatives boycotted Westminster in favour of an assembly of their own making, the Dáil Éireann. This challenge to British rule was given impetus by the volunteers of Michael Collins' Irish Republican Army, who waged a guerilla war on all servants of the Crown, civilian and military. As the police and judiciary withdrew from large areas of the country, Sinn Féin took over the administration and British rule began to wither away. In the new year of 1920, in a doomed effort to regain control, Lloyd George's government supplemented the beleaguered Royal Irish Constabulary with a large force recruited from among demobilized soldiers – they were subsequently known as the 'black and tans' by the colour of their makeshift uniforms. Later a much smaller 'auxiliary' division of ex-officers was also raised. Nominally employed for police work these forces gained notoriety by engaging in what *The Times* condemned as 'semi-official counter-terrorism'. The savage policy of 'reprisals' met with widespread denunciation in Britain, and both Violet and her father were prominent speakers on behalf of the conciliatory 'Peace with Ireland Council'. As a solution for the

---

[1] Members of parliament can resign by becoming a steward of the Chiltern Hundreds, an office in crown patronage which thus disqualifies them from sitting in the Commons. Like other public offices it was opened to women under the terms of the Sex Disqualification Removal Act of December 1919.

[2] For most of the inter-war year period there were fewer than a dozen woman MPs in parliament, less than 2 per cent of the total.

Irish question Asquith advocated early in October 1920 'dominion home rule' – giving to Ireland self-government similar to that exercised in the dominions, for example Australia. Though short of Sinn Féin aspirations this was in advance of most British thinking, and within a week Lloyd George had scotched the idea. At this point the prime minister was prepared to allow a military solution to be pursued. He explained to the diners at the Guildhall banquet on 9 November, 'by the steps we have taken we have murder by the throat ... when the government were ready, we struck the terror, and the terrorists are now complaining of terror'. His oratory delighted the audience, but drew indignation from *The Times*: 'What echo will be evoked throughout the world by his speech? None, we fear, that will not be a mockery of the British name.' Twelve days later the cycle of assassination and reprisal resulted in the killings of 'Bloody Sunday', which left twenty-six dead. To Violet, addressing the Liberal Conference at Bradford shortly afterwards, this marked 'a horror which is beyond expression.... We are witnessing in Ireland today a competition in frightfulness.' It was the urgent duty of Liberals to seek a solution, and translating her words into deeds Violet spent two weeks in Ireland in March 1921 on a fact-finding mission, using many of the contacts made through the Peace with Ireland Council.[1]

Diary – Tuesday 22 March 1921 – Kilteragh, Foxrock, Co. Dublin

Arrival at Holyhead. 'Have you any firearms with you?' Examination of luggage. Soldiers & Auxiliaries on platform. Smooth passage. Ireland lying in misty sunshine. Prisoner marched off handcuffed by squad of Auxiliaries. Sinister black uniforms. Large silent crowd looking on – above a bank of blazing gorse. Acute sense of being in a foreign country.

Arrival at Kilteragh.... Great charm – lots of polished boards & bay windows – Sir H.P. playing golf in garden. He immediately asked me to write my name in visitor's book – adding that I had written it once before but had since changed my name....[2]

[1] Unpublished memoir, and speech at 1920 Bradford Liberal conference, both Violet Bonham Carter MSS; *The Times*, 11 October, 10 November 1920; also Frank Pakenham, *Peace by Ordeal* and D. G. Boyce, *Englishmen and Irish Troubles*; for 'Bloody Sunday', see below, p. 118 and n. 3.
[2] Violet had first visited Sir Horace during a visit to Dublin in April 1910.

Diary – Thursday 24 March – Mount Trenchard, Foynes, Co. Limerick

Radiant morning. Talk with Sir H.P. before leaving – 14 deaths yesterday & that a low average for the last 4 days – 'Tell people in England that no one in Ireland doubted <u>for one instant</u> that this <u>wasn't</u> going to happen. It was inevitable after 1918 election. Irish people had been tricked by Parliament & were determined to rely on it no longer. Carson had taught them the way of force & its effectiveness. This policy & the events of the last year have made Ireland ungovernable – not only by England but by their <u>own</u> people. We shall have a terrible time to go through.' Lennox Robinson said 'It makes one so ashamed – these boys dying. Presently of course we shall get Dominion H.R. & they'll have got it for us'....[1] Sir H.P. 'All this bloodshed – & just because the B. Govt want to save their faces. Why they cld. have peace <u>to-morrow</u> & they know it'....

Got into the train at Kingsbridge. Platform crowded with troops. Soldiers & 2 sorts of auxiliary – those with black peaked caps – & funny little Glengarries. Carrying revolvers as well as rifles. Soldiers looking mere boys. Opalescent country. Great sadness about it. Small irregular fields. Snatches of bog & gorse – blue distances – white tumbledown cottages ... then on thro' strange flat country to Foynes, lying by a great wide water which I first thought was the sea – but which turned out to be the Shannon or its estuary – a great wide tidal river (1ˢᵗ thing I saw driving into [the] station was 'Up the R.I.C. – Black & Tans' in large white letters on a wall).... After 3 miles by the broad water's side we drove up through Lodge gates past ilexes & flowering bushes & palms to a grey house looking down over the water ... I went in – & found in a big chilly room (orange polished wood again), with stone arches & a gallery with an organ in it, dear old Lord Monteagle, Tom Spring Rice – Mary Spring Rice – & a cousin Miss Knox – the last 2 strong Sinn Feiners....[2]

They told me how a lorry had gone by that morning full of Black & Tans who had beaten a boy quite unprovoked about the head – fired shots after 2 old road menders who ran away – & stolen one of their coats.... Both women very extreme I can see – Miss Knox even trying to justify the Dublin murders as an act of war – which gave me my first wave of pro-English feeling since I've been here![3] I went out for a little stroll with Tom

---

[1] (Esmé Stuart) Lennox Robinson (1886–1958), dramatist; manager of the Abbey Theatre, Dublin, 1919–23.

[2] Thomas Spring Rice (1849–1926), 2nd Baron Monteagle, 1866. Thomas Aubrey Spring Rice ('Tom') (1883–1934), eldest son of 2nd Baron Monteagle; succeeded father, 1926; diplomatic service. Mary Ellen Spring Rice (1880–1924), daughter of Lord Monteagle.

[3] Miss Knox refers to 'Bloody Sunday', 21 November 1920, on the morning of which 'fourteen British officers and ex-officers living in Dublin and believed by their opponents to

Spring Rice – then rest in funny hard old bed, smelling slightly of hay – wood fire burning in chimney – bath in chilly water – dinner & much talk of Ireland. <u>Curious</u> atmosphere. They are different from us. If these things were happening to us we cld hardly speak of them – still less laugh as they do in Dublin – or seem <u>almost</u> to enjoy the hatred & the horror & the <u>whispering</u> as they do here. Perhaps one is being unjust to them. One doesn't feel it about Ld Monteagle – he is obviously riven to his very soul – suffering for his people & helpless to protect them.

Diary – Good Friday, 25 March – Mount Trenchard, Foynes, Co. Limerick

... After breakfast I set off with Miss Knox to visit Henry O'Connor, the boy who was beaten yesterday by the Black & Tans.... Great atmosphere of mystery & excitement & of a romantic fight against odds seems to brood over daily life & pervade even its most practical events. We went up a muddy path across some fields to a little farm where we found a young woman, Henry O'Connor's sister, who called him. He came out of a cowshed – a tall boy about 22 – both eyes swollen & purple, one almost shut – his nose all cut on one side & clotted with dried blood & other lesser scratches & wounds about the face. Blood stains on his shirt & clothes showing that he must have bled considerably at the time. He was apparently leading a pony along the road yesterday when the lorries drove along – they pulled up – 2 old roadmenders fled & shots were fired after them – Henry O'Connor stood his ground. They ran up – 5 or 6 of them – & attacked him – belaboured him with hands sticks etc. – & finally left him dazed & silly & bleeding in the road. Took the roadmender's coat & lunch which he had left in the road & made off with it. I asked him what caps they wore? The dark peaked caps, not the Glengarries – also whether they appeared to be under the command of any officer. He said they didn't – & whether any men intervened to stop them. He said towards the end one of them suggested that he should be left alone – but he was too dazed to notice accurately what took place. He said rather pathetically 'Ah – you'd think they hadn't any people belonging to them at all – they seem to have no

be engaged in intelligence work, and to be aiming specially at the lives of the Sinn Féin leaders, were shot in their beds, or as they were dressing, some in the presence of their wives'. That afternoon, during the Dublin–Tipperary Gaelic football game in Croce Park, a body of Crown forces drove up in lorries 'and began straightaway shooting up crowd and players'; twelve were killed, eleven seriously wounded, and fifty-four injured. 'The supporters of each country must realize that the line that their side took on this day was not incidental or exceptional (there was much that was far more cruel) but was integral to policy, as calculated to inspire fear in appropriate quarters' (Frank Pakenham, *Peace by Ordeal*, 36, 373–5).

mercy' – & I cldn't but wonder what their 'people' wld think if they saw them behaving like this to harmless innocent people in their own countryside.

Again – 'The country wld be wonderful quiet if they were gone' & when I apologized to him for my countrymen & said how ashamed I felt – 'Ah – but don't bother – you can't help it – we understand that' – with the greatest courtesy & sensitiveness. I was extraordinarily struck by the <u>apparent</u> absence of bitterness & resentment, at the humour and detachment with which he treated the whole incident. How wld an Englishman behave who had been treated like this? He cldn't speak of it with this calm – & nonchalance – aloofness. He wld be burning with a sense of the indignity of it. Did this man feel it less? – or <u>was</u> it that he had a truer sense of where the indignity really lay – that he felt it was not he who had been humiliated & degraded but his aggressors....

Miss Knox is very interesting.... I said I supposed they felt about people who didn't join up & risk everything now much as we felt about those who held back, after the War – & she said 'Yes – how can we let these boys go on dying for us?' And tho' I feel still, & passionately, that force <u>is</u> the wrong way to settle anything – what <u>is</u> one to advise them to do? They have been tricked over & over again.

Any overture on their part is treated by the Govt as a sign of weakening & surrender. There is no healing gesture from the authorities. Undisciplined hordes overrunning their country like wild beasts & cold-blooded execution of men whom they feel shld be treated as prisoners of war. Add to this the stories of torture of prisoners. What an enemy to seal any pact with.

The local teacher of Erse – to whom the place pays 150£ – is being searched out for no other reason than that he holds Irish classes – & is known to be a friend of a priest with Sinn Fein proclivities. He is now 'on the run' & his classes have to be held in secret places. This is of course just <u>absurd</u> but it drives home into the hearts of the people the sense that they are being persecuted as a nation – that Irishmen are being punished for thinking of Ireland now what Englishmen think of England....

We drove back in a very lovely light on our outside car. Back through Shanagolden & Foynes – where the poor police had been reduced to skipping in their garden for occupation – & home. We hear now that the lorry load which assaulted Henry O'Connor & stole the coat had consumed 15£ of drink in Foynes & driven off without paying for it & the landlady there is launching a complaint.

Dinner – some talk of Roger Casement whom Miss K. thinks a hero – & of the rebellion of 1916. There is no doubt that the executions, just or unjust, were a practical blunder.[1] Miss K. going to Dublin about that time

---

[1] Sir Roger Casement (1864–1916), Irish-born official in consular service, knighted (1911)

said that all in her railway carriage (3rd class) were talking of the folly of the Rebellion & those who took part in it. Coming back 3 weeks later – after the executions – the men were all heroes. Ld Monteagle said it hadn't struck him at the time as either unjust or unwise that they shld be executed, but that H.P. had always been against it. . . .

Diary – Saturday 26 March – Mount Trenchard, Foynes, Co. Limerick

I went into Limerick with Lord Monteagle. . . . It is a curious town – & reminded me strangely & irresistibly at every turn of Spain. The beauty & squalor of it – the women with black shawls over their heads – the rabble of donkeys & little low rickety carts piled with rotting vegetables – the long low buildings – <u>very</u> like tobacco factories – the towers – the wide & dirty streets – everything brought Spain back to me. We crossed the Shannon & drove along the embankment for a bit then stopped at a little house – with a small green garden in front sloping up to the front door – enclosed by a low garden wall – & gate. I gazed at the neat – safe – homeliness of it all – it was almost impossible to imagine it as the mise-en-scène of a murder.[1] We were ushered into a little drawing room where we found Mrs O'Callaghan & her sister – Mrs O'C a most remarkable looking woman – with great personality, iron will – immense strength & control & intellectual grip. Not once all the time she was with us did she deviate into irrelevance incoherence or sentimentality & though she almost broke down, kept self control throughout. I shall never forget the strength of her face. There was nothing 'broken' in any line. Very large dark eyes with strongly defined eyebrows that almost met – firm chin & cheekbones. . . .

Mrs O'C. received us with great dignity & thanked us for coming. She said 'There is nothing more you can do for me – but there are other women

for humanitarian work; captured in Kerry in April 1916 after landing from a German submarine, with intent to start an insurrection against British rule; executed for treason, 3 August 1916. Despite Casement's failure to deliver promised arms, an Irish nationalist coalition went ahead with a rebellion in Dublin, 24–29 April 1916. The 'Easter Rising' was defeated, and fifteen of its leaders executed 3–12 May.

[1] Violet visited the widow of Michael O'Callaghan, ex-mayor of Limerick, and a Sinn Féin councillor. According to an official report he was shot and wounded by armed men around 1.30 am on 7 March 1921, and died shortly afterwards. No clue was given as to the identity of the assassins, but Violet's enquiries led her to suspect two unidentified members of the 'auxiliary' force. The same men killed George Clancy, the incumbent mayor, later that night (*The Times*, 8 March 1921). When in Cork Violet took this case up with the British commander, General Strickland, who gave a sympathetic ear but could not credit the involvement of Crown forces.

you can save from this horror which I have suffered'. . . .

'The first raid happened last year. It was an official raid – authorized – & orderly – taking place under the supervision of officers, searchlight turned on outside. The 2nd which happened Shrove Tuesday (8th Feb) was what we call an unauthorized raid. The men were drunken brutal threatening & dangerous. They came in waving rifles & revolvers & blackthorn sticks. I said to Michael 'I'm sure they mean to harm you' – but he said 'Never mind – whatever they do it will all be over in a minute.' Three were specially drunken & insulting. They kept asking 'do you believe in murder?' Michael said 'No'. The Auxiliary said 'Well you'll know more about murder before you've done.' 'We'll come later next time'. . . .

'. . . The 3rd raid was 14 days later on Feb. 22nd. Again an authorized pukka raid – with a bright searchlight & women searchers. Two officers in charge & 20 police. . . .

'They very carefully explored the premises & trampled in the wooden cover of the water tank below the staircase which we had always thought of as a possible back way of escape. I noticed particularly the voice of the apparent leader this time & last – such a cultured – melodious voice I thought it cld hardly be English. You'll forgive me for saying this – but we don't think the English have beautiful voices – & I said to Michael this man must have Irish blood – the key of the gate was again asked for & again given up at the end.

'<u>On Sunday night March</u> 6th We were woken up by [a] voice calling to us from outside – It was a nice voice – the same voice. "Who lives here?" I answered "Michael O'Callaghan". "<u>We</u> <u>want</u> <u>him</u> (that's what they always say). We must see him. We're coming in anyhow. We want the key of the gate." I thought it was another raid & asked "Is there an officer in charge"? They said "One – Yes two – two officers in charge". My husband said "It's all right – don't be frightened. It's only a raid again. They did no harm before. I'll come down with you." He wld come down – tho' I had never let him. The maid or I always went to the door. I made him light the gas & we had a candle. I opened the door. Two men stood there – one wore black goggles & a thick moustache like a false one over his own – the other clear spectacles with tortoise shell rims through which I saw blue eyes. They called my husband to come out into the garden – I cried "No – No – he shall never do that". I held my arms out across [the] door between him & them – one shot him over my shoulder – & I heard Michael fall – I grappled with the man – the other slipped past me & emptied his revolver into him as he lay – again & again – again. I found the spectacles (the light ones) in my hand – I must have torn them off without knowing.

'I didn't know if Michael was alive or dead – I had never seen anyone dead. I was so inexperienced I was afraid to move him lest the blood shld flow. I got on to the telephone & tried various relations & friends but cld get no reply. At last I got the Dr – he hesitated about coming – it meant risking his life – & he had a wife too. He said "Is he dead? are you sure he is alive still?" & at last – "Since it's for you Mrs O'C. I'll come." I rang up the Barracks & asked the police to come & bring a priest – they seemed to be mocking me – they seemed to be pretending not to understand who I was – & what I wanted & so I rang off. Then they rang up again & the D.I. said he wld come & wld bring a priest.

'The Dr arrived at 1.30. All the long way to my house (tracing it on the map) he was never challenged once – <u>there were no patrols on the streets that night</u>. Why had they been withdrawn? . . .[1] He cld do nothing for my husband & he left me at 1.40 & only then on his way back did he meet the D.I. & 3 men with Father Philip, whom I had telephoned for at the same time as himself & this though he lived a mile further away. . . .'

Questioned by me 'My husband received his first death notice the day after Ld Mayor MacCurtain's funeral.[2] After that he slept away from home for nearly 6 [months]. But in the autumn he said "This is hard on you – to be alone" & came back. He received 2nd on 14th Oct. . . . I received early on Monday letters of condolence to the Corporation both written on the 7th by Gen. Cameron & Prescott Decie – both suggesting that it was done by I.R.A.'[3]

Question: 'What do you think the motive for the murder can have been?' – 'It was to stop Propaganda. My husband was not a fighting man. He belonged to the constructive – civil side of the Sinn Fein movement. He was invaluable as a speaker & as a writer. He had been one of the very earliest of the Sinn Feiners – a Sinn Feiner since 1905. During one of the raids (the drunken one) one of the Auxiliaries said "Propaganda – we'll soon put a stop to propaganda". In one Weekly Summary it was stated that the I.R.A. was breaking but the last Republican weapon was Propaganda – & still intact. My husband saw many foreign correspondents including Americans & made a Fighting speech on 31st Jan to the [city] Corporation – on resigning. The two first raids took place after that'. . . .

We said goodbye to her – 'Do your best for us' said the sister. Mrs O'C. had only been married 7 yrs. & had no children. 'I am quite strong – I'm

---

[1] Limerick was one of eight southern Irish counties under martial law by 4 January 1921; this entailed a curfew. Cork city and county were also affected.

[2] Tomás MacCurtain (assassinated March 1920), lord mayor of Cork.

[3] In the Commons on 8 March Joseph Devlin (1872–1934), nationalist MP for Falls, Belfast, asked the attorney-general for Ireland, Denis Henry (1864–1921), if the killings were 'so-called reprisals carried out by armed forces of the Crown'. Henry answered that 'the motive of these abominable crimes is very obscure', but observed that both O'Callaghan and Clancy were regarded as Sinn Féin moderates. This invited the conclusion that Sinn Féin extremists were to blame, an opinion that would be given little credence outside the ranks of his own party (*The Times*, 9 March 1921).

not broken' were the last words she said. One's heart reeled with the horror of it. One felt in a different world as one sat down to tea in a little bunshop 10 minutes afterwards with Miss Bunbury – daughter of late Prot. Bishop of Limerick – such a nice – mild woman – with gently moderate views – one wondered how they cld have survived in this atmosphere. She said the removal of Auxiliary Cadets was quite <u>essential</u> – the first condition of peace. They drink like fishes & are quite undisciplined. . . .

We walked back thro' the streets back to the station – the impression of Spain continuing strongly. Soldiers in trench helmets with fixed bayonets were walking in single file up the sides of the streets in little companies of 6 or 8 & stationing themselves at the top of the sidestreets. What practical object this manoeuvre could possibly achieve it was difficult to guess.

We travelled back to Foynes with a man of Unionist complexion who complained that the B.T.'s had begun bombing the salmon with Mills Bombs & had 70 out of the river of a friend of his by this means. Also told a story of another friend who sat fishing with a large salmon he had caught beside him on the bank. A black & tan came up & talked to him about his flies etc. & when he looked round the salmon had vanished.

Diary – Monday 28 March – Mount Trenchard, Foynes, Co. Limerick

<u>Pouring</u> rain – I stayed in all the morning writing up notes. In the afternoon a farmer N. came round to see us. Much less interesting & more like a platform hack than anyone we had seen before. Pat arguments that had often been railed about before – terrific anti-Ulster bitterness – & all the old clichés about English politicians using Ireland to climb to power on – bowing to force in Ulster etc. etc. The only thing which struck me was that being as he was a Republican & not a D.H.R. he said they had dreaded the offer of D.H.R. which wld infallibly have split them. What <u>fools</u> the Govt. are. . . .

The sensation of the day was a mysterious telegram which arrived in the course of the morning. It said 'All guests especially titled guests shld avoid all interviewers except with credentials beyond question & also avoidable journeys except with reliable escort. Do not ignore this advice which is tendered on excellent authority'. . . .[1] We thought it incredible – &

---

[1] The telegram was sent by one 'Anderson', an associate of Sir Horace Plunkett's whom Violet later met in Dublin; see below, p. 131. He wrote to Monteagle on 27 March that a proposal 'to ambush, <u>and kill</u>, Lady BC' had been turned down at British military headquarters, though the possibility of an ambush 'with intent to abduct' had not been ruled out: 'Do impress on your visitor the great necessity of caution.' Violet appears not to have taken this remarkable threat seriously.

it seemed to us quite obviously a clumsy attempt on the part of the authorities to prevent us nosing round. What a 'reliable escort' in these days in Ireland wld mean it is difficult to guess. The B. & T.'s wld certainly draw fire on one from all sides & the soldiers slightly less but still considerably. Only remains the I.R.A. We spent a last peaceful evening in the big chilly room before the wood fire – 'Tom' playing Brahms & Bach beautifully on a vile piano – then bed – before a very early start next day.

(Easter Sunday night – we wandered down through tracts of winding dark & [?]dal basement to the Servants' Hall where a dance was going on – two delightful fiddlers scraping away – a set of 4 dancing an Irish reel. We watched several different sets – <u>so</u> curiously unlike Scotch reels tho' the tempo is just the same. Absolute poker stiffness from the head down as in Morris dancing – & amazingly neat & agile feet. Afterwards we had songs – the most popular was sung by a little boy 'The felons of our land' – a most typical Irish song – it is an indictment of our administration that all their nat. sentiment flourishes in & around gaols.)

Diary – Tuesday 29 and Wednesday 30 March – written in the Metropole Hotel, Cork

... We went on to tea at the new Lord Mayor's – Stephen O'Mara. He lives in the house in which George Clancy was murdered....[1]

We were received by Mrs O'Mara – a dear little young thing – about 25 or 26 – very gay & pretty. She took me up to wash my hands & apologized for the untidiness of the house – 'The carpenters are in it'. There were bags of tools & nails at every corner. I for something to say 'What are they doing?' – Mrs O'M – with a smile 'Oh only putting iron shutters on all the windows'. One shivered at the thought of these 2 young happy careless light-hearted people having to reckon with <u>murder</u> as a possibility – in fact as I felt – as a probability – day by day & night by night. We went down to tea & then Mayor Stephen O'Mara came in – a young man – 32 or so – with eager eyes & that terrible look of controlled strain one has learnt to recognize....

He was very bitter – not unnaturally – & when I praised Strickland[2] & said he at least had shown some courage – straightness & honour he said 'He cld have saved Cork. Why did he stand by & let his men stand by

---

[1] Stephen M. O'Mara (1885–1926), member of Sinn Féin; became mayor of Limerick after assassination of George Clancy (1879–1921).

[2] General Sir (Edward) Peter Strickland (1869–1951), cr. KCB, 1919; European war, 1914–18; commander, 6th Division, Ireland, 1919–22.

when it was burning. The soldiers stood & looked on.'[1]

We told him about the plot against ourselves – & he was amused & delighted & his last words to me were 'I hope you get ambushed' & to Miss Ellis (the Quaker) 'Please come to my funeral'. <u>Poor</u> little things.

We went on to Cork the same night B & I & Francis Acland ... arrived at 8 – an hour before curfew & drove through to the Metropole.[2] We had cancelled our rooms at the Imperial which we were told was a haunt of the Military.... I suggested to Miss Ellis that we shld. ring up some of the people we hoped to see to-morrow – the deputy Ld Mayor – Professor O'Rahilly & the T.D. Liam de Roiste.[3] She smiled at me. Not one of those wld be sleeping at home. An extraordinary feature of life in Ireland nowadays – people sleeping away from their homes – & returning by day – because they are afraid not of arrest but of assassination. We therefore did nothing that night.... It was strange looking out on those deserted silent streets after Curfew – only broken at times by a Curfew lorry with a searchlight making its round.

Next morning [30 March] my head buzzing with the beginnings of an awful cold heavy upon me – we set out in the sunshine – & saw the devastations. They are very impressive & awful – a great tract in the heart of the finest part of the City – mostly big shops belonging to Unionists & 'loyalists' – whose 'loyalty' has now been rather severely shaken – & then over the river the City Hall, a really fine building, & the Carnegie Library – gutted & peering at one blindly through paneless windows – like eyeless sockets. The suggestion that the fire cld have spread from the City Hall to the other part of the City is – as is shown by the Labour report – quite ridiculous to anyone who has ever been in Cork.[4] Nothing but highly skilled incendiarism on a large scale, carried out with the help of petrol etc., cld possibly have caused the damage we saw.

Having ascertained – to our <u>great</u> disappointment that Father Philip was

[1] On the night of 11–12 December 1920 Cork city was extensively damaged by fires, soon revealed to have been the work of the Auxiliaries and the Black and Tans.

[2] (Sir) Francis Dyke Acland (1874–1939), 14th Bt, 1926; Liberal MP for N.W. Cornwall, 1910–22; Tiverton, 1923–4.

[3] Alfred O'Rahilly (1884–1969), professor of mathematical physics, University College, Cork, 1916; joined Sinn Féin, 1916; member of Cork Corporation. Liam de Roiste, alderman and Sinn Féin MP for Cork; was then working for a constructive dialogue between Sinn Féin and the British government (*The Times*, 10 March 1921).

[4] In parliament on 12 December Sir Hamar Greenwood (1870–1948), chief secretary for Ireland, had protested 'vigorously' against the allegation that Crown forces had caused the Cork fires. Relying on telegraph reports from Dublin he stated that the fires spread naturally, or else were caused by Sinn Féin. A Labour Party commission visited Cork and on 15 December sent a telegram to London asserting that Greenwood's statements were 'grossly inaccurate': the fires were undoubtedly the 'work of Crown forces' (*The Times*, 14, 29 December 1920).

not – as we had hoped – in Cork – we drove off with Miss Ellis on an outside car to see Professor O'Rahilly....

... He was a small man – much younger than I expected – about 38 or 39 I shld say – with a jaw & mouth that snapped like steel. His mind too was steel – it had a sharp bladelike quality, a kind of cold force about it. 'We are ready to negotiate at any moment – England can negotiate to-morrow if she likes – but it must be with Dail Eireann which never represented us more completely than it does to-day.... It is not a question of helpless moderates on the one hand & uncontrolled extremists on the other – of intellectuals & constructive thinkers & a murder gang. I have never carried arms in my life. I shld like to see them all at the bottom of the sea – but in this matter we are all behind each other. There is no difference of opinion as to objects or methods – only a division of functions....'

Another point he made very strongly was that there is no racial hatred between England & Ireland – 'Allow us to develop freely along our own lines of civilization – allow us to be on friendly terms with you & we shall.' I talked to him about the possibilities of coming to an agreement once negotiations started – 'Wld. the Dail be moderate in its demands?' He replied with a smile which held a touch of mockery 'Lady B.C. the Irish are really quite an intelligent people'. He told me that de Valera was an essentially moderate man & that he had seen him only 2 days ago.[1]

On 2 pts alone he seemed unreasonable. I told him what a terrible mistake from a pt of view of tactics the burning of English farms etc. was – 'Well let me tell you it is going on & it is going to get much worse.' V. 'Very bad propaganda.' O'R. 'Well we are rather tired of propaganda. It has done us so little good up to now.' He was also I thought rather bitter & obtuse about Ulster. The rest of Ireland he said wld. allow it full rights such as Swiss Cantons enjoy. But Ulster is an integral part of Ireland & must settle with Ireland & not with England.

'Can't you get the Liberal party to give up their little pug-dog H.R. schemes – they're no good to us whatever.' I pointed out that D.H.R. – with powers to raise Army & Navy suggested by Father – was anything but a 'pug dog' scheme – in fact that there was extraordinarily little practical difference between that & an independent Republic – as Dominion Status carried with it the right to secede.

His last words to me were 'Sinn Fein is the modern expression of our national consciousness' – which I believe to be profoundly true. I came away feeling the tremendous difference between the S.F.'s & the old

[1] Eamon de Valera (1882–1975), Sinn Féin MP for East Clare, 1917; president of Sinn Féin, 1917–26; president of first Dáil Éireann, April 1919; led the armed resistance against the majority acceptance of the 1921 Treaty, 1922–3.

Nationalists – a quite extinct species. The S.F.'s are far more interesting.

We got back at 12 & found the Deputy Mayor Barry Egan waiting to see us – a nice man – not half as able or interesting or intellectually distinguished as O'R – in quite a different class altogether – a very strained look.... I asked him what people felt about the <u>soldiers</u> in Cork. 'The soldiers – oh they're just inoffensive little boys – no one pays any attention to them. It is among the Black & Tans & Auxiliaries that there are some really dangerous characters. They may have been gallant soldiers & ex officers – but they are criminals for all that – & drinking away 1£ or 30/ a day....

He said that since the fire he had been for the first time in his life really proud of Cork – Cork which had been always talking – which had never done anything before – 'After the burning there was not a whimper in the whole town. A sort of cold anger seemed to run through it'. On D.H.R. he said he personally cld not trust it – he cld not feel safe without international guarantees of independence. <u>Liam de Roiste</u> – T.D. for Cork impressed me infinitely more. He had dark red hair & spectacles & an ugly amusing clever face – an excellent sense of humour – & no wish to score small debating points with people whose minds were obviously open wide & who were, as we were, only trying to prevent Egan & Daly from spoiling a fine case by using some of the worst arguments of their opponents on their own side. It gives one a real turn to hear B & T arguments from Sinn Feiners – but it often happens alas! Both sides are inoculated with the virus of force.

De Roiste made a great pt of the necessity of negotiating with the whole Dail. How cld they throw over their colleagues? They were all part of the same concern & had absolute unity of policy & direction thro' diversity of functions. He denied as all others who I have spoken to up to now have done – that Michael Collins is any more a murderer than Arthur Griffith.[1] His department is really finance & his supreme achievement the introduction into the country of the Republican loan. 'But even if he were an organizer of murder', said de Roiste – 'what right has a Govt of which H. Greenwood is a member to exclude him? We have not got a man bad enough to pair with Greenwood.' 'What is this policy leading to? If every volunteer is killed or in gaol – where are you then? Have you got a peaceful & contented Ireland – or one that you can govern.'...

---

[1] Michael Collins (1890–1922), commander of IRA during the Anglo-Irish war and bête-noire of British opinion. Arthur Griffith (1871–1922), founder of Sinn Féin, 1906; Sinn Féin MP for East Cavan, 1918–22; acting president of Dáil, 1919. Despite their differences in approach – Collins favouring direct military action, and Griffith political abstentionism – both men were pragmatists, and signed the December 1921 Treaty ending the undeclared Anglo-Irish war. Griffith went on to become president of the Dáil, and Collins commander-in-chief of the Irish Free State army.

... A most delightful man. Daly I liked much less. He was eaten up with bitterness – not unnaturally – & if one asked for evidence of anything, in order to be able to use it more effectively, obviously thought one hostile. ...

At 4 o'clock we set off to keep our appt. with Strickland at Govt. House – panted up a steep hill – & were at first refused admittance by a sentry. An N.C.O. came forward & asked our names & we got through the first gates & climbed on up, still winding uphill thro' more locked gates, guarded by plain clothes detectives, to the House perched like a fortress looking down on the town below. And there poor Strickland & his wife live like caged animals. (She had not been beyond the first gate except to canter in a field behind since September.)[1]

We were ushered into a nice light chintzy drawing room with a silver kettle humming & received by Lady Strickland – a youngish woman not at all bad looking – rather well dressed – with a hard-strained look on her face – very violent & unhappy – living in daily hourly terror that her husband will be assassinated & with nothing in the world to do but tremble for him & hate the Irish. She is not interested in the psychology of the situation – in fact interest & sympathy have been in her case as in so many others completely wiped out by fear & hatred. She regards the Irish as so many wild beasts with no human characteristics at all. She resents the Auxiliaries not because they have been brutal to the Irish, but because their disreputable conduct has compromised the Militarist régime & their disgrace is sometimes reflected on the soldiers, with whom they are confused, & they form a good pretext for people who are 'out' to make up things against us – to make excuses for the odious crimes of Sinn Fein. 'However' she said 'I daresay if they weren't there it wld all be put on us. Oh these horrible men like Kenworthy who are for ever trying to find out things against us – how I hate them.[2] People never hear what has been done on the other side. All the publicity is against us'.

I tried to soothe her telling her that but for the Daily News & intermittently the Times the whole Press solidly boycotted Irish news in so far as any outrage by the forces of the Crown was concerned. Also I begged her not to bracket her husband & the soldiers generally with the Govt. B & T's – telling her quite truthfully that I had heard nothing but good of him & of the Army since I had been in Ireland.[3] This mollified her a little –

[1] Barbara Strickland *née* ffolkes (1884–1977), cr. DBE, 1923; widow of Captain F. J. Cresswell; married General Strickland, 1918.

[2] Lieutenant-Commander Joseph Montague Kenworthy (1886–1953), 10th Lord Strabolgi, 1934; Liberal MP for Hull Central, 1919–26; Labour, 1926–31.

[3] The British army played an active but secondary role in the Anglo-Irish war, and was not regarded in the same light as the Black and Tans, and Auxiliaries: see Frank Pakenham, *Peace by Ordeal*, 53.

but she soon shot off again into a catalogue of S. F. atrocities. A baby had been trampled to death by S. F. raiders breaking into a house – a man had been dragged out of a Hospital & killed – they had shot at her husband. She had not been out of the garden except for a little riding since Sept. & was constantly getting threatening letters. 'Thank God 6 of the brutes had been shot at Cloheen the other day' (the massacre of unarmed men Egan had told us about) 'each one of those men had murdered 20 others.' She fully admitted the Aux. were a set of ruffians – but by no means all of them – 'some of them have done fine work'. I mentioned Mrs O'C. 'Oh but you can't rely on anything <u>they</u> tell you.' I told her of the boy at Foynes. 'Oh yes but those sort of people do constantly fire at soldiers.' She was very bitter poor woman – but so anxious. I tried again to soothe her by telling her the nice things I had heard said of S. 'Ah but they fire at him too.'

Meanwhile B. was talking, far more remuneratively, to Strickland, a very nice – good-looking man – tall – white haired – gentle – with the look of controlled strain one has got to know so well.... He admitted the total lack of discipline of the Auxiliaries & said the whole atmosphere of Ireland to-day was completely demoralizing. As an instance of this he told me the story of one armed D.S.O. whose conduct was such that he was dismissed even from the Auxiliaries. He then took to highway robbery on his own! telling friends who met him & asked what he was doing here that he was in the secret service! He has been arrested & tried & is now a convict....

We talked about the way a bad C.O. can establish an absolute reign of terror quite on his own in certain districts. He agreed & said stupidity was the thing he was most up against. When he arrived he found the lorries going 60 miles an hour thro' the town waving Union Jacks. He had stopped all that & now Republican flags might be shown anywhere – he had given orders they were never to be hauled down or torn off coffins. He is of opinion that the I.R.A. organization has been broken up. Here I think he is wrong. The thing which struck me most was when he said 'Even if this goes on for another 2 years the Irish are bound to get more or less what they want. We can't go on governing a country like this. And meanwhile what pure <u>waste</u> of life this all is.' A delightful man – really trying to do his best in an impossible position....

Diary – Thursday 31 March – Kilteragh, Foxrock, Co. Dublin

Strickland having asked us to lunch we resolved to stay till then. I went with Miss Ellis to see some rather dull lace-makers & saw also the worst part of the devastation – the City Hall & Carnegie Library across the river – the City Hall such a fine building – completely gutted & destroyed.... Ly

Strickland described the fire to me seen from Govt House – the great roar of the flames licking upwards & added significantly 'And the next day the B & T's were marched out'. I asked her if her husband had any <u>disciplinary</u> powers over the B & T's. She said none. 'He can move them about at will from one place to another – but he has no powers over their training or discipline.' ...

We got to Dublin about 6.30 – the station crowded with Auxiliaries & B & T's (it occurred to me that it may be partly the way their caps are pulled backwards off their foreheads that the Aux. look so very villainous – <u>as</u> they do). I motored out to Kilteragh – which seemed a haven of peace & warmth & cleanness & comfort after all our tossings & bucketings about. I felt as tho' a century had passed over my head since I was here last – but there it was quite unchanged – dear Sir Horace with his visitors' book. ...

Diary – Friday 1 April – *Kilteragh, Foxrock, Co. Dublin*

We motored into Dublin with H.P. & Gerald Heard & stopped at Plunkett House & saw Mr Anderson. He said he hoped he had not alarmed us by his telegram – but that he had had first hand information from one who had heard it direct from Crozier that the plan outlined in the letter was in contemplation – in fact had actually been put up to G.H.Q. & adopted.[1] Crozier had heard from one who was present. He added that <u>4 Generals</u> had been present when this <u>ridiculous</u> scheme was suggested.

Anderson went on to tell H.P. that Erskine Childers had come to him that morning very much shaken, as he thought that evidence against him had almost certainly been discovered at the offices of the Bulletin, which were raided a day or two ago.[2] He asked if he might sleep that night in Anderson's study! & he of course accepted. What a state of things. ...

We went in to the Arts Club where Mr Norman had invited us to lunch. ...

... I found myself sitting between Erskine Childers & James Douglas – one of the most remarkable – in fact I think the most remarkable man I met in Ireland.[3] He is a Quaker with a long narrow face & spectacles – a

[1] Brigadier-General Frank Percy Crozier (1879–1937), commander, auxiliaries to the RIC, August 1920–February 1921; at centre of a major controversy involving discipline of auxiliaries, after resigning in protest at the reinstatement of men he had dismissed for misconduct.

[2] Robert Erskine Childers (1870–1922), famous as author of *The Riddle of the Sands* (1903); a pre-war convert to home rule; Royal Navy Air Services, 1914–19 (DSC, 1916); minister for publicity in Dáil, 1919–21; fought against Treaty, captured and executed by Irish Free State forces, 1922.

[3] James G. Douglas (1887–1954), honorary treasurer and trustee of the Irish White Cross, which distributed relief in Ireland prior to the Treaty.

pacifist – hating force in any form but full of mental bite & trenchancy. He told me that if he had his way he wld. disband the I.R.A. – the first Sinn Feiner I have met who repudiates violence root & branch – even as a means to an end.

There was no <u>cant</u> about him – no loose or frothy generalizations – no platform catchwords – or debating points. A first rate sense of humour. Government not by force but by consent. A free hand within the 4 corners of Ireland. Everything outside those boundaries to be settled by negotiation. Ireland he says has seized the chance provided by the B & T's of achieving National Unity....

The gentleness & sanity of Douglas was an immense relief after the curdled – almost addled – bitterness of Erskine Childers on my left. Poor man – his intellect – if not his brain – has been <u>turned</u> by this business. He cannot smile. He has a set – pale – bitter face – a mind with no 'give' in it at any point.

He opened conversation by saying rather challengingly 'I should like to know what is in your mind about all this'. I was rather non-plussed but balbutié-d something about the wantonness & futility of it all & how easy it wld be to come to a settlement. He replied crushingly 'That was <u>not</u> what I wanted you to say'. I cldn't help smiling & said 'Oh do tell me what it was – & I will try & say it'. Without one line of his face relaxing he went on 'Do you recognize the moral right of Ireland to independence.' I. (very seriously, trying the other line) 'I think Ireland has as great a moral <u>right</u> to independence as you or I have to existence.' E.C. 'Then why don't you go back & say so.' V. 'But that doesn't necessarily mean that complete independence is the best thing for her. And even admitting that it were – the psychology of the English – however much you may despise it – is a factor one can't entirely leave out of account etc. It is part of the machinery – to put it at its lowest – thro' which Ireland will get her rights' – etc. etc.

But he wld hear nothing of compromise or adjustment – only of a frontal attack on the British public. To refuse to wave the reddest possible flag before the most irascible possible bull showed lack of courage – nothing more or less. He seemed to <u>hate</u> everyone so dreadfully. I felt hate radiating from him & turned with infinite relief to the gentleness & sanity of James Douglas.

After lunch we had coffee at the Norman's, in one of those dignified & slightly dilapidated Adams drawing-rooms (L-shaped – the whole of Dublin seems to have been built on the same day). We were introduced to a Mr Gregan who told us there had been a horrible tragedy in Tralee – a secretary of the Farmers' Union – McCarthy by name – had been murdered & he recommended us to go & see a Mr O'Hanlon the Sec. of the F.U. & hear the details. We went....

One story of O'Hanlon's made me laugh. After reciting a list of outrages on the population [of Ballyhaigne] by Major McKinnon – he told us (as a climax & a culmination) of how McKinnon had announced to a crowd of people (at Ardforth[?] I think – but I am not sure) that they cld go & tell their friends that in an hour's time he was going to motor back to Tralee by himself – so if they wanted to ambush him they wld know how to get him. 'And he went back standing up all alone in the Ford car with a bright light shining on him & a revolver in each hand. Fancy insulting a people like that – why, isn't he <u>compelling</u> us to murder him?' It was such a <u>very</u> Irish pt. of view – in fact it struck me that it cldn't possibly have been held by anyone out of Ireland. In England his action wld have struck most people as rather plucky & jarred on some as a trifle melodramatic. But the Irish saw it entirely as an insult – & as compelling them to murder him in order to wipe out the stain on their own honour....

Dinner & talk & some perusal of H.P.'s endless files of correspondence....

... H.P. has a firm belief that D.H.R. would settle things to-morrow. But it is disingenuous of the Govt to say they – the S.F. – have never asked for it. They <u>cannot</u> ask for it for fear of being given less as the Govt very well knows. De Valera in his last utterance expressly refrains from repudiating it. The irritant measures like early Curfew – with the consequent enormous financial loss involved to theatres, tramways etc. – & the inconvenience to the population generally – instead of causing impatience with & indignation against S.F. have had precisely the opposite effect & have consolidated & inflamed opinion against the Govt. The prevailing feeling in Ireland to-day – even among the opponents of S.F. – is 'Any Govt. wld be better than this' – & I must say after a fortnight in Ireland one thoroughly sympathizes with it.

Diary – Saturday 2 April – Kilteragh, Foxrock, Co. Dublin

... We got back to Kilteragh & just had time to collect our things & say goodbye to dear H.P. – & how do you do to <u>Mrs Pethick-Lawrence</u> who had just arrived! – before going straight on to the boat.[1] B. who spent all his time in Ireland in a cold sweat of anxiety lest I shld be searched & that my highly indiscreet notes wld send hundreds to the gallows insisted on my putting them in my <u>hat</u> – which I did until we pushed off from these sad shores – back into freedom again.

---

[1] Emmeline Pethick-Lawrence (1867–1954), leading suffragette and social reformer.

Epilogue: 'Ireland – as I saw it'

Violet's 'smuggled' diary was the basis for an article in the *Sunday Express*, 8 May 1921, 'Ireland – as I saw it'. Described by the paper's editorial as 'a virulently brilliant piece of dialectic', it was a damning indictment of government policy. Appearing on the page opposite was a very different perspective, 'Ireland – as I, too, saw it', written by 'An officer of the 'Black and Tans'. This depicted the nationalist movement as a 'murder gang', and commentators such as Violet as the unwitting dupes of Sinn Féin's propaganda machine. In the important battle for public opinion which this exchange exemplified Violet made a significant contribution. The day after the article appeared she addressed the Women's National Liberal Federation, arguing that negotiations to end the war could begin immediately, and that an offer of dominion home rule would be welcomed by 'an immense majority in Southern Ireland'. She believed that the existing Dáil offered the best hopes of a settlement, since the next was likely to be elected on a more extreme platform. Her statements came at an important juncture for the government which, at a special cabinet on 12 May, contemplated the options of either negotiations or escalating military conflict. A majority, including the prime minister, were in favour of the latter. Notes of caution however came from the military leaders and from the Dublin Castle administration. Public opinion, they argued, must be solidly behind any intensification of the war. They doubted that this support would be forthcoming, and perhaps by now Lloyd George did too. Despite his apparent hard line on dominion home rule, his position was fluid. The difficulty came in breaking the deadlock to negotiations with Sinn Féin. Mark Sturgis, joint assistant under-secretary for Ireland, observed: 'The P.M. will not make a definite offer so long as they ask for a Republic. They will not cease to ask for a Republic till the P.M. makes them a definite offer.' This impasse was broken in June 1921 when George V visited Belfast and in a memorable speech urged all Irishmen 'to pause, to stretch out the hand of forbearance and conciliation, to forgive and forget'. It had been written by Lloyd George's secretariat, and on 6 December 1921 the 'articles of an agreement' leading to a treaty had been signed between his government and representatives of Sinn Féin. The bloody, undeclared Anglo-Irish war, suspended by truce from July onwards, came to an end. Over a thousand lives had been lost, and immeasurable damage done. Violet wrote to Gilbert Murray: 'One can hardly believe one isn't dreaming when one sees 'Irish Peace' flapping on the posters!...

The psychology of the Tory party is really bewildering. One feels an almost insane rage when one thinks of the loss of life that might have been avoided if in 1914 they had been willing to swallow a <u>much</u> milder instalment of freedom than the present measure gives.'[1]

[1] *Sunday Express*, 8 May 1921; speech to the WNLF, 9 May 1921, Violet Bonham Carter MSS; VBC to Gilbert Murray, 9 December 1921.

SIX

Liberal Schism and Reunion
The Ruhr Crisis

October 1922–January 1924

Liberal schism : the 1922 general election

In the space of less than two years, 1922–4, there were three general elections in Britain, which collectively laid the foundation of politics in the inter-war years. They established the Conservatives as the party of government, Labour as the opposition, and relegated the Liberals to third place in a political system favouring the two strongest parties. The 1922 election came about after Conservative MPs, meeting at the Carlton Club on 19 October, voted for the break-up of the governing Coalition. Their rebellion was precipitated by Lloyd George's foreign policy, which had brought Britain to the brink of war with Turkey. Polling day was set for 15 November. At Paisley Asquith faced a straight fight against Labour, a task made more difficult by a 'sullen anti-bourgeois feeling ... swelling up like a tidal wave over the whole of the west of Scotland', which had its roots in high unemployment. In this context Asquith's success in holding the seat was highly creditable, though his majority was reduced to 316. Nationally Labour experienced its best result ever, with 142 seats; the Conservatives triumphed with 345; for Liberals there was disappointment, with only 64 'Asquithian' independents and 53 Lloyd George 'Nationals' returned. The combined Liberal share of the vote, however, was only a little less than that of Labour, and the case for Liberal reunion could not be ignored. Much depended upon the attitude of the Liberal leaders, and at Paisley there had been no sign of compromise. Asquith had treated Lloyd George and Bonar Law as the same enemy, a line of attack followed by Violet. She suggested that they differed only in presentation, and invited the electorate to choose between Lloyd George, suffering from St Vitus's dance, and Bonar Law, suffering from sleeping sickness. Between the Asquithian and Lloyd George Liberals, though, she identified fundamental disagreement. Lloyd George and his followers had betrayed their heritage, and were Liberals not of conscience but of convenience, 'who only turn to the People

*when the Carlton Club has turned them down'. On such terms,
reunion seemed a distant prospect. In fact it was effected within a year.*[1]

Diary – Monday 23 October to late November 1922 – Dorset House, Dorset Street, W.

The long impending General Election was precipitated by the Carlton Club decision – unforeseen by anyone. Parlt. was dissolved on the 23rd & when I went up to Rochdale on the 25th to speak for Ramsay Muir it was their first election meeting.... Monday [30th] was a nightmare of last preparations – & we went up by the night train.... I felt a very different atmosphere about Paisley altogether this time. There were 5,000 unemployed in the streets & great distress. Coming out of a schoolhouse meeting a woman said to me 'Could you bring up yr. children on 15/ a week?' – I said 'No I cldn't.' She said 'Well why shld you have so much & I so little?' a question to which there is obviously no answer. I never hated anything more than this 'straight fight with Labour' & the feeling that they regarded one as a sleek canting Capitalist. One might criticize their rudeness – their unfairness – their inaccuracy – their lack of good humour & of all our sense of the courtesies of a fight – but yet emotionally we felt that in their shoes we wld. have voted Labour every time. The tide of one's own emotions was – however wrongly & unreasonably – with them.

In places where there was no distress or unemployment – Huddersfield for instance – one felt quite different straightaway. There Liberalism had the democratic wind – or a gust of it – & there was no bitterness in the fight.[2]

I left Glasgow Thursday morning early [2nd November] & went to Huddersfield where I had a <u>most</u> magnificent meeting in the Town Hall – then 2 at Penistone for Pringle next day – Sunday in bed in London – an <u>appalling</u> nightmare of a meeting for Crawfurd in Walthamstow baths – up to the Spen Valley & Burnley on Wed (4 meetings) – Thursday <u>magnificent</u> meeting & overflow for Bluey at Accrington – leaving 7 next morning & speaking for B Jowitt at 3 meetings at Hartlepool that day – arriving at Glasgow at 10 o'clock at night. Women's meeting at Paisley next afternoon at which I felt quite delirious with fatigue – then a week-end in bed at Weir's[3] & two last nights at Paisley helped out by Buckmaster & a

---

[1] Stephen Koss, *Asquith*, 258; Roy Jenkins, *Asquith*, 496; Paisley addresses, Violet Bonham Carter MSS.

[2] Huddersfield was narrowly won by the Liberals in 1922: in a three-cornered contest they secured a majority of 206.

[3] William Douglas Weir (1877–1959), cr. Baron, 1918; Viscount, 1938; director of G & J

frantic day Wed. driving round the Polling stations. Our poll was to be declared at 2.30 that morning – so we sat – or rather stood on the staircase of our Glasgow hôtel watching the results go up on screen. Big Labour wins one after the other – & a hungry roar from the great crowd like the howl of a jungleful of tigers....

At about 11.30 we motored into Paisley & went to the Eadie's house where Father had been dining. McNair had predicted a doubled majority for Father – something like 5000. Everyone predicted a large increase & said Biggar had done his best in 1920. I had the strong feeling all the time that the tide was flowing against us. If what one saw with one's eyes at meetings & in the streets was evidence it certainly was. But McNair discounted these things saying the same rowdy interrupters came to every meeting – & quite truly – that a few hundred can make a big disturbance – also that his canvass was going well & scoffed at any suggestion that our majority was going down.

M. & I were not allowed up this time in the room next to the one in which the counting was going on. We sat downstairs with Mrs. Biggar – a charming woman who told us this was the last time her husband was going to contest the seat.[1] After a very long wait we went upstairs. I saw at once on Gladstone's blême face that something had happened & for a moment feared we were out – he murmured with a gasp 'three hundred' – & we rushed in to the counting room where Father looked almost for the first time in his life I thought rather shaken. He said 'the tightest fit you ever saw' – then the figures were announced & we dashed on to the Liberal Club where we all spoke amid touching enthusiasm, quite undamped I thought by the decreased majority – & home to bed by 3.30. South next day. Elizabeth met us with the news that Simon was in.... We have done badly in quantity but well in quality & most unexpectedly everywhere....

I dashed home & saw the children.... It was wonderfully comforting to tumble into bed that night knowing I shld. wake up amongst them in the morning & that not another word of any kind wld. be expected of me for ages & ages. The next weeks were very full. All the things I had neglected thro' the Election came tumbling head over heels towards me. Clothes – servants – children's winter-hats – (what a hunt! Everywhere to be met by the uncompromising 'beaver' of round upturned brim – & crowns that extinguish poor Laura's tiny pin's head & threepenny bit face!)....

Weir Ltd, Glasgow, a marine engineering firm for which Bongie once worked; married, 1904, Alice *née* MacConnachie.

[1] In fact Biggar made one more attempt, contesting the seat in 1923.

Diary – February 1923 – written in late March, at Dorset House

Cressida expressed a great desire to hear 'the truth about all the countries in the world'. I felt the limitations of parenthood – & of humanity – when I found myself asking at the local booksellers for an elementary history-book – & they were brought home to me even more vividly when 'Little Arthur's History of England' was handed over the counter. I brought it home with many misgivings as to its power of slaking the infinite thirst she had suddenly conceived – but to my amazement it was pure nectar to her. She sat with burning eyes & cheeks – drinking it in. Early Britons – Woad ... Alfred & the cakes etc. etc – interrupting me from time to time to say with tense anxiety 'Will it end happily?' – rather a difficult question to answer. Nannie tells me she has hardly had a good night since! She lives entirely in a world of Civil Wars – bishops – & beheaded Kings....

... One night when I went to see her in bed she said 'Dada's been talking to me about Parliament. Mama why is the House of Commons so much more important than the H. of Lords?' I tried to explain how one rested on votes – representing what people thought of you – & the other didn't – & tried to illustrate it by pointing out the great success Aga had always had at the Polls. 'Well poor Aga must have been a little unlucky last time.' 'Why do you say that?' – 'He got much fewer votes than before. Nannie said so.' I wasn't prepared for her to be so well up in the fluctuations of majorities. She went on 'When I grow up I'm going to speech with all my strength – because I want to go there.' I asked what she would say in her speeches & she made me quite a plausible one. 'Poor people must have nicer houses & there must be more fairness for them. If a rich man <u>should</u> take a poor woman's pram he must give her money to buy a new one. About foreign countries I won't say much. The thing about wars is to be <u>ready</u> for them. We musn't go on about the war with the Germans now 'cos it might hurt their feelings & their King's & I daresay his <u>bishops</u> gave him bad advice.' She thinks a good deal about going into the House & said to me to-day 'Who would you vote for if I was grown-up?' I left them at the end of February to go out to stay with Edgar in Berlin where I had a most deeply interesting fortnight....

'The dangerous insanity of the French – & our helplessness': the Ruhr Crisis, 1923

Under the Treaty of Versailles (1919) Germany was obliged to pay the Allies compensation for damages arising from the war. The exact figure was unspecified, and France, seeking its own security by denying Germany the means for recovery, pressed for the greatest amount possible. The British government reluctantly agreed. At

Edinburgh in March 1920 Violet stated the Liberal objections to this policy, which was neither just nor politic: 'Germany must be helped to recover.' Such advice went unheeded, as in April 1921 reparations were fixed at a level far beyond Germany's capacity to pay. When the German government defaulted on repayments in January 1923, French and Belgian troops occupied the Ruhr. The aim was to force the German government either to make good the deficit or else be cut off – perhaps permanently – from its industrial heartland. By the time that the occupation ended, nine months later, the German economy was shattered. At the end of February Violet planned to visit Berlin, and wrote to Gilbert Murray: 'One can think of nothing but the situation out there – the dangerous insanity of the French – & our helplessness'. It was a disturbing visit, and after her return she moved the resolution condemning the Ruhr occupation at the National Liberal Federation's annual conference: 'What is the good of disarming Germany, of blowing up her fortresses, of destroying her guns … when you are making an arsenal of every German heart – when you are forging in hatreds, weapons more bitter and more deadly than steel – when you are lighting in the memories of every German school-child fires that will burn while life lasts?' The Ruhr Crisis had origins in one war, and consequences in another, and Violet spoke presciently in the general election later that year: 'Now is the moment for every one of us who has a child to make a great fight for the next generation. Look at Europe to-day and think where your son will be 18 years hence….'.[1]

Diary – Thursday 1 to Friday 2 March – British Embassy, Berlin

I embarked at Liverpool St in a crowded train full of what I afterwards discovered were commercial travellers on their way to the Leipzig fair. A rather amusing row took place in the Rest car between 2 young Scotch wholesale Fish Merchants from Aberdeen & a Dutchman…. Afterwards at Harwich when I was strolling up & down the deck waiting for us to get off the 2 Scotchmen came up to me & apologized for making a row before me as I was alone…. We began talking about Scotland. I said I knew it well – my Father had represented a Scotch seat for 30 years. This filled them with curiosity 'Does he know anything about fishing?' I denied it

[1] From speeches at: Synod Hall, Edinburgh, 31 March 1920; LNU, Kingsway Hall, London, March 1921; NLF conference, Buxton, 31 May 1923; East Willesden, 1923 general election; letter from VBC to Gilbert Murray, 23 February 1923; all Violet Bonham Carter MSS.

modestly – 'Well what is he anyway?' – 'Well – he's not a Tory.' – 'Liberal?' – 'Yes' – 'Lloyd George[ite]?' – '<u>No</u>' – 'Ah – Asquith[ian].' Then followed a short talk on Ll.G.'s merits & demerits. Considering that my interlocutor had been the recipient of a life size photograph of Ll.G. during his séjour at Gairloch I thought him marvellously open to reason. . . .[1]

He pursued his interrogatory as to Father's identity – & I tried to deflect the talk on to our passage – 'Ah ya're a real artist'. Was his constituency mining? engineering? agricultural? Finally with a flash of light 'Was it anywhere near Paisley?' When he discovered it was he knelt down on the deck before me & I had great difficulty in getting him up again. We had an amusing talk in the course of which his companion told me how the Germans were cutting us out in the Herring fisheries thro' their superior craft & technique (taught in their schools) & how he had come out to buy a German boat & hire a German crew – 'I'm pro-German now – we all are. Everyone for himself'. . . .

I went below to a rocking night. Up in the grey dawn of 5.30 & into a crowded train. Dirty plush carriages 3rds 'converted' into 2nds – & 2nds into Firsts. We crawled off – very slowly – (coal being bad in quality & insufficient in quantity I was told). . . . In my carriage was a nice Englishwoman – 3 intolerable & grotesque Music Hall Americans & a rather quiet German. The Americans made me very shy by joking all the time about the Exchange – '5,000 Marks – that's [a] nickel' – 'shall I give you a million marks or so – that's 2 American dollars' etc. We got out at the frontier. . . . I changed 2£ for which I received 200,000 Marks – great bundles of paper-chase money which I cld hardly carry.[2]

We all got very hungry but the Schinkenbrötchen at the various stations were fallen upon & consumed before we cld get near them. Chocolates were sold for 7000 Marks. We got into Berlin about 10.30.[3] It was divine to arrive dirty & exhausted at the cleanliness & comfort of the Embassy. . . . Dear Tyler opened the door & I was told Helen had gone to bed after the ball last night but that Edgar was up & alone. It was the greatest fun finding him in a big delightful room. He & Helen have managed to miraculously introduce into this house some of the charm & beauty of Esher. . . .

I had dinner & then, after a short & amusing talk with Edgar, bed. . . . He is of course passionately anti-Ruhr – & thinks we ought not to have described our attitude to an adventure of which we all cordially disapprove as one of 'benevolent neutrality'. . . .

---

[1] In the summer parliamentary recess of 1921 Lloyd George took an extended holiday at Gairloch, Ross-shire, a remote location overlooking the Isle of Skye.

[2] The occupation sent post-war inflation in Germany spiralling: one dollar bought 18,000 marks early in 1923, 4.6 million in August, and 4 billion in November.

[3] Violet was travelling with her maid, Rose Law.

Outwardly everything appears absolutely normal in Berlin. There is every outward sign of prosperity. Big luxury shops full of jewels furs & flowers – just like the ones in Bond St or Rue de le Paix & with prices just as high if not higher – so there must be profiteers to buy. Under the surface, Fraü tells me, terrible quiet tragedies go on, mostly in respectable middle class homes.[1] People who starve & are shamed of starving poison themselves every day....

Diary – Saturday 3 March – British Embassy, Berlin

Fraü & I went out shopping together down the Leipziger Strasse.... Over many of the big & small shops is written 'French & Belgians need not enter here' – & I was told the Adlon Hôtel was the only one in Berlin which wld serve them with a meal of any kind.

I came back to lunch to find Helen – Edgar – General von Kluck....[2] Von Kluck I thought perfectly charming. Tho' 77 he didn't look a day older than 64. He was a vigorous & unconventional talker with a first-rate sense of humour – & a great gift of words. One felt <u>tremendous</u> vitality & energy about him & no military rigidity or conventionality. He began by talking about Joffre – & then went on to Foch who he said 'had something demonic about him. That <u>must</u> be the Fieldmarshal – he must be a demon'. He thought Haig the best of our Generals, but thought French's action in retiring [to] the Marne saved the British Army....

He was a delightfully human old boy & told with real emotion the story of a young officer who came & begged him ' "I want to go over there to the front – over there to the front where they are shooting" – he went like a child' – & directly he got there he was blown to atoms. He was badly wounded himself – got his lung full of shrapnel 'from this thing' – dangling a bit of it from his watch chain. People bothered him to write a book – he didn't want to – cldn't be bothered with all the secretaries & typists he wld need. 'There is too much blackness around now – we have to await the future – then everything is going to appear in the right proportions'.[3]

---

[1] Anne Meyer *née* Heinsius[?], the Asquith's pre-war governess, nicknamed by them 'Fraü'. She had returned to Germany shortly after the outbreak of war.

[2] Alexander von Kluck (1846–1934), Prussian general; wounded 1915; retired, 1916. Von Kluck led the German 1st Army in August 1914. The most northerly of all, it made rapid progress westwards, and von Kluck believed that he could have taken Paris had he not been ordered to fall in line with the armies to his south. According to Lady D'Abernon, 'The General can only discourse in his native tongue and his one and only topic is the 1914 advance' (Helen D'Abernon, *Red Cross and Berlin Embassy*, 104).

[3] Von Kluck must be referring to an autobiography; his memoir of the first weeks of the war, *Der Marsch auf Paris und die Marneschlacht*, had already been published (1920).

He was modest about his own part – 'I was only the carrier of thought'. Insistent on the moral effect of artillery on infantry – 'It does not matter how short they shoot, the man knows that he has the artillery behind him. Everything lies <u>in the idea</u>. That is why the tanks were so terrific. Everybody thought to himself "With the tanks I am <u>invincible</u>".'[1] He was interesting about the Germans' great lack of munitions, which we never suspected, just as they of course never suspected ours.

I drove with Edgar to the golf links after lunch.... He fulminated against the Ruhr policy & quoted someone as having said – 'Two men created the German Empire, Bismarck in 1870 & Poincaré in 1923'. He was insistent however on the necessity of keeping our troops on the Rhine....

Diary – Sunday 4 March – British Embassy, Berlin

... I went off about 4 to tea with Professor & Mrs. Moritz Bonn.[2] A dark – gloomy – untidy – & essentially <u>bachelor</u> flat in Ma[?] Kinch[?] Strasse. Mr & Mrs Bonn sitting in a comfortless little room beside a table on which there was a teapot & a little bread & butter. He is a funny looking little man – a Jew not particularly German – & very young – more like a student than a professor. Rather a sharp stoat-like face – speaking quiet lucid English.

I talked to him for about an hour & a half with rapt interest & it is rather difficult to begin to résumé what he said. First about the suffering of the people he endorsed what I had already heard about the middle-classes – officers' families – pensioned officials etc – living on capital – if they had any – or quietly starving.... He emphasized the shadow of uncertainty that hung over the whole of life & its resulting dislocation: 'I never know when I go out whether I am going to be able to pay for my meal at the Rest[aurant] – or the Hôtel. What was enough yesterday may be only half enough to-day'....

I asked him what people here expected of England – when they talked, as his wife had done to me, of England getting off the fence, what did they mean? The only gesture it still remained for us to make was to withdraw from the Rhine & this was clearly the last thing they wished us to do.

---

[1] Von Kluck suggests that, even if artillery fails to find its target, its psychological effect is still great. Tanks were first used (by the British) on the Somme in September 1916, with mixed results; notwithstanding their limitations, they made a significant contribution to the eventual Allied victory.

[2] Julius Moritz Bonn (b. 1873), professor, and financial expert; Chancellor Wirth's consultant on reparations.

He said neither Germany nor France cld possibly negotiate direct. England alone cld. find out indirectly & unofficially what Germany cld offer.... The present Govt were inexperienced politicians. He described to me again the awful sufferings of the middle classes – of the old. When I spoke of the <u>fear</u> of the French seeing a new generation of Germans growing up who might shortly come tumbling over their borders – 'Then why do they only have 2 children each?'....

Diary – Monday 5 March – British Embassy, Berlin

... Home to lunch & a talk afterwards with de Margerie, the French Ambassador, a very charming man – who Edgar says came here longing to be agreeable & loved & then had to bear the brunt of this abhorred policy. We had an amusing talk about the Conferences in London & Paris – Lloyd George, Bonar Law etc. – 'M. Ll.G. est très séduisant – mais Mr B.L. est comment dirais-je? plus gentleman'.[1] The tongue touching where the tooth ached I cldn't resist representing myself as an ardent Francophile weeping over the ruins of the Entente – 'Et cette situation ici! comme c'est triste. Vous ne savez pas combien l'opinion publique en Angleterre en est choquée etc. – etc.'[2]...

... I tried the psychological argument. <u>They</u> were psychologists – not like the Germans – they must realize that this démarche wld resuscitate & mobilize every reserve of latent Jingoism & sense of nationality in Germany. What shld we feel if a foreign nation came into Lancashire to try & work our mines. We shld fight them with sticks & stones – it wld live & <u>burn</u> in our memories for ever.

The inexorable answer 'Oui mais aussi ne refuseriez-vous pas de payer vos dettes'. He seemed curiously unselfconscious about France's debt to us! It was just what the Belgian Minister said to 'Plutôt mourir que de ne pas faire payer l'Allemagne'[3] – but I felt it was the plunging of blind exasperation rather than any clear or defined or settled purpose – or really <u>much</u> hope of bringing anything off....

... We went back to supper at the Adlon – the hôtel where the Control Commission lives & the only one which will feed a Frenchman. A very amusing atmosphere. As you come in you are faced by a romantic statue

---

[1] 'Monsieur Ll.G. is very attractive – but Mr Bonar Law is, how would I put it? more [of a] gentleman.'

[2] 'And this situation here! how sad it is. You do not know how much it shocks public opinion in England etc. – etc.'

[3] 'Yes, but then you would not refuse to pay your debts.' ... 'Better die than not make Germany pay'.

of the Kaiser with helmet & shield. When the mob stoned the Adlon in the first Revolution the old proprietor, a staunch Imperialist, stood with folded arms looking on with horror & contempt at their antics. Suddenly they caught sight of the Kaiser's statue – 'Get rid of it – down with him' etc. The old man strode forward 'And what did Lohengrin ever do to you?' – 'Lohengrin – oh – it is Lohengrin' & they drew back & thus the Kaiser's statue was saved!...

Diary – Tuesday 6 March – British Embassy, Berlin

... I dined with Colonel Norris at the Adlon.... Everyone knows everyone else by sight. The French attaché sits alone at his table. A terrible row took place there once because a Frenchman didn't stand up when 'Deutschland D. über alles' was played – Prinz Joachim attacked him – & curiously enough the waiters protected the Frenchman.

Diary – Wednesday 7 March – British Embassy, Berlin

... We went to a very clever Schnitzler play called Dr. Bernhardi – anti Anti Semite in theme – 'Prig-drama' marvellously acted by a company which might have been at our Court Theatre in the Granville-Barker days.[1] No woman appears at all except a hospital nurse in the 1st act. We stayed for 3 Acts & then an appeal for the Ruhr was made – I thought the audience apathetic compared to what our people wld have been at home. The outburst of applause after the best speech in the 3rd Act was louder & more moved. There were a lot of Jews in the theatre – (Edgar says it is very curious how the Jews are everywhere for giving way & the Christians for making a stand)....

Diary – Thursday 8 March – British Embassy, Berlin

Professor Bonn took me in the morning to see Ex-Chancellor Bauer – a very attractive Labour man of the burly solid type who was Chancellor about 1920.[2] He reminded me rather of a North-country Englishman. Very moderate & human & sound. He gave me a short elementary sketch of their political position. About 12 Communists on the extreme left – about

---

[1] Arthur Schnitzler, *Professor Bernhardi: a comedy* (1913); Harley Granville-Barker (1877–1946), renowned as an innovatory director at the Royal Court Theatre, London, 1904–7.

[2] Gustav Bauer (1870–1944), socialist Reich chancellor, 1919–20.

3 Monarchist Jingoes on the extreme right. The rest of Germany united behind Cuno's policy on the Ruhr. In reply to my question as to what England cld do – 'a firmer & more outspoken condemnation of French policy from England wld help to create public opinion in Europe. An attempt at mediation side by side with America might make a great difference'....

I came back to lunch here & met... Frau von Oheimb – an Abgeordneter des Reichstags – a very rich & well-known woman here.[1] Her vitality was immense – she was amusing & light in hand & I thought talked politically very sound sense....

She told me terrible stories about the gradual downfall of the Mittelstands which is <u>no doubt</u> the greatest tragedy that is going on here today. There are 800 Drs in Berlin most of whom are starving. Their patients can't afford to send for them. They play anything they can in the way of music at Restaurants in the evening & sell newspapers. The suicide statistics have gone up (she said 85 p.cent – but I take her figures with a pinch of salt). Students are underfed & can't afford books – lawyers are in a hopeless plight.

She said how appalling it wld be if our troops were moved from the Rhine. 'That they stay there – that I ask for every day from Ld D'Abernon and the dear Lord'.... That night we went to a big dinner at the Finns'.... One interesting incident which brought home to me a little of what the Germans are feeling to-day. I was talking French to the Italian & in the middle of what I was saying turned to the waiter & said – also in French – 'du pain s'il vous plait' – he replied in a low voice quivering with feeling 'Brot – bitte sehr'. This from a waiter – the most tolerant & international of all classes – I thought very strong.

Diary – Friday 9 March – British Embassy, Berlin

... In to lunch & hurried off directly afterwards to the Reichstag where I had an appt. with Wels the Majority Socialist.... He seemed to me honest & sensible – a <u>totally</u> different type to Breitscheid who I met that afternoon at tea – at Professor Bonn's.[2] His appearance surprised me – very tall, thin &

---

[1] According to D'Abernon, 'an important political lady' who exercised much influence in the right-wing German National People's Party (DNVP), which was dedicated to a restoration of the monarchy and opposed to the reparations terms of Versailles (Edgar D'Abernon, *An Ambassador of Peace*, ii, 169).

[2] Otto Wels (1873–1939), SPD politician, member of the Reichstag, 1912–33. Rudolf Breitscheid (b. 1874), leader of the Independent Socialists in Germany; he was associated with French socialists, had received favours from the French government, and so was considered to be pro-French.

loosely knit with a rather interesting face. Not a working man at all – an intellectual of the type you might easily meet at Ottoline's. Vain, sceptical & contrary. I was not the least attracted by him. I spoke of ... things at Bochum[1] 'All of that is exaggerated – I've just been there. The shops are not shut. The French on the whole are behaving quite well'.... 'Could Germany honestly make a repayment that would satisfy the French?' 'Yes. The French see what the great industrialists have built in the last years in the Ruhr. They put their capital into large buildings etc. so as to avoid having to pay taxes on their profits. The French look at that and very naturally expect that we pay them reparations.' 'Do you think it would be possible to have negotiations that would be successful?' 'Yes quite possible. I have spoken to a Frenchman in Düsseldorf who is Poincaré's right hand man' – etc.

I felt that if he spoke to the French in the same vein that he did to me they wld feel quite justified in the steps they were taking. He is that curious type of Pacifist who is always making excuses for Force when it is used by other nations. The same type defended Germany's invasion of Belgium – & resented our opposing it in England, as those who now in Germany defend French action in the Ruhr....

We discussed female politicians. I said our women were still apathetic & not very politically educated – 'No – not <u>even</u> Lady Astor?' – which I thought amusing.[2] He & Frau Deutsch almost came to blows over Russia. She is a passionate pro-Bolshevist – & tho' the wife of an industrial magnate & the sister of Otto Kahn is a formally affiliated member of the Socialist party.[3] Breitscheid however is passionately anti-Bolshevik....

I felt I shld have liked Breitscheid better if I'd been alone with him. The only moments when he visibly mellowed was when I offered him my cigarettes, of which he smoked two with great pleasure. I asked him what he thought of our Labour party – 'Ramsay MacDonald ist der Staatsmann – der, wie Ihr Vater sagt, sich die Krone in dem Spiegel anzieht'.[4] Bonn was very Jewish, flattering us all & trying hard to produce us all to each other.

---

[1] Bochum, an industrial city at the centre of the Ruhr region.

[2] Nancy, Countess Astor (d. 1964), first woman to take her seat in parliament; Conservative MP for Sutton, Plymouth, 1919–45; married, 1906, Waldorf Astor, 2nd Viscount.

[3] Lili Deutsch *née* Kahn, married Felix Deutsch, one of the founders of the electrical manufacturers Allgemeine Electricitäts Gesellschaft; she was the sister of Otto Kahn (1867–1934), New York banker and philanthropist.

[4] This is not idiomatic German, and the meaning is unclear. Violet did not write German as well as she spoke it, and she may have misquoted. A literal translation is 'Who, as your father says, puts on the crown in the mirror' – perhaps a reference to MacDonald's ambition and self-regard. Violet had played golf with him in 1913 and found him 'very goodlooking ... rather vain'.

Dinner in very different Company with dear General Bingham & his wife at the Adlon – the 2 Breens, Col Thompson & a very nice man called Thorburn who was at Winchester with Cys but looked years older....[1] He [Thorburn] admitted to being a pessimist but said that looking far into the future he saw a combination between Russia Germany & Japan against England & America with the Latins all nowhere. They were dying races – Italy & Spain already dead – France having this last dying flare. It is ghastly to me that all minds shld. be reaching forward to new combinations of this kind. It is significant that not once since I have been in Germany in any conversation have I heard the League of Nations mentioned as a possible factor or way out of their difficulties. To Germany, thanks to the capital blunder of her exclusion, [the League] has dropped out of the picture of European politics....[2]

Diary – Saturday 10 March – British Embassy, Berlin

Thanks to Frau von Oheimb an appalling muddle was made of my Hospital plans which resulted in my going off ... accompanied by an Abgeordneter looking like a hired mute....

We went on to the Children's Hospital.... All children – tuberculous rickety & 'heart-krank' (scrofulous I suppose?). All the direct result so they said of under-nourishment. The nice intelligent white coated Drs. said it was heart-breaking work. Directly they got the children into the Hospital & fed them up they began to mend & put on weight – then they were obliged to send them back into homes where they starved back again. The consumptives, some of them, looked fairly happy – but the rickety babies were hauntingly pathetic. Bent limbs big head – heavy tired eyes & a listlessness that seemed a kind of contradiction in terms of childhood. One little baby I shall never forget – a little starved skeleton with an old face – almost too weak to cry – lying in a cot giving a little miserable wail which ceased if one patted it as tho' a human touch made it feel a little less lonely in its misery....

No child over 2 gets milk in urban Germany. Butter is almost impossibly dear. There is no state feeding in the schools – so the Quaker Speise is really their only hope of growing up normal human beings. My one doubt was as to whether it was wise or kind to pull thro' these poor little wrecks in order to limp handicapped thro' life. It is a tour de force but is it worth

[1] Major-General Sir Francis Richard Bingham (1863–1935), chief of British section, military commission of control, Germany, 1919–24. Stephen Keith Thorburn (b. 1894), with commission of control, 1919; he was four years younger than Cys.

[2] Germany was only admitted to the League of Nations late in 1926; Hitler withdrew it in October 1933.

while? I came back tired out & harrowed to the bone....

... [After dinner] the party streamed in – Rosenberg (Foreign Minister) & his wife – Prinz & Pss Blücher – Riedl, the Hungarians etc. etc. At the end I suddenly saw Kühlmann & had quite an unexpected reflex of revulsion & desire <u>not</u> to speak to him.[1] I dodged him for a time in the full consciousness that he had recognized me, then as I sat there with Breen he came up to me & said 'Have you forgotten me?' We talked at first rather strainedly – then he began asking me about things in London & England now. I said the war had changed them a good deal. But they were changing already before the war. 'I always used to say to my poor wife (who is dead now) – that summer of 1914 had the beauty of a sunset. It was the last glorious flower of a splendour that was fading.' After a time he said 'It is such a grief to me that after struggling for 4 years against war some of my English friends still think I am in part to blame for it.' – I said 'What they say & believe is that you reported we shld not come in.' – 'I never did so. I always said from the first moment I came that Britain was very much committed to the Entente.' – 'But that last summer – didn't the Irish situation affect your point of view?' – 'No – besides I was away at the critical time.... Lady B.C. – this was as I always say a Russo-Austrian conflict – not an Anglo-German one'....

'But there was a party in Germany that wanted War – that had been preparing for War for years. Germany refused the Haldane proposals to limit the fleet. Germany refused a Conference.'[2].... I. 'Tirpitz wanted war' K. 'Tirpitz was in despair when it came. He knew we had no chance. I tell you when I came home & saw all our young fellows going off I had to cry. I knew we cldn't win.' I. 'The Kaiser didn't want it?' K. 'The Kaiser was on his yacht & directly he got the telegram reporting the Austrian ultimatum ordered them to steam for Kiel – telling the story of a Czar who saw his troops going off with flags & wreaths to the Crimea – "There goes my Army to a war I didn't want".' I. 'If E. Grey had said at once "We stand by France" – wld the knowledge we were coming in have stopped Germany?' K. 'No because no one in Germany planned or wanted War. We "stumbled" into it as Mr Ll.G. said. (2nd time this has been quoted to me) I. 'Yet you offered us certain terms to stay out – for instance not to bombard the northern coast of France.'[3] K. 'That was a last desperate clutch of a drown-

---

[1] Richard von Kühlmann (1873–1948), German diplomat as counsellor in the London embassy, 1908–14; later foreign minister, 1917–18.

[2] Haldane was sent to Berlin in 1912 to explore the possibility of a reduction in naval armaments, but could not secure German agreement to a British offer. In July 1914 Grey proposed a conference of powers to settle the troubled European scene – he was exasperated by the German veto (Viscount Grey of Fallodon, *Twenty-Five Years*, i, 316–21).

[3] Revealed to the House of Commons by Sir Edward Grey during his speech on 3 August: 'I

ing man' – raising his hands. At this pt we were interrupted. But he said 'I must see you again' & hastily arranged with Horstmann, a Jew permanent official at the F.O., that I shld lunch with them on Monday as he wanted to give me a short 'lecture'....

Diary – Sunday 11 March – British Embassy, Berlin

I was visited at 11 by Voigt, Manchester Guardian correspondent whom Breitscheid has put me in touch with[1] – a very queer clever young man in horn spectacles with a voice like Masefield, which gave me an illusion of knowing him much better than I really did. I at once took a great liking to him. He was shy & strange but obviously clever & absolutely independent & individual in pt. of view. Edgar came up while I was talking to him & we cross-examined him about the Ruhr. He seemed to think that in some places the people were breaking & trying to get employment from the French. He was by a stroke of great luck going back to the Ruhr on Monday night so I asked [him] to engage a room for me at the Düsseldorf hôtel where he stayed & suggested we might share a motor for a day or two's expedition.

... Home to rest & a long talk with Edgar & then off to see Felix Deutsch & his wife. I drove to 16 Ranch Strasse & was ushered into a typical Industrialist magnate's house. It might have belonged to a more cultured Weir or Leverhulme or Airedale. The streak of redeeming culture was Jewish – I afterwards discovered that Frau Deutsch was Otto Kahn's sister & niece of old Lady Lewis.[2]

I was ushered into the presence of Deutsch – a little short squat vehement bearded Jew – obviously very angry with this country for business reasons. After a perfunctory inquiry as to whether I was going into the Ruhr he broke into a tirade against England implying that it was her jealousy of Germany as a trade rival that had brought her into the War & that led her now to stand aside & watch Germany being trampled upon....

I assured him that whatever we might have thought in 1918 the last 4 years had taught us that our prosperity was intimately connected with that of Germany & that England's greatest need to-day was for the economic restoration of Europe. He interrupted me to say fiercely that whenever

have only heard that shortly before I came to the House, but it is far too narrow an engagement for us' (Viscount Grey of Fallodon, *Twenty-Five Years*, ii, 301).

[1] Frederick Augustus Voigt (1892–1957), renowned correspondent of the *Manchester Guardian*, based in Berlin; of German parentage; 'absolutely fearless' in pursuit of a story (*DNB*).

[2] Sir George Lewis (1833–1911), cr. Bt, 1902; solicitor, married (first) Victorine *née* Kahn, who died 1865; the Lewises and Asquiths were family friends.

German trade made a tender & got a big order there was an outcry in all the English papers that it shld have been given to Germans & not to us – I. 'In which newspapers?' 'In the technical newspapers.' Politics for him were entirely contained in a kind of industrial 'pocket' & he cldn't see beyond it.

At this point in the conversation Frau Deutsch (whose relations with Breitscheid & the Socialist party puzzled me more & more as I listened to her husband) came in dressed up to the nines in endimanché grey. She sat down & began very quietly & systematically contradicting every word her husband said – with a look of resigned endurance from which all irritation had been eliminated. She regarded him as a political lunatic. 'Nein das ist nicht so. Don't believe that Lady Bonham Carter. <u>Utterly</u> untrue.' Her contradictions petered out finally into low moans. I asked if the Govt was stable – & fairly firmly in the saddle – Deutsch: 'What we have to be afraid of is a putsch from the left' – Frau Deutsch 'A putsch from the <u>right</u> – that is the danger' etc. etc. I liked her very much – much better than at the Breitscheids' tea. She has a touch of <u>real</u> internationalism about her & real consciousness of the faults of her own country without disloyalty or bitterness or any posturing or attitudinizing about it.

I went on with them to a rather curious tea party at the house of one Sänger, an intellectual, editor of a paper called the Deutsche Neue Rudschen, a weekly political & literary – I imagine a kind of Nation or New Statesman.... Quite a good talk with Sänger – a gentle nice man – deeply unhappy about Germany. His great fear is that if the present Govt. attempted at all a moderate Peace with France the Deutsch Nationals wld kick & there wld be civil war in Germany. (I think we outsiders tend to forget the frightful domestic & internal difficulties Germany has had to cope with during the last years. Several Revolutions & no Army to cope with them.) I said it was so odd to hear people talking of possible Bolshevism in Germany & fearing disorders. One had always looked on the Germans as a people docile & orderly almost to a fault – amenable to authority – the attitude of Heine who said 'There won't be a revolution in Prussia because the police have forbidden it'. Sänger said this was a total misconception of the Germans. The Prussians had tried & for a time had succeeded in imposing their own mould on Germany.... That mould was now broken – & the real German hailing from the Danube & the Rhine was asserting himself – a much freer & less law-abiding soul....

Diary – Monday 12 March – British Embassy, Berlin

... I lunched with the Horstmanns. Exquisite Jewish meal.... I sat between Horstmann & his son & after lunch Kühlmann took me aside ... & he proceeded to explain to me map in hand the French & Belgian encircling movt. in the Ruhr – which I must say I had never before geographically realized. The Rhine, the greatest trade artery in Europe, is being blocked at every point by the French – decapitated by the Belgians – our little zone at Cologne is completely cut off....

... We left the Ruhr & got once more onto a discussion of pre-war diplomacy. He said that the war wld. certainly have been averted if Marschall von Bieberstein had stayed in England & had not died.[1] He was out for peace – as Lichnowsky also was – but he also had great prestige & weight with Berlin & they wld. have listened to him there.... [Kühlmann] seemed genuinely glad to see me & very anxious to get propaganda for himself through to England. Begged me to encourage as many English as I cld. to come to Berlin to see for themselves how things really stood there....

Diary – Tuesday 13 March – Residence of the Commander-in-Chief, British Army of the Rhine

My uneasy sleep was broken twice towards morning by French officers wanting to see my passport. I arrived about 9.30 in Cologne station & was met by two of those perfect young Englishmen one only seems to see abroad. While one of them (Gen Godley's ADC) was waiting for my luggage the other Captain Hussey came & talked to me in the motor. He began rather tentatively 'are you very Pro-French?' & on my reassuring him on this point poured out his heart to me. He was in command of the station & had the difficult task of reconciling the various authorities under him who operated there. The Germans wldn't take orders from or work with French or Belgians – & he was not surprised. He thought the French were mad – the Germans adored us. The Tommies had settled down happily & naturally into the life of the place & were universally loved....

The Godleys live about 4 miles out of Cologne in a 'Schieber's' villa 'standing in its own grounds' with a nice wide sweep of the Rhine in front of it. General Godley is quite charming – tall gaunt & lean & fair-minded with an odd echo of Kilbracken.[2] Lady Godley thoroughly tiresome & passionately pro-French. Besides the staff there was a most delightful & apparently very young man called Piggott who was Chief British Commissioner in Cologne – & his mother. Piggott sat next to me at lunch &

---

[1] Marschall von Bieberstein (1842–1912), German ambassador to Britain, May to September 1912.

[2] General Sir Alexander John Godley (1867–1957), cr. KCB, 1916; GCB, 1928; commander of British Army of the Rhine, 1922–4; first cousin of 1st Baron Kilbracken.

we had a very good talk. He is very pro German over the Ruhr business & warned me of Lady Godley's feelings in the matter.

... He spoke very highly of the Mayor Adenauer to whom I had a letter of introduction from Haspohn – & whom I went to see in the afternoon.[1] I drove in with another A.D.C. – rather timid, Fyers by name, who also asked tentatively if I was pro-French & then revealed his own sympathies in the opposite direction: 'Of course one can't talk too freely here – one so easily gets called a pro-Hun & lots of the officers here are strongly pro-French – but the Germans have been awfully amenable & easy to deal with & one can't help liking them & feeling sorry for them'....

... [I] was ushered after a short wait into Adenauer's room. He was an oldish rather tired man of great ability I thought – one of those very sad Germans one meets here.[2] I began by asking him if he wanted our troops to stay to which he answered, as they all do, that he did – & then foreseeing the reproach they all make to us, of disapproving but doing nothing, I asked what in his opinion England cld do – pointing out that we were as disarmed as they. 'You must begin arming again. France has won the war. She is to-day more powerful than she was in Napoleon's time. The balance of power in Europe has been completely upset (zerstört) by the Peace of Versailles. If you want to play a part & have a say in the counsels of Europe you must arm. You see I think we understand the French a little better than you do – & they perhaps us. You are unlike us both. You are a really peace loving people. You dislike fighting. We know what militarism feels like here & we recognize it when we see it in other nations.' I thought him a delightful man – very able – dispassionate – without violence – above all terribly sad....

V.B.C. to Helen D'Abernon   *Friday 16 March*
Commander-in-Chief's Residence,
British Army of the Rhine, Cologne

Dearest Helen

I have not had one second since I left you to write and thank you for my thrilling visit to you. Every minute of it was of <u>intense</u> interest, and I am more than grateful to you for having me....

I arrived at the Godleys' Tuesday morning, and found to my dismay that they had provisionally arranged for me to go round the Ruhr with de Boinvel, <u>French</u> Commissioner at Cologne! I explained gently but firmly

---

[1] Konrad Adenauer (1876–1967), lord mayor of Cologne 1917 and 1920; later first chancellor (1949) of Federal Republic of Germany.

[2] Adenauer was then only forty-seven, twelve years older than Violet.

that I would as soon go round the Ruhr with a Frenchman as to Ireland with a Black and Tan, or to Russia with Winston. No one would either speak to us – or even feed us! The plan was cancelled, and I left next morning for Düsseldorf, where I joined my friend M. Voigt of the Manchester Guardian, and he and I have spent some very interesting days motoring about without any difficulties (except occasionally being held up a few minutes) by the French. The situation [is] a very extraordinary one. Everything the French touch they paralyse. Chimneys are ceasing to smoke – railways are stopping – coke-ovens, which take a month to light, damping down. They are terrified out of their wits, and though armed with machine guns, tanks, and every sort of ridiculous implement of war, complain that the school children attack them, and cover the walls with placards ordering civilians to walk in single file in the middle of the street with their hands <u>turned outwards</u> so that the palms are clearly visible!...

I saw lots of miners and Trades Unionists who are determined to hold out to the bitter end. One man, who had been mobbed for resisting the war in 1914, said the French were making him see red for the first time. At Krupps, where I saw several of the Directors (but to my great disappointment none of the works) they were confident of being able to hold out for a long time. They are still taking orders, and have large stocks of raw material. Only a hunger-blockade would break the people, and this they do not think the French would dare attempt. Fifty Italian scallywag miners have been introduced into one mine and are being protected by tanks and 16 soldiers to each worker! The German retort was to switch off the electric current and plunge that part of the mine in darkness. To this the French reply by darkening other parts which they control, 'embêtement pour embêtement', and so it goes on!

A more futile and <u>frivolously</u> dangerous adventure one cannot imagine. I feel that at any moment 'an incident' might lead to frightful bloodshed. <u>Both</u> sides are so frightened. In England, the French would have been torn to bits by the women alone long before this – but the Germans are enduring – and also I feel a very <u>tired</u> people.[1] Forgive this endless letter. I shall never forget my divine visit nor cease to be grateful for it. All my love to you, dearest Helen, and to Edgar, and please let me know the <u>second</u> either of you come here. Ever yours, Violet.

'The lion and the lamb': Liberal reunion and the 1923 general election

Six months after leading the Conservative Party to victory in the 1922 general election, Bonar Law was forced to retire with terminal

[1] Lady D'Abernon commented, 'No doubt there is truth in what Violet writes, but notwithstanding wonderful intellectual and verbal gifts her judgements on men and affairs are seldom dispassionate or impartial' (Helen Vincent, *Red Cross and British Embassy*, 106–7).

cancer. His successor, Stanley Baldwin, seemed set for a lengthy term in office when, at the end of October 1923, he called a surprise general election for December. He had become convinced of the necessity of adopting protective tariffs, something that Bonar Law had pledged not to do without an election first. This came as a windfall to the Liberals, who reunited around the standard of 'free trade', behind which they had swept to victory in 1906. On 13 November a party manifesto was issued jointly by Asquith and Lloyd George, and on 24 November the two leaders shared a platform at the Clark Town Hall in Paisley. Seconding the vote of thanks on this occasion, Violet betrayed the fragility of Liberal reunion. She began by saying that since she had aired her views on the two main speakers 'so often & so freely' in the past, she would be forgiven for not doing so again. This cleverly relieved her of the obligation to praise Lloyd George, and invited her audience to remember her past criticism of him – some of it voiced in the same hall eighteen months earlier. There was a sharper barb in her concluding remarks. In the columns of *The Times* Lord Derby had observed that in approaching Lloyd George her father was like the proverbial lamb lying down with the lion, 'knowing as well as we do that he is going to be the lion's next meal'. Violet delighted her audience by turning this rebuff on its head: 'Well I confess I read that passage with a certain anxiety. I have watched them both very closely tonight – the lion & the lamb – & I have never seen Mr Lloyd George look less voracious or my father look more uneatable.' Her performance was an Asquithian victory in an unfinished war.

Asquith held Paisley in 1923 with a comfortable majority, due largely to the presence of an independent socialist who split the Labour vote. Nationally the election was another setback for the Liberals, who fielded thirty more candidates than Labour, yet secured thirty-three fewer seats, with 158. Despite a concerted Liberal effort, the gap between the two parties had widened. The overall result was to return the Conservatives to office as the largest party, with 258 seats. A dilemma now arose, for the third-placed Liberals held the balance of power. Much to the chagrin of strong anti-socialists such as Churchill, Asquith decided to vote the Tories out of office in the New Year, and give Liberal support to the first Labour government. This was constitutionally the soundest course: the electorate had not voted for a continuation of Conservative rule, and as the second largest party Labour had the right to form a government. Asquith dismissed the idea of a Liberal administration relying on Conservative votes as potentially damaging to his party and to the country. It would be a cynical denial of Labour's right, and he was certain that there could be no safer conditions under which to try the Labour experiment, since the Liberals could veto any socialist legislation. Asquith also felt that no party could avoid being damaged by being in office in the difficult circumstances of the day. Less clear was whether the Liberals could emerge with credit from opposition.[1]

Diary – late November to early December – 40 Gloucester Square, W.2

My autumn was shattered to bits by the General Election, which Baldwin with amazing folly tumbled himself & his party into. I had a big Education Meeting organized by the [Women's Liberal] Federation at the London School of Economics to preside over, so remained in London the first few days & travelled up to Paisley on Friday [23 November] in the same train as Ll.G. with whom I accidentally & rather dramatically lunched. We had an excellent talk. Having no fidelities he also has no rancours – & no embarrassment at encountering people with both. He was very amusing & exactly like himself discussing prospects 'How do you think the people will take it this time? It's a new electorate very different to that of 1906 – much less educated. I tried the arguments both ways on Megan.[2] I gave her the Protectionist case she said "That sounds very fair". I gave her the Free Trade one & she said "That sounds very complicated". Now that's what I'm afraid the masses may feel.' Elaborate receptions were planned at big stations along the route in which Sir Alfred Cope begged me to take part – a thing I didn't yet feel up to doing!

At Edinburgh he disappeared in surging crowds & I went on to Ferguslie.... Next day we had our first big meeting in the Clark Town Hall with Father & Lloyd George. I had to speak at the end – a difficult speech to make.[3] Then followed an arduous fortnight. Our position at Paisley itself was so critical that I didn't have to dash about the country but remained rooted there. It was a smaller physical strain but a much greater mental one as new stuff had to be produced daily for a very critical

[1] Violet's Paisley speeches: Violet Bonham Carter MSS.

[2] Megan Lloyd George (1902–66), fourth child of David and Margaret Lloyd George; Liberal MP for Anglesey, 1929–51.

[3] Bongie wrote to Violet, 27 November: 'The Manchester Guardian describes your speech at the Ll.G. meeting as "wistfully eloquent". I sympathize with you, sweetie, it is a bloody business to be on a platform with Ll.G. again.' She replied next day: 'I managed to avoid perjuring myself or insulting him & yet smuggled thro' a few barbs.'

audience. My only meetings outside the constituency were big ones in Glasgow (for all the 8 divisions – Jack Tennant was standing for the most hopeless)[1] & in Kilmarnock where Donald was standing. Buckmaster spoke for us, magnificently as he always does on our eve of the poll meeting. We spent the whole of the next day driving round the polling booths in <u>bitter</u> cold. We had a very stiff fight with our old opponent Biggar ... but mercifully the Labour vote was split by an extremist called Cormack. Still we were not without great qualms. We sat in the Eadie's house hearing the returns as they came out on the wireless. The Manchester victories were wonderful. When we heard <u>Masterman</u> was in by thousands we thought it looked like a landslide![2] Our result wasn't declared till 2.30. Meanwhile we sat below in the usual agonized suspense – slightly cheered by a charming porter who risked all to bring us the occasional news. 'He's leading by 3 hundred' – & finally we were allowed upstairs to hear the glorious news that he was in by 1400 – 4 times his last majority. We had a delirious scene at the Liberal Club & then all dispersed.... A very few hours in bed – & south next morning hearing more & more returns as we got south. Phillipps & Pringle & Simon being in was a real joy – Donald's defeat the worst sorrow. He fought so gallantly but had the hopeless handicap of inheriting a Coalie seat – where real Liberalism had been betrayed & scrapped since 1918. We were met at the station by a large crowd. It was heavenly to see the children again. They had all been ill almost ever since I had been away & Cressida – poor darling – looked really run down....

V.B.C. to Gilbert Murray *Friday 7 December*
Train from Paisley

Dearest Professor Murray –
You wrote me such a beloved letter just before we started – & I have been wanting to thank you – but <u>literally</u> between that Friday a fortnight ago & now I haven't had <u>one second</u> in which to read or write a line or do anything human. Only speak – & think (with a growing sterility &

[1] 'Poor little Jack is being <u>crunched</u> in Central Glasgow – Margot went to his first Meeting Monday night – he was howled at continuously. She got up & made a dramatic appeal "You must listen to him he is my <u>brother</u>" & says she got him a hearing & quelled the tigers. Jack however came out to see me next day & complained of it bitterly saying "Between ourselves M. was a confounded nuisance. Jolly for me seeing all the placards to-day 'Mrs. A. <u>rescues</u> her brother'"!!!' (VBC to MBC, 28 November 1923).
[2] At the 1923 general election the Liberals won five of ten Manchester seats from the Conservatives, but lost them all back at the next election; C. F. G. Masterman was elected at Rusholme by a majority of 2,025.

blankness) what I shall say when I speak next. It is over thank Heaven & Father safely in....

I long to see you & talk to you of so many things. This election is like Midsummer Night's Dream – as tho' dust had been sprinkled on people's eyelids & they had woken up & fallen in love at random – with the most grotesquely paradoxical results.... Then we have LlG. cartwheeling round the country with his apparatus of loudspeakers – journalists – jokes etc. etc. baiting the Tories & exchanging complimentary wires with Father!!....

Reunion has been accomplished by complete immersion <u>preceding</u> conversion – probably the only possible method. We were physically ducked under water – holding our noses – & shutting our mouths – before any change of mind or heart cld. even be attempted. As for Baldwin his only chance of recovery is to be carried upstairs again wrapped in a blanket by the Bewdley cook! Love & let me know the earliest moment we can meet – Tuesday? I do <u>pray</u> you are in   Yrs Violet

V.B.C. to Winston Churchill

Boxing Day, Wednesday 26
December
The Wharf, Sutton Courtenay,
Berkshire

My dear Winston – Thank you so much for writing. I showed your letter to Father (which I was sure you would not mind) – he & I had a long talk this morning. I think what you say about the possible Tory reaction which may result from the apparition of a Labour Govt. a very <u>real</u> danger.

But there is another (& to my mind a greater one) we must not lose sight of – i.e. the reaction <u>towards Labour</u> which wld. follow inevitably & immediately from any pact or alliance at this moment between ourselves & the Tories....

I think you tend to underrate a little the <u>immense</u> domestic difficulties & complications with which the Labour Party will be faced <u>in office</u>. They never had any inner unity or even any pretence at outward discipline or civility to their leaders in Opposition. And I think that in office these chasms will be widened rather than bridged....

... What Father feels above all is that it wld. be disastrous for almost any Party in their <u>own</u> interests to come in now & tackle this devil's cauldron (not of our own brewing) which seethes & bubbles on all sides. Let Labour have a try – & find out for themselves & show their followers & the country what the difficulties are....

A glorious New Year to you dear Winston – & a successful one to all our united fortunes – Bless you – Ever yr, Violet

I dreamt all Xmas Eve that I was discussing with you the rival merits of

Second Ballot – P.R. & Alternative Vote – & woke up <u>exhausted</u> ! & convinced that <u>all</u> wld. result in our ruin.[1]

Winston Churchill to V.B.C.   *Tuesday 8 January 1924*
                                                      2 Sussex Square, W.2

<u>Private & Personal</u>

My dear Violet,

I have thought a good deal over your letter and in the interval I feel clearer in my mind as to the future course of events and my own part, such as it is, in them. I can quite see after your father's speech, and in view of the existing circumstances, that there is no possibility of averting the great misfortune of a Socialist Government being formed. It is to what is to happen thereafter that I am directing my thoughts. . . .

It seems to me well worthy of consideration whether the Liberal Party should not be led directly into the Lobby against the Socialist Government;[2] it would thus be terminated in a single day, before it could do any mischief or undermine the commercial and business activities of the country. Even if Lloyd George and the more Socialistly-minded wing went into the Lobby with the Socialists, the only result would be a Liberal Administration, with a very great measure of freedom of action and the tacit support of the Conservative Party.

I believe this is the only chance of such a happy result. I am sure that if the Liberals keep the Socialists in office by their votes and regular attendance through the Session, a minority – maybe a small minority – of them will certainly co-operate with the Conservatives. I believe, further, that the Conservative Party will gradually gain in strength by the reaction caused in the country at the apparition of this Socialist monstrosity, and when eventually the Socialists are turned out the Conservatives will be as anxious to go to the country as Ramsay MacDonald.[3] They will be quite sure they can win sixty or seventy seats, and all chance of procuring their

---

[1] Contemplating the fact of being the third party in a two-party system, Liberal minds turned increasingly to electoral reform, and especially proportional representation ('P.R.').

[2] Churchill proposes that after voting the Conservatives out of office, the Liberals should at the first opportunity vote Labour out too, leaving a Liberal government as the only untried alternative. A Liberal administration would then govern, with Conservative support. Neither Asquith nor his daughter thought this either viable or sensible, and it shows the depth of Churchill's opposition to Labour.

[3] Churchill was right, in that both parties gained at Liberal expense at the next election, when the party's vote fell by 12 per cent, while the Conservative increased by 10.2 per cent and Labour by 2.5 per cent.

acquiescence in a Liberal Government will have passed away.....

Perhaps you will let me know, dear Violet, what you think of this: certainly show it to your father if you think it would not bore him. I should like him to know how my mind is moving, because I think that is always the right relation, and I do not believe in surprises amongst friends.... Yours sincerely, Winston S. C.

V.B.C. to Winston Churchill

Friday 18 January
Dorset House, Portman Square, W.

My dear Winston. I was on the point of answering your letter when I read your Manifesto in the paper – & now I feel there is no more to be said.[1] I am very sorry you should have published it because it is a public definition of your difference of opinion with the rest of the Party – & I rather hoped that that difference might have been bridged & reconciled by events before it was known to the world at large. But of course I recognize & respect the strength & the sincerity of your conviction – though I cannot share it.

To turn the Labour Party out a week after putting them in appears to me as a purely frivolous 'wrecking' action. We can – & already have – quite clearly defined our view of Capital Levy & Socialism – & they know that if they attempt either they will be turned out. It may be unwise for <u>them</u> to carry on on these lines, with their teeth drawn, but that is not our business.

Father's speech on Thursday was masterly – as fine a thing as I have ever heard him do. Wise – generous – courageous – & extremely dexterous & witty. The Labour men were genuinely & deeply moved. One of the Clydeside tigers said to Simon 'Well – we've got no man in our party as big as that'. Snowden was lyrical.[2] Ramsay I thought looked a little seasick when Father said, turning to him – 'Nothing but an <u>iron</u> sense of public duty could possibly have induced my Right Hon. Friend to take office under <u>such conditions as these</u>'.

... I think the Labour Govt. will suffer from the timidity & inefficiency of its members not from their violence.

I am infinitely sorry to think that you are not with us over this. Ever yrs, Violet

---

[1] The 'manifesto' to which Violet refers is probably Churchill's letter in that day's *Times*, which made his position public. It was a step on the road by which Churchill returned to the Conservative Party, which he had left over free trade in 1903.

[2] Philip Snowden (1864–1937), cr. Viscount, 1931; Labour MP for Colne Valley, 1922–31; chancellor of the exchequer, 1924, 1929–31; 'The Marxian aberration never obsessed his keen intelligence' (Winston Churchill, *Great Contemporaries*, 228).

SEVEN

Liberal Decline
Anti-Appeasement

October 1924–August 1939

Liberal decline : the 1924 general election

The Labour government that took office in January 1924 owed its brief existence to Liberal support, an uneasy arrangement which dissatisfied both parties by the autumn. Labour members felt frustrated at a veto on socialist legislation, while Liberals resented being lobby fodder for the government. When parliament reconvened after the summer recess, the Liberals were prepared to attack. The immediate cause of the government's downfall was the 'Campbell Case'. In August J. R. Campbell, communist editor of the Workers' Weekly, was charged with incitement to mutiny. The proceedings were subsequently dropped, apparently after ministerial intervention, and there were allegations of political interference with the law. The matter was made the subject of a parliamentary debate, which Ramsay MacDonald insisted on treating as a vote of confidence. When it was lost he called an election, with polling day on 29 October. Labour's links with communism, which had been an issue during the life of the government, overshadowed the campaign and polarized the debate. At Paisley Violet imagined the country 'rent by the clash of two class parties . . . crushed between the extremes of Reaction & Revolution'. Only Liberalism offered the common-sense middle way to salvation. This approach made virtue of necessity: the 1924 election confirmed the predominance of Labour and the Conservatives, who shared 82 per cent of the vote. Labour gained 151 seats, but the poll was a crushing landslide for the Conservatives, who secured 419. Liberal representation fell to just 40. In this context Asquith's defeat at Paisley was unsurprising. The previous two polls had suggested that he could be beaten, and at the age of seventy-two he faced his fourth election in less than five years, with a stiffer challenge from a new Labour opponent, Rosslyn Mitchell. Asquith campaigned vigorously, but found it difficult to adjust to the polarized nature of the debate. In more ways than one his defeat marked the passing of an era.

Margot Asquith to V.B.C.   *Saturday 4 October 1924*
                                        The Wharf, Sutton Courtenay,
                                                    Berkshire

My darling – How I wish you had been in H. of C. Tuesday (it was <u>much</u> better than Wed) father made an excellent speech listened to with the closest admiration & attention. . . .[1] Anything may happen. Ramsay might resign & the King send for Baldwin or father – or there might be a Gen. Election <u>at once</u>. I think <u>not</u> but it is all v. difficult. You shᵈ stand darling & win a seat for father. It will be our last Gen. Election & the greatest moment in our lives. Yʳ chils are at an age that cᵈ be left. You are in better health than I've <u>ever</u> seen you & it wᵈ be a wonderful joy to you to have served yʳ father – besides wʰ you'll knock all the female M.P.s & most of the male – as Raymond wᵈ have done – into puddings. A great chance in wʰ you'll distinguish yʳself beyond <u>all</u> words while you are still <u>young</u>. Adoring children as I do I wᵈ do it in yʳ place – but then we Tennants are adventurers & ambitions our only merits. . . . Love M

V.B.C. to M.B.C.   *Tuesday 7 October*
                                        Rossdhu, Luss, Dumbartonshire

Darling . . . Margot writes me a long letter urging me to stand as 'the children can easily be left at this age' (!!) & I have 'never been in better health in my life'.

Unfortunately I lack 'the ambitiousness & adventurousness of Tennants'. M. has no idea that anything more than 'adventure' is needed for standing. To her it is just a few pirouettes on a platform. She has no conception of what any sort of <u>work</u> means – let alone the aeons of drudgery involved in being in Parlt. Love . . . Yr V.

Diary – October – written in November, at 24 Hyde Park Gardens, W.2

A long tract of events to write up. Our <u>delicious</u> holiday in Scotland at Innes – Beaufort – Dalnawillan etc. left me feeling curiously tired &

---

[1] Asquith spoke on the second reading of the Irish Boundary bill, an occasion that showed him at his best: he commanded detailed knowledge of the subject, displayed statesmanlike gravity, and captured the mood of the House by supporting the bill, and at the same time suggesting that the matter had 'much better be settled in Ireland and by Irishmen' (*The Times*, 1 October 1924).

seedy – & it was all I could do to get through my two big meetings at Stirling on 10th [October] (Scottish Lib. Federation). I felt something like despair when the dissolution was announced that night – the Govt. having resigned rather than face an inquiry into the Campbell case.[1] I came south – arrived dog-tired & went on to Littlehampton next day after meeting my Executive & promising to write a Manifesto for the W.N.L.F. I felt at once the worst forebodings as to the result of the Election though I don't think I foresaw anything quite as bad as the actual result.

I had a divinely reviving Sunday with the children.... I left them on Monday morning to plunge into the fray for which I felt terribly ill-equipped physically.... Then followed a fortnight, which I look back on with something like horror, of tremendous effort against heavy physical odds. My heart was like an engine that refused to feed the rest of my machine. I felt stone-cold, breathless, & as though my head were cut off from the rest of me. All the time I realized the need not merely of keeping my end up on platforms with howling Bolshie audiences – but also of shooting a great jet of 'ectoplasm' at everyone I met. For this I felt completely unfit. Fortunately we were spared one horror – that of any sort of anxiety as to the result.

On paper our chances had never been better. Our Tory opponent McKean had withdrawn & was running in West Renfrewshire – therefore we had for the first time in our history a chance of Conservative support – & for the first time we managed to prevent ourselves from insulting them. Our machine – always a good one – was functioning for the 4th time in 5 years & had therefore attained an almost Prussian perfection. McNair reported that on a canvas of 2/3rds of the Electorate (27,000), giving every doubtful vote to Labour, we had a majority of between 3 & 4 thousand. I was comforted by this certainty & felt that it didn't matter <u>so</u> vitally whether I did well or badly. We had our usual routine of big Clark Town Hall meetings & small Schoolroom ones. As usual our excellent women's afternoon meeting in the Central Halls.

We had more rowdiness than ever before. On one occasion in the Clark Town [Hall] Father was for a long time refused a hearing – a thing which has never happened before. However our last 2 Eve of the Poll meetings with Buckmaster went off magnificently (he never spoke better) & on Wed. Father & I spent an arctic day touring the Polling booths in icy rain – our devoted workers standing on the pavements from morning to night with touching enthusiasm & endurance. We met & spoke to Rosslyn

---

[1] Violet refers to Ramsay MacDonald's decision to treat a conciliatory Liberal amendment to a Conservative motion of censure on the 'Campbell Case' as a vote of confidence. The Labour government thus determined the timing of its own demise – the debate, on 8 October, was certain to result in a government defeat.

Mitchell – our very 'preux' opponent – an ex-Liberal Glasgow solicitor – a dapper little fop with white spats & elaborate ties & a marcel wave in his hair – but (I believe) real eloquence of a kind, & a good deal of cleverness behind his tactical sob-stuff....[1] The evening we spent as usual at the Eadies' – listening to very depressing results coming in – all Manchester gone Tory – in fact the beginning of a stupendous Tory landslide. I wished I had not heard them [and] thinking 'it will be so difficult to be in as good spirits as we <u>must</u> be at the Liberal Club to-night'.

About midnight we went down to the Town Hall & sat in our little room downstairs. Father was as usual upstairs watching the counting. Our kind official murmured 'neck & neck' to us & disappeared, we hoped to bring us more news – but he never reappeared again.... At last after endless waiting with Pressmen at the bottom of the stairs I heard the doors being unlocked & flung open – there was the usual wild scamper up. I looked in vain for some of our dear friends to meet us half way, grinding our knuckles to bits. No one came. Even the official in gold buttons outside the door wldn't answer when I said 'what's the result?' – then I saw John Gladstone's white face – & the icy fear at my heart was confirmed. We were beaten.[2]

Father was standing at the table facing the Sheriff. I moved quickly to his side & took his arm – on my other side I felt Basil gripping mine in a vice of pain & sympathy. Father was absolutely controlled. He just said to me 'I'm out by 2,000' – then seconded a vote of thanks to the Returning Officer. Rosslyn Mitchell, with whom I shook hands congratulating him, was in tears & in his motion of thanks said 'the result gives me no personal satisfaction whatever'. He said to me – 'I'm so sorry – so terribly sorry this has happened.' He is obviously a man of facile emotions but for the moment I think was genuine. (He was also obviously amazed & disconcerted at getting in! – which may not suit him with Labour out – no chance of office & a prosperous Glasgow practice to desert.) The awful ordeal of the Liberal Club was before us. I shall <u>never</u> forget it. We found it – as ever – packed with our supporters ready to shout themselves hoarse with joy – having sat there waiting for hours on tip-toe – confidently expecting a great victory – dear old Grannie Walker in the first row as always – all sobbing – in floods of tears.

Father spoke to them with perfect fortitude & serenity. He has the courage of <u>real</u> philosophy & greatness – no teeth-set, tight-lipped Stoicism – something much bigger & more natural – a sort of power of seeing events immediately in scale & eliminating his own personal position completely from his perspective. I have never marvelled at him more.

---

[1] Edward Rosslyn Mitchell (1879–1965), solicitor and senior partner in family firm; former Liberal; contested Glasgow Central, 1922, 1923; Labour MP for Paisley, 1924–9.

[2] Mitchell's majority was 2,228.

McKenna spoke & the Provost. Margot said a few words with great dash & courage & I finally pulled myself together & spoke too – but I was <u>really</u> afraid of not being able to command my voice – particularly when they all sang – 'Will you no' come back again' etc. It was for <u>them</u> one minded so terribly – our splendid <u>devoted</u> friends. . . .

We left after very few hours in bed next morning – had a difficult send off at Glasgow with our old friends Dees, Mrs McDougall, Miss Jacobsen, etc. – I felt very near breaking down altogether. As the returns came in at every station & we realized that there wld be only about 40 Liberals in the next house – & all those Coalie – (every friend beaten Pringle, Phillipps, Geoffrey, Donald, etc.). I think Father at least felt a shade comforted at not being in. . . . We had a reception of dear old friends at Euston W.1 – Crawfurd, Heffer etc. etc. The children & B. were there too – I felt quite exhausted & was ordered to bed next day by Parky for 4 weeks. I have never been <u>really</u> glad to go to bed before.

Margot Asquith to V.B.C.   *Friday 31 October*
44 Bedford Square, W.C.1

My darling – all my courage has <u>gone</u>. You are young. You have got divine children (a baby <u>what a joy</u>!)[1] a new house to furnish & 1000 nursery interests & a husband happy equable sedate with a future & <u>no</u> nerves. For me all is over. Puff quite happy & busy without me. Elizabeth going back to America – father going to Egypt & Priscilla forbidden to love any one (alone in vile lodgings near a wind-swept sea). I am not young & I know & feel it in my bones that all my life is over. You are all well, young, happy & settled & can do perfectly without me. . . . But you & I have gone thro' a <u>great</u> experience together & when father has returned slowly but surely (with periodical visits from his grand children) we two will <u>remember</u> this & care for one another. . . .

Thank God I told the Press yesterday morning at Glasgow that he was well & w^d take the 1st opportunity of standing again. Phillipps told me this was read to thousands in their farewells to their weeping followers & <u>all</u> cheered to the echo, but it is bluff & he will never stand again – y^r true & loving Margot. . . .

Asquith's resignation as Liberal leader, 1924–6

In the week following Asquith's defeat at Paisley the king wrote to offer him a peerage, so as to extend an eminent parliamentary

---

[1] Mark Bonham Carter, Violet and Bongie's third child, had been born in February 1922.

career without 'further political contests, with all their attendant turmoil and unpleasantness'. Asquith's age was now a factor and he was in noticeable physical decline. He contemplated the king's offer during a six-week tour of the Middle East, and on 20 January wrote to accept. It was difficult to take leave of the Commons after almost four decades, and politically it was damaging, as Lloyd George now became party leader there. His influence grew as a result and during 1925 the tension rose between them. When confronted with opposition to his land policy, Lloyd George broke party ranks and advanced this as an independent initiative. At the same time he declined to divert his personal political fund to rescuing Liberal finances, which were in dire straits. From the upper echelons of the party there was strong pressure on Asquith to make a stand. The opportunity arose during the General Strike of 1926. When Lloyd George absented himself from a 'shadow' cabinet meeting on 10 May, on the basis that he could not concur in its unqualified condemnation of the strikers, Asquith was encouraged by his colleagues to write a strong letter of censure. Lloyd George treated this as an expulsion, and in the trial of strength that followed he gained the upper hand, his more conciliatory line on the strike finding support with party members. Asquith was outmanoeuvred, depicted as the originator of the dispute, when what the party mostly wanted was an end to the feuding. The annual conference in mid-June offered Asquith a vital chance to regain control of the situation, but he was incapacitated by a stroke the week before it started. The conference subsequently urged coexistence upon its leaders, which in Asquith's terms meant the end. He resigned the party leadership in October. Lloyd George had triumphed, and the Liberal party was now effectively his.[1]

V.B.C. to M.B.C.   *Tuesday 11 November*
                                  24 Hyde Park Gardens, W.2

Darling ... Father went off this morning after addressing his two gatherings of defeated & victorious candidates. He came to see me for about an hour between tea & dinner & said the victorious were a very hard faced lot & he felt less than ever inclined to join them. I have a curious feeling that his <u>inclination</u> is to take a Peerage – & that it is sheerly his sense of duty to the Party that makes him hesitate. The next 5 years present an

---

[1] J. A. Spender and Cyril Asquith, *Life of Lord Oxford*, ii, 351; R. B. McCallum, *Asquith*, 140–1; A. J. P. Taylor (ed.), *Frances Stevenson*, 246.

inexpressibly <u>dreary</u> prospect. No speech can turn a single vote in the H. of C. & Baldwin's Dictatorship will be as complete as Mussolini's. (In the H. of Lords I daresay he [HHA] might leave more dint.)

It is strange that for the first time since I can remember I feel no temptation whatever to read the papers. . . .

. . . Love to you Darling. I miss you & long for yr return, Yr V.

V.B.C. to Gilbert Murray   *Monday 26 January 1925*
                                 The Wharf, Sutton Courtenay,
                                                   Berkshire

Dear Professor Murray –

Thank you for your wonderful letters to us both. I have sent Father's straight on to him – (he went up to London this morning & I follow to-night). I think you & I feel just the same about this.[1] To me all the leaders in the Press to-day are like the tolling of a bell. It is the end of a glorious chapter – inevitable, as things are, but to me infinitely sad. The name is a good one – but I cannot for the life of me feel romance or dignity about a Peerage – whether created or revived.[2] If it has gone on for centuries 'meandering with a mazy motion' there <u>may</u> be a little glamour perhaps, born of sheer unbroken continuity. But Father was & is a Commoner to the <u>bone</u> – we all are – & I can't help feeling this to be a break with <u>our</u> tradition & his. I can't help feeling behind it all a streak of tawdriness & absurdity – & above all incongruity.

This <u>of course</u> only between you & me. It had to be because it was the only way in which he could go on serving the Party. It is the last – & possibly the greatest – sacrifice he has made for it. He will love your letter. Thank you for writing & for understanding –

                                  Ever yrs, Violet B. C.

---

[1] Violet refers to her father's acceptance of a peerage.

[2] At Asquith's request the king revived the earldom of Oxford, a title given by Queen Anne to her prime minister, Robert Harley. The choice was thought by some to be too grand, and the future Lady Salisbury wrote to him bluntly: 'It is like a suburban villa calling itself Versailles.' Asquith was undeterred and even amused by such remarks, but ultimately he was obliged to add 'and Asquith' to distinguish his earldom from the earlier creation (Roy Jenkins, *Asquith*, 506–8).

Gilbert Murray to V.B.C.   *Monday 7 June 1926*
                                        Yatscombe, Boar's Hill, Oxford

My dear Violet,

The last time I saw you at the Wharf the spirit descended on me to bless you for the way you had stood by your father and Liberalism, but he rather inconsiderately re-ascended before I got it said. So I say it now, and add that I think we are in for a bad beating. LG has for him not only his own supporters plus the radical sympathizers with the Strike, but all the common mass of Liberals who don't want any Liberal leader driven out. If LG attacked your father he would be utterly trodden underfoot; but he only asks to live and let live.

I think, too, if one is to face disagreeable facts, that LG will probably do very well as autocrat, with no rivals and plenty of funds.[1] Doubtless he will play for holding the balance, much as Snowden suggests....

I just write to mingle my tears with yours, but of course I do not think of any compromise, much less desire it. Ever your affectionate, G.M.

V.B.C. to Gilbert Murray   *Wednesday 9 June*
                                        3 Little Stanhope Street,
                                        Mayfair, W.1

Very dear Professor Murray ... I agree with a great deal of your letter to me – tho' I think I am not quite as despondent yet (I may end by being more so!). Our strategic position is bad – granted. If Father had acted with any strategic motive – & not simply on a respectable emotional impulse – he must have to some extent foreseen this.[2] We have against us as you say – Ll.G.'s hirelings, the muddled people who think that he alone stood for conciliation & peace in the Strike – & (what I fear most) the vast anti-split crowd – scattered all over the country – many of them Father's

---

[1] During his premiership 1916–22 Lloyd George amassed £6 million from the sale of honours, divided equally between his Conservative allies and his own Lloyd George Fund, which existed 'to promote any political purpose' of which he approved. While all governments of the day raised political funds by selling honours, Lloyd George's personal control over this wealth, and some of his nominations, aroused indignation (A.J.P. Taylor, *1914–1945*, 188). The fund inevitably became a centre of controversy between his followers and those of Asquith: National Liberals had money but lacked a party machine, while Asquithians had the machine, but lacked the money.

[2] Violet refers to her father's decision to make public his correspondence with Lloyd George over their differences arising from the General Strike. By 9 June it was apparent that this tactic had backfired on Asquith (Stephen Koss, *Asquith*, 281).

supporters – but naturally dreading fresh local rows, the withdrawal of subscribers etc.

On the other hand Ll.G.'s position is not really too happy either. He has not a single 'colleague' to his name – only salaried supporters in his immediate entourage.... I believe (as I said to you at lunch at Bedford Square) that even those who support him & are critical of Father wld. be rather afraid of being left <u>alone</u> with him as leader. They want an umbrella – & a chaperon.

It is of course a nightmare to think of him 'leading the Party' – that is to say reducing it to the status of a mere subsidized personal appendage. I don't think I quite agree that he wld do very well as an autocrat 'with funds & no rivals'. He <u>needs</u> cover & context of some kind – a bass to his treble is becoming to him. With no stick-in-the-muds to blame for putting on the brake it is difficult to appear sufficiently dashing. But it is a dark outlook whatever happens. I am sad for the Party – & all the poor bewildered people who are working for it in the dark in distant places.

What bad luck you & I have had in being born at the same time as Ll.G. He will have muddied the waters for the bulk of our political life – & mixed <u>such</u> poison in our cup....

Forgive this palsied line written in the train – Yrs ever, Violet

H.H.A. to V.B.C.   *Sunday 3 October*
Easton Grey, Malmesbury,
Wiltshire

My dearest Violet.

I have quite made up my mind to go. I met some of the faithful – the usual lot <u>plus</u> Gardiner & Spender – at Edward Grey's on Wednesday.[1] Ll.G's latest move is to offer to pay the election expenses of some 200 (?) candidates in the <u>rural</u> districts: no doubt to boost the land policy.... It is of course another stage in the process of buying the party.

I told them I should prepare & circulate among them without delay a Confidential Mem[dm] of my own: which would be of a 'grave' character: and left it for the moment at that. I will let you have a copy as soon as it is typed: so I won't recapitulate it here. It finishes with a quite unequivocal announcement of resignation.

If I was to remain, I should be forced to do one of two things: either (1) to lead a faction fight against Ll.G., who is equipped with all the sinews of war, or (2) to take part once more, under the most humiliating con-

---

[1] John Alfred Spender (1862–1942), journalist and author; editor of the *Westminster Gazette*, 1896–1922.

ditions, in the hollow farce of 'Reconciliation' and 'Restoring Unity'. Nothing will induce me to do either the one or the other, and I have of course abundant justification for going in age, health, &c.

It will be a great shock to leave excellent people: including C. Hobhouse, who writes an imploring letter, pleading for 'co-operation' without 'reconciliation' (!), which of course is pure moonshine. . . .[1]

The exact mode & time of publication requires consideration: it must be <u>soon</u>, & ought to make it unnecessary for me to go to Greenock.[2] You might think these things over & let me know your ideas. I have told no one so far but Margot, who heartily approves, but I shall tell Phillipps in advance. Ever your loving Father.

V.B.C. to M.B.C.   *Tuesday 5 October*
Lindisfarne Castle, Northumberland

Darling – I feel terribly sad & have been crying most of the morning as I have just had a letter from Father saying that he has made up his mind to go. As you know I think he is probably right but this does not lessen one's sadness that the end should come in such a way. He has told <u>no one</u> else yet (except I believe Margot) so do not breathe it. . . .

. . . I think he is right really – even apart from health reasons – but I am sure you will feel as I do that it is a tragic end – & one [that] one wld. have done anything in one's power to avoid for him. I think also that although he has many other resources – much more than most people – the Party did bulk <u>very big</u> in his life. He wasn't – as you or I wld have been – bored by addressing meetings up & down the country – & really enjoyed the devotion of the rank & file. I think he will miss it all terribly – & miss being able to poke an oar into national policy at crucial moments – tho' this I suppose he can still do. I wonder if E. Grey will take on or not? Write me all you think about it. The bitter thing is – as Father says – that the Party is being slowly <u>bought</u>. . . . Love . . . Yr V.

---

[1] Sir Charles Edward Henry Hobhouse (1862–1941), 4th Bt, 1916; postmaster-general, 1914–15.

[2] Asquith's memorandum, incorporating his resignation, was circulated early in October: 'The disintegration of the Liberal Party began with the Coupon Election of December 1918. It then received a blow from which it has never since recovered. . . .' The resignation was made public on 15 October. That night he appeared for the last time on a Liberal platform, at Greenock, with his family and closest political associates. Though the letter of 3 October suggests that Asquith wanted to avoid Greenock, it was an apt farewell which he found deeply moving (Roy Jenkins, *Asquith*, 516–17).

M.B.C. to V.B.C. *Wednesday 6 October*
64 Cornhill, E.C.3

Beloved. You are naturally feeling sad at your Father's resignation but the cause for sadness has really been there ever since L.G.'s return and this is but the inevitable end of a bitter history. He naturally must feel the sadness of the close and I quite agree that he will miss the actual business & occupation which leadership has meant. I cannot but feel relief nevertheless that the end has come to the present hopeless position.

It would have come months ago had he thought of his own interests, but now it comes with the full approval of all his colleagues whom he wished to protect. As far as his position in the country is concerned I think it probable that freedom from the party will enhance his influence & possibly his opportunity for service, and he may well find recompense in this. More and more as I write this letter I am thankful he is quit of all the dirty & degrading business which dealing with L.G. involves.... Love. B.

V.B.C. to Gilbert Murray *Wednesday 10 November*
24 Hyde Park Gardens, W.2

Private – for you alone

My Dear Professor Murray. It was nice of you to write – I thought of you more than almost anyone at the time & longed for you to be here & not away. The decision was a difficult one to make but it was – I think – right & inevitable. All through August & Sept. I wondered – without of course asking – what was crystallizing in his mind – but curiously enough I don't think looking back that he was then contemplating going.... I can't help feeling that it was the state of things in regard to <u>finance</u> revealed at this meeting which decided him (though he has never said so)....[1]

... The poor Party seems faced with two alternatives – to starve or be bought. I believe that <u>without</u> Ll.G. & his corrupting fund in the background, it could have saved itself by its own efforts & lived as the Labour Party does – more cheaply – but on democratic finance – but with doles & bribes, fantastic salaries & champagne lunches flung in all directions it cannot possibly do so.

<u>If</u> Grey were younger & had his eye-sight, if Simon were even $\frac{3}{4}$ of a man & had an ounce of courage & a few stray ounces of blood & a heart

---

[1] At the end of September Asquith met with colleagues at the house of Sir Edward Grey to discuss *inter alia* party finances. The failure of efforts to raise funds that would bring financial independence from Lloyd George created pressure for a reconciliation with him, which Asquith would not contemplate.

that beat. But these are all fairy-tale dreams. I feel – as you say – that you & I & others like us are disfranchised – perhaps for our lives.

It is <u>so</u> different from the feeling one had in 1918. Small numbers & poverty didn't matter then. The Party was <u>clean</u> – we had no Jonah on board. But to serve a Party that <u>half</u>-believes in Lloyd George – & is itself indifferent to not <u>wholly</u> believing in him (that is the sinister part – they are for the most part not even <u>honest</u> dupes – they are dupes of convenience) seems to me wholly impossible. I know I couldn't speak on a Liberal platform now if I tried except to say what I have written to you....[1] Ever yrs, Violet

'His unspoken mind': Violet and her father's death, 15 February 1928

Asquith lived for just sixteen months after he had relinquished the leadership of the Liberal Party in October 1926. The repose of his last days was overshadowed by money concerns. After Margot gave publicity to this, in the spring of 1927, a fund was organized by their friends which brought some relief. Violet, however, was deeply distressed by her stepmother's intervention. Her feelings were undoubtedly sharpened by worries about her father's health, which deteriorated rapidly. In the new year of 1927 Asquith suffered a stroke, and for periods that spring and summer he was incapacitated. By the end of the year he was unable to move without difficulty and in his last weeks, when Violet was constantly at his side, he swung between periods of lucidity and of confusion. He died at the Wharf on the evening of 15 February 1928. Cyril Asquith afterwards wrote to his sister expressing thankfulness that after their father's death she remained, 'like Brunhilde to Wotan, his unspoken mind'. It was a perceptive remark, and within months Violet was living up to it, defending her father in a brief controversy with Churchill over the content of a posthumously published collection of Asquith's letters. The affair ended amicably enough, but it gave a telling indication of the force of Violet's feelings. At the time Churchill was preparing the text of his obituary notice of Asquith, in which he described Violet as a 'champion redoubtable'. They were qualities to which he could personally testify.[2]

---

[1] Violet had written to Bongie on 6 October 1926: 'Poor party – is it really going to become a paid & kept appendage of Ll.G.? It is <u>tragic</u>. All decent Liberals will go out of public life....'
[2] Stephen Koss, *Asquith*, 282–3; Cyril Asquith to VA, 23 February 1928.

V.B.C. to M.B.C. *Tuesday 26 July 1927*
Stockton House, Codford St Mary,
Wiltshire

Darling – Enclosed <u>appalled</u> me.[1] What <u>does</u> it mean? that Margot's begging has borne fruit? How has it got into the Press? I really think if anything of the kind is on foot you & Oc shld. get in touch with its promoters & see that it is in some sort of way secured on Father & subject to <u>conditions</u> if possible. It is monstrous that other people shld. be made to foot Margot's bridge-bills (40£ last Sunday) in <u>his</u> name. I mean that he should be made the decoy-duck to induce generous people to defray the cost of her completely irresponsible extravagances. Is Rufus the instigator do you suppose? I know Margot went to him.

I am horrified by the publicity only because <u>everyone</u> knows how <u>she</u> lives & will think it scandalous that she should be further subsidized in his name to do so. <u>How</u> she has dragged his name through the mud! I can't bear to think of it.... <u>Love</u> Yr V.

V.B.C. to Gilbert Murray *Wednesday 4 January 1928*
The Wharf, Sutton Courtenay,
Berkshire

<u>Private</u>

Thank you for your letter – I know you realized a little of the terrible sadness of the days & hours we are living through when you came over last – & things have been much worse since then. To watch Father's glorious mind breaking up & sinking – like a great ship – is a pain beyond all my imagining. I did not know life could be as cruel as this. At times he is terribly sad – aware that he is as he says 'sick in mind & body'. If only that <u>knowledge</u> could be spared him I could bear anything – for it would be the inmost circle of the Inferno to him to realize any loss of mental power. Sometimes again he is a prey to strange & terrible delusions – as that either he or those around him must be mad – & to believe <u>either,</u> as he said to Bongie, is Purgatory. There are moments again when he is his old self – but these <u>alas!</u> seem to me to become rarer & more fleeting. Last night he talked to me about the Parnell Commission & the whole Irish

---

[1] Enclosed was a cutting from the previous day's *Daily News*, 'Lord Oxford – Provision for his future – Old friends' gift': 'A number of Lord Oxford's friends have arranged among themselves to present him with a gift in the form of financial provision for his future. Lord Oxford is not, and never has been, a wealthy man.' A similar notice appeared in *The Times* of 30 July.

situation at that time with <u>all</u> his old vigour & power & brilliancy.[1] I wld. like to have written down every word he said – but then he seems to vanish again into a strange hinterland of dreams – to toss for hours on seas of unquiet thought & find no anchorage. If I could choose the moment I wld. <u>beg</u> you to come & see him – but I cldn't bear you to come at a time which wld. make <u>you</u> deeply unhappy & not really bring happiness to him.

I wld. love to see you myself. If I cld. get away to-morrow I will telephone & suggest coming up for $\frac{1}{2}$ an hour sometime if I may. This letter is for you <u>alone</u> – & I do trust you not to tell anyone now or afterwards about this time. I wld. like their memory of him to be untroubled by this bewildering sadness. You love him enough to know.

Ever yrs, Violet

Margot Asquith to V.B.C.   *Wednesday 8 February*
The Wharf, Sutton Courtenay,
Berkshire

My dear darling ... I feel somehow as if I was not equal to what has happened – not good, or <u>great</u> enough. I have an old fashioned feeling that there is some purpose in all this – that life is <u>not</u> a hazard, a throw of dice that anything may turn up: it is firm & deeper than this. Father has played his part nobly for 75 years – it is for me to play mine.

I don't think I am playing mine well. I've been morbidly <u>afraid</u> of the Press, & of sympathy but not so much for myself – tho' this sounds sly – but I've long felt that his great brain <u>might</u> go & it would be a humiliation for <u>anyone</u> to know this. That he is ill past recovery was enough – but the other is past all bearing. I see it coming slowly but surely & I am determined <u>no</u> one shall see him again (except all of us).... I know father does not belong to me. It didn't hurt me when you said it. I can stand the truth but don't forget you are young & have everything. I am not young & I am ill: not physically, but ill in soul & mind. My heart has a prop – my prop has gone. I s^d be on my knees with gratitude that I have had it so long: but I'm not....

... We are crying the same tears, praying at a lost shrine – we must be patient with one another darling   y^r Margot

[1] Asquith had made his name during the Parnell Commission of 1888–9, in which he had contributed to the defence of the Irish nationalist leader with a devastating cross-examination of a key witness.

Gilbert Murray to V.B.C. *Friday 17 February*
League of Nations Union,
London S.W.1.

My dear Violet,

The Executive tell me to write to you to express their sympathy, & it is true that your father's death is the greatest loss that the cause of the League has ever had. One of the innumerable hardships of the last ten years has been that, just as the man who could have made the peace was not allowed to touch the peace treaty, so the man who could have directed & built up the League was never allowed even to see it working, much less to direct British policy with regard to it.[1] To think how immeasurable the difference in Europe would have been if your father had been Prime Minister & Grey Foreign Secretary since the war!

The newspapers make me sick. And I am glad that there is to be no funeral at Westminster Abbey with Lloyd George and Baldwin and Ramsay as pall-bearers. He was so absolutely sincere, as simple & kind as he was great, and the solemn humbug would have jarred on one. My dear, I am so sorry for you. Yours ever, G.M.

V.B.C. to Winston Churchill *Monday 28 May*
28 Sussex Square, W.2

My dear Winston –

On receiving your letter I immediately searched the Daily Telegraph of the 24th for any reference to you & could only find one – in the sentence 'The corpses of the slain include a number of renegades – Winston, Hamar Greenwood, F. Guest, Montagu, Kellaway'.[2] Is this what you object to so strongly? If so I am amazed – as it would never have struck me as particularly 'opprobrious' or 'offensive'. You are not in any way singled out for special criticism, but bracketed with many others, whom in those days certainly you would have regarded as excellent company.

The word 'renegade' I understand as meaning one who has seceded from his old faith – & surely it was no secret to anyone that my Father regarded Coalition Liberals as having seceded from Liberalism as he understood it? He thought the Coalition Govt.'s policy (Black & Tans etc.)

[1] Shortly after the Armistice Asquith had an interview with Lloyd George where he made known his desire to attend the Paris peace talks as a British delegate. Lloyd George then gave no answer, and Asquith played no part in the deliberations that led to the Versailles Treaty.

[2] Violet refers to a sentence written by her father, and which appeared in the serialization of his posthumously published *Memories and Reflections, 1852–1927*.

<u>illiberal</u>. In this view he may have been right or wrong, just or unjust, but it is not necessary to delve into diaries or extracts from private letters to discover that he held it. He expressed it freely & forcibly in all his public speeches at the time.

I am infinitely sorry that anything he has said or written should have hurt you – but I should have thought that in this particular instance his opinion was well-known to everyone....

I must I feel add one personal word – as between you & me. Though we do not meet very often nowadays I have never ceased to count you as one of my closest & truest friends. This year has held the greatest sorrow that can ever come to me. You sent me no word – or sign – of sympathy – & tho' I was a little surprised I was not hurt – because I know what a busy & absorbing life yours is – & I thought it <u>very</u> natural that in its strain & stress you should have forgotten me.

But that your first – & only gesture towards me at such a time – & after such an experience – should be the letter I received on Friday is quite unworthy of your heart. It makes me almost regret that you should now have remembered me. Ever yrs, Violet Bonham Carter

Winston Churchill to V.B.C.   *Friday 1 June*
                                                         Chartwell

<u>Private</u>

My dear Violet,

I was sorry to have written the letter the moment it had gone: & the same reproachful reflection wh you make in yr closing sentences rose in my own mind. I was angered by reading quite unexpectedly an offensive & abusive term applied to me publicly through the dead pen of one for whom I have always had a deep regard, & who had never in his lifetime publicly engaged in such forms of controversy. Moreover I have always repressed my own abiding sense of having been thrown to the wolves about the Dardanelles & left in a defenceless position to bear the whole blame, while the chief whose personal decisions I was carrying out sailed on at the head of a new Administration. It was not I who failed to support yr father. He dismissed me. I have never indulged in any recrimination upon the treatment I received in May 1915, because I understood how gt his difficulties were at that time: but never in his lifetime wd I have allowed an expression such as I now complain of to be applied by him to me without rejoinder. I understood from Margot that you had edited these memoirs, & I yielded to the impulse of the moment.

As it happened I had just been writing a brief tribute of sympathy with all of you & of respect to yr father – wh I hope some day you will read, &

it was in this mood that I received the crude, & as I hold unjustified taunt to wh I have referred.[1] Pray make allowances for this. It is in defence of what I wrote – but not in defence of having written it to you. For that I am truly sorry.

I never for a moment forgot you & I am ashamed that I did not set out my feelings in a form wh will reach yr consciousness. In the circumstances you are quite right in what you say. Yours ever, W

V.B.C. to Winston Churchill   *Monday 11 June*
                                        Stockton House, Codford St Mary,
                                                           Wiltshire

My dear Winston – Thank you for your most sweet & generous letter. It was entirely like you to write it. I saw representatives of Father's publishers in London last week & asked them as a personal favour to myself to leave out the passage you take exception to from the book – & they have agreed to do so....[2]

I don't think Father ever accused you of deserting him. Certainly I never heard him do so. He <u>terribly</u> minded having to yield to the Conservative demands in 1915 – not merely in regard to you & the Admiralty – but still more in agreeing to leave Haldane – his oldest friend – out of the Govt. altogether. Nothing wld. have made him do it – but what he (rightly or wrongly) felt to be a stringent national necessity....

He never receded from his view that the Dardanelles was the one brilliant <u>idea</u> of the war (it was the Fisher-rows – not the Dardanelles policy surely that made the Tories demand a change at the Admiralty?) & I know he always felt that your séjour at the Duchy – had you stayed there would have been a very short one – & that you wld. soon <u>inevitably</u> have been in high office again.

I believe I shall see you at Taplow next month – so I won't write more except to thank you again for writing to me as you did – Ever yours, Violet

V.B.C. to Hilda Currie   *Monday 15 November 1929*
                                        Stockton House, Codford St Mary,
                                                           Wiltshire

My dearest Hilda – It seems so terribly ungracious to refuse anything you

---

[1] Churchill's tribute to Asquith, the basis of a chapter in *Great Contemporaries* (1937), first appeared as an obituary in *Nash's Magazine*, August 1928.

[2] The word 'renegades' was omitted; *Memories and Reflections*, ii, 205.

ask me – most of all this <u>tiny</u> little service – the seconding of a vote of thanks! – but the truth is that I do not want to do any flag-waving or flag-wagging just now (not even run up that sober Jolly Roger Lady Bryce!).

I feel the state of the Party is terribly bewildering – & tragic. I can't see daylight for it anywhere at present – because even if we of the Liberal Council make our 'clean cut' where is the money & where is the <u>spirit</u> to come from that will revive it? with Ll.G. still there – still inextricably entangled in its Fate & 'good' – so far as I can see for another 15 years at least? Of course I welcome the sale – or any step that will help what is left of the Party to stand on its own feet – & I shouldn't the least mind saying this – but if I wag <u>one</u> flag I shall immediately be handed another. I feel the strongest inclination to remain a political trappist until there is something which can really usefully be said. Forgive me & do understand this state of mind. I am sure you <u>do</u> really.

Ever yr loving, Violet

'The years when England slept': Violet Bonham Carter,
anti-appeasement and the 1930s.

There is no diary for the 1930s, nor have many letters survived. This was a period, though, of great activity and importance in Violet's public life. The following account draws heavily on the transcripts of the speeches that she gave in these years, when she was prominent in the anti-appeasement movement led by Winston Churchill.

Introduction

In the latter part of the 1920s Violet became less active in politics, largely through disillusionment with the Liberal Party over its links with Lloyd George. When her fourth child Raymond was born in June 1929 she took the opportunity that this gave to withdraw from party councils. For several years afterwards her horizons shortened to the nursery and the home. The journals and letters of the period are concerned mostly with domestic life. But as her young family grew up she found time again for politics, and she became increasingly absorbed in the issues of foreign policy that dominated the decade. Violet regarded the rise of Nazism as a sign of the breakdown of the post-war world order that her generation had hoped would save its successors from future conflict. Central to this breakdown was the eclipse of the League of Nations as a peace organization regulating the affairs of the international community. She came to believe that a second world war was inevitable unless Britain stood by the League, and against international aggression. Successive British governments, though, did neither, adopting instead the conciliatory diplomacy of 'appeasement'. Violet campaigned vigorously against this, first under her own banner and later as part of a cross-party alliance led by Winston Churchill. The course of events ultimately vindicated the anti-appeasers, but during the 1930s they were in a minority, and Violet later remembered these as 'the years when England slept'. Society had been neither ready nor willing to accept the message that, in defence of freedom and peace, there must be readiness for war.

Appeasement, which evolved as the policy of the British government during the 1930s, aimed at the avoidance of war by negotiation and compromise. In practice it meant averting threatened conflict by placating the aggressor. To its advocates it was a realistic approach to foreign relations that greatly lessened the prospect of conflict between the major powers. To its critics it was a surrender to force, which because it rewarded aggression greatly increased the likelihood of war. It compelled the weak to pay tribute to the strong, but never at Britain's expense. In Violet's phrase, appeasement bought peace at a price that someone else could be made to pay. Proponents and opponents of the policy had in common the experience of the Great War, the legacy of which was a sense of responsibility for the avoidance of future conflict. Where they disagreed was on how best this could be achieved. Violet put her faith in the League of Nations, which aimed at deterring war by providing for 'collective security' among its members. Article XVI of its founding Covenant gave the League power to impose economic, and even military, sanctions on any member guilty of aggressive action. Since the League was a voluntary movement 'collective security' inevitably depended upon the cooperation of the member states. This was a potential weakness in the eyes of the British government, which as a major power was in any case accustomed to pursuing an independent foreign policy. While ministers publicly pledged support for the League, the strength of British commitment to 'collective security' would not be clear until it was actually tested.

In the years following the Great War it was both natural and easy to support the principle of the League. At its conference in January 1925 the Liberal Party adopted a manifesto that included a clause expressing its commitment to 'the ideal of the League of Nations'. Violet, though, proposed that this be amended. She wanted to omit the phrase 'the ideal of': 'She said the League had suffered from people who supported the ideal instead of the fact.

What was wanted was not burned incense but active service.'[1] The resolution was unanimously adopted, but the fact that it had been raised at all indicates Violet's early concern that a noble idea, to which it was all too easy to subscribe, was not translating into reality. In truth the organization had been undermined at its inception. Neither the United States nor the Soviet Union would join, while the defeated powers were not allowed to. Violet regarded the admission of Germany and Austria as 'absolutely essential', since without them it became 'a League of victors ... both morally and practically paralysed'.[2] Their inclusion was necessary to their own rehabilitation, upon which depended the peace of Europe. But the prevailing sentiment in Britain and France in the immediate post-war years was against anything that might strengthen Germany. Violet witnessed first hand the consequences of this punitive approach when she visited the Ruhr during the French occupation in 1923. As she told the delegates of the National Liberal Federation after her return:

> In Germany to-day one feels there is always a revolution in the offing, if not in full swing. A new and unsteady Democracy is struggling on to its feet, and we've got to keep it there: we've got to help it and back it up: we who fought the War not to wring the uttermost farthing from the defeated, but for the liberty of the democracies of the world. French action in the Ruhr is threatening with extinction this new spirit which is struggling for life, and if the German workers are defeated in their fight against militarism it may have far-reaching and disastrous international consequences, for which our children and the children of all the world will have to pay.[3]

The rise of Nazism and the defence of German Jews, 1933–4

A decade after Violet's speech in May 1923, the 'new and unsteady Democracy' of the Weimar Republic was dead, and the fears that she had then expressed were beginning to be realized. In January 1933 Hitler became Reich chancellor, and inaugurated a campaign of political violence that was intended to make permanent his own dictatorship. The principal targets were the communists and Jews,

---

[1] *The Times*, 30 January 1925.

[2] Address to the LNU, Manchester, 3 December 1920; address to the WNLF, 11 May 1926.

[3] Address at the NLF conference, Buxton, 31 May 1923; resolution condemning French occupation of the Ruhr.

and reports of what was happening in Germany soon began to appear in the British press. The *Manchester Guardian* of 27 March carried an account of Nazi stormtroopers assaulting Jews on the streets of Berlin, and the killing of a Jewish lawyer by stormtroopers that weekend was widely reported in British newspapers the following Monday.[1] Violet read this news with horror, and wrote somewhat penitently to Gilbert Murray: 'The German atrocities make me feel quite ill with rage & shame. They also make me feel foolish at having been so steadfast a Pro-German ever since they became under-dogs'.[2]

What had made her a 'steadfast Pro-German' had been a strong sense of fair play. She brought intense moral conviction to politics, and this now led her publicly to oppose Nazism. It is characteristic that in doing so she was also prepared to acknowledge Britain's share of the responsibility for problems that it faced. On 18 May 1933 at the Liberal conference at Scarborough she assessed the consequences of the first three months of Nazi rule:

> In Germany freedom as we conceive it seems to have perished in the last few weeks, in the twinkling of an eye, almost without a struggle, & given place to a nightmare reign of force whose horror we can hardly conceive.... We ask ourselves with horror how this nightmare can have arisen – how it has become possible. The answer is that one fact & one fact alone has made it possible – the extinction of Liberalism, & the extinction of Liberalism in Germany – let us remember that we have some responsibility. Hitlerism, that monstrous portent, was born of an illiberal peace treaty & of the bludgeoning of a Liberal Germany that vainly tried to struggle to its feet in a hostile world. It is a dangerous, a threatening portent.

The danger, she told her audience, came not just from the black and brown shirts of fascism, but also the red of Soviet dictatorship. They all denied people their liberty, and at a time when Liberals were electorally at their lowest ebb, democracy had the most urgent need of their services: 'Our function is not exhausted. We have before us perhaps the greatest task in all our history to perform. The odds against us are great – but so is our spirit.'[3]

Doubtless some thought that her warnings about Nazi brutality

---

[1] Martin Gilbert, *The Holocaust*, 32–5.
[2] VBC to Gilbert Murray, 4 April 1933.
[3] 18 May 1933, Scarborough, Liberal Conference.

were exaggerated, but the continuing reports in the British press for the remainder of 1933 proved otherwise. On 23 August, for example, *The Times* reported that a young woman had been forced to parade through Nuremburg with a placard around her neck declaring that she had offered herself to a Jew. She was described as being 'small, fragile, and in spite of her shaven head and condition, obviously pretty'. Her circuit through the town's hotel lobbies and cabarets was followed by a jeering crowd estimated at 2,000. Violet was enraged at this latest incident, and wrote to Bongie: '[it] really makes me feel the Germans are an uncivilized people. I wld. like to boycott them in every <u>possible</u> way.'[1] In a public speech next month she warned that the Nazi system threatened 'not merely the soul of a people, but the peace of the world'.[2] Even she was surprised, though, by the pace of events. On 14 October there was the 'thunderbolt' of Germany's withdrawal from the League (to which it had finally been admitted in 1926), as well as from the World Disarmament Conference in Geneva. This double blow undermined collective security and disarmament, the two strongest pillars to peace. Violet wrote disconsolately to Bongie: 'It really does look dark for Europe with only 3 Great Powers left in the only peace organization that exists. My only feeling of relief is that Germany shld have shown her mad-dog hand so soon ... instead of waiting for strength to reveal herself.'[3] She did not then imagine that the British government's response to this militarist regime would be a conciliatory one.

As political and religious persecution in Germany increased so did the flow of refugees leaving the country, and by December around 60,000 were being looked after by the League in Geneva. The great majority were Jews, and towards the end of that month an appeal was launched at a women's luncheon at the Savoy Hotel, in aid of the resettlement of Jewish women and children.[4] Perhaps because of her early public condemnation of Nazism, Violet was invited to second the appeal. She began by reviewing recent events in Germany, as they affected the Jewish community:

I want to make clear my profound conviction that this is not

---

[1] VBC to MBC, 25 August 1933.

[2] 16 September 1933, Perth: tribute to Viscount Grey of Fallodon (Sir Edward Grey) on his retirement.

[3] VBC to MBC, 15 October 1933.

[4] *The Times*, 6 December 1933. Around 300 guests attended the luncheon, paying £10 each for a simple meal, and in all more than £8,000 was raised for this cause. Among the guests were Margot Asquith and Clementine Churchill.

a matter which concerns the Jewish community alone. It concerns all who believe in justice and in our common humanity.... I want to say – speaking not for myself alone, but for countless others who, like myself, though outside the Jewish community are deeply stirred by these terrible events – we wish to stand by your side in taking up this challenge.... I can truthfully say that nothing within my political memory has ever moved me more deeply to horror and indignation than recent events in Germany. We in this country have looked on with dazed astonishment at this nightmare. We have seen libraries burnt. We have seen monuments erected to murderers. We have seen faith and race persecuted and proscribed, thought and art forbidden unless confined in the strait-jacket of State control. We have seen Germany banish and despoil many of her greatest and most distinguished sons, men whose high achievements in every field of endeavour have brought her honour throughout the world. And these are perhaps the happiest. For countless nameless ones are suffering imprisonment and worse to-day, are suffering gross and cruel injustices, simply because they happen to be what we here should call Liberals, or to belong to the Jewish race and persuasion. I suppose if this were Germany most of us would be behind barbed wire. I can only say for myself that I should be ashamed to be anywhere else....

Violet had no doubts that the Jewish faith would survive this trial, as it had survived others in the past, but she despaired for the fate of the young unless they were removed from persecution and replanted 'in a soil in which they can grow to freedom and happiness'. She spoke more as a mother than as a politician in wondering what could be the human consequences of such injustice: 'Children instinctively give back to life what life has given to them. What sort of a world are these children going to build? How can these child-victims of blind racial persecution lay the foundations of that new order of international brotherhood and understanding which, we are told and truly told, is the only hope of the future?'[1]

---

[1] The speech was printed the following year as a pamphlet, 'Child Victims of the New Germany – A Protest'. It included an appendix of details of the 'Cruelties and Humiliations' inflicted on Jewish children, drawn from reports in the German press, and also the *Manchester Guardian*, *Daily Telegraph* and *Jewish Chronicle*.

Italy, Abyssinia and the League, 1935–6

Violet did not doubt that the 'monstrous portent' of 'Hitlerism' was destined one day to be exported beyond the boundaries of the Reich, and she watched anxiously throughout 1934 and 1935 as Germany rearmed, building an air force and introducing conscription. This made British rearmament inevitable, a fact that Violet reluctantly accepted. But after years of advocating international disarmament she could only contemplate increased British defence spending as a contribution to international 'collective security'. Whether this was ever a viable defence option, given the equivocal attitude of British governments to the League, is questionable. The Abyssinian crisis of 1935–6 however put the issue beyond doubt.

Mussolini had long entertained ambitions of colonial expansion in Africa, and during 1935 tension increased along the border between Italian Somaliland and Abyssinia. Violet saw a parallel between the circumstances of Belgium in August 1914 and of Abyssinia two decades later. With an eye on Nazi Germany, she wrote to *The Times* at the end of August:

> I believe that war can be prevented now if every nation still within the League is prepared to carry out its obligations. War is inevitable sooner or later if this cold-blooded experiment in international anarchy is successfully carried through before a watching world. It is an example which some will not be slow to follow, and Europe may be their playground instead of Africa.'[1]

Just as in 1914, Britain's moral duty and ultimately its own self-preservation lay in upholding the rights of a 'small nation'. When the invasion came on 3 October Violet was touring the Continent, and Bongie wrote to her of the reaction in Britain. France had been tepid in its response, and Bongie detected the beginnings of a diplomatic surrender: 'It seems very flat and disappointing but I am sure we cannot act alone. Yet at least one would like us to give with all sincerity and purpose a strong lead and I do not think we shall. In any case the League mills grind slowly and it seems likely that the teeth will be very blunt.'[2] In the short term the British government made strong declarations in favour of the League, and undertook to adopt such sanctions as would be necessary to reverse

---

[1] *The Times*, 29 August 1935.
[2] MBC to VBC, 4 October 1935.

the aggression, stopping short of anything that would lead to war. This, though, was a highly significant qualification, since it was only by contemplating force that the League was likely to win through. Violet grasped the nettle firmly at a League of Nations Union meeting at the Albert Hall at the end of October, which had been called to rally support for sanctions:[1]

> I can conceive no greater, no more appalling danger than the death of the League, the collapse of the whole collective system, and nothing less is at stake to-day. For unless the League can here and now wield the will of the world with irresistible effect, unless it can defeat those who have defied its authority, unless it can protect those who have invoked its help, it cannot survive as a living force. It lives by the trust of the weak, and by the respect of the strong. Therefore, if economic sanctions should fail, which Heaven forbid, if they should fail, we cannot on that account accept the failure of the League. Still less could we accept any peace which would bring it dishonour. We should not, to my mind, rule out in advance any form of sanction, any form of action whatsoever, within the collective will of the Covenant that may be necessary to assure its victory. We can be content with nothing less.

There was an obvious difficulty in raising the prospect of war before an audience that supported the League precisely because it was an instrument of peace. Violet surmounted this by asking what kind of peace was to be contemplated:

> It is true that the League was made to maintain peace. To seek peace, and to ensure it, that has been, that is to-day, its constant, its unswerving aim. But as our Chairman has told us, peace cannot be built on a defiance of law. Peace cannot be founded on a betrayal of right, peace cannot be bought by the abject surrender of justice to brute force. And those who counsel us to-day to be content with gestures and with half-measures are in effect advising us to yield to blackmail. Yes, and to pay its price, not with our own lives, not with our own possessions, but with those of others, for whom as members of the League we stand trustees. Let them make no mistake. Collective security cannot be applied piecemeal.

---

[1] The occasion was only briefly reported in *The Times*, and this account is based on the transcript from which Violet delivered her speech.

One law for the strong, and another for the weak, one law for the white and another for the black, one law for ex-allies and another for ex-enemies. We cannot make licensed brigandage in Africa the price of peace in Europe. We cannot toss backward peoples into the expansionist maw to save our own skins. Abyssinia, her wrongs, her sufferings, and her dead are very far away, but to those who have eyes to see they are our own. In Abyssinia's fate let every nation read its own destiny, and let those who seek to break or blunt the sword of justice now realise, that if they succeed to-day, it may never again be drawn in their defence.

She concluded by urging her audience to prove that although they loved peace, they had the courage to contemplate war. Without the League there was nothing 'but the blind anarchy of force. A world made safe for gangsters'.

There was acceptance in Britain of such a message. In June of that year the League of Nations Union declared the results of its 'Peace Ballot', showing that almost 60 per cent of $11\frac{1}{2}$ million respondents endorsed the principle of military sanctions. With the Abyssinian crisis the hypothetical situation put forward in the Ballot became a reality. The government though was not planning to avail itself of this support, but instead was preparing to abandon collective security. In December Samuel Hoare and Pierre Laval, the British and French foreign ministers, met in Paris and agreed a secret plan to appease Italy. About a half of Abyssinia, including strategically and economically the best land, was to be ceded to Mussolini. When the 'Hoare–Laval plan' was made public in Britain, after being leaked to the French press, there was a storm of indignation. Hoare was forced to resign. This did not, however, signal a change of policy. Economic sanctions were allowed to drift on ineffectively, and in May Italy annexed the whole of Abyssinia. The crisis was over. In June economic sanctions were finally scrapped and Samuel Hoare, the sacrificial lamb, was resurrected as first lord of the admiralty. The League had failed its vital test, having been undermined by the '3 Great Powers' on which Violet had pinned her hopes in October 1933 – Britain and France, the unwilling defenders, and Italy, the aggressor.

Before the crisis had been played out, Hitler posed another test for 'collective security'. On 7 March he sent German troops into the Rhineland, an area of great strategic importance that had been demilitarized under the terms of the Versailles treaty. It is now known that Hitler had executed a major bluff, and that he would have withdrawn had Britain and France offered resistance. They did not, lacking both the will and the military preparedness. The fact that Hitler had accompanied the remilitarization with an offer to negotiate Germany's relations with its neighbours seemed to justify the conciliatory approach adopted. To opponents of appeasement, though, the Rhineland action gave Germany a much stronger military footing in Europe, and was another milestone passed along the route to catastrophe.

The Freedom Focus, 1936–7

One of the lessons of the Abyssinian crisis had been that public support for the League could not effectively be turned into political pressure. This realization stimulated the formation in the spring of 1936 of the Focus in Defence of Freedom and Peace, a loosely organized anti-appeasement coalition under the leadership of Winston Churchill. Churchill had emerged as the predominant figure in the opposition to the government's foreign policy. He saw the Freedom Focus as a way of mobilizing public opinion, and of building a political consensus in favour of the League. Despite its failure over Abyssinia, he still regarded that organization as offering the best prospects for co-ordinating international action against aggression. Churchill particularly sought the participation in the Focus of trade unionists and politicians of the left, and Violet was included at his special request. The nucleus of the group comprised less than two dozen prominent individuals, drawn from a cross-section of politics. Leading figures included Sir Walter Citrine, secretary-general of the TUC; Sir Robert Mond, industrialist; Hugh Dalton, chairman of the Labour Party; Duncan Sandys, Conservative MP; Philip Guedalla, historian and lifelong Liberal; Henry Wickham Steed, ex-editor of *The Times*; and Sir Norman Angell, Nobel Peace Prize laureate.[1]

The early work of the group culminated in a public meeting at the Albert Hall on 3 December 1936, at which Churchill was the main speaker. He addressed the dangers to world 'freedom and peace' represented by Nazism and Bolshevism, in response to which Britain must rearm, gather allies and stand squarely by

---

[1] Sir Walter McLennan Citrine (1887–1983), cr. KBE 1935; Sir Robert Mond (1867–1938), chemist; (Edward) Hugh Dalton (1887–1962), Labour MP for Bishop Auckland and chairman of the Labour Party 1936–7; Duncan Sandys (1908–87), Churchill's son-in-law and Conservative MP for Northwood; Philip Guedalla (1889–1944); Henry Wickham Steed (1871–1956), active supporter of the League of Nations; Sir (Ralph) Norman Angell (1872–1967), cr. Kt 1931, publicist.

the Covenant of the League. Violet was one of three supporting speakers:[1]

> It needed a great cause to bring together on one platform the men you see before you here to-day – Conservatives, the great Trade Unionists, Liberals and last but not least Mr Winston Churchill – that brilliant political phenomenon who eludes all categories and defies classification. One cannot label dynamic forces. What has brought them here together? Not a great cause alone, but what we feel to be a vital emergency. Whatever our differences may be we feel the common need to declare a common faith, to defend that which is the common heritage of us all – the Freedom we have won, and mean to keep, in the teeth of every challenge from within and from without, and Peace which alone makes such freedom possible. Now there are 2 kinds of peace and there are 2 ways of getting them. You can get peace, of a kind and for a time, by a surrender to violence. That is the peace which is sincerely advocated by non-resisters at home, and as sincerely welcomed by Dictators abroad. Or you can get peace by the resolute enforcement of law based on justice. That is the peace for which we stand to-night....
>
> After the war I was one of those who thought, who hoped, who believed that Force had had its day, that Armies and Navies and Air Forces would dwindle away and disappear – discarded like broken toys that men had outgrown. But to-day – look at the world. To-day we see a world which has put back the clock, a world which is reeling backwards away from law, away from freedom, back to the blind anarchy of force. Wherever we look we see nations turning into armies before our eyes.... We have watched the triumph of the aggression of Italy – and the agony of its victim. In that struggle the public opinion of the whole civilized world was solidly ranged against the aggressor. What was the use? Public opinion proved powerless against poison gas. And I think the lessons we have learned from these defeats of law is that it is no good passing judgement unless you are ready to enforce it. It is no good giving a great moral lead if it is to be followed by a rapid physical scuttle. Justice cannot rule this

---

[1] *The Times*, 4 December 1936. Gilbert Murray wrote to VBC, 4 December 1936: 'I found people at the LNU in a state of lyrical enthusiasm over your speech at the Albert Hall. Mill said Winston was dull & only you made the meeting worth while.... Miss Glazebrook & Miss White say it is the best Albert Hall speech they have ever heard.'

world armed with the scales alone – in her other hand she must hold a sword. Unless we, the free democracies of the world, who are still loyal members of the League, are prepared to stand together and to take the same risks for Justice, Peace and Freedom as others are prepared to take for the fruits of aggression – then our cause is lost – and the Gangsters will inherit the earth.

But that day is not yet. We have not come here to-day to bewail the past. We have come to meet the challenge of the future.... Let us prove, as prove we can, that Democracy – that great Army that needs no uniform – is not played out. That those who love peace above all things do not lack the will and the courage to defend it. Let us remember that the great, enduring victories of all time have not been won by mercenaries or slaves – but by free men who cld. draw the sword of the spirit, free men united as one soul in a great cause. The cause is here. For some of us it is the one cause still left worth dying for. For all it is worth living for – and winning for to-day.

At the end of the meeting a woman in the audience shouted 'God Save the King', a reminder that it was the Abdication Crisis, and not the Focus meeting nor even fascism, that was then dominating the news. Against this the Focus could not compete for public attention, and in general it faced difficulties in counteracting what Violet later remembered as the 'perverse optimism or deliberate escapism' of the day.

The Czech crisis, 1938

The decisive factor in changing public opinion came with the Munich conference in September 1938. At the time Munich was seen as the ultimate triumph of appeasement, but quite soon it became synonymous with its bankruptcy. At issue was the fate of more than three million 'Sudeten' Germans living in Czechoslovakia, a state created after the Great War, and which included substantial numbers of Czechs, Slovaks, Germans, Hungarians, Ruthenians and Poles. Hitler wanted to redraw its boundaries, 'reuniting' the German-speaking peoples with the Reich. The government in Prague naturally resisted this claim, and received faltering support from Britain and France. In the second half of September Chamberlain attempted to negotiate an agreement, whereby the issue of sovereignty in the disputed regions would be determined by a plebiscite of the inhabitants. Hitler however demanded immediate occupation of the Sudetenland, to which British opinion apparently would not accede. In London preparations were made for war.

Then on 28 September news came that in response to Mussolini's mediation Hitler had postponed mobilization of the German army, pending the results of an international conference at Munich. Germany, Italy, France and Britain were to be represented. Significantly, Czechoslovakia was not. Chamberlain received the news in the Commons and at once relayed it to the expectant chamber. There were emotional scenes, and Harold Nicolson recalled an instant of absolute silence followed by a 'roar of cheering'. When Chamberlain sat down the whole House 'rose as a man to pay tribute to his achievement'. Nicolson did not record that he was one of a small number who remained seated, instinctively registering their mistrust at what was taking place.[1] Baffy Dugdale, a stalwart supporter of the League, heard the news over the radio and her initial reaction too was of 'incredible, almost stunning, relief'. This quickly turned to doubt, and she became sceptical of the Commons' response. The next day, 29 September, she attended a meeting of the League of Nations Union and talked with several members who had been present in the chamber:

> saw Archie Sinclair, Philip Baker, and other M.P.s, who had not felt enthusiastic themselves, but had met the impact of the enthusiasm. They were like men who had been bruised. Violet Bonham Carter, hard as steel, took Archie Sinclair, her leader, to task in front of us all for having said nothing.[2] He and Philip both assured us that it would have been *physically* impossible, but Violet was implacable. Parliament, on which we had set such hopes, had failed her. She would not even join in a very critical resolution, because it began: 'While sharing the universal relief'. . . .[3]

While the League of Nations Union meeting was taking place Chamberlain arrived in Munich. By chance the Focus group had planned a luncheon meeting, and at the Savoy Hotel feelings ran strongly against the Chamberlain mission. Churchill decided that

[1] Harold Nicolson, *Diaries and Letters 1930–1939*, 370–2; the next day he wrote that he felt 'ashamed' of the conduct of the House, likening it to 'a Welsh Revivalist meeting'.

[2] Sir Archibald 'Archie' Sinclair (1890–1970), Liberal MP for Caithness and Sutherland, 1922–45, and leader of the Liberal Party, 1935–45; see biographical notes.

[3] Mrs Edgar Dugdale, *née* Blanche 'Baffy' Balfour (d. 1948), member of the executive committee of the LNU; the extract is from *Baffy: the diaries of Blanche Dugdale*, 107.

a telegram should be sent to the prime minister to the effect of 'No more concessions at the expense of the Czechs'. It was to be signed by half a dozen prominent figures, including himself, Anthony Eden, Archie Sinclair and Clement Attlee. Violet later recalled the despair when this initiative failed:

> Archie of course consented at once, Anthony (on the telephone) refused,[1] George Lloyd (present) was willing,[2] P. Noel Baker had to telephone to his [Labour] colleagues who characteristically replied that they cldn't get a mandate from their Party until after the next meeting at Blackpool or some other watering place. W. was in tears. I came away with a lump in my throat and met Eddie [Marsh] coming jauntily in on the ball of the foot with bristling eyebrows 'Isn't it glorious?' he piped 'we are not going to be bombed after all.' I replied with fury 'Glorious? Where do you see glory? You think of nothing but your own skin' – the only unkind word I had ever said to Eddie and it made me feel afterwards as if I'd hit a child. There followed a dinner of the Other Club for which W. stayed and at which there were such rows that people said there were grounds for 3 duels – Garvin, Duff and Walter Elliot screamed and were screamed at.[3] Duff was still in the Govt. and defending it. After midnight when the early editions of the papers came in Colin Coote ran out to get them and read out the terms. Duff became suddenly silent – next day he resigned.[4]

Under the Munich terms the Sudetenland was to be ceded to Germany over a ten-day period, and the integrity of the reduced Czech state guaranteed by the four Conference powers. Whatever shame most Britons felt about the inconsistency of British policy – for at Munich Hitler gained what had been denied him a week

[1] Eden apparently feared that his action would be interpreted as a personal vendetta against the prime minister, from whose government he had resigned earlier in the year. Violet, though, doubted the strength of his commitment to the anti-appeasement movement.

[2] George Ambrose Lloyd (1879–1941), cr. Baron, 1925; former Conservative MP and a steadfast critic of Chamberlain's foreign policy; made colonial secretary in Churchill's 1940 Coalition.

[3] James Louis Garvin (d. 1947), editor the *Observer*, 1908–42. Walter Elliot Elliot (1888–1958), Conservative MP for Kelvingrove, Glasgow, 1924–45; minister of health, 1938–40; director of public relations, war office, 1941–2.

[4] Colin (Reith) Coote (1893–1979), ex-Coalition Liberal MP; journalist, and later managing editor of the *Daily Telegraph*. Duff Cooper resigned from his post as first lord of the admiralty. The extract is from Violet's diary for 14 May 1957.

previously – it was lost in relief that war had been averted. Chamberlain was given a tumultuous reception on his return from Munich on 30 September. On the morning of his departure he had approached Hitler with a written statement of 'the desire of our two peoples never to go to war with one another again', which the Führer had willingly signed. Chamberlain therefore brought back to Britain not just 'peace with honour', but 'peace for our time'. He was acclaimed as a national saviour, and appeared with the King and Queen on the balcony of Buckingham Palace before a cheering crowd. In the words of one admirer, he had shown 'superb courage and persistence' in averting a war over a state 'which, in the opinion of one great Judge, "ought never to have been created at all"'.[1]

Violet, who had visited Czechoslovakia in 1935, took a very different view. She saw no prospect of peace, no mark of honour, only a 'final betrayal' in the Munich terms. A young democracy that Britain had helped to create had been abandoned to a brutal dictatorship. Germany gained by threats what it might never have achieved by war. It was, in Churchill's words, 'a total and unmitigated defeat' for British diplomacy. On the morning after the conference Violet was visited at her home by Jan Masaryk, son of the first president of Czechoslovakia, who told her that his government would resign rather than accept the terms. She later recalled, 'I can still see the anguish in Jan's eyes and feel my own burning shame.' But Munich galvanized the resistance to appeasement. In the subsequent Commons debate a distinguished group of thirty Conservatives registered their opposition by abstaining. Though the government won by a large majority, it was 'rattled'.[2] Violet made her contribution to the mounting pressure with a Liberal Party address at the Caxton Hall in London later that month:

> We meet in a very dark hour. The events of the last 3 weeks have shattered what remained of that new world-order which some of us have hoped & worked & striven to build for 20 years. They have done more. They have broken a great & honourable tradition of English foreign policy to which this country has adhered through changing Governments & changing parties for centuries. The keystone of that policy has been the refusal to truckle to the strong at the expense

[1] The view of George Lambert (1866–1958), Liberal National MP for South Molton 1931–45, quoted in *The Times*, 5 October 1938.

[2] Harold Nicolson, *Diaries and Letters 1930–1939*, 376.

of the weak. We have consistently thrown the whole weight of our power behind justice for the weak – against the domination of any single power. This policy to which the smaller states of Europe have owed their freedom & their existence has been renounced to-day. When the Prime Minister signed the Munich Agreement he renounced for us all claims to moral leadership. We ceased to be the trustees of a standard of justice & decency in international relationships. We made our formal submission to the rule of Force – & that rule with the acquiescence & sanction of our Government is the only rule that runs in Europe to-day. All this is hailed as a triumph by its supporters. I do not believe that any Peace worthy of the name can be built upon an act of flagrant injustice backed by Force.'[1]

The culmination of a year of great activity for her was a speech at the Albert Hall on 1 December 1938, at a 'National Demonstration Against Religious and Racial Persecution':

I speak only as an English woman – of no importance – one of the many thousands in this country who to-day are stricken with horror, and who long to hold out a hand to those who are enduring suffering, which is outside our own experience and perhaps beyond the reach of our imagination. In our name I would like to say to the Jewish Community, if any words of ours can reach them: 'We honour your race, whose genius has given so much to the world; we revere your faith from which our own was born; we share your suffering; we salute your courage. But there is one thing that you cannot share with us, our shame – shame that the government of a nation which for centuries has at least called itself a Christian nation, should outrage justice, gentleness and mercy, should violate every canon of our Christian faith.' As Christians, and as English citizens we repudiate this hideous persecution whether of race or creed, this madness to which neither faith, nor age, nor sickness, nor childhood even, is sacred.... Let us prove that this great Christian country is still worthy of its heritage of freedom and of tolerance, that we can still make sacrifices for the faith we stand for.'[2]

---

[1] 20 October 1938, Caxton Hall, London; Liberal Party Organization Lecture on Collective Security.

[2] Among the letters of praise that she received for this speech was one from Jimmy

That autumn Violet had given practical effect to such utterances by trying to secure the passage to Britain from Czechoslovakia of a Jewish family, the Buchwalds. In March 1939 Frau Buchwald and one of her two young sons arrived safely in England, to be followed next month by her husband and other son. She sent Violet a letter of thanks and a small gift in appreciation of her efforts on the family's behalf. This arrived three days after German troops had entered Prague, and Violet replied:

> I am so deeply touched by your letter & by the beautiful gift you sent me this morning. Of course I could not keep it. You must hand it on to your little son so that he also may pray over it on Friday nights & thank God for the courage of his parents & (I hope) the deliverance of his people. This terrible tyranny & oppression surely cannot last – our children must live to see the dawn of another day – & to grow up in freedom, justice & tolerance. If not – one would rather they were dead. This is what I feel about mine. . . .[1]

Stafford Cripps and the 'united front', 1938–9

In the post-Munich atmosphere traditional rivalries were dissolved and news alliances forged. On the international front Violet called for a rapprochement with the Soviet Union: 'We must cease to treat her as a pariah nation – good enough for us to "stand by" at the 11th moment of the 11th hour – but not good enough to take into the Conference Room'. Closer to home she backed the steps that were taken towards extending to a national level the informal political consensus of the Focus group. Violet had considered the idea of a 'united front' as early as 1935, during the Abyssinian crisis.[2] In the winter of 1938 the Liberals had pulled down their own candidate at three by-elections in favour of an 'anti-appeasement' candidate.[3] But the impetus that elevated this consensus to the

Rothschild, 1 December 1938: 'Your speech was the most moving and the most eloquent I think I have ever listened to, and I wanted just to send you a line of real gratefulness. It is good to have such a champion as you.'

[1] VBC to Frau Buchwald, 18 March 1939.

[2] Campaigning during the General Election she called for a cessation of Liberal–Labour hostilities, and for genuine national unity, not the sham of the 'national' government: 'The vital necessity at the moment is not to extinguish Liberalism – not to defeat the Labour Party – but to show a united front to Italy.'

[3] At Oxford in October the Liberals supported A. D. Lindsay, the master of Balliol; in November, Vernon Bartlett at Bridgwater; in December, the Duchess of Atholl at Kinross and West Perthshire. Only Bartlett was elected, though in its way each of the campaigns was a success.

level of a national campaign came from a most unexpected quarter.

Towards the end of the year Violet was contacted by the publisher Victor Gollancz on behalf of Sir Stafford Cripps, who wanted a meeting with her.[1] Cripps was a leading member of the Labour Party who Violet had regarded as a doctrinaire socialist and an uncompromising pacifist. He fell into her category of the hypocrite who was a pacifist abroad and a 'class jingo' at home. She had been especially alarmed at his plans in the early 1930s to reform parliament into a single chamber, and wrote in the October 1933 issue of the *Westminster Newsletter* that if he succeeded Britain would 'not be far from the system which Hitler has established in Germany'. Cripps' approach was thus an interesting one:

> Of course I told Victor I shld be delighted to see him & he duly arrived. I liked his finely cut, austere face. He went straight to the point. 'You will be surprised' he said 'by my visit & still more by what I am going to say to you. As you know I have always been a Socialist & a Pacifist. I was a Pacifist during the Italian attack on Abyssinia. I know how differently you reacted. I have come to tell you that I have changed. There is only one thing to be done now – to save Europe from Hitler – by any means one can, including force. This shld be the supreme aim of men of all parties – & those of us who believe in it – however much we may differ about other lesser things – shld form a United Front & work together & refuse to oppose one another at by-elections. Wld the Liberal Party consider such a plan?' I said it wld have my fervent support & that I felt confident I cld persuade Archie Sinclair to agree to it.[2]

During that winter Cripps prepared to put the case for a 'united front' to the Labour Party executive. In January 1939 it was rejected by a large majority. Cripps' colleagues believed that only the Labour Party could defeat Chamberlain's government, and when he continued to propound the united front he was expelled. To Violet it was an example of Labour shortsightedness, which was laden with danger:

> From the tragedy of Europe there is one lesson we can learn ourselves to-day. In Germany, in Italy, in Spain Fascism only snatched its victory because the forces of Freedom were not

---

[1] Victor Gollancz (1893–1967), left-wing publisher and writer; helped found the wartime 'national committee for rescue from Nazi terror', of which Violet was a member.

[2] Autobiographical note, Violet Bonham Carter MSS.

united. Are we going to let that happen here? Barcelona is falling. As the ramparts of freedom fall one by one it is cold comfort to some of us to know that Transport House still stands – exclusive – undefiled. I am proud to share a platform with Sir Stafford Cripps who is prepared to face ... even the polluting presence of a political Untouchable like myself. To save a cause greater than all the parties that ever were – to save the soul of freedom for humanity.[1]

She wholeheartedly endorsed Cripps' 'national petition' calling for a union of all anti-government forces, and in March recommended this to the National Liberal Club in London:

In the great Petition asking for Co-operation between the 3 progressive parties – Liberal, Labour and Co-operative – launched by Sir Stafford Cripps, I see the first definite hope for the forces of progress. I was relieved to see that you none of you jumped out of your skins when I mentioned Sir Stafford Cripps. I watched you very carefully. I know that his name sometimes causes alarm.... I am not concerned to explain or to defend what Sir Stafford Cripps has said in the past – nor can I answer for what he may say in the future. My only concern is that in this hour when all we care for is imperilled, he has had the courage and the common-sense to face realities, to put first things first, the substance before the shadow. He has had the vision to recognize and the courage to proclaim that there are moments in the history of mankind when even the bye-laws of the Socialist Party must go by the Board....

The last weeks of peace, July–September 1939

Cripps' campaign to raise awareness in Britain of the need for political consensus happened at a vital time. In mid-March the rump Czech state disintegrated, and Nazi Germany was the major beneficiary. The Munich agreement was now worthless, and so too was the Anglo-German understanding that it had epitomized. Chamberlain bowed to the inevitable and took steps to guard against future Nazi aggression. At the end of the month Britain entered into an alliance with Poland, which was thought to be Hitler's next target. In April the government announced that it was to introduce conscription. Appeasement, however, was not

---

[1] Speech at the Queen's Hall, London, 25 January 1939.

quite over. The long-awaited German attack on Poland came early in the morning of 1 September. There seemed only one possible British response. When Chamberlain appeared in the Commons the following evening, Saturday the 2nd, the House expected to be told that an ultimatum had been delivered to Germany. Instead it heard of the prospect of an international conference that would explore ways of resolving the crisis. This was reminiscent of Munich, and Chamberlain's statement shocked many even on his own side of the House. It fell to Arthur Greenwood, the deputy Labour leader, to demand that Britain at once make its promised stand in defence of Poland. When he rose to speak there were cheers of support and cries of 'Speak for England' and 'You speak for Britain' from the Tory benches. 'It was an astonishing demonstration. Greenwood almost staggered with surprise.'[1] After the session he informed Chamberlain privately that if war was not declared the next morning Labour would turn all of its efforts towards opposing the government in the House. An ultimatum was duly sent to Germany at 9.00 a.m. on 3 September, to expire two hours later.

The event that Violet had dreaded for much of the previous two decades had finally come to pass. She later recalled that for those who had been active in the work of the Freedom Focus the declaration of war brought no sense of triumph: 'To us it came as a relief to know that the retreat was over, and that our country which throughout its history had held the line of freedom, was true to its traditions and itself.' This account has naturally concentrated on her contribution to the anti-appeasement movement, but she would have been the first to point out that she was only one of a number – by no means the only, still less the most important, critic of appeasement. Her role was a supporting one, and in her eyes, and to many of those who worked alongside her, the undoubted leader of the movement was Winston Churchill.

Her final efforts in the weeks before war was declared were dedicated to putting pressure on Chamberlain's government to admit him to its councils. Violet later reflected with pride and amusement that in their common struggle against appeasement she and Churchill had drawn fire from all sides. Churchill attracted criticism from fellow Tories for his support for the League, and was ironically dubbed a 'pacifist', while her support for collective security led to her being branded 'bloodthirsty' by fellow Liberals. They were thus marginalized as trouble-making 'bloodthirsty paci-

---

[1] Harold Nicolson, *Diaries and Letters 1930–1939*, 419.

fists', who threatened to disturb the post-war equilibrium. In fact they were pioneers in a political coalition that carried Britain successfully through the war, leaving a legacy that greatly changed the face of British society in the post-war era.

THREE

The Second World War

1939–1945

CHRONOLOGY OF EVENTS 1939–1945

1939	August	23/24 – Nazi–Soviet non-aggression pact; 25 – formal treaty of mutual defence between Britain and Poland
	September	1 – German attack on Poland; 3 – Britain and France declare war on Germany; Churchill enters government
1940	April	8 – German occupation of Denmark and Norway
	May	7–8 – Commons debate on Norway – government majority falls to 81; 9 – German invasion of Low Countries; 10 – Chamberlain resigns, succeeded by Churchill; formation of Coalition Government; 27 – 'Operation Dynamo' – Dunkirk evacuation (to 3 June)
	June	10 – Italy declares war on Britain; 14 – Germans enter Paris; 17 – surrender of the French army; 22 – Franco-German armistice
	August	13 – battle of Britain (to 15 September)
	September	7 – beginning of the 'Blitz' (to May 1941)
1941	June	22 – German invasion of Russia
	July	12 – Anglo-Soviet agreement signed, pledging 'mutual assistance' against Germany and no separate peace
	August	12 – Atlantic Charter
	December	7 – Japanese attack American fleet at Pearl Harbor, and begin invasion of Malay Peninsula; war widens – Britain and United States at war with Japan; Germany and Italy at war with America
1942	February	15 – fall of Singapore to Japanese
	June	20 – fall of Tobruk to Germans
	October	23 – battle of El Alamein (to 4 November)
	November	8 – 'Operation Torch' – Allied landings in French North Africa; 11 – German army occupies Vichy France
	December	1 – publication of the 'Beveridge report' on *Social Insurance and the Allied Services*

1943	February	2 – surrender of German army at Stalingrad; 16–18 – Beveridge report debate – Labour amendment calling for stronger government approval defeated 335–119
	March	16 – start of Montgomery's attack on the Mareth Line
	July	10 – Allied invasion of Sicily
	September	3 – Allied invasion of Italy; 8 – unconditional surrender of Italy
	November	28 – Teheran Conference (to 2 December)
1944	June	5 – Allies enter Rome; 6 – 'Operation Overlord': D-Day landings on Normandy beaches
	October	9–19 – Moscow Conference: Churchill meets Stalin
1945	February	4–11 – Yalta Conference
	April	25 – beginning of San Francisco conference on the United Nations organization; 29 – surrender of German forces in Italy
	May	7 – unconditional German surrender; 8 – VE-Day; Churchill proposes continuation of the Coalition; 23 – resigns, signalling end of Coalition government, and beginning of 'caretaker' government
	July	5 – general election; 26 – declaration of the poll: 393 Labour, 213 Conservative, 12 Liberal; Attlee becomes prime minister
	July	17 – Potsdam Conference (to 2 August)
	August	atomic bombs dropped on Hiroshima (6) and Nagasaki (9); 14 – Japanese surrender

EIGHT

The Home Front

September 1939–December 1942

Towards the end of her life Violet was asked her impressions of the reaction in Britain to the outbreak of war in September 1939, compared with August 1914. 'It couldn't have been more different,' she replied. Her generation had not known war and consequently greeted it with 'romantic exultation', whereas in 1939 'people did know more what war was, and I don't think there was exultation ... all that feeling was absent'. The contrast was made sharper because in 1914 major battles began within weeks of the outbreak, and public attention was immediately engaged, while in 1939 almost eight months elapsed before serious fighting took place. In this period of 'phoney war' British forces were mobilized, but public opinion was not. Boredom and apathy overtook the nation, which Violet regarded as more dangerous to morale than the fear of defeat itself. From the outset both she and Bongie were active on the 'home front', working as air-raid wardens. For them, as for parents of their age throughout Britain, there was a grim sense of repetition. Where previously they had worried about their brothers and friends being killed, they now worried about their eldest son, and his friends, who were either of military age or close to it. Less than a fortnight after Mark Bonham Carter's eighteenth birthday, Violet addressed a meeting of Liberals in London: 'We know what War is. We have seen our own generation broken on the wheel. We have seen their victory thrown away. To-day we see the world they died to save, in ruins at our feet – and we must bind our children to the wheel to save it once again.' If a feeling of resignation replaced the moral fervour of an earlier era, there was no lack of moral conviction. This was a war in defence of civilization itself, of 'the rights of men and nations, great and small, of every race and class and creed, to live their individual lives in peace and liberty – the right of men to think their own thoughts, pray their own prayers, to call their souls their own ...'. Above all else, it was a Liberal's war.[1]

---

[1] Harris interview; TSS of speech at the Queen's Hall, London, 24 February 1940; Violet Bonham Carter MSS.

V.B.C. to R.B.C. *Saturday 2 September 1939*
40 Gloucester Square, W.2

Darling Ray – We are expecting war to begin here to-day.[1] Bongie sat up nearly all night at the Air-Raid Warden's centre – we had a <u>complete</u> black-out – one had to grope one's way about the streets. To-day the balloon barrage is up all round London – most of the shops are shut – the streets very empty. London seems to be holding its breath.

I am 'mobilized' & went to my First Aid centre this morning at 10 & have been working there. It is in the Garage of St. Mary's Hospital. Everything seems terribly unready & in a muddle. Men are hammering up water-pipes & lights. We have been taught to give morphia injections & anti-tetanus.... Love & blessings, Yr Mama

V.B.C. to R.B.C. *Thursday 7 September*
40 Gloucester Square, W.2

Darling Ray ... We had another Air-Raid alarm this morning at $\frac{1}{4}$ to 7 – our 3rd since War began. I was sitting up – as my 'shift' was 4–8 – & I woke Bongie & the other Warden who lives in our house – & Bongie slipped on his French mechanic's overalls over his pyjamas & put on his shell-helmet & they all rushed into the street blowing their whistles & getting people into the crypt of St. John's Church. We didn't get the 'All Clear' till 9 o'clock. I see in the paper that enemy bombers were sighted off the East Coast but failed to get through our defences.

I long for you to see our house – all sandbagged up & with paper strips across the windows. It looks like a fortress. Bongie goes his rounds every night round his 3 Sectors – hammering at people's doors if he sees a chink of light. You must be having lovely weather at Fellside. It is such a waste of these beautiful days to be in London & at war. All my love my darling – Ever yr. <u>Mama</u>

V.B.C. to Desmond MacCarthy *Friday 8 September*
40 Gloucester Square, W.2

Dearest Desmond – I was so deeply touched by your lovely letter. Watching beloved Oc dying through those 3 weeks & knowing oneself quite powerless to help or save him was pain unspeakable. I was thankful to be with

---

[1] Mark and Raymond Bonham Carter spent Easter and summer of 1939 at Fellside, a shooting lodge in a hamlet in the Cumberland fells, two miles from Caldbeck.

him to the very end. From what you write about him I see that you know what he was – & what he was to me (which matters less). I think he was one of the most perfectly & unselfconsciously <u>good</u> people I have ever known. His courage was cold courage. He <u>hated</u> fighting & never – even when he joined up – romanticized the War. I remember a talk with him & Rupert (Brooke) at Downing St one evening before they left – when Rupert said he felt he had been born for just this hour – to go & free Constantinople from the Turks etc. – & Oc said very prosaically through his teeth that he just considered the whole thing 'a <u>beastly</u> duty'. But he made it more than that by his humanity – which gave him his great powers of leadership....

—— —— —— —— ——

Now Armageddon is upon us. We have at <u>long last</u> done the honourable thing – but because we have waited so long to do it the odds against us seem to me immeasurably great. I can never remember a moment between 1914–1918 when I had a doubt of victory. To-day – alas! – I feel the most <u>probable</u> end is a long drawn out stale-mate. There are two windfalls Heaven <u>might</u> send us to prevent this – disruption in Germany itself – or American intervention.

Mark & Raymond are safe (tho' alone) in Cumberland, & Laura & her baby in St. Andrews.[1] Bongie & I are in this dark – tent town which seems to be holding its breath....

... The pitchy darkness at night is less inky than that of the newspapers under the yoke of the Censorship. The Censors have got drunk with power & are behaving with something like <u>insanity</u>. Apart from arousing grave fear, suspicion & mistrust here they are <u>outraging</u> American correspondents – & doing us great harm in neutral countries. No news & no criticism is apparently to be allowed. The 'War Cabinet' is alas! the 'old familiar faces' – plus Winston – who has been harnessed to an office to keep him quiet & occupied – with departmental routine.[2] I fear that mediocrities & yes-men are still being appointed to every post....

Your present to Cressida & Bubbles is so terribly generous.... Poor darling! she is frozen at the thought of Bubbles being taken from her & thrown into this cauldron of horror. It is so <u>much</u> – much worse than last time. I long for the great ghosts to come back & lead us – instead of these small men.

[1] Laura and Jo Grimond's first child, Andrew, had been born the previous year.

[2] Chamberlain's war cabinet comprised nine ministers, seven of whom had served in the 1937–9 administration; Churchill and Hankey (minister without portfolio) were the newcomers.

Dearest Desmond – please keep in touch with me. Your letter made me feel less lonely – I know we feel alike. B. & I are very tired from want of sleep with all this work – & missing the children – & fearing for them – Bubbles & Mark & Jo. Bless you & thank you for writing – & forgive the length of this letter. There is so much I want to say to you. Ever your, Violet

P.S. You ask about Margot – alas! she is still <u>possessed</u> to the exclusion of all else – all human feeling almost – by her extraordinary views – & wrote me a long violent controversial letter on the day of Oc's funeral at Clovelly to tell me that he agreed – or wld. have agreed – with her! I try & think it is old age – but there are moments when one is vulnerable – even to her.[1]

V.B.C. to Betty Asquith[2]

Wednesday 27 September
40 Gloucester Square, W.2

Darling Bett – Do forgive me for being so slow in sending you this – & thank you a thousand times for dropping the vacuum cleaner here. It will be such a comfort. I think of you so often in this lovely autumn weather & am thankful that at least you are in the country. Somehow inanimate things are the only peace & comfort in these days when everything <u>human</u> hurts.

Here even Kew Gardens has been shut – till last Sunday – & when we went there people were being forbidden to take in their Kodaks! I think the civilian public will get demoralized unless <u>something</u> is done soon to make an appeal to their courage & imagination. Everyone has lost their peace-jobs & can't get war-jobs – they feel idle & ruined, & useless into the bargain. There is no light – no intercourse – no food for the mind or spirit – above all no <u>news</u>! It is somehow easier to be heroic when faced with big events – however catastrophic – than a mass of small petty aggravations.

Winston made a marvellous speech in the H. of C. yesterday & cheered everyone up – after Neville Chamberlain had rumbled out a dreary 'read'

---

[1] Harold Nicolson recalled: 'Violet Bonham Carter rings up. She had been down to the funeral of her brother Oc at Clovelly and on her return had found a letter from Margot Oxford saying "If only people like you had rallied behind Chamberlain at the time, this would never have happened." She is hurt by this stupidity and insensitiveness on Margot's part' (Harold Nicolson, diary, 30 August 1939).

[2] The widow of Oc Asquith.

statement – as Harold Nicolson said to me 'like the Secretary of the Undertaker's Association!'[1]

Write me a line about all of you & what you are doing. The boys went back to their schools last week after 2 nights here. All my love – & blessings – Yr <u>Violet</u>

Margot Asquith to V.B.C.   *Sunday 22 October*
                                                44 Bedford Square, W.C.1

My darling ... I have read – not <u>all</u> of it – the book you told me to read, & I'm very glad you spoke of it, as I <u>doubt</u> if I w^d have read it otherwise. It has <u>convinced</u> me that the war will be even shorter than I thought (I may of course be talking <u>nonsense</u>!) I feel that it will be over very shortly after Xmas. I will tell you <u>why</u>. Because the day Russia & Germany shook hands – Ribbentrop & Stalin – I felt in my bones that Russia w^d fight <u>our</u> war.[2] I have had long talks with men who <u>know</u> Russia & they <u>all</u> say the same thing. I, of course know <u>nothing</u>, I only <u>feel</u> it, & your book has confirmed me. Stalin is a more astute, & even <u>viler</u> man than Hitler, & to judge by Hermann Rauschning,[3] the Munich Visit, so far from being what the P.M.'s opponents trumpet – a <u>failure</u> – was the reverse. This is old history, but of one thing I'm <u>quite</u> certain: if we had made up to Russia, unless we had done it in 1918, we w^d have had the whole of Europe against us, instead of <u>with</u> us: all these Autumns w^h I've spent abroad, I've been <u>amazed</u> at the <u>hatred</u> w^h Russia has inspired: 'We prefer the Germans – even <u>Hitler</u>, to Stalin's Russia'; was said to me by every Balkan I met. My one fear <u>now</u> is what sort of Peace we can make. <u>I</u> am no judge, but I w^d not make <u>one</u> step towards Peace till we have won the war, & <u>not</u> on battle-fields. 'The spirit of man is the candle of the Lord'. Will the spirit of man be equal to making a noble Peace? – or are we to have another Ll.G. Versailles Treaty?

It is now 4 A.M. so I'll <u>try</u> & sleep. Love – ever yr Margot

---

[1] '[Chamberlain] is dressed in deep mourning relieved only by a white handkerchief and a large gold watch chain. He reads out his statement exactly as if he were the secretary of an undertaker's Association reading the minutes of the last meeting. One feels the confidence and spirits of the House dropping inch by inch' (Harold Nicolson, diary, 26 September 1939).

[2] Margot refers to the Nazi–Soviet non-aggression pact, signed by von Ribbentrop and Molotov on the night of 23–24 August 1939, which cleared the way for the German attack on Poland.

[3] Hermann Rauschning, *Germany's Revolution of Destruction* (1939).

Diary – Thursday 2 to Tuesday 14 May 1940 – written c. 14 May, at 40 Gloucester Square, W.2

Re-reading a few of the notes I kept in this book about the last War made me wish that I had kept a short record of this one since the start.[1] It is too late to go back now – when the storm is bursting over our heads – so I will jot down a brief skeleton account of the last fortnight.

On Thursday 2nd May I had my usual 'Venusberg' lunch after the L.N.U. Committee with Baffy – Bruce Lockhart – Colin Coote & a young man called Sanderson. Bob Boothby came in half-way through.[2] The Norwegian situation looked bad.... What was my horror to hear at luncheon from Colin Coote & Bob that we had already evacuated Andalsnes & were withdrawing from Southern & Central Norway altogether – only leaving a small force at Narvik.[3] Awful details followed about the muddle & inefficiency with which the force had been equipped & sent. All the Anti-Aircraft guns on one ship, which had been sunk etc. – no air protection for our troops – no snowshoes – raw semi-trained Territorials sent to accomplish this impossible task etc. I felt completely 'winded' with horror & amazement – for we had heard nothing from Govt. spokesmen but the most optimistic forecasts & reports. We discussed the possibility of the Govt. falling on it next week – & Bob assured us that 40 Conservatives wld. vote against the Govt. But he has told us that so often & up to now it has usually resulted in 3 abstentions, so I went away not much cheered....

On Tuesday (7th) I dashed down to Leicester to lecture & got back just in time to dine with Harold Nicolson at H. of C. Party: Baffy, Sybil Colefax, Hugh Walpole & a young man called Forbes who had been to Finland & seemed to know the Admiralty ropes well.[4] They were all agog over Roger

---

[1] The book in question is Violet's diary for 1915; about a third of its 500 pages had been used when, in May 1940, she began a new diary in it by using the blank pages at the back.

[2] John Harold Bruce Lockhart (1889–1956), headmaster of Sedbergh School, 1937–54. Robert John Graham 'Bob' Boothby (1900–86), Conservative MP for East Aberdeenshire, 1924–58; under-secretary at ministry of food, 1940; later staff officer, RAF, and with Free French. The informal 'Venusberg' luncheons were organized by Violet on behalf of a small group of friends, who often brought along guests. There was much discussion of current affairs.

[3] The failed British attempt to eject the Germans from Norway involved campaigns in Narvik and Trondheim. The latter was to be attacked in a pincer movement, after landings at Namsos and Aandalsnes, respectively north and south along the coast. German air power proved decisive in this ill-fated venture: Namsos and Aandalsnes were evacuated on 2 May, while the forces at Narvik held out until 8 June.

[4] Sybil Colefax *née* Halsey, a famous hostess in London society. Sir Hugh Seymour Walpole (1884–1941), Kt, 1937; novelist. Alastair Forbes, Royal Marine, later attached to the Free French.

Keyes' speech which had apparently been the sensation of the debate. He spoke in Admiral's uniform which he had never worn in the House before, & this, as Harold said, wld have been a ridiculous gesture from a vain man like Beatty, but done by Keyes was simple & moving.[1]

He read his speech but gripped the House with every syllable. He indicted the Govt. & the Admiralty for refusing to let the ships go for Trondheim. He said he had offered to conduct the operation himself & took full responsibility for it. The P.M. by all accounts had been very poor & never held the House at all. Amery was called – as usual – in the dinner hour – but I had no ticket to go in & hear him. He made a remarkable speech ending up with the Cromwellian peroration 'In the name of God go'.[2]

Oliver Stanley wound up – very badly I am told.[3] Next day I had a seat in the Speaker's Gallery & listened to the most dramatic debate I have almost ever heard in my whole Parliamentary memory. Morrison opened – quite unremarkably. Sam Hoare followed – <u>so</u> bad that he emptied the House. It was like a maiden speech – people cld hardly listen even to tales of the feats of Gladiators on frozen lakes.[4] I went out to have tea with Percy Harris who assured me that not more than 13 Conservatives wld. vote against the Govt. that night. There was an exciting scene when Morrison announced that the Labour Party were going to divide the House. Chamberlain jumped up & with affected surprise (for he <u>must</u> have known beforehand),[5] & real indignation, said that he welcomed [the] challenge – & appealed to his friends – 'for I have friends in this House' – to

---

[1] Admiral Sir Roger John Brownlow Keyes (1872–1945), cr. Bt, 1919; Baron, 1943; Conservative MP for Portsmouth North, 1934–43; liaison officer to King of Belgium, 1940; 'I come to the House of Commons to-day in uniform for the first time because I wish to speak for some officers and men of the fighting, sea-going Navy who are very unhappy ...' (*Hansard*, vol. 360, 1125). David Beatty (1871–1936), cr. Earl, 1919; admiral of the fleet.

[2] Leopold Charles Amery (1873–1955), Conservative MP for South Birmingham, 1911–45; secretary for India, 1940–5. Amery repeated Oliver Cromwell's injunction to the Rump Parliament in 1653: 'You have sat too long here for any good you have been doing. Depart, I say, and let us have done with you. In the name of God, go!'

[3] Oliver Frederick George Stanley (1896–1950), Conservative MP for Westmorland, 1924–45; president of board of trade, 1937–40; secretary for war, 1940; served army, 1940–2; secretary for colonies, 1942–5.

[4] Hoare described the desperate struggle to establish a fighter presence in Norway, involving a squadron of obsolescent Gladiator biplanes. These were chosen for their ability to operate from makeshift landing grounds, such as that constructed on the frozen Lake Lesjaskog. Within a week of becoming operational, though, the Gladiator squadron had been put out of action by enemy fire. Hoare was forced to admit that the airfield had no anti-aircraft guns with which to resist Luftwaffe bombing (*The Times*, 9 May 1940; Denis Richards, *Royal Air Force 1939–45*, i, 89–92).

[5] The Opposition only decided to press for a division earlier that morning, and it is *not* clear that Chamberlain had known beforehand.

support him. This unfortunate phrase, which got him a Party cheer at the time, became the 'leit motif' of his ruin. Anyone else might have said it with impunity – but it was so profoundly, fatally characteristic to make this tremendous issue a matter of who were, & who were not, his friends.

When I came back from tea Ll.G. was speaking. He made the best & most deadly speech I have ever heard from him – voice – gesture – everything was brought into play to drive home his indictment. Material was not lacking. The House was profoundly shaken. Only once – when he said our 'promissory notes were rubbish in the market' was he interrupted. He had just overreached himself (as he almost invariably does) but the effect of his speech was devastating.[1]

Stafford Cripps spoke – well as he always does – but made too legalistic a point. Duff made an <u>extraordinarily</u> good & decisive speech – saying he was going to vote against the Govt. On their side old George Lambert – Sir A. Southby – & the usual woodlice crept out from under their stones as in the Munich debate.[2]

Not one of them cld sway a thought or a vote. I went home to have a hurried meal & returned to hear Alexander – quite good – & Winston's winding-up.[3] His was of course the <u>only</u> speech on the Govt. side – but he had no case to make & even his peroration sounded conscientious & forced. He <u>cldn't</u> throw all his weight in it. He had an unfortunate brawl with the Labour Party at the very end – because Shinwell interrupted him & W. accused him of 'skulking' & they appealed to the Speaker as to whether 'skulk' was or was not a Parliamentary expression! & he was a good deal interrupted in his last 10 minutes.[4] Then the House divided. We

---

[1] 'Could anyone doubt that our prestige has been impaired? It was only necessary to read friendly American papers to find that out. We had promised Czechoslovakia, we had promised Poland, we had promised Finland. Our promissory notes were now rubbish in the markets.' There were loud cries of 'shame' from the ministerial benches, to which Lloyd George replied, amid cries of 'hear, hear', 'Tell me one country that would be prepared to stand up to the Nazis upon a mere promise from ourselves. What is the use of not facing facts?' (*The Times*, 9 May 1940).

[2] Commander Sir Archibald Richard Southby (1886–1969), cr. Bt, 1937; Conservative MP for Epsom, 1928–47.

[3] Albert Victor Alexander (1885–1965), Labour MP for Hillsborough, Sheffield, 1922–31, 1935–50; first lord of the admiralty, 1929–31, 1940–5.

[4] Churchill's attempt to paint a positive picture of the débâcle in Norway met with cries of 'Oh' from one MP – Violet identified the Labour MP Emanuel Shinwell (1884–1986). Churchill replied: 'Yes, I dare say the Hon. Gentleman does not like it. He would rather that I have a bad tale to tell. That is why he is skulking in the corner.' When called upon to withdraw this remark Churchill refused, and the Labour MP Neil Maclean (d. 1953) appealed to the speaker for a ruling. To the general levity of the House the speaker judged 'skulk' to be a parliamentary word 'if ... used accurately'. Uproar followed as Maclean protested, and Churchill stood shouting angrily at the Labour benches (*The Times*, 9 May 1940).

all sat tensely waiting for the figures – my hopes quite low though in the Debate the Opposition (on all sides) had had it all their own way. In a crowded – bumper House they were announced – 'Ayes to the Right 281 – Noes to the Left 200'.

The Govt. majority had fallen to 81. Then followed a scene I shall never forget – Cheers – shouts of 'resign' – 'Go' – Prim respectable Conservatives like Harold Macmillan – with his high white collar & tightly fixed pince-nez yelling 'Go! Go! Go!' like inspired baboons. I went down to the Liberal Whips' room & talked there to Archie, Percy Harris & Wilfrid Roberts till nearly 1 o'clock.[1] We all agreed the Govt. must go – that Neville Chamberlain cldn't carry on at such a moment after such a demonstration from within his own Party. We all made our choice of P.M.'s – Winston – Halifax & Ll.G. being the candidates – & all gave Winston our 1st vote tho' some thought Halifax more probable. Archie alone envisaged the possibility of Ombrello being asked & consenting to serve under Winston – a thought which chilled us all.[2]

B. went to Rugby next day (Thursday 9th May). Negotiations & meetings went on all day – & it was quite clear that reconstruction was impending & that neither of the Opposition Parties wld. consent to serve under Chamberlain.

V.B.C. to Winston Churchill

Thursday 9 May
40 Gloucester Square, W.2

Dearest Winston –

I know what a heavy strain the last month must have been & what a heavy burden you have been bearing. I have made no sign, for I know that you cannot have had a spare moment for anything outside your work. I have sat through the debate, & I think you know where my hopes have lain. I wish that your present ship may sink – & I look forward to the launching of a greater one, of which you will hold the supreme command. There is a great tide flowing which <u>you</u> can direct. My hope & trust go with you. Later on I shld like to see you someday – Ever yrs, Violet

[*diary continued*] <u>Friday 10th May</u> B. got through to me on a trunk call from Rugby before I was called. He said 'Have you heard the news?' I said 'No – has Chamberlain resigned?' He replied 'Holland & Belgium were invaded early this morning.'

[1] Wilfrid Hubert Wace Roberts (1900–91), Liberal MP for North Cumberland, 1935–50.
[2] Chamberlain ('Ombrello') in fact became lord president in Churchill's cabinet; he retained significant Conservative support and his inclusion was necessary to national unity.

There was not a word yet in the papers – but the wireless had announced it at 8 & reports came through during the day that the Dutch & Belgians were fighting hard – in spite of bombing attacks & parachute troops – helped out by [a] Fifth Column in Holland. We had an immediate meeting of Air-Raid Wardens & B. & I took the 8–12 watch at the Post & decided not to go away for Whitsuntide as we had intended. At 9 o'clock I went downstairs & listened in & heard Chamberlain make a very dignified resignation speech – & say he had recommended the King to send for Winston as his successor. What a moment to take on!

He will indeed have to ride the whirlwind & direct the storm. If any man can he will, but he has as a heritage the years that the locust has eaten. How different if he had been allowed to take a part during the last 5 years in preparing for the peril which he so clearly foresaw. On Sat. (11th) I went down for the day to see Ray compete in the 'Sports' at St Ronan's. He received me glowing with happiness & excitement. . . .

The first event was the hurdles which he won by miles. . . . We then watched the Senior Long Jump which gave him a breather & he then went down to the start for the 100 yds. I stood up at the tape. He got a splendid start & was easily leading about $\frac{3}{4}$ of the way down the course when he quite suddenly fell out sideways off the course. I thought he felt faint & rushed across to him. He had torn a muscle in his thigh! probably a result of the hurdling. It was the most poignant disappointment – for he was quite disabled & cldn't go in for any other event. B. arrived just as the 'sister' & I were taking him in to lie down. I didn't know any personal thing cld be so harrowing – with the world in flames around us. But it was certainly the greatest blow he has ever sustained in his life – & in spite of great courage – he shook all over with quite dry sobs & I didn't know how to comfort him. Next year's Sports seemed so far away. . . .

Archie's appt. to the Air Ministry was announced on Sat. night. He will have the toughest job of anyone after Supply. B. went round to Brooks's Sat. night & had a long talk with him. Production is going to be given to a separate dept. which will immensely lighten his labours. It is said that Winston has offered it to Beaverbrook.[1] They both come into a difficult heritage. The rest of the Govt. as at present announced is Anthony – War Office, Alexander – Admiralty, Morrison – Supply, Bevin – Labour (all good) but the War Cabinet itself is deplorable & seems to have been entirely dictated by Party exigencies – Winston, Halifax, Attlee, Green-wood, Ombrello – symbolic sexagenarians. Not an executive instrument

[1] There was a precedent in the creation of the ministry of munitions in 1915, which relieved the war office of the responsibility of production, allowing it to concentrate on strategy. Despite a show of reluctance Beaverbrook was at work even before formally accepting on 14 May (A. J. P. Taylor, *Beaverbrook*, 411–13)

nor even a good shop-window. Winston will of course run it – but the others do not even present a surface on which a mind cld. <u>strike</u>. Fortunately his has more power of self-ignition than most of ours.

Archie told B. the Tory pressure on W. had been tremendous & that he had even been obliged to give <u>Kingsley Wood</u> the Exchequer to get him out of the War Cabinet. Simon is going to the Woolsack instead of to the scrap-heap. Hoare is out thank Heaven. Archie ought of course to have been in the War Cabinet but this wld. have ruled him out from having a fighting dept. B. said that while they were talking at Brooks's Eddy Devonshire came up & said to Archie 'I consider you quite unfit for the Air Ministry. I wldn't even make you sub-agent of one of my properties'. He then went on to twit him with taking away his boys from Eton.[1] B. said Archie took it all very good temperedly but finally said 'Look here Eddy, do you want to quarrel with me?' on which he went away. B. afterwards spoke to Eddy who said he thought Winston, Archie & most members of the new Govt were 'hysterical' which Chamberlain was not....

Frightful news of bombing in Holland & Belgium – I don't see how the Dutch can hold out. Rotterdam is said to be a ruin – Brussels has been declared an open town. The House met (Monday 13th) & Winston made a short & moving speech with the Garibaldian theme 'I have nothing to offer those who join my Govt but blood, toil, tears & sweat'. Some said that a great organized reception was given to Chamberlain & a markedly cooler one to him. I wasn't there.

<u>Tuesday 14th</u> – the Dutch capitulated having lost 100,000 of their Army. There are ghastly stories of the bombing of open towns. Rotterdam is said to be almost rased to the ground – refugees are streaming away....

Diary – Wednesday 15 May – 40 Gloucester Square, W.2

We dined with Stinnes – Warburg & a man called Lucas from M.E.W. at Brown's Hôtel.[2] All anxious that we shld. show greater ruthlessness & less scruple – Lucas fearing a move in M.E.W. to call off contraband control in the Mediterranean in order to placate the Italians – who are assaulting members of our Embassy in the street – plastering the Embassy & other buildings with insulting placards & generally behaving insufferably. Marigold came to see me at tea-time. She has come up to find a flat for Archie.

---

[1] Edward William Spencer Cavendish (1895–1950), 10th Duke of Devonshire, 1938; a parliamentary under-secretary, 1936–45.

[2] Sir Siegmund George Warburg (1902–82), German-born banker; left Germany, 1933, and settled in England (naturalized, 1939); began New Trading Co. Ltd (changed name to S. G. Warburg & Co. Ltd).

I spoke to him on the telephone before going to bed. He sounded in good spirits – trying to get the bearings of his new & complicated office. The full German pressure is now focused on Belgium. I don't see how we can save it. Our troops had a wonderful reception when they swept in – but the Germans are over the Albert Canal – & I don't know what line we can hold there. Liège & Namur are still holding out.

Diary – Thursday 16 May – 40 Gloucester Square, W.2

It was hard to concentrate on L.N.U. & on an endless discussion between Bob & Victor Lytton on the future constitution of the League.[1] Lunch at Venusberg.... Discussion on new Govt. etc. – but all overshadowed by the news of a terrible German thrust in the direction of Leiden with super-tanks, which seem invulnerable to the ordinary anti-tank guns, & fleets of bombers.[2] For the first time the awful fear that our line might break crossed the frontier of my mind....

Diary – Saturday 18 to Sunday 19 May – written on Wednesday 22 May, at 40 Gloucester Sq.

We spent a week-end of amazing & unreal beauty at Mottisfont with Gilbert & Maud....[3] The loveliness of this Spring will remain in memory an unforgettable part of its tragedy. Never have I seen such a burst of blossom, flowers, birdsong....

The news did not improve. The Germans had reached Rethel on Friday evening – 70 miles from Paris. We listened in at 1 & 6 & 10 – Duff gave a good broadcast on Sat. night & Winston a most moving one on Sunday – ending with a fine text from Maccabees.[4] It was difficult to gather exactly what was happening but it seemed clear that the German tank advance, protected by heavy bombers, had taken the French by surprise & though

[1] Victor Alexander Lytton (1876–1947), 2nd Earl, 1891; at ministry of labour, 1942–5.

[2] The defending forces were poorly equipped to deal with the German Panzers, lacking not just anti-tank guns but also the tactics to confront tank divisions, in the development of which the Germans were pioneers.

[3] Gilbert Byng Alwyne Russell (1875–1942), banker; married Maud *née* Nelke 1917; old friends of Violet and Bongie.

[4] 'Arm yourselves, and be ye men of valour, and be in readiness for the conflict, for it is better for us to perish in battle than to look on the outrage of our nation and our altars. As the will of God is in Heaven, even so let him do' (*The Times*, 20 May 1940; 1 Maccabees 3). It was Churchill's first broadcast to the nation as prime minister, and he warned that the full force of German aggression would soon be turned towards Britain.

slowed down had not been halted. Open fighting was taking place. In some places German tanks were behind our lines – in others we were behind theirs. My terror is lest our force, which had advanced almost unopposed into Belgium, shld be cut off by a drive towards Calais & driven into the sea. . . .

Diary – Tuesday 21 May – written on Wednesday 22 May, at 40 Gloucester Square

The papers told one little – on the whole the impression given was that things were faintly better – but acute anxiety gnaws every minute – like the fox at the little Spartan's body – hidden under his clothes.[1] Cys came to see me in the morning. Little Hallands is one mile from Newhaven. He is convinced that there will be attempts at invasion. If the Germans get the Channel ports they can reach London with Artillery fire – quite apart from the air. They are as good as in this country. . . . I went down to the H. of C. after luncheon & sat in the Strangers' Gallery. The new Ministry looked a strange jumble on the Front Bench. Winston between Attlee & Chamberlain – Bob Boothby – Ellen Wilkinson – Archie – Anthony etc.[2] I thought Winston looked better than when I had seen him last. The House was in a rather foolish-rollicking mood – possibly from nerves. Every new Minister & Under-Secretary got a 'reception' when he rose to answer questions. . . . It was difficult to feel they realized the gravity of the situation.

I came back to tea & Laura & I switched on the news at 6. It was appalling. Amiens & Arras have fallen. Reynaud revealed in a speech to the Chambre that owing to 'incredible folly which will be severely punished' the bridges over the Meuse were not blown up & the Germans streamed over them. It was a weak part of the line & was left to the defence of inferior officers & troops – the better ones having gone to Belgium. He ended by saying 'If I am told that France can only be saved by a miracle then I reply that I believe in miracles – for I believe in France'.

The Germans claim Abbeville also – & looking at the map I feel that our force must be cut off. . . . At 9 the same news in rather greater detail was repeated – followed by an excellent broadcast from Duff – in which he used the words which I hung onto like a life-line through sleepless hours 'There is no cause for serious alarm or panic' – 'Serious alarm' <u>surely</u>? Yet

[1] A story told in old school books to illustrate the incredible stoicism of the Spartans: the fox was concealed, but the boy did not cry out and reveal it, even though he was being eaten.

[2] Ellen Wilkinson (d. 1947), Labour MP for Jarrow, Durham, 1935–47; parliamentary secretary, ministry of home security, 1940–5.

he must know more than we do. I spoke to Morhange after 11.[1] He thought things were as black as they could be & that there was no doubt that our Force was now cut off. Air-raid alarm (yellow warning only) at 1.15 – I got up & dressed in full paraphernalia. White came through at $\frac{1}{4}$ to 2. The only bright spot in the day [was] a remark by Mrs White my cook – 'I thought things must be hopeless when Mr Churchill started quoting Scripture'.

Diary – Wednesday 22 May – 40 Gloucester Square, W.2

Another day stretched on the rack – living from 'news' to 'news' – 1–6–9– midnight – waiting always for the French counter-attack that never comes. 'Arras retaken' was in the evening papers – but apparently it had never really been occupied by the Germans. If they are really at or near Abbeville I don't see how we can keep our communications.

The French are fighting near Cambrai on the other hand. If only they cld. counter-attack in force the Germans' vulnerable salient wld be squeezed. I feel alas! the struggle this time is not man against man or I shld be more confident. It is machines against men – & the Germans have more & better machines. Maud Russell, Van & Serita lunched with me. Van terribly depressed désoeuvré & bitter.[2] We asked him about the English Quislings mentioned ... in the Whitehall News Letter. Do they – can they really exist? When Edith had left the room he told us that Maule Ramsay, Tory M.P. for Peebles, was one of them – & had given at meetings lists of people he wld. have shot – including Van himself....[3]

Diary – Thursday 23 May – 40 Gloucester Square, W.2

No further news this morning. Winston went over to France again yes-terday – & back. Lunch with Baffy, Walter Elliot.... W.E. looking very depressed. It must be a great blow to be out of office at such a moment – after making such long concessions of principle to remain in. He had given up his seals that morning & said the King told him he had said to

[1] Alfonse 'Toto' Morhange (1893–1976), assistant to financial attaché of French embassy, May–July 1940; afterwards with the Free French in London; see biographical notes.

[2] Robert Gilbert Vansittart ('Van') (1881–1957), cr. Baron, 1941; as permanent under-secretary at the foreign office he had warned constantly of the dangers posed by Nazism, but had been given the empty role of chief diplomatic adviser to the foreign secretary, 1938–41. On coming to power Churchill did not change this, which 'Van' had hoped he would.

[3] Captain Archibald Henry Maule Ramsay (d. 1955), Conservative MP for Peebles, South Midlothian, 1931–45; detained in Brixton prison May 1940–September 1944 under regulation 18B, (see below).

Winston 'You are <u>my</u> Prime Minister you know – you mustn't become the P.M. of France as well' – & that W. had replied that he was afraid he must fly over again next day....[1]

I have just listened to 6 o'clock news. We (the B.E.F.) have held all our positions on the Scheldt except at Oudenaarde where the enemy forced the river. In the gap between Arras & Bapaume some mechanised forces have got through. The Germans have taken Abbeville & fighting is reported to be going on in & round <u>Boulogne</u> – all one's worst fears realized. Maule Ramsay of whom Van spoke yesterday has been arrested & taken to Brixton prison – & the offices of the B.U.F. raided & all their papers seized.

A bill was introduced in the House yesterday conscripting all labour & property & passed without opposition. As the Evening Standard says to-night, had such a measure been passed 9 months ago perhaps a million lives might have been saved. The blind, smug inertia of Neville Chamberlain & his followers, their refusal to believe in war, to prepare for it, or even to meet it when it came is criminal. It is not they who are paying the penalty but the innocent young whom they have sacrificed & betrayed. On the 9 o'clock broadcast the news came through that Oswald Mosley had been arrested & 8 of his fellow Fascists – the one bright spot in a dark evening.[2] No French counter-offensive yet.

Diary – Friday 24 to Monday 27 May – 40 Gloucester Square, W.2

On Friday evening we heard that the Germans had taken possession of Boulogne. Calais is clearly threatened. The Germans are at Ghent – threatening Ostend – so Dunkirk remains the only port through which we cld feed – or if necessary – re-embark the B.E.F. ... Anthony made an appeal at night for volunteers against parachutists.

I had tea with Mrs. Huntington who said that all her American friends were crowding onto the President Roosevelt to get away – even wives &

---

[1] In fact Churchill next flew to France on 30 May. He pursued his goal of keeping France in the war up to the last, only cancelling his sixth journey across the Channel on 16 June when he learned that Pétain was seeking an armistice.

[2] As many as eighty members of the BUF were arrested that day under regulation 18B, amended the previous evening to allow the detention of members of fascist or pro-fascist organizations, on the assumption that they constituted a security risk with a German invasion threatening (see Robert Skidelsky, *Oswald Mosley*, 447–9). Violet was not immune from the obvious general anxiety about a British fifth column, but she became increasingly concerned about the manner in which regulation 18B was applied, and in 1941 urged tighter controls over the powers given to the home secretary under its terms.

children of Embassy officials.[1] I cld. see that she herself had a real needle about invasion which one cannot rule out as a possibility....

I am worried about R. at Worthing & Harry's suggestion of moving the school to Frensham – 15 miles from Aldershot – does not commend itself to me at all![2] Happily he has now heard of a place in Devonshire which he is going down to see. On Saturday we had a lovely day of accidental reunion – as Mark came up for the day – Laura & Jo arrived from Aldershot & Bubbles also turned up in the afternoon – with incredibly short hair, red face & shining eyes – in battle-dress. He was in amazing form & spirits – amused by his companions – suffering no great discomfort except sweet tea in the canteen & passionately anxious to take back nails (on which to hang things) empty bottles & rags for cleaning equipment....

Sunday morning (26th May) B. & I went to the Canon's church for the service of intercession.[3] It was packed out (there were 700 even at our sleepy old St. John's). The Canon made a magnificent sermon of the most militant kind on the text 'Thou shalt have no other Gods than me'. He spoke of the Litany, in which we had just called ourselves 'miserable sinners' – of the blind complacency of our statesmen saying 'Peace–peace' where there was no peace – of that cowardly & fatal slogan 'Safety First'. I saw him for a moment after the service & thought how beloved Frances wld. have loved his sermon. He is the best example I know of the 'Church Militant'.

... Calais is still held. The stories of the unbelievable chaos in Boulogne during the German entry & our evacuation continue to pour in. B. heard from someone that in one café there were French Belgian – English & German soldiers – all trying to snatch food at the same time. I feel what Harold calls a 'stale ache' all the time at the thought of our force – in that narrow strip between the Germans & the sea.

Diary – Monday 27 May – 40 Gloucester Square, W.2

No news – except of our epic air exploits – moving & almost incredible stories of heroic encounters against terrific odds & almost invariable

---

[1] Mrs Huntington, wife of Constant Huntington, chairman of Putnams publishers; their daughter Alfreeda had become friendly with the Bonham Carters at Fellside in the summer of 1939.

[2] W. B. ('Harry') Harris, headmaster of St Ronan's. The threat of an invasion caused the school to be moved from Worthing, on the south coast. Aldershot, a military base, was also a likely target of enemy action, and the school was finally moved to South Devon.

[3] Reverend James Owen Hannay (1865–1950), vicar of Holy Trinity, Kensington Gore, 1934–50; formerly rector at Mells, 1924–34, and a close friend of Frances Horner, mentioned below; a prolific novelist under the pseudonym George A. Birmingham.

victory. Archie said that he had been begged to issue more credible communiqués – as people cld. not believe that 5 of ours invariably attacked & brought down 15 of the enemy. But he said 'I can only reply that these are facts'.[1] The morale of our pilots & their consciousness of the immense superiority of their machines makes them feel on top all the time. . . .[2]

Diary – Tuesday 28 May – 40 Gloucester Square, W.2

I was woken this morning by a telephone call from Veronica Morhange – asking me 'Do you know what has happened?' in a voice of breathless horror. I said no – & she told me that the whole Belgian Army had surrendered. Of all the blows we have suffered in the last 6 weeks this seemed the worst – & the most completely unexpected. Only last night at midnight we heard that the Belgians were being heavily attacked & that the B.E.F. were going to their rescue. . . .

. . . Winston made a statement in the House in the afternoon in which he said we must suspend judgement. The Belgian Army had fought bravely. The position of our force hemmed in on 3 sides & exposed to violent air-attack was very perilous. Duff gave a courageous broadcast at 9 in which he used the word 'withdraw'. Does this mean that we can get some of them at least away by sea?[3] The 2 awful alternatives of massacre & surrender stare one in the face. B. thinks they might make a kind of Verdun stand – but how can we feed & munition them? The Belgian surrender has opened the road to Dunkirk.

Diary – Wednesday 29 May – 40 Gloucester Square, W.2

The thought of our troops . . . with their backs to the sea gnaws at one day & night. Perhaps one shld be grateful for the sea – the one element

---

[1] Neither side produced accurate statistics: it has been estimated that during the 'battle of Britain' later that year the British exaggerated by 55 per cent (i.e. 40 kills, 62 claimed) and the Germans by 234 per cent (i.e. 40 kills, 133 claimed) (Asa Briggs, *The War of Words*, 261–2).

[2] Violet refers to the air fighting over Dunkirk which took place mostly below 2,000 feet, conditions that favoured the Spitfire. At higher altitudes its adversary the Messerschmitt 109e was 'decidedly superior' because of its engine design (J. E. Johnson, *Wing Leader*, 49). In fact the planes were 'extraordinarily evenly matched' throughout the war (Hugh Dundas, *Flying Start*, 34). Morale varied, depending greatly upon the leadership qualities of individual squadron leaders and their flight commanders.

[3] 'Operation Dynamo', the Dunkirk evacuation, had begun the previous day, when 7,000 men were transported across the Channel; see below, pp. 221–3.

which has always been our friend. But how many can we get away? & what will happen to those who are left?

I went to hear Archie speak at one of Nathan's Dorchester lunches.... I sat next [to] Benes. Stafford Cripps is going to Russia – which I have <u>always</u> wished – & I asked him how hopeful he felt about the results of this mission.[1] He was not very hopeful I cld. see – as he said the ground had been insufficiently prepared, also the Russians are Orientals who are impressed by a display of power – & they will attribute such a mission at such a moment to weakness rather than to strength. Eddie Winterton sat opposite to me. I drove away with Jan [Masaryk]. It was a comfort to see & talk to him. No one has suffered more for his country & with greater courage – & he understands one's suffering now. He told me – in strict confidence – that Maule Ramsay had been in touch with the enemy through a Secretary at the <u>American Embassy!</u> who had also been arrested....[2]

Morhange & Veronica dined. M. says he thinks our force in Flanders is about 150,000 strong & the French about the same. The Germans by talking Lille have now driven a wedge between us. He thinks the French have <u>no</u> chance but will try & draw off the fire from our men & enable as many as possible to get to the sea. He says that <u>no</u> warning was given to either of us of the Belgian intention. It is serious for France that she has lost all her coal-fields. Also the timber (& the paper) situation is bad for us both. Our evacuation of Boulogne was heroically carried thro' under most frightful conditions. Our men remained till the last to blow up the harbour – station – cranes – everything that cld. be of use to the Germans.

Diary – Thursday 30 May – 40 Gloucester Square, W.2

Venusberg lunch – Walter Elliot – Baffy – Bob Boothby – Cressida – Rosemary Hinchingbrooke – Namier[3] – Bob in marvellous form. He said he had seen Roger Keyes the day before – who after a fortnight's liaison work with the King [of Belgium] had returned from Belgium a shattered man. He was in tears when he spoke of the horror raging over there – incomparably greater than anything in the last War – & said no one must pass judgement on the King. Walter Elliot had seen a man, Scott by name,

---

[1] Cripps had visited Moscow in a private capacity in February 1940 and gained valuable experience there. In May Churchill offered him the post of ambassador, and he departed that month.

[2] See below, p. 223.

[3] Lewis Bernstein Namier (1888–1960), historian; professor of modern history at Manchester University, 1931–53; a close friend of 'Baffy' Dugdale.

who had been with the Duke of Gloucester & said during a bombing raid they both lay down on the ground which heaved under them.[1] It was like an earthquake – the noise alone shattered every sense. They were quite unhurt but felt good for nothing afterwards. Our men were getting away – under terrific bombing – but better than we had expected. . . .

We discussed the next German move. Walter Elliot thought it wld be an assault on Paris. Namier said Hitler wld. go for London. He said that ever since 1918 the Germans had been brooding over the mistakes they made last time. One of the principles of Clausewitz was: 'If you have one enemy go for its capital. If you have 2 cut their communications'. In 1914 the Germans made the great mistake of going for Paris instead of taking the Channel ports. This time they will know better. They will try & sever the communications between this country & France & then strike at the capital – London. Compared to which Paris is a mere provincial town. Bob Boothby said it was quite inevitable that the Italians wld. come in within the next 10 days.[2] He & W.E. left having a violent argument about milk.

Diary – Friday 31 May – 40 Gloucester Square, W.2

It appears that we are getting unhoped of numbers off from Dunkirk. Figures like 80,000 are mentioned – one dare not believe them – but the men are coming home. The sea is black with 'craft' of all sorts & sizes from battleships to small yachts & fishing boats who are 'nosing' their way in to the beach – where thousands are waiting. The men swim & wade out to the boats – under a torrent of bombs from the sky. B. heard from a man called Marsham in the City that his son had come back that morning – but that Ld. Erne & [the] Duke of Northumberland had been killed & the Duke of Norfolk was very badly wounded.[3] We had our watch at the Post.

Diary – Monday 3 June – 40 Gloucester Square, W.2

Law told me Sat. morning that she had read in the paper that Kim had

---

[1] Henry William Frederick Albert (1900–74), 3rd son of George V, cr. Duke of Gloucester, 1928; chief liaison officer between British and French armies, 1939–40.

[2] Boothby was only one day out: Italy declared war on 10 June.

[3] John Henry George Crichton (1907–40), 5th Earl of Erne, 1914; with Royal Horse Guards; killed 23 May. Henry George Alan Percy (1912–40), 9th Duke of Northumberland, 1930; lieutenant, Grenadier Guards; killed 21 May. Bernard Marmaduke Fitzalan-Howard (1908–1975), 16th Duke of Norfolk; major, Sussex Regiment; survived.

been killed.[1] It is just a fortnight since he went out. Marigold saw him at the Berkeley & he said to her 'I am off to the races on Friday'. I cannot write about it. One feels an almost impersonal horror & grief. He was I suppose one of the 'predestined'.

I went down with B. to see little Ray. They are 'evacuating' on Monday to go to Ld. Clinton's house at Exeter [Bicton]. He was overcast & quiet – & obviously minded pulling up his roots & leaving St. Ronan's. He took me to see his garden & said rather sadly 'The roses are just coming out'.... We went back in the evening to Beb & Cynthia's – Cynthia warned me that Beb was unwell – she feared high blood-pressure. The last 3 weeks of fighting over the same ground – the same names & places – had re-opened all his old war-wounds that seemed so miraculously healed by Sullington....[2] The weather was incredibly beautiful – hot sun, cloudless skies & summer glory everywhere. We heard a nightingale singing on our way up the drive. Has the piercing beauty of this spring been sent to mock or to console us?

We went in to St. Ronan's for the service in the chapel on Sunday.... Next day I went to see them off – & found them 'queued' up in the garden each with a small suit-case & a paper bag containing their luncheon ration for the day – looking poignantly like 'evacuees'. I went in the bus to the station with them & after a long wait on the platform saw them off ... & felt a disproportionate tightening of the heart. R. had in the button-hole of his grey flannel coat a faded rose from his garden. I lunched with Beb & Cynthia on the shingle in the sun & got back here about 6 – 335,000 have been evacuated from Dunkirk! an <u>incredible</u> figure.[3] One feels boundless relief – & thankfulness.

Diary – Tuesday 11 June – 40 Gloucester Square, W.2

I have not written for a whole week. Last Tuesday Winston made the greatest speech in my memory – one of the greatest speeches in history. Its candour & its courage were alike admirable. He admitted that we had

[1] Rose Law, Violet's maid (below, p. 258). (Ian) Kim Muir (d. 1940), 10th Hussars; a keen falconer, he became friendly with the Bonham Carters when they stayed at Tilshead, in Wiltshire, where he kept his hawks.

[2] Beb and Cynthia Asquith were then staying at Sullington, West Sussex. In April 1917 Beb had fought at Arras, the scene of an armoured engagement between the British and Germans in May 1940.

[3] The public had been prepared for a disaster: Churchill spoke in the House of Commons on 28 May of 'hard and heavy tidings' to come, and he was then expecting to get perhaps 20,000–30,000 men away. But the evacuation proved 'a miracle of deliverance', and 338,226 men were rescued (Martin Gilbert, *Churchill*, 650–6; A. J. P. Taylor, *1914–1945*, 486).

had in Flanders a colossal defeat. We had lost enormous quantities of material – over 1,000 guns. Wars were not won by evacuations. But we shld fight to the end – if necessary alone. On the beaches – on the hills – in the fields – & even if part of England were invaded & subjugated – our Fleet & our Dominions wld bring the new world to the rescue of the old. This was only a breathing space. We must expect a new blow at any moment.

On Wed. 5th June the new blow fell. A tremendous German offensive in France set in – from Abbeville down to Rethel. The size & violence of the battle exceeded anything in the last war. ... Much the same tactics seem to have been employed. Infiltration of tanks – low flying dive bombers etc. The French fought splendidly – but the Germans have gradually reached Rouen – & yesterday they crossed some bridge-heads on the lower Seine. ... The Germans appear to be closing in round Paris. They are 2 to 1 at least in numbers & seem to have an even greater superiority of equipment. There is little we can do to help them – as though we have men – we have lost guns – tanks – & transport in Flanders.

Georges Boris turned up here on Friday & asked us for a bed. He has been all thro' the Flanders campaign as liaison officer attached to a British regiment & got off from Dunkirk. He looks like a haunted man – a shadow of his old self. He hadn't had a bath for 6 weeks & his feet were covered with plaster & blisters. He is in agony about France – & I find him straying in pyjamas round the wireless like an âme-en-peine after we have sent him up to bed with a sleeping draught. I am so terribly sorry for him. He said the Territorials & Militiamen stood bombing better than some of the Regulars – & what shocked us – that the English regiment he was with systematically looted the French Chateaux they were staying in – ransacking drawers carrying off silver etc. – loading things into trucks – & unable of course to take anything away [from Dunkirk] – often not their kit. His regiment did not suffer much. ...

Cys & I had an amusing luncheon [Saturday 8th] with Raymond Mortimer in his delicious rooms. The N.S. is now absolutely 'sound'.[1] He said he had heard a meeting of the P.P.U. denouncing this Govt. in the street as the beginning of Fascism in this country. Desmond came to see me & told me that Tyler Kent (from the American Embassy) who was arrested was their professional decoder – & had transmitted all our most confidential messages to America which is rather sinister.[2] I spent Sunday quietly alone

---

[1] (Charles) Raymond (Bell) Mortimer (1895–1980), literary and art critic for the *New Statesman* and the *Sunday Times*. The *New Statesman* had supported the dismemberment of Czechoslovakia in September 1938.

[2] Tyler Kent, a code clerk in the American embassy in London, was responsible for passing coded telegrams to the Germans; American security was seriously compromised.

here – trying to prepare a broadcast on England for the B.B.C. . . .

[Monday 10th] . . . at 6.30 I went off to the Post for our meeting. Coming out of it Clive (our head-bore) said to me 'I wonder what is going to happen to all the Italian waiters?' I said – 'when Italy comes in?' He replied 'Italy has just declared war on us – Erlanger heard it on the news'. It came through apparently at the very end – the first intimation being the reception of Mussolini's broadcast at 6. It was inevitable – & I only regret the large leak in the blockade all these months – & the humiliating attempts that have been made to placate them.[1] Kites – jackals – vultures – who do not even kill their own prey – but wait for it to be killed for them before they batten on it.

Duff made a fiery broadcast at 9 which was well worth hearing. One cld literally feel his veins swelling at the microphone. It contained one deplorable lapse, of taste & I think of judgement, when he flung Caporetto in their face & accused their Army of cowardice there.

To-day I had tea with Clemmie at the Admiralty, from which they have not yet moved. It was looking cool & delicious – full of flowers – & all their lovely pictures lit up. Clemmie was absolutely her normal self – chirrupy – <u>very</u> sweet – & always a little more amusing than one expects to find her. She talked a lot about the move – which is being delayed partly because of all the private wires which have got to be installed for Winston & which necessitate taking up floors etc. Apparently Chamberlain never even had a telephone in his bedroom. She told me 2 things of interest. One – that W. had said that if anything happened to him he thought the only person who <u>cld</u> possibly carry on the war here was <u>Beaverbrook</u>. Secondly – that Kingsley Wood – whom I criticized strongly for his admin-istration at the Air Ministry, was one of those who <u>before</u> the change of Govt. used to come to W. to say he thought things 'cldn't go on like this'. That when Chamberlain felt he wld. have to go he began by sending for W. & saying 'I shall ask the King to send for you'. Next day however he saw W. & Halifax together & said 'I don't know which of you I ought to ask the King to send for' – W. was silent – as it was difficult for him to say what he felt. Halifax said 'I think I shld be rather a fish out of water'. According to Clemmie it was largely Kingsley Wood who persuaded Chamberlain to recommend the King to send for W.

I can't help suspecting that the old boy was feathering his future nest in advance – & I can't believe that Ed. Halifax wanted it. But Clemmie says she thinks Dorothy H. did. Clemmie also said that a great section of the Tory Party were not behind Winston & had received his great speech

---

[1] It was in British interests to keep Hitler and Mussolini apart, and Churchill had previously recommended (6 October 1939) that the government find ways of doing this.

of last Tuesday even in sullen silence. She said 'I wish I cld say it was not so – but it is'....

Diary – Wednesday 12 June – 40 Gloucester Square, W.2

... In the evening Boris dined & seemed slightly more himself – but when we listened in again to the wireless at midnight he relapsed into despair. The Germans are closing in round Paris & it has been declared an open town. Boris thought they wld. contest it step by step – & fight in the streets. He wld. rather it had been destroyed than that it shld surrender. He is going to Scotland to-morrow to address Munitions workers in Glasgow & Edinburgh – with a heavy heart.

Diary – Friday 14 to Monday 17 June – written a.m. Monday 17th, 40 Gloucester Square, W.2

I went to Winchester on Friday to spend Mark's leave-out day with him – & stayed at the Firths' till Sunday afternoon.[1] He met me at the station & after dropping luggage etc. we strolled out into Meads together & sat there till lunch. The beauty & the peace of Winchester seemed like a mirage – incredibly unreal against the nightmare background of facts – & yet stabbing one like a sword. It was a radiant day. The buildings rose in silvery beauty from amongst the trees – every tree a different green – willows – poplars – planes. The stream along the edge of Meads flowed crystal clear. Boys passed through War Memorial – raising their straw-hats as they went. Very old dons crawled about in the sunshine. All unchanged – & seemingly unaware. We lunched at school-shop on buttered eggs & strawberries. The young waitress bringing in the strawberries suddenly said to us with a bright uncomprehending smile on her face 'The Germans have entered Paris'.

Mark & I walked in the hot sunshine to St. Cross & sat by the edge of the river – an old pensioner with his Holbein hat & silver cross pottering nearby – stunned with the pain we cld. hardly accept or believe. Yet we saw it – Paris, where we were all together[2] – the Seine – the Champs Elysées – the Arc de Triomphe – fountains & lilac & spreading trees –

[1] John d'Ewes Evelyn 'Budge' Firth (b. 1900), Anglican priest (1930), fellow of Winchester, 1922; master of the house through which Mark and Raymond Bonham Carter passed, and a good friend of Violet and Bongie.

[2] Violet had taken Cressida, Mark and Raymond to Paris in 1938, to stay with Toto and Veronica Morhange at their apartment in Avenue Foch.

grace – beauty – freedom – gaiety – civilization. The Germans tramping in – the Swastika flying over it all. We walked back by the other side of the river – had some iced coffee at school shop – where people of all ages were laughing & eating unconcerned – showed the Cathedral to a charming Canadian passing through – who said 'We have got cathedrals in Canada, but nothing like this' – & who knew that Winchester was Camelot.

... Mark feels that Oxford in these conditions wld. be unreal & useless & that he ought to join the young 18–19½ Defence Force. I have written to Ned Grigg asking whether they have equipment & training facilities for them.[1] I went to watch cricket in Meads. The Bank of England playing Winchester. I sat there in a kind of dream. Hills – Meads – Chapel Tower – & the boys playing what seemed like 20 games of cricket in the sunshine – watched by old Trant-like figures – living in some safe, remote & happy past.

Mark was not well on Sunday & I went to Chapel with Mrs Firth & sat with him after luncheon in the sick-wing before going back to London. I shall never forget Winchester as it was these days.

Diary – Monday 17 June [p.m.] – 40 Gloucester Square, W.2

Veronica rang me up in tears. She spoke of Chartres where Toto's people are. The morning papers give the sinister news that Reynaud's Govt. has resigned & that he has been succeed by Pétain. Weygand & Darlan are in the Ministry & thank Heaven the rumours that Bonnet & Flandin are included are not true.[2] Still it does not look good. Why did Reynaud go. It must mean weakening.

At 1 o'clock sitting alone here I switched on the news. Even the announcer's preamble seemed to me to lack its usual Robot confidence – & then it came – the worst – the very worst of all. The French A

The Fall of France – 17 June 1940

Violet's second diary entry for 17 June ended abruptly in mid-sentence, exactly as it is transcribed above. The news that she could not bring herself to record was that Marshal Pétain had ordered

---

[1] Sir Edward William Macleay Grigg (1879–1955), cr. KCMG, 1928; 1st Baron Altrincham, 1945; served with Grenadier Guards during Great War, MC 1917, DSO 1918; Conservative MP for Altrincham, 1935–45; joint parliamentary under-secretary for war, 1940–2.

[2] Maxime Weygand (1867–1965), in command of French army, 1940; favoured armistice; Vichy governor-general in North Africa, October 1940. Jean Louis Darlan (1881–1942), collaborationist admiral and politician; see below, pp. 247–50.

Violet Bonham Carter, photographed by Cecil
around the time of her marriage, November 1915.

'I do really think that some of the boys should enlist. Father will be asked why he doesn't begin his recruiting at home.' (VBC, 31 August 1914) Top, Cyril ('Cys') Asquith, Queen's Westminster Rifles, c. 1915. Bottom, Raymond Asquith, Grenadier Guards, c. 1916.

'Do not care much what happens to me or what I do. When I give thought to it at all, I hate people – people I like – to care for me.' (Rupert Brooke, 4 March 1915) Rupert Brooke, photographed by Sherrill Schell, 1913.

'We have got extraordinarily fond of all the Old Hoods and as each one goes it hurts like nothing else.' (Bernard Freyberg, 12 September 1915) Officers of the Hood Battalion, Royal Naval Division, at Blandford in February 1915. Back row, extreme left, 'Oc' Asquith; middle row, second left, Rupert Brooke; fourth left, 'Johnny' Dodge; fifth left, Denis Browne; front row, third left, Bernard Freyberg; centre, Lt. Col. John Quilter.

'withdrawn safely from that cauldron of horror' (VBC, 2 June 1915): Arthur ('Oc') Asquith (on left) and Bernard Freyberg recuperating from Gallipoli wounds, pictured with Violet in Alexandria, June 1915

'such talks are of great value in keeping L-G sweet' (MBC, 31 December 1915):
H. H. Asquith and David Lloyd George, pictured at the Wharf, 1916.

Low Attends a Women's Meeting at Paisley.

'The Paisley people were wonderful material to work upon - an extraordinary combination of cool heads and warm hearts' (VBC, January 1920): scenes from the Paisley by-election, January-February 1920: (top) 'Mrs Asquith sympathizes with an ex-prisoner of war'; (bottom) Low depicts Paisley politics.

(top) Violet seeks the support of Paisley milliners - most of them still too young to vote; (bottom) the Asquith camp savours victory after the poll, undeterred by the peasemeal thrown at their car by boisterous electors.

Sir Maurice Bonham Carter, or 'Bongie', with his dog 'Butter', late 1920s or early 1930s.

Mark Bonham Carter, while at Winchester.

Bongie, Cressida and Laura
Bonham Carter, pictured at Stockton

Walking on the Downs
– Cressida, Laura and
Violet, early 1930s.

Mark and Raymond at Stockton, 1932

Violet with Raymond and Laura at Stockton

Xmas
1941

'After dinner I listened alone to W's broadcast – in a way the most moving I have ever heard him make' (VBC, 13 May 1945): Violet and wireless set, c.1945.

Churchill, Christmas 1941; a photo kept by Violet.

'He looked well – very thin – amazingly alive' (VBC, 26 October 1943): Mark Bonham Carter with his parents, October 1943, following his escape from a POW camp in Italy

'Back home & then on to meet Beveridge at Dingle Foot's. We handled him quite well I think' (VBC, 23 May 1944): Violet with Sir William Beveridge (left) and Dingle Foot, February 1945

'The "Chair" is not my spiritual home – & I hate "official" positions' (VBC, 29 March 1944): the new president of the Liberal Party, pictured at her desk, April 1944

"WHICH ONE OF US IS SHE GOING TO RESCUE?"

'It all arose out of a speech of Violet's!' (Diana Sandys, 10 April 1945) : David Low's cartoon heralds the return of party politics after the Liberal Assembly, February 1945

'It continues quite lovely up here' (MBC at Balmoral, 6 October 1945): picnic at Balmoral, clockwise: George VI, Taw-Taw Gilmour, [unidentified], Princess Margaret, Queen Elizabeth, Mark Bonham Carter, [unidentified].

the surrender of the French army. The Germans had thus achieved what they had been unable to accomplish a quarter of a century before, and defeated the Allied armies in the field. Only the Channel barred an invasion of Britain. The psychological impact on the British public was immense – it elicited one of Churchill's most stirring speeches the following day. Though the threat of invasion was real, it was not immediate. The speed of the German advance necessitated a pause and it was only on 16 July that Hitler gave orders to his chiefs of staff to prepare for invasion – 'Operation Sea Lion'. Later that month he authorized an all-out air offensive, to begin in August, as the necessary preliminary to a Channel crossing in September. The Luftwaffe, however, was denied air superiority in the 'battle of Britain', and the planned invasion was postponed, before being cancelled on 12 October. By this time German efforts were directed at breaking civilian morale through the bombing of London and other cities. Violet and Bongie worked tirelessly as air-raid wardens during the 'Blitz', which is one reason why the diary so abruptly ended in June was not resumed later that year. It was not until January 1942 that Violet began to keep a journal again, writing short entries in the narrow columns of an engagement book. In the intervening months she was busier than perhaps she had ever been, accepting in March 1941 an invitation to become a governor of the BBC, work that she had to combine with her duties as president of the Women's Liberal Federation.[1]

V.B.C. to Winston Churchill   *Tuesday 10 September*
Clovelly Court, Devon

Dearest Winston – I must write you one line of gratitude for your speech.

There is no adjective I can apply to it. They are all pale & inadequate, & shrivel on the pen. Your sentence about the Air-War – 'Never in the history of human conflict has so much been owed by so many to so few' – will live as long as words are spoken & remembered.[2] Nothing so simple, so majestic & so true has been said in so great a moment of human history. You have beaten your old enemies 'the Classics' into a cocked hat! Even my Father would have admitted that. How <u>he</u> would have loved it! (My

[1] John Colville, *Fringes of Power*, 161; Martin Gilbert, *Finest Hour: Winston S. Churchill, 1939–1941*, 566, 570–1; Craig, *Germany 1866–1945*, 722.

[2] Churchill's famous speech came in a review of the first year of war, in the Commons on Tuesday 20 August, when he praised especially the courage of the RAF airmen.

brother Cys, writing to me about your speech, pointed out that even that cocoa-blooded old Munich-ite Spender referred to it as 'thrilling'! The first time Spender has ever been 'thrilled' in his still-life!)

I am entreating Clemmie to restrain you from going to front-line places like Ramsgate in a tin hat. It may be fun for you – but it is terrifying for the rest of us. Please realize that for most of us this war is a One-Man Show (unlike the last) & treat your life as a guarded flame. It does not belong to you alone but to all of us. I look forward to seeing you when I get back to London in 10 days or so. I hope you aren't too tired. Ever yrs, Violet

V.B.C. to M.B.C.   *Tuesday 10 September*
                                        Clovelly Court, Devon

Darling – I am <u>slightly</u> comforted by your departure by the fact that it is <u>pouring</u> with rain to-day – the first real rain we have had since our arrival here on 2nd August.... There seems to have been quite a bad Raid again last night – tho' the German planes down – 52 – is much better. They say 'bombs in the West-end'. Remember that this bulletin <u>will</u> make me <u>very</u> nervous now you are back & try & keep me in some sort of daily touch – i.e. <u>send a wire in the morning if you have failed to get through the night before</u>.

Love & bless you. <u>Take no risks</u>   Yr V.

M.B.C. to V.B.C.   *Saturday 14 September*
                                        Boodle's, St James's Street, S.W.1

We had an exciting night, which you would have enjoyed very much. The usual raid started round nine o'clock and continued intermittently through the night. I dined at this club where we are being received while Brooks's is shut, and after dinner went with John Christie to Grosvenor House where he is living and we went up on to the roof to see what was to be seen.[1] It was a lovely night the moon being nearly full and from the height of Grosvenor House it was possible to see for miles, but there was little going on except two fires, one in the city or that direction and the other beyond Victoria. So I went home and in due course went to bed – things had meantime livened up a bit and the drone of enemy aircraft above could be heard....

I had undressed and just gone to bed when I heard a noise outside,

---

[1] John Christie (1882–1962), co-founder, with his wife (m. 1931, Audrey *née* St John-Mildmay, a gifted soprano), of the Glyndebourne Opera; see below, p. 242.

which was not more than a slight clatter. I thought it might be an incendiary bomb, or more probably a large bit of shrapnel in the road below, but I got out and went down and found Blackman on the doorstep. He had been watching from there and had heard a noise which he thought was a bomb or one of our shells passing over & falling beyond St John's Church. At that moment three tin hatted men came running down Southwick Place past our door & round the corner into Hyde Park Square. So after them we went and there we found the square lit up by incendiary bombs, one in the square, several at the entrance to Connaught Street and one near Hyde Park St. . . .

. . . The wardens were very pleased with themselves, no rules were followed, no reports were made, no one was recognised as being in charge but all went well. I must post this. Morhange is now working with de Gaulle and is very bored. Love always, B.

M.B.C. to V.B.C. *Sunday 15 September*
Boodle's, St James's Street, S.W.1

I had an excellent night last night as we had only intermittent raids and I spent at least nine hours in bed and slept until tea this morning. Today we saw a thrilling fight over London. I say 'we' because thousands of people must have seen it. It was a morning of sun and fleecy cloud, and a raid was on and no firing from our guns, so it was clear that our fighters were up.

I was in Somers Mews and found a crowd with glasses gazing up into the sky almost above our heads. There, thousands of feet up, was clearly to be seen the lean dark shape of a German bomber and seemingly far above it, wheeling in circles like transparent white sunlit moths, some four or five of our fighters. Suddenly one dived down in a great swooping curve on the tail of the bomber and down went its head in a straight fall through the cloud. It is said to have fallen in bits near Victoria Station. A round white shape was to be seen floating in the sky, which was said to be a parachute, but this has not been confirmed. The crowds cheered as when the first Zeppelin was brought down and how they enjoyed the show. . . .

I have just heard that one of our fighters was brought down this morning so I trust the parachutist was the pilot. Love, B.

Clementine Churchill to V.B.C.   *Saturday 26 October*
                                                 10 Downing Street,
                                                 Whitehall, S.W.

Dearest Violet

The bomb on the Treasury was very bad and, alas, killed two Civil Servants and two messengers. Their bodies were retrieved only last night. We have a very comfortable shelter at No.10. We do not hear much noise, but I fear it is not safe as it is on a level with the garden. But it makes one feel safe and that is a great thing.

I think it very courageous of you to be a Warden, and what you tell me about Bongie fills me with admiration. Please give him my love. I should very much like to see you soon, but we have been 'blown' out of Downing Street and are living in two rooms – one of them your former sitting-room looking on to the garden. We have no gas or hot water and are cooking on an oil stove. But as a man called to Winston out of the darkness the other night, 'It's a grand life if we don't weaken!' Yours very affec^ly, Clemmie

---

A meeting with Stafford Cripps, Friday 13 June 1941

S.C. began by telling me that he thought war between Germany and Russia was imminent, and might break out within the next few days.[1] The Germans would make – if they were not already making – demands on Russia. I asked if he meant economic demands. No, political demands. They might demand the Ukraine and Baku outright.[2] The Russians would concede everything they could, but his belief was that the Germans would try and make it impossible for them to comply – because they wanted to attack them.

This seemed incredible to me, and I said the obvious things about war on two fronts – and how much to our advantage such a development would be. He disagreed, and clearly thought that Russia had little chance of standing up to a German attack. In this new kind of warfare the

[1] Early in June 1941 Cripps was recalled from the Soviet Union for talks in London, against the background of a build-up of German forces along the Russo-German frontier. Churchill had been given intelligence reports in March that pointed to an imminent German attack, but his warnings to Stalin in April were ignored. The Soviet leader was unprepared for war and, as Churchill later observed, 'must have tried very hard to preserve his illusions about Hitler's policy' (Winston S. Churchill, *The Second World War*, iii, 326).

[2] Baku, capital of Azerbaydzhan; Caspian Sea port with access to the Soviet oilfields in the Caucasus.

Germans had only got to send their mechanised divisions in, and once behind the Russian lines they would be paralysed. The country was perfect for tanks and mechanised divisions – flat, wide plains which they could sweep across. . . . He then gave a terrifying picture of a German conquest of Russia, and exploitation of Russia's natural and industrial resources. She could build up there a productive machine equal to America.

How would they force the Russians to work for them? By letting them starve. They could seize the nerve centres of the country – oil, etc. – and have the people at their mercy. (The Russian people have, I reflected, always been at the mercy of someone – whether Czars or Soviets.) . . .

Had the Russian hostility to us been dictated all the time by fear of Germany or by mistrust of ourselves? Both – mainly fear of Germany, but mistrust of this country persisted. They knew there were many people here who still preferred Germany to Russia, and would be quite prepared to take this opportunity, if it materialized, to make peace.

I asked about Stalin. He had seen him only once. He was on a big scale. He did not believe that Germany would win. He believed in sea-power. He said to S.C.: 'You cannot conquer Europe without sea-power'. The Army and Navy were pro-English and disliked the Germans. (This surprised me.)

I asked about their views of Winston, etc. He did not know. It is impossible to know what they think about anyone because one never talks to them. There are only official interviews. They never have dinner or any meal with anyone – no social intercourse is allowed.

Was life there very grim? No, not exactly grim. *Did the people look happy? Were they ever gay?* Well, no – not gay. The children looked happy and well-cared for. Much was done for them. *Was it all communal? Was there any home life?* Again he did not know. They could not see the inside of any Russian home. Lady Cripps had tried in vain to get a permit to visit a factory. I asked him whether he lived there like a diver in a bell – and he admitted it.[1] They saw only the members of the few remaining friendly Embassies – Americans, Turks, Iranians (!) etc. . . . *Had people stopped thinking in Russia?* No, he did not think so, but it was impossible to know what they thought. There was only one official school of thought. . . .

About things here, he realised the obvious truths. Winston was the only man. He had not time to give to the Home Front, and its problems did not challenge his imagination. We agreed that he had made a great mistake in making a 'symbolic' Government instead of one based on intrinsic individual merit. I pointed out that Chamberlain's necessary inclusion in his first Government had made this difficult. . . .

---

[1] As ambassador Cripps found Moscow 'an unfriendly place'; he was tied to official routine, at a time when relations between Britain and the Soviet Union were markedly cool (Colin Cooke, *The Life of Stafford Cripps*, 267).

V.B.C. to Winston Churchill   *Friday 25 July*
                                        40 Gloucester Square, W.2

<u>Invective and Abuse</u>

I am a lover of strong language – and frequently use it. Indeed I have received in my day the high tribute of an appeal from you – a fellow-addict – to 'draw it mild'. (This was, I think, after a slightly disparaging remark from the platform directed at your dear old pal Lloyd George.)

Personally I prefer violence to vulgarity, and vitriol to dirt. (That is a matter of taste.) But I think that (as a Master of the Art) you will agree that the <u>first</u> rule of invective and abuse is that it should hurt the other fellow more than it does you. The object of a verbal assault is to hit your enemy between the eyes, and not to make your own side sick.

'Cassandra's' broadcast has failed in the first object, and achieved the second.[1] It has 'built up' P. G. Wodehouse into a figure (which he never was) and made our own side sick, both here and in America. (I have ample evidence of this – and not from squeamish or cocoa-blooded highbrows – but from all quarters and classes. For instance – a Mess of young air-men flying nightly over Germany express their profound shame and disgust.)

It was generally regarded as an outrage on decency – and therefore deflected condemnation from P.G.W. to Cassandra. (Lying is also usually bad policy. The statement that he did not pay his income tax in America has already, to our detriment, been proved to be untrue there.) It was not on aesthetic grounds alone, but as a piece of rotten and <u>self-defeating</u> propaganda that I opposed it, and regretted that 'full editorial control' over the B.B.C. should be exercised by those who have so little 'ear for music' where the British public are concerned.

I have told Clemmie that if, after hearing it, you can honestly say that this is the voice in which you think England should speak to the world, I will give you £10 – not for a Spitfire Fund – but to spend on a few cigars and some of the classic masterpieces of abusive English prose (which will certainly include several of your own speeches).

Ever yours – still red in tooth and claw – battle ready but gutter-shy – Violet

---

[1] Violet objected to the content of a propaganda broadcast by 'Cassandra', directed against the novelist P. G. Wodehouse (1881–1975). Wodehouse had lived in France and been interned by the Germans in 1940. On his release in 1941 he made five radio broadcasts in a comic vein to America from Berlin. These aroused hostility in Britain, where he was portrayed as having bargained for his release by broadcasting for the enemy. Cassandra's comments were nevertheless considered libellous by the BBC's lawyers, and Duff Cooper, who had insisted upon the broadcast, was compelled to promise the board, which had opposed it, that he would take full responsibility.

V.B.C. to M.B.C.　　　　　　　　　　　　　　　*Saturday 2 August*
　　　　　　　　　　　　　　　　　　　　　　　Clovelly, Devon

Darling – Berwick is naturally a great disappointment – as I think it would have been an ideal seat ... & it seems a wasted opportunity for the Party not to have got in <u>someone</u> (not necessarily <u>me</u> of course!) who wld. have cut a little more ice for the Party in Parlt. & outside.[1] (I daresay I shld. have cut far less in Parlt. than people wld. have expected of me.) However it is quite clear that no more could have been done – & I should have hated to go to a place where I was not acceptable & welcome – or on which I had been in any way 'thrust'. (It seems a little hard that my pitch shld. have been queered by Mrs. Hilton Philipson!! but women are still judged collectively & men on individual merits.[2] I must admit that women have so far been rather disappointing in Parlt.) I think Mark & Raymond are even more disappointed than I am! As you know I am not a very ambitious woman – but I shld. have liked to be in this particular Parlt. which may have the shaping of the conditions in which peace will be made....

We all wish you were here.... All my love. I must recast the future in my own mind. I fear I had counted too certainly on the prospect of Berwick & it is a 'nice thought' gone – Ever yr V.

V.B.C. to M.B.C.　　　　　　　　　　　　　　　*Sunday 3 August*
　　　　　　　　　　　　　　　　　　　　　　　Clovelly, Devon

Darling – I write you a line to enclose in Mark's. We have had another lovely day of sun. Church in the morning. In the afternoon Mark, Ray & I walked towards Mouth Mill ... now after supper Raymond is dancing like a 'Jitterbug' to the Polish National Tunes before the News. He & Mark are <u>most</u> sweet together. Ray really adores him – & roars with delicious laughter & Mark is divine to him. I hate to think how much separated they are going to be in the years immediately to come when Mark will be in the Army – & his short leaves will rarely coincide with Ray's holidays....

I feel an increasing, rather than diminishing, disappointment about

---

[1] Berwick became vacant with the elevation of the Liberal Sir H. M. Seely to the peerage. Under an electoral truce agreed September 1939 by the three main parties, the seat would remain Liberal, unless won by an independent. George Grey, a near contemporary of Mark Bonham Carter at Winchester, was selected and returned unopposed on 18 August.

[2] Mrs Hilton Philipson, *née* Mabel Russell (1887–1951), had been Conservative MP for Berwick, 1923–9.

Berwick. I had counted on it with <u>far</u> too great certainty. . . . I feel also that my expectations must have been partly based (tho' I did not consciously realize it) on over-rating my own attempts at service to the Party – a pitfall I did not think <u>I</u> shld. be likely to fall into. Of course I have always realized that my relationship to Father was the main source of any 'goodwill' I reaped – but this also was an element which I felt might have carried some weight in this emergency. What I don't quite understand is why the Executive put my name forward <u>at all</u>. . . . All our love – & longing to see you – Ever yr V

V.B.C. to Gilbert Murray

Saturday 3 January 1942
The Manor House, Mells, Somerset

My dear Gilbert . . . Every New Year wish to you & Lady Mary & all yours. My family, like most, are widely scattered, Mark – who left Balliol in June – is now a full-blown Grenadier – Cressida's husband Jasper Ridley is in Libya (60th Rifles). She started a baby on his last 'embarkation' leave – which makes her happy. Laura is in Scotland – also expecting a baby. (Brave children to enter this world at this moment! – but I know they are right.)[1] My little Raymond (12) is with me on 'holidays' & still a passionate politician. I am sometimes sad to think I shall not live to watch his progress through the new world.

All my love dear Gilbert. I am very sad at this temporary severance from L.N.U. My B.B.C. work is fairly exacting & alas! we meet that day from 1 o'clock (sometimes to 8 or 9!) Ever yrs, Violet

Diary – Sunday 8 February – 40 Gloucester Square, W.2

Streets a sheet of ice over snow – skating going on on the Serpentine when B. & I went out for a short walk in the afternoon. Otherwise work indoors – reading Intelligence Reports & listening in to excellent B.B.C. Programme – 2nd Dorothy Sayers play – not so good as the first – but good. <u>First-rate postscript by Stafford Cripps.</u>[2] B. saw Jasper after tea who said he <u>feared</u>

---

[1] Cressida had a son, Adam, on 14 May, and Laura a daughter, Grizelda, on 27 February.

[2] Cripps gave a graphic account of the hardships endured in Russia in a common cause, infinitely worse than anything experienced in Britain, and questioned: 'Are we going "All Out"?' (*Listener*, 12 February 1942, 195–6). Violet later recalled that the talk made 'a deep impression': 'It was a calm broadcast – delivered in his very beautiful voice. It was a change from the war-like broadcasts we had been inspired by – & it coincided with a critical mood which had set in here.' Churchill had not broadcast in the previous six months, and Cripps' postscript greatly enhanced his own position: 'in some quarters there were murmurings that Cripps might be an alternative P.M.'.

Bubbles' regiment was in action.[1] Singapore Dock flooded. Bombs & shells falling in the town.[2] No news of Libya. Mark looked in on way back from Amberley.

A meeting with Winston Churchill, Wednesday 11 February

I lunched at 10 D. St. Went there early at Clemmie's request to see her <u>first</u> alone. I spoke at once about the plight of Singapore – & she said that W. cld. not understand our troops falling back there – as we had 100,000. To my amazement she expressed doubt as to whether they cld. be <u>fighting</u>. Later I mentioned Stafford Cripps. She said she had liked his Postscript to the News on Sunday but that W. had thought it <u>awful</u>! taking special exception to the passage in which he urged every one to do his share – having himself refused to take a job in the Govt.[3] She clearly did not like S.C. personally ('My dear I think he's an odious man – & very ambitious') & said she felt sure he wld. not hit it off with W. temperamentally. With his ascetic teetotal & vegetarian habits he wld be censorious of W.'s cigars & brandy. I said 'No – W. wld. be censorious about Cripps's raw grated turnip diet – but not vice versa.'

 . . . W. came in – dressed in his siren-suit. He looked disturbed I thought – almost tears in his eyes. His first words were 'The Evening papers are running the <u>Japanese</u> news in their head-lines.' I said – 'Are things not as bad in Singapore as they say. Is there a chance that we can hold it?' He said 'How many troops do you think we have got there? Now have a guess.' I said Clemmie had told me there were 100,000 – & their quality must be good – the Australians. 'Yes not only Australians – but some of our finest British troops. They outnumber all the Japs in the Malay Peninsula. They shld. be able to hold it.' – I said 'But what about aircraft? isn't that the trouble as it was in Crete? Haven't we only one airfield out of gun-range?' He said that was true but that in the last war in France we had held on against artillery fire & shelling when we had only 2 rounds a day

---

[1] By 'Jasper' Violet here refers to Jasper Ridley senior, father of her son-in-law Jasper 'Bubbles' Ridley.

[2] Singapore was Britain's principal naval base in the Far East, and of great strategic importance. It was threatened by the Japanese invasion of Malaya in December 1941. Though a substantial number of troops were committed there, insufficient attention was paid to its defence.

[3] On 26 January, three days after Cripps returned from Russia, Churchill offered him the ministry of supply. Cripps rejected this unless it was accompanied by a seat in the war cabinet, since he regarded the department as being under the control of the minister of production, Beaverbrook. Churchill rejected this demand (A. J. P. Taylor, *Beaverbrook*, 508).

to fire back – & not given way....[1] I was disturbed by the fact that W. seemed to have hopes of holding Singapore <u>not</u> shared by the uninformed. He girded at the Press – the headlines 'grave disquiet exists' etc. I said that I thought the Press had on the whole behaved well to him – & that he was very blessed compared to my Father who had had the whole of the Northcliffe & Beaverbrook machines mobilized against him. He said 'Not Beaverbrook – Max hadn't got any papers yet. He didn't buy the Daily Express till much later.[2] But your father fell because he was stabbed in the back by Ll.G. I never stabbed Neville Chamberlain in the back. I supported him'. I agreed – & did not add that it was not <u>Ll.G.</u> whom the Press had attacked for his personal treachery – but my Father, who was guiltless of it....

W. talked about the composition of the War Cabinet. He defended Greenwood on the grounds that his heart was sound – & that he had 'spoken for England' – on the famous occasion in the H. of C.... He then said 'You are a friend of Cripps's aren't you? You wrote to me about him when he was here last, urging me to take him in (to the Govt). Well I made him an offer – a very good one – & he turned it down. Why shldn't he accept Supply? He has no administrative record at all.' I asked why he had refused – 'Because he wanted to be in the War Cabinet. Lots of people want to. You cld fill the Albert Hall with people who want to be in the War Cabinet.' I said I did not think Cripps was actuated by personal ambition in his refusal. I thought he had great intellectual integrity – whatever might be said or thought of his judgement. If he had refused it was probably because he felt the whole arrangement to be unworkable.[3] W. seemed unconvinced by this – 'What has he ever done? What post has he ever held? He wasn't a success in Russia. Stalin didn't care about him. Stalin never even said goodbye to him. He behaved most discourteously to Cripps.' (This with feigned shockedness but actual relish!) ...

From time to time he said 'I'm fed up'. On criticism – 'I feel very biteful & spiteful when people attack me.' – 'I don't want to be surrounded in the War Cabinet by a lot of people who want to beat me up. How can I cut the Labour Ministry in two – as they want me to do.' etc.

[1] Violet later discussed Churchill's depressed spirits with Harold Nicolson: 'underneath it all was a dreadful fear, she felt, that our soldiers are not as good fighters as their fathers were'. Nicolson shared this fear: 'Our men cannot stand up to punishment.... And yet they are the same men as man the merchant ships and who won the battle of Britain. There is something deeply wrong with the whole morale of our Army' (Nicolson, diary, 12 February 1942).

[2] Churchill was mistaken; Beaverbrook (Aitken) acquired control of the *Express* almost three weeks before Asquith's resignation (A. J. P. Taylor, *Beaverbrook*, 99–100).

[3] Violet later recalled: 'I continued to urge him to offer Cripps another more compatible job. But he only grunted resentfully. As we came out of lunch Clemmie whispered to me: "Go on at it. You are making an impression. He will have to do it in the end." '

Again & again he said rather wearily 'I'm fed up'. Then cheered up a little when we talked of Walter Sickert's death & gave a very amusing account of W.S. coming down to Chartwell to teach him to paint.[1] W. rushing in out of the garden where sunlight was blazing & begging W.S. to tell him how to transfer the marvellous greens & purples he saw onto the canvas – & W.S. refusing to put his nose out of doors. He sang a song which Sickert had crooned at dinner over his wine (of which he drank as much as possible) ending with the refrain 'Charlie Dilke, he spilt the milk – Out of the Gladstone Bag'. Bright interlude from Clemmie about her youthful adventures with Sickert when 16.

Back to business again. He said he was urged to add talent to his Govt – 'but where is the galaxy?' He became sombre again – & my heart went out to him when he said to me again & again 'I can't get the victories. It's the victories that are so hard to get'.

Diary – Friday 13 February – 40 Gloucester Square, W.2

Awoke thinking of nothing but Singapore – to read in headlines that the Scharnhorst & Gneisenau had <u>sailed down the Channel</u> – & thro' the Straits of Dover.[2] Their presence was only reported when they had reached Boulogne – too late for the Navy to intercept them. They were attacked by aircraft & destroyers but reached port in Heligoland Bight. We lost 42 Aircraft. Every beard in England will feel singed. I am <u>sorry</u> for Winston. This is a further blow. Lunched with S. Warburg at Browns Hôtel. Deeply disturbed about production position – slowness of decisions – mediocrity of Govt personnel etc. Instanced absurd arrangement in defence of aero-dromes (defending force to be dressed in Khaki when on duty – in A.F. uniform for 'walking out' & on ceremonial occasions!) Went with Griffin to see 'Citizen Kane' at the Elephant & Castle Cinema. Far the most remarkable film I have ever seen in my life – by a young man in the 20s called Orson Welles who produced & also acted it. Written round the life of Hearst. Cldn't sleep for excitement.

[1] Sickert had died on 22 January 1942, aged eighty-one. Painting played a cathartic role in Churchill's life and he had first taken it up in 1915 in the weeks following his loss of the admiralty.

[2] The warships sailed from Brest to Germany. The *Gneisenau*, crippled by torpedo and bombs the previous year, was irreversibly damaged during this journey, while the *Scharnhorst* was sunk in December 1943.

Diary – Sunday 15 February – 40 Gloucester Square, W.2

C. got a cable from Bubbles saying he is safe – thank Heaven – sent 7th Feb. Warmer day with gleams of sun.... Clear reactions of public shock thro' escape & Channel passage of German ships – which won't be helped by fall of Singapore when it comes.[1] Went for 2 walks – Cony Benck-endorff & Nathalie came to tea. Cony thinks Peter Masefield is right in suggesting the ships tho' sea-worthy were not battleworthy & therefore chose the Channel route. But the reflection on our Air Reconnaissance & Intelligence Service is inevitable.

A meeting with Stafford Cripps, Thursday 19 February

Stafford Cripps and his wife were coming to dine with us alone. After careful inquiries about his bizarre diet I extracted from her the concession that we should be allowed to give him cooked instead of raw carrots for a change. The thought of offering him a raw turnip on this Arctic night sent a shiver down my spine. After my last week's talk with W. and the breakdown of their negotiations I didn't feel we should have a very cheerful evening – and anticipated wringing our hands together and wondering where we should go next.

He came in looking very cheerful with those strangely bright and pierc-ing eyes. His first words were: 'Well – what do you think of the new Government?' I gasped – and he then told me that he was in the new War Cabinet and Leader of the House....[2] He said the whole thing happened in the last two days. W. had been very nice about it. He had received him quite friendlily yesterday.... W. had asked whether he wished to wind up the debate on Tues & Wed. but he had said no. He was going to keep quiet & learn about the H. of C. first.

---

[1] Singapore fell that day; 62,000 empire troops were taken prisoner. That evening Churchill broadcast to the nation: 'Here is another occasion to show – as so often in our long story – that we can meet reverses with dignity and with renewed accessions of strength.... Let us move forward steadfastly together into the storm and through the storm' (*Listener*, 19 February 1942, 239).

[2] Churchill's cabinet restructuring in mid-February reflected recent criticism of the govern-ment, and there were important changes. Attlee became deputy prime minister and dominions secretary, and Cripps succeeded him as lord privy seal. Arthur Greenwood (on 22 February) and Kingsley Wood left the war cabinet, though the latter remained chancellor. Oliver Lyttelton (1893–1972), Conservative MP for Aldershot, 1940–54, became minister of war production, 1942–5 (in war cabinet, 1941–5). Beaverbrook, whom Lyttelton replaced at production, 12 March, declined Churchill's offer of ambassador in Washington (A. J. P. Taylor, *Beaverbrook*, 508–17).

... [Cripps] Very critical of W's broadcast – his allusions to millstone – bickering – national unity etc. – 'What wld he have said if I had said I had got Russia into the war?' Asserted that W. had been a flop in America. Said that apart from fan-mail he had innumerable letters congratulating him on not going in to the Govt – & urging him to stay out & form a possible alternative. He said he wld get many letters of abuse to-morrow for joining it. ...

V.B.C. to Winston Churchill   *Sunday 22 February*
                                          40 Gloucester Square, W.2

Dearest Winston – One line of love & congratulation on your new cast. I welcome some of the departures ... as much as the new arrivals Stafford Cripps & Oliver. I feel sure that you will feel your burden lightened by the change.

As to possible divergence of opinions, you may have more to contend with. But friction breeds sparks. Unanimity may become a comfortable slough. Cripps's mind is a keen-edged & finely tempered instrument which I am sure that you can use to advantage – & I think he has absolute intellectual integrity (& the further advantage of being unhobbled by any party allegiances).

Also though he feeds on raw turnips & other unpalatable cattle-fodder he contrives to keep burning what Carlyle called 'fire in his belly' – & this is a rare & useful quality nowadays – when so many stomachs seem to be lined with asbestos. (I was relieved to see he smoked a cigar when he dined with me on Thursday!) The changes have had a great reception – & I am sure you were wise & right in making them. The pole-axe is painful to wield I know for one of your affections & loyalties. I wish you had a greater 'galaxy' of untried stars to choose from – I always remember your saying to me at a dinner at Mary Elcho's – at which I first met you – 'We are all worms – but I do believe that I am a glow-worm'. You never said a truer word – but oh! for more glow-worms!

Godspeed to your new team. Swimming far behind you – but always behind you – 'into the storm & through the storm'. Ever your B.D., Violet

Diary – Friday 6 March – 40 Gloucester Square, W.2

... Tea with Isabel Cripps & very interesting talk. Beaverbrook has not gone to U.S.A. & there are baleful rumours that he may not go. W. is so overburdened & overtired that he finds it difficult to make decisions involving risk. Ministry of Supply needs cleaning up – as it is at present a close corporation of I.C.I. & the Air Ring. She feels the effect on W. of the public's sudden coldness & the Hallelujah Chorus with which S.C. is being hailed & fears it may queer the pitch of their relationship. . . .[1]

Diary – Tuesday 10 March – 40 Gloucester Square, W.2

. . . Terrible statement by Anthony on the Japanese atrocities in Hong Kong. Our soldiers & officers tied hand & foot & then bayonetted to death. Appalling treatment of civilians. No Protecting Power or Red X allowed to intervene. What a nightmare – & for those who have sons there what agony.

Diary – Sunday 21 June – 40 Gloucester Square, W.2

. . . Listened to 6 o'clock news & to my horror heard that the Germans & Italians have announced the fall of Tobruk & 25,000 prisoners.[2] The blackest possible news. Is Bubbles back at the frontier?

Diary – Monday 22 June – 40 Gloucester Square, W.2

Lunched H of L with ʊ̀. In the evening went to BBC Maida Vale where the Leningrad Symphony by Shostakovitch was being given for the 1ˢᵗ time in this country (written during the siege of Leningrad). Maiskys & Cripps's came. Sat between Mrs Maisky & Stafford Cripps. S.C. told me fall of Tobruk was completely unexpected – Auchinleck thought he cld hold it.[3] Sitting in the boudoir about 11.30 I thought I heard front door bell ring. Later it pealed again insistently. B. went down to answer it – I went on telephoning to Cys. When I had stopped B. stood before me & said 'The telegram has come.' I said 'Bubbles?' – 'Yes' – 'Killed?' – 'No – Missing –

---

[1] Harold Nicolson recalled conversation in the BBC canteen the previous week: 'It is generally agreed that Winston's position has been much shaken. [Vernon] Bartlett puts it well: "Winston could not get rid of Stafford Cripps but Cripps could get rid of Winston"' (Harold Nicolson, diary, 26 February 1942).

[2] Tobruk fell to the Germans on 20 June. Violet gives a conservative estimate of the number of prisoners, which may have been more than 30,000; in addition large quantities of supplies were captured.

[3] Field Marshal (Sir) Claude John Auchinleck (1884–1981), cr. GCB, 1945; commander-in-chief in India, 1941, 1943–7; in Middle East, 1941–2.

since May 26th.'[1] Night of unforgettable agony wondering how to tell C.

Diary – Tuesday 23 June – 40 Gloucester Square, W.2

... At 3 o'clock B was just starting for Mockbeggars when Ly Ampthill rang me up. She said that some names had just then 5 minutes before come thro' from Geneva – as prisoners of war – amongst them Jasper Ridley with an Army N°. I telephoned W.O. & found from Army List there was no other J.R. in the Army. Overwhelming & unspeakable relief. Telephoned C – who poor darling not knowing the background was very dashed to hear B. was a prisoner. With Rommel driving on thro' Libya & 8th Army lining up for a fearful battle on the frontier I am thankful that his life at least is safe.

Diary – Monday 6 July – 40 Gloucester Square, W.2

Back by 7.10 train. Lunched with Maynard Keynes at Univ. Club. Very well & excellent company as ever. Thinks large reinforcements of material have arrived in Egypt which are being poured in by Auchinleck now. Thinks the war cannot last 2 more winters – & that in the next 6 months we shall at least know how it is going to end.... Winston hates being criticized or bored – but if stood up to reacts well. More sensible than anyone else if he can be reached: not always possible. Even if the Germans reached the Caucasus oil they wld find great difficulties in transporting it. Stafford Cripps' shares have gone down rather with his colleagues. He makes statements which he cannot thoroughly substantiate (surprising this). 'Hate-love' relationship had always existed between him & the government.

Diary – Thursday 8 October – 40 Gloucester Square, W.2

Very long Bd meeting. Demonstration of Eye-Witness account of Parlt (by Ryan) most amusing – but terrified Harold! who seems to regard MP's as

---

[1] Bubbles' unit had been involved in the battle of the Gazala line, which began 26 May; German and Italian forces struck at, and captured, this major defensive position of the 8th Army, before going on to take Tobruk.

sacrosanct – & appears to ignore our duty to interest public in Parlt.[1] Sat till nearly 7 o'clock.... Stalingrad still holding – R.M. thinks it will hold out – & that the Germans lost the War 6 weeks ago when they failed to take it. Griffin thinks war will only be won by German casualties....

Diary – Friday 9 October – Glyndebourne, East Sussex

Went down with B to Glyndebourne to stay with his friend John Christie – one of the best Queeriboos I have ever met.... Delicious place.

Diary – Saturday 10 October – Glyndebourne, East Sussex

I was rather surprised (as we eat out here in the chauffeur's cottage) to find our host in full evening dress. Even more surprised to find that he comes down in it to breakfast in the morning. Sheets of rain over this lovely downland country. 100 sweet children in the Nursery School in the house – happy scuttling about in little coveys – laughing – mobbing me like small birds – <u>beautifully</u> looked after. Walked in woods in the rain with B. in the afternoon. J.C.'s Manager – a nice, sad Austrian called Bing & his Russian wife our only fellow-guests.[2] Saw the Opera House – stage décors etc.

Diary – Sunday 11 October – Glyndebourne, East Sussex

Lovely day of sunshine. Sat out all the morning writing an article on F.A.'s for the Star. Walked on the downs with B. to an old earthwork camp. Lovely views over the country below – the Ouse winding thro' it – back to talk to our host about Opera – B.B.C. & the Nat. Conscience. Eat marvellous grapes & peaches & B. drank '1st Folio' wines. We are manacling German prisoners as a reprisal & they are now going to manacle 3 times as many

---

[1] The mock-broadcast of parliamentary business, by the news-editor A. P. Ryan, began 'Under the blaze of four hundred lights, the House of Commons today discussed fuel economy.' Harold Nicolson preferred objective to subjective reporting: 'I argued that the moment you got comment or colour, you were bound to cause offence. Violet argued that the House of Commons is the worst House we have had for a century, and that they ought to be exposed to criticism. Why should they be protected?' (Harold Nicolson, *Diaries and Letters 1939–1945*, 247–8).

[2] Rudolf Bing (b. 1902), Austrian-born impresario, and general manager of the Glyndebourne Opera, 1936–49; married, 1929, Nina *née* Schelemskaja.

of ours. Foolish policy. We can't compete with them in horror – nor deter them by it.

Diary – Monday 12 October – 40 Gloucester Square, W.2

Back to-day. Our host this morning dressed in Tyrolean clothes – white woollen stockings – shorts – white cricket boots – & a curious leather harness across his chest. Coped with domestic complications & found [that] the parlourmaid, who had refused to come on our terms, wld consent owing to the cook being an R.C. Gaffed her for to-morrow. Sent off my article. Talk on Fire Fighting at the post. . . .

Diary – Thursday 15 October – Fulling's Mill, Winchester

Interesting B.B.C. Bd. Got them to reject fatuous recommendation of Music Committee about 'Enemy Composers'. Considered Chief M.O.H.'s request for a broadcast on the terrible spread of T.B. & V.D. – 40 p.c. increase in latter on pre-war; 70,000 new notified cases this year. Felt that it was a matter for Govt. advice. Major question of policy. Health of troops here (including Americans) to be weighed in the balance against use which wld be made of it in Germany – & in U.S.A. Morrison rumoured to be taking steps towards compulsory examinations. Left by 5.30 train for Winchester. . . .

Diary – Thursday 22 October – 40 Gloucester Square, W.2

Rather an amusing B.B.C. meeting. Fraser back from U.S.A. – <u>intact</u> – having learnt & forgotten nothing – only put on 10lbs in weight.[1] As usual he raised the point of pinkish & leftish Broadcasters – Vernon Bartlett being considered particularly dangerous to the Troops![2] His most priceless remark to me was 'But Lady Violet you want to reform things – you live in a little world of your own'. . . .[3]

[1] Sir Ian Fraser (1897–1974), Conservative MP and governor of the BBC; see appendix of biographical notes. He and Violet disagreed on most things political.

[2] (Charles) Vernon (Oldfield) Bartlett (1894–1983), Independent Progressive MP for Bridgwater, Somerset, 1938–50; journalist with *News Chronicle*, 1934–54.

[3] 'Fraser tries to defend the view that right wing people ought to speak merely because they are right wing and irrespective of whether they have anything to say. Violet objects. He says to her "But Lady Violet you live in a tiny world of people who believe in reforms. We don't believe in reforms"' (Harold Nicolson, diary, 22 October 1942).

Diary – Wednesday 28 October – 40 Gloucester Square, W.2

Maud lunched with me. I went afterwards to the Home Office to a deputation to Herbert Morrison led by Archbishop of Canterbury, Cardinal Hinsley & Whele[?] the head of the Free Churches to ask for the admission of 2000 Jewish children from Unoccupied France into this country to prevent them from being shipped off to Germany.[1] Morrison spoke for $\frac{3}{4}$ of an hour from a dusty departmental brief & refused <u>everything</u>. I have never seen a deputation so mishandled & so angry. They cld have torn him to bits. Bill Astor intervened rather well....[2]

Diary – Monday 2 November – 40 Gloucester Square, W.2

Winston's remark: 'I have had many heavy crosses to bear in this war – but perhaps the heaviest of all has been the Cross of Lorraine'. Keynes to Jasper: 'The only man who cld succeed W. as P.M. if some catastrophe happened to him is the Archbishop of Canterbury'. Came back in time for lunch – worked all the afternoon. Summoned to meet Mrs Roosevelt at M. of I. to-morrow afternoon....[3]

Diary – Tuesday 3 November – 40 Gloucester Square, W.2

... Went to M. of I. at 2 o'clock to receive Mrs Roosevelt in a large room which gradually filled up with a monstrous Regiment of Women. Mrs R. arrived about 2.15. She is as ugly as sin but made a <u>very</u> good speech natural – easy – personal – well-delivered. Tentative – not confident & overwhelming. No 'figure-head' here cld have done it as well. Delicious dinner with Betty at the Lansdowne Club & excellent talk. Christine very pretty. Bett angelically gave us a chicken – dozen eggs, pot of jam & some pears.

[1] William Temple (1881–1944), archbishop of Canterbury, 1942–4. Cardinal (Arthur) Hinsley (1865–1943), Catholic archbishop of Westminster, 1935–43. 'Unoccupied' France means the area under Vichy control.

[2] William Waldorf Astor (1907–66), Conservative MP for East Fulham, 1935–45.

[3] The first lady arrived in London on 23 October, the guest of the king and queen, with whom she stayed at Buckingham Palace.

Diary – Thursday 5 November – 40 Gloucester Square, W.2

Last night sitting alone in the boudoir working I chanced to switch on the Wireless at 11 o'clock at what shld have been the end of the Gaelic News. To my amazement I heard a special announcement being broadcast in English – describing a great victory in Egypt. The 8th Army had driven two wedges into the Germans, taken 9,000 prisoners & 2 German Generals & were still advancing. It seemed too good to be true. We claim 600 Aircraft destroyed – 300 in the air & 300 on the ground.[1] Board Meeting. Mark rang up to say that he had had sudden orders to leave Pirbright & report at Wellington Barracks.

Diary – Friday 6 November – Mottisfont Abbey, Hampshire

Went to see Stafford Cripps at 12.15 to talk to him about prisoners & our deputation to Morrison about refugee children. He was sympathetic & helpful about the deputation but put up a bad case about the prisoners. We had to 'react' to the German action. If we hadn't done it people wld have complained the other way, etc. A wedge had been driven between Hitler & the High Command by our action, etc. . . .

Diary – Saturday 7 November – Mottisfont Abbey, Hampshire

This place lovely as ever. Day opened wet but became lovely – warm & sunny. Trees glowing like burning bushes. Beeches beacons of red & gold. . . . Egyptian advance continues 20000 prisoners, 350 tanks, 400 guns. We are just south of Mersa Matruh with mobile units. Terrible bragging interview with Montgomery in Daily Telegraph. Pity our 1st victorious general shld be a bounder of the 1st water![2] Spoke to Mark on the telephone last night. . . . To his surprise & ours he was told he was to go out to Libya almost immediately to join the 6th [Battalion]. He is to have a fortnight's leave to get equipment. Rather a shock to me. He seemed excited & quite pleased tho' he wld have preferred the 3rd with Nigel.[3]

---

[1] The battle of El Alamein was won on 4 November, when Rommel's Afrika Korps retreated westwards from Montgomery's advancing 8th Army; it marked a turning point in the North Africa campaign.

[2] A week later Violet wrote in her diary: 'Further nauseating utterance by Montgomery! "Good hunting" has succeeded "in the bag" as his favourite phrase.'

[3] Nigel Nicolson (b. 1917), younger son of Harold; at Balliol; with 3rd Battalion Grenadier Guards, North Africa and Italy (captain; despatches, 1944).

Diary – Sunday 8 November – Mottisfont Abbey, Hampshire

Woke in the morning & asked housemaid if there had been any news on the Wireless. She said she thought there had been an American landing in N.A. B. listened at 10 on European News & it was confirmed. They had landed at several ports – Oran – Algiers – Casablanca & Gen Giraud had made an appeal on the Algiers Radio for the French to help. There had been a rising in Morocco – suppressed according to Vichy. This is the news we had been waiting for 2 months.[1] In Egypt 40,000 prisoners – 500 tanks. Advance continues. Lovely day. Short walks in sunshine under autumn leaves with Conrad.[2] Heard Hitler's speech – also de Gaulle & Roosevelt in French.

Diary – Wednesday 11 November – 40 Gloucester Square, W.2

Mark & I lunched H. of C. with Victor & Keynes whom I had asked.[3] K. in excellent form. Talked of planning – Archbishop (of whom Maynard is a strong supporter), the Beveridge scheme (not yet out) & the present situation. What our next move shld be – occupation of Sardinia – Sicily. The Germans have moved into unoccupied France. German air-born troops have arrived in Tunis. Got a seat in B.B.C. box by a miracle & heard Winston's speech. Quite excellent. No flights of rhetoric & no undue exhilaration over victory....[4]

Diary – Thursday 12 November – 40 Gloucester Square, W.2

Mark & I lunched at N° 10 with Winston who was in splendid form – very confident that we shld wipe out Rommel with his force altogether in N.

[1] The Allied invasion of French North Africa, 'Operation Torch', began in the early morning of 8 November. In an attempt to extinguish the resistance from French forces loyal to Pétain, the Allies turned to the Vichy general, Henri Giraud (1879–1949). Giraud appealed for a French ceasefire, in return for Allied recognition as the supreme commander of all forces in the region. The Allies, however, had miscalculated on his influence and his appeal was ignored. In Roosevelt's estimation, a 'dud' (Charles Williams, *Last Great Frenchman*, 192–7).

[2] Conrad George Edward Russell (1878–1947), Balliol contemporary of Raymond Asquith; stockbroker turned farmer.

[3] Lieutenant-Colonel Victor Alexander Cazalet (1896–1943), Conservative MP for Chippenham, 1924–43; political liaison officer to General Sikorski and a good friend of Violet.

[4] In his account of El Alamein Churchill echoed the sober message he had delivered at the Lord Mayor's luncheon the previous day: 'Now this is not the end. It is not even the beginning of the end. But it is, perhaps, the end of the beginning' (*The Times*, 11, 12 November 1942).

Africa. He was very interesting about his visit to Stalin (who said he had had a far worse time with the Kulaks than he was having at present). Also about the reasons which led him to bump off Auchinleck – & the assembly of the great Armada of ships that carried out the invasion of N. Africa. Darlan had given no orders to the French Fleet as yet.[1] It was at Toulon with the French Army round it in a ring fence. He had a marvellous sentence about democracy's duty being not to conceal but to confuse – 'not the silence of the oyster serene in its grotto – but the smudge & blur of the cuttlefish'. Bd Meeting.

Diary – Sunday 15 November – 40 Gloucester Square, W.2

Cold foggy day spent indoors working at my confounded Lecture. Darlan has to my horror been recognized by Eisenhower as a plenipotentiary in Northern Africa. Giraud accepts appt. from his unclean & Vichy-tainted hands & ends a proclamation to the troops bracketing the name of Pétain with that of France – 'Curiouser & curiouser' – & not at all pleasant. Mark returned late after spending Sunday with Ray.

Diary – Friday 27 November – 40 Gloucester Square, W.2

Shopping for Mark – sandgoggles, steel looking glass, etc.... Borises to dinner & talk about the French situation. At 9 o'clock dramatic announcement most movingly told that the French Fleet had scuttled itself when at 4 o'clock in the morning German troops entered Toulon & attempted to seize it. Admiral de Laborde gave the order.[2] André Philip has been seeing Roosevelt, who said to him – 'I welcome de Gaulle. I welcome Giraud. I welcome Dakar for Darlan & wld welcome Paris for Laval.'[3]

[1] The Vichy admiral, Darlan, had arrived in Algiers shortly before the Torch landings, and entered into negotiations with the Allies. In return for recognition as 'high commissioner for North Africa', Darlan agreed to announce an armistice covering French forces in the region. His authority was widely respected, where Giraud's had not been. The military benefits to the Allies of the 'Darlan deal' had to be balanced with the political cost of making a pact with a Vichy leader (Charles Williams, *Last Great Frenchman*, 195–206).

[2] Darlan was unable to deliver the French fleet at Toulon to the Allies, and on 25 November the Germans attempted to seize it. The order was then given for it to be scuttled; 170 ships were destroyed (Charles Williams, *Last Great Frenchman*, 200).

[3] André Philip (1902–70), French academic, socialist deputy and resistance leader. Roosevelt pragmatically defended the 'Darlan deal', saying that he would make an alliance even with the Vichy chief minister Pierre Laval (1883–1945) if it secured Paris. When Philip saw Roosevelt, though, the president was already in the process of abandoning Darlan.

Diary – Thursday 3 December – 40 Gloucester Square, W.2

Arctic day – B.B.C. Discussion of Beveridge Report which is (amusingly) being 'plugged' Overseas for its propaganda value – & so cannot be altogether overlooked at home.[1] Beveridge broadcast last night on Bracken's suggestion – my colleagues having been very timid & said that of course he cldn't be allowed to go to the microphone to expound his own scheme. Fraser excelled himself by saying that Darlan stood for Fighting France!

Diary – Monday 14 December – 40 Gloucester Square, W.2

Committee at 1 at Gayfere St – shopping for Mark. Got him morphia & other drugs at Savoy & Moore. (Fortnum's luxury altars were covered with W.C. paper!) ... Back to wait for Mark who arrived just before 8. Dined at Causerie. He said to me 'One can't take in the big things. I realize the dentist so clearly – but not that to-morrow I shall be gone'. Saw him off at Paddington 12.5 – 'As many farewells as the stars in Heaven'.

Diary – Tuesday 15 December – 40 Gloucester Square, W.2

Attended L.P.O. Executive at 2 & went on to Beveridge's wedding party at the Dorchester. The bridal pair were there – hot from the altar with a vast gathering of guests – Maisky – Winant – Keynes – Layton – etc. Frank Pakenham master of ceremonies.[2] Speeches. Rather a long shy-making & elaborate one from her son who had a complete black out in the middle. Then Brendan – very good – & finally Clem Davies. Champagne beakers in which their health was drunk – then they replied – Beveridge good & simple as ever – Mrs Mair perfectly composed. I had a short interchange with Clemmie over Darlan in which she – to my amazement – completely lost her temper & nearly emptied a glass of champagne over herself & me saying 'I used to think you were an intelligent woman'![3] Last telephone

[1] Publication of Beveridge's report on *Social Insurance and Allied Services* had been delayed until 1 December because members of the cabinet thought it 'too revolutionary' (José Harris, *Beveridge*, 419). Violet later noted that it was 'acclaimed by [a] Hallelujah chorus of praise on all sides' (diary, Wednesday 9 December).

[2] John Gilbert Winant (1889–1947), American ambassador, and a friend of the Churchills. Sir Walter Thomas Layton (1884–1966), cr. Kt, 1930; chairman, News Chronicle Ltd, 1930–50. Francis Aungier Pakenham (b. 1905), cr. Baron Pakenham, 1945; Beveridge's personal assistant, 1941–4.

[3] The Darlan episode was deeply embarrassing to Churchill, who had to reconcile an outraged de Gaulle to the deal.

talk with Mark. He passes thro' to-night & leaves from St Pancras – but told us not to come.

M.R.B.C. to V.B.C. *mid-December*
pre-embarkation camp

Dear Mama,

Forgive this letter being in pencil, but at the moment the facilities for writing, or indeed for anything other than eating & sleeping, are distinctly mediocre. I don't at the moment feel particularly inspired & this letter is one which I must scratch off before going. I write perched on my bed in a small room with six other officers. Their qualities or defects I have not yet had time to analyse as so far I have only seen their baggage.

I read your letter, & I thank you for it. I will keep it with me. It is as you say a wrench to leave but my imagination is so weak that I can't really convince myself that next weekend I won't be taking my ticket for London, & spending it with you & the others at Gloucester Square. I cannot here & now recapitulate all the delicious things I remember or the many familiar things to which I hope to return, but they are always in my mind. It is funny to think that I will not see you & Dada & everyone for at least two years, so odd & unnatural that I cannot imagine it. But it is exciting to be going on a journey, not in an entirely casual manner, but for a purpose which one can understand, & with which one can agree. I wish I could have come to Bev's party. It must have been amusing. I hope you gave him my love....

... Thank you once more for your letter, & thank you always for everything. I have always had every opportunity, now I must see if I can use what I have learned. All my love, to you & everyone, <u>Mark</u>

Diary – Christmas Day, Friday 25 December – Clovelly Court, Devon

Got up in the dark & went to early service with Ray, B., Christine.... The windows of the church looked lovely, glowing amber thro' the dark – candles lit within. Back to breakfast & <u>church-bells</u> – rung for the 2nd time since the War. R. very happy with his stocking & silver snake-chain gift from B. We went to church again at 11 & then I had a short breather. On my way in to lunch I passed the door of what is now the Hospital Staff dining-room. I overheard their wireless 1 o'clock saying something about Darlan – rushed in to listen. <u>He was assassinated</u> yesterday afternoon by a young man of unknown nationality! What a niblick shot out of the bunker! Fate has been kind for once.[1] Cavendish family to lunch. Then listened to King's speech, better delivered than usual. Walk to Gallantry Bower – Tea – Carols & Xmas Tree with the soldiers.

Diary – Thursday 31 December – 40 Gloucester Square, W.2

Took R. to bad picture Exhibition at Academy. Then on to Bd Meeting. Dined in with Toto & Diana Grey. Toto interesting about Darlan assassination. The assailant was a Free Frenchman & <u>may</u> not have been executed he thinks.[2] Wire of good wishes from Winston – & Clemmie! First letter from Mark – written before embarkation. Held up a fortnight.

---

[1] Darlan was assassinated in Algiers on 23 December by a young Gaullist, Fernand Bonnier, who had Free French and British backing (Charles Williams, *Last Great Frenchman*, 201–5).

[2] Bonnier had been executed, after a summary court-martial, on the morning of 26 December.

NINE

Mother and Son

1943

I was born the third child and the first son of my parents on February 11th 1922. My mother, who was a woman of Gudrunish emotional force, directed much of this at me, a fate I shared with my elder sister Cressida & which was largely avoided by my second sister Laura and my brother Raymond, who was seven years younger than me. She invested in me many ambitions & many of the high hopes which for her, as for so many of her generation, had been frustrated by the slaughter in the trenches.... She loved passionately, cared meticulously & had the highest expectations of her children.

Mark Bonham Carter, autobiographical fragment

Mark is – he has been all his life – the light of my eyes, my pride & hope & Morning Star. Even if in these skies his star has set, I am still greatly blessed to have possessed him. He felt passionately about the issues of the war & bent all he had – a brilliant mind & a nature in which gentleness & power are strangely blended – to the task of fitting himself to fight for them.

Violet Bonham Carter to Winston Churchill, 6 April 1943

Diary – Friday 1 January 1943 – 40 Gloucester Square, W.2

Started the New Year by a very barren Committee meeting at Gayfere St. from 10.15 onwards on the 'Structure of Industry'. Back to lunch & on with Ray & Sir Ian Hamilton (aged 90 a fortnight ago) to a vast splendid Pageant at the Albert Hall. Massed Guards bands – British Legion – all the Allies & their banners – every 'Service' male & female – the Merchant Marine got far the biggest reception, & the Soviet Union a much better one than U.S.A. Four magnificent prelates appeared at one moment on thrones among the flags – the Archbishop in purple, the Cardinal in Scarlet, the Moderator & Rabbi in black. The only flaw a <u>very</u> long speech by Stafford Cripps – read from a copybook in a pulpit voice. One cannot turn over pages standing among flags at the Albert Hall....

After the Albert Hall we went back to tea with Sir Ian & Mrs Shields (his Secretary?). The table made us blink. Never as Ray said – even in peacetime or on a film – had we seen such a tea. <u>Three</u> iced cakes & one plum! Pyramids of sandwiches with little flags labelled 'foie gras' 'shrimp & salmon' – piles of short-bread – 2 pots of jam – hot tea – cakes. Sent Mark a telegram to Durban.[1]

Diary – Sunday 3 January – 40 Gloucester Square, W.2

Bright cold day. . . . George Grey came to see me for an hour in the morning. Talked about future Liberal policy, possibility of Stafford Cripps adhesion . . . future Liberal economic policy, American lack of co-operativeness – suggestion that I shld succeed Ld. Meston as Chairman of L.P.O. (which I certainly shld not welcome!). . . .

Diary – Wednesday 6 January – 40 Gloucester Square, W.2

Lunch at N° 10 with W., Clemmie, 2 Crippses, High Commissioner for S.A. (Waterson) & talkative wife – & Garvin with the most rolling migrant eye I have ever seen.[2] W. greeted me by saying 'Well you were glad about Darlan.' I said 'It was the making of my Xmas day – my Xmas stocking.' He said 'I believe you wld have done it yourself' – very smiling & mellow. I sat between Cripps & Garvin. Cripps & W. will never be 'Buddies', <u>that</u> is certain. W. talked of S. Africa – the greatness of Botha & Smuts who were big enough to <u>accept</u> self Govt. in the spirit in which it was given. Ireland cldn't. I said it was offered too late. He talked of India – 'I'm pro-Moslem – the only quality of the Hindus is that there's a lot of them & that's a vice' – of the Empire 'One cld defend it against everyone except the British – always wanting to despoil themselves – decry themselves etc. Why shld we be hailed before the bar to defend our own record? We are fighting this war for our lives. The old ways were good ways – decent ways.' – Cripps – 'Wars always lead to change' – Waterson – 'They are a kind of world General Election' – Winston – 'Well let's make sure we have the right register.'

I talked to W. afterwards about the Jews – about which I had written him a letter – & told him what I thought of Morrison – which he took well. Then we talked about Darlan – he <u>half</u>-defending. He said 'One must

[1] The sea journey by which Mark Bonham Carter was to join his regiment in Egypt meant going via South Africa, with stopover in Durban.

[2] Sidney Frank Waterson (1896–1976), high commissioner for South Africa in London, 1939–42; married, 1924, Hilda *née* Markus.

have a bull's eye. We are fighting this war against Hitler' – I said 'No – against <u>evil</u>'. Clemmie very mellow & conciliatory.

M.R.B.C. to V.B.C.   *early January*
                                     On board a troop ship,
                                     en route *for Egypt*

Dear Mama ... We spent new year in port – a delicious & very appropriate introduction to Africa, although we were not allowed ashore owing to beriberi (due to eating <u>polished</u> rice) malaria yellow fever etc, & in consequence I had to watch it through Dada's telescope. It was I must say all that I expected. A blue sea, with flying fish twiddling their gills, black negroes, <u>very</u> black, in boats diving for pennies, huts & bungalows on a malarious shore & behind, romantic Persian blue mountains covered with 'scrub'. I was so excited by it that for some days after I was quite sure that all I wanted to be was a Colonial Civil Servant. My imperialistic instincts are, I may say, on the march. The tantalizing view from my ship, made me long to, & determined to, see more of the Brit Empire (particularly African & S. American)....

It's very odd to think that one day this journey will be a blurred & indistinct memory, that I will find it difficult to remember some of the people on this ship, & that I will forget the sequence of events. At the moment it seems so very distinct, & different, like a silhouette in clarity, against the background of everything else up to now. It's also very odd looking over the side of the ship, & seeing land, & thinking that at that point Africa begins & the sea, which is much the same here or in England, ends. It seems surprising that it should start so suddenly, & that it should be so clearly defined....

I hope you had a delicious Christmas holidays at Clovelly. I do envy you that, it must have been delicious. I must say there are two things I yearn for, one to go for a walk in the country & to be able to walk without turning round every few yards, & the other is to sleep in a large high Victorian room, with a vast bed, & a kind of mahogany smell about it. However the first of my desires is I trust about to be satisfied, the second can very well wait as it is neither very acute, very important, or very necessary, & as it is in any case quite premature, for I am living & sleeping in perfect comfort as it is.

I trust you can read this. Give my love to one & all & tell Toto his pouch is exquisite, Miss Law & Nana that their socks are excellent. All Love Mark

Diary – Wednesday 27 January – 40 Gloucester Square, W.2

The long expected news of the meeting between Roosevelt & Winston was announced at 3 o'clock this morning in our European Service. I had <u>felt</u> W. was out of the country for some time (he leaves a vacuum which I am always aware of) & besides this Transocean & other Axis wireless stations have been saying for the last 10 days that he was in Washington. Toto told me 2 days ago that the rumour at French H.Q. was that he was in Morocco. B. thought Roosevelt wld not be allowed to leave the country. Giraud & de Gaulle have also met. Toto said de Gaulle seemed very cheerful last night – slightly less so today. . . .[1]

V.B.C. to M.R.B.C.

Thursday 28 January
40 Gloucester Square, W.2

Darling Mark – We had quite a noisy air-raid here on the night of 17th–18th just before Ray went back to school – & a bad day one which killed a lot of children in a school.[2] Reprisals for Berlin – otherwise all quiet. The Casablanca meeting is now announced, also de Gaulle's with Giraud which everyone hopes will clear the air.[3] The Russian successes are dazzling & the German wireless to their own people incredibly sombre. The change is very sudden & makes one feel things <u>may</u> be worse there than we know. . . . Are you basking in sunlight I wonder & eating fruit?[4] We rang up Arthur Penn yesterday but he had no news of you to give us.[5] Love Mama

---

[1] Roosevelt and Churchill met at Casablanca 14–15 January to decide on strategy after the conquest of North Africa. A key issue was who should be recognized as the leader of the French forces of national liberation, and with what powers they should be accorded. Far from resolving these questions, Casablanca made clear the difficulties ahead, not least in reconciling the diverse strong characters involved – Roosevelt, Churchill and de Gaulle (Charles Williams, *Last Great Frenchman*, 209).

[2] At the time Violet thought that around thirty children had been killed, but the final figure was near sixty, with around fifty injured (*The Times*, 22 January 1943).

[3] De Gaulle and Giraud were then locked in a struggle to determine who would command the Free French forces. By the autumn of that year, de Gaulle had won. Casablanca did little to settle their differences (Charles Williams, *Last Great Frenchman*, 212–14).

[4] Mark Bonham Carter was probably near Cairo, waiting to join the 6th Battalion on its journey to Tunisia where it would participate in the 8th Army's attack on the Mareth Line.

[5] Arthur Horace Penn (1886–1960), regimental adjutant Grenadier Guards, 1941–5.

Diary – Saturday 30 January – 40 Gloucester Square, W.2

Hitler will not speak today – the 10th Anniversary of his Accession to Power. For him to be 'sealed lips' shows he must be on a sticky wicket.... Heard Goering's speech which was delayed an hour by a daylight raid of our Mosquitoes.[1] It dealt entirely with the Eastern Front – the horrors of Bolshevism etc. England only mentioned once as having betrayed Europe.... Heard Goebbels.[2] Amazed by beauty of his voice.

Diary – Tuesday 2 February – 40 Gloucester Square, W.2

Committee all day ... Woman Power at H. of C. 4 to 6. Passed a resolution in which I spoke strongly about Refugees (Jewish). Mrs Tate & Nancy Astor thoroughly unsound – trying to shelter behind Anti-Semitic feeling in this country.[3] I told them it was a thing to be fought, not kow-towed to – a disgrace to this country – representing a victory for Hitler. When I got home to my <u>delight</u> I found Mark's 1st letter awaiting me on the slab. It is 7 weeks today since he left. It was undated – & held no clue to where it was sent off & he said that censorship prevented his saying anything he wanted to. They had had a very rough journey – in circs. of great discomfort. Very different from Bubbles's luxury liner. He had not <u>been</u> sick but felt it for several days. Midnight news announced final capitulation in Stalingrad area.[4]

Diary – Thursday 18 February – 40 Gloucester Square, W.2

Afternoon spent at B.B.C. – Beveridge Debate still raging.[5] Kingsley Wood's speech had a disastrous effect & the Lab. Party & our people are in revolt. Archie has met them twice with no effect. A. Greenwood withdrew his name from his motion & moved another expressing dissatisfaction on

[1] Hermann Goering (1893–1946), commander-in-chief, Luftwaffe; president of the Reichstag, and Hitler's designated successor.

[2] (Paul) Josef Goebbels (1897–1945), director of Nazi propaganda.

[3] Mavis Constance Tate *née* Hogg (d. 1947), National Conservative MP for Frome, 1935–45.

[4] The German 6th Army under the command of Field Marshal Friedrich Paulus (1890–1957) surrendered on 2 February 1943, ending the six-month siege of Stalingrad; the Germans lost more than 250,000 men, killed or captured, in what proved to be one of the decisive engagements in the war.

[5] The Beveridge debate lasted three days, 16–18 February. It concluded with a vote on a Labour amendment that called for a stronger government endorsement of the report; though defeated by 335 votes to 119, this marked a substantial rebellion against the government.

which he divided the House. Our people all voted against the Govt. with the exception of Graham White & Jimmy Rothschild.[1] G.W.'s vote is to me quite unaccountable as he is a man of conscience & courage I shld have thought. Division – 119 voted against Govt. All the Young Tories caved in. Quintin Hogg after roaring like a lion voted like a lamb.[2] Worked late recasting my speech for Oxford.

M.R.B.C. to V.B.C.   *Thursday 18 February*
                                           6th Bn Grenadier Guards, M.E.F.

Dear Mama,

Thank you for three airgraphs & an air letter card I received today.... I have joined the battalion after a very brief wait. Only Jack A[llsopp] & I have, the others remain at my previous address. It is an almost entirely Etonian battalion, & in consequence I know very few people here, & none at all well. This makes the initial immersion rather more alarming, particularly as all the military staff is new to me as well.

My company (No 1) is commanded by Peter Evelyn, age 34?, appearance older, demeanour at first stern, mentally fox hunting, general character rather attractive, very kind, sense of humour $\alpha\beta$, military ability I should say excellent though not inspired.[3] Second in Command Nic Villiers, other members – John Wiggin, Nicholas Durham, a nice R.C.[4] Forgive this squirmy pencil, but I have no pen here, & the facilities are rude. My first few days were I must say alarming, rather like going to school again, only the people more humane. It made it much better having a platoon & therefore something to do, rather worse being the first newcomers to the Bn for nearly a year....

... Owing to the energy of my Coy Comdr we live very well here, plenty of food & drink, & perhaps what I most lack is time to read, & a slightly

---

[1] (Henry) Graham White (d. 1965), Liberal MP for Birkenhead East, 1929–45. James A. de Rothschild (d. 1957), Liberal MP for Isle of Ely, 1929–45.

[2] Quintin McGarel Hogg (b. 1907), fellow of All Souls, Oxford, 1931–8; Conservative MP for Oxford, 1938–50; commissioned Rifle Brigade, 1939. Hogg had stated that the report 'deserved warmer support than the Government had in fact given it': 'If they did not give the people social reform the people would give them social revolution' (*The Times*, 18 February 1943).

[3] Peter G. Evelyn (d. 1943), major, 6th Battalion, Grenadier Guards; died of wounds after being taken prisoner during Horseshoe battle, Mareth Line, 17 March 1943. Evelyn's wife wrote to VBC, 3 May, 'The first time I heard of him [Mark], Peter was rather disgusted at having his Old-Etonian party marred by a Wykehamist!'

[4] J. H. Wiggin, (later) captain, Grenadier Guards; MC, 1946. Nicholas J. R. J. Durham, lieutenant, killed during Horseshoe battle, 17 March 1943.

more intellectual companion.... As you say it's so boring having no time limit, no days to tick off, no end of term. I can't say that I want to stay here longer than I need, but I do feel very well, & look rather like a prawn.... I wrote Raymond a very dull airgraph. I'm glad Budge enjoyed the Joys. I yearn for the ballet – Love Mark

Diary – Friday 19 February – The Master's Lodgings, University College, Oxford

Went to Oxford & was met by a young man Dunn from New College who gazed at me a very long time but made no attempt to find out who I was. Changed like lightning at the Beveridges'. 'Bev' was attempting to put up black-out on the top of a very high cupboard when I arrived, with Simian agility. Dined at the Randolph [Hotel] with Dunn, Miss Park & the Pres. of the Union. Audience of about 60 I shld say including Christine & Jean & B. Spoke for over an hour (to my horror).[1] Then back to coffee at the Randolph. Long talk with the Bevs when we got back about the debate etc. His feelings are natural but he is very reticent as he has to hold them up for an impending article in the Observer. He says that he is now bored with his Report & wants to get on to something new. They have no servants at all. Spring-like evening – lovely sky with towers & spires grey on red.

V.B.C. to M.R.B.C.[2]   ***Sunday 28 February***
40 Gloucester Square, W.2

Darling – Not much news since I wrote last.... Excellent article in Observer by Beveridge pointing out in crystal clear & icily dispassionate language that the Govt. have jettisoned the central idea of his whole Report – i.e. the right of everyone to a minimum subsistence level. Both Archbishops have weighed in publicly for the Report which will I imagine be the signal for 'wigs on the green' for those who think the Church ought to be a kind of Civil Service – dumb about, & indifferent to, social issues....
    I had quite an interesting lunch tête-à-tête with Kenneth Clark on Fri.

---

[1] At the Oxford Union, Violet attacked the 'New Conservatism' recently proclaimed by Quintin Hogg in the *Spectator*: 'It has taken a world-war to educate him & many like him. The education of the Conservative Party has been & is going to remain an expensive business for this country. It costs us a great deal more than the Beveridge Report....'.

[2] Returned marked 'Missing 17.3.1943'.

at Bucks Club.[1] He <u>is</u> I think clever & has done an immense deal for art & young painters. He is also politically enlightened. George Grey made a good speech in the Debate (Beveridge) very badly reported. I haven't seen him since. Yesterday was little Sigele's 1st birthday! – I thought of her arrival in Edinburgh this time last year – of Laura & I driving out of the hôtel in the dark of early morning crunching over the snow in the silent streets. I am occasionally aware in the blurred time-table of the war of the extraordinary speed of passing years. I expect that to you time is <u>crawling</u> now – because you are doing so many new things. I long to know if you are still quite static or whether a move is approaching. . . .

The Canon came to tea with me yesterday – in <u>excellent</u> form & breathing fire – tho' nearly 80 he tells me. Miss Law is collecting <u>money</u> for you against yr. return! For this purpose she has boned a fund of 9/8 which we had collected 2 years or more ago for Refugees! & on yr. birthday told me she had added 5/ of her own to it. No protests from me as to misappropriation of funds raised for charity wld. move her an inch! She just replied obdurately: 'No – that's for Mark. 'E can 'ave it – better than them Refugees'.[2] Love & blessings, Mama

Diary – Wednesday 3 March – 40 Gloucester Square, W.2

I took the Chair for Bev. at Caxton Hall lunch-hour meeting.[3] I was never more surprised than when I drove up. The street outside was seething with a mob of people who were being turned away literally in hundreds. Their fury & despair was a new experience – after these years of political apathy & indifference. Here was <u>something</u> which people passionately longed to hear about. Bev. arrived & was made to sign numerous caricatures etc. of himself – then we went 'on' & addressed a <u>packed</u> Hall. He spoke very well – tho' being a <u>lecturer</u> & not a platform speaker he didn't end on his

---

[1] Sir Kenneth Mackenzie Clark (1903–83), cr. KCB, 1938; director of the National Gallery, 1934–45; controller, home publicity, ministry of information, 1939–41.

[2] Rose Law was a cockney, and a great figure in the lives of all of Violet's children. Jo Grimond remembered: 'Had she chosen to desert Violet she would have made a fortune on music-halls. . . . She and Violet engaged in a long-running "turn", Violet barking at her and Miss Law shrugging her shoulders . . . before with perfect timing producing like a conjuror whatever Violet had lost' (*Memoirs*, 95).

[3] The first in a series of lunch-hour talks organized by the Liberal Party for those living and working near Westminster. Violet introduced Beveridge as one of the '6 most famous' men in the world, 'counting in Hitler, which perhaps it is only fair to do': he was 'the first & perhaps the only man who in this war has given people hope – definite hope – that on the other side of victory there lies a new & fairer, freer world – & told us in plain terms how we may win & build it for ourselves' (Violet Bonham Carter MSS).

top-note.[1] He was photographed outside 'chatting' to soldiers – & at St Ermin's Hôtel we were again photographed repeatedly for Picture Post during a (disgusting) lunch!. . . .

Diary – Thursday 4 March – 40 Gloucester Square, W.2

Board Meeting all afternoon as usual. Good altercation with Ian Fraser. When denouncing the B.B.C. for having allowed the freedom of the Air to L.N.U., New Commonwealth, etc. in pre-war days he says 'It never gave us Winston'. I pointed out with some force that W. was the last person he & his Party had wanted – that they had howled him down – that it was the left which had supported him. Terrible accident in Bethnal Green Shelter where 175 people were killed. A woman fell on the stairs & a man on the top of her – pressure from behind flung one on the top of the other in heaps & they were all asphyxiated.[2]

V.B.C. to M.R.B.C.[3]
Sunday 7 March
40 Gloucester Square, W.2

Darling – I forget if I told you that the Canon who came to tea with me (& has a grandson in Irish Guards) was lyrical about the Guards & said 'They are just like an old order of chivalry'. I had a telegram from Winston to-day thanking me for a letter & small bunch of violets I sent him; also a letter from Laura – well & grappling with both children alone quite successfully. Just back from a Sunday walk in the Park with Dada – Forsythia & Almond in full bloom & countless sea-gulls circling over the Round Pond & Serpentine. I went yesterday to see a short news-reel film of the capitulation of General Paulus at Stalingrad. It is one of the most indescribably painful things I have ever seen – Paulus twitching with nerves & embarrassment opposite the Russian General who is interrogating him – in the glare of the cinema apparatus which is playing on him. Also the unspeakable misery & hardship with which the faces of the German prisoners are steeped. Paulus ought of course to have died. I can imagine

---

[1] 'The street outside was a seething crowd of people trying in vain to get in & being turned away in hundreds. I haven't seen such a sight since before the last war. He spoke very well – tho' he is not of course a "platform" speaker – & does not work up to a climax & sit down on it' (VBC to MRBC, 5 March 1943).

[2] The Bethnal Green underground station was being used solely as an air-raid shelter; 178 were killed and 60 injured in this tragedy (*The Times*, 5, 6 March 1943).

[3] Returned marked 'Missing 17.3.1943'.

no worse torture for Hitler than to see this film. The sneering commentary which accompanied it made me feel ashamed. I am longing for more news of you but realize that I have no right to expect it as yr. last letter arrived (with incredible speed) on the 1st March. I do hope you are feeling more at home & discovering some unsuspected affinities – or that new ones are rolling up.... Dada sends his love. All mine – send as much news as you can – Yr Mama

Diary – Wednesday 10 March – 40 Gloucester Square, W.2

... On the day after the American reverse in Tunisia a friend of Griffin's going thro' Covent Garden met a coster who said 'Good news today Sir', to which he asked: 'Have the Russians done well?' 'No – the Americans have got the knock.'[1] This was a universal reaction.

M.R.B.C. to V.B.C.   *Friday 12 March*
6th Battalion Grenadier Guards,
8th Army, Tripoli

Dear Mama,

Note this new address, & note also that air letter cards are the most satisfactory form of communication. For the last few days I have been so busy that I really haven't had a moment to write or even to think. We took part in a successful action & suffered hardly at all, but I am back with my platoon.[2] The journey we came was extraordinary & interesting. We drove all the way from Cairo through all the famous battlefields – familiar names, Sollum, Bardia, Tobruk, Derna etc....[3] My first experience of battle consisted mainly of being shelled & bombed. Mainly the first. It was fairly

[1] On 20 February the American 1st Army lost the Kasserine Pass in Tunisia to Rommel's Afrika Korps; it was a significant, but not decisive, reverse for the Allies.

[2] Mark Bonham Carter participated in the battle of Medenine, on the morning of 6 March. The Grenadier Guards played only a supporting role and it was the Scots Guards who bore the brunt of the German attack, which ended after the loss of fifty-two tanks. The victory persuaded Montgomery to press ahead with his plan to attack the Mareth Line on 20 March (Nigel Nicolson and Patrick Forbes, *The Grenadier Guards in the War of 1939–1945*, ii, 295–6).

[3] The 6th Battalion had left Qatana in Syria on 7 February, arriving at Medenine on 2 March after an epic drive of 2,200 miles. Within four days of arrival the Battalion was in its battle position facing the Mareth Line: 'There are few who took part in the desert drive who do not retain of it an impression of mounting excitement' (Nigel Nicolson and Patrick Forbes, *The Grenadier Guards in the War of 1939–1945*, ii, 290, 294).

alarming in a mild sort of way, but for us anyhow, it was impersonal. The result was highly satisfactory.

There is I am sure more to come – so far I have seen no one outside the Bn & my life has been a whirl of activity. It seems a long time since I saw you all, though really I suppose it is ridiculously short compared with those who have been here six years. I often think of Gloucester Square, London & Tilshead with nostalgic pleasure & I hear of Russian & Allied success with prospective pleasure. Give my love to everyone, here I am very happy with my fellow officers & my pl. Thank you for your many letters, I enjoy them all –

Love Mark

Diary – Saturday 13 March – 40 Gloucester Square, W.2

Went to Desert Victory with C & B – wonderful & moving war-film. I <u>think</u> the best that I have ever seen. It came to life to me thro' thinking all the time – <u>this</u> is the country Mark is travelling through – at this moment – the way that he may have to fight. . . .

'Baptism of Fire': the 6th Battalion Grenadier Guards
and the battle of the Horseshoe, 16–17 March 1943

Violet followed with immense interest and pride the progress of the Grenadier Guards through North Africa, and she later went to great lengths to establish the details of the confused engagement in which her son Mark went missing on the night of 16–17 March. The battle was a part of a concerted Anglo-American bid to win an outright victory by defeating the German and Italian armies in Tunisia. Barring the advance of Montgomery's 8th Army from the east was the Mareth Line, a French-built fortification defended by the Afrika Korps. Before the main attack on this could begin on 20 March a small group of hills in a horseshoe three miles to the south had first to be taken. These were not thought to be strongly defended, and Montgomery decided to blood the Guards Brigade newly arrived from Syria. He assured the 6th Battalion shortly before the battle: 'When I give a party, it is a good party. And this is going to be a good party.' On this occasion his renowned self-confidence was misplaced. While the Germans had forewarning of the attack, which began in darkness at 7.30 p.m. on 16th, the Guards were unaware of the existence of two dense minefields in their path. Heavy German artillery combined with exploding mines to make the battlefield a bewildering place. After crossing the first minefield Mark Bonham Carter literally collided with his company commander, Peter Evelyn, who asked: 'Do you suppose this always happens in battles?' Showing great resolve, three companies of Grenadiers took their objectives in the hills, but soon discovered that they were isolated. Most were evacuated the following morning, but a shortage of space in the transports meant that a small contingent was left behind, including Evelyn and Mark Bonham Carter. Before the inevitable surrender later that day Evelyn had been mortally wounded, and another officer, Nicholas Durham, killed. Mark Bonham Carter was the only officer from his company to survive. The regimental history endorses Montgomery's verdict that despite not attaining its objective the engagement was 'on the whole a great success'. Churchill came to a different conclusion, regarding it as 'unsuccessful and costly'. A fortnight after the battle, on 30 March, Violet was informed that her son was missing. Later that day she attended a meeting of the BBC board and Harold Nicolson recorded in his diary: 'Poor Violet, she is in a dreadful state. She says to herself, "On that day, at that hour, we were drinking coffee and listening to the wireless.".... She spoke so calmly, and then she broke down. Now, when silly people cry, I am merely irritated. But to see a strong person, and one whom I so deeply admire, break down and sob, is to me a real anguish.'[1]

Diary – Thursday 25 March – 40 Gloucester Square, W.2

Long altercation at Bd. Meeting as to whether it wld or wld not be in the national interest for Beveridge to broadcast – as he offered me on Monday to do. Harold & I supporting & the rest against. An ingenious motion of the Chairman's staved off a division. I have come to the conclusion that Millis is an even more rigid reactionary than Fraser – whose very cynicism gives him flexibility![2] No news from Tunisia except that fighting continues – 'Artillery Duels' reported....

[1] Nigel Nicolson and Patrick Forbes, *The Grenadier Guards in the War of 1939–1945*, ii, 295–309; Mark Bonham Carter, 'Baptism of Fire', in the *Observer*, 4 April 1993; Winston S. Churchill, *The Second World War*, iv, 686; Harold Nicolson, *Diaries and Letters 1939–1945*, 288. For the German view see the aptly named chapter 'Hell in the Mareth Line' in Heinz Werner Schmidt's, *With Rommel in the Desert*.

[2] Sir (George) Allan Powell (1876–1948), chairman of the BBC, 1939–46. Charles Howard Goulden Millis (1894–1984), managing director, Baring Bros. & Co. Ltd, 1933–55; vice chairman, BBC, 1937–45.

V.B.C. to M.R.B.C.[1]   ***Thursday 25 March***
                                      40 Gloucester Square, W.2

My Darling – We are thinking of you all the time & wondering whether you are in this battle & how you are faring. It is so strange to lie in bed here safe & sound, between sheets, with a hot water bottle & the prospect of being called by Law with tea in the morning, & think of you – perhaps in a howling sandy waste – or worse. It is horrible to know so little & feel so out of reach but I must say that the post has been kind to us for yr. letters have usually reached me in a fortnight since you 'got there'. We are all of course very dashed by yesterday's news that we have lost our bridgehead in the Mareth Line – probably dearly bought. To-day's news is only of artillery duels. I have no idea whether you are in reserve, in the line, or in the outflanking movement. From all accounts the battle has been fiercer even than El Alamein.... Darling – all this must seem so distant & unreal to you if you are in this terrible cauldron I read about. Pray God you are not.

My thoughts – love & prayers never leave you – Yr. Mama

Diary – Tuesday 30 March – 40 Gloucester Square, W.2

When I came in from my luncheon with Mallon[2] to meet a steel expert called Elliot at the Ritz I found B. & Ray in the library – I said to Ray 'Have you written yr letter to Mark to go by air with Toto's friend?' B. said 'I had better tell you at once. I have a telegram to say that Mark is missing'. It was from Gilbert Talbot at G.H.Q. M.E.F. We have been able to find out nothing – except that they have been all thro' the fighting on the Mareth Line & that on the 17th–18th there was much confused night fighting & that many officers were missing, some having since walked in.[3]

Diary – Wednesday 31 March – 40 Gloucester Square, W.2

A leaden day following a leaden night. Efforts to get news of Mark from Casualty Dept of W.O. ... from the Grenadiers. No lists in yet – George Grey very kind – & doing everything he cld to help.... At 10.30 the

---

[1] Returned: 'It is regretted that this item could not be delivered because the addressee is reported prisoner of war.'

[2] James Joseph Mallon (1875–1961), warden of Toynbee Hall, 1919–54; on board of governors of BBC, 1937–9, 1941–6.

[3] Violet and Bongie had been misinformed about the date of the battle.

telegram from the War Office came, as with Bubbles. He has been missing since 17th – the day we were told the reconnaissance in force took place.

Winston Churchill to V.B.C.

Monday 5 April
10 Downing Street,
Whitehall, S.W.

Dearest Violet,

I am profoundly grieved to learn that Mark is missing & at all the sorrow & anxiety you feel. Please accept my deepest sympathy in yr distress. On the other hand you shd by no means despair. By far the greatest number of 'missing' are alive as Prisoners of War. I asked the War Office for their latest information, but all they cd give me was the enclosed.[1] With heartfelt sympathy to you both, I remain, Yours affect. W

V.B.C. to Winston Churchill

Tuesday 6 April
40 Gloucester Square, W.2

My dearest Winston –

I was deeply touched by your letter – & by your sparing time & thought from your heavy cares to write to me – & I do thank you for it from my heart, & for the inquiries you have made about Mark at the War Office.

I have heard more about the action now from various sources – i.e. that it was an attack by night by the Brigade of Guards on the north end of the Mareth Line – in which the Grenadiers (fortuitously) bore the worst brunt. There was fierce hand-to-hand fighting & they suffered heavily, losing 26 officers killed, wounded & missing. I have a letter from a friend of Mark's at G.H.Q. M.E.F. (sent by air) in which he tells me that to reach their objectives they had to cross a large-ish Wadi which was found to be full of mines, many of them anti-personnel, & to be accurately covered by mortar-fire. Two Companies are <u>known</u> to have got across on to the objective. I am proud to think that Mark's was one of these – & I gather that these are missing. Some of them have of course been killed. News of two more dead came in yesterday. (Their bodies were recovered.)

Mark is – he has been all his life – the light of my eyes – my pride & hope & Morning Star. Even if – in these skies – his star has set – I am still greatly blessed to have possessed him. He felt passionately about the issues

---

[1] Churchill enclosed a typescript statement to the effect that Mark Bonham Carter was reported missing in the attack which the Guards Brigade made on the Mareth Line, 16–17 March.

of the war & bent <u>all</u> he had – a brilliant mind & a nature in which gentleness & power are strangely blended – to the task of fitting himself to fight for them. If he is a prisoner of war I can only pray for <u>his</u> sake that either by recapture or escape he may be freed to fight for them again, for I can imagine no <u>bitterer</u> disappointment or frustration for him than to be a passive captive for the rest of the war. I cannot <u>ask</u> Fate for that – though it may be the best she has to give. It is hard, & strange, to be unable to reach him with my love, wherever he may be. But I <u>trust</u> his young & ardent spirit to remain unbroken – either by life or death.

God bless you dearest Winston – & thank you for your thought of me – Ever yr Violet

Diary – Tuesday 6 April – 40 Gloucester Square, W.2

... In the evening was rung up by Pamela McKenna to say she had a letter from Barbara – I asked her to read it to me down the telephone.[1] She did so & then brought it round by taxi. She (B.) had seen Mark's Colonel Archer-Clive who is wounded in the jaw in Cairo. He was most hopeful about Mark – who he said was wounded in the arm. He thought he must be a prisoner. The bodies of young Trenchard & Jack Allsopp have been found[2] – so all day long I felt that every ring at the bell might mean that Mark's had been found. This was therefore an immense relief – tho' there is no <u>certainty</u>.

Diary – Monday 12 April – 40 Gloucester Square, W.2

'The days come up like beggars one by one.' No news. Letter from Eddie S.W. congratulating us on Mark being a prisoner.[3] Rang him up – & he referred me to his sister Ly Romily ... who had heard it at a concert with Billy Jolliffe yesterday from a young Grenadier. Rang up Billy at Pirbright

[1] Pamela McKenna and Barbara Freyberg (1887–1963) were sisters (*née* Jeykll), and childhood friends of Violet.

[2] Hon. Hugh Trenchard, elder son of Viscount Trenchard, marshal of the RAF; lieutenant, 6th Battalion; killed 16 March. J. R. Allsopp, captain, 6th Battalion; killed 17 March.

[3] Edward Charles Sackville-West (1901–65), first cousin of Vita; worked for features and drama department of the BBC during the war. Mary Herbert wrote in mid-April: 'it is such an agony waiting & I can feel what you are suffering because I've been through it – though I know it must be a thousand times worse when your communications are so cut off. When it was France in the old days, there was always someone to see – some information to glean.'

who said the young Grenadier who spoke to them was David Wedderburn.[1]
Rang up David Wedderburn who denied having said anything except that
he had heard Mark was wounded.

M.R.B.C. to V.B.C.[2]

Monday 12 April
P.O.W. Camp 38, Poppi, Italy

Dear Mama – I regret your anxiety only less than my general position. I
live in a villa overlooking 'noble' vineyards, mountains & a fine river –
most beautiful now. Conditions v. good.... My luck was incredible, my
experience bloody. I was taken near Mareth. Tell Penn – John Wiggin,
Arnold Vivian are prisoners unwounded, Brabourne prisoner slightly
wounded:[3] Peter Evelyn after amazing courage badly wounded, taken with
me. They promised to send ambulance for him, & did I think. I gave him
morphia. Nic Durham fellow-subaltern in Coy of 39 yrs, delightful, killed.
I alone saw it. Write to his wife or mother for me, also to Jack Allsopp's
wife. I hear (confirm it) that he was killed. He had children, I came to like
him very much. Send paints etc. if possible, suède shoes of mine, & some
Chutney (sliced mango!). Masses seen, done, experienced, & felt – much
rather disillusioning, much I long to discuss with you & tell you. Think
now that I enjoy the army v. much up till now. Weighing my present
mates in the balance. They look a little light. Am well, living in beautiful
surroundings, morale high, food OK   MARK

Diary – Wednesday 14 April – Clovelly Court, Devon

Travelled with Ray to Clovelly. Good journey – lovely day. Everything out
as we drove from Bideford – primroses – blossom – lambs in the fields – &
red cascades of rhododendrons as we turned in by the stables.

Found Bett, Christine & Sue finishing tea & walked out with Bett to the

[1] David Michael Alexander Wedderburn (1922–60), a Balliol contemporary of Mark Bonham
Carter.

[2] This letter was forwarded to VBC at the Manor Farm, Stockton, 30 August, via Rome and
Lisbon. Mark Bonham Carter was first at 'PG 38', a prisoner of war camp at Poppi, roughly 25
miles east of Florence. Early in June he was moved to 'PG 47', a camp at Modena in northern
Italy, 'a vast place filled mainly with South Africans and New Zealanders'.

[3] Norton Cecil Michael Knatchbull (1922–43), 6th Baron Brabourne, 1939. He and Arnold
G. Vivian, lieutenants with the 6th Battalion, were captured at the Horseshoe battle and
imprisoned in Italy. They were later shot 'in cold blood' by the Germans for trying to escape
while being transferred to a prison camp in Germany (Nigel Nicolson and Patrick Forbes, *The
Grenadier Guards in the War of 1939–1945*, ii, 307).

cliffs afterwards. When I got back Ray said to me in a very quiet matter-of-fact voice – 'Mama – Bongie rang up to say that Mark is a prisoner, in Italian hands. The B.B.C. got it off the Italian Wireless.' B. rang up later to confirm this. A monitor had picked Mark's name off a Vatican broadcast – with Army N° correct & my name & address as next of kin & sent it straight in to Mrs Fuller. To his humanity & initiative we owe this heaven-sent reprieve. I asked B. to inquire at once for the 7 other names.

Diary – Thursday 15 April – Clovelly Court, Devon

Day of summer heat & really burning sun. We went to Hartland by bus & picnicked on the cliffs.... Thinking of Mark all the time. Is he plunged in abysmal gloom, frustration & disappointment. Does he realize how narrowly his life has been saved? Is he lonely & longing to get in touch with us – can he feel our thoughts reaching out to him? All the beauty here which he loved so dearly brings back my holidays alone with him & Ray. If only I cld change places with him – & let him get back to action in these years of youth. I can't bear to think of him eating his heart out behind barbed wire. Sheaves of telegrams, from Winston & many others....

Diary – Saturday 17 April – Clovelly Court, Devon

Another burning day – B. & Betty gardened in the intervals of blood transfusions which went on all day. Everyone giving blood including Mr Cavendish who didn't seem to have too much to spare.... Tried to answer some of my hundreds of letters. How strange that I shld not be <u>sure</u> whether Mark was alive or dead.

V.B.C. to M.R.B.C.[1]

Monday 19 April
Clovelly Court, Devon

My own Darling. You will know the immeasurable inexpressible joy & relief brought by your message. It was narrowly preceded by news from a B.B.C. monitor who picked yr. name off a Vatican broadcast. But for the

---

[1] Between April and October Violet sent more than two dozen letters to her son, whose mail, like that of all prisoners of war, was strictly rationed. To maximize the space available on the 'Prisoner of War Post' aerogrammes that had to be used, Violet had her letters typed. Luckily she kept the manuscript originals, on which these transcriptions are based.

268 *Champion Redoubtable*

Vatican we shld still be on the rack. I am almost tempted to join its fold.... I wrote last week to you on the off-chance, telling you of our great pride in yr. achievement, of yr. C.O.'s high praise, of all yr. friends' anxiety & messages ... & of our grief for your losses.... I still don't know how many of those still missing are safe with you. That you shld all join Bubbles wld be, I suppose, too good to be true....[1] I realize so poignantly the crushing disappointment you will be feeling & the gloom at the boredom & frustration stretching ahead. But events are moving rapidly, <u>you are alive</u>, & there are other fields to conquer beyond battlefields.... Languages are one obvious thing to tackle if amenities exist.... Writing from Clovelly & fear to describe it lest it shld. wring your heart with nostalgia. Everything at its loveliest & all thinking of you – from Cruses to Cavendish. Primroses out – buzzards hovering – Gallantry Bower aflame with gorse. To all this you will now certainly return darling & to much more beside. Though space is so opaque & sundering you are held closer to us by our thoughts, every passing hour, than you have ever been before. Be sure of this. God bless & keep you.

Jo Grimond to V.B.C.
Sunday 25 April
8 Abbotsford Crescent,
St Andrews, Fife

Dear Violet,

I am so glad Mark is safe. What a relief it must be to you. It is the best that could be hoped for. I am sure the Italians are the best people to be a prisoner among and the climate of Italy will be reasonable even in a prison camp.

I do feel on the other hand extraordinarily sorry for Mark. To be a prisoner at all must be hell, but at 20 when he ought to be at Oxford it is a dreadful fate. It is so distressing that no one can make up their lost time, I feel very Housmanish about him & Bubbles 'And of my threescore years & ten'.[2]

On the other hand I selfishly & possibly ignobly heave a sigh of gladness when any of my friends are out of harm's way. I have no Spartan feelings, enough of 'those whom the gods love die young', and if he had been

---

[1] After his capture Bubbles was interned in POW camp '21' at Chieti, midway down Italy and 8 miles from the east coast, a considerable distance from Mark Bonham Carter's camp near Florence.

[2] From A. E. Housman's *A Shropshire Lad*, 'Loveliest of trees, the cherry now / Is hung with bloom along the bough....'.

killed it would have been a ghastly repetition of the last war, another loss of the best. I feel that Mark may be something rather special as Toto would say. My friends are a bit fine spun, I doubt if Con or Bubbles will ever engage very closely in the cogs of the world.[1] Not that they want to do so. Those that might do so among my contemporaries are often too stupid to turn the wheel over – at least in the right direction. Mark I feel has probably an intellect sufficiently like Bubbles, allied to an easier personality more likely to impinge on the world. I think he might do very well in politics and shows every sign of wanting to do so....

Laura and children are on the whole well, slightly afflicted by colds & tooth-cutting.... Love to you all, yr Jo

V.B.C. to M.R.B.C.   ***Thursday 29 April***
40 Gloucester Square, W.2

My own Darling. It is hauntingly horrible to feel that while spring beauty is spread about us here & our every want supplied you are without any essential from toothbrush to books & news. I think of you from morning to night, wondering if you are clothed or bare, hungry or satisfied, & feeling dismally certain that however yr. body may be faring yr. mind is crucified with boredom. The only life-line to clutch at is the <u>miracle</u> of your being alive, for 2 more were reported found dead last week – Strang Steel & Haden.[2] Have just heard Wiggin is safe with you. No news of Evelyn or Durham yet. You will know their fate whatever it is.... In general yr survival from the holocaust has marked you out as a 'Man of Destiny' – a part you will now be obliged to fill, willy-nilly. Loving you & thinking of you unceasingly, Mama

M.R.B.C. to V.B.C.   ***Monday 3 May***
P.O.W. Camp 38, Poppi, Italy

I wonder how this life affects my character? Clearly it makes one egotistical (whence this question). Equally clearly it tends to make the irritable more so, & the indolent more indolent. It arouses the minor vices to a frenzy of activity. So far I have been so sunny to my fellow prisoners that I must vent my spleen about them. I will snap at them. This camp is small, &

[1] Con O'Neill (1912–88) and Jasper Ridley were Jo Grimond's Eton and Balliol contemporaries, and close friends; Con was in the Intelligence Corps, 1939–45.

[2] J. Malcolm Strang Steel and W. C. Haden, both lieutenants with the 6th Battalion, Grenadier Guards, killed during the Horseshoe battle.

half of its dwellers are majors, & lieutenant-colonels. They wander around like old maids carrying either their red cross parcels (very good food) or useless little trinkets made out of their tins – elaborate and leaking mugs, & ungainly eyeshades of cardboard. They live for the next parcel, or game of bridge, & in between they spend their time not unprofitably learning Italian or discussing Dorothy Sayers books. The Library here is not bad, if you look you can find quite amusing books, hidden between the Londsdale Library for 'sports' & wood carving for beginners.... I suffer from a lack of female society – a need that the old maids cannot, & doubtless, would not, assuage. My love to Raymond, Morhange, & Budge – an odd trio! Mark.

Diary – Saturday 22 May – Winchester

Rainy day – but cleared enough for cricket in the afternoon. Sat in Meads watching Toye Pot. As I was talking to Leeson who shld come by but 'Monty' (here to see his boy).[1] I expected to be blasted out of Meads by his 'binge[?]' but found him quite quiet & without the Kruschen quality I feared. He is tiny in stature – lean – with a face like a bird. I asked about the Guards' action – & he said how well they had done & how he had written to the King about it – & when I said 'But they cldn't hold the position' he said 'But they drew off the Germans for the main attack.' I was not completely convinced. Ray came back to tea & we went to Evening Chapel where Monty appeared....

V.B.C. to M.R.B.C.

Friday 4 June
40 Gloucester Square, W.2

My Darling ... Gruyère made a characteristically good comment about one of our 'organizers of victory' (who you will recognize) 'Irrepressible in defeat, insufferable in victory'.[2] The last stricture is extraordinarily inappropriate to the nation as a whole. The sobriety & decency of their bearing in these days of success is as creditable as their 'even keel' during disaster. In one of the reports I get I came upon the comment that it was

[1] Spencer Leeson (1892–1956), headmaster of Winchester, 1935–46; ordained, 1940; later bishop of Peterborough; Violet later observed that Leeson was 'drowned in a mystical culte' for Montgomery, whose only child, David Bernard (b. 1928), was at the school.

[2] 'Gruyère' is Churchill, and the 'organizer of victory' General Montgomery.

'hard luck for the Germans not to be able to Dunkirk as we cld!'[1] As tho' the rules of the game had not been drawn quite fairly for them. I don't know whether it is a strength or a weakness that we find it so impossible to hate. We just can't do it. It arises partly I suppose from a lack of imagination & a desire not to believe in the existence of things we hate. It has been made easy for us by the fact that we have always been able to keep them at arm's length from our own shores & soil. When you feel desolate & homesick remember that you have helped in this, & that thanks to you & others they are waiting, safe & unchanged, for you to come back to. How terribly I look forward to that moment darling.... Longing for another letter from you. Tell me all you feel even if inky. Love – which never leaves you – Mama.

... Trust you have got some letters, one Vatican cable & spectacles by now.

Diary – Tuesday 22 June – 40 Gloucester Square, W.2

... Went to a party given by Masaryk to meet the Benes. He just back from his journey to Russia & America. As usual very optimistic, saying 'Italy in 3 months – Germany in a year'. He said 'You see I have been right' – I felt inclined to say 'you must be sometime'! (for last year the dear old boy told me the Russians might give Germany a knock-out that winter).... Alert between 2 & 4. No Gunfire or Bombs.

V.B.C. to M.R.B.C.

Saturday 26 June
40 Gloucester Square, W.2

My Darling – No letter from you since 26th April. Every morning when I wake & every time I come in I wonder 'will there be a letter'? & alas! there never is. It is so tantalizing to know you have written. If only I felt sure that you get mine regularly I shld be happier.

The repatriated say they got nearly all their letters from home but that only about $\frac{1}{2}$ of those they wrote arrived. Therefore repeat any important need. I'm sending books regularly but possibly the wrong ones. Your action on the Mareth line was broadcast, dramatized, in the 'Into Battle' series a few nights ago. I wished you cld have heard it. We all felt very

---

[1] When the German and Italian armies in Tunisia were cornered on the Cap Bon peninsula they had no opportunity of seaborne escape, as the British and French armies had had at Dunkirk in May–June 1940. After 3 May the Axis forces there surrendered in increasing numbers, in all around 275,000.

proud. Ray was 14 on Sat. & wrote to me 'How Bong will revel in the fact
that I no longer take a half'! (ticket.)[1] (You know B.'s passion for spending
double what he need on very dull things like railway tickets.) Ray joins
J.T.C. this autumn which is a funny thought....

I am wondering if Bubbles will be moved from his area in present circs.
C's great fear is that he may be parted from his cello. We never go to the
Joys now. Without you or Bubbles it wld be too nostalgic. There was a
good B.B.C. P.S. last night in which a Scotchman, Welshman & Cockney
all said why they loved this country. The Scotchman much the best of
course, but the Cockney (a costermonger) also quite first-rate. He had so
obviously adored every moment of his life in the London streets & said 'if
I was to die to-morrow & St. Peter was to meet me at the gates & ask me
what I wanted there's only one thing I cld say "I want my barrow" I'd say
"You give me that, & the run of the streets, that is if they're anything like
London"'. It made me feel how unimaginative social reformers (of all
shades) are. They have a 'utility' conception of happiness. There is a
lovely Picasso on view here which I long for you to see called 'La Belle
Hollandaise'. I will try & send you a photograph of it. Law is still collecting
money for you. She is selling rags for pennies to add to your 'box'. I miss
you inconceivably. Absence plus silence are like sub-conscious toothache
all the time. But the tooth will be out before long. When I think of all the
others who are dead, & poor Mrs Evelyn (still knowing nothing) I know
how lucky we really are. God bless & keep you. Love without end – Mama

Diary – Thursday 1 July – 40 Gloucester Square, W.2

... On to International Youth Centre where packed like sardines in boiling
heat I had to listen on my legs to a very boring speech by Stafford Cripps
without one glint of humour, originality, warmth, humanity. Jan Masaryk
followed with an excellent one – to which they all warmed at once.
Coming in I saw with my heart in my mouth a stack of Air Mail Letters
on the table. Were they delayed ones from Mark from Italy? They were 9
of my own to him – returned from Africa with 'Missing 17/3/43' written
across them.

Diary – Friday 9 July – Winchester

Tiring day – Caldere fitting – lunch at Selfridges. Hair washing – dash to
93 Park Lane to see amazing stereoscopic Air photographs of the results of

---

[1] i.e. Raymond was now required to pay a full adult fare.

our Raids on the Ruhr in Peregrine Churchill's office there. They are shattering photographs. In Düsseldorf there is literally not a roof on any house for something like 5 miles. The only one that <u>shocked</u> me was Elbenfeld S^t – a <u>purely</u> residential Area – devastated. On to <u>Winchester</u> – working at my speech all the way. Ray came to dinner looking radiantly well.

Diary – Saturday 10 July – 40 Gloucester Square, W.2

I woke early & vaguely heard on the Wireless downstairs the words 'General Eisenhower'. It flashed thro' my mind almost subconsciously – 'Has the invasion of Europe begun?' ... B – who was getting up early to breakfast with Ray – came into my room & said – 'The invasion has started. We've landed in Sicily'.[1] We turned on the European News at 10 o'clock & heard that we had landed on a 100 mile front between Syracuse & Catania.

Diary – Saturday 17 July – Cliveden, Buckinghamshire

Last day of Lib. Conference – Archie spoke in the morning. Quite well – but for one extraordinary reference to 'Homes for Heroes' – & <u>poor</u> Ll.G's inability to build them for lack of the Liberal Party – which he had just murdered. Lunched between him [Archie] & Walter Layton at Walter Rea's.[2] W.L. told me Winston had asked him to back Lib. Reunion in the News Chronicle as he envisaged the Lab. Party breaking away after the war & wanted a coalition with a strong Lib. Party....

Diary – Sunday 25 July – 40 Gloucester Square, W.2

The end of to-day held one of the most exciting moments of my life. We had had a peaceful eventless day sitting out in the square in the sunshine – writing to Mark & Winston & reading the papers. After dinner I listened to the wireless most of the evening ... suddenly just after 11 they 'broke programmes' & the announcer said in a very quiet matter-of-fact voice 'Mussolini has resigned. The King of Italy has accepted his resignation'. I rang up News Chronicle & B.B.C. who told me the King of Italy had sent

---

[1] The invasion of Sicily began 10 July with an Anglo-American amphibious assault; initial success in capturing Syracuse and key airfields was not followed up, and though the island fell, the Germans managed to evacuate most of their forces across the Straits of Messina.

[2] Walter Rea (1873–1948), cr. Baron, 1935; former Liberal chief whip.

for Badoglio who had accepted office.[1] The midnight news announced this with the Proclamation. It did not mention the German Alliance tho' it said 'We fight on'. It was also significant that it wasn't dated '21' (the year in the Fascist Calendar). Harold rung me up. He thinks it is the end in Italy & so do I.[2] What will Mark be feeling – & Bubbles? I can think of nothing else. I let Marigold know – & Cressida.

V.B.C. to M.R.B.C.   *Tuesday 27 July*
                                          40 Gloucester Square, W.2

My Darling. Listening to music on B.B.C. last night it was suddenly interrupted to announce Mussolini's resignation. My 1st thoughts flew to you & Bubbles, & I felt all our hearts bounding up together. You can guess our feelings for yr. own. Much more will have happened before you get this. Still no news as to whether & where you have been moved, so I duplicate this letter.... I live for the day when I shall hear that you have heard from us. (You surely <u>must</u> have done by now?) All news here eclipsed by last night's announcement. Optimism even before that was rampant, & fully justified by events....

Nigel also has been back to yr. old battlefield still strewn with wreckage of cars & still lethally dangerous from mines. He is not engaged in present operations. I long to know more about yr routine of life, whether you have a chance of learning languages, whether any books have reached you yet. Fear dislocation of transport may cause a hold-up. It seems centuries since you left us & for you it must seem longer still because of the aeons of experience you have passed thro'. But once you are back it will all shrink & become a strange dream. <u>Everything</u> here is as you left it but for the sense that we are getting nearer, <u>much</u> nearer to the end. Desmond was here last week & brought a lovely selection of books to send you which I am holding up till certain of yr. camp. Long to share background of yr. thoughts. So far both our letters have been 'services' into the void with no return. God bless & keep you. Unceasing love & instancy. Yr Mama.

---

[1] Supported by a vote in the Fascist Grand Council, King Victor Emmanuel III dismissed Mussolini, 25 July, replacing him by General Pietro Badoglio (1871–1956); this signalled the collapse of the Italian Fascist Party, but not immediately of the Italian war effort.

[2] Nicolson recalled, 'For her it means Mark's release' (Nicolson, *Diaries and Letters 1939–1945*, 308).

M.R.B.C. to V.B.C. *Saturday 31 July*
P.O.W. Camp 47, Modena, Italy

Dear Mama, I can hardly write coherently – things are happening so fast, &
so well – it's like a dream come true. I hang on the next edition. By the
time you get this all will be well. How marvellous everything is! Give my
love to everyone, Balogh & Martin.[1] Mark

V.B.C. to M.R.B.C.[2] *Tuesday 3 August*
Manor Farm, Stockton, Wiltshire

My own Darling ... You can guess the pure delight it is to be here, pure
but for the gigantic flaw of yr absence. I miss you, & seem to see you, at
every turn, just eluding me round one of the big planes in the College
Garden, or ahead of me & just out of sight in the jungle of loose-strife &
willow-herb on the path by the river-side. . . . I was called in to attempt to
interpret for 4 Italian prisoners who are living in Witt's cottage, as free as
air, but rather 'lost' after a well-organized camp at Shaftesbury. I tried to
find out their most urgent needs & wants in my best 'pidgin Italian'. They
pointed wildly at Witt's ceiling & I gathered they expected a shower-bath!
After that, macaroni & radio. I said they might come & listen to mine, but
I doubt if they wld enjoy what they hear at present. We are living from
hour to hour, from one 'news' to the next. Events are moving so fast & yr
immediate fate is so intimately bound up with them. Fascism has collapsed
like a house of cards. What will take its place?? How I long to know the
reactions at yr end. I have just sent another air-parcel of books, praying
they may never reach you. Love goes out to you not from us 3 alone but
from the downs & woods & watermeadows you love & which await yr
sure return to them. Laura, Jag, Griselda have just arrived & send you their
dear love & missing. Yr Mama

Diary – Wednesday 11 August – 40 Gloucester Square, W.2

Went to London by early train from Wylye (8.2). Found stacks to do
there – 3.30. Negotiations reported to Archie at Air Ministry. Once again I
felt his thorough unsoundness about a free General Election. He is clearly

---

[1] Thomas Balogh (1905–85), Hungarian-born political economist (naturalized, 1938); lec-
turer, Balliol College, 1939–45; a friend of the Bonham Carters.

[2] Returned undelivered by the censor, because of Violet's references to Italian prisoners of
war staying in Stockton.

ready for a Lib–Tory Coalition against Labour. I think it wld be the end of
the Lib Party & so does Dingle Foot with whom I drove away. He says it
wld mean going 'right' quite definitely....

Diary – Thursday 19 August – 40 Gloucester Square, W.2

Went to Miss Rathbone's Nazi Victims Committee – Eric Perth there &
very useful – also Frank Pakenham – otherwise all Jews except for me & E.
Rathbone.[1] Left with F. Pakenham. On to luncheon at Grosvenor House
with [B.B.C.] Bd. to meet Haley M.G. director & director of Reuters, another
candidate for 'Editor General'. Nice man with great integrity & probably
great efficiency in his own world of journalism but not <u>apparently</u> possessed of any aesthetic judgement or discrimination. No University background. Long discussion at Bd in which Harold & I both voted against his
appt. I shld have infinitely preferred Maud. My colleagues dread & suspect
brilliance & think it inherently unsound.[2]

V.B.C. to Arthur Mann[3]   *Sunday 22 August*
The Manor Farm, Stockton, Wiltshire

Dear Mr. Mann – Many thanks for your letter & suggestion that we shld.
meet....

I was profoundly depressed by our (<u>far</u> too hurried) decision & even
more by the discussion which preceded it. I think we <u>may</u> have missed
the last big chance which will fall to us as Governors of raising the artistic
standards of the B.B.C. to the level which (you & I & Harold Nicolson at
least) aspire to. I agree with John Christie that 'every contact between the
B.B.C. & the public is a matter of Art' & that 'it is vitally important that
the man in the supreme position shld. understand Art & Artists'.

I do not know enough of Haley to make a final judgement (we none of
us do) but there is no <u>evidence</u> whatever to prove that he possesses artistic

---

[1] Eleanor Rathbone (d. 1946), Independent MP for Combined English Universities, 1929–
46; vice chairwoman, national committee for rescue from Nazi terror.

[2] Haley was appointed editor-in-chief, and the evidence suggests that the decision had been
taken even before the board 'interviewed' him (Andrew Boyle, *Poor Dear Brendan*, 303; see,
too, correspondence of VBC and Harold Nicolson). The decision brought Violet and Harold
Nicolson close to resignation. They had favoured John Maud (1906–82), master of Birkbeck
College, the first (and only other) candidate to be interviewed.

[3] Arthur Henry Mann (1876–1972), editor of the conservative *Yorkshire Post*, 1919–39;
member of the board of governors of the BBC, 1941–6; a forceful critic of appeasement.

susceptibilities, discrimination or judgement; & it is in this field that we need direction & reinforcement.

The Board itself is already overloaded with business capacity (the Chairman, Millis – Managing Director of Barings, Foot – 25 years of Gas Light & Coke.)[1] None of these 3 have any sense of intellectual or aesthetic values, or much interest in, or respect for, the things of the mind as such. Fraser is frankly & militantly a-cultural. His avowed intention is to avoid stirring the minds of people into any kind of activity or vitality. 'Shrewdness', 'negotiating ability', & business success are the qualities our colleagues understand & look for.... Their whole outlook is worse than Philistine, for they hardly apprehend or understand the things they are opposed to. They just feel a blind fear & mistrust of the 'high-brow' or 'academic'. Not one of them has a flicker of feeling for literature, poetry, or music. We are in fact, as a Board, lamentably unfit to direct the B.B.C. – the greatest educational instrument of our democracy.

Its national fortunes are to-day in the melting-pot, & if, when the Charter expires in 1947, it is either taken over by the Govt. or broken up into commercial units we shall bear a large part of the responsibility for its fate, because we shall have failed in our Trustee-ship....

Hoping to see you on Wed. afternoon. I am yrs very sincerely – Violet Bonham Carter

V.B.C. to M.R.B.C.   *Wednesday 1 September*
Manor Farm, Stockton, Wiltshire

My Darling – Yr. 1ˢᵗ letter of 12ᵗʰ April just arrived! with list of yr. needs, & news at last of Evelyn & Durham – the 1ˢᵗ authentic news we have of them. I will at once tell Penn & Red X & write to Mrs. E. (with whom I have often corresponded – poor, poor woman) & with Durham's people. I terribly fear that E. must have died of wounds, but no report has ever come thro' about him. How well I realize the truth of what you write 'Masses seen, done, experienced & felt' & how I long to share it with you. Keep it safe for me, do not let it become blurred or faded before you return. You add 'much rather disillusioning'. Can you indicate in letters the nature of this?... I long for you to be here every hour. I know how the leaden hours must creep from you darling but here we do now feel the end in sight, & the end for you we feel might come any moment. Constant love, missing & instancy – Yr. Mama

---

[1] Robert William Foot (1889–1973), general manager Gas Light & Coke Co., 1928–41; joint director, BBC, 1942–3; director general, 1943–4.

Diary – Friday 3 September – Manor Farm, Stockton

The first <u>autumn</u> day. Mists & stillness & in the afternoon sunshine. We have had lovely sunsets every evening which light up our little dining-room while we have supper. I wrote letters all the morning & went out just before 1 to post some letters & try & get some more eggs. As I went down the village I suddenly heard – on one of the many 'Wirelesses' which now shout down the swallows in the eaves, that we had invaded Calabria – between Reggio & San Giovanni – British & Canadian troops – at 4 o'clock this morning....[1] Laura & I went to National Day of prayer service in the church here. Very thin attendance alas! Lovely service.

Diary – Wednesday 8 September – Manor Farm, Stockton

The best day of the war for us! It opened with a glorious day of sunshine & stillness.... At $\frac{1}{4}$ to 6 the telephone rang. It was Toto – who said he had news for me – <u>Unconditional surrender by Italy</u>! Mark must know to-night – & Bubbles. Later at 6 they broadcast Eisenhower's statement & Badoglio's proclamation. At 9 they put on Eisenhower's voice which sounded strangely unimpressive after John Snagge! – & revealed the fact that the Armistice was agreed on Friday when we landed.[2]

> *'We didn't think you looked like Italians': the escape of Mark Bonham Carter and Tom Butler from Modena prisoner of war camp, September–October 1943*
>
> In the widespread confusion that followed the announcement of the Italian armistice on 8 September, 50,000 Allied prisoners of war effected what has been called 'the greatest mass-escape in history'. They left their camps and disappeared into the Italian countryside, from where they attempted to reach either the Allied lines in the south or the safety of Switzerland. Many elected to lie low and wait for the battle to pass over them. Virtually all were assisted by ordinary Italians, many of whom risked their lives in

[1] On 3 September, the fourth anniversary of the war, British and Canadian troops crossed the Straits of Messina and landed in Calabria, beginning the invasion of Italy. Further landings were made at Salerno, the most northerly beach within fighter range of Sicily, on 9 September.

[2] John Derrick Mordaunt Snagge (1904–96), the voice of the Oxford–Cambridge boat race, 1930–80; presentation director, BBC, 1939–45. The Allies had been negotiating with Badoglio's government for an armistice since Mussolini's fall, and it had been signed before the Calabria landings on 3 September. To Violet the Italian surrender meant the liberation of her son and son-in-law; her hopes were soon dashed.

so doing. According to the terms of Italian surrender, prisoners of war were to be assisted in reaching safety, but insofar as this happened it depended entirely upon individuals. In some camps prisoners were free to leave, in others they were detained and handed over to the German army. At Modena the Germans occupied the camp quickly and moved its inmates north, and only around 200 of the 1,200 there escaped. Among them were Mark Bonham Carter and Major Tom Butler, a Grenadier who had also been captured at the Horseshoe battle in March. They hid in a suffocatingly small hole for two days, waiting for the camp to be emptied. They then scaled the perimeter wall and began walking, trying as hard as they could to look like locals. Avoiding all roads and bridges they took a circuitous route through difficult terrain to reach the Allied lines about 100 miles east of Rome. It took thirty days to cover more than 400 miles. The last steps were among the most dangerous, but they finally came upon a British gun battery 'as large as life, and true to life – for they were brewing up', to whom they declared themselves to be two escaped English officers. 'That's a good show,' came the reply. 'We didn't think you looked like Italians. We thought you might be Germans.' Fewer than 5,000 of the 50,000 who escaped in September had made a successful 'home run' by the end of the year. Success required courage, good judgement and luck, all in generous portions, and for their efforts Mark Bonham Carter and Tom Butler were later mentioned in despatches, 'in recognition of gallant and distinguished services in the field'.[1]

Diary – Wednesday 15 September – 40 Gloucester Square, W.2

Very sadly left Stockton by early train – 8.2 from Wylye. Sun just breaking thro' from a lovely day as we stood on the little platform waiting for the train. B. saw in someone's paper that the Germans claim to have re-taken Salerno. It is clear that things aren't going well there.[2] On arrival here found letter & card from Mark.... Card 31st July full of pathetic joy & excitement over Mussolini's fall. He writes 'It's like a dream come true'.

[1] Roger Absalom, *A Strange Alliance: Aspects of Escape and Survival in Italy 1943–45; Household Brigade Magazine*, Spring 1944; supplement to *The London Gazette*, 13 June 1944.

[2] The expected American–British amphibious assault on Salerno met with stiff resistance from the German forces under Kesselring, and six days of intense fighting followed before decisive support arrived from advance units of the 8th Army to the south.

Poor poor darling – the disappointment will be so bitter. I dare not think of it....[1]

Diary – Sunday 19 September – Manor Farm, Stockton

... Bad news on 9 o'clock news about the prisoners. The Germans claim to be moving 25,000 of them to Germany from Northern & Central Italy. They say many had been released by the Italians but most have been 'rounded up'. Poor poor Mark – & Bubbles.

Diary – Tuesday 21 September – 40 Gloucester Square, W.2

A whole day with the Liberals & I came away feeling fairly sick of them. Some of them have very little sense of proportion & so many are obsessed with a desire to be 'on the left' at all costs. Suddenly arctically cold. Had a bun & coffee for lunch at Lyons on Westminster Bridge....

Diary – Tuesday 28 September – 40 Gloucester Square, W.2

Breakfasted at 9 o'clock at the Dorchester with <u>Ld Baldwin</u>. He received me with his nice old face full of pig-charm – & a stiff leg & a stick. Talked of the Abdication nostalgically – (his 'finest hour'!).[2] The King [Edward VIII] having accused him of hypocrisy in being indifferent to his <u>living</u> with Mrs S. but shocked at his marrying her – & his answer 'We allow Kings great licence because in their marriages they can't be choosers. The people must have a say in who is to be their Queen'. He quoted the remark of a Yorkshire yokel '<u>You</u> can marry a whore & <u>I</u> can marry a whore. But the King can't. Because the King is not a man but a job'. He said he had had 3 hours with W. & we discussed his lack of vanity, greatness of heart, & lack of great colleagues. We both deplored Beaverbrook's return....

[1] Violet's mood changed rapidly in the week after 8 September, when the Allies were held at Salerno, and German airborne commandos rescued Mussolini. After the Italian surrender she had written to Harold Nicolson 'I am walking on air', but by 13 September she shared his despondency: 'I see little hope of Mark being rescued now' (Harold Nicolson, diary, 13 September 1943).

[2] 'S.B. has handled the whole affair with dignity, calm and efficiency quite superb. Even people like Violet Bonham Carter are loud in his praise. She told me this weekend that she even concluded he had handled it better than her father would have done' (diary of Victor Cazalet, December 1936, quoted in Robert Rhodes James, *Victor Cazalet*, 187).

Diary – Monday 11 October – 40 Gloucester Square, W.2

Left [Stockton] in thick mists with 25 lbs of onions, flowers & luggage. Lunched at Chinese Embassy.... Talked to Beatrice Eden – Anthony is in Russia. She says he hates going abroad & she feels claustrophobia in England. I cldn't bear to be out of it. Very bad news from Ly Brabourne. Four S. Africans have written to S.A. House from a transit camp in Southern Bavaria saying they were moved there from Camp 47 after a terrible 3 days' journey in cattle trucks & found others from the camp who had made the same journey. I feel despair about Mark's chances.

Diary – Wednesday 20 October – 40 Gloucester Square, W.2

... Lunched at the Connaught Hôtel.... Sat between Vincent Massey & Air Marshall Leigh-Mallory – Archie opposite.[1] L.M. very pessimistic about the Russians – thinking they have a tacit entente with the Germans & will sit down on the Polish frontier & occupy Persia, half the Balkans & Constantinople, & that the Germans will buy them off on any terms from getting into Germany. That they do not want England & U.S.A. to end the war strong – but exhausted....

Diary – Friday 22 October – 40 Gloucester Square, W.2

Lunched with Cyril Radcliffe at Cotton Grill.[2] He was more optimistic about Russia & her intentions. Thinks W. wld be an impossible post-war P.M. either as the head of a Coalition or of the Tory Party. His 'invincible pugnacity' had been invaluable thro' the war, but wld not be helpful afterwards. I pointed out the dearth of substitutes – but he seemed to think more good men might be thrown up by a real social convulsion – if as I suggested 'the mould was broken'. He thinks Beaverbrook entirely evil & his re-emergence as sinister. Eden not a leader....

[1] Vincent Massey (1887–1967), high commissioner for Canada in UK, 1935–46. Air Chief Marshal Sir Trafford Leigh-Mallory (d. 1944), cr. KCB, 1943; air commander-in-chief Allied expeditionary air force, 1943–4.
[2] Cyril John Radcliffe (1899–1977), cr. KBE, 1944; distinguished QC; director-general, ministry of information, 1941–5.

Diary – Saturday 23 October – 40 Gloucester Square, W.2

... Met Jack Churchill in St James's Park & he took me in to Downing St with his pass.[1] He said of the Russian advance 'It is going almost too fast' implying that we are not ready for it. I spoke of the slowness of our Italian advance. He said 'We have never been up against the Germans except when we were 3 to 1 against them & Montgomery can't afford to lose men. Manpower is our great difficulty.'....

Diary – Monday 25 October – 40 Gloucester Square, W.2

Telegram from Ly Wiggin saying she had had a card from John. He was in a Stalag on the borders of Yugoslavia & Hungary. I telephoned to her later on & she read it to me.... No mention of Mark – so they have been separated. I rang up Ly Brabourne after dinner. She told me (absolutely in confidence) that a W.O. friend of hers said there <u>had</u> been some escapes from Modena (something like 150) & that one of these had telegraphed from Switzerland....

Diary – Tuesday 26 October – 40 Gloucester Square, W.2

<u>The happiest day of my life</u> – without any doubt or comparison. Little Andrew came thro' in the morning from Scotland. I lunched with him & went out afterwards to shop. When I came in & went into Miss T.'s room she looked as if she had seen a ghost. She said 'Lady V. who do you think telephoned <u>3 minutes ago</u>? <u>MARK</u>. He said he was in England & wld probably be home to-night. He has escaped.' About an hour later he walked in – I heard his voice in the hall saying 'Is her Ladyship in?' – & then he ran up the stairs. He looked well – very thin – <u>amazingly</u> alive. He had walked 500 miles – from Modena to Termoli – right thro' the German lines & joined our forces. It is a miracle. Poor Warburg walked in unsuspectingly to tea – & vanished as quick as possible. We dined at Claridges – with Laura – Morhange & Sue. Mark talked to me till nearly 3. I lay awake all night tense with the greatest happiness I have ever felt.

---

[1] John (Strange Spencer) 'Jack' Churchill (1880–1947), younger brother of Winston, with whom he lived during the war after being bombed out of his own home.

Diary – Wednesday 27 October – 40 Gloucester Square, W.2

Mark was 'interrogated' all today by every kind of military authority & when we both came in at tea-time the house was stiff with Pressmen – & their cars parked outside. They didn't leave us till 10 o'clock at night! Mark had been forbidden to 'make any statement' & they were ravening for news. Another night of sleepless happiness.

Diary – Friday 29 October – 40 Gloucester Square, W.2

Unthinkable indescribable happiness continues. Too happy to sleep – so very tired – but <u>thankful</u> that I can't. It wld be a waste of happiness. I am afraid of getting used to it. Lunched at Venusberg. Mark still being 'interrogated' all day long by the various Intelligence Authorities.... Talked to Mark for hours & hours on end. We never go to bed till 3. I have never known his mind better or more active. He is very good on Economics – thrilled by South Africa & much stimulated by all the S.A.'s he met there.

Diary – Saturday 30 October – 40 Gloucester Square, W.2

Mark had his medical yesterday & to-day went out to see the Adjutant General. He lunched with Desmond & when Laura & I came in from seeing a film (Rebecca) he & Desmond were both fast asleep. Desmond on the sofa & Mark in a chair. I think he is very tired. He said 'I hate "excitement" & people who say they like it have never felt excited' – à-propos the excitement of his journey. Nathalie came to tea.

V.B.C. to Gilbert Murray   *Monday 1 November*
                                40 Gloucester Square, W.2

Dear Gilbert. The joy is unbelievable. I don't think I have ever been <u>quite</u> so happy in my life! We had <u>no</u> hope – because we knew his camp had been moved to Germany in cattle-trucks (a 3 days' journey). Many had already written from there – & I had written 3 times to him in Germany already.

He took just a month to cover the 500 miles – never touching a road or crossing a bridge – (wading or swimming the rivers) & spent 2 days getting thro' the German lines. Till then Italian Fascists were the greatest risk – because one cldn't tell a man's <u>ideology</u> by looking at him – whereas one did know a German when one saw one. The only safe friends to go to he said were the poorest of the poor. They were always on our side & never failed him. We mustn't fail them now. Ever dear Gilbert, With my gratitude – yrs Violet

Diary – Wednesday 3 November – 40 Gloucester Square, W.2

... on to our 2nd meeting with Nat. Libs. at St Ermin's Hôtel.[1] Felt even more defeatist about Reunion than last time – Shakespeare & Hutch made it quite clear that they intend to pledge themselves to a post-war Coalition in advance.[2] None of them is the least interested in 'politics' or ideas – & they all frankly admit that they 'lean to the right'. B & Mark went to Winchester to see Ray. How I <u>long</u> to see their meeting.

Diary – Tuesday 9 November – 40 Gloucester Square, W.2

'Women in the State' Committee at Gayfere St in the luncheon hour. Mrs Ethel Wood came & I think may be helpful. I went on to see Walter Rea at his request & he pressed upon me the Presidency of the L.P.O. in succession to Lord Meston – an invitation which I feel an intense disinclination to accept. The Chair is not my spiritual home.[3] H. of C. Committee on Nazi oppression victims – then met Mark at Gayfere St – where Wilfrid Roberts was pressing him to stand for Richard Acland's seat Barnstaple for which he might well get in.[4] Two difficulties (1) Money (2) I don't know whether he shld be pinned down to the H. of C. so young.

[1] The first meeting of the Liberals and National Liberals to discuss reunion had been in August. Violet was one of the six Liberal negotiators, and had written to Mark Bonham Carter: 'as you can imagine I spoke very frankly. They have no policy, fear Labour, & wld sign on any "dotted line" which wld enable them to keep safe seats under cover of a "Coupon"'. Meetings eventually broke down in 1944 over the Liberal Nationals' desire to maintain the Churchill-led Coalition after the war.

[2] Sir Geoffrey Hithersay Shakespeare (1893–1980), cr. Bt, 1942; Liberal National MP for Norwich, 1931–45, and former private secretary to David Lloyd George. Major-General Robert Hutchinson (1873–1950), cr. Baron, 1932; former Scottish Liberal National MP.

[3] Violet was also concerned that she could not take on another Liberal commitment, as she was already serving on some six committees, and devoting almost as much time again to the BBC.

[4] Sir Richard Thomas Dyke Acland (1906–90), 15th Bt, 1939; Liberal MP for Barnstaple, Devon, 1935–42; and as leader of the Common Wealth Party, 1942–5. Barnstaple would be a difficult seat to win: from 1918 to 1935 the seat was Conservative-held, mostly on very small majorities; Acland had won it for the Liberals in 1935 with just 454.

Diary – Thursday 11 November – 40 Gloucester Square, W.2

Bd meeting. Haley still very new & his only contribution when I was pressing for a broadcast on help to the Jews – to commemorate the demonstration in Parlt on 17ᵗʰ Dec. last – very disappointing.[1] The usual excuse – fear of arousing Anti-Semitism. Harold's account of his Swedish visit thrilling. They expect the German collapse in a matter of weeks. They say Germany is like a pear – not mouldy or rotten but filled with fluid corruption & only held together by a rind which a prick cld pierce at any moment.... He made us feel how tremendously much Sweden – & indeed Europe expects of us. America they feel does not know Europe & they are terrified of Russia....

Diary – Friday 19 to Saturday 20 November – Manor Farm, Stockton

... [Mark] had an audience at 12.30 at Buckingham Palace with his female Col-in-Chief – Princess Elizabeth.[2] He cldn't find a shirt at the last moment (he is still without a garment in the world!) but fortunately one of Morhange's fitted him. Then came a desperate hunt for a collar. He came down in Morhange's looking too ridiculous but luckily we found one 'Van Heusen' which wld fit him. He joined us at Stockton at luncheon on Sat & described his interview. He was ushered in by Arthur Penn & then left quite alone with her. He said she had quite amazing 'ease' – & was far less 'Royal' than he had imagined she wld be. Also much prettier than she looks in photographs as she has a very good skin. The only political 'note' she struck was when she said 'Of course Mussolini did a lot of good to begin with didn't he' – to which Mark replied 'I think that is all eye-wash'. He ran into the Queen going back into Arthur Penn's room & had a few words with her. Winston described our progress up Italy as 'crawling up Italy like a harvest-bug'.

[1] On 17 December 1942 Anthony Eden informed the Commons that the Allied governments were in possession of 'numerous reports' which indicated that the Germans were 'carrying into effect Hitler's oft repeated intention to exterminate the Jewish people in Europe'. The Allies together reaffirmed 'their solemn resolution to ensure that those responsible for these crimes shall not escape retribution' – a declaration issued that day in Moscow, Washington and London. At the conclusion of the discussion that followed William Cluse (1875–1950), Labour MP for South Islington, asked the speaker if the House might rise in silence 'in support of this protest against disgusting barbarism'. The speaker replied: 'That should be a spontaneous act by the House as a whole,' on which 'Members of the House then stood in silence' (*Hansard*, vol. 385, 2082–7).

[2] In fact the colonel-in-chief of the Grenadier Guards was the princess's father, George VI; Princess Elizabeth was the regiment's colonel.

Diary – Wednesday 24 November – 40 Gloucester Square, W.2

... Demonstrations everywhere against Mosley's release.[1] Nat. Council of
Lab. has passed resolution dissociating themselves from it. Crowds tried
to get in to H. of C. The whole thing has been grossly mishandled but it
seems to me lots of Liberals are getting off on the wrong foot about it. We
do not imprison people here for their opinions & 18B is a Security & not
a punitive measure. I was amazed to hear that Baffy had signed a petition
against the release.

Diary – Wednesday 1 December – 40 Gloucester Square, W.2

... Went on to debate on Mosley's release in H. of C. Morrison made a
good & unanswerable speech.[2] It was crucifixion to me to hear the Lib.
view left to be stated by him & by the Tories. Silence from the Lib.
benches. Percy had spoken earlier – very woolly I am told. The Lib. Press have gone
terribly wrong over this issue....

Diary – Saturday 11 December – 40 Gloucester Square, W.2

Mark returned from Windsor this morning. He had the most perfect Gala
Night there. At dinner he sat next to his Colonel & he danced the 1st
dance with her. He danced the last with the Queen. He also danced another
with Pss Elizabeth & 2 with Pss Margaret who he says is full of character – &
very 'tart' in her criticisms.... Pss E. liked Smuts & said they had asked
him to say a word or two in Chapel to the soldiers 'But I suppose a P.M.
can't say a word or two. He spoke for $\frac{1}{2}$ an hour'. He says she is above the
average intelligence & has above all great character. He drew her out on
the subject of Stalin. She thought he wasn't perhaps a very nice man – but
must be very efficient. He said the food was exquisite & rivers of cham-

---

[1] In response to the marked deterioration in Sir Oswald Mosley's physical condition he and
his wife were released from prison for 'humanitarian' reasons on 20 November and placed
under house arrest. There was a storm of protest from the political left and from the public,
who thought that Mosley had been given preferential treatment because of his social class
(see Robert Skidelsky, *Oswald Mosley*, 461–2). Harold Nicolson thought the affair had 'widened
the class breach' providing 'a nasty reminder of the prejudice and passion of the proletariate'
(Harold Nicolson, diary, 3 and 1 December 1943).

[2] 'This policy is based not on the inexpediency of making martyrs of persons who do not
deserve the honour ... but on the general principle that these extraordinary powers of
detention without trial must not be used except in so far as they are essential for national
security' (*The Times*, 2 December 1943).

pagne were flowing. They had a marvellous band & a sit down supper. They were not 'sent for' but asked the Princesses to dance quite freely....

Diary – Thursday 16 December – 40 Gloucester Square, W.2

I went as usual to the B.B.C. – & started our sandwich luncheon with Millis & Mallon & the Chairman. Fraser came in & said his chauffeur had told him Winston was seriously ill – he had heard it on the news.[1] We sent at once for the news & found that Attlee had announced to the Commons that W. had been laid up with a cold for some days & had now developed a patch of pneumonia in the left lung. I rang up Clemmie's secretary – She knew no more but said that he was in the sun – evidently in N. Africa which gave him a better chance than being here. My heart stands still as I think of his life & all that hangs on it. It is only 10 months since he had his last pneumonia. Apparently he had a cold when he went out. The evening bulletin said his condition had slightly improved.

Diary – Monday 20 December – 40 Gloucester Square, W.2

... Good bulletins of Winston thank God. His temp. is normal. Mark goes off to Barnstaple to-morrow to interview the Lib. Assoc. who want him to stand at the next Election instead of Richard Acland.

Diary – Christmas Day, Saturday 25 December – Manor Farm, Stockton

Xmas Day Everyone's stocking a success.... We also went to church – Mark, Laura, Ray B & I & sang the Xmas hymns. No sermon. Laura secured a Turkey for lunch! a real triumph. I listened alone to the King's speech – & then took Gelda out. Sykes & Tristram came to the tree & a nice American Lorentzen who was here before & is the one American always asked out, because he can be trusted to go! Our little tree looked lovely. Dinner all together. Rang up Cressida who poor darling is terribly worried about Bubbles as the Germans have threatened reprisals on English & American

---

[1] Churchill had a punishing itinerary in the last weeks of 1943, and was taken seriously ill at Carthage in the second week of December. By 12 December his temperature was 101, and his doctors feared for his life.

prisoners on a/c of the Kharkov Trials.[1] 'Alice in Wonderland' on the wireless.

Diary – New Year's Eve, Friday 31 December – Manor Farm, Stockton

... Telegram from Georgie Tennant to say one John Verney had last seen Bubbles at Sulmona on 30th September when he was well.[2] We all sat up to see the New Year in – Laura, Jo, Mark, Ray & self (B. alas! kept at Wells). No bells but on the B.B.C. Where shall we be this time next year? This year has held heights & depths of suffering & happiness undreamed of. Is it to keep – or only lent for a while?

---

[1] At Kharkov, in the Ukraine, on 15 December, four members of the SS were brought to trial accused of murdering Soviet civilians; all were found guilty, and publicly executed four days later.

[2] Sulmona is about 25 miles south-south-west of the Chieti camp where Bubbles was held; by 30 September the inmates of Chieti were being moved north and Sulmona was probably a transit base.

TEN

Reconstruction

1944

Diary – Sunday 2 January 1944 – Manor Farm, Stockton, Wiltshire

Cold wind with burst of sun from a grey sky streaked with gold. Church with Ray & B. ... No news except of another Berlin raid. Stasis in Italy thro' frightful weather. Russians still advancing – 27 miles now from the Polish border. Mark brought me from London another letter from Walter Rea – pressing me insistently to accept the Presidency of the L.P.O. I feel the utmost reluctance to do so – & my conscience doesn't prick me very <u>hard</u> – only feebly & at rare intervals. Delicious gay evening of laughter with all the children. B. very funny – Ray shaken with heavenly giggles – Laura doing marvellous sketches of Mark & Jo – 12.30 now & talk still going on in bathrooms & passages. All happiness now seems on loan & not a sure possession. Precariousness gives a sharper edge to it. ...

Diary – Saturday 8 January – Manor Farm, Stockton, Wiltshire

... I felt some bitterness reading the papers in the train to see the romances woven around the Whittle Engine – 'The men who saved Whittle from despair' etc. & no mention at all of B's part or his 8 years hard work on it. ...[1] Ray said to me after reading my Public Information Report 'Mama – what <u>is</u> war-weariness?' He cannot guess what it means! A good deal of firing & explosives went on this morning.[2]

---

[1] The jet engine had been developed at Power Jets Ltd of Rugby, of which Bongie was a director. Its inventor Frank Whittle (1907–97), then an RAF group captain, had been working on the project since 1937.

[2] British and American military exercises took place in the Stockton area in the months before D-Day, 6 June 1944.

Diary – Tuesday 11 January – 40 Gloucester Square, W.2

... Mark arrived from Claydon having had his call-up. He goes to Windsor on Thursday. He will be at the Castle which may be fun.[1] He feels terrible 'accidie' at starting all over again – which I well understand. I asked him what he wld like best in the world to do – & he said some regular intellectual work in one place – Oxford wld be perfect.

He & I & Diana & Brigid dined in – B & Toto (back from U.S.A.) at Brooks's & joined us afterwards.[2] The Americans have made a huge daylight raid on Germany 700 strong – & lost 60. Ciano was <u>shot</u> by the Germans this morning with de Bono & 3 others.[3] The thought of that jaunty cocky absurd figure being shot gives one a strange sense of horror – the incongruous mixture of the trivial & the terrible. He was not worth fate's while. Will they all shoot each other & save us the trouble? The Germans have established a precedent for execution for a purely political offence – voting against Mussolini was Ciano's – which might have dangerous reactions on some [of] their own fates.

Diary – Monday 17 January – 40 Gloucester Square, W.2

Cony greeted us at breakfast with the news that there had been a smash on the railway at Ilford yesterday evening in which 15 people had been killed & 30 injured. It was a head-on collision in the fog. It was the 4.40 – the train I had decided to go on & in which he had adjured me to get into the <u>front carriages</u>! I should feel a 'woman of destiny' after this miraculous escape if I were a little younger. We got up [to London] just in time for lunch.... Found a telegram from W. thanking me for my letter ... & congratulating B. on Whittle. Also a long letter from Mark from Windsor where he is living in the lap of luxury in a lovely bedroom in one of the Towers & feeding on partridges chickens port & sherry, surrounded by innumerable servants. (He calls them 'waiters' in one passage – so long have we been removed from 'civilization' of that kind.) ...

[1] Mark Bonham Carter was assigned to the garrison at Windsor Castle, before rejoining his regiment at the end of the year.

[2] Brigid Balfour and Diana Grey were paying guests at 40 Gloucester Square; Brigid qualified as a doctor during the war.

[3] Count Galeazzo Ciano (1903–44), son-in-law of Mussolini; Italian foreign minister 1936–43; voted against Mussolini in the Fascist Grand Council meeting of 24–25 July 1943; tried for treason and executed, 11 January 1944. Executed with him were Emilio de Bono (1866–1944), Italian general, and three other members of the Fascist Grand Council – Marinelli, Gottardi and Pareschi.

Diary – Wednesday 19 January – 40 Gloucester Square, W.2

Very interesting & amusing luncheon with Keynes & Lydia at Antoine's in Charlotte St. The 4th was an old girl called 'Auntie' (whose, I never made out). Eat <u>tripe</u> for the 1st time in my life. Maynard in excellent form. He says America has <u>no</u> future in the long-run as they are a race of sub (or super) dagos, speaking no known language intelligently, with no roots anywhere & no power to stay in one house even for as long as 3 months. He loves Winant & the old traditional Americans but says they have ceased to represent or control the country. He is not bullish about immediate 2nd Front results as it will have to be done so largely by untried American troops. He was rather amusing comparing K. Wood & John Anderson – his 2 chiefs. He thought K.W. very astute ... seeing more of the wood & less of the trees than J.A. J.A. had seen W. at the station & thought him looking rather white & puffy – as if he had been living in a hot-house & on very rich food (which no doubt he has). I regret Beaverbrook's presence during his convalescence as I think he has a bad personal as well as political effect on W. – like a bad cocktail – immediate kick & deleterious hang-over.

Maynard told me one amusing story about Stalin & W. on the Moscow visit when things weren't going too well over the 2nd Front. Stalin said goodbye to him when he went back one night & added 'I have carried out an old rite of Russian hospitality & put a pretty girl in yr. bed.' – W. rather embarrassed replied 'I shld prefer a good cigar'. When he got back he found a little girl of 4 with a placard round her neck on which was written 'I shall be ready as soon as the 2nd front'. Maynard thinks the Russians – whose propaganda & diplomacy have so far been flawless – have made a bad mistake over Poland. He says it is not a question of frontiers but of the Polish Govt. whom they are practically ordering to liquidate itself. He says this will be the trouble all along the line. They will not ask for territory but will insist on the setting up of subservient puppet Govts 'friendly to the Soviet Union'....

Diary – Friday 21 January – 40 Gloucester Square, W.2

Lunched with Baffy at Venusberg. Dull party – Rob Bernays, Namier (king-leach – lethal blood sucking bore), dreary F.O. man called Allen.[1] Talk

---

[1] Robert Hamilton Bernays (1902–45), Liberal National MP for Bristol North, 1936–45; captain, Royal Engineers, 1945. Sir Isaiah Berlin knew Lewis Namier well, and recalled: 'those who met him were divided into some who looked on him as a man of genius and a dazzling talker and others who fled from him as an appalling bore. He was, in fact, both' (*Personal Impressions*, 70).

entirely on Russo-Polish situation – & Pravda incident.[1] Namier defending the indefensible thro' thick & thin – completely anti-Pole & 'my Soviet right-or-wrong'. Came away after a very short time as I had heard from intelligent orderly at Windsor Castle – whom I rang up with a message for Mark – that he was coming up for a few hours this afternoon. He arrived soon after I got back & we had a delicious cosy afternoon together discussing everything. He had a <u>very</u> nice letter from Dick Acland giving him his blessing at Barnstaple. He had slept out of doors last night in a sleeping bag somewhere near the White House above Windsor Park – & I must say looked much better than when he went away. He says they breakfast à quatre every morning with 2 footmen circling round them, another bringing in food & a 4th sitting outside the door! Never less than 3 at lunch. He goes to Singleton to-morrow for a week's course. Dingle Foot came to tea & we talked over the Party situation, reorganization at Gayfere St, my Presidency of the L.P.O. etc. then went on to Electoral Reform Committee at Gayfere St.... Driving back with Dingle he was rather gloomy about immediate war-prospects. He thinks the Germans will give us a terrific crack when 2nd Front begins & also stage big air attacks on this country & that the Americans may mind their losses a good deal. Perhaps we are living in a fool's paradise – dreaming of the end this year. The Russian cloud is far bigger than a man's hand.

Diary – Sunday 23 January – 40 Gloucester Square, W.2

A Sunday spent by B. & me mainly in doing 'housework'. Our house is filthy as we cannot by hook or crook get a char or man of any kind to clean it. B. spent the morning cleaning out the area in a boiler suit – & the evening doing the windows in dining-room & library & the front door & doorstep. I worked for 1½ hours in the night-nursery on the windows & window ledges which were grimy beyond words. I think I emptied something like 20 or 30 buckets of inky water. It was a slight satisfaction to see it coming off but my hands were quite disgusting afterwards. Sue came in for half-an-hour after luncheon & told us more about Clovelly fire. I see she thinks it never will be rebuilt.[2] Walter Layton dined & we had a good talk about the future & present. He thinks the

---

[1] Violet had noted in her diary, 16 January: 'The Russians are behaving very oddly – publishing in "Pravda" a canard that Ribbentrop has been negotiating in Cairo for a separate peace. It is suggested that this is to "tick us off" for welcoming the very reasonable Polish note.'

[2] Clovelly Court, the home of Violet's sister-in-law Betty Asquith, was badly damaged by a fire in 1944; it was later rebuilt – see appendix of notes on houses.

Party Truce shld be lifted for by-elections & I agree – but meanwhile we shldn't break it....[1]

Diary – Tuesday 25 January – 40 Gloucester Square, W.2

... Went on a bus to Toynbee Hall to Children's Theatre Committee. I love driving thro' the City – & seeing the tide of ruin & devastation stop at the very steps of St. Paul's as though some divine power has stayed it.... Ly Clark mercifully gave me a lift back as far as Charing X where I got a taxi to H. of C. 'Liaison Committee' in Percy's room.... By-election situation discussed. Even Dingle (far the most in touch with Lib. thought & feeling of any member of the Govt.) is living in a fool's Paradise so far as Party Truce is concerned. We cannot 'hold' the situation as it is, beyond the next Assembly, I am sure. I spoke plainly to G. Mander about Archie's lack of leadership & its results.[2]

Diary – Wednesday 26 January – 40 Gloucester Square, W.2

... Toto rang up to say a Col. Archdale, who had just heard from his son in Germany, said that his son had been at [camp] 21 & that something like 1,000 of those from that camp were still loose in Italy. I wonder if there can be hope that Bubbles is among them. His name has not yet come through from Germany. Russia has refused America's offer of mediation between her & Poland. I feel very blue about future prospects in Europe. Diana's sister (working in the Admiralty) knows the date of the invasion....

Diary – Thursday 3 February – 40 Gloucester Square, W.2

Board Meeting. Millis in the Chair which improved matters considerably. I like him better & better. His laconic <u>straightness</u> is a relief after the Chairman's slippery discursiveness. As Eddy S.W. says 'crookedness is almost an occupational disease at the B.B.C.' ... I was on duty. We had quite a heavy raid – or rather 2 – one at 8.15 – & another at $\frac{1}{4}$ to 5 in the morning. I felt <u>very</u> loath to get up & go out. There was quite heavy gunfire – & a big fire in the direction of the docks. Some wardens heard

---

[1] Pressure was growing, particularly at the grass roots of the Liberal Party, to break the electoral truce that had been agreed in September 1939.

[2] (Sir) Geoffrey Le Mesurier Mander (1882–1962), cr. Kt, 1945; Liberal MP for East Wolverhampton, 1929–45; parliamentary private secretary to Sir Archibald Sinclair, 1942–5.

one bomb drop. Pinto says that we are instructed to expect heavy attacks <u>with</u> gas when 2nd front begins. The gas being prepared is a mixture of phosgene & Lewisite – persistent and non-persistent – not pleasant to deal with.[1] Back to bed <u>very</u> cold at 6.30.

Diary – Thursday 10 February – 40 Gloucester Square, W.2

Lunched at Savoy at 1 with Archie, Dingle, Crinks, Percy, Gwilym Ll.G., G. Mander, Wilfrid Roberts. . . .[2] Then we got to the business for which we had met – Electoral Truce. My impression of the whole discussion was that the Lib 'Ministers' – with the exception of Dingle – were remote from all Lib. opinion. The furthest A. cld contemplate going was making a speech to say we wld fight the Election as an ind. Party – but even on this he was doubtful. Dingle said he wld be making a virtue of necessity – as Libs wld certainly stand, with or without official support. A. said 'But they wldn't have a chance of success if the Lib Ministers didn't support them?' . . .

Diary – Tuesday 15 February – 40 Gloucester Square, W.2

Got up & went in a taxi to Gayfere St to L.P.O. meeting – where my willingness to stand as President had just been announced. . . . The die is cast – I do not feel exhilarated by the prospect which faces me. There are too many lunatics & pathological cases in the Party – Clem Davies & Horabin[3] – also rather small people bulking larger than they deserve because of the size of the Party. We badly need an infusion of new blood.

Diary – Thursday 2 March – 40 Gloucester Square, W.2

. . . Back to find Mark here. Had a delicious dinner with him & Cressida at the Causerie. Met Harold Macmillan & Richard Law & had a long &

---

[1] Phosgene was a colourless poisonous gas used during the Great War, and lewisite an irritant that caused blisters.

[2] Harcourt 'Crinks' Johnstone (1895–1945), Liberal MP for Middlesbrough West, 1940–5. Gwilym Lloyd George (1894–1967), younger son of David Lloyd George; Liberal MP for Pembrokeshire, 1929–50; minister of fuel and power, 1942–5.

[3] Clement Davies (1884–1962), Liberal MP for Montgomeryshire, 1929–62. Thomas Lewis Horabin (1896–1956), Liberal MP for North Cornwall, 1939–47. The following year Davies became party leader, and Horabin chief whip.

interesting talk with them.[1] Mark told Richard Law – extraordinarily vividly & well – what he had found in the way of political psychology among the Italian peasants. No feeling for democracy – free speech etc. meaning nothing to them – but a great feeling for equality. I asked him [Law] whether he thought we were not back in the region of power politics again – with Russia jumping her claim to what she needed & waiving the principle of settlement by negotiation which <u>we</u> were fighting for. He said it might be wishful thinking but he tried to think otherwise. I asked if we <u>were</u> back to power politics, whether we also ought not to create power for ourselves in a Western bloc. He was against this – said the Western nations should look to us – but didn't seem very clear for what. I liked him nevertheless.[2]

Diary – Tuesday 14 March – 40 Gloucester Square, W.2

The worst raid we have had since the Blitz. The siren went about 11 & B. went to the Post. I dressed & made Diana go downstairs as the gunfire was intense & for a time too much Flak was falling for me to get to the Post. I looked out into darkness one moment & the next when I opened the door found the Square in brilliant white light I cld have read a book by. Literally hundreds of incendiaries were falling in the Square & on the houses all around & soon the red light of the fires was in the skies in all directions. I went round to the Post where I met Blackner who said 'Pinto's hurt – in Somers Mews'. I got a stretcher & some blankets & Toto & I took it to Somers Mews. In the Archway I found Pinto lying on the cobbles in great agony. His leg was hurt. There were big fires in Somers Mews – Sussex Gardens – Southwick St.... After an endless wait got him off to St. Mary's in an ambulance. His leg was amputated above the knee. He refused morphia.[3] Back to deal with fires.

Diary – Wednesday 15 March – 40 Gloucester Square, W.2

Liberal Council Meeting. Most unpleasant. 'Radical Action' behaving as

---

[1] Richard Kidstone Law (1901–80), younger son of Andrew Bonar Law; Conservative MP for South West Hull, 1931–45; minister of state, 1943–5.

[2] In the 1960s Violet thought this a 'strange verdict to look back upon', remarking 'How he has changed!'

[3] Violet visited Pinto in hospital at St Mary's in May and found him 'looking very ill & still in great pain – tho' it is nearly 8 weeks since he lost his leg'.

badly as possible.[1] Lancelot Spicer even went so far as to attempt to quote from what he himself described as 'a private conversation' with me – I have not the foggiest recollection of ever having had one with him in my life. This à propos of the only condition I made in accepting nomination for the Presidency. I said I shld be delighted to tell the Council what it was. I asked from my colleagues an assurance of 'loyalty to decisions reached in common'. It was really jarring to see people behaving so badly after the carnage of the night before.

Diary – Wednesday 22 March – 40 Gloucester Square, W.2

... Dined at Claridges – our guests Richard Law to meet Edgar Mowrer....[2] I like Richard Law – who has great virility – modesty – & a supple kind of wisdom.

About Russia he said that he thought we had established about 80 p.c. understanding & confidence & that it was growing rather than waning. That there was no object to be served by having a 'show-down' with them now – for we were in no position to enforce anything. In fighting for Poland, Poland herself might be lost. She [Russia] was having great military successes & we weren't. She saw the 2nd Front in terms of common sacrifice. About its chances he seemed to me not enormously sanguine. He still thinks it possible for us to lose the war. When I asked how? he said 'If the 2nd Front went wrong – the Russians made peace – & the Americans grew discouraged'. Mowrer thinks disaster wld be the one thing to rouse his compatriots....

Diary – Sunday 26 March – 40 Gloucester Square, W.2

Heavenly sunny spring day. It has come so suddenly after 8 weeks of bitter cold....

... George Grey came to tea. He was in very good form. Cripps, who he has been keeping in touch with, is apparently meaning to resign after the 2nd Front & George seems to think there is a good chance of his joining us. He wld like to get Beveridge too. He says Winston rags Cripps about his red nose & says, after tossing off his 8th Brandy – 'I drink the brandy Stafford & you get the nose'....

---

[1] Radical Action was a Liberal ginger group, which consistently pressed for an end to the electoral truce between the parties. Lancelot Spicer (1893–1979) was the group's chairman.

[2] Edgar Ansel Mowrer (1892–1977), distinguished American journalist; *Chicago Daily News* correspondent in Rome, Berlin and Paris between the wars.

... Winston broadcast for $\frac{3}{4}$ of an hour – the worst I have ever heard him do. The war-part with which it opened was not inspiring – & the second part he slanged his critics over Planning & described a temp. house in the minutest detail – as Mark said like Knight Frank Rutley.[1]

V.B.C. to Gilbert Murray   *Wednesday 29 March*
                                   40 Gloucester Square, W.2

My dear Gilbert –

Thank you for your thought of me. I shall need <u>every</u> wish you can make for me – at wishing-wells & elsewhere – in my new job. I fought against it for months – & only finally capitulated after having entreated everyone else I could think of to do it instead – but all in vain! The 'Chair' is not my spiritual home – & I hate 'official' positions. I wld. far rather be an untrammelled free-lance. But there it is – I must try & do it not <u>too</u> badly. I went up to Lancashire on Monday to speak at Bolton – & was amazed at finding a hall holding 1500 packed out – & hundreds (literally 2 or 3 hundred) turned away at the door. I really think there <u>is</u> a Liberal tide flowing. If only we had the men to ride on it. Archie Sinclair is alas! completely absorbed in his Dept.

Mark is still in this country. He means to stand as a Liberal & is on the verge of being adopted. He is only 22 – & has no money – but he is passionately politically minded – & I feel no spark shld be quenched by caution in these days. We must all live dangerously – if we are going to live at all.

I wish I saw you sometimes? I am working very hard with B.B.C. & Liberal Party by day & Air Raids at night again – quite bad ones. (We had 56 'incidents' & 36 casualties in our tiny 'sector' the other night – & one of my fellow-Wardens lost his leg.) I wasn't happy about W.'s last broadcast. He doesn't recognize the 'dualism' in the public mind about himself or

[1] Speaking for the first time since his illness that winter, Churchill betrayed anger at recent criticism: 'The harshest language is used, and this National Government, which has led the nation and the Empire, and, as I hold, a large part of the world, out of mortal danger ... is reviled as a set of dawdlers and muddlers.' His description of the prefabricated dwellings, built to cope with the severe housing shortage, had echoes of the estate agent: 'not only have they excellent baths, gas or electric kitchenettes, and refrigerators; but their walls carry fitted furniture – chests of drawers, hanging cupboards, and tables ...' (*The Times*, 27 March 1944).

the Govt. – & it is such a <u>sound</u> public attitude really.[1] My love to you & to Lady Mary – Ever yrs, Violet

Diary – Saturday 1 April – 40 Gloucester Square, W.2

Lunched with Dingle Foot (or rather he with me) at Claridges. Discussed Govt & Party situation. He also is not too sanguine about Second Front prospects. He is <u>very</u> critical of Anthony at the F.O. & wants him to go....

He thinks the Tank situation bad – & that the American Air Force is making a greater contribution than our own by its daylight precision bombing. He thinks that in the autumn Harris & the Govt were too sanguine as to the effects of our bombing of Germany.[2] They believed the German people wld break under it. In spite of unimaginable suffering they haven't done so. They have got a kind of 'strength thro' Apathy.' They have nothing to lose....

Diary – Monday 10 April – Manor Farm, Stockton

Frank Sykes drove us up to Yarnbury this morning (B. Ray Jag & self).[3] It was a grey day with misty distances & one couldn't see faraway landmarks from the top of the great walls – but there was great beauty in the cloudy shapes that hung about the circle of the horizon where land & sky met. I was <u>horrified</u> to find that the down had been ploughed up & <u>barley</u> sown (to make an American holiday!) quite near the ring & when I asked Frank Sykes how long it wld take to return to its original downland he replied to my despair '<u>500 years</u>'. The thought of that <u>timeless</u> turf with its carpet of milk-wort & wild orchis being replaced by <u>grass</u> such as one cld find in Essex or Hertfordshire is a nightmare. I see that agriculture is going to do more to ruin Wiltshire than military operations. The rash of huts &

---

[1] Harold Nicolson had sensed a change in public mood earlier in the year: 'I fear that Winston has become a liability now rather than an asset.... In the station lavatory at Blackheath last week I found scrawled up "Winston Churchill is a Bastard". I pointed it out to the Wing Commander who was with me. "Yes" he said "the tide has turned. We find it everywhere." "But how foul" I said, "How bloody foul." "Well you see, if I may say so, the men hate politicians." Winston a politician. Good God!!!' (Harold Nicolson, diary, 7 February).

[2] Sir Arthur Harris (1892–1984), cr. KCB, 1942; air chief marshal, 1943; commander-in-chief, bomber command, 1942–5. Harris controversially persisted with night-time 'area bombing' of German cities until April 1945, though as early as February 1944 long-range fighter cover made daylight 'precision' bombing possible (A. J. P. Taylor, *1914–1945*, 551–3, 570–2, 591–2).

[3] (Arthur) Frank (Seton) Sykes (1903–80), farmer; married Barbara *née* Yeatman Biggs.

camps will be swept away & vanish – but the disappearance of the downs themselves for 500 years! This is irreparable. . . .

Diary – Monday 17 April – 40 Gloucester Square, W.2

Up to London from Codford by the 10.4 & at Westbury got into a 1ˢᵗ in which there was one empty seat & found there my dear M. Prytz.[1] We talked the whole way up to London. Very critical of W.'s broadcast. Bullish about the war situation, thinking the longer 2ⁿᵈ Front is held up the better, as with the Russian advance & our bombing Germany might collapse before – whereas an initial success in repelling it might stiffen them up. Quoted amusing remark of a neutral (I think Turkish?) friend on the decline in the quality of Foreign Secretaries. They used to be formidable men like Salisbury & Grey – & are now young sleek well-dressed 'eldest sons' like Eden & Ciano! He obviously has not a very high opinion of Eden. . . .

Diary – Friday 21 April – 40 Gloucester Square, W.2

Met Geoffrey Crowther at United Univ. Club to have a talk about Lib. policy – & as quid pro quo B.B.C., in which he is passionately interested.[2] He wants Brendan to put him on the Commission which will consider the revision of the Charter. We only had half an hour together so I didn't have time to milk his udders of much Lib. policy. I then buzzed on to meet Morrison & Ellen Wilkinson at Fothergill's invitation.[3]

We met in a voluptuous room overlooking the river at the Savoy – bottles plunged in ice-pails etc. Ellen W. arrived first – very maquillée (odd on her mug!) & gasping from some affliction – she said bronchitis – but I thought asthma. She hardly uttered. Morrison arrived next – full of bonhomie – with his well eye beaming – very 'avenant' & accommodating & ready to meet one ½ way on every point. I led off with the Party Truce issue & he admitted (off the record) that the present plan was bad for the nation & that he personally thought my plan quite feasible. Later we got on to the future chances of Lib–Lab co-operation & discussed the possibility of a Govt. centred on the left & containing Labour Libs & perhaps a few left-wing Tories. He said (rather amusingly) that it was very

---

[1] Björn Prytz (1887–1972), Swedish envoy in London, 1937–44.

[2] Geoffrey Crowther (1907–72), editor, *Economist*, 1938–52.

[3] (Charles) Philip Fothergill (1906–59), merchant; later a president of the Liberal Party Organization.

awkward when Libs – & even young Tories – tried to get to the left of Labour. (I <u>didn't</u> retort, which I well might have done, that it was almost impossible to get to the right of them!) He also said that Libs. were undisciplined & voted all over the place & that it was difficult to rely on them in a Coalition. I reminded him of the 'patient oxen' days when we tramped thro' the lobbies to keep them in, while they denounced us on every platform in the country. He admitted the folly of Ramsay's suicide on the Campbell case – & said he never knew if it was due to miscalculation or not. It had put the Tories in for 25 years.[1] He obviously sees the faults of his own people – & feels the relief of working with others – who are not class-bound. I told him I cld never join Labour – sign on the dotted line – & ask permission of Transport House to go & speak at by-elections.

I also told him how badly I thought they treated their intellectuals – which he admitted, tho' saying they were very tiresome! He envisages an election immediately after the end of the European war (tho' he says he thinks it ought to wait a year) & that it will be fought on Party lines. We agreed there was a strong left tide flowing – & he said it was a tragedy that there was no one in their Party who cld take it. Left for Stockton by 5 train.

Diary – Tuesday 25 April – Manor Farm, Stockton

Frank Sykes drove us into Salisbury & told us that yesterday 3 Germans had parachuted down from a crashing plane. One had landed at Tytherington – one at Boyton ... & one at Sutton Veny. The Tytherington one went to a cottage where the woman recognized him as a German & slammed the door on him in terror. However a farm labourer called Burt came along with a prong & escorted him up the village street, menacing him the while with his prong, & then telephoned the police. How I wish one had come down in this garden!...

Diary – Wednesday 26 April – 40 Gloucester Square, W.2

Went up early to London on a lovely <u>cold</u> bright morning.... I talked to Bracken about the Election. He evidently thinks it may be rather a rough business. He said half the present Tory members wldn't stand again. I don't think even this will save them. He said he thought Bobbetty Cranborne wld make a better P.M. than anyone else – significant as showing his attitude

---

[1] Liberal votes had kept Labour in office during 1924; for this, and the 'Campbell Case', see above, p. 161.

to Anthony. I don't see Bobbetty in that rôle much as I love him. I went to tea with Cyril Radcliffe at the M. of I. We 1ˢᵗ discussed B.B.C. shop – then politics. He thinks there will be an anti-Tory landslide at the next Election & that even Victory & Winston will be powerless to save them. He was <u>very</u> critical of W.'s broadcast & thought its failure was fully appreciated at Nᵒ 10. . . .

Diary – Saturday 6 May – Manor Farm, Stockton

. . . Mark arrived at tea-time. He had a lovely ball at Windsor on Friday night. Sat between the Queen & Pss. Margaret at dinner & danced from 9.15 to 4.30. The Queen charming as ever. Danced twice with his Colonel who said to him, à propos of her new activities, 'I feel it's <u>started</u>' which seemed to me to show some imaginative perception of what the rest of her life was going to be. . . .

Diary – Sunday 7 May – Manor Farm, Stockton

. . . After luncheon having borrowed the Yetters' pony-trap & Ray's old pony Tinker we went for a heavenly picnic to Gt Ridge Wood – only marred by Ray's absence. It cldn't have been lovelier. At the entrance to Longdene Bottom 30 or 40 grim looking American vehicles were parked – lorries – tanks – guns – which we had to circumvent. . . .

As usual in Gt. Ridge Wood 'no birds sang'. I didn't even hear a jay. Its silence is part of its character. It was pure happiness to be back there & find it unchanged – except that a vast clearing had been made in Fox Alley – but only I <u>think</u> of conifers. (Here the bluebells grew thick in the open.) On our way back we found that in the 2 hours we had been away an American bull dozer had arrived & was busy making a road over the down from the Longdene Bottom end! How many years will it take for this country to recover from the war? I can't <u>bear</u> to see what the Americans are doing to it. . . .

Diary – Sunday 14 May – Manor Farm, Stockton

. . . After lunch the sun shone brilliantly & B & I went a most lovely walk to Stockton Wood where we had heard the wild lilies of the valley were out.

We went up Long Hedges & straight ahead so as to enter the wood at the extreme <u>west</u> end by the big beeches – but on reaching the down outside found 2 huge guns planted there – one in [the] course of being erected – the other with a camouflaged net over it & the crew (English) assembled under it – which suddenly began to fire making vast flashes. A charming young officer told us it wasn't blank & wld fall 14 miles away in Lark Hill. We went on into the wood – which was full of bluebells – spurge – yellow archangel – & entered the main ride to look for the lily of the valley. We then saw a most extraordinary sight. The whole wood was alive with Americans – squatting under the trees – round fires ... drying washing – their vehicles parked & camouflaged everywhere. It was like some strange dream.

When we came to what we thought was the lily of the valley ride B. said – 'But we can't look there – they're on top of them – it wld be like going into someone's bedroom'. It was so unimaginable that the solitude of these ageless woods shld suddenly be so peopled. What must the oaks have thought? We found the lilies – in great profusion & on our way back found the gun blazing away. The Bulldozers have done their work with horrible thoroughness – great wide roads stretching thro' the untrodden green. I lay down above the junipers near Barnard's cottage while B. cut the most wonderful bough of blossoming whitebeam I have ever seen almost.

Diary – Tuesday 23 May – 40 Gloucester Square, W.2

Up by early train from Codford in freezing cold – hectic hour at G.Sq. dealing with letters. Then off to luncheon at News Chronicle office.... Back home & then on to meet Beveridge at Dingle Foot's. We handled him quite well I think. It is clear that he wants to stand, & means to do so. As what? 'Radical Independent' he tentatively suggests. I told him that to be an Ind. is futile – & that you cannot be politically effective without an organization behind you. He agreed & admitted that he cld never possibly join the Labour Party.[1] I said the great weakness of the Left was in men. It was almost impossible to put together a Cabinet of the Left that cld govern – unless some more significant figures cld be recruited. He agreed again – & is going to think things over & then meet us again. Italian offensive going well....

---

[1] In fact Beveridge had had talks with senior Labour figures about joining the party earlier in the year, and following his defeat at the 1945 general election he made clearer to Violet how close to Labour his sympathies actually lay (WB to VBC, 31 August 1945).

Diary – Wednesday 24 May – Manor Farm, Stockton

... Foreign Affairs debate summary on the wireless. Good speech by Winston – with <u>inexplicably</u> <u>bad</u> passage about Spain – & Franco – puffing & boosting them – & saying in one breath that we cld not allow our enemies to set us Fascist Govts, & in the next that the internal affairs of other countries was not our concern. I was really shocked by its inconsequence as well as by its bad doctrine. There were fine passages in the rest of his speech....[1]

Diary – Sunday 4 June – Manor Farm, Stockton

... It was clear from the news throughout the day that we were nearing Rome & it looked as if the Germans didn't mean to fight for it. On the midnight news came through 'Rome lies open to our Troops'. If only I thought Bubbles was near there. I fear he must be much further north....

Diary – Monday 5 June – Manor Farm, Stockton

Rome has fallen. The Germans are still shelling at long-range & many of those who rushed out to welcome our incoming tanks were killed by shell-bursts & splinters.

I spent the morning finishing against time an article for the Star then rushed off to the B.B.C. luncheon for Sir H. Wood – a great function at which he formally bequeathed the 'Proms' to the B.B.C. It was held in the big ball-room at Claridges.... Finally Bracken proposed the health of the Chairman & went completely off the (right) deep-end in advocating freedom of discussion of controversial issues by the B.B.C. I <u>longed</u> for Fraser to have been there – & hope there was a short-hand note. He told me to disregard Parliamentary criticism. I had had a word with him first – but never expected such a reaction! I also had a word with him about W. & Franco. He said that W. wanted to please the Spanish people. I pointed out that Franco had put most of them in prison....

[1] Churchill praised Spain for not breaking its neutrality, when this might have gravely threatened the Allies, and distanced himself from criticism of General Franco in the British press. Confronted by Emanuel Shinwell with the inconsistency of a policy that cultivated relations with fascist Spain while forbidding a fascist restoration in Italy, Churchill observed that the latter had proved a threat to Britain, which the former had not (*The Times*, 25 May 1944).

Diary – Tuesday 6 June – 40 Gloucester Square, W.2

... just before 10 – Toto rang me up & said that someone in his office had told him that parachutists had been landed in the Seine Valley. Cld it be true? I rang up the B.B.C. who confirmed that the invasion had started early this morning. The 1st official news was given out at 9.30 – but the Germans had announced it earlier, before 8 o'clock. Miss Tunnard's friend heard it from them. We have landed between Le Havre & Cherbourg.... The impediments in the sea were less bad than we expected. Montgomery is in command – so it is clearly not a feint!

I listened hourly till luncheon – & after. Went to Women Power Committee at H. of C. Met Harvie-Watt coming out & asked after W.[1] He said he was rather 'nervy'. He spoke in the H. of C. this morning & again at 6.30 this evening. Everything seems to be going as well as it possibly can so far. Howard Marshall who had waded ashore thro' 5ft of water after his landing craft struck a mine did a very good commentary.[2]

Diary – Wednesday 7 June – 40 Gloucester Square, W.2

3 Beach-heads secured & heavy fighting inland – at Caen & near Bayeux. More airborne troops being rushed across. Wounded are already being landed here & trainloads are said to be going thro' East Anglia. Spent the morning working & listening to news bulletins. Went to H. of C. at 5.30 & met (in Percy's room) the negotiating Committee – Geoffrey Mander, Wilfrid Roberts & Gilpin. Discussed the Nat Libs document – which I think any Tory cld easily subscribe to. I am personally against the whole enterprise – whatever they agree to – I think they have only re-opened negotiations because they feel a free Election may be inevitable. No change in the evening news except that the Germans are re-inforcing heavily. Mark telephoned from Aldershot. 'War-Review' after the News on the B.B.C. is quite excellent. Our war-reporting unit has really risen to the occasion.

---

[1] Sir George Steven Harvie-Watt (1903–89), Conservative MP for Richmond, Surrey, 1937–59; parliamentary private secretary to Churchill, 1941–5.

[2] Howard Percival Marshall (1900–73), director of war reporting and war correspondent, BBC, 1943–5. The invasion of Europe was covered by a specially trained War Reporting Unit, whose members were charged with producing graphic, quick and accurate news. Their broadcasts were highly popular on *War Report*, first transmitted after the 9 o'clock evening news on D-Day (Asa Briggs, *The War of Words*, 591–8).

Diary – Thursday 8 June – 40 Gloucester Square, W.2

London seems to have become suddenly empty of soldiers. All the ones behind us in Hyde Park Square are packing up & clearing out. Jo's batman called this afternoon & left his suit-case – which I felt to be rather ominous. One listens every hour for the news. It sounds very precarious still but we are holding the attacks – tho' the weather is <u>cruelly</u> against us. Cold north winds blowing – rough seas & to-day hard rain all day.... Missed the 9 o'clock news. We are in Bayeux. Caen alas! in flames.

Diary – Monday 12 June – 40 Gloucester Square, W.2

... Back at 4.30 to have tea with G. M. Young & Mark.[1] I liked G. M. Young & his views astonished me. He wants a 'Left' Govt in after the war with a strong intelligent & tolerant 'Right' Opposition. He doesn't think Winston cld be a post-war leader – or that he wld command votes as such. Walked with Mark to the Ballet & took tickets for to-morrow.

Supped at Causerie with Mark. The 6th Battn. is now broken up & he doesn't know what his future will be – W., Smuts & Brooks have been over to France – Alexander driving up Italy – oh for news of Bubbles! Dined with Mark at the Causerie.

Diary – Wednesday 14 June – 40 Gloucester Square, W.2

... W. has been heckled in the H. of C. very properly on the de Gaulle issue & non-recognition of his Nat. Committee as the Provisional Govt of France. I imagine it is Roosevelt's fault & that he is showing real personal obstinacy about it. It is to my mind <u>insane</u> policy – & personal issues shld not affect it. We must recognize & accept the <u>fact</u> – that de Gaulle stands for France – all that resists & stands.[2]

---

[1] George Malcolm Young (1882–1959), historian; fellow of All Souls, Oxford.

[2] Churchill was not badly heckled, and *The Times* thought that the House was right to question the government's coolness towards the only regime 'compatible with the dignity and just aspirations of France' (*The Times*, 15 June 1944). Violet was correct in thinking Roosevelt the main obstacle, though de Gaulle did not then enjoy Churchill's support either, the latter telling him two days before D-Day, 'every time I have to choose between you and Roosevelt, I shall choose Roosevelt' (Charles Williams, *Last Great Frenchman*, 252).

Diary – Thursday 15 June – 40 Gloucester Square, W.2

Dashed to H. of C. to see private exhibition of Air photographs. Our execution of devastation in France appals me – Amiens – Limoges – Toulouse – look as bad as Berlin & Frankfurt. It is a tragic irony that it is we not the Germans who are devastating France materially. On to Board Meeting. An interesting Board – I raised again the question of controversial broadcasts on which I had circulated a paper – supported by one from Haley which gave a good historical background. Bracken's speech lent power to my elbow. Fraser was good-tempered & didn't fight tho' he admitted that he was opposed to the idea. Millis cautious – Mallon also – Mann supporting. The B.B.C. has excelled itself this week & knocked the press completely out of the picture. Mallon reports the strange collapse from enemy air action of a railway bridge in the East End. No trace of aircraft. Was it a secret weapon?[1]

Diary – Friday 16 June – 40 Gloucester Square, W.2

Last night an Alert was sounded at about 20 to 12 – B. went out but I waited before changing to see if they meant 'business'. Terrific rocket-gun fire started a few minutes afterwards so I changed & went out with Toto just before midnight.

As we went out of the door I heard a most extraordinary sound over-head – completely different to that of any plane I had ever heard before. It was very low – & had a strange rolling reverberation – quite unlike the tone or rhythm of ordinary aircraft. I said to Toto – 'I believe this to be the Pilotless Plane'.[2] On arrival at the post I found B. had seen one go down coming from the Park & passing over the church – losing height very rapidly. It showed a flame & ended with an explosion. I asked MacKenzie what his theory was. He said 'the pilotless plane' – my own idea. Then followed a very long all-night alert with long periods of complete silence & bursts of intense fire. I went to bed at 2.30. The alert was still 'on' this morning – & after an all clear at 10 we had repeated Alerts all thro' the day tho' without much gun-fire. One started just before

[1] The first 'V1' flying bomb fell on London on 13 June 1944. Between then and 29 March 1945 around 8,000 were launched from bases in France and the Low Countries, causing more than 23,000 casualties in Britain. The 'pilotless plane' was one of a number of 'secret weapons' that the Germans were developing in the latter stages of the war.

[2] The 'V1' had a 'ramjet' propulsion system, which worked intermittently, giving it a distinctive sound. The rocket fell when its engine cut out at a predetermined point, and it would descend silenty in a steep glide to earth, detonating a 2,000lb warhead on impact.

Raymond's train was due & I went up to Paddington to meet him with 2 steel-helmets....

Diary – Saturday 17 June – 40 Gloucester Square, W.2

B. was up all night. Ray & I went to a news-reel of the Invasion – very good. Then after lunch we saw him off at Waterloo. Thronged station & packed train. A nice porter secured him a place. Vast queues. Back home & sat in the Square – in a little sun – Wind still blowing.... As we had been up 2 nights running we resolved to have one good night. I took a sleeping draught & we went to bed. I even undressed. Towards 5 in the morning I heard the strange – unmistakable noise very near – then a flash & terrific bang. It had fallen. The whole house shook to the foundations – but no windows broke. B. went out. It had fallen in Bayswater Rd just opposite the Convent. Very mercifully it caught in the trees on the edge of the Park & exploded there instead of in the street. The poor nuns were bombed for the 2nd time....

Diary – Sunday 18 June – 40 Gloucester Square, W.2

We went out in the morning to look at the damage. <u>Everywhere</u> strewn with glass – & every door blown out of the back of Connaught Square – Albion St etc. The very few remains of the wrecked plane still in the street. 16 slight casualties – mostly cut with glass. Nothing serious. B. left for Bristol after lunch. I sat in the Square & worked & read. Gave old Percy Harris tea & briefed him with Bev.'s excellent Post-Script criticising Govt.'s White Paper. Hope he will make good use of it. It is a brilliant brief. I wish we had a better performer to put it across.

I was on duty. Alert lasted all day. All clear at 8 & another alert soon after. At 9 a Robot flew up Radnor Place – pursued by a Spitfire. Met A[?] outside the Sector Post between 1 & 2 A.M. He told me the Guards' Chapel had been hit at 11 o'clock that morning just when it was full for the Morning Service & nearly everyone had been killed – Ld Edward Hay, Ivan Cobbold, Dodds were the only 3 names I heard.[1]

---

[1] The chapel in Wellington Barracks took a direct hit from a V1 and sixty-three service personnel and fifty-eight civilians were killed. Perhaps because of the implications for morale this catastrophe was not reported in *The Times* until 10 July (Martin Gilbert, *Churchill*, 779; *The Times*, 10 July 1944).

Diary – Thursday 22 June – 40 Gloucester Square, W.2

... Violet [Modiste] was in Westminster Cathedral when the P.P. passed over which destroyed the Guards' Chapel. She heard the machine switch off just above them & thought they were doomed – but it drifted as far as the Guards' Chapel before crashing. She had just been to see the Gilliat boy's coffin there – with 50 others. About 150 were killed. G. Wyndham told me that as it passed over Westminster Abbey the clergyman who was reading stopped & the whole congregation shouted 'Go on'.

At 6.30 Bev. & Dingle came here.... We had a very interesting talk. Bev. is torn between 2 alternatives. The easy & simple course of being elected as an Ind. Progressive for London Univ. & keeping his Mastership at Oxford – with an entrée to all 'left' Parties & responsibility for none – & the far bigger & more ambitious possibility of cutting the hawser with Oxford – taking the plunge & building up a Radical Party of the Left – an 'alternative' Party – & Govt. He is tempted by the big stake & game – but fears tying himself up with us as (1) he might lose influence with other groups thro' being labelled & (2) he doesn't know where we shall stand after the next Gen. Election. He fears that Archie & Crinks will want to remain in the Govt., or rather to rejoin it after the Gen Election. I cannot honestly say that I think his fears are groundless. I feel sure that Archie's one desire is to remain with W. & continue to work in much the present set-up....

Just before dinner we saw marvellous flights of Bombers in the sky, returning from bombing Cherbourg defences, for 80 minutes on end. Very comforting & impressive sight.

Diary – Friday 30 June – 40 Gloucester Square, W.2

Went out to lunch at the Air Ministry & as I got into Oxford St a flying bomb fell far ahead & a huge column of smoke rose. Took the tube at Marble Arch but was turned out at Piccadilly & found Piccadilly Circus a sea of glass. Huge bits like ice & smaller fragments & everywhere above the traffic the scrunch of its being swept up. The P.P. had hit the Regent Palace Hôtel. Lunched with Archie, Marigold & Dingle. Marigold who was slightly flown & whose tongue was certainly loosened burst into a violent diatribe against the Americans saying 'Of course they're not men – they're just monkeys – you can't treat them as human' & Archie pained & monitory 'Marigold, Marigold you mustn't say such things. No two nations have ever co-operated so closely in such unbroken harmony & perfect unity towards a common end' etc. Dingle rubbed in the embarrassment that W.'s Franco speech had caused him in U.S.A. He said he was there at the very worst moment – <u>after</u> W.'s speech & before the Flying Bomb.

We then took Archie on about the Election – was there any truth in the rumour that the Tories mean to 'pull' one with 'Victory in sight' but not attained? Archie appeared quite ignorant but said Beaverbrook might be working towards that end. Then the problem of Bev. & the Party's post-war plans. On this he put up quite a good case. It was impossible for us to commit ourselves now. If the Tories got a clear majority they cld do without us. If Labour got a small one they might want other Parties in. If the Tories got a small one – ? That wld be the difficult situation I think. I heard another Flying Bomb which passed over us fall with a crash. When I got home I found Miss Tunnard very much shaken having been blown over on the pavement by it, & seen & helped to bandage many people cut with glass. It fell in Aldwych on the blast wall between Bush House & the Air Ministry.

I have since heard 40 B.B.C. 'personnel' were hurt – 9 seriously. Left for Winchester by 5.30 & found Ray looking very well....

Diary – Monday 3 July – 40 Gloucester Square, W.2

One of the worst nights ever. Flying Bombs falling 2 or 3 in 5 minutes. They sounded near but were not in fact within the Paddington area, until one fell somewhere in Westbourne Grove at $\frac{1}{4}$ to 8 in the morning. B. & I went out for a few hours between 12 & 2.30 or so. Then as things seemed quieter tried to sleep again. I may have slept $1\frac{1}{2}$ hours in the whole night.

Went to see Brendan open an Exhibition of War Photography by the Daily Express.... Flying Bombs falling in a desultory way throughout the day. Storms of tropical rain – the streets a deluge. Awful for our offensive in France. The fall of Minsk announced in the 9 o'clock news. Germans must know they are doomed.

Diary – Friday 7 July – 40 Gloucester Square, W.2

... Telephoned to Jasper when I got back. It is almost unbearable to see the Daily notices in the Times 'safe in Allied hands' ... & still no news of Bubbles. Jasper told me of one strange development – C. has received a post card addressed to Bubbles from an old fellow-prisoner in [camp] 21 now in a German prison-camp.... [This] is the 1st <u>authentic</u> news we have had that B. was out & 'at large'. How I pray every hour of every day that we may get news of him. Jasper is going to the W.O. with the p.c. Mark arrived & will be here till Sunday. Gilbert Talbot has been killed – a real tragedy. He was in Normandy. Also poor little Persse in Italy.[1]

Diary – Sunday 9 July – 40 Gloucester Square, W.2

Grey wet day. <u>Never</u> has there been such a summer – nor one in which
the weather fought so cruelly against us. Again no flying will be possible
in Normandy & the low grey clouds help the Flying Bombs here (though
that is <u>relatively</u> unimportant). I had the <u>worst</u> Public Information Report
from the M. of I. I have had since the war. It gave me a shock to realize
<u>how</u> morale had been shaken by this thing – even in salted old Blitz
veterans. . . .

. . . As I write a Flying Bomb is circling overhead. Slept upstairs in perfect
peace. Fall of Caen announced on 9 o'clock news.

Diary – Sunday 16 July – Manor Farm, Stockton, Wiltshire

Church with B. & a large American party with the Y.B.'s afterwards (new
Americans – the old ones have moved off). They are the bravest people in
the world (the Y.B.'s I mean) still teaching Americans croquet from 8 a.m.
onwards. . . .

Diary – Wednesday 19 July – 40 Gloucester Square, W.2

. . . <u>Terrible news</u> brought by B. from Jasper about Bubbles.[2] I cannot realize
or accept it. It has taken all the meaning out of life. I feel it is final – tho'
he still feels there may be a loophole of hope.

I wld rather be crucified ten thousand times over than think of Cressida.
Her whole life is in the minefield with him.

---

[1] Gilbert Seymour Talbot (1921–44) and John Henry Persse (1922–44), Winchester contemporaries of Mark Bonham Carter, were both serving in the Rifle Brigade, and both killed
on 20 June – Talbot, a captain, near Bayeux, and Persse, a lieutenant, near Perugia. Talbot was
perhaps Mark's greatest friend at the school, and Persse a fellow member of Trant's house.

[2] Bubbles had been killed on 13 December of the previous year, in a minefield near Castel
di Sangro, about 80 miles south-east of Rome. He had escaped from captivity in northern
Italy, while being transferred to Germany with the other inmates of the Chieti camp.

Diary – Thursday 20 July – 40 Gloucester Square, W.2

Nathalie came round to see us in the morning. Jasper told her last night. She is a heroic woman. She feels it is final. She said 'I cannot grudge him for this cause. It is the only cause – the only war that has ever been worth fighting'. She is thinking of Cressida. We all felt she shld be told ... she may get a letter any day from Bubbles. Nathalie will go down tomorrow & B. will follow on Saturday....

Went to see Mr Weston at W.O. Intelligence Branch – in Curzon St – nice – sympathetic man. I can see he has no hope.

Diary – Friday 21 July – 40 Gloucester Square, W.2

The attempt on Hitler's life announced last night is the great news to-day. A time bomb went off at his Conference of Generals & he went to the microphone to denounce a conspiracy of a small clique of criminal Generals. Every sort of wild rumour was circulating of civil war in Germany – purges – executions etc. Himmler has been put in charge of everything.[1] Hitler was <u>slightly</u> bruised & burned & scratched. Von Stauffenberg placed the bomb. Beck has been executed.[2]

Lunched with Cys at Shelley's Dive. I can think only of Bubbles & Cressida's future. I felt every hour today – these are the last <u>happy</u> hours of her life. Nathalie will soon be telling her. Put out the light – & then put out the light.[3]

Diary – Sunday 23 July – 40 Gloucester Square, W.2

A long grey sad day spent alone here. Diana in to some meals. Went to R.C. Cathedral in the afternoon. Occasional Alerts. Wrote to Cressida. Telephoned to Mark just back from Barnstaple. Poor darling I had to tell him – B still at Mockbeggars. He says Cressida is <u>wonderful</u> & little Adam a great solace & occupation. How Bubbles wld have loved him.

[1] Heinrich Himmler (1900–45), Reichsführer-SS, head of Gestapo; minister of interior, 1943–5.

[2] The bomb plot of 20 July aimed at Hitler's 'Wolf's Lair' headquarters in East Prussia, and was the focal point of a widespread conspiracy in which army generals and leading civilians were implicated. Chief among the conspirators was Count von Stauffenberg (1907–44), who planted the bomb. He and General Ludwig Beck (1880–1944), regarded as a potential head of state after a successful coup, were summarily executed that night. Thousands of Germans were subsequently killed in Nazi retribution.

[3] '... I know not where is that Promethean heat / That can thy light relume': *Othello*, V, ii.

Bubbles' letter to her arrived yesterday morning – a few hours after Nathalie had told her – only just in time. B. says it is poignant beyond words in its impatience. He cldn't wait – & yet poor – poor darling waited too long. For if he had started south ... & gone by a lucky route he wld have reached our lines about the same time as Mark did – when the German lines were still thin & easier to get through.

Diary – Tuesday 25 July – 40 Gloucester Square, W.2

Two Committees – Blanket Bill at 1 & Liaison at 4.15 in Percy's room at H. of C. Went thro' all the seats & candidates in England – & was depressed by the tracts of Liberal wasteland.[1] Leaden heart & find it difficult to work or concentrate. Telephoned Nancy Morse for news of Cressida which she gave me. I am thankful she is there – she said they had had a 'good' day – & that she still can't realize or believe it – she has such a 'happy' feeling about Bubbles. I have lost faith in hunches....

Diary – Tuesday 1 August – 40 Gloucester Square, W.2

Up by the early train & lunched with Winston. Party: Clemmie, Sylvia, Barbie Wallace, Gen. Spears, Beaver, Eddie Marsh.[2] Eddie rushed up to me when I arrived & said 'How's Bubbles?' & when I told him burst into tears. I was so touched. W. came in looking <u>pinker</u> than I had expected – & tho' fairly puffy not unwell.

I said he was looking much better than I thought he wld & he replied, to my surprise 'But I am not really well. My inside worries me – even when I eat next to nothing.' I asked him whether going to Normandy had been bad for him. He said 'no that had done him good'. In spite of the good news his mood was not <u>sanguine</u> (this also surprised me). He talked of secret weapons quite apprehensively – tho' agreeing they <u>cld</u> make no difference to the outcome of the war. I believe that what is really weighing on his mind is the prospect of peace-making, with all its difficulties. He said to me 'When I was at Teheran I realized for the 1st time what a very <u>small</u> country this is. On one hand the big Russian bear with its paws

---

[1] Liberal Party constituency associations had suffered from a progressive decline, greatly exacerbated by the Asquith–Lloyd George schism. Despite its declared ambition of forming a government after the next election the party could field candidates in only 307 of 640 constituencies.

[2] Major-General Sir Edward (Louis) Spears (1886–1974), cr. CBE, 1919; KBE, 1942; Conservative MP for Carlisle, 1931–45; first minister to Syria and Lebanon, 1942–4.

outstretched – on the other the great American Elephant – & between them the poor little British donkey – who is the only one that knows the right way home'.[1]

He said (probably truly) that directly the war was over everyone wld begin behaving as badly as possible. There wld be strikes & mutinies. The Govt which he had tried to hold together wld. break up: 'I shall be attacked by Crinks – & Herbert Morrison perhaps.' 'What sort of an Election must we have after the war & when?' – I said 3 or 4 months after the end – & that it must be a free Election – without Coupons – & reminded him of the excellent account he had given of 1918 in the 'Aftermath'.[2] He appeared not too pleased with this compliment & said 'I don't want any raking up of the past – none of that "Your M.P." stuff.'[3] I said 'The past is very relevant to the future – & some of us are not going to allow the Tory past to be forgotten. You remember it as well as I do'. He said 'The war has washed all that out.' – I said the young who had died in the war had done nothing to shrive Sir Horace Wilson or Patrick Hannon of their sins.[4] He said 'well everyone made mistakes – the Liberals only came along in the last 2 years.' – I reminded him that we had moved for a Ministry of Supply in 1936 – before anyone else – & rubbed in the familiar fact that the present Parlt. had been elected on a trick.[5] We then agreed on Baldwin's record & complete harmony was re-established!

He asked me how I thought things were going in the country. I said I thought a strong tide was flowing left – tho' not in the direction of any particular left Party. He asked me what I thought wld be a fair way of

[1] At Teheran Churchill faced American–Soviet pressure to formalize plans for 'Operation Overlord'. This he was reluctant to do, fearing that it would be at the expense of the Allied advance in Italy, to which British forces were heavily committed.

[2] Winston S. Churchill, *The World Crisis: The Aftermath* (1929), the fifth and final volume in his history of the Great War. Of the 1918 'Coupon election' he wrote: 'I was a consulted and consenting party.... But when the Election came it woefully cheapened Britain' (*Aftermath*, 40–1).

[3] Gracchus Tiberius (pseud.), *Your M.P.* (1944). Violet recommended the book to the Oxford University Liberal Club on 3 June, when condemning the Tory record of the 1930s: 'If any of you want to refresh yr own memories ... read "Your M.P." – a book of which I see your own M.P. Capt. Hogg bitterly complains.... "It is an attempt" he says "to pillory a group of politicians by publishing their less-considered statements". Wld. Capt. Hogg I wonder have welcomed the inclusion of his own Election Address – which was presumably a carefully considered statement? I remember it very vividly & think it well worthy of a place.'

[4] Sir Horace John Wilson (1882–1972), cr. GCB, 1937; official head of civil service, 1939–42, greatly valued by Chamberlain. Sir Patrick Joseph Hannon (d. 1963), cr. Kt, 1936; Conservative MP for Moseley, Birmingham, 1921–50.

[5] Baldwin had promised 'no great armaments' during the 1935 campaign, but the following year made statements apparently contradicting this, and suggesting that he had decided upon this as early as 1933; see A.J.P. Taylor, *1914–1945*, 385, 387.

allocating broadcasts between the Parties – & that he thought one way of giving the Libs. a fair deal wld be to do it on a basis of votes cast last time – rather than seats gained. Clemmie piped up with great courage & said 'W – I think you shld resign the leadership of the Tory Party before the Election. You shldn't use your great prestige to get them in again. They don't deserve it.' – for which I gave her good marks! He took me out alone & was most sweet about Bubbles & took me into his Secret Map Room – a room whose walls were entirely covered by maps, with all the divisions operating marked in flags – Guards Armoured Division etc. Three eminent Khaki-clad figures hovered about – saying 'Yes Sir' most deferentially at intervals. . . .

W. gave me the impression of being a very tired man – as tho' the last pull up the hill was an immense effort – & the grasshopper had become a burden. He once used the wrong word 'armisticed' instead of 'abdicated' about the King (Edward VIII) which was unlike him. Above all I didn't feel the exultation in approaching victory I had expected. He thinks a terrible world lies ahead of us – & said to me 'You will see it – thank God I shan't'.

Diary – Sunday 6 August – Manor Farm, Stockton, Wiltshire

Very hot radiant day. Church with Ray B. & Laura. . . . Long hot lazy afternoon in the garden. After tea Ray Laura & Jag went off to bathe in the pool at Fisherton De-la-Mare. The war news is dramatically good. The Americans have overrun & cut off the whole Brest Peninsula & we are across the Orne. The Russians do not claim to be in East Prussia yet but they must be very near. It looks like the real beginning of the end.

I am so ashamed to feel so little exhilaration – & to realize how much my impatient longing for victory centred in Bubbles' return – how empty it all seems without him – how narrow & personal one's outlook is – how one's human perspective is limited by the intensity of one's human relations.

Diary – Friday 11 August – 40 Gloucester Square, W.2

Travelling up in the train yesterday as we got near London a fellow traveller lent me his Daily Telegraph. The 1st thing that caught my eye in small type at the bottom of the page was 'Captain George Grey M.P. for Berwick killed in action.' I am so numbed with pain over Bubbles that I hardly can register sorrow any more. George Grey is a tremendous loss. I loved him & so did Mark – & their future political companionship wld have been of <u>inestimable</u> value to each other & the Party. I think he is the greatest loss the Party cld have sustained. He wld most certainly have led it one day.... Curiously enough neither Mark nor I thought of him as amongst the 'predestined'. I felt he had a lucky star & wld survive. Worked all day till I left with B. by 5 o'clock for Stockton. <u>Very</u> hot journey – arrived late. Ray doing agricultural work on Frank Sykes's farm. He & B. sleeping out.

Diary – Tuesday 15 August – 40 Gloucester Square, W.2

Up by the early train & L.P.O. Committee at 2.15. Have written to Bev. to ask if he wld consider Berwick vacancy if offered it.[1] Dingle drove me back. He is passionately anxious that <u>I</u> should take it – but as I have told him <u>they do not want me</u> – which is the deciding factor. He suggested that I might take it up to the General Election & then – if they wished it – make way for a young Service candidate. I said that if I went into the House at all it shld be for more than 2 or 3 months. He said 'I am sure that once there they wld wish to keep you.' But I feel very clearly that one's relationship with one's Constituency shld be – indeed <u>must</u> be – a romantic one – & not a marriage de convenance....

Diary – Wednesday 16 August – 40 Gloucester Square, W.2

... On to see Wilfrid – mainly about Berwick. He wanted my view – which is exactly <u>his</u> – i.e. that Beveridge wld be the greatest asset to the Party if he took it, as it wld get him committed as a Liberal 'pur sang' before the Election – which might have a quite incalculable effect on our party fortunes in swinging votes elsewhere. He told me that Hugh Seely is averse to Bev. & has gone up to stay with Allendale to oppose the idea – shld it be suggested.[2] He wants <u>Mark</u> to stand there! (Archie I gather also favours Mark.) It is all very flattering to Mark – but I feel that it wld be quite wrong for him to leave Barnstaple where he has just been adopted. Mark came up for the night & quite agrees with me. He was looking really well – having had a more healthy outdoor life than usual. His presence I find the most <u>comforting</u> of all – because I know that he is suffering in exactly the same way as I am.

[1] Berwick became vacant with the death of George Grey. Beveridge wrote to Violet on 21 August to say that he would accept the candidature.

[2] Hugh Michael Seely (1898–1970), cr. Baron Sherwood, 1941; Liberal MP for Berwick-upon-Tweed, Northumberland, 1935–41; additional under-secretary of state for air, 1941–5. Wentworth Henry Beaumont (1890–1956), 2nd Viscount Allendale, 1923; president of Northern Liberal Federation, 1925–49.

Diary – Thursday 17 August – 40 Gloucester Square, W.2

Met Cressida & Adam at Liverpool St – the first time I have seen her. Her face moved me more than I can say – in its indescribable suffering – & at the same time what Nancy called 'sublime acceptance'. She looked very white & ill – & is not well. . . . I am haunted by her words – 'the unbeaconed future' – that is what she faces – every hour. Oh that I cld go as Orpheus did to Hades – & bring back Bubbles & stay there myself instead.

Diary – Tuesday 29 August – 40 Gloucester Square, W.2

. . . Percy Harris rang me up after dinner & gave me a disquieting account of the Lib Shadow Cabinet lunch at which Beveridge's candidature was discussed. Archie, Sherwood & Crinks were dead against him – also Gwilym Lloyd George on the grounds that he wld be too critical of the Govt, & wanted undertakings from him that he wld support the Govt & even be prepared to take the Govt Coupon Letter. Dingle was admirable in the other sense – & Wilfrid strongly supported him & displayed some anger I was glad to hear. Percy himself was absolutely sound. Poor Allendale sat by, listening to these divided counsels. They broke up on a note of discord. Advance in France continues.

Diary – Wednesday 6 September – 40 Gloucester Square, W.2

. . . B & I alone in the house which feels strange. It is the 1st time for so long. Brigid is gone, Toto in U.S.A., Diana ordered by her husband to leave London because of Flying Bombs. There has been an almost unbroken lull in these since last Friday. End of Blackout on Sept. 17th announced on 9 o'clock News. Also suspension of Home Guard Drills etc. It is strange that I feel so little exhilaration at the coming of Victory & Peace. There is too much for which there can be 'no return'.

Diary – Wednesday 13 September – 40 Gloucester Square, W.2

. . . back to hear the news of Bev. Goodwin came through at 5.0 to say that the Berwick Executive had invited him 'to address their Association with a view to his possible adoption as a Liberal candidate'. This sounded rather guarded – but it is obviously essential to appear to safeguard the rights of the Berwick Association & not seem to rush them. I hastily drafted a message for the Press – then went off to my meeting at the Nat. Liberal

Club....[1] I went straight from there to the Dorchester where Bev. Ly Bev. & her 2 sons-in-law had just finished dinner. He had had a Press Conference & was in good spirits. Publicity obviously gives him a kick. I do think he is showing immense enterprise & courage to join the smallest poorest Party at such a moment in its fortunes & in his life – when he cld have safely sailed in as an Independent almost anywhere & almost any day....

Diary – Friday 6 October – 40 Gloucester Square, W.2

Very full day.... I had to hare back by bus to meet Desmond here. I hadn't seen him for months & we went together to a dramatization of the Last Chronicles of Barchester. Not really well acted but extraordinarily enjoyable. The interesting thing was that the whole audience sat spell bound through the Trollope dialogue. Desmond & I discussed what it cld be which had led to this extraordinary renaissance of Trollope during the war.[2] He thought it wasn't entirely 'escapism' – but a longing for a world with some fixed standards of value – in this shifting quicksand world. Back to find a wire from Bev. saying 'Contest on – will you speak eve of poll 16th Alnwick & Amble'. Went to R.A.C. with Desmond where we cld get no food but Spam sandwiches. Talked to him about Bubbles....

Diary – Wednesday 1 November – 40 Gloucester Square, W.2

Mark & I lunched at N° 10. When we arrived Clemmie explained rather excitedly to me that Corbin was coming! & when I expressed surprise entreated me not to quarrel with him as she said (falsely!) that I had done with de Margerie! I promised to treat him with 'cool civility' – which indeed I did when he came in looking more wretched & undergeared than ever....[3]

Winston looked a different being since his return from Russia. He had

---

[1] Beveridge was duly adopted and won the seat comfortably against an independent candidate, but with less than a quarter of the electorate voting.

[2] Vera Wheatley's adaptation of Trollope's *The Last Chronicle of Barset* (1867), *Scandal at Barchester*, played at the Lyric Theatre in London October–December 1944; the Trollope renaissance was stimulated before the war by the OUP publisher Humphrey Milford.

[3] Violet regarded Charles Corbin and Roland de Margerie, diplomats, as agents of Vichy, and they were consequently *persona non grata*. Corbin was ambassador in London during May–June 1940 but returned to France, telling de Gaulle 'You are right, but I'm an old civil servant. Outlawry is too much for me.' De Margerie (1899–1990), Reynaud's private secretary, served Pétain but 'wanted nothing to do with Vichy' and so arranged for himself the post of chargé d'affaires in Peking (Don Cook, *Charles de Gaulle*, 81).

obviously enjoyed his time there tremendously & told good stories after we left the room about the 'scabrous Lublin Committee' – a species of invented Quisling – whom he had 'tortured a little' & of how Grabski made Stalin cry by his (Russian) eloquence – but how Stalin still said 'no' through his tears. Also how maddening was the incapacity of <u>our</u> Poles to <u>make up their minds</u> – to cut their losses & give up Lwow – when time was racing against them & they might lose more with the Russian advance.[1] After lunch he made a violent attack to me on the B.B.C. Announcer's foreign pronunciation – 'Why do they call Aix la Chapelle "Aachen"! that guttural expectoration'. He wants all names Anglicized. I pointed out it wld be difficult to keep pace with him.[2] When they had all gone he talked about the Election – & asked if I was satisfied with his statement.[3] I said I thought everyone was. He said 'Well I suppose we shall all be slanging each other in 6 months' time.' I said it might be a great advantage to him to lose a few of his Die-Hards. He said 'But things don't happen that way. They will keep their seats & the Progressives will be mown down if anyone is.'

He amused me by making a passionate personal appeal to me (!) not to try & get rid of all the Kings! 'Now look here my dear do keep these Kings!' 'But Winston – I don't bother about Kings one way or the other. I have nothing against King Haakon or the Queen of Holland. The King of Greece – well his own people don't seem to care much about him. I shld prefer a Restoration in Spain to Franco.' 'Now why do people say I praised up Franco?' – 'Because you did.' Short altercation on this. Then some ragging with Clemmie about Corbin – after which he said to me – 'My dear – there must be some worms in this world for you & me to tread on'! As we went upstairs together he reeled out a long magnificent sentence &

---

[1] The communist-controlled 'Lublin Committee', a Soviet-backed provisional government for Poland, took its name from the city that it declared the temporary capital. Professor Grabski was a leading member of the alternative exiled 'London Government'. Lwów, in the Ukraine, had been annexed by the Soviet Union in 1939 but was subsequently captured by the Germans. It was liberated by the Red Army in July 1944 and thereafter controversially remained in the Soviet Union.

[2] The B.B.C. board had originally defended the use of Aachen on the grounds that it was the version preferred by the press and the Allied command, but that, as Harold Nicolson recalled, did not satisfy Churchill: 'So incensed was he that he asked Violet to lunch and gave her a tremendous talking-to' (Nicolson, *Diaries and Letters 1939–1945*, 409–10).

[3] In the Commons on 31 October Churchill moved the second reading of the bill to prolong the life of parliament by another year. Sensing 'the odour of dissolution in the air' and the resurfacing of party rivalry, he hoped to cement the coalition until the defeat of Nazism. He promised that there would be no 'khaki' election, saying that a decent interval should elapse after victory 'while we are all rejoicing together and rendering thanks to God for our deliverance' (*The Times*, 1 November 1944).

said – 'Now remember <u>that</u>. I shall never say it so well again'.[1] Stalin had given him 2 absolutely <u>hideous</u> cut glass contraptions with zinc & aluminium bears, warriors & other objects at either end. Russian hospitality hadn't tired him & he said he hadn't drunk more than usual because they used 'conjurors glasses' half-filled up. Of Archie he said 'Poor Archie! he'll be very sad to leave the Air Ministry. With him the Air comes 1st – the Lib. Party 2nd – & poor Marigold – nowhere!' He had had a great reception at the Ballet in Moscow & Stalin who had never attended since the War went with him & joined in the applause. I was happy to see him looking <u>so</u> much better than last time. Literally a new man. I think now that he will 'stay the course' – to victory & after.

Diary – Friday 3 November – 40 Gloucester Square, W.2

Beveridge's Maiden speech in the House. I sat above the clock with Ly Bev. & a daughter-in-law. He followed Butler & was obviously nervous when he started but got well going with a joke about 'paternity' & a maiden-speech – which is just the sort of thing the H. of C. enjoys – & the rest went off well.[2] We went down afterwards to luncheon with her & Dingle & he was plied with sherry & surrounded by a court of admirers & congratulations. . . .

Diary – Monday 6 November – 40 Gloucester Square, W.2

. . . Straight to the Agenda Committee – long controversy over Dingle's Foreign Policy resolution in which I found myself at friendly loggerheads with Bev – who sees the international field thro' rosy spectacles of ideal & quite impracticable solutions. This war, which has brought me down to earth with a bump (the <u>fact</u> of Russia), has made him raise his claims. . . .

Diary – Saturday 11 November – Winchester

. . . Ray tells us that 'Monty' was here 2 days ago & addressed the school for an hour in his most typical form. 'This is a very interesting map – because it is the map <u>I</u> held in <u>my</u> hand when <u>I</u> landed on D Day'. It is

---

[1] Re-reading her diary in the 1960s Violet noted 'Alas! I have forgotten it!'

[2] 'The admitting of paternity is always a slightly delicate operation; perhaps it is a particularly delicate admission in what is a maiden speech.' Beveridge spoke in the debate on the government's social insurance scheme (*The Times*, 4 November 1944).

interesting that his ego-centricity is glaringly obvious to the whole school & that he is <u>not</u> a hero to them tho' he cultivates them so assiduously....

Diary – Wednesday 15 November – 40 Gloucester Square, W.2

... Went to luncheon for International Youth Centre given by Lord Bennett (with Stafford & Isabel Cripps & myself as joint hosts)....[1] I sat between Stafford Cripps & Ld Bennett – & talked all thro' lunch to Stafford. I said I saw the Labour Party were pulling down their candidate against him at Bristol. He said 'that depends on whether I am going back to the Party or not.' I thought it was settled. He said he hoped we shldn't run candidates against each other. I asked him what he thought of Beveridge. He said 'I think he is a very good <u>Liberal</u> economist' stressing the word Liberal as a mitigating factor. He said he thought Bev. a strong supporter of Private Enterprise. I said we weren't doctrinaire about it either way. We were empiricists. He thinks it doubtful whether the Labour Party will allow their members to go back into a Coalition after the war even if majorities were very narrow. Jan Masaryk spoke well. Cripps efficiently but dully....

Diary – Thursday 16 November – 40 Gloucester Square, W.2

Bd. Meeting. Discussed output report – disability & other things. Came home to find Mark had arrived for his embarkation leave. I feel an awful knell sounding for us all. To go back to this horror in cold blood after a year at home is very difficult – & in this weather! Snow on all the fronts. I thought of what he must be feeling as we listened to War Report – the fighting in Holland – mines – machine guns – flame throwers etc.[2] He was very tired having had a beano & been up all last night. Papers full of rumours that Hitler is mad – ill-ordered.

Diary – Tuesday 21 November – 40 Gloucester Square, W.2

Sir Clifford Heathcote-Smith of the I. Refugees Committee (our rep. in Italy) came to see me this morning to urge me to urge the Govt to take

[1] Richard Bedford Bennett (1870–1947), cr. Viscount, 1941; Canadian politician, appointed chairman of the London advisory committee of the Canadian Red Cross Society.

[2] After rejoining his regiment early in December Mark Bonham Carter was kept in England until 30 January, when he joined the 1st Battalion of Grenadier Guards in Belgium.

further action to save the 11 million 'threatened' people still in German hands.[1] The facts he gives about the death-trains leaving with the regularity of Bradshaw – human beings packed 80 at a time into sealed trucks where they are left for 4 days & nights & arrive with dead & living & dying jammed together & are then driven to gas-chambers & slaughter houses is too terrible. He says truly that as we have 7 skins & only feel with one or two top ones – so these things do not penetrate to the deeper layers of our thought & feeling. I don't know what I can do – except write what he says to Bracken. He wants more warnings – by broadcasts & leaflets dropped on Germany....

Diary – Thursday 30 November – 40 Gloucester Square, W.2

Interesting Board Meeting. Haley behaved with great spirit to the Americans who broadcast to Germany a most <u>horrible</u> account of 2 German spies being executed, with their last words, confessions etc. 'live' – the loading of guns, firing squad etc. It was quite revolting & Haley sent a message to say that if it was repeated all B.B.C. personnel – engineers etc. wld be withdrawn. Fraser typically defended it – <u>if</u> it was well broadcast!...

Diary – Sunday 10 December – 40 Gloucester Square, W.2

... Dingle came to lunch here & we had a long political jaw in the afternoon about Party Finance etc. He said (truly) that Bev. is 1st rate on Full Employment & Social Security – much less good on Electoral reform & International policy & begged me to curb him on this terrain – saying that I had created this Frankenstein & must now control it!...

Diary – Saturday 16 December – 40 Gloucester Square, W.2

Memorial Service for beloved Bubbles at St Bartholomew's Smithfield where he & Cressida were married. A grey wet day – Laura arrived about 2 & she & I & C. went together by Underground – & found Mark, Ray & B., Nathalie, Jasper, Patrick & Constantine there.[2] I had not been there since the June day when they were married. We walked down the same narrow stone passage leading to the church & I remembered them coming

---

[1] Sir Clifford Heathcote-Smith (1883–1963), cr. KBE, 1943; representative in Italy of inter-governmental committee on refugees, 1944–5.

[2] Patrick and Constantine were Bubble's brothers.

out into the sunlight & C.'s beauty – in her lovely dress & the radiance & gravity in Bubbles's face – & the crowd & the cameras clicking – –

The Service was infinitely lovely & moving.... I sat between Mark & Ray. Cressida sat between Jasper & Nathalie. Her face had the beauty of stone.... She walked away alone.... When she got back she told me she had walked back all thro' the City past their house in Mecklenburgh Square & found a void where it had stood. It had been destroyed by a bomb.

Diary – Boxing Day, Tuesday 26 December – Manor Farm, Stockton

One of the most beautiful days I can remember in my life. The whitest – hardest frost – unimaginable. The beauty of Long Hedges frozen into white coral is a thing I shall remember always. It was more beautiful than snow – for every line had an exquisite – feathery delicacy. The whole world seemed the work of a master draughtsman – Ingres or John or Dürer – not a painter. Frank Sykes fetched us at 11.30 – Laura Ray Gelda Jag & self – & took us to the meet at Heytesbury. We went by car to Tytherington & then changed into the Pony Trap where I sat in front with the 2 children & Frank & Laura & Ray on the floor behind. We drove thro' white watermeadows, white willows [and] white poplars glittering in still sunshine & crystal air, over frozen puddles to Heytesbury where there was a small meet of a dozen people in the village street. Barbara & Tristram 'whips'. Then we drove up the steep hill round Siegfried's wood which the hounds were 'drawing' & heard them baying through it – & then as we walked down the hill saw them all plunging out through the cover into the sunshine below us & back into the wood again.[1]

Back to lunch at $\frac{1}{4}$ to 2. Then out again with Frank B & Ray & Jebb & a pottering shoot round the copses in Stockton Park.... Out of the sunshine it was icy cold – but in it heavenly. The frost was so hard that the white beauty remained till the very end of the day – & the Jack Frost on my bedroom window-pane <u>un</u>thawed to-night.

On the Wireless in the 9 o'clock news I heard to my amazement that W. & Anthony Eden are in Athens![2] When they arrived I don't yet know

[1] Siegfried Sassoon (1886–1967) lived at Heytesbury House in Wiltshire; he and Violet had become good friends during the period when the Bonham Carters stayed at nearby Stockton.

[2] Churchill and Eden had flown to Athens on Christmas Day, leaving England early in the morning with a small staff. Their aim was to bring the parties in the Greek civil war then raging to the conference table. Churchill hoped that this initiative, backed up by a British military presence, would give rise to a coalition government that would save Greece from communist domination. It was a dramatic mission, involving considerable discomfort and some risk, and several times during the three-day visit Churchill's party came under fire from communist forces.

as I missed the news last night when Frank & Barbara dined with us – & we have had no papers for 2 days. I must say Winston is a dauntless man. At his age & with his burdens & 2 major illnesses, to undertake such a journey at such a moment.

Diary – New Year's Eve, Sunday 31 December – Manor Farm, Stockton

A very lovely last day of the old year. It froze again tho' not so hard – & we walked to church in early sunshine down a hard dry village road. After luncheon Ray & I & B & Jag went 'wooding' up at Stockton Wood.... Dinner here – B & I & Laura & Ray. Listened to the Wireless Programme (Robert Donat very good as narrator) ending with a Watch Night Service in St Paul's. The News announced that Hitler was speaking. I switched on & heard him for $\frac{1}{2}$ an hour or so. Quite changed & subdued. No shouting. Strange end to the year.

ELEVEN

Victory and Defeat

1945

Diary – Sunday 7 January 1945 – 40 Gloucester Square, W.2

Ray came into my bedroom fully dressed in battle dress & covered with packs & various appurtenances slung around his not-very-big form – rather a touching sight. He hurried off to catch his train at 11 from King's Cross going by underground. I hope his journey isn't as vile as yesterday's & that the camp & course is all his fancy pictures.[1] Mark came down late & looking very sleepy but well. He said that walking home last night about 2.30 (from the '400') down Edgware Rd he heard 2 short explosions – much smaller than 'V2' & saw a wonderful red glow all over the sky.[2] He & I spent a peaceful day together at work in front of the boudoir fire – broken only by one short <u>icy</u> walk in Ken. Gardens which was worth doing because it made one so glad to get back. He left about 6.30. He came up on Wed. to dine with the Dss of Kent.[3] He had a nice party on Xmas night at the Castle. He said the King had a long outburst to him about the W.O. – adding with a hoarse Hanoverian chuckle 'And after all I am the head of the Army – aren't I?' Mark didn't know whether he ought to assent <u>seriously</u> – or laugh!...

Diary – Friday 26 January – 40 Gloucester Square, W.2

... When I got home I heard that Mark had rung me up. He got through later & told me that he had just had orders (the day before) to <u>go abroad next Tuesday</u>. This was a body blow to me. He had no idea of going for

[1] Raymond left for a junior military training course at Catterick army base, where he was much the youngest to take part.

[2] The 'V2' rocket was a ballistic missile, a forerunner of the later long-range weapons. First used on Paris on 6 September 1944, more than 1,300 were subsequently fired at Britain, the last in March 1945. Like the V1 it carried a 2,000lb warhead but, unlike the V1, there was no defence against it.

[3] Princess Marina, HRH Duchess of Kent (d. 1968), youngest daughter of HRH Prince Nicholas of Greece and Denmark; married, 1934, HRH the Duke of Kent (killed on active service, 1942).

he had arranged to 2nd the Peace Resolution next week at the [Liberal] Assembly & hoped to get down to his constituency again. I spent a leaden-hearted hour being photographed by 'Pictorial Press' in this house – Ray being a great help. Then B. & I dined with the Mowrers at the Dorchester. Winant our only fellow-guest – except their nice boy just back from an Antarctic convoy. Enjoyed it enormously. Mowrer is <u>quite</u> delightful – simple & quite un-'ébloui' by all he has shared. He gave a very amusing a/c of his Moscow visits. He thinks Stalin a gangster but very remarkable & with a real grip on things & very quick wits. When W. said that England was getting rather pinker he replied 'That's a sign of good health' & when W. toasted 'The Proletarian masses' he retorted by toasting 'The Conservative Party'. He gave an amusing description of Montgomery spending a whole day in the desert talking about himself....

Diary – Saturday 27 January – 40 Gloucester Square, W.2

Mark arrived early – before I was up – on another icy day. He looked ill & shivery being full of 3 inoculations – typhoid typhus & tetanus. Ray & he went out for a bit & then he sat rather drowsily by the fire. Ray left after lunch for Winchester – quite happy & looking better – B. saw him off. We spent the rest of the day by the fire – Mark dozing & reading – obviously feeling ill.... It is <u>horrible</u> looking at flasks – morphia & other objects for Mark to take away. There is something more sinister than usual about setting out away from home & fires into this freezing world.

Diary – Sunday 28 January – 40 Gloucester Square, W.2

A sad Sunday spent sitting by the fire with Mark – broken only by 2 short outings.... It was horrible to feel that it was our last Sunday. It was so exactly like the rest – & I had felt so confident that they were going on – & so I think had he. I thought him <u>very</u> depressed. He has no illusions about what is before him. This time there is no glamour – no voyage of discovery into the unknown – not even a lovely journey under strange sunny skies round Africa. Just a short transit across an icy sea with cold horror at the other end. I think also that he minds terribly leaving things here – his constituency – his undelivered speech at the [Liberal] Assembly – his new friends (Dss of Kent etc!). We looked out socks & boots. He wrote innumerable letters & went off by the $\frac{1}{4}$ to midnight train back to Windsor. He passes through for the last time on Tuesday.

Diary – Tuesday 30 January – 40 Gloucester Square, W.2

Thaw began today & the roads were a sea of brown slush tho' much snow
is still lying. I spent the morning trying to get gloves for Mark & succeeded
at last in finding <u>one</u> pair of the sheepskin kind he wanted at Gieves –
after ringing up 10 shops – many of whom (Fortnum for instance) hadn't
a <u>single</u> pair of any kind. He arrived soon after lunch with his soldier
servant & spent most of the afternoon packing & getting things together –
Iodine, morphia, flasks etc. stood on the table like preparations for an
operation – <u>parting</u> – the major operation in life. . . . B & I & he went out
thro' the snow to dine at Claridges – where we dined so rapturously on
the night of his return – the happiest night of my life. Cobb fetched us
8.15 & we picked up his luggage here & then Bong drove with him to St.
Pancras – & saw him off. He got a sleeper. He is bound for Harwich. Hitler
spoke at 10.15. Very bad transmission. I cld hardly hear anything. The
beginning was the old stuff about Jewish Bolshevikness – the end a com-
mendation to the 'Gnade' of God.

> *'The "bow & arrow" men were defeated by overwhelming majorities'*
> *– the Liberal Party Assembly, 1–3 February 1945*

With a general election expected after the defeat of Germany,
the 1945 Liberal Assembly assumed a special significance. It was
inconceivable to Violet that the coming election could be anything
other than a free fight between the parties, and that notwithstanding its great success the wartime coalition would end. As
she pointed out in her presidential address, the electorate had
been 'disenfranchised' for ten years, and millions had never had a
chance to vote. It was the duty of Liberals to ensure not just that
they had that chance, but that they were not forever condemned
to a choice between Conservative and Labour, 'between two rotten
apples . . . between the two evils of Tory stagnation and the Socialist
strait-jacket of control'. With this speech the battle lines of renewed
political conflict were drawn. None of those gathered at the Kingsway Hall in London could have been under any illusions as to the
difficulty of the task ahead. From an inter-war peak of 159 seats in
1923, the party's representation had fallen to just 21 in 1935. Violet
believed that if the Liberals were to reverse this trend they must
take the offensive – 'to be defensive is to be defeatist' – and without
rejecting a glorious past she advocated 'twentieth-century
methods' for 'twentieth-century problems'. The embodiment of
this forward-looking approach was Sir William Beveridge, who was
welcomed to the assembly as the party's 'latest & greatest recruit'.

He was given a central role in proceedings, and on the second day introduced a motion calling for 'full employment'. Violet regarded this as 'the most vital resolution' of the hour, 'the acid test by which all political Parties in this country are going to be judged'. Only weeks before, Beveridge's *Full Employment in a Free Society* had been published, and he spoke as an acknowledged expert. There were only four dissenting votes to his proposal, and these came from what Violet disparagingly called the 'bow and arrow men' of the party, reactionaries who would not embrace necessary change. She was encouraged that the vast majority supported fully the ambitious programme of social reconstruction endorsed by the party executive. The assembly had been positive, even buoyant, but *The Times* registered a note of scepticism. The previous year's White Papers on social security and full employment showed, it suggested, that policies the Liberals claimed as their own already commanded the assent 'of liberals in all three parties' and also of 'the liberal-minded majority of the nation as a whole'. But while there was a 'liberal' consensus, this did not translate into 'Liberal' votes, and herein lay the Party's dilemma. To exploit their undeniable electoral potential Liberals had to appear as a credible instrument of government, an almost impossible task given their standing at inter-war polls.[1]

Diary – Monday 5 February – 40 Gloucester Square, W.2

Monday spent in a turmoil of letters – still feeling very tired. I was rung up in the evening by Fothergill who had had a talk with Morrison that morning. He was enthusiastic about my speech & said he was going to get it printed for distribution in his own Party. At the end of their talk, & separated from all this by a decent interval, he said it wld be very helpful if we did not run a candidate in East Lewisham – (his own constituency!)....[2] Low had an <u>excellent</u> cartoon in the Evening Standard of me dressed as a knight of old in armour riding thro' a wood with Bev. ambling behind on a mule towards 3 figures – one (tied to a tree)

[1] VBC to Arthur Mann, 4 February 1945; *The Times*, 2, 3, 4 February 1945.

[2] Violet had received a warm and congratulatory letter from Morrison the previous day, praising her performance at the Assembly. She wondered what significance to attach to the note, marked '<u>Private</u> & Personal', but while Morrison flirted with the idea of a Liberal–Labour alliance his commitment went no deeper.

labelled 'People' & 2 card-players labelled 'Tory Party' & 'Labour' – with the caption 'Which one of us is she going to rescue?'[1]

Diary – Tuesday 6 February – 40 Gloucester Square, W.2

Letters all day. Woman Power Committee at 4 – very dull. Thelma & Summerskill approached & congratulated me simultaneously – Summerskill saying 'I am so glad you called the Tory Party "Rotten apples"' – Thelma: '<u>Some</u> people regret that you said that.' Point completely missed by both.[2]

Diary – Thursday 8 February – 40 Gloucester Square, W.2

Amusing Board Meeting – at which I had one of the clashes with my colleagues which I thoroughly enjoy. Haley suggested that it might be a good thing to lay before the country in a series of broadcasts the policies for which the different Parties stand <u>before</u> the Election. I was of course strongly in favour of this course & said so. Fraser was of course passionately against. Mann, Mallon & Harold all wobbled & stressed the difficulties. I finally said that if I were in a minority of one I shld formally move [a resolution calling for broadcasts] that enlightened the public on these issues before the Election – & that I wished it to be put on record that I had done so. The Chairman said he thought there was a general agreement with Fraser – at which Harold, Mann & Mallon got nervous & protested – & I mocked their alarm. Mallon begged me to postpone my motion for a fortnight & after a pretence at indecision I consented to do so.

---

[1] David (Alexander Cecil) Low (1891–1963), New Zealand-born political cartoonist, with *Evening Standard* from 1927. Low's cartoon plays on the central theme of Violet's presidential address to the Assembly, that the Liberal Party could free the people from the thrall of Tory and Labour dominance. The cartoon was popular among Liberals, and Violet signed twenty copies for auction for the Party's 'Fighting Fund'; it is reproduced above.

[2] Edith Clara Summerskill (1901–80), Labour MP for West Fulham, 1938–55. Thelma Cazalet Keir (1899–1945), younger sister of Victor Cazalet (married, 1939, David Keir); Conservative MP for East Islington, 1931–45. Violet's point was that the two extremes represented by Summerskill and Cazalet Keir were equally unattractive (see above, p. 326).

M.R.B.C. to V.B.C.   *Friday 9 February*
                                                          50 R.H.U. B.L.A.

Dear Mama,

I feel rather apologetic as I might have written sooner & I am convinced that you think I might be thrown into a bloody engagement on arrival as it happened last time. It couldn't however be further from the truth as I am drifting about in this very quiet backwater.[1] I read intermittent reports of the Liberal Assembly....

Will you forward all my letters on to me at the above address. I trust that I won't be here too long but I think I may be here long enough to get letters. I would also welcome a monthly parcel of 6 ozs of Players Medium Navy Cut (not mixture) tobacco, & a weekly Times or Manchester Guardian.... Let me know the news of the Assembly – I'm glad you raised £7000 – it's a good start.[2] Love Mark

P.S. I really think that there might be a little English propaganda out here, bearing in mind one's views on a Western bloc. In the very short time I've been here I can't pretend to have seen many newspapers, but all the News Films are American, & so are the Interest films.

Diary – Wednesday 14 February – 40 Gloucester Square, W.2

... Wrote innumerable letters – then went off to a very amusing Women's Press Club behind the Law Courts which was being opened by Brendan. Had a word or two with him about Mark – also about W. who did have a cold at Malta but is now better. Saw Ellen Wilkinson who congratulated me on my speech with far more fervour than any Liberal has done! The passage about Winston & the Women & Children was what chiefly delighted her. She said 'You have exploded this huge land-mine under them 6 months before they meant to use it'.[3] She cldn't have been more friendly & enthusiastic.

[1] Mark Bonham Carter had joined the 1st Battalion at its base at St Trond, 45 miles east of Brussels, where it was preparing for the attack on the Rhine that would mark the final phase of the war in Europe.

[2] This sum was promised to the Liberal 'Fighting Fund', opened at the Assembly to finance the party's campaign at the general election.

[3] 'He [WSC] is not only the leader of the Nation. He is also the leader of a Private Army – the Conservative Party – an Army in whose numbers we desire to see a considerable reduction – to put it mildly.... They cannot claim immunity at our hands – they cannot expect to deflect our aim by driving Mr Churchill in front of them – as tho' he were the "Women and Children" (& there is nothing that he less resembles) & shouting "You know it's very dangerous to fire at us. You might hit our great Leader by mistake – and that would be most ungrateful – & very

Diary – Thursday 15 February – 40 Gloucester Square, W.2

... On to H. of C. where I went to a Committee Room taken by Eleanor Rathbone to hear evidence of 3 Poles who had been deported by the Russians – imprisoned & sent to forced labour. Terrible eye-openers as to what lies ahead of us. The woman was most remarkable – & rather beautiful – with a look of <u>intense</u> suffering. Brigid came in to see us.

Diary – Saturday 17 February – Winchester

Went to Winchester by 11.30.... walked down towards the Southgate & met Ray & Bong coming up to meet me. Back with them to a late lunch & then we went to see the Yalta News Reel – terribly funny – Winston in his fur-hat & British Warm – Roosevelt looking wasted & beautiful – Stalin like a neat Commissionaire....[1]

Diary – Monday 19 February – 40 Gloucester Square, W.2

... De Gaulle has refused to meet Roosevelt on his way back from Yalta. <u>Most</u> foolish I think. Thomas thinks right. To stand on one's dignity is like a servant – trying to keep his 'place'. Thomas thinks (rightly) that we are behaving badly to France....

Diary – Tuesday 20 February – 40 Gloucester Square, W.2

... After dinner I heard on the wireless with bale that Ll.G. is showing signs of great weakness. The bulletin sounded as if he were dying. Just what I feared! before Beveridge's promised visit! De Gaulle's refusal to meet Roosevelt is now officially announced. W. said 'It was <u>too</u> good an opportunity for de Gaulle to miss! after Roosevelt had sent 500,000 Americans to liberate his country'. No word of Mark.

unpatriotic into the bargain".' The difference between the 'two Winstons' was a profitable line of attack for Liberal and Labour at the general election in July.

[1] The 'big three' met at Yalta in the Crimea, 4–11 February, and discussed among other things the post-war settlement of Europe.

Diary – Thursday 22 February – 40 Gloucester Square, W.2

Long & animated Board Meeting – & good dog fight over my motion.[1] Harold pulled up his socks & seconded it. Fraser tried to circumvent it by a (as he thought) wily amendment. Mann with his usual muddle-headedness seconded the amendment. I refused to accept it. It was carried by 1 vote – Millis Mann & Fraser voting for it, Harold & I against it, & Mallon abstaining. It was so nonsensical in form that the Chairman himself (tho' he voted for it – I think most irregularly) proposed an amendment – i.e. that Haley shld go & consult with the political parties about their Election broadcasts, & the desirability of putting out the policies of Parties after the end of the war with Germany or before. As the negotiations will be in Haley's hands I agreed to this....

Diary – Saturday 24 February – 40 Gloucester Square, W.2

A lovely bright day with clear cold air & sunshine. Went out with B. on the vain quest (as it seemed at one moment) to buy a pair of shoes which I badly need. There is about one pair in one size in one colour in each shop.... At Fortnums by supreme luck I found a pair – not exactly what I wanted – but black, comfortable & wearable – tho' how long they will last I can't guess. Back by Bumpus where we looked in vain for a German dictionary for Mark. Lunch alone together & a short turn in the park.

The offensive in the West has begun – mostly the American 9th Army in the Aachen sector. I was visited at 4.30 by a man called Palyi – American of German extraction – sent to me by the M. of I. He stayed 3 hours but was really rather interesting. He was obviously very anti-Russia & said that he had been profoundly shocked by the 'hardboiledness' of people in this country about Poland. Cripps had shocked him by denying that foreign policy shd have any moral or ethical basis (I remember he once did the same to me when we were talking about Lithuania & Estonia). He was quite interesting about the German future – & obviously had a very soft spot still left for his own country. Able & rather pathetic. Anti-Roosevelt – saying that he wasn't taken seriously by his own country so far as foreign policy was concerned.

---

[1] This refers to Violet's proposed motion regarding BBC policy on pre-election broadcasts on the political parties; see above, p. 328.

Diary – Monday 26 February – 40 Gloucester Square, W.2

I had a very nice & most encouraging letter from Arthur Hobhouse telling me exactly what I wanted to know about Wells.[1] I feel strongly tempted to have a shot at it. Worked all the morning – had my hair washed (a rare luxury!) in the afternoon. I had a letter from Mark which only took 4 days. Still at R.H.U. 40. He describes hideous, flat, dull country – poor ugly people – thin small children. No beauty of line or colour anywhere. The English also vile! particularly the officers – who sleep with vests under their pyjamas & scrub their faces & red necks with cold water in the morning. I also had a nice letter from Jo – about Cressida amongst other things. The Americans are 14 miles from Cologne – & the German resistance is said to be becoming 'disorganized'. Up at the Canadian end on the other hand it is stiffening. There has been the biggest raid yet on Berlin. What hell it must be. Unimaginable.

Diary – Monday 5 March – 40 Gloucester Square, W.2

The Midnight news tells us of American tanks in Cologne – & the Germans withdrawing over the Rhine in some disorder – 60,000 prisoners taken altogether. German casualties estimated at 100,000. Most of the bridges blown up. We are fighting up near Wesel. Less agreeable news came with the revelation of the Dumbarton Oaks voting formula.[2] The Russians have clearly carried the day – for in order to take any action against an aggressor the 5 great powers must be unanimous – which means that no aggressor will ever be forcibly restrained. We are not afraid of aggression by Peru or Paraguay. The mastodons will be sitting on the heads of the aggressive mice. It is a most cynical decision. . . .

[1] Sir Arthur Lawrence Hobhouse (1886–1965), cr. Kt, 1942. Hobhouse had been Liberal MP for Wells, 1923–4. Despite Violet's positive thoughts about contesting Wells, it was a difficult seat for a Liberal to win, having been Conservative throughout the inter-war years with the exception of Hobhouse's brief tenure. The Conservative majority in 1935 was comfortably large, 7,621.

[2] Representatives of America, Britain, China and the Soviet Union met at Dumbarton Oaks, in Washington DC, 21 August–7 October, to discuss the United Nations organization. The Soviet Union demanded that the permanent members of the security council – the four powers present and France – should have power of veto. Violet was in agreement with Sir William Beveridge in thinking this 'the short way to a third world war', since it would compel the smaller states to seek protection from the permanent members, and divide the world into hostile power blocs (*The Times*, 7 March 1945).

Diary – Thursday 8 March – 40 Gloucester Square, W.2

The 9 o'clock news announced that the Americans are across the Rhine between Bonn & Coblentz – Gen Bradley's Army.[1] (How Monty will mind!) Things really do seem to be moving rapidly. The photographs of the ruins of Cologne are <u>appalling</u>. . . .

. . . Harold was back from Paris – where he said all those who had played an inglorious rôle (Jean Cocteau etc.) were full of explanations & long stories – & the real heroes said nothing. He said the French were very skinless & one's fingers felt all thumbs talking to them. (Bang! A very near V2 has just fallen.) I forgot to mention that Desmond told me Winston at the Other Club was very amusing describing his own attempts to explain Parly Govt to Stalin – who remarked at the end – 'But wldn't it be much simpler to just have <u>one</u> Party?'

Diary – Friday 9 March – 40 Gloucester Square, W.2

Lunched at the Air Ministry with Archie, Marigold, Percy, Angus, B & self. Violent altercation afterwards about Dumbarton Oaks Security Council Voting Procedure in which Archie as usual toed the Govt. line & showed no Liberal reactions of any kind. We had a good struggle of voices in which I was almost as un-interruptable as him. . . .

Diary – Monday 12 March – 40 Gloucester Square, W.2

. . . Lull on the Western Front. Laura writes me that she has heard from Jo '& even he admits the war can't last more than 6 weeks now'. Astonishing opinion from one on the spot – but which I find it difficult to share. <u>Letter from Mark</u> – still at R.H.U. 40. He has been to Brussels & had a tremendous blow-out Oysters – sirloins – wine etc.[2] It is horrible that all this shld exist side by side with starvation. He says a man's suit costs £75 & the shops are full of fur-coats, electric trains & other intricate electrical devices – all at fabulous prices.

---

[1] General Omar Nelson Bradley (1893–1981), commander of American armies in France, 1944.

[2] The Grenadiers' base at St Trond was only an hour by road from Brussels, and a return journey for dinner was a popular recreation among the officers.

Diary – Sunday 18 March – 40 Gloucester Square, W.2

A really loud V2 shook up the house at 9.30 this morning. It felt – & in fact was – much the nearest one we had had. It fell just where the orators hold forth near Marble Arch – killing 2 people & injuring about 20. The windows of the Post were broken. We lost none. No glass left in the Cumberland [Hotel] of course or down Bayswater Rd. B. & I walked down to see the crater – which was roped off. All the trees were intact except one which was down. It cldn't really have fallen in a much better place. Lunched alone with B. & had our usual walk to the Round Pond – grey with sails & birds. . . .

Diary – Saturday 24 March – Clovelly Court, Devon

. . . on to Bideford with Baker. On arrival there I was shot into the house of a Liberal called Mr Cock where I had a very secret tête-à-tête assignation with Mr Chubb – V. President of the local Labour Party. He is anxious not to oppose Mark. He fought with Oc in the Naval Division – is of old Liberal descent & says his T.U. followers don't want to present the seat to the Tories either. There are however other Labour elements who may think it their duty to fight unless they receive orders to the contrary from Transport House. I advised him to apply for orders there direct – resolving to communicate with E.W. myself. On to a 'Social Event' at Bideford – where I again had to speak & where songs & recitations followed – ending up with a marvellous tea. I felt utterly exhausted at the end of it all & was never more glad to arrive <u>anywhere</u> than at beloved Clovelly. . . . Too 'lively-minded' to sleep really well tho' I took a draught – but heavenly peace descended on me. On the 9 o'clock news the thrilling announcement was made that we are across the Rhine. The Germans left one bridge unblown up which had enabled the Americans to get across & now we had forced it higher up & were streaming across. I have never heard a more <u>thrilling</u> War Report. . . .

Diary – Tuesday 27 March – 40 Gloucester Square, W.2

Our deputation to Anthony Eden was put off as he has laryngitis. We met at the H. of C. instead with Percy Harris, Eric Drummond, Gilbert Murray, Andrew McFadyean – & discussed our brief.[1] Eric showed far more edge,

---

[1] Sir Andrew McFadyean (1887–1974), cr. Kt, 1925; joint treasurer, Liberal Party Organization, 1936–48.

bite & biffo than I expected of him. Gilbert looked tired & discouraged – tho' he did say in his gentle voice that this was the 'consecration of injustice'. We shall clearly get nothing out of Anthony when we do go – but we must do it as a gesture – & after doing it we can fight publicly....

Diary – Wednesday 28 March – Manor Farm, Stockton, Wiltshire

... Headlines in the early evening editions at Salisbury say 'Monty's Armour running wild'. It looks as tho' the whole German front were collapsing all along the line. We have 8 bridges over the Rhine. The Guards Armoured Brigade is mentioned in the stop press but not the Guards Armoured Division. The Germans have no reserves & I don't see what can stop us. The best they can do is some hedgehog defence which wld be encircled or sealed off....

Diary – Wednesday 4 April – Manor Farm, Stockton, Wiltshire

... At last Mark's whereabouts are revealed. The G. A. Division is striking north along the Ems Canal to cut off the Germans in Holland who are reported to be streaming out. The Canadians are striking N.W. at the same time. The 53rd Division seem to be following up the Guards. One's hopes were so high – so keyed up by Security black-out curtains & assurances that when it was at last lifted we shld be dazzled & amazed by results, that one can't help being a little disappointed with the pace of events. Patton is meanwhile still steaming ahead.[1] His methods are described – rather enviously I thought – as 'daring & unorthodox'....

Diary – Monday 9 April – 40 Gloucester Square, W.2

Travelled up by 4.8 from Codford. Met Wickenhauser during a long wait at Westbury – B. met me at Paddington. He told me Elizabeth's death was reported in the Times today. The F.O. rang up Puff on Sunday night & he

---

[1] General George Smith Patton (1885–1945), commander of the American 7th Army in Tunisia and Sicily, 1943; 3rd Army, 1944–5; his forces crossed the Rhine on 22 March. 'Laura got a letter from Jo – full of amusing schadenfreude at Patton having stolen a march on Monty by nipping across the Rhine ahead of him without any fuss or ballyhoo!' (diary, 3 April 1945).

broke it to Margot. Priscilla read it in the paper.[1] It is tragic – but perhaps less tragic than her life. The pathetic thing is her severance all these last years from all she loved – & that she shld have died just when return wld have been possible. Mercifully she knew that we had won the war. I am terribly sorry for Margot.

Diary – Tuesday 10 April – 40 Gloucester Square, W.2

Deputation to Anthony Eden on Yalta Formula[2] – Percy, Eric Perth, Beveridge, Herb. Samuel, Andrew McFadyean, Ly Rhys Williams, self.[3] We had half an hour's wait then Percy introduced us. Eric opened – I followed rubbing in the point that this was appeasement enshrined in an International Charter.[4] Bev. followed up – Herb. Sam never uttered.

Anthony did not seek to defend the formula in any way whatever. He simply said the Russians wldn't look at anything less – & they had had great difficulty in screwing them up to this point. He said they were being very difficult to deal with at this moment. . . . This was the only condition on which we cld get them in <u>at all</u>. It was thought best to do so – in the hopes that improvements might gradually be inserted later. I asked if we shld be free, if not to initiate amendments at least to support them if proposed by others. On this he was not very clear. He said we cld go to the Russians & say 'You see which way the wind is blowing'. It was clear from what he said that he was feeling the draught of Dominion opinion. (They are sitting here now.)[5] I went away feeling that all criticism wld be helpful & strengthen their hands – but very depressed about the way things were going.

[1] Elizabeth Bibesco died in Rumania, aged forty-eight. Margot had not seen her since the beginning of the war and was 'completely crushed' (Daphne Bennett, *Margot*, 390).

[2] At Yalta Roosevelt proposed a modification to the 'Dumbarton Oaks' formula for security council voting. It effectively confirmed the veto power of the permanent members, and therefore did nothing to allay Liberal concern (Winston S. Churchill, *The Second World War*, vi, 181–6, 309–12).

[3] Lady (Juliet Evangeline) Rhys Williams (1898–1964), cr. DBE, 1937; honorary secretary, WLF, 1943; chairman, publicity committee of Liberal Party, 1944–6.

[4] Violet attacked the veto proposal in a speech at Birmingham the following month: 'There were 2 things the world had a right to expect from our Victory. One was Security, the other Justice. I can find in these proposals no promise of either. This is the policy of so-called Realism. Why if we ourselves had practised the Realism we are at present preaching to the rest of the world we shld never have gone to war in 1939.'

[5] Dominion and Indian statesmen were then gathered in London to consider the response of the British Commonwealth to the San Francisco deliberations on the United Nations organization.

On to Ll.G.'s Memorial Service. I sat very near Winston who looked extraordinarily well – young & buoyant. He sat in the 1st Choir Stall quite near us. They sang the hymns to Baptists' Tunes. All the family were opposite us including Miss Stevenson in Widow's Weeds.[1] Megan looking very pale & stricken. I hear she feels it deeply that Ll.G. has left all his papers to Miss S. Lunched with Dingle at the House. He told me that coming out of the Abbey with Diana Sandys he commented to her on the Bevin–Bracken hammer & tongs interchange – & she replied 'Well you started it. It all arose out of a speech of Violet's'! What did she mean?....[2]

Diary – Thursday 12 April – 40 Gloucester Square, W.2

Very full & deeply interesting day. Jan Masaryk came to see me at 11 – straight from Moscow. Most depressing account of the International situation – all my worst fears confirmed. He is utterly miserable. His country in the grip of Russia – & helpless. 'They gave me sitzbads of caviare – but what's the use of that to me. I don't want caviare & vodka. There are certain values I can't give up while there's life in my carcase'. He & Benes will try their best – & if they can't preserve these values they will go. What is terrible for them is that they are now 'on the wrong side of the table'. He told me countless instances of Russian bad faith. He was never told the Poles were in Moscow while he was there – never told the diplomats going to Czechoslovakia were not allowed to sail when he had made all arrangements that they shld – was forbidden – is forbidden to take one reputable British or American journalist with him to Czechoslovakia.... He told me Stalin had asked him whether he trusted him. Jan said 'Why shldn't I?' Stalin said 'There is every reason why you shldn't. We tried to foment revolution in yr country for the last 20 years. But you can trust me now.' I said to Jan 'And do you?' He replied 'No'. I am deeply sorry for him....

---

[1] Frances *née* Stevenson, Countess Lloyd George (d. 1972); private secretary to David Lloyd George, 1913–43; she had married Lloyd George in 1943, and was thus styled 'countess' from the time that he became an earl, 1 January 1945.

[2] Diana Sandys *née* Churchill (1909–63), Winston and Clementine's first child; married Duncan Sandys, 1935. On Saturday 7 April Ernest Bevin had publicly attacked the pre-war record of the Conservative Party, and the following Monday Bracken retaliated against 'Mr Bevin's Blitz'. This exchange has been seen as marking the beginning of the return to party politics. Diana's suggestion, though, is that Violet's speech at the Liberal Assembly earlier had first opened the political debate (*The Times*, 9, 10, 13 April; see above, p. 326).

M.R.B.C. to V.B.C.   *Sunday 15 April*
                                                      1st Battalion Grenadier Guards,
                                                                          B.L.A.

Dear Mama,
Thank you for your letter – I got one from Laura & Cressida today too. At
the moment I am in a small German farm-house – we have just packed
off a Frenchman & a Polish girl.[1] The whole country is stiff with slaves.
These Germans make the 'no fraternisation' order particularly difficult.
They treated the Frenchman very well indeed & he affirms that in this
district there were hardly any Nazis. They all offer food & eggs to us &
they have just done my laundry for me which was most necessary. I would
say that 50% of the Germans are docile sheep, 25% are positively glad to
see us, & 15% are unspeakable – but it is difficult to assess.[2] The soldiers
are patchy – though most of them fire their weapons, they pack up when
you get close to them. Some of them do more than that & some less. . . .
Roosevelt's death makes San Francisco even more gloomy – the thought
of Truman as President does fill me with despondency.[3] I think Aunt
Libby's death very tragic – Love <u>Mark</u>

Diary – Thursday 19 April – Manor Farm, Stockton

Papers full of appalling accounts & photographs of Concentration Camps
which have been liberated – Buchenwald – Celle – Nordhausen – Belsen.[4]
Even to me who had no illusions they have brought a shock of indescribable horror. Men have eaten grass – eaten each other. The scale of
brutality – & dehumanization is unimaginable. What can be done with,
or to such people? . . .

---

[1] i.e. they were liberated.

[2] MRBC expressed no opinion on the missing 10 per cent.

[3] Harry S. Truman (1884–1972), 33rd president of the United States, 1945–52. Vice president
in Roosevelt's final term, Truman had been in office for only eighty-two days before becoming
president, on the eve of the San Francisco Conference, and was perceived as lacking the
necessary experience.

[4] One of the first accounts to reach the public came from the CBS war correspondent
Edward R. Murrow (1908–65) who entered Buchenwald, near Weimar, on 12 April. His report
was broadcast on the 15th. The first report in *The Times* appeared on 16 April. Three days later
Richard Dimbleby's graphic account of conditions in Belsen was broadcast. By 'such people'
Violet means the Nazi camp guards.

M.R.B.C. to V.B.C.   ***Sunday 22 April***
                                      1st Battalion Grenadier Guards,
                                                                B.L.A.

Dear Mama,

I must apologise for the paucity of the information I have given & the fewness of my letters. The fighting has been tiresome in the extreme, simply because it has all been such nonsense – they have already lost the war & they are merely prolonging the agony for themselves & postponing the pleasure for us. Our part has been particularly irritating in this way. All the way up since we crossed the Rhine on the famous Bailey Bridge we have met resistance which has been overcome in each case but which has reappeared five or ten miles further on.[1] The roads have been cratered & blocked, the little villages held, & in the woods there have been these parties of Germans with Bazookas. Until recently we had met little artillery except for a few S.P. guns – now we are getting a bit more. How long the particular pocket in which we are engaged will last I have no idea, but there is no particular reason why it should collapse immediately.

A tragedy occurred to me – I have somehow lost Mansfield Park – if you could let me have another I would like it very much. My only other requirement is cigarettes – 400 a month would be very welcome. Thank you for your many letters – your life seems to grow daily more hectic, give my love to everyone & I will write again as soon as I can. The general news seems very good – though Buchenwald & the other places do not bear thinking of. . . .

I don't much like the Germans – though the children are sometimes pathetic & rather sweet in a good Aryan way. The population are very docile & obedient. Love <u>Mark</u>

I found this rather 'Ritzy' paper in the village we are holding

Diary – Sunday 29 April – Manor Farm, Stockton

<u>Arctic cold</u>. Never in winter have I felt an icier wind. Church with B. Jag &

---

[1] The Guards crossed the Rhine at Rees early on the morning of 30 March, and headed towards Bremen, encountering dogged German resistance. The regimental history has observed that there were 'two wars raging in Northern Germany during April'. That to the south of the Grenadiers involved 'infrequent casualties', and was 'almost enjoyable'. That which the Grenadiers experienced, however, 'was neither exciting nor stimulating, not a light-hearted adventure but a calculated slogging match, the kind of fighting that wastes lives' (Nigel Nicolson and Patrick Forbes, *The Grenadier Guards in the War of 1939–1945*, 225).

Ray – & Sherry with the Y.B.'s.[1] I feel convinced that Hitler is dead. Wild rumours that he has had a cerebral haemorrhage – that he is mad, that Goering is mad & paints his toe-nails red etc. & dresses in a Roman toga. No hard news except Truman's statement that Germany has not surrendered – & that we are not yet at peace. This as a corrective to wild rumours in the U.S.A....

Diary – Tuesday 1 May – 40 Gloucester Square, W.2

I was rung up by Walter Layton at $\frac{1}{4}$ to 10 to-night to say that the German Wireless had just announced Hitler's death. They pretend that he died the Hero's death fighting against the Bolsheviks. I have been convinced that he was dead ever since Himmler's offer came through. He has apptd Admiral Doenitz his successor who has issued an order to all ranks to fight on.[2] As it is mainly the Marine & Naval Forces which are offering such stiff resistance now this may be obeyed by them (I rang up Marigold who of <u>course</u> knew nothing!). Went to Bev.'s Press Conference for the Campaign Committee. He uses the personal pronoun too much.

M.R.B.C. to V.B.C.   *Wednesday 2 May*
                                              1st Battalion Grenadier Guards,
                                                                      B.L.A.

Dear Mama,

I've just heard the news tonight – unconditional surrender in Italy, the death of Hitler, the new Führer Doenitz, etc. – it really looks as though the war can't [last] any longer. Today, for the first time since we started, nothing much has happened – the immense physical pleasure of sleeping for nine hours & being dry (it has poured incessantly for the last four days) almost makes one forget the discomforts of the last few weeks. The death of poor John Moller was tragic – so near the liberation of Denmark – he was killed taking a little village – shot through the head.[3]

---

[1] William Huyshe Yeatman Biggs (1878–1952), Winchester contemporary of Bongie; married, 1905, Muriel *née* Swann; they lived at Long Hall in Stockton.

[2] Himmler negotiated to secure an armistice in the west, and Anglo-American support for a continuation of the war against the Soviet Union. The Allies dismissed the offer, 22 April, reiterating their demand for an unconditional surrender. Karl Doenitz (1891–1980), admiral; commander-in-chief of the German navy, 1943; supreme commander of all German armed forces on the death of Hitler. He established an acting Reich government on the Danish border, and also sought unsuccessfully a separate peace with America and Britain.

[3] John C. Moller, lieutenant; killed in action, Dalum, 9 April 1945.

A few days ago, as you will have heard from the news, we freed a concentration camp.[1] There were 14,000 prisoners of war & 7,000 political prisoners. The prisoners of war were in quite good shape – the political prisoners were no longer human, a sight which I will never forget, & which I am sorry I have ever seen. They were pale, haggarded, fevered ghouls – emaciated & starved, dying at the rate of a hundred a day. The first day we got there 500 were buried in a mass grave. We attacked the place without much difficulty though on the way a small village was set on fire. That night I went back to bring up some transport, as I passed through this village I saw these ghoulish ghostly figures dressed in their striped clothes digging among the smouldering ruins for the scorched remains of dead cows, pigs & sheep. I saw a group go off carrying a blackened & gory limb – they asked me for cigarettes & I gave them five, they fought among themselves over them. The ordinary prisoners were of every nationality – mainly Russian & French. I met a Polish boy of twelve, captured in Warsaw. Another Pole came up to Mervyn Vernon when we had captured the place & thanked him effusively – he finished up by saying 'I must tell you though, that the Russians are <u>escaping</u>'!! The French were pathetic in their desire to help. When I brought up the transport, one of them came up with a tiny glow-worm of a torch – he asked to help & said 'this torch is very useful – very useful'. Others gave us coffee out of red cross parcels, & they told us the most horrifying stories about the arrival of 'les politiques' – loaded in railway carts & tipped out manacled, the dying & the dead, promiscuously. When I asked what we should do to these S.S. – all of whom had escaped – they said – 'You cannot treat them as they have treated the political prisoners, there is only one thing to do, to shoot them. It is not civilized to do anything else.' But I will never forget these people – degraded, & all vestiges of humanity except the wasted outline of their limbs removed. Among these political prisoners the Germans mixed the most degraded criminals.

... Give my love to everyone. Love, <u>Mark</u>

[1] The liberation of Sandbostel, on the River Oste, was virtually the last action of the Grenadiers during the war. The camp was 'a minor Belsen', in which 2,500 had died in less than a month after it was partially taken over by the SS, 5 April, to house political prisoners. The contrast between the 'military' and 'political' sections was marked, with Red Cross parcels in the former, starvation and disease in the latter (Nigel Nicolson and Patrick Forbes, *The Grenadier Guards in the War of 1939–1945*, 245).

Diary – Thursday 3 May – 40 Gloucester Square, W.2

Never was there such a day of news as yesterday. Surrender of the whole German Army in Italy – one million men. Fall of Berlin. Death of Hitler & Goebbels – & yet what is so odd is that one feels no wild excitement, no exhilaration or kick – no desire to throw one's hat into the air – only the sense of having reached a long foregone conclusion – at last. One never, even in the blackest hour, had any doubt of the end....

'A left tide flowing' : the general election of 5 July 1945

With the resumption of domestic political hostilities in April, and the advent of victory in Europe in early May, the demise of the wartime Coalition seemed imminent. Yet on 18 May Churchill proposed to extend its life until after victory against Japan, perhaps another eighteen months away. The suggestion reflected his desire to preserve the wartime consensus, which he believed was essential to social and economic reconstruction. But this ran counter to expectations that he had himself raised – that after victory in Europe there would be a clean break, and a clean electoral fight. Neither the Liberal Party nor the Labour Party was prepared to accept the proposal, which they believed was designed to force on them the unpopular decision of breaking up the government. They contended that there was less consensus on policy than the Conservatives allowed, and that the electorate must be given a chance to decide between the alternatives. And as Archie Sinclair put it, democracy in Britain needed 'to get some exercise' after years of enforced idleness. Both parties favoured an autumn poll, which would give servicemen full opportunity to vote, and signal continued unity of purpose at a difficult juncture in international affairs. This, however, was not on offer. Churchill argued that if the Coalition must end before the defeat of Japan then it should be at once, otherwise government would be rendered impotent by infighting. Again his opponents detected a trick – the Conservatives sought to exploit his status as a war leader in a 'khaki election': in Violet's phrase, 'the Peace-with-Honour men of 1938 are bidding to become the War Profiteers of 1945'. It was with Churchill, however, that the initiative lay, and he resigned at noon on 23 May, bringing the Coalition to an end. Until the dissolution of parliament on 15 June he would lead a 'caretaker' government, nominally 'national', but effectively Conservative. Polling day would be 5 July, with the declaration on 26 July, to allow time for overseas votes to be included. At this election the

Liberals were battling to survive. There was a severe shortage of funds, and of organizational capacity too. Violet's own campaign at Wells in Somerset was typical in that it was lacking in resources, if not in effort or ideas. She had been convinced for some time previously that there was a 'left tide flowing' in politics, and hoped that her party would be the beneficiary. In fact the 1945 election saw what she afterwards identified as an 'anti-Tory tidal wave', and instead of carrying votes to the Liberals, this swept them to Labour.[1]

Diary – Friday 4 to Saturday 5 May – Wells, Somerset

Started for Wells where I am to be adopted to-morrow. Went to Bristol where I spent the afternoon at Aero Engines – & went round the Works. Then we motored on to Wells with Wickenhauser thro' most lovely country – stayed at the Swan [and] went after dinner with Wickenhauser to the local films where we saw Western Approaches & the news-reel film of the horrors of Belsen & Buchenwald. Unspeakably horrible – quite short. (Too many M.P.s – above all too much Mrs Tate.) In the middle of the Film came a News Flash announcing the surrender of all German Forces in Holland Germany Denmark to Montgomery – over a million men.[2]

Started $\frac{1}{4}$ to 11 [Saturday] for Glastonbury with Major Rowe Evans & B. for my Adoption Meeting. Arrived in rain at the rather bleak Assembly Rooms.... We then went into the meeting where there were – I shld think – about 200 people. There were first business preliminaries & then an endless speech by the dear old Chairman who rambled about among 'Umbrellas' & other symbols & ended by laying Excalibur at my feet![3] I then spoke for just over half an hour. The audience were kind & welcoming – but distinctly elderly as all Liberal Associations are in these days alas! Very few questions....

[1] *News Chronicle*, 31 May 1945; *The Times*, 4 February 1945; speech at Liberal Candidates Conference, 8 September 1945.

[2] This was a 'battlefield surrender', which came into effect at 8.00 a.m. on Saturday 5 May; it applied to forces in north-west Germany, rather than the whole country.

[3] In a speech the previous winter the Labour ex-minister Arthur Greenwood had invited Liberals to 'take shelter' under the Labour 'umbrella': with Chamberlain's nickname in mind ('Ombrello') Violet had then ridiculed it as 'an ill-omened symbol'.

Diary – Monday 7 May – 40 Gloucester Square, W.2

<u>Unconditional Surrender</u> took place early this morning in Rheims....[1] At 7.40 I switched on accidentally & by sheer fluke heard the announcement that 'V.E. Day' wld be held to-morrow – that Winston wld make an announcement at 3 o'clock & that the King wld broadcast at 9. Goebbels' body has been found poisoned – with that of his wife & children. An order signed by Himmler has been found saying that no prisoners in Dachau are to be left alive to fall into Allied hands....

Diary – Tuesday 8 May – Manor Farm, Stockton, Wiltshire

A wonderful crashing thunderstorm raged for about 2 hours in the night. It was almost like a portent from Heaven – or an Ersatz Blitz. Lightning playing constantly. Sweet little Adam came into my room in the morning. He is really <u>beautiful</u> now I think – quite apart from his knock-down charm. Lunched with Bartholomew of the Daily Mirror at Carlton Grill – Wilf the host & Bev. the fellow-guest.[2] The streets <u>fairly</u> full of people with rattles & paper hats – but not really crowded even in Whitehall – where I dropped a note at Downing St. There were people bunched round the bottom of the street & some perched on the window-ledges etc. down Whitehall.... After dinner B & I & C. & Nathalie & Jasper & Patricia Manners went out across Hyde Park where a few mild squibs were exploding.[3] We sat under the trees & Nathalie (whose courage moves me deeply) lit a little dirty paper to make a tiny bonfire. Then we went on down Constitution Hill to Buckingham Palace where a little <u>very</u> mild roistering was going on. I saw no one drunk – or even really excited. People were sitting all over the Queen Victoria monument waving flags. The Palace was floodlit & looking its very best – & Big Ben – lit up again – peeped thro' the trees in the distance. Jasper said from time to time 'I'm glad I'm not a German'. After a <u>far</u> too interminable wait the King & Queen came out at $\frac{1}{4}$ to 12 & showed themselves. They shld have done this <u>sooner</u> & <u>oftener</u>. Then we walked home across the Park again. I wondered what Mark was doing & feeling in Germany.

---

[1] General Jodl, German chief of staff, signed the instrument of surrender at Eisenhower's headquarters in Rheims; fighting was to cease at midnight on 8 May.

[2] H. G. Bartholomew, editorial director of the *Daily Mirror*.

[3] Patricia Manners, a paying guest at Gloucester Square, the daughter of Lord and Lady Manners.

V.B.C. to Winston Churchill   *Tuesday 8 May*
40 Gloucester Square, W.2

Beloved Winston –

On this day of days the love & immeasurable thankfulness of the whole nation goes out to you. You have led, inspired, sustained us <u>as</u> <u>no</u> <u>other</u> <u>could</u> <u>have</u> <u>done</u>. This war began long before 1939. You were leading us then – & I am proud to have been with you from the start to this our Journey's End.

May God bless & keep you. None prays this more fervently than your devoted <u>Violet</u>

Diary – Wednesday 9 May – 40 Gloucester Square, W.2

A day of great heat – dusty streets full of flying paper – trampled bunting – bits of red white & blue ribbon – dirty caps. I spent the morning at Campaign Committee – where to my surprise I found Archie, Bev., Percy, Megan, Herb. Samuel, Graham White, Wilf & Geoffrey Mander. We discussed the Election date & were unanimous in our opposition to a July election on the grounds of the very severe handicaps it wld impose on servicemen. They haven't a chance by then of knowing anything about the issues involved – or being reached. Archie tells us there are great technical difficulties about the people in Burma (14th Army) voting at all in time for July. This wld rule it out if it were true. Archie seemed much more on the spot....

M.R.B.C. to V.B.C.   *Thursday 10 May*
1st Battalion Grenadier Guards,
B.L.A.

Dear Mama,

This is I fear, a rather long overdue letter. I can plead no excuse as we have been doing absolutely nothing for the last week or so, though now we have started to polish, & paint & drill, etc. fiendishly.[1] I heard the BBC V.E. day broadcast – I thought live recordings of the crowds very exciting.

---

[1] Between 8 and 22 May the 1st Battalion of Grenadier Guards was based at Stade and Freiburg, villages on the Cuxhaven peninsula, between Bremen and Hamburg. The days following the German surrender of 5 May were spent mostly polishing and cleaning: 'In fact, by VE Day there was little to show that any of the Battalions had ever taken part in a campaign at all' (Nigel Nicolson and Patrick Forbes, *The Grenadier Guards in the War of 1939–1945*, 249).

Monty's broadcast was typical, & the King's much better than usual – Atty commented that there was too much God about it, 'I do like to feel that I have done something towards winning the war'.[1]

At the moment I am living in a most luxurious villa not far from the sea, with H & C in every room, a charming little 'suntrap' in which to sit, & comfortable beds. The weather is divine & conditions are altogether satisfactory. I have applied to come home & they are merely waiting now for written authority to come through so I expect to leave fairly soon.[2]

The Germans remain revoltingly, though luckily, docile – no werewolves so far. . . .[3] Give my love to everyone, Mark

Diary – Sunday 13 May – 40 Gloucester Square, W.2

. . . Lunched with Archie & Marigold – & drove with them down the route to the Thanksgiving Service at St Paul's. The crowd was very moving – very patient – children in the front rows with tiny Union Jacks. I went to my lowlier seat in the side aisle – & sat next a nice A.B. It was a nice democratic audience – full of 'services' of various kinds. W. & Clemmie came in – he looking very pink & smiling – the Royal Family were heralded by a marvellous fanfare. They were all in pale blue of various shades – Queen Mary pastelle – the Queen chocolate box – Pss E. forget-me-not with a white hat – Pss M 'dove-grey'. Everything to match – very typically royal. . . . After dinner I listened alone to W's broadcast – in a way the most moving I have ever heard him make. It was slowly, hesitantly delivered – he sounded tired & his utterance was at times thick & indistinct. But his passage at the end about the blurring of our war-aims – about the police state in Europe – a clear warning to Russia – was magnificent.[4]

[1] Hon. Thomas Anthony 'Atty' Corbett (b. 1921), 2nd son of 2nd Baron Rowallan, and cousin of Jo Grimond; lieutenant, 1st Battalion, Grenadier Guards; twice wounded; MC, 1946.

[2] All servicemen who were bona-fide parliamentary candidates were to be given special leave so that they could campaign in their constituencies prior to the general election.

[3] An allusion to 'Undertaking Werewolf', an organization for conducting guerilla warfare, secretly established by Himmler. In fact it was never intended as a resistance movement, to become operative after German defeat, which itself could not be contemplated. Rather, it was a paramilitary force, designed to fight behind the Allied lines. When the Germans surrendered, Admiral Doenitz ordered the 'Werewolves' to cease their activity in the West, which they did (Hugh Trevor-Roper, *The Last Days of Hitler*, 48–51).

[4] 'On the continent of Europe we have yet to make sure that the simple and honourable purposes for which we entered the war are not brushed aside or overlooked. . . . There would be little use in pursuing the Hitlerites for their crimes if law and justice did not rule, and if totalitarian or police governments were to take the place of the German invaders' (*The Times*, 14 May). The broadcast marked the fifth anniversary of Churchill's premiership.

Diary – Wednesday 16 May – 40 Gloucester Square, W.2

... off to a party at the Soviet Embassy – where I talked to David Low, Prytz, Ld. Moran & Clemmie.[1] Ld Moran said he thought the coming landslide (which he appeared to assume as a matter of course) wld be the most terrible blow to Winston – as he wld feel it <u>personally</u> as a sign of ingratitude. I talked to Clemmie about Russia. She told me that the reason Winston had had to put off his broadcast was because she was not yet out of the country. She had of course longed to get back but cldn't – as it wld have been assumed that the difficulties between us & them were the cause of her going. She said the poverty & want was extreme but coupled with great dignity & burning patriotism.[2] Came back & found a letter from Mark saying he was coming back in 5 days! It might be to-morrow.

Diary – Thursday 17 May – 40 Gloucester Square, W.2

Mark suddenly arrived this morning about 11.30! I heard Bongie shouting for me & went down to find him in the hall – a beret on his head – very sunburnt & well-looking & the hall a sea of luggage – tin boxes & vast Khaki 'valise'. It was terribly exciting – & I cldn't 'settle down' to anything else all day. I haven't begun to hear all his news yet. He says the Germans are terribly servile & docile. The soldiers take out pictures of Hitler & shoot at them & they just say 'gut' & smile. All the little boys salute them in the street. They were living in a Dr's house & the Dr & his wife who were turned out come every day to clean it – ask if they are all right & put flowers in. They expected to have to feed all those who were billeted on them. He was nearly killed 2 days before V.E. Day – with Atty in a small car by Bazookas which hit the car & wounded the driver.[3] We all lunched together C & Adam & he & I – & spent the afternoon together. ...

---

[1] Charles McMoran Wilson (1882–1977), cr. Baron Moran, 1943; Churchill's physician, the president of the Royal College of Physicians, 1941–50.

[2] At the end of March 1945, at the invitation of the Russian Red Cross Society, Clementine Churchill undertook a five-week visit to the Soviet Union; she travelled widely, visiting hospitals, and was received by Stalin; she was still there on 9 May, which the Russians celebrated as Victory Day.

[3] Another of Mark Bonham Carter's company had been killed just weeks before the end of the war. Terence C. Reeves, lieutenant, had died of wounds on 24 April 1945. He was only twenty. Mark Bonham Carter wrote to his mother that it was 'unspeakably tragic & makes all rejoicing seem hollow'.

Diary – Friday 18 May – 40 Gloucester Square, W.2

... I received an urgent call from Geoffrey Mander saying that I must
come & see Archie on business of the highest priority. I went at 5.30 &
met him, Wilfrid, Jimmy, Hugh [Lord] Sherwood, G. Mander. He showed
us a letter from Winston the gist of which was that he turned down an
autumn Election but that i̱f we wld continue to work with him till the
end of the Japanese War it wld be a great relief to him. We had a long
discussion & different views were expressed. General opinion was that it
was an astute move to put upon us the onus of breaking up the Govt &
refusing to finish the job.... Mark said truly that it wld probably – if
accepted – split every party except the Tories.

R.B.C. to V.B.C.

Sunday 20 May
Bramston's House,
Winchester College

Dear Mama,
   ... As you will have guessed, I expect, the Great Man is staying here.
Budge told me yesterday that he saw Him and the headmaster walking
together in meads. He said with a twinkle in his eye that the headman
was in ecstasy.[1]
   HE held a sort of 'press conference' in the headmaster's drawing room
to which the senior House Prefects were invited last evening. He
announced that he was our member on the Commission for governing
Germany. He said he would lecture to us on the crossing of the Rhine and
the race to the Baltic. Race because it was essential for us to get into
Denmark and across the Kiel Canal in sufficient strength before the Russians. Otherwise the Russians would have occupied both Denmark &
Norway and would never have gone out.
   He described his banquet with Zhukov (or was it Konev?) at which he
said he broke his golden rule and (a) drank alcohol (vodka) and (b) drank
too much.[2] Guise (our senior prefect who attended this 'Press Conference')
said Monty had brought with him boxes of cigarettes which he had been
given by the Russian Generals. Also some he had been given by the
President of Turkey. Not the ideal present for Monty?[3]
   Throughout this discussion people asked questions etc. & argued with

---

[1] For Spencer Leeson's appreciation of General Montgomery, see above, p. 270.
[2] Marshal Georgy Zhukov (b. 1896), commander-in-chief, and Ivan Konev (1897–1973),
general, were central figures in the Soviet invasion of Germany 1945.
[3] Montgomery abhorred cigarettes.

him, especially Dr. James who regarded everything from the aspect of science and continually criticised him.[1] HE sees as the only method of stopping war, the division of the world into the Anglo-American bloc & the Russian bloc, each so strong that they dare not attack each other. That is a very gloomy idea and as far as I can see, purely the essence of fascism in the world sense, power politics and totalitarianism all put together.... Much love, Ray

Diary – Tuesday 22 May – 'The Swan', Wells, Somerset

I left by 9.15 this morning for Wells – suffering from fibrositis which has been bothering me for some days now. Worked hard in the train at my speech or speeches – changed at Chippenham & Witham – was met by Rowe Evans at Wells 1.42. Went to the Swan – unpacked – & on with him to a meeting of really old cats at the house of one Mrs Hill. Dear old Chairwoman – well over 80. Mrs Hewlett, the only non-dodderer there ... the others cld hardly totter – let alone canvass. The men's Association had decayed – & fallen into bits years ago. There were two very old men there – one almost in his grave. They were all very sweet & welcoming – but how to breathe the breath of life into them, with what bellows to create sparks, passes my imagination....

V.B.C. to Winston Churchill

Friday 1 June
40 Gloucester Square, W.2

My dearest Winston –

One line to say how sad I am that we shall be fighting this Election under different flags. You do not need me to tell you that though I am not a 'Woman of Goodwill', towards you my 'goodwill' (to put it mildly!) can never change. But I could never go into action side by side with Sir Herbert Williams & Co. – and you know 'the reasons why'.[2] You know them perhaps even better than I do. You have never been 'one of them' and the only action of yours (except one) I have ever regretted since you took office was your decision to become their leader. You should have remained a National Leader – above the battle, and then we could all have followed you into the peace. You needed no 'machine'.

---

[1] Eric John Francis James (b. 1909) was science master at Winchester, 1933–45.

[2] Sir Herbert Williams (1884–1954), cr. Kt, 1939; Conservative MP for South Croydon, 1932–45; he had attacked Churchill's government during the vote of confidence debate of 27 January 1942 (Harold Nicolson, *Diaries and Letters 1939–1945*, 208).

I said 'except one'. My only other regret is the timing of this Election. This not for Party reasons (<u>no one</u> is 'ready') but because to my untutored, ignorant eye the international scene looks graver and more critical than it has been since 1939. I may be wrong, but I think on this account alone we should have held together till the autumn or winter. An indefinite commitment – up to 18 months – were goods which it would have been difficult for any Party to deliver without being split from top to toe.

Well – there we are – on opposite sides of the line, we who have felt and fought and thought together – in fair weather and foul – but especially foul. And ranged behind you I see – Thelma Cazalet! (poor, dull, industrious goose! who junketed at Nüremberg) and all the old appeasers, and that Vermiform Appendix, the National Liberals – which I do not grudge you. (Dear Lord Moran will tell you, if you ask him, that it is an anatomy which has outlived its usefulness in the higher forms of animal life – but that it still performs a vital though mysterious function in rabbits.) Their new leader, Harry Rosebery (who has played no part whatever that I know of in the political life of this country), claims for his followers the virtue of 'reliability' – and rightly so.[1] Even in the Norwegian Division they supported Chamberlain almost to a man – with the reliability of Robots.

Past history? <u>You</u> have reminded us that 'the past must be studied if the future is to be successfully encountered'. They have not changed their spots – nor has your Bloody Duck changed her feathers. My unchanging love to you. Ever your devoted, <u>Violet</u>

P.S. <u>How</u> dark & tangled is the European scene!

Diary – Monday 4 June – Wells, Somerset

Left London feeling ill & in a state of very bad morale after a bad night.... Endless business to discuss & a horrifying series of meetings ahead. Home now & have just heard W's broadcast which really does lay it on a bit thick! – suggesting that if Socialism came to pass in this country a Gestapo wld be the inevitable result![2]

[1] Albert Edward Harry Primrose (1882–1974), 6th Earl of Rosebery, 1929; son of the Liberal prime minister 1894–5; a pre-1914 Liberal MP, and president of the National Liberal Party, 1945–7.

[2] 'I declare to you from the bottom of my heart that no Socialist system can be established without a political police.... No Socialist government conducting the entire life and industry of the country could afford to allow free, sharp, or violently-worded expressions of public discontent. They would have to fall back on some form of Gestapo, no doubt very humanely directed in the first instance.' Churchill's broadcast, the first of the election campaign, came against the background of Soviet incursions in eastern Europe (*Listener*, 7 June 1945, 629–32).

Diary – Wednesday 6 June – Wells, Somerset

Again heavy rain & no air. Attlee gave a good & dignified & reasoned & constructive reply to Winston.[1] I believe Winston's broadcast may be a terrific liability to live down. Very good evening – 4 outdoor 'meetings' & one very good indoor one at Wooky. The people are all so nice. Took my 1st plunge with the loud speaker – & gradually got inured to it. In bed now having missed Herbert Samuel's broadcast. Must read it to-morrow. Feeling better & higher morale.

Diary – Thursday 7 June – Wells, Somerset

... spent the afternoon preparing my speech for the Wells Town Hall meeting in the evening. To my amazement we had a marvellous meeting. Packed out. There wasn't standing room. Ly Hobhouse in the chair & Mary Waldegrave & Anthony Clarke on the platform.[2] Archie was due at 7.45. He didn't turn up till 9.15! I spoke for nearly an hour. Had a lot of questions – Ly Hobhouse was marvellously ingenious in holding the fort for Archie. He arrived at last & made a rather ragged speech which went quite well. They say they never had a meeting like it in Wells before. It certainly was an amazing success in this stickiest pool in the Division.

Diary – Wednesday 13 June – Wells, Somerset

Spent the afternoon with Konradin Hobhouse paying calls in Castle Cary & addressed the women waiting in the Food Office for their ration books from outside – with loud speaker. Tea at Hedspan – more calls in villages on the way back – 2 open air meetings at the Horsingtons – then back to tidy before the Brains Trust at the Town Hall which was packed.... The Labour man delivered himself rather badly into my hands by saying the Liberal Party was a Peter Pan which had never grown up & had taken 18

[1] 'When I listened to the Prime Minister's speech last night in which he gave such a travesty of the policies of the Labour Party, I realized at once what was his object. He wanted the electors to understand how great was the difference between Winston Churchill the great leader in war of a united nation, and Mr Churchill the party leader of the Conservatives. He feared lest those who had accepted his leadership in war might be tempted out of gratitude to follow him further. I thank him for having disillusioned them so thoroughly. The voice we heard last night was that of Mr Churchill, but the mind was that of Lord Beaverbrook' (*Listener*, 14 June 1945, 656–50).

[2] Mary *née* Grenfell, Countess Waldegrave; wife of Geoffrey, 12th Earl Waldegrave. Konradin *née* Jackson, Lady Hobhouse; married Sir Arthur Hobhouse, 1919.

years dying. I was easily able to explode this mixed metaphor – & say that when the Labour Party cld point to a record of achievement comparable to ours it cld claim political maturity. Not before. We were there from 8 till nearly 10.

Diary – Saturday 23 June – Wells, Somerset

My broadcast. Day of travail & final accouchement at Bristol – Mr. Beadle (Controller) was not allowed to coach or criticize. This was the universal rule for the Election. <u>Never</u> have I felt such a needle. My first try-over was – B. said – the worst I'd ever done! <u>So</u> difficult not to read. I was terrified by the thought that I might let down the Party – & the agony of waiting while the clock ticked ever nearer zero hour, & the red light went on, was worse than any fear I have ever experienced. I was <u>literally</u> trembling in every limb when I started off.[1] But it was the best production I have given & I came back reassured. Miss Iredale rang me up to say it was a chef d'oeuvre – perfect in every way & that she was proud to be working for me!

Diary – Tuesday 26 June – Wells, Somerset

Mark & I started at 9.30 in his car & motored to Barnstaple – stopping at the Liberal Club.... The whole place seemed seething & humming with election Fever. Colours – posters – everyone greeting Mark – & he <u>terribly</u> good at greeting them & obviously beloved by them all.

He is a <u>first-rate</u> candidate – which I am not. I find it so much easier to fight for others than myself. We went on to the Friends – delightful people who Mark is staying with at a <u>charming</u> house just outside Barnstaple – <u>terribly</u> luxurious with h & c etc. We lunched on <u>chicken</u> – then he went off to Farmers at Bideford & another meeting & I rested & prepared my speech for the evening. Then off I drove with Mr Dunn to Ilfracombe where we had a magnificent meeting in a large hall with a stage. Packed out. Mark spoke first for 20 minutes or so very forcibly & well & answered questions – excellently. Then he went off to Bideford. I made the long speech & followed. The audience which was a mixed one with a good many Tories & open-minded people got warmer & warmer & gave me a

---

[1] 'That which has made this country what it is, that which has made us great, has been our Liberalism.... remember that a Britain without Liberalism would be a Britain that had lost its soul. And if you want to keep that soul alive, then give us power. Vote Liberal on the 5th' (Violet Bonham Carter MSS). Violet's was one of four Liberal election broadcasts.

great reception at the end. I then followed to Bideford where I arrived about 9.15. Terrific crowds in the Market Place. I shld think about 1200 packed together – standing like herrings. Marvellous audience & great enthusiasm & cheering. Mark answered questions admirably. The cheering was tremendous & crowds in the streets came & saw us off in the car. Bett & Mrs Cruse were on the platform. Back to the Friends to supper.

Diary – Wednesday 4 July – Wells, Somerset

The very last day! Plans for doing a grand tour somehow broke down. Spent the morning answering letters & preparing my Eve of the Poll speeches. Out with Arthur Hobhouse in the afternoon for a lovely drive – not very remunerative quà results as it consisted largely in waving to stray people – & talking to one or two. No pre-arranged calls.

    ... Tea, wash & change & then on to my 4 Eve of Poll Meetings. Tiny one in Mary Waldegrave's house – very good one at Glastonbury where Ethel Wood was speaking – then the big one at Street where I had the chance of answering some Labour questions fairly smashingly. I was amazed by their ignorance & ill-informedness. Finally the last at Evercreech.

Diary – Thursday 5 July – Wells, Somerset

Started at 8.45 on a radiant morning to tour the Polling Stations in a rather uncomfortable car with B., Christopher Morland & Anthony Clarke & hustled round some 50 Polling Stations. Workers & supporters waiting to greet us at many of them.... Labour making a great show. Lots of red rosettes everywhere. Crossed Boles very often in the Blue districts. Liberal Colours showing best in the towns – Street especially where a large Labour crowd thronged the pavement in front of the Polling Station. Got home about 8.30.... Telephoned Mark who had had marvellous Eve of Poll Meetings – 3000 at Barnstaple & 1500 at Ilfracombe with 300 outside listening to loud speaker relay. He seemed very confident thank Heaven. Thank Heaven also it is all over!

Diary – Saturday 7 July – Wells, Somerset

Quiet day. Body blow from an extraordinary letter from Scott Stokes – steeped in pessimism. Mark arrived in the evening – looking rather tired but having obviously wildly enjoyed his Election & had marvellous audiences & enthusiasm. Toto & Patricia here.

V.B.C. to Gilbert Murray   *Saturday 7 July*
                                              40 Gloucester Square, W.2

My dear Gilbert –

Thank you and bless you for your letter – which brought such balm & encouragement to me in the midst of my scrimmage. You know there is no one whose praise I am more humbly proud to earn than yours. I was dead-tired – & am now dead-tired-er after 120 meetings in the Division in 4 weeks – & a few outside helping Mark, Vernon Bartlett & others. I don't think I shall get in. Time & space were against me – & had 123 villages & 8 towns to cover – & very little organization. In the villages politics had to be simplified to a very elementary degree – & there was not one big hall in which I cld get people together & arouse a surge of feeling.

I am full of hope that Mark will get in for Barnstaple. A wrecking Labour candidature was run there – really inexcusably – they didn't fight last time & forfeited their deposit in '31.[1] And Stafford Cripps whom I helped & stood by over the United Front – & fought many battles for with Winston since – went & spoke against Mark – & for the Labour man whose candidature cld. only help the Tory. Aren't they extraordinary? I wld rather eat meat than my principles!

My love dear Gilbert, & to Lady Mary. . . . Ever yrs, Violet

Diary – Tuesday 10 July – Wells, Somerset

. . . No one has any idea of results – or of whether they are in or out. Dined (B & I & Mark) with Roger Fulford & his wife. He fought Holderness where he says he did very badly. Both terribly funny about their Election. They had an Agent who they afterwards discovered to have been marked by the Labour Exchange 'unfit for any work involving contact with human beings'. He bought a kettle costing £9. Bev. failed to turn up at their biggest effort – a meeting numbering 2,000. . . . Fulfords distributed Bev. leaflet with 'Please turn over & you will see something important to all Liberals'. And what was it? 'We didn't have time to put anything' – ! All their special

---

[1] In March Philip Fothergill, for the Liberals, and Ellen Wilkinson, for Labour, had included Barnstaple in their discussion of constituencies where there might be electoral accommodation between their parties; no agreement was reached.

message to the Forces beginning 'We miss you – the Election is dull without you' were distributed to a garden suburb by mistake.

Diary – Thursday 12 July – 40 Gloucester Square, W.2

... Mark went to Winchester. We follow to-morrow. General opinion is that Tories will get in with very small majority. Winston cld have swept the board if he had behaved with dignity & ordinary common-sense....

Diary – Sunday 15 July – 40 Gloucester Square, W.2

Crashing thunderstorm & lightning all night. Chapel. Visit to Bluey – & short walk with him – Winchester looking marvellously green – leafy & bosky. Stifling lunch at Norman Mede. Then long visit to the Bin who says that Monty's last visit & disquisition shocked even the Head-Master. He thinks we must arm to the teeth against a possible war with Russia. To divide the world into 2 blocs – both so strong that they daren't attack each other is the only hope. Back with Mark by 4 train & home by $\frac{1}{4}$ to 7.

Diary – Tuesday 17 July – 40 Gloucester Square, W.2

... I can hardly bear to wait to hear the result of Mark's Election. It will determine the whole future course of his life. For if he is in, it will mean home – the H. of C. & a career starting at once. If out he will be back in the Army. How I pray he is in. My own result means nothing to me in comparison. The 'Big 3' are now meeting at Potsdam – in conditions of profound secrecy.[1] On 9 o'clock news – the King George V & a British squadron are with the American Fleet bombarding Japanese coast-line at 10 mile range. Long telephone talk with Walter Layton. Much impressed by Liberal resurgence in the country – & feels on Gallup survey that

---

[1] The 'big three' – Churchill, Stalin and Truman – met at Potsdam, south-west of Berlin, 17 July–2 August, to discuss the continuation of the war against Japan and the post-war settlement in Europe. The meeting exposed large areas of disagreement, notably over the borders of Poland. In the middle of the proceedings the results of the British general election became known, and Churchill was replaced by Attlee at the conference table.

anything is possible from small Labour majority to Tory majority of 60.[1] I
wld plump for Tory majority much smaller than 60 – say 30. Stalemate
wld put us in an awkward though powerful position.

Diary – Saturday 21 July – 40 Gloucester Square, W.2

Mark & I went down to the Laytons for the day.... We talked all day about
Election prospects & what we shld do if – as a tiny group – we had to hold
the balance of power. Who shld we put in – what terms shld we make?
Walter Layton thinks it quite <u>possible</u> that Labour might equal the Tory
vote or even have a tiny majority. According to Gallup Polls they have
much increased their vote.... Dear Lord Bob came to tea. Quite
unchanged – as amusing as ever – seeing absolutely eye to eye with us
about the General Election. He thinks Winston's great mistake was ever to
become leader of the Tory Party. When he did – that all the rest followed....

Diary – Sunday 22 July – 40 Gloucester Square, W.2

... Dingle came to tea & we had a good 2 hours' crack. He said Winston
was becoming more & more autocratic & went on wiring to S. Francisco
to Eden & Attlee to come home at once & finally threatened to dissolve
Parlt. unless they returned immediately.[2] He said that at Cabinets it frequently took him 2 hours of rhetoric to find his way to a quite simple
solution – which when Attlee was in the chair cld be reached in 5 minutes
(instance of relief to France & Belgium – when shipping space was the
only issue – & he perorated with matchless eloquence about what was
done to this country)....

---

[1] The *News Chronicle* of 4 July 1945 published the results of a Gallup Poll conducted 24–27
June, predicting a 47 per cent Labour vote, 41 per cent Conservative and 10 per cent Liberal.
The paper however would not forecast the crushing Conservative defeat that these figures
suggested – and instead reflected general thinking that the result was likely to be close. In fact
the poll proved remarkably accurate (R. B. McCallum and Alison Readman, *General Election of
1945*, 242–3, 277).

[2] Eden and Attlee were members of the British delegation at the conference on the United
Nations, convened at San Francisco 25 April.

Diary – Thursday 26 to Saturday 28 July – Wells, Somerset

Early breakfast on dark day of pouring rain. Went to the Town Hall with Arthur Hobhouse at $\frac{1}{4}$ to 10 – much too early but we had been told results wld be out by 11 owing to 8 hours sorting the day before. Neither of the other candidates were there. Long tables covered with votes. Scrutineers of the 3 parties opposite. Votes in bundles of 100 stacked in open pigeon-holes on a deal table with 3 compartments. I saw at once that Boles was leading by a largish head – Morgan & self neck to neck with the advantage to Morgan. Watched in agony the stacks piling up.... Realized with icy certainty that we were well behind Labour.

Final result – Boles 13,000 (odd) – Labour 10,500 – Self 7,910.[1] Very bad indeed. Declaration by Returning Officer. Speeches (very short) on dripping balcony.

Then back to lunch at Swan – all feeling very dashed. In the afternoon we 'toured' to thank the workers at Street, Glastonbury, Shepton, Milborne Port (dear Milborne Port), Cary, Wincanton, Bruton. Everyone touchingly nice – & the dear gloomy schoolmaster at Bruton, Mr. Crowther, made a really very good & thoughtful speech. Back to dinner very tired & gloomy. The hammer-blow reached me at Street – a telegram from Mark saying he was out & Peto in by 4000.[2] This really knocked the heart out of me. I didn't care about myself – but the thought of Mark's victory had buoyed me up. It was my great personal stake in this Election – & his whole future hinges on it. Meanwhile the astounding Election results came rushing in. By lunchtime there were only 24 Conservatives in – & 85 Labour – Bracken, Sandys, Amery, Grigg,[3] Harold Macmillan – Dick Law out – (Hatchie of course) & then the astounding news that not only Dingle & Beveridge (which I feared) but Archie also had lost his seat. This last seemed to me to be incredible. He was bottom of the poll at Thurso of all places. Like the monarchy falling.[4] By nightfall Labour was in with a clear majority of 288. Our Libs reduced to 12 – Grahame White, Mander & Percy out. (The

[1] The official result was: Boles (Conservative) 13,004, C. Morgan (Labour) 10,539, Violet Bonham Carter 7,910. The 2,465 majority was considerably smaller than was gained at the 1931 and 1935 elections (5,271 and 7,621 respectively).

[2] C. H. M. Peto (Conservative) 17,822, Mark Bonham Carter 13,752, I. A. J. Williams (Labour) 10,237; the 4,070 majority was the biggest in the constituency since before the Great War.

[3] Sir (Percy) James Grigg (1890–1964), cr. KCB, 1932; secretary for war, 1942–5; National MP for East Cardiff, 1942–5.

[4] The voting at Caithness and Sutherland, the constituency of Sinclair's home town of Thurso, was incredibly close: E. L. Gandar-Dower (Conservative) 5,564, R. I. A. MacInnes (Labour) 5,558, Sinclair (Liberal) 5,503. Sinclair had held the seat since 1922, being unopposed in 1923, 1924 and 1931.

only amazing thing – Jo – who telephoned me after dinner – only beaten in Orkney & Shetland by 329 votes! He nearly won it in 3 weeks campaign – with a Tory agent & <u>no</u> organization!) He told it me very quietly & modestly – after condoling with Mark & me.

To bed terribly tired & cldn't sleep. Home next day from Bristol. Long telephone talk with Walter Layton who told me that Bevin who he had seen Wed. night didn't even feel sure <u>he</u> was in – & a Tory candidate, Clarke by name, offered Walter £1 for every seat <u>under</u> 320 the Tories failed to win! He wld have made £150 or more. W. issued a rather moving message to the nation. Extraordinary Maelstrom – incredible to foreign eyes. The Nation differentiating between W. as a War-Leader & the Tory Party. <u>Saturday</u> Mark arrived with the Friends for the night at 6.30 – looking tired poor darling. Very sweet & quite brave but obviously bitterly disappointed by his result as his meetings had been so <u>marvellous</u>. Puff rang up in the morning to say that Margot had died in her sleep. I went round to see him – & her. . . . He was crying like a child. I asked him if she had longed to live till the very end. He said she had. This was the indomitable thing in her. She wanted life always – & at any price. Death held no <u>peace</u> for her. The house was so like her – with all the family's treasures – each in the perfectly right place. Her eye was impeccable. These were all <u>so</u> full <u>of</u> memories. Dinner with Mark & the Friends.

Diary – Monday 30 July – 40 Gloucester Square, W.2

Went to Gayfere St after lunch & saw [Clem] Davies there. Ly Rhys Williams came in. Everyone's morale seems excellent considering all things. Wilfrid came to tea looking more elongated & cadaverous than ever (B. described him as a Wolf in Worm's Clothing!) & we had a long & rather gloomy talk about the Election in which he said that he wondered how many Liberals like himself were longing to climb on to the Labour band-waggon. I said this was the one moment when one <u>cldn't</u> join them. He said 'Oh I know – the opportunity for ratting is past'. He has a good sense of humour. . . .

Diary – Tuesday 31 July – 40 Gloucester Square, W.2

A sad day. Drove down with Priscilla & B. to Margot's funeral at Sutton Courtenay – all thro' Maidenhead Thicket & past Templecombe Golf Links – the familiar route I used to drive with Father every Saturday of my life. The toll-gate on Culham Bridge had gone. Some villagers were standing round the church – Puff & Peter Russell were there & an old parson who just read through the sermon quite tonelessly & very rapidly. No

singing or music. We went out to the grave – where the coffin was lowered
with one big bunch of roses on it. It was not beside Father's or under his
stone – which I think she wld have minded. I drove straight back to the
end of the Campaign Committee.... Bev. looks a broken man. I am <u>so</u>
sorry for him. His innocent vanity as well as all else is stabbed to the core.[1]

Diary – Monday 6 August – Manor Farm, Stockton, Wiltshire

Greyer day with intermittent sun & rain. After tea went up to Stockton
Wood with B & Mrs Y.B. & sat in High Grove which is now thick with
<u>clover,</u> looking out at that infinitely lovely view to the downs beyond the
Valley. It was a day of light & shades – the woods looked almost black on
the greys & greens & blues of distant downs – with flecks of gold where
corn was growing. Sky piled high with vast white clouds – softer than
snow & vaster than any mountain. B. & Muriel hunted meanwhile for
more flowers in the wood below & found some. We went back thro'
Stockton Wood & looked for deer in vain. I have hardly ever seen the
down so thick with flowers.

On the 9 o'clock news came the announcement of the dropping on
Japan of the first atomic bomb – an amazing discovery on which English
scientists have been working all thro' the war. Each bomb is as powerful
as <u>2000</u> 10 ton bombs. A V-1 was 1 ton. Germany was at work on the same
problem – & we just won – 500 millions were spent on developing it in
U.S.A.[2] One troubles for the future of the world. Thank Heaven it is in our
hands now – but how long will it remain in them? Poor Winston! What a
blow for him to have been out when this triumph ripened. His own
statement prepared for the occasion was read.

Diary – Friday 10 August – Manor Farm, Stockton, Wiltshire

Lovely day of heat & sun with fresh wind blowing – Mark bicycled to
Yarnbury with C & Nancy in the afternoon. Laura & I & Gelda went to
see Ray at work in the harvest-field beyond Long Hall after an early tea &
as we passed, Diana's Frank, who was standing outside, said 'Do you know
the war is over?' He said it had been on the 1 o'clock news. It was the

---

[1] The result at Berwick was: R. A. F. Thorp (Conservative) 12,315, Beveridge 10,353, J. Davis
(Labour) 5,782.

[2] The first atomic bomb was dropped on Hiroshima at 8.15 a.m. local time; the final death
toll approached 140,000. It had been developed in the United States by scientists from America
and Britain. Their work began mid-1941 and was both top secret and urgent.

end – really the end. A second wave of numb relief – this time the final one. How wonderful that at last our prisoners will be freed – that the men in Burma can come home – that it is <u>all over</u>. My secondary 1st thought was '<u>Poor</u> Winston!' This shld have been his triumph too – & he has handed it to Attlee. We cld have 'finished the job' all together & had the autumn Election if only Beaverbrook hadn't driven him on into the mad course he pursued.[1] <u>How</u> bitter for him!...

Diary – Saturday 11 August – Manor Farm, Stockton, Wiltshire

Another lovely day. Ethel Sands & Stephen came over to tea from Wilsford.[2] Stephen looking really more 'extreme' than I have ever seen him – rouged up to the eyes – with drops in them & peroxide tinted hair. <u>Much</u> stronger & 'weller' looking – & really very good looking but for his make-up. Gold bangle on his wrist – white socks & sandals & Laura said exuding a marvellous scent. Ethel beautifully dressed & very like herself. Ray had a friend over from Larkhill – Pyman by name – who must have been astonished! Stephen was very sweet & amusing – & appreciative as ever.... Horrible head-lines saying 2nd Atom Bomb was an improvement on the 1st! Russians still advancing.[3]

Diary – Tuesday 14 August – 40 Gloucester Square, W.2

Margot's Memorial Service at St Margaret's at 12 today. Mark came up at 11 from Windsor (all his medal ribbons on for the 1st time – General Service & German Campaign as well as his Africa Star) & he & I & B went away early so that they could usher. There were already quite a lot of people in the church. I went to the vestry to speak to the Canon & Canon Marriott (from North Berwick) who did the service. The Canon gave a very brave & moving address round the line from Adonais 'He is safe from

---

[1] Beaverbrook was widely regarded as 'the adviser of Mr Churchill and director of the Tory campaign', an image propagated by his own newspaper, the *Daily Express*. His influence was probably not as great as Violet imagines (see R. B. McCallum and Alison Readman, *The British General Election of 1945*, 209–10).

[2] Ethel Sands (1873–1962), painter; aunt of Archie Sinclair; friend and pupil of Sickert. Stephen James Napier Tennant (b. 1906), nephew of Margot Asquith; painter and aesthete.

[3] The second atom bomb was dropped on Nagasaki, 9 August; the death toll approached 50,000. The day before, Russia had declared war on Japan, and invaded Manchuria. Japan finally surrendered on 14 August, accepting in essence terms set out by the Allies at Potsdam.

the contagion of the world's slow stain'.[1] He said that stain had never touched Margot – & in a sense this is quite true. She remained always completely free from the bonds of conventional values. He grasped the nettle of her attitude towards money with extraordinary courage – pointing out that to her it was a thing of no account. She didn't seek security from it – to her it was just a medium for living freely & openhandedly....

Went back to lunch with Mark – finished necessary work. Unable to catch early train so took the 5 o'clock. No answer still from the Japanese on 9 o'clock news.... At 11 we were told to listen for important news at midnight. Ray made me call him & he & I & Laura then listened together & heard the Japanese surrender announced by Attlee. One thought '<u>how</u> hard for Winston! & how differently he wld have done it!' A faint noise made us go to the window. It was a very distant 'All Clear' <u>in intention</u> – but in actuality a Siren! perhaps the last we shall ever hear.

Diary – Tuesday 21 August – Manor Farm, Stockton, Wiltshire

Motored into Salisbury with Frank Nancy & Laura – & out to Wilsford from the station in Janet Bailey's car. Enjoyed seeing the unfamiliar & lovely valley between Salisbury & Amesbury. Found Stephen in bed – with shivery – flue-ish chill he said – but added that he thought it was the fatigue of having guests in the house. I sat with him & in a characteristically fantastic bedroom panelled with looking-glasses – pink marbled paper & festooned with extravagant curtains. Shells – lay everywhere. An elaborate dressing table – white satin – black lace mirror inlaid. Books & sheaves of paper on the floor. Stephen in a nice plain white shirt & tie in bed – but alas peroxided hair which terribly vulgarizes him. We eat some pigeon together & drank <u>claret</u> & then some <u>melon</u> (rare treat!) then he read me some of his poems & I drove home $\frac{1}{4}$ to 3 after a short stroll round the garden – by that loveliest road that goes past Stonehenge & Yarnbury. It was a day of cloud & sun & shadows. Infinite beauty of colour & line on the downs – & stubble-fields....

Diary – Saturday 25 August – Manor Farm, Stockton, Wiltshire

Another grey day with occasional rain. Spent mostly writing letters & working in a desultory way....

After dinner B & I & Ray went to the V.J. ball in the barn for which B.

---

[1] 'From the contagion of the world's slow stain / He is secure ...': Shelley, 'Mourn not for Adonais'.

had given the band. It was packed out with soldiers & other outsiders – the village not much en évidence. I shld think about 150 were there – great heat & scrum in which Ray joined with intrepidity & gusto – dancing with Colonel Harrison (the Brigadier)'s very nice 16 year old daughter. Ray has not yet returned (midnight) so he is evidently having fun. We found Jo here when we got back. He gives a frightful account of U.N.R.R.A.'s task & of the plight of Europe. The Russians on the lines of communication are he says just savage children – wearing wrist-watches up to their shoulders in rows – filling their pockets with alarm-clocks which terrify <u>them</u> when they go off – raping right & left & mistaking lavatories for shower-baths so that they put their heads in them & then pull the plug! They have torn up all the telephones in Vienna by the roots to take to Russia & stacked them in the market-place where they are still rotting to this hour.

Diary – Wednesday 5 September – 40 Gloucester Square, W.2

... Went on to tea with old Percy in the small Restaurant near Gayfere St. He is a pathetic old boy – his whole raison d'être ravished from him after 40 years. He bravely pretends not to mind – says 'I am my own master now – thinking of writing a book etc.' but I know he feels like a lost dog. He says there is no hope of Gwilym taking any active part in the affairs of the Party. He & Megan have both been left very poor by Ll.G. & only given empty farms & country houses 'in trust'. Miss Stevenson has got away with the whole swag. Went with Ray to film to which I was asked by Soviet Embassy – the capture of Berlin & Moscow Victory Parade. Though documentary I thought it <u>very</u> dull – & it contained not one allusion to the part played in the war by Russia's Allies!

Diary – Wednesday 19 September – 40 Gloucester Square, W.2

... Leon Blum & his wife came to dinner[1] – Toto – Veronica & Cressida were the rest of the party. He is an enchanting man – simple – natural with infinite charm & a 1st rate sense of humour – <u>very</u> superior to most Frenchmen's. He told us the whole of his experiences in captivity at Dachau etc. – where he was kept with about 150 key-hostages. There was a défilé of them in front of his cell the 1st night. First <u>Schacht</u> whom he had last seen at the Hotel Matignon in Paris: 'Je crois que vous auriez été encore plus étonnés que moi si je vous avais dit que nous nous reverrions

---

[1] Léon Blum (1872–1950), French socialist leader; premier, 1936–7 and 1938.

à Dachau' he said to Schacht.[1] Then 'Vous ne me connaissez pas. Je suis Dr. Schuschnigg' said the next – then Best – the British Secret Agent who was pulled over the frontier at the beginning of the war.[2] Then Kalei – Hungarian P.M. – 'avec un paquet de ministres Hongrois' – then the Thyssens with very smart luggage – 'de Pullman'. Asprey leather with gold initials which they were always packing & repacking because they were afraid of losing it on their many moves. Falkenhayn – von Halder – the Stauffenberg Family – all who had been suspects in the attempt on Hitler.[3] There were only 6 French amongst them 'L'évèque de Clermont- Ferrand – le Prince de Bourbon-Parme – Ma femme et moi – et un communiste du Nord'. Every day the German General Staff officers spread out a map & marked it with flags & arrows – one saying 'They are at Augsburg – they will be here in 10 days.' Another 'No they will make a wide encircling movement round Munich & won't reach us for 4 weeks'. Whenever the guns sounded near they were all moved – until they ended up on a peak in the Dolomites. The Blums were 1ˢᵗ alone with poor Mandel – who was taken away to be murdered – on Laval's orders.[4] He knew he was going to his death & they knew it too & were half-ashamed & guilty not to be taken with him. I asked them how soon they thought the Germans <u>knew</u> they were beaten. They said not till Rundstedt's counter-offensive failed.[5] They were as overjoyed over D-Day as we were – thinking that we were bound to be destroyed.

Blum said de Gaulle cldn't last more than 8 months at longest. When he saw Cressida he said quite simply shaking hands with her 'Quels yeux'! He said that he <u>had</u> been going to lunch with Winston on Friday but had been put off because on Dr's orders he was staying abroad a little longer.[6] He said he believed his health was not good. I fear for him the sudden deflation of Peace – plus loss of power.

[1] Hjalmar Schacht (1877–1970), German financier dismissed as head of Reichsbank 1939 over opposition to rearmament expenditure; later charged with high treason and interned. 'I think you would have been even more surprised than me if I had told you that we would see each other again in Dachau.'

[2] Kurt von Schuschnigg (1897–1977), chancellor of Austria, 1934–8; interned by Nazis. Captain Payne Best, one of two British agents abducted by Germans from the Dutch border town of Venlo, 9 November 1939.

[3] For the 20 July 1944 attempt on Hitler's life, see above, p. 311.

[4] Georges Mandel (1885–1944), French minister for colonies, prior to 18 May 1940, when made minister of interior; imprisoned by Vichy government and, as a Jew, subsequently handed over to the Germans.

[5] Gerd von Rundstedt (1875–1953), field marshal; led the German counter-offensive in the Ardennes, beginning 16 December 1944, known as the 'battle of the Bulge'. Initially successful, the advance was halted, and reversed, within a month.

[6] In September 1945 Churchill took an extended holiday in Italy and southern France: 'Sunshine is my quest' (Martin Gilbert, *Churchill*, 859).

Diary – Wednesday 3 October – 40 Gloucester Square, W.2

... Back to tea with G. M. Young – who wld tell the Russians <u>now</u> to retire behind their 1939 frontiers or Atom Bomb them. Heroic prescription – possibly in the long-run wise – but our morals are not up to it....

Diary – Friday 5 October – 40 Gloucester Square, W.2

Spent the morning in Livingstone Hall with Gollancz, Eleanor Rathbone, Crossman ... & a lot of Labour M.P.s to draft resolution for the meeting on Monday.[1] Very interesting account of Germany given by Crossman. Refugees are flooding into our zone 10,000 a week. We are concentrating on getting something going – & not being too particular about the ideology of those whom we employ to do it. We are the best 'zone' quà humanity – tho' not perhaps quà politics. The Russians of course care nothing about humanity & everything about ideology. They are creating a deliberate wilderness – & liquidating everybody they do not want by expulsion....

M.R.B.C. to V.B.C.   *Saturday 6 October*
                                                        Balmoral Castle

Dear Mama,

Thank you so much for your letter. It continues quite lovely up here – really hot & delicious. Yesterday & the day before I went out stalking. On the first day I got two stags – with two shots! The King told me that when Aga came up here he got two with two & refused ever to stalk again. Yesterday I got one. Two days' stalking, combined with a dance, left me rather stiff & today we went out for a picnic lunch at the Queen's Marie Antoinette cottage, & walked on the hills afterwards. Most of the guests have gone.... The food is magnificent – & the comfort very great. There are infinite opportunities for good sluicing. The house has I think been changed a bit since old days, though there is still quite a lot of tartan about. The pipers come screaming round after dinner. Love <u>Mark</u>

Diary – Monday 8 October – 40 Gloucester Square, W.2

... Went to Conway Hall meeting on 'Save Europe Now' – stopping the expulsions & sending more transport – food & cargo shipping. Gollancz

---

[1] Richard (Howard Stafford) Crossman (1907–74), Labour MP for Coventry East, 1945–74.

in the Chair. Crossman & Barbara Ward made the long speeches moving & seconding the resolution.[1] Gerald Gardiner – a Quaker – & I supported.[2] Audience of long haired highbrows....

Diary – Monday 22 October – Clovelly Court, Devon

Radiant morning which dimmed as day went on. Spent it trying to write ... in a little sunny bedroom....

Started 'Oliver Twist' for the Chimney Sweep scene & <u>cldn't</u> put it down. Know I shall read it all night. News cld hardly be worse. In the French Elections the Communists are the biggest single Party. No Party has a clear majority. (They hate de Gaulle – & are hated by the Socialists & most other Parties for they applaud Moscow even when Stalin vetoes the presence of France in international Conferences!) America has reduced the figure of her proffered loan to us from 1200 million to 1000 million & increased the interest rate![3] More British troops are landing at Haifa.[4]

Diary – Thursday 25 October – Clovelly Court, Devon

... I received a letter (in reply to mine) from Winston. I had asked if he wld like to be entertained by the remains of the old 'Focus'. His reply is that of a sulky child! thanking me but refusing on the ground that he doesn't want to be involved in 'tiresome arguments' & that in the remote

[1] Barbara Mary Ward (1914–81), assistant editor, *Economist*.

[2] Gerald Austin Gardiner (1900–90), barrister; served with Friends' Ambulance Unit, 1943–5. Violet spoke of the pressing need for international unity: 'In Europe where we've had to blast our way to victory we have created a great void. Europe to-day is like a great bomb-crater – roped off. And we stand round the ropes & gaze into this void which is at once our danger & our tremendous opportunity....'.

[3] In August John Maynard Keynes had been sent to Washington to negotiate a financial arrangement with the American government, following the termination of lend–lease. The best that he could achieve was a loan of $3,750 million, repayable at 2 per cent: in American eyes a generous settlement, it was received with profound disappointment in Britain (Kenneth Harris, *Attlee*, 274).

[4] In September the British government was made aware of the likelihood of Jewish armed resistance to the administration of its mandate in Palestine. Additional troops were sent in anticipation of trouble.

future things may be 'easier'. He is clearly aggrieved & bitter – as Horatia had told me he was.[1]

Diary – Wednesday 7 November – 40 Gloucester Square, W.2

Committee at Gayfere St at 11 o'clock to discuss Finance & <u>Archie</u> – whom it is generally agreed we must get south by hook or crook if any progress is to be made with money getting. Back to luncheon – work on my speech & then off to the Soviet Embassy Party. I was there only during the early & unfashionable 'jam' – & saw no one but rather grim & joyless Russians clinking Vodka glasses. The celebration was the 28th Anniversary of the glorious Soviet Revolution. I only saw Leith Ross, Garvin, Low, Professor Dent – & Clemmie just arriving as I left. She gave me a rather 'guarded' wave!...

Diary – Thursday 8 November – 40 Gloucester Square, W.2

Busy morning clearing up odds & ends shifting furniture etc. Read the Debate on Atomic Bomb. Winston's was a definitely <u>bad</u> speech I thought – saying the Russians cld have no grievance if it was true that they cld make the bomb themselves in a short time & demanding that we get bombs for ourselves <u>at once</u> – as the M.G. puts it – in time for Xmas. Bevin's speech was an amazingly outspoken & <u>personal</u> anti-Russian outburst – full of simple touches like 'why shldn't I make friends with the neighbours in my own street? etc.' & accusing Russia of trying 'to cut right across the throat of the British Empire'. It is strange how Palmerstonian Labour Ministers become directly they go to the F.O....

---

[1] Horatia Seymour, a Liberal friend of the Churchills, had told Violet that Clementine 'is terribly bitter about the Liberals'. Violet wondered in her diary 'Why – God knows' (17 October). Harold Nicolson, with whom she discussed the Focus invitation, would have been able to elucidate: 'I doubt myself whether [Churchill] will ever for one moment agree to speak to Violet or Archie again. She seems blissfully unaware that the policy of the Liberal Party at the last election was not only foolish and ill-considered in itself, but was extremely selfish and unpatriotic' (Harold Nicolson, diary, 20 September 1945). Churchill had levelled special criticism at 'the Sinclair–Beveridge Liberals' in his first election broadcast. Like Labour, they chose 'to put Party before country'. Unlike Labour, they had no substantial disagreement with the Conservatives, and their opposition could not be justified (*Listener*, 7 June 1945, 629–32).

Diary – Wednesday 28 November – 40 Gloucester Square, W.2

Attended the 1st meeting of the Liberal Shadow Cabinet at H Samuel's room in the H of Lords – Clem Davies presiding. Discussed Foreign Affairs, Atomic Bomb, Palestine etc. Nothing very new said or decided. Clem very 'agreeable' & full of blarney to <u>Megan</u> – whom he had so hotly abused to me! I can't understand these Welsh! but perhaps they understand each other!...

Diary – Saturday 1 December – 40 Gloucester Square, W.2

Tried on at Caldere's. She had a nice new Schiaparelli model which I regretted not having seen before. Off to the Candidates Conference after luncheon which happened in the City & at which Clem Davies made a highly emotional Welsh speech lasting <u>one hour</u>. 'Er ist nir widerlich.' When I got back Mark had arrived & he & I arranged the drawing-room together. It looked <u>quite</u> lovely with glistening curtains & covers. At 8 we had our 'ball-dinner' – the first since the war. It felt so odd putting on an evening-dress – literally for the 1st time for 5 years or more.... We found a vast throng already crowding in Enid's house – dancing with floodlights & spotlights. I was unfortunately buttonholed by Bernard who sat with me against a deafening band – & I had to roar into his deaf ear while he said 'Do you remember Stanley Bay Violet? I was very fond of you Violet? Did you realize it? I was very sentimental Violet – you laid my unsophisticated Colonial heart quite flat etc.' – etc. – I was utterly exhausted![1] B. took me to recover in the flat – which was a haven of peace. Later Enid came up & we had a good talk. I admired her complete detachment from her ball & its cares.... We came back about 2 – in a very expensive car!

Diary – Monday 10 December – 40 Gloucester Square, W.2

Discussed [American] Loan at H. of L. with Liberal Party Committee. Clem Davies in the Chair. He asked me to speak 1st – I said I thought we <u>had</u> to support it. The political reasons for it outweighed the economic disadvantages.... The coming years wld be of unparalleled austerity without it. This we might contemplate with equanimity but the country wldn't. Megan spoke next & disagreed. She thought we were not so weak – that our social reform schemes might be interfered with & that if we sank U.S.A. wld be obliged to rescue us in the long-run, as Germany was rescued

---

[1] See above, p. 65.

in the last war. I pointed out that if we had to be rescued in the long-run it was better this shld be done before our heads were under water. Everyone else welcomed it with varying degrees of emphasis – Herbert Samuel I thought unduly lyrically.

Diary – Wednesday 12 December – 40 Gloucester Square, W.2

... Loan Debate in H. of C. – where Bob Boothby scored a tremendous personal success by describing it as our economic Munich & accusing the Govt of selling this country for a packet of cigarettes. The Tories abstained from voting as they objected to the word 'welcome'. Very weak – as they certainly wld not have taken the responsibility of refusing it.

Diary – Friday 14 December – 40 Gloucester Square, W.2

... When I got back I found Mark here back from Barnstaple where he had had a very busy week but I gathered quite enjoyed himself. I had <u>luckily</u> ordered him a new shirt for his B.P. party for the King's birthday & he went off in this & his old Winchester short coat – looking I thought all right (Alistair Wedderburn said to B. the other night 'I saw Mark dancing with Pss Elizabeth & he was the worst dressed man in the room. A soft collar etc. – well I suppose it may be all right for Mark'!) He has decided to take his All Souls exam in May – rightly I think.

Diary – Wednesday 19 December – 40 Gloucester Square, W.2

Last day here & very busy. Wanted to go to Maurice [Baring]'s Memorial Service but was prevented from doing so as Eric Mieville[1] rang up from B.P. to ask Mark to go to a play & dinner with the Princesses on Thursday & I had to get through to Barnstaple where I was luckily able to speak to him. He had a dance engagement at Ilfracombe the following night & felt it wld be such a disappointment to the local Liberals that he decided to refuse. <u>Very</u> good of him – <u>& right</u> – I don't think I shld have done it. Lunched with Ray at Allies Club – & shopped with him a little, quite successfully – got a <u>fountain-pen</u> (they are extinct) for Mark at Websters – 'under the counter'....

[1] Sir Eric Charles Mieville (1896–1971), KCVO 1943; assistant private secretary to the king, 1937–45.

Diary – New Year's Eve, Monday 31 December – Manor Farm, Stockton, Wiltshire

... A long happy evening – with Ray – Mark & Cressida – all together except for B. in London – Laura & Jo – & the gap that never closes – & never can – <u>Bubbles</u>.

We listened to the MacNeice programme on B.B.C. which was good – & to the watchnight service – Auld Lang Syne – Toast to the New Year – & have only just gone to bed (1.30). We looked back & Ray said he had only been one year at St Ronan's when war broke out. Mark was only 17 – <u>one</u> year older than Ray is now. It seems incredible. We all felt that the war-years oughtn't to be allowed to 'count' to us in age – that we ought to start from scratch from where we left off then. It seemed incredible that Laura was now 27 – & that when Jo married her he was only one year older than Mark is now. It makes me realize what a very short time is left to B. & me to <u>live</u> – for the years race past at an ever accelerating tempo – & yet I don't really feel any <u>older</u> than I did 20 years ago – & in some ways more active & <u>un</u>tired physically.

I wish I felt as much confidence about the future as I did this time last year – when Victory was clearly in sight – & one did not look much beyond it. Now we are facing forces far more incalculable & uncontrollable than the Germans alas!

APPENDIX A: *Glossary*

An explanatory list of words, phrases and abbreviations appearing in the text. Foreign words, and notably French adjectives, are given as they appear in the original.

400, the – a second world war London nightclub

Abgeordneter – a member of the Reichstag

accidie – laziness, apathy

accouchement – delivery, childbirth

acharné – staunch, fierce, extremist

A.F. – Air Force

affairé – busy

agréable – pleasant, agreeable

Allies – in 1914–18 war, principally Britain (and Empire) and France; in 1939–45, Britain (and Commonwealth), France, (from December 1941) America (= the 'Western Allies'), and the Soviet Union

âme en peine – soul in despair

Anzac – Australian and New Zealand Army Corps; also 'Anzac cove', the beachhead between Cape Helles and Suvla Bay, secured on 25 April and afterwards defended with great distinction by the Anzac forces

Archie Gordon Club – see 'Club, the'

Arlesienne, the – the cruel woman of Arles, the central character in Alphonse Daudet's play *L'Arlésienne*, who is a constant but unseen presence; a failure when first performed in 1872, it became a staple in French repertory after being revived in 1885

army – military force consisting of a number of corps, under a general or lieutenant-general, with upwards of 250,000 men

A.R.P. – air-raid precautions

A.T.S. – Auxiliary Territorial Service (British women's army corps)

Auxiliaries/aux – a supplement to the Royal Irish Constabulary 1920–1, raised from among ex-officers, who were paid a pound a day; officially the 'auxiliary division', they were commonly known as 'auxis', and identifiable by their dark-blue uniforms and distinctive glengarry caps

avenant – personable, prepossessing

Bailey bridge – prefabricated bridge made of lattice steel, used during military operations in the second world war; after the designer, Coleman Bailey

balbutié-d – muttered

battalion – army unit of 600–1,000 men, under command of a lieutenant-colonel

Bd/bd – see 'Board, the'

B.D. – see 'Bloody Duck'

B.E. – an aeroplane (B.E.2) used by the Royal Flying Corps in France in 1914; a capable reconnaissance aircraft, it was soon superseded as a fighter by advanced German models

beano – holiday, or 'day out'

B.E.F. – British Expeditionary Force

B.L.A. – British Liberation Army (later British Army of the Rhine)

Black and Tans – a supplementary force to the Royal Irish Constabulary, 1920–1; the first recruits joined in the new year of 1920 and arrived in Ireland in March, where they were given makeshift uniforms of khaki and dark green, with black leather belts and peaked caps; on their appearance in Limerick they were dubbed the 'black and tans' after a local pack of hounds; recruited from among demobilized soldiers, they were paid ten shillings a day

black-out – during the second world war, the compulsory extinguishing of lights as a precaution against air raids

blême – wan, deathly pale

Bloody Duck – Violet's occasional soubriquet in letters to Churchill: when invited by Churchill to serve on the board of governors of the BBC in 1941, Violet had replied 'can a bloody duck swim?', and thereafter she sometimes signed herself 'bloody duck' or 'B.D.'. She was consciously echoing his own reply to Baldwin in 1924, when on being offered the 'chancellorship' after several years out of office, Churchill had thought he was being given the chancellorship of the duchy of Lancaster; when Baldwin made clear that it was the exchequer, he was unable to contain himself

Board, the – (chapters 8–11) BBC Board of Governors; (elsewhere) the board of the admiralty, which advised the first lord

Bolshie – Bolshevik, ill-mannered

Bradshaw – colloquial term for *Bradshaw's Railway Guide*, a timetable of all trains running in Britain, first produced 1839 ('with the regularity of Bradshaw')

Brains Trust – popular radio programme, first broadcast on New Year's Day 1941, in which a panel of five answered listeners' questions on a variety of topics; originally factual, these later extended to the general and speculative; the British public avidly took up the idea of a panel of experts answering questions, and 'Brains Trusts' proliferated

brigade – army unit of 4,000–8,000 men, comprising a number of regiments or battalions, under a brigadier or a brigadier-general

British Warm – British army overcoat issued to officers

B.T. – Black and Tan[s], see above

B.U.F. – British Union of Fascists

Bulletin – the *Irish Bulletin*, a weekly Sinn Féin propaganda news-sheet, printed in Dublin and aimed, in part, at the foreign press; Erskine Childers, an adept publicist, became editor in 1921

Bumpus – J. & E. Bumpus, renowned London bookseller

Bystander – social and current affairs magazine

capital levy – the levying of tax on capital to reduce or eliminate the national debt, Labour Party policy after the Great War, it was abandoned during the 1922 election campaign

Caporetto – scene of a humiliating reverse for Italy during the Great War, when an Austro-German attack 24 October 1917 resulted in the collapse of the Italian line; the situation was saved only by Allied reinforcements

Carlton Club – London Conservative Club

carted – let down, deceived, betrayed

Castle, the – Dublin Castle, centre of the British administration in Ireland prior to the signing of the 1921 Anglo-Irish Treaty

Causerie – a restaurant in Claridge's Hotel which offered a moderately priced smorgasbord, from which diners could eat as much as they liked

Cavendish world – of the social milieu at 20 Cavendish Square, London W., the Asquiths' home for fifteen years, before the family moved in to Downing Street in 1908

Central Powers – Germany, Austria–Hungary, Turkey (1914–18)

chef d'oeuvre – masterpiece

Club, the – the Archie Gordon Club, a boys' club founded by Violet in Hoxton, an impoverished area of East London, in the autumn of 1910. She received enormous help from Bongie in this venture, which was a living memorial to their friend the Hon. Archie Gordon, who died in December 1909 after a motor-car accident

Coalie[s] – Coalition or 'National' Liberals, followers of Lloyd George

company (Coy) – army unit of 100–150 men, under a captain or major

Compulsion Bill – bill to introduce conscription in Britain during Great War

corps – army unit comprising a number of divisions, around 75,000–150,000 men, under a lieutenant-general or major-general

Coupon – in the context of the 1918 general election – a letter signed by Lloyd George and Bonar Law, and sent to all parliamentary candidates of whom they jointly approved. The aim of the letter was to formalize and to extend into peacetime, through an electoral alliance, the wartime political alliance between Unionists and Lloyd George Liberals. The letter was withheld from any Liberal who had proved hostile to Lloyd George and it was derisively dubbed 'the coupon' by Asquith

C.P.O. – Chief Petty Officer

Creamery – dairy (Ireland)

Cuckoo – a term coined by Cynthia Asquith 'for the flitting from temporary roof to temporary roof, forced on her by lack of permanent home – she had not, as the saying went, "married a country house".' (Cynthia Asquith, *Diaries*, xiii)

Dáil Éireann – Gaelic, meaning 'assembly of Ireland'; the Irish Parliament instituted in 1919, following the election of seventy-three Sinn Féin members at the 1918 general election, who refused to take their seats at Westminster

Dardanelles – narrow channel dividing Asia Minor and the land mass of Europe, and connecting the Aegean with the Sea of Marmara; strategically, a gateway to Constantinople from the west

démarche style of walking; to undertake a walk (faire des démarches)

désoeuvré(e) idle, at a loose end

D.H.R. – see 'dominion home rule'

D.I. – District Inspector (Ireland)

division – army unit comprising a number of brigades, with around 9,000–20,000 men in total, under a major-general

dominion home rule – a term that gained currency 1918–22 to describe the kind of self-government to be offered to Southern Ireland; a term with considerable potential for ambiguity, it came to mean 'dominion status' – implying the wide powers of self-government possessed by the dominions (Australia, New Zealand, South Africa and Canada); it marked a dramatic advance on the powers implicit in 'home rule' (see below) and even held out the possibility of a republic

doe – woman

D.S.O. – Distinguished Service Order

Duchy – Duchy of Lancaster

Duty – air-raid warden duty – Violet and Bongie undertook this regularly throughout the 1939–45 war

Earl's Court – in central London, the site of a permanent funfair in Edwardian times

embêtement pour embêtement – this is not a phrase in French, but in the context used it means 'blow for blow' ('embêtement' = annoyance)

endimanché Sunday best [adj.]

Ersatz – substitute or imitation; the German for 'replacement', 'Ersatz' was a British colloquialism that acknowledged the German ability to produce remarkable substitutes, reducing their dependence on imported raw materials

Erse – the Gaelic language

Etat désespéré – 'hopeless state'

F.A.['s] – family allowances

F.C.N.L. – French Committee for National Liberation

flak – anti-aircraft fire

flying bomb – see 'pilotless plane'

F.O. – foreign office

Focus – the Focus in Defence of Freedom and Peace, or simply Freedom Focus, a loosely organized anti-fascist group that formed under Churchill's leadership in the mid-1930s and of which Violet was a founder member

Fortnums – Fortnum and Mason, superior London provisions store

Free Liberals – or 'Wee Frees'; 'uncouponed' or 'independent' Liberals at the 1918 election, who afterwards supported Asquith against Lloyd George in the party schism 1918–23

free trade – central tenet of British Liberalism, the belief that trade should move freely between countries, without the inhibition of protective tariffs; see 'protection'

full employment – central tenet of Beveridge proposals; defined as the existence of more paid jobs than men and women seeking jobs; Liberal Party policy at the 1945 general election

Gallantry Bower – a beautiful man-made walk along the coast high above Clovelly, in North Devon

Gallipoli – the Gallipoli Peninsula, rocky and mountainous land mass to the north of the Dardanelles Straits, part of Turkish territory in Europe; also refers to the military campaign there, 1915–16

gauleiter – Nazi district commander

Gayfere St – a Liberal Party headquarters in central London

G.B.E. – Dame (or Knight) Grand Cross of the Order of the British Empire

Gestapo – Nazi secret police: Geheime Staatspolizei

G.H.Q. – General Headquarters

Giorgione[sque] – resembling the style of the Italian painter Giorgione Barbarelli (1478–1510)

Gnade – grace, mercy (German)

Gudrunish – emotionally intense, after Gudrun Brangwen, one of the central characters in D. H. Lawrence's *Women in Love*

h. & c. – hot and cold (water)

H. of C. – House of Commons

heygate – conventional (of manners, attitudes, etc.); the word carried a negative connotation

Holbein. . . – of a hat or coat, [prob.] after the style of those featured in the portraits by Hans Holbein the younger, court painter to Henry VIII

home rule – the policy, favoured by Liberals and opposed by the Unionists pre-1914, of re-establishing in Dublin a parliament that would legislate for the internal affairs of Ireland; it was advanced in three bills – which differed on points of detail – in 1886, 1893 and 1912–14; derisively thought of as 'gas and water' devolution by those who demanded greater powers of self-government – see 'dominion home rule'

hôtel-de-ville – town hall

House, the – the House of Commons

H.R. – see 'home rule'

Hullo Ragtime – music-hall show featuring American 'ragtime' music, and popular in London shortly before the Great War

instancy – urgency; occasionally used by VBC in signing off her letters to MRBC, when he was a prisoner of war in Italy in 1943; it conveys the pressing nature of her feelings for him

I.R.A. – Irish Republican Army; in this context, the unified pre-1922 (i.e. pre-Irish Civil War) movement, led by Michael Collins.

Joys, the – 'Ridgeway's Late Joys' – a Victorian-style cabaret, and a popular late-night venue with performers in other West End shows; originally in a top-floor location at Covent Garden it was moved during the war to a basement in 23 Albermarle Street

J.T.C. – Junior Training Corps, preparatory youth training for the army

K.B.E. – Knight Commander of the Order of the British Empire

K.C.B. – Knight Commander of the Order of Bath

K.C.M.G. – Knight Commander of the Order of St Michael and St George

K.C.V.O. – Knight Commander of the Royal Victorian Order

Kia Ora – exclamation of good will – 'good health!' or 'be well!' (Maori)

Knight Frank Rutley – well known firm of London estate agents

Krithia – village about six miles from the tip of the Gallipoli Peninsula, to the west of the Achi Baba heights; one of the initial objectives of the invasion of 25 April it was never taken, despite three major offensives

K.R.R.C. – King's Royal Rifle Corps (the 'Rifle Brigade')

Kruschen quality – irritating and exaggerated well-being; after 'Kruschen's salts', a patent medicine that claimed to infuse energy and a feeling of vigorous good health; the salts were advertised under the slogan 'that Kruschen feeling'

Kursaal – public building provided for the entertainment of visitors, especially at a German spa

L.D.V. – Local Defence Volunteers; formed by Anthony Eden, this uninspiring title was later changed to the 'Home Guard'

League – see 'League of Nations'

League of Nations – organization for international co-operation and peace, established by the victorious powers after the Great War; a League Covenant was formulated at the Paris Peace Conference in 1919 and was subscribed to by the Allies; the organization's headquarters were in Geneva

League of Nations Union – founded in Britain in October 1918 from two wartime peace organizations, the League of Nations Society (1915) and the League of Free Nations Association (1917); its aim was to encourage, mobilize and direct public opinion in support of the League of Nations, and the cause of world peace generally; almost 407,000 annual subscriptions were collected in 1931, but the popularity of the movement declined as the League's authority in world affairs diminished; it was led by Lord 'Bob' Cecil, a founder of the League itself, 1923–45, and Violet was an active member, serving on its executive

Liberal Council – a policy-making group within the Liberal Party, formed in 1927 under the presidency of Lord Grey; it reflected the internal party struggle between the followers of Lloyd George and Asquith – Violet, who was a vice president, defined it as 'a rallying ground for Liberals who refused to compromise the freedom and independence of the Party'

L.N.U. – see 'League of Nations Union'

Lohengrin – knightly central figure of Wagner's opera of the same name

loyalists – pre-1922, Irish opponents of Home Rule (i.e. those 'loyal' to the parliamentary union with Britain)

L.P.O. – Liberal Party Organization – created in 1936, it was intended to be the central policy-making body of the Liberal Party, replacing the National Liberal Federation in the reorganization suggested in Lord Meston's report

Lyons – popular teashops serving light refreshments, owned by the London based firm of J. Lyons & Co. Ltd; there were also 'Lyons Corner Houses', the best known of the larger London restaurants

maquillée – 'made up', in the sense of wearing make up

marconigram – a wireless telegraph, after the name of the inventor

Meads – the field at Winchester College, used for second XI cricket, which opens from the direction of War Memorial Cloister and chapel

M.E.F. – Mediterranean Expeditionary Force

mesquin – mean, petty

M.E.W. – Ministry of Economic Warfare

Mexican handkerchief – a cold remedy using a hot potion applied by handkerchief [?]

M.G. – *Manchester Guardian*, national daily newspaper (became, 1960, *The Guardian*)

Midlothian (campaign) – famous electoral campaign waged by Gladstone 1879–80 in the Scottish county constituency of Midlothian, around Edinburgh

Mills bomb – an egg-shaped time-fused hand grenade, introduced to the British army in 1915

mise en scène – setting, background

M. of I. – Ministry of Information

M.O.H. – Medical Officer of Health

Mulberries – Mulberry Harbour, code name for the prefabricated harbour used on D-Day June 1944; a term thereafter applied to any artificial harbour

Nazi – National Socialist German Workers' Party (N.S.D.A.P.)

National Liberals – Liberals who supported the national governments of the period 1931–45

National Service – a term used for conscription during the Great War

N.L.C. – National Liberal Club

N.L.F. – National Liberal Federation

N.S. – *New Statesman*, a weekly current affairs magazine

O.M. – Order of Merit

Ombrello – Neville Chamberlain, after the umbrella that he carried during a diplomatic visit to Italy

open town – in reality, 'open city'; a term used in time of war to denote a city unfortified and undefended, and thus under international law exempt from enemy bombardment

Other Club – cross-party parliamentary dining club, founded May 1911 by Winston Churchill and F. E. Smith, partly with the aim of dissipating the party bitterness engendered by the 1909 budget, etc.

O.U.P. – Oxford University Press

Paynims – pagans or non-Christians – chiefly Muslims or Saracens

P.C. – Privy Councillor

piano – subdued

pilotless plane – German 'V1' flying bomb, commonly known to British public as the 'doodle-bug' (see also 'V2')

platoon – group of 25–30 soldiers, under command of a junior officer – lieutenant or 2nd lieutenant

Post – observation point and meeting place for air-raid wardens

pounce – card game, better known as 'racing demon'

P.O.W. – prisoner of war

P.P. – see 'pilotless plane'

P.P.S./p.p.s. – parliamentary private secretary

P.P.U. – Peace Pledge Union

preux – valiant

Proms – the 'promenade' concerts held annually at the Royal Albert Hall

protection – policy advocated by the Conservative Party from 1903, favouring the imposition of tariffs on imported goods to protect home industries; often linked with 'Imperial preference', by which countries within the Empire are given more favourable treatment in respect of tariffs than those outside; see 'free trade'

P.S. – a 'Postscript' programme, a feature of BBC broadcasting during the war, made famous by J. B. Priestley

Quaker Speise – food, possibly in the form of a soup-kitchen, supplied by the Society of Friends during the Ruhr occupation, 1923

Queeriboo – a term used by Violet to mean 'eccentric'; it had no sexual connotation

quincunx – an ostentatious way of indicating a group of five; used by Sir Thomas Browne c. 1658 in *The Garden of Cyrus or The Quincunx*

Quisling – a traitor, or fifth-columnist; after Major Quisling, leader of the Norwegian Fascist Party, who proclaimed a puppet government in Norway the day after the German invasion of the country

R.A.M.C. – Royal Army Medical Corps

R.C. – Roman Catholic

réclame – appeal

relevé – to raise, take note, or given an account of something in conversation [adj. or past part.]

reparations – the compensation levied by the Allies on Germany for damages arising out of the Great War; the final sum of £6,600 millions was agreed by the Reparations Commission in April 1921; under the terms of the Young Plan of 1928 it was reduced to £1,850 millions

R.H.U. – Regimental Holding Unit

R.I.C. – Royal Irish Constabulary

R.N.D. – Royal Naval Division – infantry force around 15,000 strong, consisting of three brigades, one 'naval' and two 'marine', each with four battalions

Ruhr – industrial region in north-west Germany, on the banks of the river of the same name; in inter-war years the Ruhr was one of the largest single concentrations of industrial capacity in the world

Safety First – Conservative slogan at the 1929 general election, which Violet associated with Stanley Baldwin, disarmament and appeasement

Schadenfreude – malicious pleasure (of another's misfortune) (German)

Schinkenbrötchen ham roll

Scophony [Ltd] – company making projectors and transmitting equipment, and of which Bongie was chairman

Season, the – the period when society assembled in London to enjoy the entertainment of dinners and dances; the summer months of May, June and July

Second [2nd] Front – in the 1939–45 war, the opening by the Allies of an offensive front in Western Europe through an invasion of France; it became an issue in Anglo-American relations with the Soviet Union, which wanted the 'second front' opened as soon as possible to take pressure off Russia in the east

senti – heartfelt

serviable – helpful

Shell Shock – medical term describing nervous breakdown under artillery bombardment; in medical use in 1915, thousands of cases were reported during the massively heavy bombardments of the Somme offensive the following year; early on, when not properly understood, it carried connotations of cowardice

Sinn Féin – Gaelic, meaning 'ourselves alone'; in this context the movement c. 1918–22, when it was the majority party in Irish politics

Sitzbad – hip-bath (German)

Skat – a three-handed card game, with bidding

sluicing – drinking, in a social sense; at parties one 'browsed and sluiced' – ate and drank

S.O.E. – (British) Special Operations Executive

S.P. gun – self-propelled artillery gun; the generic name for a type of artillery gun, mounted on a tracked, half-track or wheeled chassis, and used either

S.P. gun – *contd.*
as an assault gun in support of
infantry, or as a defensive anti-tank
weapon; widely used by all of the
major belligerents during the second
world war

Spam – 'spiced ham' tinned meat
product; an unappetizing but
ubiquitous sandwich filler, endured
by the British public during the
1939–45 war, when fresh meat was
scarce

Spectator – weekly political and current
affairs magazine

S.S. – Nazi special police: Schutz-Staffel

Suvla [Bay] – Allied landing point (6
August) at northern end of Gallipoli
Peninsula

taoiseach – prime minister of Eire
[Gaelic – 'chief, leader']

tapis – tapestry or covering; 'on the
tapis' – under consideration

Taube – a centre-wing monoplane, used
in early aerial bombing raids and in
reconnaissance; became the generic
name used by British soldiers for
German aircraft (German, 'Dove')

T.D. – Tealto Dáil – a member of the
Dáil Éireann

tent[ly] – a word of Violet's invention,
mixing 'tense' with 'taut', it suggests
anxiety, expectation

Toye Pot – trophy (i.e. a 'pot') awarded
at Winchester for inter-house
competition in junior boys cricket;
there were a number of such trophies
to be won, each named after a master

Transport House – building near the
Houses of Parliament, constructed in
the inter-war years under the auspices
of the Transport and General
Workers' Union, and housing the
headquarters of that organization,

and also of the Trade Union Congress
and the Labour Party

Trant – of, or like, the Reverend John
Trant Bramston (d. 1931), master of
the house at Winchester to which
Beb, Oc and Bongie all belonged

Troad – the mountainous north-
western corner of Asia Minor,
forming a geographical unit
surrounded on three sides by the sea;
the name derives from the belief that
the area was once under Trojan rule

Turcos – Turks

un-ébloui – 'not overcome',
'unimpressed'

Unionists – those upholding the union
of Great Britain and Ireland
enshrined in the Act of Union of
1800; until the creation of Éire, i.e.
until 1921/2, the term described
British Conservatives as well as Irish
opponents to Home Rule; see
'loyalists'

U.N.O. – United Nations Organization

Unsittlichkeit – immorality (German)

V2 – German 'V2' rocket, successor to
the 'V1' flying bomb, or pilotless
plane (see above)

V.A.D. – Voluntary Aid Detachment –
nursing organization operative
during the Great War

Venusberg – a regular political
luncheon party, almost a luncheon
club, organized by Violet and held at
the Chandos Street Restaurant; each
of those present paid a set three
shillings for the meal; the name
derives from a private joke referring
to the unlikely friendship formed
there between Walter Elliot and Baffy
Dugdale

Verdun – longest and costliest
engagement of the Great War,

February to December 1916; a determined attempt by the Germans, under Falkenhayn, to 'bleed' the French army to death; it was equally determinedly resisted, and around 650,000 were killed (from both sides)

Versailles – city south-east of Paris, and home to the Louis XIV palace in which the Treaty of Versailles was signed, 1919, putting in place the peace settlement following the Great War

Vichy – the French government established under Marshal Pétain after the armistice with Germany, June 1940; taken from the name of the town in which the government was based; 'Vichy' France consisted of about a third of the country – the Germans having occupied the whole of the Channel and Atlantic coasts

wadi – a dry [often rocky] watercourse in riverbed [Arabic]

War Memorial – cloister in Winchester College, built 1922–4 in memory of the Wykehamists who fell during the Great War; sited at a busy thoroughfare, through which most of the boys pass several times a day; among the names engraved on its walls are those of Raymond Asquith

and Guy Bonham Carter

W.C. paper – water-closet (toilet) paper

Weekly Summary – a four-page propaganda news-sheet, produced by the Dublin Castle administration for consumption by the Crown forces

Wharf, the – the Asquiths' home at Sutton Courtenay, on the Thames in Oxfordshire

W.L.F. – Women's [National] Liberal Federation

W.N.L.F. – Women's National Liberal Federation

W.O. – War Office

Woman Power Committee – unofficial non-party and parliament-based committee, concerned with the wartime employment of women and with women's rights

Woolsack – the office of lord chancellor, so called because of the wool-stuffed seat on which the lord chancellor sits in the House of Lords

W.V.S. – Women's Voluntary Service (now W.R.V.S., Women's Royal Voluntary Service)

Y.W.C.A. – Young Women's Christian Association

zerstört – destroyed, ruined, wrecked

APPENDIX B: *Biographical notes*

For the most part these biographical notes have been confined to cover the period 1914–45 only. Names in square brackets are commonly used nicknames, and those in rounded brackets are unused given names. The colleges identified are Oxford, unless otherwise stated. All unattributed quotations are of Violet and come from the Violet Bonham Carter MSS.

Aitken, William Maxwell – see Beaverbrook, Lord.

Asquith, Anthony [Puffin/Puff] (1902–68), second child of Margot Asquith, Violet's half-brother and godson; godfather to Raymond Bonham Carter; educ. Winchester and Balliol; founder member of the Film Society in London; film director: *Tell England* (1930–1), *Pygmalion* (1938), *The Way to the Stars* (1945).

Asquith, Arthur Melland [Artie/Oc] (1883–1939), third son of H. H. Asquith, Violet's older brother, and godfather to her daughter Cressida; married, 1918, Hon. Betty Constance *née* Manners; educ. Winchester and New College; early career in Sudan Civil Service; joined RND September 1914; served Gallipoli and France (DSO and two bars, 1917); severely wounded, December 1917 (lost his leg, and invalided out of active service); retired, honorary brigadier-general, 1918; controller, trench warfare department, 1918; controller, appointments department, ministry of labour, 1919; company director; died of leukaemia, 25 August 1939. 'Whenever I met him I was aware of his strength & sweetness of his nature; his generosity, sound judgement, fidelity & modesty. He represented in himself what makes us love our Country' (Desmond MacCarthy to VBC, 1 September 1939).

Asquith, Cynthia *née* Charteris (1887–1960), eldest daughter of Lord Elcho, 11th Earl of Wemyss; married, 1910, Herbert Asquith, three sons; educated privately; private secretary to J. M. Barrie, 1918–37; novelist, biographer and diarist.

Asquith, Cyril [Cys] (1890–1954), Violet's younger brother, the youngest child of H. H. Asquith's first marriage; married Anne Stephanie *née* Pollock; educ. Winchester and Balliol; served with Queen's Westminster Rifles (captain), 1914–18; barrister, 1920; KC, 1936; judge of high court of justice, King's Bench, 1938–46.

Asquith, Herbert [Beb] (1881–1947), second son of H. H. Asquith, Violet's older brother; married, 1910, Lady Cynthia Charteris, three sons; educ. Winchester and Balliol; served with RFA (captain), 1914–18; poet and novelist: *The Volunteer* (1915), *Wind's End* (1924), *Roon* (1929), *Youth in the Skies* (1940).

Asquith, Herbert Henry (1852–1928), cr. Earl of Oxford and Asquith, 1925; Violet's father; born in Morley, Yorkshire; married, (1) Helen Kelsall Melland (d. 1891),

1877, four sons, one daughter; (2) Margot Tennant, 1894, one daughter, one son; educ. City of London School and Balliol; barrister, 1876; MP for East Fife, 1886–1918; prime minister 1908–16 (and secretary for war, March–August 1914); MP for Paisley, 1920–24; resigned leadership of Liberal Party, October 1926; died 15 February 1928. 'Rarely have a father and daughter been united by such a perfect, unbroken love and understanding' (Arnold Ward to VBC, 16 February 1928).

Asquith, (Emma Alice Margaret) Margot *née* **Tennant** (1864–1945), Countess of Oxford and Asquith; Violet's step-mother; 6th daughter of Sir Charles Tennant, Bt; married H. H. Asquith, 1894, one daughter, one son; died in London, 28 July 1945. Margot was a woman of tremendous style and élan, with great character and considerable social courage. She was also extravagant and could be insensitively candid. Her relationship with Violet was chronically strained, though there was warmth mixed in with the inevitable misunderstanding. Violet remembered her as: 'Entirely devoid of caution, or what some might have called discretion, contemptuous of convention, unaware of public opinion. She went through life just as she rode to hounds, with reckless audacity, absolute courage, complete self-confidence but no vanity.'

Asquith, Raymond (1878–1916), first child of H. H. Asquith, Violet's eldest brother; married, 1907, Katharine *née* Horner (1885–1976; godmother to Laura and Raymond Bonham Carter), two daughters, one son; educ. Winchester and Balliol; barrister, 1904; adopted Liberal candidate for Derby, 1913; junior counsel to Inland Revenue, 1914; 2nd lieutenant, Queen's Westminster Rifles, December 1914; transferred 3rd Battalion Grenadier Guards, July 1915; lieutenant; died of wounds near Trônes Wood, during Somme battle, 15 September 1916. 'I am joining the army, because the alternative is to spend the rest of my life explaining why I did not.'

Asquith, Violet – see Bonham Carter, (Helen) Violet.

Attlee, Clement Richard (1883–1967), educ. Haileybury and University College; Labour MP for Limehouse Stepney, 1922–50; chancellor of the duchy of Lancaster, 1930–1; postmaster general, 1931; leader of the Labour Party, 1935–55; member of war cabinet, 1940–5; lord privy seal, 1940–2; dominions secretary, 1942–3; lord president, 1943–5; deputy prime minister 1942–5; prime minister, 1945–51.

Baker, Harold Trevor [Bluey] (1877–1960), educ. Winchester and New College; a contemporary of Raymond Asquith, and a lifelong friend of Violet; Liberal MP for Accrington, 1910–18; contested Accrington, 1922; fellow of Winchester College, 1933; warden, 1936–46.

Baldwin, Stanley (1867–1947), cr. Earl, 1937; Conservative MP for Bewdley, 1908–37; president of the board of trade, 1921–2; chancellor of the exchequer, 1922–3; prime minister, 1923–4 and 1924–9; lord president, 1931–5; lord privy seal, 1932–4; prime minister, 1935–7. 'If Baldwin were a slyer man one wld think it [Protection] was a deliberate red herring to take people's eye off the ball – (i.e. Europe) but the worst of it is I think he really is honest – – & the measure of his honesty is his stupidity. But I thought he had real charm – porcine charm. A charming pig' (VBC to Gilbert Murray, 9 November 1923).

Balfour, Arthur James [AJB] (1848–1930), cr. Earl, 1922; educ. Eton and Trinity College, Cambridge; Unionist MP for City of London, 1906–22; first lord of the admiralty, 1915–16; foreign secretary, 1916–19; lord president of the council, 1919–22, 1925–9.

Beaverbrook, Lord – William Maxwell Aitken (1879–1964), cr. Baron Beaverbrook, 1916; born Maple, Ontario; educ. in New Brunswick; Unionist MP for Ashton-under-Lyne, 1910–16; minister of information, 1918; member of war cabinet, 1940–2; minister of aircraft production, 1940–1; minister of supply, 1941–2; lord privy seal, 1943–5; owner of *Daily Express, Sunday Express, Evening Standard*; author of *Politicians and the War* (2 vols. 1928–32). A severe critic of Asquith in office, Beaverbrook was one of the first and most generous subscribers to the fund raised to assist him financially in his last years; in the second world war, 'he performed miracles of production and made a major contribution to winning the Battle of Britain. Later in the war he was markedly unhelpful, upsetting any applecart in sight.' (John Colville, *Fringes of Power*, 732).

Beneš, Eduard (1884–1948), Czechoslovak statesman: president, 1935–8; president of government in exile, France and later England, 1939–45; returned to Czechoslovakia, 1945, re-elected president, 1946; resigned after communist coup, 1948.

Beveridge, Sir William Henry (1879–1963), cr. KCB, 1919; married, 15 December 1942, Janet 'Jessy' Mair, his second cousin by marriage; educ. Charterhouse and Balliol; director, London School of Economics and Political Science, 1919–37; master, University College, 1937–44; Liberal MP for Berwick-upon-Tweed 1944–5; author of the seminal report on *Social Insurance and Allied Services* (December 1942).

Bevin, Ernest (1881–1951), largely self-educated; general secretary of the TGWU, 1921–40; Labour MP for Central Wandsworth, 1940–50; minister of labour and national service, and member of the war cabinet, 1940–5; foreign secretary, 1945–51.

Bibesco, Elizabeth Charlotte Lucy *née* **Asquith** (1897–1945), daughter of Margot Asquith; Violet's half-sister; novelist; married, May 1919, Prince Antoine Bibesco (1878–1952), Rumanian diplomat; lived abroad thereafter, with infrequent visits to England; died in Rumania, April 1945.

Bonar Law, Andrew (1858–1923), born in New Brunswick; educ. in Hamilton, Ontario, and High School, Glasgow; Conservative MP for Bootle, 1911–18; for Glasgow Central, 1918–23; leader of the Unionist Party 1911–21; colonial secretary, 1915–16; chancellor of the exchequer, 1916–18; lord privy seal and leader of the Commons, 1919–21; resigned, March 1921; returned as Conservative leader, October 1922; prime minister 1922–3.

Bonham Carter, Cressida – see Ridley, (Helen Laura) Cressida.

Bonham Carter, Laura – see Grimond, Laura (Miranda).

Bonham Carter, Mark Raymond (1922–94), third child and elder son of Violet and Maurice Bonham Carter; educ. Winchester and Balliol, 1940–1 and 1945–6; joined Grenadier Guards, August 1941; 2nd lieutenant, 1941; lieutenant, 1942; with 6th Grenadier Guards, 8th Army, Libya; captured at Mareth Line battle, March 1943; prisoner of war, Arezzo and Modena, Italy; escaped and returned to England, 1943; captain; despatches; with 1st Grenadier Guards, Northern Europe, February–May 1945; contested Barnstaple, 1945 general election.

Bonham Carter, Sir Maurice [Bongie] (1880–1960), cr. KCB, 1916; KCVO, 1917; Violet's husband, youngest of the eleven sons of Henry Bonham Carter; a close friend of Violet's brothers; married Violet, 30 November 1915, two daughters, two sons; educ. Winchester and Balliol; private secretary to H. H. Asquith, 1908–16; assistant secretary, ministry of reconstruction, 1917; air ministry, 1918; director, Blackburn & General Aircraft Ltd; chairman of Aero Engines, Bristol; Power Jets, Rugby; air-raid warden, 1939–45. 'Bongie's goodness, unselfishness and capacity for devotion are qualities such as to be, to those that know them, grotesquely undervalued by any word ransacked from my ill furnished vocabulary...' (Edwin Montagu to VA, 1 July 1915).

Bonham Carter, Raymond Henry (b. 1929), fourth and youngest child of Violet and Maurice Bonham Carter; educ. St Ronan's preparatory school, Winchester and Magdalen College; 'I have a wild hope that my new child might bring me back some echo of Father. I feel so strongly that where children are concerned one is not a creator – but just the most passive of transmitting mediums – that any far-away current might flow through one' (VBC to Gilbert Murray, 9 April 1929). 'His temperament is very like Father's. I have never – except in him – known such stability of keel – such a marvellous "temper" – both intellectual & otherwise – such philosophy & complete lack of introspection, self-pity & irritability' (diary, 22 May 1944).

Bonham Carter, (Helen) Violet *née* Asquith (1887–1969), born 15 April 1887, in Hampstead, London, fourth child and only daughter of H. H. Asquith by his first wife, Helen Melland; privately educated; fluent in French and German; married Maurice Bonham Carter, 30 November 1915, two daughters and two sons; president of the WLF, 1923–5, 1939–45; member of the executive, LNU; member of Churchill's 'Freedom Focus', 1936–39; governor of the BBC, 1941–46; first woman president of the Liberal Party Organization, 1945–7; contested Wells, 1945 general election. 'She was in many ways Edwardian in spite of her achievement in coming to terms with each turn of the modern world.... Violet shared a good deal of Margot

Asquith's liking for worldly success and had a deep interest in people of all sorts and in ideas. She was also intensely loyal and generous-minded.... In spite of or probably because of her sophistication she was curiously innocent...'(Jo Grimond, *Memoirs*, 72, 86–7).

Boris, Georges, married to Germaine; he stayed with the Bonham Carters at 40 Gloucester Square during the war; socialist journalist and newspaper editor; one of the first Free French to join General de Gaulle in London; appointed head of press relations of Free France; on learning of his appointment Boris asked Geoffroy de Courcel, 'Does the General know I am a Jew? He must be told.' De Gaulle's response was, 'You are a French soldier'.

Bracken, Brendan (1901–58), educ. Sedbergh; became managing director, the *Economist*, 1929; Conservative MP for North Paddington, 1929–45; for Bournemouth, November 1945–50; parliamentary private secretary to the prime minister, 1940–1; minister of information, 1941–5; first lord of the admiralty, 1945. 'In the years immediately before the war, and during the war itself, he was a bright comet sweeping across the skies, afraid of nobody, jolting Churchill out of melancholy or intemperate moods, and proving a strikingly successful Minister of Information ...' (John Colville, *Fringes of Power*, 733–4).

Brooke, Rupert Chawner (1887–1915), second of three sons of William Parker Brooke, master at Rugby School, and Mary Ruth *née* Cotterill; educ. Rugby and King's College, Cambridge; published, 1911, *Poems*; fellow of King's, 1912; travelled in North America and South Seas, 1913–14; contributed to *New Numbers*, 1914–15, in the last issue of which his five 'war sonnets' appeared; joined RND as sub-lieutenant, September 1914; served Antwerp, October; sailed for Gallipoli, 28 February 1915; died of septicaemia, on board the French hospital ship *Duguay-Trouin* off Skyros, 23 April 1915. 'His beauty, which was very great, is difficult to describe in terms of line & feature.... The things which chiefly stand out in one's physical memory are the directness & intensity of his expression, the rare beauty of his voice, the extreme gentleness – & above all his youth.'

Carson, Sir Edward (1854–1935), cr. Baron, 1921; educ. Portarlington and Trinity College, Dublin; Unionist MP for Dublin University, 1892–1918; Duncairn, Belfast, 1918–21; attorney-general, 1915; first lord of the admiralty, 1916–17; member of war cabinet, 1917–18; lord of appeal in ordinary, 1921–9; leader of Ulster resistance to home rule.

Chamberlain, (Arthur) Neville (1869–1940), son of Joseph, half-brother of Austen; educ. Rugby and Mason College, Birmingham; Conservative MP for Ladywood, Birmingham, 1918–29; for Edgbaston, Birmingham, 1929–40; minister of health, 1923, 1924–9, 1931; chancellor of the exchequer, 1923–4, 1931–7; prime minister 1937–40; resigned premiership 10 May 1940; lord president of the council, in war cabinet, May–October; resigned due to ill health, October; died November 1940.

'Then, of course, when Munich came ... that opened some eyes. But still all too few. Chamberlain, as you remember, was acclaimed by vast cheering crowds when he returned waving his scrap of paper. And by many he was hailed as a Saint and a Redeemer – out to save the souls of the dictators by Christian charity, strangely inverted, turning the other cheek of other people ...' (interview with John Connell, *Lady Violet Remembers*, broadcast 27 August 1965).

Chamberlain, (Joseph) Austen (1863–1937), son of Joseph, half-brother of Neville; educ. Rugby and Trinity College, Cambridge; leading Unionist politician, secretary for India, 1915–17; member of war cabinet, 1918; chancellor of the exchequer, 1919–21; lord privy seal, 1921–2; foreign secretary, 1924–9; first lord of the admiralty, 1931.

Churchill, Clementine Ogilvy Spencer *née* Hozier (1885–1977), daughter of Sir Henry and Lady Hozier; married Winston Churchill, 1908, four daughters, one son; educ. at Berkhamsted High School for Girls and privately; president of the YWCA Wartime Fund, 1941–7; chairman of the Red Cross Aid to Russia Fund, 1941; GBE in victory honours list in recognition of her war work. '[Clemmie] was without exception the wisest political wife I've known in my experience. Most political wives, I mean, if they're interested in politics at all, are apt to be fanatical supporters of their husband's opinions.... But Clemmie always had an absolutely independent mind. Her mind, it was so different to Winston's. That was the lucky thing, that the spokes in his great powerful wheel didn't catch in hers and whirl them round. She revolved at a little distance and she saw things independently and often with great wisdom.'

Churchill, Winston Leonard Spencer (1874–1965), elder son of Lord Randolph Churchill; married, 1908, Clementine *née* Hozier, four daughters, one son; educ. Harrow and Sandhurst; Liberal MP for Dundee, 1908–18; Coalition Liberal, 1918–22; Constitutionalist MP for Epping, 1924–31; Conservative, 1931–45; for Woodford, 1945–64; first lord of the admiralty, 1911–15; chancellor of the duchy of Lancaster, 1915; battalion commander, 6th Royal Scots Fusiliers, France, 1915–16; minister of munitions, 1917–19; secretary for war (combined with air), 1919–21; colonial secretary, 1921–2; chancellor of the exchequer, 1924–9; left shadow cabinet over proposed reforms to government of India, 1931; first lord of the admiralty and member of war cabinet, 1939–40; succeeded Chamberlain as premier, 10 May 1940; prime minister and minister of defence, 1940–5; became leader of the Conservative Party 9 October 1940, following Chamberlain's retirement due to illness; godfather to Cressida, Violet and Bongie's first child. 'I was absolutely devoted to him. I couldn't have loved him better but I wasn't in love with him' (VBC in interview with Kenneth Harris, 1967).

Cranborne, Viscount [Bobbetty] – Robert Arthur James Gascoyne-Cecil (1893–1972), educ. Eton and Christ Church; married, 1915, Elizabeth Vere (d. 1982), daughter of Lord Richard Cavendish; Conservative MP for South Dorset, 1929–41;

secretary of state for dominions, 1940–2, 1943–5; lord privy seal, 1942–3.

Cripps, Sir Richard Stafford (1889–1952), cr. Kt, 1930; married 1911 Isabel *née* Swithinbank; educ. Winchester and University College, London; Labour MP for East Bristol, 1931–50, solicitor-general, 1930–1; expelled from Labour Party, January 1939 (readmitted, March 1945); ambassador to Russia, 1940–2; lord privy seal and leader of the House of Commons, 1942; member of the war cabinet, 1942; minister of aircraft production, 1942–5; president of the board of trade, 1945–7. In early 1942 Cripps was seen as a possible rival to Churchill as premier. In fact the latter had helped to make Cripps' reputation, by generously acknowledging his contribution towards improving Anglo-Soviet relations in June 1941, in recognition of which Cripps was made a privy councillor. His challenge did not materialize (Colin Cooke, *Stafford Cripps*, 270, 272–3).

Currie, Sir James (1868–1937), who married, 1913, Hilda Beatrice *née* Hanbury; Currie was a senior figure in the administration of the Sudan, during Oc Asquith's time in the Sudan Civil Service; he and his wife Hilda became friendly with Violet from that time, and the acquaintance was renewed in Wiltshire between the wars – when the Bonham Carters lived at Stockton, and the Curries at Aldbourne; they were active in Wiltshire Liberalism, and he contested Devizes as an Asquithian at the 1918 general election.

Curzon, George Nathaniel (1859–1925), cr. Earl, 1911; Marquis, 1921; educ. Eton and Balliol; lord privy seal in May 1915 coalition; lord president and member of war cabinet, 1916–19; foreign secretary 1919–24; lord president, 1924–5.

de Gaulle, General Charles André Joseph Marie (1890–1970), educ. Saint-Cyr Academy; captain, 1914–18 war – wounded three times, and spent two years eight months as a prisoner of war; temporary brigadier-general and commander 4th French Armoured Division, 1940; invited by Reynaud to join government, 5 June, as under-secretary for war; sent to London to negotiate with British, and made immediate and favourable impression on Churchill, 9 June; left for England after Pétain's accession; made famous appeal from London, 18 June, to compatriots to continue the war, and assumed leadership of the 'Free French'; tried *in absentia* by French military court and sentenced to death, 2 August 1940; moved headquarters to Algiers, 1943, ultimately becoming sole president of the French Committee of National Liberation; returned to Paris as leader of provisional government, 9 September 1944.

Drummond, Eric – see Perth, Lord.

Duff Cooper, Alfred (1890–1954), educ. Eton and New College; married, 1919, Lady Diana Manners; served European War, 1914–19 (DSO); Conservative MP Oldham, 1924–9; St George's, Westminster, 1931–45; secretary of state for war, 1935–7; first lord of admiralty, 1937–8; minister of information, 1940–1; chancellor of duchy of Lancaster, 1941–3; ambassador to Free French 1943–4; to France, 1944–7.

Edward VIII (1894–1972), Edward Albert Christian George Andrew Patrick David; educ. Osborne, Dartmouth and Magdalen College; succeeded his father, George V, 20 January 1936; fell in love with, and determined to marry, Wallis Simpson (1896–1986; later Duchess of Windsor), an American divorcee; faced with opposition from the political and religious establishment, he abdicated 11 December 1936, becoming the only British sovereign voluntarily to renounce the throne; created Duke of Windsor by his younger brother, who succeeded him as George VI; married Wallis Simpson, June 1937, thereafter lived in exile, mostly in France.

Eden, (Robert) Anthony (1897–1977), educ. Eton and Christ Church; with KRRC 1915–19; Conservative MP for Warwick and Leamington, 1923–57; lord privy seal, 1934–5; minister without portfolio, with responsibility for League of Nations affairs, 1935; foreign secretary, 1935–8; resigned January 1938 over disagreement with Chamberlain on conduct of foreign policy; dominions secretary, 1939–40; secretary for war, May–December 1940; foreign secretary, December 1940–5. 'There was a time when I hoped that Anthony Eden would have come out & lead a great new progressive party. But he would not go "over the top" – even to the extent of associating himself fully with Winston – let alone with the rest of us' (VBC to Arthur Mann, 23 April 1941).

Fisher, Admiral John Arbuthnot (1841–1920), cr. Baron, 1909; entered navy 1854; first sea lord 1904–10; recalled to the admiralty by Churchill, October 1914; resigned, 15 May 1915. After resigning he produced a remarkable memorandum setting out six conditions on which he would stay and 'guarantee the successful termination of the war': he would not serve under either Churchill or Balfour; the former would have to be excluded from the cabinet; etc. 'This document convinced Asquith that he was dealing with a megalomaniac, and he let him go without further remonstrance' (Roy Jenkins, *Asquith*, 359).

Foot, Dingle (Mackintosh) (1905–78), educ. Bembridge School (IOW) and Balliol; Liberal MP for Dundee, 1931–45; parliamentary secretary, ministry of economic warfare, 1940–5; a close Liberal associate of Violet's during the second world war.

Fraser, Sir (William Jocelyn) Ian (1897–1974), cr. Kt, 1934; educ. Marlborough College and RMA Sandhurst; Conservative MP for North St. Pancras, 1924–9, 1931–6; Lonsdale, Lancaster, 1940–50; governor of the BBC, 1937–9, 1941–6. Served with King's Shropshire Light Infantry during Great War, and was blinded during battle of the Somme; afterwards championed the cause of ex-servicemen and the blind.

French, Field Marshal Sir John (1852–1925); cr. Viscount, 1916; Earl of Ypres, 1922; educ. RN naval cadet; commander-in-chief BEF, August 1914–December 1915; of home forces, 1916–18; lord-lieutenant of Ireland, 1918–21.

Freyberg, Sir Bernard (1889–1963), cr. KCB, 1942; born in Richmond, Surrey, his family emigrated to New Zealand, 1891; married, 1918, Barbara *née* Jeykll (1887–1973), widow of Hon. Francis McLaren; educ. Wellington College, New Zealand; served 1914–18 war, RND and 29th Division (DSO and two bars; VC, 1916; brigadier, 1917); GOC New Zealand Forces, 1939–45 (third bar to DSO, 1945); commander-in-chief Allied forces, Crete, 1941. Fought alongside Oc Asquith at Gallipoli and in France, thereafter a lifelong friend of the Bonham Carters and Asquiths, and godmother to Laura Bonham Carter. 'The salamander of the British Empire.'

George V (1865–1936), George Frederick Ernest Albert, cr. Duke of York 1892; second son of Edward VII and Queen Alexandra; married, 1893, Princess Mary of Teck; RN, 1883–92; educ. Dartmouth and RN College, Greenwich; succeeded father, May 1910; opened Northern Ireland parliament, 22 June 1921: 'I appeal to all Irishmen to pause, to stretch out the hand of forbearance and conciliation'; began Christmas Day broadcast to the empire, 1932.

George VI (1895–1952), Albert Frederick Arthur George, cr. Duke of York, 1920; second of five sons of George V and Queen Mary; married, 1923, Lady Elizabeth Angela Marguerite Bowes-Lyon (b. 1900) – two daughters, Princess Elizabeth Alexandra Mary (b. 1926), Princess Margaret Rose (b. 1930); educ. Osborne, Dartmouth and Trinity College, Cambridge; RN, 1913–18; RAF, 1918–19; the death of his father and the abdication of his brother, 1936, led to his accession, 11 December.

Godley, (John) Arthur (1847–1932), cr. Baron Kilbracken, 1909; educ. Rugby and Balliol; distinguished former civil servant, the father of Violet's close friend Hugh Godley.

Godley, Hugh John (1877–1950), 2nd Baron Kilbracken, 1932; a close friend and contemporary of Raymond Asquith and of Bongie; married (1) 1919 Helen Monteith (diss. 1936); (2) Leonora Taylor; educ. Eton and Balliol; assistant parliamentary counsel to treasury; member of the central control board, 1917–21; counsel to the chairman of committees (House of Lords), 1923–44. Hugh was one of Violet's closest friends. They had been close to marrying one another in 1909, when the adverse opinion of Violet's father had probably been instrumental in deciding her against. She could not, though, exclude Hugh from her life then or later, and for many years afterwards it seemed as if their friendship might result in marriage.

Greenwood, Arthur (1880–1954), educ. Victoria (later Leeds) University; Labour MP for Wakefield, 1932–54; minister without portfolio in war cabinet, 1940–2; deputy leader of the Labour Party, 1935–45. Greenwood deputized for Attlee, who was ill, during the critical days leading up to war in September 1939.

Grey, Sir Edward (1862–1933), 3rd Bt, cr. Viscount Grey of Fallodon, 1916; educ. Winchester and Balliol; Liberal MP for Berwick-on-Tweed, 1885–1916; foreign secretary, 1905–16; Violet knew Grey well, and admired him greatly; he was godfather to her daughter Laura; 'a man of sorrows', he experienced great personal misfortune, which culminated in the loss of his sight. He was greatly saddened at the failure of his foreign policy to avoid war, August 1914. Of his famous speech on 3 August, Violet has commented: 'That speech has often been described as a personal triumph. But it was not a triumph. It was the culminating point of a poignant personal tragedy.'

Grey, George Charles (1918–44), educ. Winchester and Hertford College; Liberal MP for Berwick-on-Tweed, 1941–4; captain, Grenadier Guards; evacuated at Dunkirk; killed in action near Caumont, 30 July 1944. A near contemporary of Mark Bonham Carter at Winchester. 'He had a very [rare] degree of political instinct & judgement & a tremendous sense of <u>essentials</u>. He was curiously mature in that he never attempted to be "clever" or say "good things" or stalk an epigram.... I shall think always of the gravity & modesty of his eyes – which concealed such confidence & drive & humour.'

Grimond, Joseph [Jo] (1913–1993), Violet's son-in-law; married Laura Bonham Carter, 1938, three sons, one daughter; educ. Eton and Balliol; barrister, 1937; served Fife and Forfar Yeomanry, and on staff 53rd Division, 1939–45 (major); director of personnel, European Office of UNRRA, 1945–7.

Grimond, Laura Miranda, *née* **Bonham Carter** (1918–93), Violet and Maurice Bonham Carter's second child, born 13 October 1918; educated privately; married, 31 May 1938, Joseph Grimond, at St Margaret's, Westminster; three sons, one daughter. 'Of <u>all</u> the young men who have loved her in the last 18 months (& they have been many & various) I like him far the best – so I am overjoyed. My only regret is her youth (<u>just</u> 19). I hoped she would go on "shaking a loose leg" (as Father called it) for many years more – & I shall <u>hate</u> losing her so soon' (VBC to Beb Asquith, 27 November 1937).

Haldane, Richard Burdon (1856–1928), cr. Viscount, 1911; educ. Edinburgh and Göttingen Universities; Liberal MP for Haddingtonshire, 1885–1911; secretary of state for war, 1908–12; lord chancellor, 1912–15, and 1924 (in first Labour government); one of Asquith's oldest friends, the brusque manner of his dismissal from office in May 1915 was 'the most uncharacteristic fault of Asquith's whole career' (Roy Jenkins, *Asquith*, 362).

Haley, William (John) (1901–87), educ. Victoria College, Jersey; director, *Manchester Guardian* and *Evening News*, 1930–43; director of the Press Association and Reuters, 1939–43; editor-in-chief, BBC, 1943–4; director general, 1944–52; after the initial awkwardness caused by the nature of his appointment at the BBC, he became a close friend of Violet. 'He thought of the BBC as the world's greatest educational institution' (*DNB*).

Halifax, Lord – Edward Frederick Lindley Wood (1881–1959), cr. Baron Irwin, 1925; 3rd Viscount Halifax, 1934; cr. Earl, 1944; educ. Eton and Christ Church; married, 1909, Dorothy *née* Onslow; leader of the House of Lords, 1935–8, 1940;

foreign secretary, 1938–40; member of war cabinet, 1939–45; ambassador to United States, 1941–6. Supported appeasement: 'He went so far as to suggest that *we* might satisfy the Germans by letting them have the *Portuguese* colonies' (John Colville, *Fringes of Power*, 746).

Hankey, Maurice Pascale Alers (1877–1963), cr. Baron, 1939; educ. Rugby; joined Royal Marine Artillery, 1895; secretary to committee of imperial defence, 1912–38, to Dardanelles Committee 1914–16, and to war cabinet, 1916–19; minister in war cabinet, 1939–42. Highly valued for his judgement 1914–18: in the opinion of Balfour, 'Without Hankey we should not have won the war'.

Harris, Sir Percy Alfred (1876–1952), cr. Bt, 1932; educ. Harrow and Trinity Hall, Cambridge; Liberal MP for South West Bethnal Green, 1922–45; chief Liberal whip, 1935–45, and deputy leader, 1940–5.

Herbert, Hon. Aubrey Nigel Henry Molyneux (1880–1923), eldest son of the 4th Earl of Carnarvon, by his second marriage; married, 1910, Mary Vesey (b. 1889; lifelong friend of Violet, godmother to her daughter Cressida); educ. Eton and Balliol; Unionist MP for South Somerset, 1911–18; Yeovil, 1918–23; joined Irish Guards, August 1914; afterwards intelligence officer in eastern theatre. Aubrey's method of volunteering was characteristically irregular. Aware that poor eyesight would disqualify him from military service, he had the Irish Guards uniform of his wife's cousin Tom Vesey copied, and wearing this fell in with the regiment as it left Waterloo Barracks for France, 12 August 1914. His enlistment was accepted as a *fait accompli* on the Channel crossing, and he afterwards served with distinction in France and Gallipoli, finishing the war as temporary lieutenant-colonel (Margaret Fitzherbert, *Greenmantle*, 128–9).

Hitler, Adolf (1889–1945), Austrian-born dictator of Germany, 1933–45; founder (1920) and leader of the Nazi Party (NSDAP); Reich chancellor, 1933–45; committed suicide as Soviet forces closed on Berlin, 30 April 1945.

Hoare, Sir Samuel John Gurney (1880–1959), 2nd Bt, 1906; cr. Viscount Templewood, 1944; educ. Harrow and New College; secretary for air, 1922–4, 1924–9; secretary for India, 1931–5; foreign secretary, 1935; first lord of the admiralty, 1936–7; home secretary, 1937–9; lord privy seal and member of war cabinet, 1939–40; secretary for air, 1940; ambassador to Spain, 1940–4.

Keynes, John Maynard (1883–1946), cr. Baron, 1942; educ. Eton and King's College, Cambridge; married, 1925, Lydia *née* Lopokova; treasury official, 1915–19; principal representative of treasury at Paris Peace Conference, January 1919; resigned, June; fellow and later bursar of King's College; editor, *Economic Journal*, 1911–44; treasury adviser, 1940; leader of British delegation which negotiated American loan in Washington, September–December 1945.

Kilbracken, Lord – see Godley, (John) Arthur.

Kitchener, Horatio Herbert (1850–1916), cr. Earl, 1914; educ. in France, and at RMA Woolwich; British agent and consul-general, Egypt, 1911–14; secretary for war, 1914–16; drowned in sinking of HMS *Hampshire*, 5 June 1916. Raymond Asquith wrote to his wife the following week: '[I] can't help still suspecting that Kitchener will stroll into the House of Lords combing the seaweed out of his hair as strong and silent as ever' (John Jolliffe, *Raymond Asquith: Life and Letters*, 268).

Lister, Charles Alfred (1887–1915), only surviving son of 4th Baron Ribblesdale; educ. Eton and Balliol; a childhood friend of Violet and her brothers, and a Balliol contemporary of Cys Asquith; with the Hood Battalion of the RND, September 1914; severely wounded at Gallipoli, 25 August 1915; died of wounds on a hospital ship off the peninsula, 28 August.

Lloyd George, David (1863–1945), cr. Earl Lloyd-George of Dwyfor, 1945; educ. Llanystumdwy Church School and privately; Liberal MP for Caernarvon Boroughs, 1890–1931; Independent Liberal, 1931–45; chancellor of the exchequer, 1908–15; minister of munitions, 1915–16; secretary for war, 1916; prime minister, 1916–22; leader of the Liberal Party, 1926–31; died 26 March 1945. Of him, Violet has written: 'His mind had no anchor. And yet emotionally he was consistent. He was a democrat – before all things a man of the people; the champion of the underdog and disinherited – dauntless, resourceful, ready to fight their battle against all comers and against any odds....'. 'He needed in order to deploy his great gifts, a great stage, footlights and above all an audience. But he wasn't an actor. He was a medium. He lived and fed on his immediate surroundings.... I remember in those early days of my youth asking Maynard Keynes ... "What do you think happens to Lloyd George when he's alone in the room?" And Keynes replied "When he's alone in the room there's nobody there".'

MacCarthy, (Charles Otto) Desmond (1877–1952), educ. Eton and Trinity College, Cambridge; literary editor *New Statesman*, 1920–27; wrote for the *Sunday Times*, 1928–52; an old friend of the Asquith family, and of Violet in particular.

MacDonald, James Ramsay (1866–1937), educated at a board school; leader of the Labour Party, 1911–14, 1922–31; prime minister and foreign secretary, 1924; prime minister of Labour government, 1929–31; of National government, 1931–5; lord president of the council, 1935–7.

McKenna, Reginald (1863–1943), married 1908, Pamela *née* Jeykll; educ. King's College, London, and Trinity College, Cambridge; Liberal MP for North Monmouthshire, 1895–1918; home secretary, 1911–15; chancellor of the exchequer, 1915–16.

Macmillan, (Maurice) Harold (1894–1986), educ. Eton and Balliol; served 1914–18 war with Grenadier Guards; Conservative MP for Stockton-on-Tees, 1931–45; parliamentary secretary, ministry of supply, 1940–2; parliamentary under-secretary for colonies, 1942; minister resident at Allied headquarters, North West Africa,

1942–5. 'And there was a newsreel before the film which showed Chamberlain, driving through the streets of Rome, not to very great acclaim, in an open barouche with Mussolini. And the crowds were crying, not very enthusiastically, "Ombrello, Ombrello", you see. But one didn't hear that as it was a silent film. But Harold Macmillan who was sitting beside me [i.e. VBC] in the stalls with a nest of his Conservative friends all round, and who looked very conventional with a very high stiff collar, suddenly began shouting in this still theatre "Ombrello, Ombrello" at the top of his voice. I thought I'd never see such an act of moral courage. I forged friendship with him from that moment onwards.'

Marsh, Sir Edward Howard [Eddie] (1872–1953), KCVO, 1937; educ. Westminster and Trinity College, Cambridge; private secretary to Winston Churchill when in office, 1905–29; of independent means, Marsh combined the role of civil servant with that of patron of the arts; edited *Georgian Poetry*, anthology of modern verse in five volumes, 1912–22, dispersing profits among contributors, including Rupert Brooke; published Brooke's *Collected Poems*, with a memoir, 1918; trustee of Tate Gallery, 1937–44.

Masaryk, Jan (1886–1948), son of Thomas (1850–1937; first president of Czech republic); Czech diplomat and statesman, minister in London, 1925–38; foreign minister in the Czech government in exile in London, 1940–5; later in Prague, 1945–8; thought to have committed suicide when the communists took control of the government, March 1948.

Montagu, (Beatrice) Venetia *née* Stanley (1887–1948), youngest child of the 4th Baron Stanley; educated privately; married, July 1915, Edwin Montagu; one daughter. Her special relationship with Asquith began early in 1912; Asquith's love for her was paralleled, and rivalled, by that of Edwin Montagu, who first proposed to her that summer.

Montagu, Edwin Samuel (1879–1924), second son of Samuel Montagu, 1st Baron Swaythling; married, July 1915, Hon. Beatrice Venetia Stanley, one daughter; educ. Clifton College, City of London School, and Trinity College, Cambridge; Liberal MP for Chesterton, Cambridgeshire, 1906–22; financial secretary to the treasury, 1914–15; privy councillor, 1915; chancellor of the duchy of Lancaster, January 1916; minister of munitions, June–December 1916; secretary of state for India, 1917–22. Edwin's father had died in 1911 leaving the bulk of his fortune in trust for his children, with a proviso that they would be excluded if they either abandoned the Jewish faith into which they were born, or married outside it. Without this money, Edwin's income was small (M. and E. Brock, *H. H. Asquith: Letters to Venetia Stanely*, 6). 'He did in the end resign with most of Mr Asquith's liberal colleagues, but he had no intention of being permanently entangled in the fallen fortunes of the prime minister' (*DNB*).

Montgomery, Field Marshal Sir Bernard Law (1887–1976), cr. KCB, 1942; married,

1927, Elizabeth *née* Hobart, one son; educ. St Paul's School and Sandhurst; with 1st Warwickshire Regiment, 1914–18 (severely wounded, Le Câteau); south east command (England), 1942; commander 8th Army, North Africa, Sicily and Italy, 1942–4; commander-in-chief, British group of armies, Northern France, 1944; commander 21st Army Group, 1944–5. 'Before Sicily was invaded he had taken some leave in London where he found himself a popular hero, an enjoyable discovery which made him less and less amenable to subordination or advice. He had come to regard himself as the greatest fighting commander alive. He was ready to lay down the military law and he had no hesitation in criticizing anyone' (*DNB*).

Morhange, Alfonse [Toto] (1893–1976), cousin of Georges Boris; married Veronica, an Englishwoman; head partner of a Paris bank; sent to London by French government, September 1939, becoming assistant to financial attaché of French embassy, May–July 1940; afterwards with department of finance at Free French headquarters; from March 1944, director of finance with European office of UNRRA. 'His courage, already proved by the Medaille Militaire in the 1914–18 war, was shown again by his unhesitating choice of exile among the Free French in the second' (Jo Grimond, obituary).

Morrison, Herbert (1888–1965), educ. at elementary schools; Labour MP for South Hackney, 1929–31, 1935–45; East Lewisham, 1945–51; minister of transport 1929–31; minister of supply, 1940; secretary for home office and home security, 1940–5; member of war cabinet, 1942–5; lord president of the council, 1945–51.

Murray, (George) Gilbert (Aimé) (1866–1957), born in Sydney; married, 1889, Lady Mary Howard, eldest daughter of 9th Earl of Carlisle; educ. Merchant Taylors' and St John's College; fellow of New College, 1905; regius professor of Greek, University of Oxford, 1908–36; South African delegate to League of Nations assemblies, 1921 and 1922, and British delegate 1924; chairman, LNU, 1923–38; unsuccessfully contested Oxford University as a Liberal at all the general elections, 1918–29. Violet knew Murray from her early youth – he was a friend of her father and Sir Edward Grey. As chair of the LNU, 'He was incapable of ruthlessness, and never learned to turn a deaf ear in the right direction.' 'Even in his indignation there was never a shrill or bitter note. His sense of humour and his common sense remained invulnerable. I have often wondered how it was possible to combine such ardour with such tolerance.'

Mussolini, Benito (Amilcare Andrea) (1883–1945), Italian dictator; founder of the Italian Fascist Party; prime minister of Italy, 1922–43; dismissed from office, 24 July 1943, following a meeting of the Fascist Grand Council; subsequently arrested and imprisoned by forces of the Italian government; freed from captivity by Germans, and installed as a puppet dictator in northern Italy; shot and killed by Italian partisans, 28 April 1945.

Nicolson, Harold (George) (1886–1968), married, 1913, Hon. Victoria Mary ('Vita')

Sackville-West (d. 1962), two sons; educ. Wellington and Balliol; early career in foreign office – on British delegation at Peace Conference, Paris, 1919; resigned when at embassy, Berlin, 1929; on editorial staff, *Evening Standard*, 1930; National Labour MP for West Leicester, 1935–45; parliamentary secretary to minister of information, 1940–1; governor, BBC, 1941–6; preceded VBC as president of the London Regional LNU, May 1941. Nicolson was influential in persuading Duff Cooper to appoint Violet to the board of governors of the BBC, in March 1941; he later joined her on the board, and they grew to be good friends and close allies.

Northcliffe, Lord – Alfred Charles William Harmsworth (1865–1922), cr. Baron, 1904; Viscount, 1917; Dublin-born, largely self-educated; founded the *Daily Mail* (1896); chief proprietor of *The Times* (1908) and other papers; greatly distrusted by Asquith. He became in 1915 a leading advocate of conscription and mobilized his papers behind this cause, which became a vehicle for his implacable opposition to Asquith. 'The European War transformed Northcliffe from the anxious newspaper proprietor, working in the background, into the public figure seeking the limelight of the stage.... He placed himself at the head of all the popular movements of the moment' (*DNB*).

Perth, Lord – (James) Eric Drummond (1876–1951), 16th Earl of Perth, 1937; educ. Eton; entered foreign office, 1900; private secretary to H. H. Asquith 1912–15; to foreign secretary, 1915–19; first secretary-general to the League of Nations, 1919–33.

Pétain, (Henri) Philippe (Omer) (1856–1951), first world war French general, hero of the siege of Verdun; marshal of France, 1918; made vice-premier by Reynaud; succeeded Reynaud, 16 June 1940, and sought armistice with Germans, signed 22 June; led Vichy government 1940–4; convicted of treason and imprisoned after war.

Plunkett, Sir Horace (Curzon) (1854–1932), cr. KCVO, 1903; educ. Eton and University College; organizer of co-operative dairies in southern Ireland, 1889–91; commissioner, congested districts board of Ireland, 1891–1918; Unionist MP for South County, Dublin, 1892–1900; founded Irish Dominion League, 1919; senator, Irish Free State, 1922–3; became an advocate of home rule, and an opponent of partition; leading force in Ireland for agricultural and economic improvement through farming co-operatives.

Reynaud, Paul (1878–1966), French conservative politician and statesman, and opponent of appeasement; minister of finance, 1938–March 1940; premier March–16 June 1940; made de Gaulle his under-secretary of state for war; tried to keep France in the war, but outnumbered by defeatist colleagues, and resigned; later arrested and imprisoned by the Germans for duration of war.

Ridley, (Helen Laura) Cressida *née* Bonham Carter (b. 1917), eldest child of Violet and Maurice Bonham Carter, born 22 April 1917; educated privately; married,

June 1939, Jasper Ridley (d. 1943), at St Bartholomew-the-Great, Smithfield; one son, Adam (b. 1942).

Ridley, (Maurice Alexander) Jasper [Bubbles] (1913–43), Violet's son-in-law, and an exact Balliol contemporary of her other son-in-law, Jo Grimond, to whom he was best man; married Cressida Bonham Carter, 1939; educ. Eton and Balliol; barrister, 1938; joined army May 1940; with KRRC, November 1940; lieutenant, 1941; MEF, December 1941; captured June 1942, Gazala battle, Libya; POW Chieti camp, Italy; escaped, and was killed 13 December 1943 in a minefield near Castel di Sangro while trying to reach Allied lines.

Rommel, Erwin (1891–1944), field marshal, commander of the Afrika Korps, February 1941–March 1943; thereafter given commands in Italy, and France, where he organized the defence of the Channel coast. Convinced by June 1944 of need to seek armistice with Allies he was implicated in the July 1944 bomb plot attempt on Hitler's life, and chose suicide to a public trial and execution, October 1944.

Roosevelt, Franklin D[elano] (1882–1945), 32nd president of the United States, 1933–45, who married, 1905, his distant cousin (Anna) Eleanor *née* Roosevelt (1884–1962); the only president re-elected three times, he died shortly into his fourth term, 12 April 1945. Eleanor Roosevelt shared her husband's political drive, and was prominent in the campaign for civil rights in America, and undertook morale-raising trips to forces overseas during the war; in 1942 she visited Great Britain: 'Her voice is familiar on the wireless; her writings are as widely read as those of any journalist in the United States. They are the expressions of a powerful and independent mind' (*The Times*, 24 October 1942).

Samuel, Herbert (1870–1963), cr. Viscount, 1937; educ. University College School and Balliol; president of local government board, 1914–15; postmaster-general, 1915–16; home secretary, 1916, 1931–2; high commissioner of Palestine, 1920–5; leader of the Liberal Party, 1931–5.

Simon, Sir John Allsebrook (1873–1954), cr. Viscount, 1940; educ. Fettes and Wadham College; attorney-general 1913–15; home secretary 1915–16; foreign secretary in the national government, 1931–5; home secretary, 1935–7; chancellor of the exchequer, 1937–40; lord chancellor, 1940–5.

Sinclair, Sir Archibald Henry Macdonald [Archie] (1890–1970), 4th Bt, 1912; married, 1918, Marigold *née* Forbes (godmother to Raymond Bonham Carter); educ. Eton and Sandhurst; Churchill's second-in-command with 6th Royal Scots Fusiliers, 1916; personal secretary to Churchill at war office, 1919–21; Liberal MP for Caithness and Sutherland, 1922–45; leader of Liberal Parliamentary Party, 1935–45; secretary of state for air, 1940–5; 'His wife, Marigold ... had a stronger character than her husband and was a pleasant, if alarmingly determined, woman' (John Colville, *Fringes of Power*, 770–1).

Stalin, Joseph (1879–1953), secretary general of the Communist Party of the Soviet Union, 1922–53; premier of the Soviet state, 1941–53. Gladwyn Jebb, a senior British diplomat at Yalta, recalled that of the 'big three', Churchill, Roosevelt and Stalin, the latter 'had the greatest natural authority, and while recognizing him for the appalling tyrant that he certainly was, one was bound to admit that it was not only his unparalleled ferocity but also his sheer political ability that enabled him for thirty years to be the undisputed Tsar of all the Russias' (Ted Morgan, *FDR: A Biography*, 753).

Stanley, Venetia – see Montagu, (Beatrice) Venetia.

Vincent, Sir Edgar (1857–1941), cr. Baron d'Abernon, 1914; Viscount, 1926; married, 1890, Lady Helen *née* Duncombe (d. 1954), daughter of 1st Earl of Feversham; educ. Eton; diplomatic service; ambassador to Berlin, 1920–6; former Unionist MP who became a Liberal over tariff reform; a close friend of the Asquith family, and godfather to Cressida Bonham Carter.

Wood, Sir Howard Kingsley (1881–1943), cr. Kt, 1918; educ. Central Foundation Boys' School, London; Conservative MP for Woolwich West, 1918–43; secretary for air, 1938–40; lord privy seal, 1940; in war cabinet, 1940–2; chancellor of the exchequer, 1940–3.

APPENDIX C: *Notes on houses and places mentioned in the text*

The following descriptions are based on information to be found either in the Violet Bonham Carter MSS, or the relevant edition of Nikolaus Pevsner's *The Buildings of England* series (arranged by county). The information here is mostly restricted to the period 1914–45.

I. *Houses outside London, and abroad*

Balmoral Castle (*Aberdeenshire*) – private residence of the monarch; a nineteenth-century castle in the Scottish baronial style, built on the banks of the River Dee; used as a summer residence, with access to grouse shooting, stalking, highland games, etc.

Beaufort Castle (*Inverness-shire*) – the home of Lord Lovat, near Beauly; a red sandstone Scottish baronial mansion, built in the nineteenth century; Bongie spent summer holidays there.

Bicton House (*Devon*) – on an estate owned by Lord Clinton, Bicton was the site of St Ronan's School during its wartime evacuation from the south coast; remembered by Raymond Bonham Carter as 'a beautiful large Georgian house ... with an arboretum said by some to be second only to that at Kew'.

British Embassy, Berlin – 'A big house built rather on the lines of Chesham House (the Russian Embassy) at home with the converging double staircase'.

Chartwell (*Kent*) – the favourite home of Winston Churchill for forty years; two miles south of Westerham, it was purchased in 1922 for £5,000, and almost completely rebuilt in 1923.

Cliveden (*Buckinghamshire*) – home of the Astors, Waldorf and Nancy; a beautiful nineteenth-century country house, built by Sir Charles Barry on a bend of the River Thames.

Clovelly Court (*North Devon*) – seat of the Carys and Hamlyns, and then the home of Betty and Oc Asquith; built in the eighteenth century, the house was largely burned out in 1944, though afterwards it was rebuilt; it was a favourite visiting place of the Bonham Carters, standing on a rugged stretch of the North Devon coast high above the beautiful fishing village of Clovelly, which nestles in a deep cove leading to the sea.

Colerne House (*Kent*) – home of the Dickson-Poynders, Lord and Lady Islington, near Sandwich; he was an ex-Liberal MP and retired governor-general of New Zealand.

Dalnawillan (*Caithness*) – the home of the Sinclairs, Archie and Marigold; Bongie enjoyed spending time at this shooting lodge near Altnabreac, where there was grouse shooting to be had, and salmon fishing on the Thurso river.

Easton Grey (*Wiltshire*) – the home of Margot's sister, Lucy Graham Smith; a late eighteenth-century manor house on the Avon, near Malmesbury, 'grey, like its name, standing among tall elm trees'.

Esher Place (*Surrey*) – the home of Lord and Lady D'Abernon (Edgar and Helen Vincent); it was 'a very large Frenchy mansion' built for Lord D'Abernon 1895–8, on a site with buildings going back to the fifteenth century; with a sunk garden designed by Lutyens.

Fulling's Mill (*Hampshire*) – house belonging to the de Stein family, on the River Itchen near Winchester.

Glyndebourne (*East Sussex*) – the home of John Christie, and the location of Glyndebourne Opera; a sixteenth-century house on the South Downs just east of Lewes, extensively rebuilt in Victorian times; in 1933 Christie added a 311-seat opera house, joined to the main building by a music room; the opera house was designed by Edmund Warre.

Hartfield (*Sussex*) – home of Lord Kilbracken (South Hartfield).

Kilteragh (*Co. Dublin*) – home of Sir Horace Plunkett, near Foxrock in County Dublin; it was burned down by political extremists in 1923, when Plunkett was visiting the United States; Violet remembered it as 'like some hybrid cross between Lutyens and the Danish Pavilion at Overstrand'.

Lindisfarne Castle (*Northumberland*) – owned by O. T. Falk, a friend of the Bonham Carters and a business partner of Bongie; built on Holy Island, it was a sixteenth-century fort renovated in the early twentieth century by Lutyens.

Manor Farm (*Wiltshire*) – a beautiful farmhouse in the village of Stockton, built in the late sixteenth and early seventeenth centuries, and taken by the Bonham Carters during the war; the farmhouse is close to the east gates of Stockton House.

Manor House (*Somerset*) – home of Katharine Asquith, near Mells; a beautiful Elizabethan manor house, extensively restored early in the twentieth century.

The Master's Lodgings, University College (*Oxford*) – the home of Sir William Beveridge during his time as master of the College, 1937–44; a nineteenth-century building in Jacobean style, built by Bodley.

Mockbeggars (*Suffolk*) – home of Jasper and Nathalie Ridley, near Claydon.

La Mortola (*Italy*) – a fine old Italian villa, or *palazzo*, on the coast at Ventimiglia just north of Monaco; restored in the late nineteenth century by Sir Thomas Hanbury, a famous botanist, who created a beautiful tropical garden containing thousands of species of rare plant.

Mottisfont Abbey (*Hampshire*) – home of Gilbert and Maud Russell; a thirteenth-century abbey, rebuilt in the eighteenth and twentieth centuries on the River Test about eight miles west of Winchester.

Mount Trenchard (*Co. Limerick*) – home of Lord Monteagle, near Foynes.

Penrhôs (*Anglesey*) – home of Lord Stanley, father of Venetia; of Tudor foundation, now a ruin.

Stanway (*Gloucestershire*) – seat of the Earl of Wemyss (Charteris family); a late sixteenth- and early-seventeenth century house, near the north Cotswold village

of Winchcombe; Violet wrote to Bongie in August 1914: 'It is heavenly here –
the greenest sleepiest most remote & lulling place you can imagine – divine
Elizabethan house covered with orange lichen. I can feel the moss growing on
me as I write.'

Stockton House (*Wiltshire*) – owned by O. T. Falk, and used by the Bonham Carters
for Easter and summer holidays between 1927 and 1934; a fine square Elizabethan
house in the village of Stockton in the Wylye valley, some ten miles north-west
of Salisbury; the children had ponies kept at Stockton, which was set in beautiful
downland countryside.

Taplow Court (*Buckinghamshire*) – home of the Grenfell family (Lord Desborough);
a large four-storey house set in 3,000 acres on the Thames just above Maidenhead.

Vice Regal Lodge (*Dublin*) – seat of the lord-lieutenant of Ireland.

Walmer Castle (*Kent*) – a sixteenth-century castle, converted into living accommodation in the eighteenth century, and now the official residence of the Warden
of the Cinque Ports.

The Wharf, Sutton Courtenay (*Oxfordshire*) – the Oxfordshire home of the Asquiths from 1912 to 1931/2, when it was sold by Margot; a moderate-sized Thames-
side house, originally of eighteenth-century construction, but converted and
enlarged by Walter Cave after its purchase; Violet and Bongie regularly visited
for weekends and longer holidays – sometimes for Christmas and part of the
summer; they often took the children with them, who stayed with their nannies
in the Mill House across the road.

Wilsford Manor (*Wiltshire*) – near Salisbury, the seat of Lady Glenconner, wife of
Lord Glenconner (Sir Edward Tennant, Margot's elder brother).

Yatscombe (*Oxfordshire*) – home of Gilbert Murray; on Boar's Hill, about three
miles south-west of the centre of Oxford.

II. Houses in London

44 Bedford Square, W.C.1 – previously belonging to Ottoline Morrell, and pur-
chased by the Asquiths in 1920 after the sale of 20 Cavendish Square; set in a
Georgian Square of simple four-storey brick houses in Bloomsbury, next to the
British Museum.

Dorset House, Portman Square, W. – Violet and Bongie's first married home,
situated between Oxford Street and the Marylebone Road, and north-east of
Hyde Park; the lease, which was taken in July 1915 at a cost of £4,000, was a
wedding gift from Bongie's brother Gerard; described by Bongie as 'quiet, sunlit,
Georgian, [with an] open space with trees at the back, detached, in condition
almost fit to go into now without a scrap of paint or varnish. It looks outside
like a doll's house, flat brick four-storeyed.'

40 Gloucester Square, W.2 – Violet and Bongie's home from the autumn of 1935
until 1952, when the property was converted into flats, one of which they

subsequently took; a large house, on the fork between two roads, just north of
Hyde Park.

24 Hyde Park Gardens, W.2 – Violet and Bongie's home from 1924 until 1934;
the lease was bought from the Church Commissioners, but it was an expensive
house to run, and so it was sold; it was nearly always let for the Season, when
the family stayed in the country, and Bongie would live in Brooks's Club in St
James's; situated directly north of Hyde Park, not far from Marble Arch.

III. Places

Claydon (*Suffolk*) – village home of Cressida Ridley's parents-in-law, Jasper and
Nathalie.

Glymenopoulo (*Egypt*) – on the outskirts of Alexandria, about half an hour out by
tram, and near, although not on, the sea: 'it is a plantation of villas – rather
White City, architecturally, they look all cardboard & coloured shutters'. Violet
and Oc stayed at the Summer Palace Hôtel, 'clean – rather bare – understaffed –
good food – unluxurious baths (a meagre, intermittent trickle instead of a gushing
Niagara) a good terrace to sit out on'.

Yarnbury Castle (*Wiltshire*) – between Warminster and Amesbury; 'a vast prehistoric earthwork on one of the high downs.... It is a circular camp about a
mile round, guarded by a triple rampart of green walls and belonging ... to the
Early Iron Age.'

SELECT BIBLIOGRAPHY: *a note on sources and further reading*

I. Manuscript sources

The manuscript material published in this volume is drawn from the Violet Bonham Carter MSS, with the exception of the following: Winston Churchill to Violet Asquith : among the Chartwell Papers at the Churchill Archives Centre, Cambridge; Violet Asquith to (Lady) Ettie Desborough: among the Desborough Papers at Hertfordshire Record Office, HRO D/ERv; Violet Asquith to/from Arthur Melland ('Oc') Asquith: private collection; VBC to Arthur Mann: among the Arthur Mann Papers at the Bodleian Library, MS Eng. c. 3276 (box 3) fols 1–344; VA to Ottoline Morrell: among the Morrell Papers at the Harry Ransom Humanities Research Centre, Texas.

II. Printed sources

The Times has been the main contemporary printed news source. The relevant volumes of *Who Was Who* and *The Dictionary of National Biography*, arranged chronologically, have been the principal sources of biographical information. All references to speeches and broadcasts made by Violet Bonham Carter have been taken from the Violet Bonham Carter Papers, unless otherwise attributed. The 'Harris interview' refers to the transcript of an interview given by VBC to Kenneth Harris, the basis of a BBC television programme celebrating her eightieth birthday. A. J. P. Taylor's *English History 1914–45* (Oxford, 1990 edition) has been the principal general history used. Full references of all other books quoted in footnotes to the text are given below (place of publication is London, unless otherwise stated). Also included are some memoirs of special relevance.

Absalom, Roger *A Strange Alliance: Aspects of Escape and Survival in Italy 1943–45* (Florence, 1991)
Asquith, Cynthia, *Haply I May Remember* (1950)
– *Remember and Be Glad* (1952)
– *Diaries, 1915–1918* (1968)
Asquith, Herbert, *Moments of Memory* (1937)
Asquith, H. H., *Memories and Reflections* (2 volumes, 1928)
Asquith, Margot, *Places and Persons* (1925)
– *Lay Sermons* (1927)
– *More Memories* (1933)
– *Myself When Young* (1938)
– *Off the Record* (1943)
Benckendorff, Constantine, *Half a Life* (1954)
Bennett, Daphne, *Margot: A Life of the Countess of Oxford and Asquith* (1984)

Berlin, Sir Isaiah, *Personal Impressions* (1980)

Blake, Robert, *The Unknown Prime Minister: The Life and Times of Andrew Bonar Law* (1955)

Bonham Carter, Mark (ed.), *The Autobiography of Margot Asquith* (1995)

Bonham Carter, Mark and Pottle, Mark (eds), *Lantern Slides: The Diaries and Letters of Violet Bonham Carter, 1904–1914* (1996)

Bonham Carter, Violet, *Winston Churchill as I Knew Him* (1995)

Boyce, D. G., *Englishmen and Irish Troubles: British Public Opinion and the Making of Irish Policy, 1918–22* (1972)

Boyle, Andrew, *Poor, Dear Brendan* (1974)

Briggs, Asa, *Governing the BBC* (1979)

– *The History of Broadcasting in the United Kingdom*, vol. iii, 'The War of Words, 1939–1945' (Oxford, 1970)

Brock, M., 'The Eternal Lack of Motive: Raymond Asquith's Buried Talents', in R. Custance (ed.), *Winchester College: Sixth Centenary Essays* (Oxford, 1982)

Brock, M. and Brock E. (eds), *H. H. Asquith: Letters to Venetia Stanley* (1985)

Brown, Malcolm, *The Imperial War Museum Book of the Western Front* (1993)

Bullock, Alan, *Hitler and Stalin: Parallel Lives* (1991)

Carlton, David, *Anthony Eden* (1981)

Cassar, George H., *Asquith as War Leader* (1994)

Chamberlain, Austen, *Down the Years* (1935)

Churchill, Winston, *The World Crisis: The Aftermath* (1929)

– *Great Contemporaries* (1937)

– *The Second World War* (six volumes, 1950–54)

Colville, John, *The Fringes of Power: 10 Downing Street Diaries, 1939–1955* (1985)

Cook, Don, *Charles de Gaulle* (1984)

Cooke, Colin, *The Life of Richard Stafford Cripps* (1957)

D'Abernon, Edgar Vincent, Viscount, *An Ambassador of Peace* (1929–30)

D'Abernon, Helen Vincent, Viscountess, *Red Cross and Berlin Embassy, 1915–26* (1946)

David, Edward (ed.), *Inside Asquith's Cabinet: From the Diaries of Charles Hobhouse* (1977)

Dugdale, Blanche E., *Baffy: The Diaries of Blanche Dugdale, 1936–47* (1973)

Dundas, Hugh, *Flying Start: A Fighter Pilot's War Years* (1988)

Fitzherbert, Margaret, *The Man Who Was Greenmantle* (1983)

Freyberg, Paul, *Bernard Freyberg, VC: Soldier of Two Nations* (1991)

Fry, James W. and McMillan, Thomas, *The Complete History of the Royal Naval Division* (1919)

Gilbert, Martin, *Churchill: A Life* (1991)

– *The Holocaust: The Jewish Tragedy* (1986)

– *First World War* (1994)

– *Finest Hour: Winston S. Churchill, 1939–1941* (1983)

Grenfell, Ethel, *Pages from a Family Journal* (privately printed, Eton, 1916)

Grey of Fallodon, Viscount, *Twenty-Five Years* (2 volumes, 1925)

Grimond, Jo, *Memoirs* (1979)

Haldane, R. B., *An Autobiography* (1929)

Hamilton, Sir Ian, *Gallipoli Diary* (1920)

Harris, José, *William Beveridge* (Oxford, 1977)

Harris, Kenneth, *Attlee* (1982)

Hart-Davis, Duff (ed.), *End of an Era: Letters and Journals of Sir Alan Lascelles, 1887–1920* (1986)

Hassall, Christopher, *Rupert Brooke: A Biography* (1964)

Horner, Frances, *Time Remembered* (1933)

James, Robert Rhodes, *Victor Cazalet: A Portrait* (1976)

Jenkins, Roy, *Asquith* (1964)

Jerrold, Douglas, *The Royal Naval Division* (1927)

Johnson, J. E., *Wing Leader* (1979)

Jolliffe, John (ed.), *Raymond Asquith: Life and Letters* (1980)

Koss, Stephen, *Asquith* (1976)

Levine, Naomi B., *Politics, Religion and Love* (1991)

McCallum, R. B. and Readman, Alison, *The British General Election of 1945* (Oxford, 1947)

Miles, Captain Wilfrid, *Military Operations: France and Belgium, 1916* (2 volumes, 1938)

Morgan, Ted, *FDR: A Biography* (1985)

Mosley, Nicholas, *Julian Grenfell: His Life and the Times of his Death 1888–1915* (1976)

Munson, James (ed.), *Echoes of the Great War: The Diary of the Reverend Andrew Clark, 1914–1919* (1985)

Nicolson, Nigel (ed.), *Harold Nicolson: Diaries and Letters, 1930–1939* (1966)

– *Harold Nicolson: Diaries and Letters, 1939–1945* (1967)

Nicolson, Nigel and Forbes, Patrick, *The Grenadier Guards in the War of 1939–1945* (2 volumes 1949)

Pakenham, Frank, *Peace by Ordeal* (1962)

Ponsonby, F., *Recollections of Three Reigns* (1951)

Ponsonby, Sir Frederick, *The Grenadier Guards in the Great War* (1920)

Richards, Denis, *Royal Air Force 1939–45: The Fight at Odds* (volume one, 1974)

Ridley, Jane and Percy, Clayre (eds), *The Letters of Arthur Balfour and Lady Elcho 1885–1917* (1992)

Schmidt, Heinz Werner, *With Rommel in the Desert* (1997)

Skidelsky, Robert, *John Maynard Keynes: The Economist as Saviour, 1920–1937* (1992)

– *Oswald Mosley* (1990)

Spender, J. A. and Asquith, Cyril, *Life of Herbert Henry Asquith, Lord Oxford and Asquith* (2 volumes, 1932)

Spier, Eugen, *Focus* (1963)

Taylor, A. J. P., *Beaverbrook* (1972)

– *The Struggle for Mastery in Europe, 1848–1918* (Oxford, 1971)
– (ed.), *Lloyd George: A Diary by Frances Stevenson* (1971)
Weinberg, Gerhard L., *A World at Arms* (Cambridge, 1994)
Williams, Charles, *The Last Great Frenchman: A Life of General de Gaulle* (1993)

INDEX

An asterisk signifies those individuals who are listed in the appendix of 'Biographical notes'. An italicized page number indicates the location of a biographical footnote. A superscript cross identifies houses listed in the appendix of 'Notes on houses'. Entries are sub-divided chronologically rather than alphabetically.

Abdication crisis, 189, 280 & n. 2
Abyssinia, Italian invasion of (1935), 184–6, 187, 194, 195
Acland, Sir Francis, *126*
Acland, Sir Richard, *284*, 287, 292
Adenauer, Konrad, *153*
Agar-Robartes, Hon. Thomas, *80*
Aitken, William Maxwell *see* Beaverbrook, Lord
Albert Hall, 185, 187, 193, 251–2
Alexander, Albert, *210*, 212
Alexander, Gen., 305
Allendale, Viscount, *315*, 316
Allsopp, Jack, 256, *265*, 266
Altrincham, Lord *see* Grigg, Sir Edward
America *see* United States of America
Amery, Leopold, *209*, 357
Anderson, John, 291
Angell, Sir Norman, *187*
Antwerp, falls to German army (1914), 10, 14, 44
Anzac, 46, 64–5, 72, 74–5
appeasement, 178–198, 336, 350
Archie Gordon Club, 37, 49, 79 n. 4, 89–90
Asquith, Anthony ('Puffin'/'Puff')*, 51, 165, 335–6, 358
Asquith, Arthur ('Artie'/'Oc')*:
  prepares for Gallipoli, 26, 27, 28; *en route* to Gallipoli, 30, 34, 36; and death of Rupert Brooke, 41–2, 59; at Gallipoli, 45–7, 71–2, 74, 76; wounded, 47–8; Violet visits him in Alexandria (June 1915), 48–9, 55, 57–8, 60, 64–6; 'it is simply a choice between being killed & being disabled', 69; 'Our Iliad is over: our Odyssey beginning', 91–2; and death of Raymond Asquith, 94; fights to avoid staff post in France, 61 n. 1, 95–6; his character and response to the war, 38, 205; his death, 204–5, 206; mentioned: 11, 14, 15, 16, 18, 19, 20, 23, 29, 32, 62, 63, 67, 99, 173, 334; correspondence: AMA to VBC, 41–2, 45–7, 71–2, 73–4, 84, 91–2, 94, 95–6; VBC to AMA, 36–7, 72–3, 75, 77–9, 80–1, 106–7
Asquith, Betty, 107, 206, 244, 249, 257, 266, 267, *380*; correspondence: VBC to BA, 206–7
Asquith, Christine, 244, 249, 257, 266

Asquith, Cynthia*:
  her thoughts on Violet's marriage, 67, 84–5; response to bereavement during Great War, 81 n. 3; mentioned: 9 n. 3, 11, 19, 36 n. 2, 65 n. 1, 99, 222
Asquith, Cyril ('Cys')*:
  war service, 16, 80; on Violet and their father, 172; on J. A. Spender, 228; mentioned: 7, 14, 15, 17, 25 n. 1, 31, 34, 52, 61 n. 1 & 2, 148, 215, 223, 240, 311
Asquith, Elizabeth *see* Bibesco, Elizabeth
Asquith, H. H.*:
  public: and outbreak of war, 5; visits Western Front, 61–2; accused of being pro-German, 68, 110; press campaigns against, 35, 92; and drink question, 35–7; conscription, 74, 75; on his colleagues, 35, 88 n. 1; and Lloyd George, 35, 90, 156, 158, 166; and May 1915 coalition, 49, 52–5, 57, 59, 176–7; contemplates taking war office (Oct. 1915), 82; 'clutch not in', 83; resigns as premier (1916), 92–3, 97–9; defeated at 1918 election, 99–100, 105; and Paisley elections (1920–3), 105, 108–114, 136–8, 141, 155–8; and Ireland, 105, 111, 116–17, 127, 162, 173–4; and first Labour government, 155–60; and defeat at Paisley (1924), 161, 163–6; takes peerage, 165–7; resigns Liberal leadership (1926), 165–72.
  personal: and Margot Asquith, 54–5; and death of Raymond Asquith, 92–5; and Violet, 51, 55, 67, 69, 85–8, 93, 112, 164, 173–4; and death of Rupert Brooke, 41; and Montagu marriage, 49, 51, 62, 63; financial worries in retirement, 172–3; decline and death, 172–5; mentioned: 5, 7, 8, 15, 17, 19, 36, 47, 68, 73, 78, 139, 227, 234, 236, 358–9, 364; correspondence: HHA to VBC, 85–6, 87–8, 169–70; VBC to HHA, 9–14, 86–7
Asquith, Helen, 80
Asquith, Herbert ('Beb')*:
  'England expects...' (Aug. 1914), 8; visits hospitals at front (1914), 9–11; affected by war, 75, 80, 99, 222; mentioned: 9 & n. 3, 10–11, 16, 19
Asquith, Jean, 257

Asquith, Julian, 80 n. 1
Asquith, Katharine, 33, 36, 80, 83, *381*;
and Montagu marriage, 63 n. 2; and
Violet's marriage, 67; and Raymond
Asquith, 80
Asquith, Margot*:
public: views on Lloyd George, 62 n. 2;
on Northcliffe, 62 n. 2, 75 n. 1; lobbies
on conscription, 74, 75 n. 1; accused of
being pro-German, 68; at Paisley
elections (1920–4), 110, 113–4, 138,
165; 'rescues' brother at Glasgow poll
(1923), 157 n. 1; defends Chamberlain's
record (1939), 206.
personal: and death of Elizabeth
Asquith, 336 & n. 1; and Asquith, 54–
5, 63, 162, 165, 174; and Violet, 27 n.
1, 43 n. 1, 47 n. 2, 63, 67, 69, 86, 162,
165, 172–3, 206, 361; and Montagu
marriage, 63; 'extravagance' of, 69, 81,
173; death of, 358–9; memorial service
for, 360–1.
mentioned: 14, 27, 36, 47, 54, 55, 84,
97, 107, 108, 170, 176; correspondence:
MA to VBC, 62–3, 86, 162, 165, 174
Asquith, Perdita, 80
Asquith, Raymond*:
war service, 33, 79, 80; character, and
death of, 92–5; mentioned: 6 n. 1, 36,
61 n. 1, 96 n. 1, 99, 162, 246 n. 2
Asquith, Susan, 266, 282, 292
Asquith, Violet *see* Bonham Carter, Violet
Astor, Ava, 33
Astor, Nancy (Countess), *147*, 255
Astor, Waldorf, 147
Astor, William ('Bill'), *244*
Atholl, Duchess of, 194 n. 3
Atomic bomb, 359 & n. 2, 360 & n. 3, 364,
366, 367
Attlee, Clement*, 191, 212, 215, 238 n. 2,
351 & n. 1, 356, 360, 361
Auchinleck, Field Marshal, *240*, 241, 247
'Auxiliaries' *see* Ireland, 'Auxiliaries' in

Badoglio, Gen., *274*, 278
'Baffy' *see* Dugdale, Mrs Edgar
Baker, H. T. ('Bluey')*, 137, 355
Baker, Philip Noel, 190
Baldwin, Stanley*, 155, 158, 162, 167, 175,
280, 313 & n. 5
Balfour, Arthur James ('AJB')*, 35, 51 n. 2,
57, 82, 97
Balfour, Brigid, *290*, 316, 330
Balmoral Castle†, 106–7
Balogh, Thomas, *275*, 330
Baring, Maurice, *10*, 368
Barrie, J. M., 93
Bartholomew, H. G., *344*
Bartlett, Vernon, 194 n. 3, 240 n. 1, *243*,
354
Bauer, Gustav, *145*
Beatty, Earl, *209*
Beauchamp, Earl, 40 n. 2

Beaverbrook, Lord*:
'only possible' successor to Churchill
(1940), 224; thought 'evil', 281;
'blamed' for timing of 1945 election,
309, 360 & n. 1; Violet's poor opinion
of, 280, 291; mentioned: 212, 236, 238
n. 2, 239–40, 309, 312
Beck, Gen. Ludwig, *311*
Belgium:
and Great War, 7 n. 1, 8; and Ruhr
invasion (1923), 140, 142, 152; and
Second World War, 211–5, 219, 220;
mentioned, 184
Belsen, 338 n. 4, 343
Benckendorff, Constantine ('Cony'), 290
Beneš, Eduard*, 220, 271
Bennett, Lord, *320*
Berlin, Isaiah, on Lewis Namier, 291 n. 1
Bernays, Robert, *291*
Best, Capt., *363*
Beveridge, Lady (Janet), 257, 317, 319
Beveridge, Sir William*:
and 'Beveridge report' (on *Social
Insurance and Allied Services*), 246, 248 &
n. 1, 255–6, 257, 258, 262, 307; popular
reaction to, 258–9; and Labour Party,
302 & n. 1; and Liberal Party, 296, 302,
308–9, 317, 326–7; and Berwick
candidacy (1944), 315–7; maiden
speech, 319; and 1945 Liberal
Assembly, 326–7; and Dumbarton Oaks
formula, 332, 336; and 1945 election,
345, 357, 359; Churchill afterwards
aggrieved with, 366 n. 1; Violet's
impressions of, 317, 319, 340, 359;
mentioned: 249, 309, 320, 330, 340,
354
Bevin, Ernest*, 212, 337, 358;
'Palmerstonian' at foreign office, 366
Bibesco, Elizabeth*, 68 n. 2, 83, 108, 138,
165; death of, 335–6, 338
Bibesco, Priscilla, 165, 336, 358
Biggar, J. M., *114*, 138
Bing, Rudolf, *242*
Bingham, Maj.-Gen. *148*
Birdwood, Field Marshal, *74*, 75, 92
'Black and Tans' *see* Ireland, 'Black and
Tans' in
Blum, Léon, *362*-3; on de Gaulle's future
(1945), 363
Boer War, 6, 32 n. 1 & 2
Bonar Law, Andrew*:
and May 1915 coalition, 49, 52, 54 n. 2,
57; and Dec. 1916 coalition, 97, 98; and
1918 general election, 99; Asquithian
view of (1915), 82 n. 1; compared with
Lloyd George, 136, 144; retires, 154–5;
mentioned: 19, 73
'Bong[ie]' *see* Bonham Carter, Sir Maurice
Bonham Carter, Cressida *see* Ridley,
Cressida
Bonham Carter, Frederick, *79*
Bonham Carter, Guy, *62*

Bonham Carter, Laura *see* Grimond, Laura
Bonham Carter, Mark*:
  at Winchester, 225–6; begins war
  service, 233, 234, 245, 247, 248, 249,
  251; with Grenadiers in North Africa
  (1943), 252, 253, 254 & n. 4, 255, 256–
  7, 260–66; missing in action, 263–6;
  prisoner of war in Italy, 266 & n. 2, 267,
  269–71, 274, 275, 278, 279, 280; escape
  from POW camp, 278–9, 312; returns
  to England, 282–4; adopted
  parliamentary candidate for Barnstaple,
  284, 292, 297; with Windsor Castle
  garrison, 286–7, 290, 292, 301, 315,
  324; on Churchill, 297; and death of
  George Grey, 314–5; rejoins Grenadiers
  (1944), 320; with Grenadiers in Europe
  (1945), 324–6, 329, 332, 333, 335, 338,
  340–1, 345–6; and liberation of
  Sandbostel, 341; describes Germans at
  end of war, 338, 339, 346, 347; returns
  from war, 347; contests Barnstaple at
  1945 election, 334, 352–4, 355, 357,
  358, 368; on timing of 1945 election,
  348; at Balmoral (Oct. 1945), 364;
  Violet's feelings for, 248, 251, 262, 264–
  5, 267, 282–3, 325; mentioned: 165 and
  passim from 203; correspondence:
  MRBC to VBC, 249, 253, 256–7, 260–1,
  263, 266, 269–70, 275, 329, 338, 339,
  340–1, 345–6, 364; VBC to MRBC, 253,
  254, 257–8, 259–60, 267–8, 269, 270–1,
  271–2, 274, 275, 277
Bonham Carter, Sir Maurice ('Bongie')*:
  public: (1914–18) volunteers for
  military service, 17 n. 1, 99 & n. 1; on
  Gallipoli campaign, 24; visits Western
  Front (1915), 61–2; knighted (1916),
  97–8; impressions of Asquith, 56, 59,
  62, 82, 171; of Balfour, 82; of Churchill,
  56–7, 83–4; of Lloyd George, 39, 68, 70,
  77, 83–4, 90, 171; (1919–39) visits
  Ireland, 130; and Anglo-French reaction
  to Italian invasion of Abyssinia, 184;
  (1939–45) air raid warden, 204, 205,
  212, 227, 228–30, 295, 306, 307; and
  invention of jet engine, 289–90.
  personal: and Montagu marriage, 62–3;
  feelings for Violet, and marriage, 38–9,
  41, 49, 56–9, 67, 68, 69, 70–1, 84–90.
  mentioned: *passim*; correspondence:
  MBC to VBC, 7, 9, 38–9, 41, 56–7, 58–
  9, 61–2, 68, 69–70, 77, 82, 83–4, 90, 97,
  156, 171, 184, 228–9; VBC to MBC, 8,
  55, 57–8, 60–1, 68–9, 83, 110–111, 156,
  162, 166–7, 170, 182, 228
Bonham Carter, Norman, 99
Bonham Carter, Raymond*:
  describes Gen. Montgomery, 319–20,
  348–9; begins junior military training,
  324; mentioned: 178 & *passim* from 204;
  correspondence: RBC to VBC, 348; VBC
  to RBC, 204

Bonham Carter, Violet*:
  public: (1914–18) and outbreak of war,
  5, 7–8; considers nursing, 8, 15, 26, 33,
  48; visits Western Front (1914), 9–14;
  on Asquith's war leadership, 83; on
  Asquith's resignation (1916), 98–9;
  apprehensive about post-war world,
  99–100; (1919–39) and 1920 Paisley
  election, 105, 108–14; contemplates
  standing for parliament, 115–6, 162;
  visits Ireland (1921), 116–35;
  threatened during visit, 124–5, 131;
  1922 Paisley election, 136–8; visits
  Germany (1923), 139–54; 1923 Paisley
  election, 154–8, 161; views on a first
  Labour government, 158–60; 1924
  Paisley election, 161, 163–5;
  disillusionment with Liberal party, 171–
  2, 178; anti-appeasement activist, 178–
  98; joins calls for 'united front' (1938–
  9), 194–6; (1939–45) and outbreak of
  war, 197, 203; ARP work, 293–5, 297;
  governor of the B.B.C., 227, 232, 234,
  242 n. 1, 243, 259, 262, 276–7, 285, 284
  n. 3, 287, 306, 320, 328, 331; and
  Berwick candidacy (1941), 233–4, 315;
  and Liberal Party, 234, 280, 284, 289,
  294, 296; presidency of the LPO, 252,
  284, 289, 292, 294, 297, 326–7; and
  Wells candidacy (1945), 332, 343, 349,
  350–8; critical of Conservative Party,
  349–50; on Labour Party, 299–300, 351–
  2; and social reform, 272; thoughts on
  end of war, 313–4, 316, 342–3, 360; and
  United Nations, 332 & n. 2, 333, 336;
  supports united Europe, 364–5;
  apprehensive about post-war world,
  319, 365, 369.
  personal: feelings for Bongie, and
  marriage, 43, 49, 55, 56–8, 60–1, 67,
  70–1, 79, 82, 83, 84–90; her children
  when young, 96, 109, 113, 114–6, 138,
  163, 165; her family during war, 287–9,
  321–3, 344, 368–9; and christianity, 49,
  50, 193; love of Wiltshire countryside,
  298–9, 301–2, 322, 359, 361; described
  by others, 154, 190, 251, 262.
  speeches: (1920–39) L.N.U., Dec. 1920,
  180; N.L.F., May 1923, 180; W.N.L.F.,
  May 1926, 180; Liberal Conference,
  May 1933, 181; Liberal meeting, Sep.
  1933, 182; Savoy luncheon, Dec. 1933,
  182–3; L.N.U., Oct. 1935, 185–6; L.P.O.,
  Oct. 1938, 192–3; 'Against Religious and
  Racial Persecution', Dec. 1938, 193;
  N.L.C., Jan. 1939, 196; (1939–45)
  Liberal meeting, Feb. 1940, 203; Oxford
  Union, Feb. 1943, 257; Oxford Liberals,
  June 1944, 313 n. 3; Liberal Assembly,
  Feb. 1945, 326–9, 337 n. 2; Birmingham
  Liberals, May 1945, 336
Bonn, Julius Moritz, *143*, 146
Boot, Sir Jesse, *98*

Boothby, Robert ('Bob'), *208*, 214, 215, 220, 221, 368; and American loan (1945), 368

Boris, Georges*, experiences fighting in Flanders (1940), 223; prefers destruction to surrender of Paris, 225; 247

Brabourne, Lord, *266*

Bracken, Brendan*, backs Beveridge broadcast (1942) 248; predicts Tory electoral difficulties, 300; advocates discussion of controversial issues on B.B.C., 303, 306; controversy with Bevin, 337; mentioned, 299, 309, 321, 329, 357

Bradley, Gen. Omar, *333*

Breitscheid, Rudolf, *146*–7, 150, 151

Bridges, Robert, *15*, 16, 48

British Broadcasting Corporation (B.B.C.): and 'Cassandra' broadcast (1941), 232; appointment of William Haley, 276–7; covers 'D-day' landings, 304–6; 'crookedness an occupational disease', 293; and discussion of political subjects, 303, 306, 328, 331, 241–2; pronunciation of foreign names, 318; mentioned: 224, 234, 240, 243, 246, 248, 259, 262, 273, 274, 287, 299, 320

British Expeditionary Force ('B.E.F.'), (1914) 5, 7, 8 n. 1; (1940) 217, 218

British Union of Fascists (B.U.F.), 217 & n. 2

Brooke, Alfred, *59*

Brooke, (Mrs) M. R., and death of Rupert, 44, 59; correspondence: MRB to VBC, 44, 59

Brooke, Rupert*:
'hated the idea of war', 44; romantic approach to Gallipoli campaign, 24, 26, 205; departs for Gallipoli, 28–31; offered staff post, 32, 37; illness and death, 37–8, 40–44; appearance, 27, 28, 37; character, 23, 24, 28–9, 31, 44, 47–8; Violet and, 28–9, 31, 32–4, 43, 48, 65, 77, 81; mentioned: 14, 27, 34, 47, 78; correspondence: RCB to VBC, 16, 17–18, 20–21, 22, 26, 31, 37–8; VBC to RCB, 15–16, 16–17, 19–20, 21, 23, 28–9, 32–4

Browne, Denis, 14, *16*, 27, 30, 38, 42, 59, 69, 78

'Bubbles' *see* Ridley, Jasper (jnr.)

Buchenwald, 338 n. 4, 339, 343

Buchwald family, 194

Buckmaster, Stanley, *112*, 137, 163

'Budge' *see* Firth, John

Bulgaria, and Great War, 80

Burns, John, 40 n. 2

Butler, Maj. Tom, 278–9

Cameron, Gen., 123

'Campbell case,' the, 161, 163, 300

Campbell, J. R., 161

'Canon, the' *see* Hannay, Revd. James

Caporetto, 224

Carden, Admiral, *23*

Carmichael, Alec, 79

Carson, Sir Edward*, 58, 97, 98, 118

Casablanca meeting (1943), 254

Casement, Sir Roger, 120–21

'Cassandra', 232

Cazalet Keir, Thelma, *328*, 350

Cazalet, Victor, *246*

Cecil, Lord Edward, *64*

Cecil, Lord Robert ('Bob') Gascoyne-, *106*, 356

Chamberlain, Austen*, and May 1915 coalition, 57; mentioned: 73

Chamberlain, Neville*:
and appeasement, 189–98, 207; and Norwegian debate (May 1940), 209–11; resigns as premier, 211–3; in Churchill's cabinet, 215, 231; without telephone in bedroom, 224; Violet's criticism of, 193, 206 n. 1, 207, 208–9, 217; mentioned: 205 n. 2, 236, 343 n. 3, 350

Charteris, Hugo ('Ego'), *65*

Charteris, Yvo, 81

Charteris, Evan, *36*

Childers, (Robert) Erskine, *131*-2

China, and United Nations organization, 332 n. 2

Christie, John, *228*, 242–3, 276

Church of England, 64, 257

Churchill, Clementine*:
defends Churchill during May 1915 crisis, 57; and living in 10 Downing Street, 224, 230; on Chamberlain, 224; thinks Cripps 'odious', 235; urges Cripps inclusion in government, 236 n. 3; thinks Churchill should resign leadership of Conservative Party, 314; visit to Soviet Union (1945), 347; described by Violet, 224; relations with Violet, 248, 250, 253, 317, 318, 366; mentioned: 19, 22, 27, 62, 228, 232, 237, 252, 287, 312, 346; correspondence: CC to VBC, 230

Churchill, John ('Jack'), *282*

Churchill, Lady Gwendeline, *19*, 22, 78

Churchill, Winston*:
(1914–18) reaction to war, 25; the Curragh mutiny, 56; and Kitchener, 25, 34; and Royal Naval Division, 14, 19, 22, 25, 27; and Gallipoli, 25, 34, 45, 72–3, 176–7; and conscription, 83–4; and admiralty crisis (May 1915), 49, 51–4, 56–7, 62–3, 177; fall of Asquith (1916), 236; (1919–39) fear of Bolshevism, 154; opposes first Labour government, 155, 158–60; and anti-appeasement, 178–9, 187–8, 197–8; (1939–45) in Chamberlain's government, 205, 210, 211; loyalty to Chamberlain, 236; becomes premier, 211–3, 224; position threatened by Cripps, 234 & n. 2, 240

n. 1; critical of Cripps, 235–6; includes Cripps in government, 235 n. 3, 238; relations with Cripps, 235, 238, 252, 296; becomes premier, 214, 215, 216–7; and fall of France, 219, 227–8; and fall of Singapore, 235–7; and 'Darlan deal', 248, 252–3; Casablanca meeting, 254 & n. 1; and Mareth Line battle, 262; 'impossible post-war P.M.', 281; illness of (1943), 287; March 1944 broadcast criticized, 297–9, 301; 'praises' Fascist Spain, 303, 318; and D-Day, 304; not a post-war leader, 305; and Teheran, 312–3; on post- war politics, 273, 313–4, 318; in Athens, 322–3; at Yalta (1945), 330; and end of war, 344, 346, 356; and 1945 general election, 342, 347, 348, 350–1, 355, 358; and Conservative Party, 210–11, 259, 329 & n. 3, 351 n. 1; lacks Conservative support, 213, 224–5; should distance himself from Conservatives, 313–4, 349–50, 356; post-election, 359, 360, 363; on de Gaulle and Free French, 254 & n. 1, 330, 244; on Archie Sinclair, 319; and Stalin, 291, 318, 319, 333; on democracy, 247, 252; on Empire and the dominions, 252; on the 'Russian bear [and] American Elephant' (1943), 312–3; character, 25, 52, 57, 108, 241, 280; and painting, 82, 237; meets Henry James, 21 & n. 1; mentioned: 77, 106, 230, 250, 267, 270, 273, 285, 290, 308, 337, 354.

and Violet: disagreement over first Labour government, 158–60; dispute over Asquith's memoirs, 175–7; the Freedom Focus, 178, 187–8, 190–1, 197–8; Violet senses his absence, 254; Violet critical of (1944) 297–8, 303; Violet visits, (Nov. 1942) 246–7; (Aug. 1944) 312–4, (Nov. 1944) 317–9; and 1945 election, 349–50, 355; (post-1945 election) 359, 360, 361, 363, 365–6, 366 & n. 1; correspondence: VBC to WSC, 158–9, 160, 175–6, 177, 211, 227–8, 232, 239, 264–5, 345, 349–50; WSC to VBC, 159–60, 264

speeches and broadcasts (1939–45): May 1940, 214; June 1940, 222–3, 227–8; Feb. 1942, 238; Nov. 1942, 246; Mar. 1944, 297, 299, 301; May 1944, 303; June 1944, 305, 308–9; Oct. 1944, 318; May 1945, 346, 347; June 1945, 350–1

Ciano, Count, *290*, 299
Citrine, Sir Walter, *187*
Clancy, George, *121* n. 1, 123, 125
Clark, Sir Kenneth, 257-*8*
Clovelly†, 253, 266–8, 292 & n. 2, 334
Club, the *see* Archie Gordon Club
Cluse, William, *285* n. *1*
Coates (maid), 48
Cocteau, Jean, 333

Colefax, Sybil, *208*
Collins, Lt.-Col., *47*, 68
Collins, Michael, 116, *128*
Conservative Party:
   during Great War, 54; and May 1915 coalition, 56–7; and 1916 coalition, 97; and Ireland, 134–5; 1922 general election, 136; 1923 general election, 155; 1924 general election, 161, 164; pro-Chamberlain and anti-Churchill, 210, 211 & n. 2, 213, 224–5, 259; during 1939–45 war, 256, 257 n. 1, 276, 299–300, 309; 1945 general election, 342–3, 357; and American loan, 368
Constantine, King of Greece, 80
Coote, Colin, *191*, 208
Corbett, Thomas ('Atty'), *346*, 347
Corbin, Charles, *317*, 318
Cork, burning of (1920), 123 n. 1, 125–6, 128, 130–1
Cranborne, Viscount ('Bobbetty')*, 81, 300–1
Crewe, Lord, *39*, 57
'Crinks' *see* Johnstone, Harcourt
Cripps, Lady (Isabel), 239–40, 252, 320
Cripps, Sir Richard Stafford*:
   and 'United Front', 194–6; ambassador to Soviet Union, 220, 230–1, 234, 236, 239; and Stalin, 231, 236; critical of Churchill, 231, 239; his Feb. 1942 'Postscript', 234 & n. 2, 235; rivals Churchill, 234 & n. 2, 235, 239, 240 & n. 1; in Churchill's government, 238–9, 241, 245, 296; relations with Churchill, 252, 296; on Beveridge, 320; and Liberal Party, 252, 296; and Labour Party, 320; advocate of realpolitik, 331; Violet meets, (June 1941) 230–1; (Feb. 1942) 238–9; Violet supports, 234, 235–6, 239; Violet critical of, 251, 272, 354; mentioned: 210
Cromwell, Oliver, quoted (May 1940), 209 n. 2
Crossman, Richard, *364*
Crowther, Geoffrey, *299*
Crozier, Brig.-Gen. *131*
Cunard, Nancy, 33
Currie, Lady (Hilda)*, 177–8; correspondence: VBC to HC, 177–8
Curzon, George*, 25, 53, 58, 73, 77, 83, 97
'Cys' *see* Asquith, Cyril
Czechoslovakia, crisis of 1938, 189–194, 196, 197, 207, 210, 223 n. 1 *see also* Beneš, Eduard; Masaryk, Jan

'D-day', anticipated (as '2nd front'), 291–2, 296, 298, 299; undertaken, 304, 319; viewed by Germans, 363
D'Abernon, Lord/Lady *see* Vincent, Sir Edgar/Lady Helen
Dachau, 344, 362–3
Dáil Éireann, 116, 127, 128, 134

Daily Chronicle, 85
Daily Express, 236, 309
Daily Mail, 62, 75
Daily Mirror, 113, 344
Daily Telegraph, 183 n. 1, 245, 314
Dalton, Hugh, *187*
Dandys, Diana, *337*
Dardanelles *see* Gallipoli campaign
Darlan, Admiral Jean, *226*, 247 & n. 1, 2, 248; assassination of, 249–50, 252–3
Davies, Clement, 248, *294*, 367
de Bono, Emilio, *290*
de Gaulle, Gen. Charles*, and Churchill, 248 n. 3, 305; and Gen. Giraud, 254 & n. 3; and Roosevelt, 247, 305, 330; mentioned: *229*, 246, 317 n. 3, 363, 365
de Laborde, Admiral, *247*
de Margerie, 144, *317*
Dent, Professor, 366
Derby, Earl of, *89*, 155
de Roiste, Liam, *126*, 128–9
Desborough, (Lady) Ettie, 61 n. 2
Deutsch, Felix, *147*, 150–1
Deutsch, Lili, *147*, 150–1
de Valera, Eamon, *127*, 133
Devlin, Joseph, 123 n. 3
Devonshire, Duke of, *213*
Dimbleby, Richard, 338 n. 4
Dodge, John ('Johnny'), *26*
Doenitz, Admiral, *340*, 346 n. 3
Donat, Robert, 323
Douglas, James, *131-2*
Drummond, Eric *see* Perth, Lord
Dublin, 131, 132 *see also* Easter Rising; Ireland, Bloody Sunday
Dudley, Rachel, 48
Duff Cooper, Alfred*, resigns over Munich, 191 and n. 4; during Norwegian debate (May 1940), 210; makes rousing broadcasts, 214, 215, 219, 224; and Cassandra broadcast (1941), 232 n. 1; mentioned, 33
Dugdale, Mrs Edgar ('Baffy'), *190*, 208, 216, 220 & n. 3, 286, 291
Dumbarton Oaks (U.N. voting formula), 332 n. 2, 333, 334, 336 & n. 2, 3
Dunkirk, evacuation of (1940), 208–9, 219–20, 221, 222–3, 271
Dunn, Sir James, 9 n. 3, *11*, 13 & n. 3, 29
Durham, Nicholas, *256*, 262, 266, 269, 277

Easter Rising (Dublin, 1916), 111 n. 2, 120 n. 1
Eden, Anthony*, and Munich agreement 191 & n. 1; criticism of, 298, 299, 300–1; Dumbarton Oaks, 336; mentioned: 215, 240, 281, 285 n. 1, 322, 334, 335, 356
Eden, Beatrice, 281
Edward VIII*, 280, 314
Egan, Barry, 128, 130
Eisenhower, Gen., 247, 273, 278

El Alamein, battle of (1942), 245, 246, 263
Elcho, Lady, *7*, 8, 239
Elcho, Lord, *7*, 8, *see also* Charteris, Hugo
Elizabeth, Princess, 285, 286–7, 301, 346, 368
Elizabeth, Queen, 285, 286, 301, 344, 346, 364
Elliot, Walter, *191*, 216, 220, 221
Erne, Earl of, *221*
Essex, Lady, 25, 33
Evelyn, Peter, *256*, 262, 266, 269, 277
Evening Standard, 217

Fallodon, Viscount Grey of *see* Grey, Sir Edward
Farrer, Reginald, 67
First World War *see* Great War
Firth, John, *225*, 257, 270, 348
Fisher, Admiral John*, deserts admiralty (May 1915), 49–51; Churchill on, 54, 177
Foch, Gen., 10, 142
'Focus in Defence of Freedom and Peace' *see* Freedom Focus
Foot, Dingle*, and Beveridge, 308–9, 315, 316, 319; against a Liberal–Tory alliance, 276; and party truce (1944), 293, 294; critical of Churchill, 356; mentioned: 292, 298, 302, 337, 357
Foot, Robert, *277*
Forbes, Alastair, *208*
Fothergill, Philip, *299*, 327
France:
    and outbreak of Great War, 5, 39–40, 149–50; army during Great War, 7 & n. 1; Violet visits (Oct. 1914), 9–14; territorial ambitions of, 35; and Ruhr crisis, 139–40, 142, 144–7, 153–4, 180; 'last dying flare of', 148; and Abyssinia, 184, 186; and Czechoslovakia, 189–90; German invasion (1940), 211–26; surrender of army (June 1940), 226–7; devastated by Allied bombing (1944), 306; elections in (Oct. 1945), 365; mentioned, 365; *see also* North Africa (French); Vichy regime
Franco, Gen., 303 & n. 1, 308, 318
Fraser, Sir Ian*, critical of Violet, 243 & n. 3; VBC critical of, 248; they disagree, 259, 328, 331; mentioned, 287, 303, 306
Freedom Focus, 187–9, 194, 197–8, 365, 366 n. 1
French, Field Marshal Sir John*, 'absolutely changed in appearance', 10; 'amazingly optimistic', 17; 'constantly at loggerheads' with Kitchener, 52, 53; loathed by George V, 106; saves British army at Marne, 142; mentioned, 9, 12, 14, 80 n. 3, 88
Freyberg, Barbara, 265, *387*
Freyberg, Sir Bernard*:
    early career, 27–8; friendship with Rupert Brooke, 65–6; at Gallipoli, 46,

72, 73, 90–1; thoughts on leaving
Gallipoli, 90–1; post-Gallipoli, 96;
Violet's impressions of, 27–8, 65–6;
reminisces (1945), 367; mentioned: 14,
41, 42 n. 2, 96; correspondence: BF to
VBC, 75–6, 90–1; VBC to BF, 96
Freyberg, Oscar, *66*, 69
Fulford, Roger, 354–5

Gallipoli campaign:
   early stages of, 23 n. 1 & 2, 25–6, 32–3,
   34, 36–7; planning of, 34, 45, 51;
   underestimation of Turkish strength,
   24–5, 32–3; Turks 'playing low tricks',
   65; Turk 'is a clean fighter', 74; first hand
   accounts of fighting, 45–7, 71–6; Violet's
   impressions of, 60, 64–6, 68–9;
   evacuation of peninsula, 90–2;
   mentioned: 24, 88, 176–7
Gardiner, Gerald, *365*
Garvin, James Louis, *191*, 366
general elections: (1918) 99–100, 105,
   116, 170 n. 2, 313 & n. 2; (1922) 136–
   8; (1923) 154–8; (1924) 159, 161, 162,
   164, 165; (1935) 313 & n. 5; (1945 –
   anticipated during war), 300–1, 308–9,
   312, 313, 318 & n. 3, 329 & n. 3; (1945 –
   campaign and outcome), 342–3, 346 n.
   2, 348, 349–50, 355–8
General Strike, 166, 168
George V*:
   pledges abstinence during Great War,
   36; pro-Kitchener, 51–2; supports
   Haldane in May 1915 crisis, 56; at
   Balmoral (1919), 106–7; and Labour
   Party – 'They may want to get rid of me',
   106–7; loathing of Gen. French, 106;
   intervenes over Ireland (1921), 134;
   offers Asquith peerage, 165–7;
   mentioned: 27, 162
George VI*, greets Chamberlain after
   Munich, 192; invites Churchill to form
   government, 212, 224; and Churchill,
   216–7; angry at War Office, 324; and
   V.E. day, 344, 346; mentioned, 270, 285
   n. 2, 364, 368
Germany:
   and outbreak of Great War, 5, 149–50;
   army during Great War, 6 n. 1, 7 n. 1, 9
   n. 2, 10 & n. 3; and Versailles treaty,
   139–40; post-war British attitudes
   towards, 140–1, 150, 152–3; and
   reparations, 139–40, 147; Violet urges
   conciliation towards, 180–5; and
   League of Nations, 148 n. 2, 180, 182;
   Nazi Party in, 178, 180–3; position of
   Jews in, 145, 180–3, 285 n. 1; and
   demise of Czechoslovakia, 189–94;
   alliance with Soviet Union, 207;
   invasion of Poland, 197; attacks Soviet
   Union, 230–1; Allied fears of German
   armistice with Soviets, 281; invasion of
   Low Countries and France (1940), 211–

226; concentration camps in, 338 & n.
   4, 339, 341, 343, 344; post-war, 364;
   mentioned: 254
Giraud, Gen., *246*, 247, 254
Globe, 68 n. 2
Gloucester, Duke of, *221*
Glover, Ronald, 37
Glyndebourne†, 242
Gneisenau, 237, 238
Godley, Gen. Sir Alexander, *152*, 153
Godley, Arthur *see* Kilbracken, Lord
Godley, Hugh*:
   on Great War, 6, 94; on Raymond
   Asquith, 93–4; offers Violet financial
   help (1916), 97; mentioned: 17, 97, 240;
   correspondence: HG to VBC, 6, 70–1,
   93–4; VBC to HG, 70, 95, 97–8, 107–8
Goebbels, Josef, *255*, 342, 344
Goering, Hermann, *255*, 340
Gollancz, Victor, *195*, 364
Grabski, Professor, *318*
Granville-Barker, Harley, 16 n. 2, *145*
Great War:
   comparison with Second World War,
   265; conscription issue, 74–5, 78, 81–2,
   83–4, 89, 90; drink question, 35–6, 37;
   London during, 75, 78; munitions
   issue, 35, 39; responses to, 5–8, 37, 39–
   40, 63, 81, 82, 93–5, 99, 147, 179, 205;
   shell shock during, 96; and *passim* 5–
   100
Greece, and Great War, 80, 84, 88
Greenwood, Arthur*, 197, 212, 236, 238
   n. 2, 255; offers Liberals an 'umbrella',
   343 n. 3
Greenwood, Sir Hamar, *126*, 128, 175
Grenadier Guards, (1914–18) 92–3; (1939–
   45) 261–2, 264, 270, 333 & n. 2, 335,
   339 n. 1, 345 & n. 1
Grenfell, Billy, *81*, 93
Grenfell, Julian, *61-2*, 81
Grey, Diana, 250, *290*, 293, 295, 311, 316
Grey, Sir Edward*, and outbreak of war, 5,
   39 n. 3, 149; and cabinet secrets (1915),
   74; mentioned: 19 n. 4, 51 n. 2, 97, 169,
   171, 175, 182 n. 2, 299
Grey, George*, on Stafford Cripps, 252,
   296; death of, 314–5; mentioned: 233
   n. 1, 258, 263
Griffith, Arthur, *128*
Grigg, Sir Edward, *226*
Grigg, Sir James, *357*
Grimond, Andrew, 205 n. 1, 275, 282, 314,
   322, 323, 339, 344
Grimond, Grizelda, 234, 258, 275, 287,
   322, 359
Grimond, Joseph ('Jo')*:
   on Mark Bonham Carter, 268–9;
   predicts end of war, 333; and 1945
   general election, 358; mentioned: 205
   n. 1, 206, 218, 288, 289, 305, 332, 335
   n. 1, 346 n. 1, 362, 369; correspondence:
   JG to VBC, 268–9

Grimond, Laura*, birth, 109; mentioned
    passim from 205
Guedalla, Philip, *187*
Guest, Flora, 29

Haden, W. C., *269*
Haifa, British troops sent to, 365
Haig, Gen., 142
Haldane, R. B.*, mission to Berlin (1912),
    149; pledges abstinence during Great
    War, 36; and May 1915 coalition, 52–3,
    56–7, 177; appearance, 64; mentioned,
    106
Haley, William*, 285, 306, 328, 331;
    appointed editor-in-chief B.B.C., 276–7
Halifax, Lord*, potential premier (May
    1940), 224; mentioned: 211, 212
Hamilton, Sir Ian, appointed c-in-c
    Gallipoli campaign, *32*; and Rupert
    Brooke, 37–8, 41, 42; praises RND, 63;
    recalled from Gallipoli, 91; mentioned,
    47, 251–2
Hankey, Maurice*, on Gallipoli, 74, 75;
    mentioned 34, 72, 73, 82, 205 n. 2
Hannay, Revd. James, *218*, 258, 259, 360
Hannon, Sir Patrick, *313*
Hardy, Thomas, *The Dynasts*, 16
Harris, Air Chief Marshal Sir Arthur, *298*
Harris, Sir Percy*:
    and Norwegian debate (1940), 209, 211;
    and party truce, 294; supports
    Beveridge's candidature at Berwick
    (1944), 316; and 1945 general election,
    362; Violet's opinion of, 307;
    mentioned: 286, 293, 304, 312, 333,
    334, 336, 345, 357
Harris, W. B., *218*
Harvie-Watt, Sir George, *304*
Heathcote-Smith, Sir Clifford, *321*
Henderson, Arthur, *58*
Henley, Sylvia, *69*
Henry, Denis, 123 n. 3
Herald, 85
Herbert, Hon. Aubrey*, on Violet's
    marriage, 67; mentioned: 6, 9;
    correspondence: VBC to AH, 81–2
Herbert, Mary, 9, *390*, 265 n. 3
Himmler, Heinrich, *311*, 340, 344, 346 n.
    3
Hinsley, Cardinal, *244*, 251
Hitler, Adolf*:
    and League of Nations, 148 n. 2; takes
    power, 180–1; and Rhineland (1936),
    186–7; and Czechoslovakia, 189–92;
    and Poland, 196; preferred to Stalin in
    Balkans, 207; Namier predicts will take
    London before Paris, 221; and invasion
    plans, 227; British attempt to divide
    from his high command, 245; July 1944
    bomb plot against, 311 & n. 2, 363;
    rumoured mad, 320; death of, 340, 342;
    speeches heard in Britain, 246, 255, 323,
    326; mentioned: 184, 195, 230, 253,

258 n. 3, 260, 347; *see also* Germany,
    Nazi Party
Hoare, Sir Samuel*, 186, 209 & n. 4, 213
Hobhouse, Sir Arthur, *332*, 351 n. 2, 353,
    357
Hobhouse, Charles, 39 n. 2, 54 n. 1, *170*
Hobhouse, Lady (Konradin), *351*
Hogg, Quintin, *256*, 257 n. 1, 313 n. 3
Holland, and Second World War, 211–3
Home Rule *see* Ireland, Home Rule
Hood Battalion *see* Royal Naval Division
Horabin, Thomas, *294*
Horner, Edward, *61* & n. 2
Horner, Frances, 218 & n. 2
Housman, A. E., *A Shropshire Lad*, 268
Howard, Geoffrey, 50, 165
Humphrey, Milford, 317 & n. 2
Huntington, Mrs Constant, 217-*8*
Hutchinson, Maj.-Gen. Robert, *284*

Ireland:
    Anglo-Irish treaty (1921), 127 n. 1, 128,
    134–5; 'Auxiliaries' in (1920–1), 116,
    117, 118, 122–3, 124, 128, 130, 131;
    'Black and Tans' in (1920–1), 116, 118,
    124, 125, 128, 131, 132, 134, 153, 175;
    Bloody Sunday (1920), 117, 118–19;
    British army in (1920–1), 126, 128,
    129 & n. 3; and dominion home rule,
    117, 118, 124, 127, 133, 134; and Home
    Rule, 56, 116–17, 127; and Ulster, 124,
    127; and *passim* 116–35
Irish Boundary Bill (1924), 162 n. 1
Irish Republican Army (pre-1922), 116,
    123, 125, 128,130, 132
Isaacs, Sir Rufus, *48*, 90, 173
Italy:
    and Great War, 53, 80, 89; predicted
    demise of, 148; and Abyssinia, 184–6;
    and Second World War, 213, 221, 224,
    273–4, 278–9, 290 & n. 3, 303

James, Eric, *349*
James, Henry, 21 & n. 1
Japan, during Second World War, 342,
    348, 355, 360 n. 3, 361
Jewish Chronicle, 183 n. 1
Jews, 'Samuel memorandum' on (1915),
    35; (and Judaism) Violet's attitudes
    towards, 49–50, 54, 147, 150, 151;
    Violet's defence of, 180–3, 244, 245,
    252, 255, 285 *see also* Germany, position
    of Jews in; Vichy regime
Joffre, Gen., 142
Johnstone, Harcourt ('Crinks'), *294*, 308,
    311, 316

Kahn, Otto, *147*, 150
Kaiser (Wilhelm II), 19, 145, 149
Kelly, Frederick ('Cleg'), at Gallipoli, 46,
    73; post-Gallipoli, 91 n. 3, 96; death of,
    96; mentioned: *27*, 28, 29, 38, 42 n. 2,
    69

Kent, Duchess of, *324*, 325
Kent, Tyler, 220, 223
Kenworthy, Lt.-Cmdr., *129*
Keyes, Admiral Sir Roger, *209*, 220
Keynes, John Maynard*:
 The Economic Consequences of the Peace,
 107–8; view of Lloyd George, 107; on
 Churchill, 241, 244; on social planning,
 246; on America and Americans, the
 Soviet Union and Poland, 291;
 negotiates US loan (1945), 365;
 mentioned: 108, 248
Keynes, Lydia, 291
Kharkov, trials (1943), 288
Kilbracken, Lord*, advises Violet to stand
 for parliament, 115–16; mentioned:
 152; correspondence: Kilbracken to
 VBC, 115–16
Kilteragh†, 117
Kitchener, Lord*:
 and recruiting, 8 n. 3; and India, 25;
 pledges abstinence during Great War,
 36; 'culpably apathetic' about
 munitions, 35; rows with Lloyd George,
 38–9; secrecy of, 39; 'constantly at
 loggerheads' with French, 52, 53;
 blamed by Liberals for May 1915
 coalition, 55; 'rattled & tired', 82;
 'strongly in favour' of Gallipoli
 campaign, 34; delays troops to Gallipoli,
 34 & n. 3; asks Churchill to assess
 Gallipoli, 73 n. 1; described, 17;
 mentioned: 10 n. 3, 32 n. 1, 51 n. 2,
 75
Kluck, Gen. von, 14 n. 1, *142*-3
Konev, Gen., *348*
Kropotkin, Prince, *36*
Kuhlmann, Richard von, on outbreak of
 war and post-war settlement, *149*-50,
 151–2
Labour Party:
 problems facing a first government,
 106–7; commission visiting Ireland
 (1921), 126; 1922 general election, 136;
 1923 general election, 155; first
 government of (1924), 155–60, 161;
 1924 general election, 161; and 'United
 Front', 195; outbreak of war (1939), 197;
 and downfall of Chamberlain, 209;
 during 1939–45 war, 255 & n. 5, 299,
 302; possibilities of Lib-Lab alliance,
 299–300, 334; 1945 general election,
 342–3, 357, 366 n. 1; post-war politics,
 273, 276, 309, 320; mentioned: 171
Lambert, George, *192*, 210
Lambourne, Lord, *109*
Laval, Pierre, 186, *247*, 363
Law, Richard, 357; on Soviet Union, *295*-
 6
Law, Rose, 141 n. 3, 221, 253, *258*, 263,
 272
Layton, Sir Walter, *248*, 273, 292, 340,
 355–6, 358

League of Nations, 175, 178–98 *passim*;
 and Abyssinia, 184–6, 187
League of Nations Union (LNU), 186, 188
 n. 1, 190, 208, 214, 234, 259
Leeson, Spencer, *270*, 355
Leigh-Mallory, Air Chief Marshall, *281*
Lewis, Sir George and Lady, *150*
Liberal Action, 295–6
Liberal Council, 295–6
Liberal Party:
 and May 1915 coalition, 54, 56; 1916
 coalition, 97; post-war schism and
 reunion, 108, 110, 136–7, 154–6, 158;
 1922 general election, 136; 1923
 general election and first Labour
 government, 155–7, 161; 1924 general
 election, 161, 165; leadership of, 1926,
 171–2; and League of Nations, 179–80;
 and 'United Front', 194–6; during 1939–
 45 war, 255 & n. 5, 258, 273, 276, 280,
 286, 293 & n. 1, 294, 299, 309, 312 &
 n. 1, 313–4; possibility of Lib-Lab
 alliance, 299–300, 334; 1945 assembly,
 324–9, 337 n. 2; 1945 general election,
 342–3, 345, 348, 354–8; after 1945
 general election, 366, 367; and
 American loan, 367–8; *see also* National
 Liberals
Liberal Party Organization (LPO), 248,
 252, 284, 289, 290, 299 n. 3
Limerick, 121, 123
Lindsay, A. D., 194 n. 3
Lindsay, Henry, 81
Lister, Charles*:
 character, 38; at Gallipoli, 46, 71–2, 73,
 75–6; death of, 76, 77–8, 80, 81;
 mentioned: 14, 25 n. 1, 41, 42, 61 n. 1,
 69
Lloyd George, Countess, *337*, 362
Lloyd George, David*:
 on outbreak of Great War, 149; rows
 with Kitchener, 39; rows with
 McKenna, 35, 90; and May 1915
 coalition, 49; and munitions, 35, 39,
 70; and conscription, 77, 83; backed by
 The Times against Asquith, 62, 68, 97;
 1918 general election, 99; described by
 Keynes, 107 n. 4; compared with Bonar
 Law, 144; and Ireland, 108, 116–7, 134–
 5; and Liberal Party finances, 168 & n.
 1, 169–70; and Liberal leadership
 (1926), 166, 168; attacks Chamberlain
 (1940), 210; considered a candidate for
 premiership (1940), 211; Violet on, 98–
 9, 108, 136–7, 155, 156, 168–9, 171–2,
 178, 210, 232, 273; memorial service
 for, 337; mentioned: 48, 51, 141, 158,
 159, 175, 207, 232, 236, 330, 362
Lloyd George, Gwilym, *294*, 316, 362
Lloyd George, Megan, *156*, 337, 345, 362,
 367; and American loan (1945), 367–8
Lloyd, Lord, *191*
Lockhart, John, *208*

Loos, battle of (1915), 80 n. 3
Low, David, 327-*8*, 347, 366
Lusitania, 48
Lwów, 318
Lyttelton, Oliver, *238* n. *2*, 239
Lytton, Victor, *214*

McCallum, Sir John, 105
MacCarthy, Desmond*, 106, 223, 274, 283, 317, 333; correspondence, VBC to DM, 204–6
McCracken, W. J., *42*
MacCurtain, Tomás, *123*
MacDonald, James Ramsay*, 147, 159, 160, 161, 162, 163, 175, 300
McFadyean, Sir Andrew, *334*, 336
McKean, 109, 111, 163
McKenna, Pamela, 19, 52, 265
McKenna, Reginald*, rows with Lloyd George, 35, 90; mentioned: 19, 52, 57, 69
Mackenzie, Compton, *Sinister Street*, 15–16
McKenzie Wood, Maj., *109*
Maclean, Sir Donald, *110*, 114, 157, 165
Maclean, Neil, *210*
Macleod, Sir Reginald, 82
McMahon, Col. Sir Henry, *64*
McMahon, Lady, *64*
Macmillan, Harold*, 211, 294, 357
McNair, T. Dun, 110, 113-*114*, 138, 163
MacNeice, Louis, 369
Mallon, James, *263*, 287, 306, 328, 331
Manchester Guardian, 150, 154, 156 n. 3, 181, 183 n. 1, 366
Mandel, Georges, *363*
Mander, Sir Geoffrey, *293*, 294, 304, 345, 348, 357
Mann, Arthur Henry, *276*, 306, 328, 331; correspondence (VBC to AHM), 276–7
Manners, Diana, 33
Manners, John, *6-7*, 9, 81, 93
Manners, Lady, 9
Manners, Patricia, *344*, 354
Mareth Line, battle of (1943), 254 n. 4, 256 n. 3 & 4, 260 n. 2 & 3, 261–2, 263, 264, 266, 271–2
Margaret, Princess, 286–7, 301, 346
Marsh, Sir Edward ('Eddie')*: and Rupert Brooke, 41, 43, 78; reaction to Munich agreement, 191; mentioned: 16, 21, 22, 25, 27, 28, 37, 59, 83, 312; correspondence: EM to VBC, 40; VBC to EM, 76–7, 88–9
Marshall, Howard, *304*
Marvell, Andrew, 21
Mary, Queen, 36, 346
Masaryk, Jan*, view of Stalin and Soviet Union (1945), 337; mentioned: 192, 220, 271, 272, 320
Masefield, Constance, 36, 47–8
Masefield, John, and death of Rupert Brooke, 47–8; mentioned: *36*, 106, 150

Massey, Vincent, *281*
Masterman, C. F. G., 157
Masterton-Smith, James, *51*, 52, 62
Maud, John, *276*
Mells†, 81
Meston, Lord, 252, 284
Meyer, Anne, 142
Mieville, Sir Eric, *368*
Millis, Charles, *262*, 277, 287, 293, 306, 331
Mitchell, Rosslyn, 161, 163-*4*
Moller, John, *340*
Mond, Sir Robert, *187*
Monro, Gen. Sir Charles, *91*
Montagu, Edwin*: objects to Jewish homeland, 35; marriage to Venetia Stanley, 49–50, 51, 54, 59, 63 & n. 2; and 1916 coalition, 97; relations with Asquith, 108; Violet's disapproval of, 49–50, 108; mentioned: 30, 33, 36, 77, 90, 175
Montagu, Venetia *see* Stanley, Venetia
Monteagle, Lord, *118*, 119, 124 n. 1
Montgomery, Field Marshal Bernard*: and Mareth Line battle (1943), 260 n. 2, 261–2, 270; and Soviet Union, 348–9, 355; 'his ego-centricity is glaringly obvious', 319–20, 325; mentioned: 245 & n. 2, 282, 304, 333, 335, 343, 346
Montgomery, David Bernard, *270*
Moore, Arthur, 8 n. 1
Moran, Lord, on effect of 'coming landslide' on Churchill (May 1945), *347*; mentioned, 350
Morhange, Alfonse ('Toto')*, gloomy about outcome of fighting in Flanders, 216, 220; works for de Gaulle, 229; ARP work of, 295, 306; breaks news of D-Day, 304; mentioned: 225 n. 2, 226, 250, 253, 254, 263, 269, 270, 282, 285, 290, 316, 354, 362
Morhange, Veronica, 219, 220, 225 n. 2, 226, 352
Morley, John (Lord), on outbreak of war, *39–40*
Morrell, Ottoline, 5, 147
Morrison, Herbert*, on possibility of Lib-Lab cooperation (1944–5), 299–300, 327 & n. 2; defends release of Oswald Mosley, 286; mentioned: 209, 212, 243, 244,252, 313
Mortimer, Raymond, *223*
Mosley, Sir Oswald, arrest (1940), 217; controversy surrounding release (1943), 286
Mowrer, Edgar, describes Stalin, 325; mentioned: *296*
Muir, Kim, *222*
Munich agreement *see* Czechoslovakia, crisis of 1938
Murray, Gilbert*: on Asquith, 175; condemns Dumbarton Oaks formula, 334–5; mentioned: 106,

181; correspondence: GM to VBC, 111, 168, 175, 188; VBC to GM, 108–9, 113, 134–5, 140, 157–8, 167, 168–9, 171–2, 181, 234, 283–4, 297–8, 354
Murray, Lady (Mary), 234, 298, 354
Murrow, Edward R., *338*
Mussolini, Benito*, 167, 184, 224 & n. 1, 273–4, 278 n. 2, 279, 285

Namier, Lewis, *220*, 221; 'my Soviet right-or-wrong' (1944), 291–2
Nannie (Ada Bentley), *110*, 111, 113, 114, 139, 253
Nathan, Sir Matthew, *43*
National Liberals, and Liberal reunion, 284 & n. 1, 304; mentioned, 350
New Statesman, 223
News Chronicle, 273, 302, 356 n. 1
Nicholas, Grand Duke, *52*
Nicolson, Harold*:
  governor of the B.B.C., 241–2, 262, 276, 318 n. 2, 328, 331; on fall of Singapore, 236 n. 1; Churchill's position threatened by Cripps, 240 n. 1; describes Violet, 206 n. 1, 262; on release of Oswald Mosley (1943), 286; on Churchill's unpopularity (Feb. 1944), 298 n. 1; on Churchill's anger at Liberals after 1945 election, 366 n. 1; mentioned: 190, 192 n. 2, 207, 208–9, 240, 274, 285, 333, 357
Nicolson, Nigel, *245*, 274
Norfolk, Duke of, *221*
North Africa (French), Allied invasion of (1942), 246–50
Northcliffe, Lord*, agitates against Asquith, 62, 70, 75, 97; and conscription, 75, 78, 81; mentioned: 236
Northumberland, Duke of, *221*
Norway, British invasion of (1940), 208–9

Observer, 257
'Oc' *see* Asquith, Arthur
O'Callaghan, Michael, *121*–3
O'Callaghan, Mrs, *121*–4, 130
Oheimb, Frau von, *146*, 148
Oliver Twist, 365
O'Mara, Stephen, *125*
'Ombrello' *see* Chamberlain, Neville
O'Neill, Con, *269*
O'Rahilly, Alfred, *126*, 127–8
Orpen, Sir William, 11 n. 1
Other Club, the, 191, 333

Paisley elections, (1920) 105, 108–114; (1922) 136–8; (1923) 154–8; (1924) 161–5
Pakenham, Francis, *248*, 276
Palestine, 365 n. 4, 367
Paris, captured by Germans (1940) 221, 223, 225–6; after liberation (1944), 333; mentioned, 247

Paris, Maj.-Gen., *22*
Parkinson (Dr), 48, 109, 165
Parnell commission, 173–4
Partington, Oswald, 54 n. 1
Passchendaele, battle of, 99
Patton, Gen., *335*
Paulus, Field Marshal, *255*, 259–60
Peace Pledge Union (PPU), 223
Peel, George, *27*, 30
Penn, Arthur, *254*, 266, 277, 285
Persse, John Henry, *310*
Perth, Lord (Eric)*, 77, 276, 334–5, 336
Pétain, Marshal*, 226, 246 n. 1, 247
Pethick-Lawrence, Emmeline, *133*
Peto, Ruby, 33
Philip, André, *247*
Philipson, Mrs Hilton, *233*
Phillipps, Vivian, *109*, 114, 157, 165, 170
'Pilotless Plane' *see* 'V1' flying bomb
Plunkett, Sir Horace*, 117, 118, 121, 124 n. 1, 131–2, 133
Poland, 196–7, 207 n. 2, 289, 291, 292, 293, 294, 318, 330, 331, 355
Ponsonby, Arthur, *40*
Ponsonby, Cyril Myles, *80*
Potsdam meeting (1945), 355 & n. 1
Powell, Sir Allan, *262*, 277, 287, 293, 328, 330
Price, Alfred, 37, 79; correspondence, AF to VBC, 79; VBC to AF, 89–90
Prytz, Björn, *299*, 347
'Puff[in]' *see* Asquith, Anthony

Quilter, Colonel, *19*, 20, 21, 27, 38, 46, 78

Radcliffe, Cyril, *281*, 301
Raleigh, Sir Walter, *15*, 17
Ramsay, Archibald Maule, *216*, 217, 220
Rathbone, Eleanor, *276*, 330, 364
Rauschning, Hermann, *Germany's Revolution of Destruction*, 207
Rea, Walter, *273*, 284, 289
Reading, Lord *see* Isaacs, Sir Rufus
Reeves, Terence C., 347 n. 3
Revelstoke, Lord, *107*
Reynaud, Paul*, 215, 226
Ribbentrop, Joachim von, 207
Ridley, Adam, 234, 311, 316, 347
Ridley, Constantine, 321
Ridley, Cressida*, birth, 96, 99; quizzes Violet on politics, 139; and mentioned *passim* from 205
Ridley, Jasper, *63*, 235, 241, 244, 309–10, 311, 321–2, 344
Ridley, Jasper ('Bubbles')*:
  missing in action in North Africa (1942), 240–1, 264; prisoner of war in Italy, 255, 268 & n. 1, 272, 274, 278, 280, 287, 288, 293, 303, 305; death of, 309–12, 314; memorial service for, 321–2; Violet's grief at his death, 310–12, 314, 316, 369; mentioned: 205, 206, 218, 234, 235, 238, 240, 268, 269, 317, 369

Ridley, Nathalie, *63*, 238, 283, 311, 321–2, 344

Ridley, Patrick, 321

Roberts, Wilfrid, *211*, 284, 294, 304, 315, 316, 345, 348

Robinson, Lennox, *118*

Rommel, Erwin*, 241, 245, 246, 260 n. 1

Roosevelt, Eleanor, 244, *395*

Roosevelt, F. D.*:
and 'Darlan deal', 247 & n. 3; and Gen. Giraud, 246 n. 1, 247; and de Gaulle, 247, 254, 305, 330; mentioned: 330, 331, 338, 254

Rosebery, Lord, *350*

Rothschild, James A. de ('Jimmy'), 193 n. 2, *256*, 348

Royal Air Force, 218–9, 232

Royal Irish Constabulary, 116, 118

Royal Naval Division:
departs for Gallipoli, 28–31; at Gallipoli, 45–7, 63–6, 68–9, 78; evacuation from Gallipoli, 90–2; post-Gallipoli, 91–2, 96; mentioned: 14, 17, 18, 19, 22, 24, 25, 27, 37 n. 1, 38

Ruhr, occupation of (1923):
inflation arising from, 141, 143; social distress during, 142, 143, 146, 148; expectations of British mediation, 143–4, 146, 153; mentioned: 180; and *passim* 140–54; *see also* France; Germany

Runciman, Walter, *36*, 83

Rundle, Sir Leslie, *32*

Rundstedt, Field Marshal von, *363*

Russell, Bertrand, 88

Russell, Conrad, *246*

Russell, Gilbert, *214*

Russell, Maud, *214*, 216

Russell, Peter, 358

Russia, and Great War, 9 n. 2, 34, 35, 36, 52, 75; *see also* Soviet Union

Ryan, A. P., 242

Sackville-West, Edward, *265*, 293

St Paul's, 34, 43, 293, 346

Salonica *see* Greece

Samuel, Herbert*, memorandum proposing Jewish homeland (1915), 35; mentioned: 194 n. 2, 336, 345, 351, 367, 368

San Francisco conference (1945), 336 n. 5, 338, 356

Sandbostel (concentration camp), 341 & n. 1

Sands, Ethel, *360*

Sandys, Duncan, *187*, 357

Sassoon, Siegfried, *322*

Sayers, Dorothy, 270

Schacht, Hjalmar, *363*

Scharnhorst, 237, 238

Schell, Sherrill, 44 & n. 1

Schlesinger (Dr), 65–6

Schnitzler, Arthur, *Professor Bernhardi*, 145

Schuschnigg, Kurt von, *363*

Scott, Lady, *43*

'Second Front' *see* 'D-Day'

Second World War:
air raids, (on Britain) 204, 216, 227–30, 254, 259 & n. 2, 293–5; (on France) 306; (on Germany) 272–3, 290, 298 & n. 2, 332, 333; comparisons with Great War, 265; threatened invasion of Britain, 215, 222, 227; London during, 204, 228–9, 293, 305, 307, 308; outbreak of, 196–8, 203, 205; public mood during, 271, 292, 297; and *passim* from 203

Seely, Sir Hugh *see* Sherwood, Lord

Serbia, Prince Paul of, *52*

Sex Disqualification Removal Act (1919), 115–6

Seymour, Horatia, *366*

Shakespeare, Sir Geoffrey, *284*

Sharp, Clifford Dyce, *106*, 108

Shaw-Stewart, Patrick, character, 28–29, 38; mentioned: 14, *25*, 27, 30, 42, 66, 91

Sherwood, Lord, opposes Beveridge's candidature for Berwick (1944) *315*, 316; mentioned, 348

Shinwell, Emanuel, *210*, 303 n. 1

Sicily, invasion of (1943), 273 & n. 1

Sickert, Walter, 237 & n. 1, 360 n. 2

Simon, Sir John*, on John Morley's resignation, 40; mentioned, 108 n. 2, 138, 157, 160, 171–2, 213

Simpson, Wallis, 280

Sinclair, Sir Archibald ('Archie')*:
at air ministry, 212–3, 219; and Beveridge's candidature for Berwick (1944), 315–6; leadership of Liberal Party, 255, 273, 293, 294, 297, 308–9, 319, 345, 348, 366; contemplates Liberal–Tory alliance, 275–6; bottom of poll at Thurso (1945), 357 & n. 4; Churchill aggrieved with (1945), 366 n. 1; argues with Violet over Dumbarton Oaks, 333; mentioned: 190–1, 195, 211, 215, 220, 342, 346, 351

Sinclair, Lady (Marigold), on Americans, 308; mentioned: 213, 222, 274, 308, 319, 333, 340, 346, *395*

Singapore, fall of (1942), 235–6, 237, 238

Sinn Féin (pre-1922), 111 n. 2, 116, 118, 120, 123, 126, 127–8, 129–30, 132, 133, 134

Smuts, Gen., 286, 305

Snagge, John, *278*

Snowden, Philip, *160*, 168

Somme, battle of, 79 n. 2, 91 n. 2, 92–4, 96

Southby, Sir Archibald, *210*

Soveral, Marquis de, *39*–40, 107

Soviet Union:
and Britain, 106, 108, 207, 231, 234, 281, 282, 291, 295, 346, 347, 348, 364, 366; British attitudes towards, 148, 181, 194, 251, 260, 281, 282, 291, 292, 293, 295, 296, 299, 319, 348–9, 355, 364,

366; Churchill and, 154, 291, 312–3, 317–8, 346; Sir Stafford Cripps and, 220, 230–1; and Czechoslovakia, 337; European fears of, 207, 285; alliance with Germany, 207; attacked by Germany, 230–1; and League of Nations, 180; and Poland, 291–2, 293, 296, 318, 330, 331, 355; and Second World War (military), 254, 259–60, 261, 289, 348, 360; and United Nations organization, 332, 336; post-war world, 362, 364, 366; mentioned: 147, 181, 220, 251, 255, 260, 261, 271, 319, 331, 341

Spain, 121, 148, 303 & n. 1, 318
Spears, Maj.-Gen. Sir Edward, *312*
Spectator, 257 n. 1
Spender, J. A., *169*, 228
Spicer, Lancelot, *296*
Spring Rice, Mary, *118*
Spring Rice, Thomas Aubrey, *118*, 125
Spring Rice, Thomas *see* Monteagle, Lord
Stalin, Joseph*:
    'even viler man than Hitler', 207; preserves illusions about Hitler, 230 n. 1; Cripps view of, 231; ignores Cripps, 236; 'far worse time with the Kulaks', 247; performs 'old rite of Russian hospitality' for Churchill, 291; gift to Churchill, 319; refuses Grabski, 318; 'a gangster', 325; and parliamentary government, 333; and Jan Masaryk, 337; mentioned: 286, 330, 365
Stalingrad, siege of, 242, 255 n. 4, 259–60
Stamfordham, Lady, *106*
Stamfordham, Lord, *106*
Stanley, Oliver, *209*
Stanley, Venetia*:
    character, 50, 63; Asquith's feelings for, 55, 59, 62, 63, 69; marriage to Edwin Montagu, 49–50, 51, 54, 59, 63 & n. 2; correspondence: VBC to VS, 7–8
Stauffenberg, Count von, *311*, 363
Steed, Henry Wickham, *187*
Stevenson, Frances *see* Lloyd George, Countess
Stockton, 275, 289 n. 2, 359
Stopford, Gen., 73 n. 3, 75
Strachey, Lytton, *107*
Strang Steel, Malcolm, *269*
Strickland, Gen., 121 n. 1, *125*, 129–30
Strickland, Lady, *129-30*
Sturgis, Mark, 134
Summerskill, Edith, *328*
Sunday Express, publishes article by Violet on Ireland (1921), 134
Swaythling, Lord, 49, 50
Sykes, Barbara, *298*, 322, 323
Sykes, Frank, *298*, 300, 315, 322, 323, 361

Talbot, Gilbert, 263, 309-*10*
Tate, Mavis, *255*, 343
Teheran conference (Dec. 1943), 312–3

Temple, William, *244*, 251, 257
Tennant, Edward, *79*
Tennant, John Amherst, *79*
Tennant, Stephen, *360*, 361
Thorburn, Stephen, *148*
Tiberius Gracchus (pseud.), 313
Times, The, 'Amiens dispatch' (1914), 8 & n. 1; on Great War, 22, 62; reports battle of the Somme, 93 n. 2; praises Reginald McKenna, 69; backs conscription, 75; backs Lloyd George, 68, 97, 155; on Violet at Paisley (1920), 110 n. 3, 112 n. 1; on Ireland (1920–1), 116–17, 129; reports Nazi repression in Germany (1933), 182; Violet writes to, 184 (Aug. 1935); on liberation of concentration camps (1945), 338 n. 4; mentioned: 23, 64 n. 2, 309, 327, 335
Tobruk, fall of (1942), 240
'Torch', Operation *see* North Africa (French), invasion of
Tories/Tory Party *see* Conservative Party
'Toto' *see* Morhange, Alfonse
Tree, Viola, 33
Trenchard, Hugh, *265*
Triumph of Time, The, 31
Trollope, Anthony, wartime renaissance of, 317 & n. 2
Truman, Harry S., *338*, 340
Tunnard, Miss, 304, 309
Turkey, threat of war with (1922), 136; *see also* Gallipoli campaign

'Undertaking Werewolf', 346 & n. 3
'United Front', 194–6
United Nations organization *see* Dumbarton Oaks
United States of America:
    and Great War, 19–20, 48; and Ireland, 123; and Germany, 141, 146; and League of Nations, 180; and Second World War, 205, 217, 220, 223, 231, 243, 246, 281, 285; 287–8, 296, 330, 349; (military) 260, 261, 290, 292, 298, 314, 331, 332, 333, 334, 355; American troops in Britain during, 298, 301–2, 310; British attitudes towards, 251, 260, 291–2, 308, 312–3, 321, 329, 349; and United Nations organization, 332; post-war loan to Britain, 365 & n. 3, 367–8; mentioned, 146, 340, 359

'V1' flying bomb, 306–10, 316, 359; its effect on public morale, 310
'V2' rocket, 324, 333, 334
Vansittart, Robert, *216*
'V.E. Day' (and celebration of), 344–6
Venizelos, 80
Verdun, 219
Versailles, treaty of, 105, 139–40, 153, 175 n. 1, 181, 186, 207
Vichy regime, 246–7, 248; and Jews in, 244, 363 n. 4

Index

Vincent, Sir Edgar*, 17, 52, 54, 139, 141, 142, 143,144, 145, 146
Vincent, Lady Helen, 141, 142, *396*; her assessment of Violet, 154 n. 1; correspondence: VBC to Lady Helen,153–4
Vivian, Arnold G., *266*
Voigt, Frederick, *150*, 154

Waldegrave, Countess, *351*, 353
Walpole, Sir Hugh, *208*
Warburg, Siegmund, *213*, 237, 282
Ward, Barbara, *365*
Waterson, Sidney, *252*
Wedderburn, Alistair, 368
Wedderburn, David, *266*
Wedgewood, Eliza, 7, 8
Weir, William, *137*-8
Welles, Orson, *Citizen Kane*, 237
Wells, H. G., 15
Wels, Otto, *146*
Wemyss, Earl of *see* Elcho, Lord
'Werewolf' *see* 'Undertaking Werewolf'
Westminster Newsletter, 195
Weygand, Maxime, *226*
Wheatley, Vera, 317 & n. 2
White, Graham, *256*, 345, 357
Whittle, Frank, *289*
Whittle jet engine, 289–90

Wiggin, J. H., *256*, 266, 269, 282
Wilkinson, Ellen, *215*, 299–300, 329, 334
Williams, Lady Rhys, *336*
Williams, Sir Herbert, *349*
Wilson, Sir Arthur, *53*, 57
Wilson, Sir Horace, *313*
Wimborne, Lady, 21, 27
Wimborne, Lord, *62*
Winant, John, *248*, 291, 325
Winchester College, 225–6, 270, 355
Wodehouse, P. G., *232*
Women, and Paisley elections, 105, 111, 112, 163; and parliament, 115–16, 147, 162; Violet's views on, 36, 64, 147
Wood, Sir Henry, 303
Wood, Sir Howard Kingsley*, and appointment of Churchill as premier, 224; mentioned: 213, 238 n. 2, 255, 291
Wyndham, Percy, 6-7

Yeatman Biggs, Muriel, *340*, 359
Yeatman Biggs, William, *340*
Yeats, W. B., 48
Young, George Malcolm, and post-war politics, *305*, 364
Your M.P. (1944), 313

Zeppelin, raid on London (1915), 78; 229
Zhukov, Marshal, *348*